ENHANCING
JUSTICE
REDUCING BIAS

SARAH E. REDFIELD
Editor

AMERICAN BAR ASSOCIATION
Judicial Division

Cover design by Elmarie Jara/ABA Design

The materials contained herein represent the opinions of the authors and/or the editors, and should not be construed to be the views or opinions of the law firms or companies with whom such persons are in partnership with, associated with, or employed by, nor of the American Bar Association or the Judicial Division unless adopted pursuant to the bylaws of the Association.

Nothing contained in this book is to be considered as the rendering of legal advice for specific cases, and readers are responsible for obtaining such advice from their own legal counsel. This book is intended for educational and informational purposes only.

Printed in the United States of America.

21 20 19 18 17   5 4 3 2

Library of Congress Cataloging-in-Publication Data

Names: Redfield, Sarah E., editor.
Title: Enhancing justice : reducing bias / edited by Sarah E. Redfield.
Description: Chicago : American Bar Association, 2017.
Identifiers: LCCN 2017014776 (print) | LCCN 2017015090 (ebook) | ISBN 9781634258388 (epub) | ISBN 9781634258371 (book)
Subjects: LCSH: Discrimination in justice administration—United States. | Denial of justice—United States. | Bias (Law)—United States.
Classification: LCC KF384 (ebook) | LCC KF384 .E446 2017 (print) | DDC 347.73—dc23
LC record available at https://lccn.loc.gov/2017014776

Discounts are available for books ordered in bulk. Special consideration is given to state bars, CLE programs, and other bar-related organizations. Inquire at Book Publishing, ABA Publishing, American Bar Association, 321 N. Clark Street, Chicago, Illinois 60654-7598.

www.ShopABA.org

Contents

Judge Karen Arnold-Burger, Kansas Court of Appeals
Jean Mavrelis, Chief Executive Officer, Kochman Mavrelis Associates
Attorney Phyllis B. Pickett, Lawyer and Mediator, Raleigh, North Carolina

Judge Kevin Burke, Hennepin County, Minnesota
Judge Steve Leben, Kansas Court of Appeals

Professor Victoria C. Plaut, University of California, Berkeley,
    School of Law
Deputy District Attorney Christina S. Carbone, Contra Costa County,
    California

Professor Cynthia Lee, The George Washington University Law School

Dr. Patrick S. Forscher, University of Wisconsin-Madison
Professor Patricia G. Devine, University of Wisconsin-Madison

Dr. Lindsay M. Perez, Data Analytics Consultant, Reno, NV
Professor Monica K. Miller, University of Nevada, Reno
Dr. Alicia Summers, Independent Court Consultant, Reno, NV
Professor Shawn C. Marsh, University of Nevada, Reno

Judge Sophia H. Hall, Circuit Court of Cook County, Illinois

Judge Jeremy D. Fogel, Director, Federal Judicial Center

Preface

Judge Theodore McKee

At the dawn of the 20th century, noted sociologist, activist, and scholar W.E.B. DuBois told those assembled at the first Pan-African conference in London, "The problem of the Twentieth Century is the problem of the colour-line."[1] Now from the perspective of the 21st century, we see that our society and our institutions have clearly made dramatic progress since DuBois's pronouncement in 1900, but the problems of the color line persist. To be sure, the kind of explicit overt discrimination and racism associated with the era of Jim Crow and DuBois's time is no longer the social norm.[2] Yet, our society is still plagued by inequalities and inequities. The glaring disparities in our institutions that are committed to education and justice reveal that various bias-derived divides persist.[3] The disparity appears as early as elementary school, where disparate treatment is visited upon children because of entrenched biases. These differences increase potential exposure to, and inclusion in, the criminal justice system. Researchers call this the "school-to-prison pipeline" because poor children and children of color are funneled from school disciplinary systems into prisons by the time they are in their teens.[4]

Outcomes like these based on race, ethnicity, gender, socioeconomic level, and other differences among people are well known and all too common. We need to ask ourselves how and why these disparities persist and why they are so common, despite decades of commitment to diversity and equality. As Professor Philip Atiba Goff puts it,

> How does one explain persistent racial inequality in the face of declining racial prejudice? This riddle, which I call the "attitude-inequality mismatch" question . . . is the fundamental problem facing contemporary scholars of race in the United States. . . . A related and equally provocative question, however, is this: Why have we not answered this question yet?[5]

Professor Goff—and many others—suggest the possible (albeit partial) answer lies in the emerging understanding of implicit bias, the subject of this book.

Having been a judge at the trial or appellate level for over 30 years, I can attest to the fact that, as a singular profession, we judges want our decisions to be based only on the unbiased application of the law to the facts or the record before us. We view fairness and objectivity as our hallmark and continuously work to ensure that our decisions are devoid of any improper influence. Yet, a substantial body of research casts doubt on our ability to do this because, like everyone else, we harbor biases of which we are not even aware.

As Daniel Gilbert, Professor of Psychology at Harvard University, has explained, "Judges . . . strive for truth more often than we realize, and miss that mark more often than they realize. Because the brain cannot see itself fooling itself."[6]

Numerous studies have shown that even though we may not be aware of the bias that lurks within, our acculturation results in implicit bias in each of us that is imprinted onto our subconsciousness and is as intractable in its placement as it is pervasive in its influence. This bias is present in all jurisdictions, at all levels of our justice system, and in all types of cases. It affects our judgment as well as our actions and thereby infects the very institution that we depend upon for fairness and the just resolution of disputes: the courts.

In speaking for a plurality of the U.S. Supreme Court in *Parents Involved in Community Schools v. Seattle School Dist. No. 1*,[7] Chief Justice Roberts opined that "[t]he way to stop discrimination on the basis of race is to stop discriminating on the basis of race." Yet, research shows that our neurological circuitry does not include an on/off switch that, when tripped, disables the bias that has accumulated in our subconscious mind. Rather, the most we can hope for is that each of us will be sensitized to our own unconscious bias and then consciously guard against allowing it to affect our attitudes or behavior. As Harry Edwards, the former Chief Judge of the U.S. Court of Appeals for the District of Columbia, has advised, "[O]ne's personal beliefs should be consciously, rather than subconsciously recognized."[8] Judge Edwards explains, "The real threat that a judge's personal ideologies may affect his decisions in an inappropriate case arises when the judge is not even consciously aware of the potential threat."[9]

Surely we all can agree that the most fundamental principle of any judicial system is fairness. Judges, no less than lawyers, victims, and defendants, want and expect equal treatment from courts. Like everyone else, judges abhor the notion that our actions are affected by any kind of bias. As Professor Gilbert correctly opined, we see ourselves as striving for fairness and giving equal treatment before the law. For us judges, that is the source of considerable pride as well as personal and professional satisfaction.

However, judges are not the only actors in the judicial system. Police exercise tremendous discretion in deciding whether to make the initial arrest that is the entree into the criminal justice system.[10] Prosecutors must decide whom to charge and what to charge them with, and jurors must decide who is telling the truth if the initial arrest results in a trial.

Police, prosecutors, and jurors all strive to be fair. During the decade I served as a trial judge, I was always struck by how seriously jurors tried to be fair as well as how earnestly they attempted to follow my instruction to find the facts based on the evidence before them and apply the law as I explained it to those facts. And yet, despite the good intentions and best efforts of those involved in our system of justice, there is significant evidence of bias in the system. Studies have found bias at every level of the judicial system, from the initial encounter with police to the judge who imposes the sentence. People of color have higher rates of conviction in contested matters, tend to get longer sentences even when controlling for all other factors, and tend to more often have children removed from the home in child welfare matters.

It is therefore not surprising that communities of color have much lower trust and confidence in the justice system. Recent studies find that even those who identify as a member of an ethnic majority often receive a different level of justice. Decisions about whom to arrest, whom to charge, whom to convict, and the appropriate sentence are all affected by implicit bias. Given this unpleasant truth, it is understandably difficult for some members of our society to embrace the courts as champions of the rule of law. Such skepticism is understandable when the actions of courts and judges adversely impact people based (at least in part) on their race, ethnicity, or gender. Since we are not aware of the extremely subtle—yet powerful—subconscious bias that dwells within each of us, we cannot be aware of its influence on us, our actions, or our judgments. Rather than the insight most of us assume and hope that we have, our wiring contains a "blindspot" that conceals the underlying attitudes that are actually influencing, and even controlling, our actions,[11] just as Professor Gilbert has explained.

I submit that this is particularly true of judges, and research bears this out.[12] Our very identity is inextricably intertwined with the notion of fairness and the belief that our minds are as free of bias as are our rulings and judgments. That is our job, and we dedicate our professional (and often our personal) lives toward that end. We also set the tone for the proceedings we preside over, and we are therefore primarily responsible for ensuring the fairness of the judicial system.

It is therefore particularly difficult for us to acknowledge that, like everyone else, our human frailty conditions us to be unwitting hosts to what Mahzarin Banaji refers to as "mind bugs." Mind bugs, she explains, are small cues, such as implicit biases, that can have a powerful impact on our decision making. "Mind bugs operate without us being conscious of them." Banaji further explains that "[t]hey are not special things that happen in our heart because we are evil."[13] But assumptions lead to attitudes, and attitudes lead to choices that, in the context of the judicial system, can have lasting, far-reaching consequences. It is especially difficult for those of us who are judges to recognize this frailty.

However, nothing suggests that we must accept or tolerate bias in our judges, ourselves, or our institutions. Rather, as Judge Edwards counseled and as research has confirmed, we can take steps to neutralize and control that bias if we recognize its existence and consciously struggle to negate its influence. Fortunately, steps are being taken to do precisely that. For example, the National Center for State Courts is actively engaged in helping judges recognize and neutralize implicit bias.[14] The Federal Judicial Center is integrating the concept of implicit bias into the curriculum for all new federal judges and ensuring that the subject is being discussed at national judicial workshops for federal judges. In the words of Judge Jeremy Fogel, Director of the Federal Judicial Center, "[B]eing able to recognize implicit bias and deal with it is one of the core competencies of being a judge."[15]

While these and other constructive steps are being taken by the judiciary, our success can only be measured over time. Moreover, although judges do set the tone for the system, the fate of those caught up in it is also determined by the initial decision to arrest, the severity of any charge that is filed, the conclusion of jurors, and the crime of which one is ultimately convicted. As I noted at the outset, within the judicial system, important decisions are also being made by lawyers, parties, prosecutors, juries, and court personnel that can be unwittingly influenced by bias.

This book helps explain how so many who pride themselves on being fair can be part of a system that is so widely seen as unfair by those who have historically been the victims of bias and prejudice, as well as by others. It is the result of an effort undertaken by the American Bar Association to address the ubiquitous problem of subliminal bias and its impact on the judicial system. It was written by an exceptional and diverse team of authors, all with expertise relevant to understanding and ameliorating implicit biases. Judges, lawyers, social scientists, professors, and experienced trainers worked together to bring cutting-edge research and thinking to this effort. The result offers both perspective and practical advice from their disciplines and their collaboration. While not all the authors would agree on each possible approach, the focus is on best practices, as we know them today, which can enable courts to lessen the impact of implicit bias. As Drs. Devine and Forscher describe, we seek to "break the bias habit" by increasing knowledge and awareness of implicit bias, improved understanding and practice of procedural fairness and of culturally competent communication across cultures, and a sustained commitment to mindfulness.

While each chapter can be read and used on its own, there is a method to this book's organization that should prove helpful. The first two chapters are introductory. Chapter 1, "Decision Making, Implicit Bias, and Judges: Is This Blindfold Really Working?," is authored by Judge Chad Schumacher and his colleague Joseph Sawyer from the National Judicial College and serves to orient us to the task of reading and using the book. These lifelong educators offer a "pre-test" to spark our interest and thinking (and they suggest we revisit the test at the end of the book). Chapter 2, "Framing the Discussion," written by Judge Bernice B. Donald and Professor Sarah E. Redfield, also orients us to the rest of the book. These women were part of the American Bar Association's early entry to the field of implicit bias and are well-regarded thinkers and trainers on the topic. They share their own personal reflections on implicit bias and its ramifications, and then provide an introduction to the basic vocabulary of implicit bias, group identity, micromessaging, and debiasing. This chapter provides the scaffolding upon which the rest of the book builds in more depth and with more nuance.

The next three chapters introduce us to social science and its relationship to fairness in the judicial system. Chapter 3, "Implicit Bias: A Social Science Overview" by Professors Justin D. Levinson, Laurie A. Rudman, and Danielle

M. Young, provides the social science overview in the legal context. Chapter 3 is powerful in its review of the science, showing us how even the best-intentioned among us may, because of implicit unconscious bias, be making decisions with which we would honestly and explicitly disagree. Chapter 4, "Manifestations of Implicit Bias in the Courts," is authored by Judge Mark W. Bennett, and Chapter 5, "Implicit Bias in Judicial Decision Making: How It Affects Judgment and What Judges Can Do about It," is by Judge Andrew J. Wistrich and Professor Jeffrey J. Rachlinski. These men are all pioneers in the field, known for their theoretical work, empirical research, and practical application of those to the actual courtroom and on-the-ground practices. Their chapters address the issue of implicit bias from the perspective of courts and judges and offer specific suggestions, grounded in law and science, for next steps.

The next two chapters consider the issues of implicit bias and group preference from additional perspectives. In Chapter 6, "When Myths Become Beliefs: Implicit Socioeconomic Bias in American Courtrooms," Professor Michele Benedetto Neitz discusses implicit bias as it plays out around socioeconomic status and adds another valuable layer to our understanding. While much of what is written about implicit bias deals with race, this chapter reminds us that implicit bias is triggered by many associations and it negatively affects many groups. It is a dynamic that operates on and negatively affects "the other," however that other might be defined. In Chapter 7, "With Malice toward None and Charity for Some: Ingroup Favoritism Enables Discrimination," we reproduce a thought-provoking piece by two renowned psychologists, Professors Anthony G. Greenwald and Thomas F. Pettigrew. While Professor Greenwald is sometimes called the father of the Implicit Association Test (IAT—the most common method used to measure implicit bias), in this chapter he and his colleague draw our attention away from this topic to a related—they would say more important—area: group favoritism. Professors Greenwald and Pettigrew suggest that issues we thought of as outgroup hostility are better construed as ingroup favoritism and that this favoritism grounds much of the discriminatory behavior we see.

The next two chapters move us toward an understanding of what we can *do* to ameliorate the negative impacts of implicit bias or group favoritism. These chapters harken back to concepts we have seen before—cultural competence, community relations, and procedural fairness—and connect these ideas with the new thinking on implicit bias and how we might overcome such biases. Chapter 8, "Hearing All Voices: Challenges of Cultural Competence and Opportunities for Community Outreach," is authored by an exceptional interdisciplinary team—Kansas Court of Appeals Judge Karen Arnold-Burger, cultural competence expert Jean Mavrelis, and attorney and mediator Phyllis B. Pickett. These experienced and expert authors provide strong insight into culture, communication, and community. Their discussion of hypothetical encounters offers an excellent opportunity to improve in these areas in a practical way. Chapter 9, "Procedural Fairness," brings us the expertise of two absolute leaders in this field, Minnesota District Judge Kevin Burke and Kansas Court of Appeals Judge

Steven Leben. Here they provide important and practical steps for improving fairness and the perception of fairness while at the same time reducing the likelihood of implicitly biased decision making.

The next four chapters hone in further on ways to become aware of and ameliorate implicit bias and its negative impacts. Chapter 10, "Considering Audience Psychology in the Design of Implicit Bias Education," is written by two social scientists/lawyers. Professor Victoria C. Plaut and her colleague Contra Costa County Deputy District Attorney Christina S. Carbone present best practices for designing and implementing implicit bias training. Recognizing there is still much to learn and assess, their examination of the issues of whether and how to train ourselves offers an excellent primer for next steps. Chapter 11, "Awareness as a First Step toward Overcoming Implicit Bias," is authored by Cynthia Lee, a professor of criminal law who has written extensively about race, gender, and sexual orientation norms, particularly how these identities can influence verdicts in self-defense and provocation cases. Here, she focuses on the significance of awareness as a necessary step to other training. Chapter 12, "Knowledge-Based Interventions Are More Likely to Reduce Legal Disparities Than Are Implicit Bias Interventions," is written by Dr. Patricia G. Devine and her colleague Dr. Patrick S. Forscher, both highly regarded social scientists. They offer their analysis of knowledge-based interventions as the preferred way to break the prejudice habit as they call for us to move our attention from the narrow focus on implicit bias and the IAT to a more established and sustainable focus grounded in the science of habit breaking. Chapter 13, "Assessing Interventions to Reduce Judicial Bias: Fighting Implicit Bias—What Judges and Lawyers Can Do," is again a chapter crafted by a diverse team of lawyer/scientist authors. Drs. Lindsay M. Perez, Monica K. Miller, Alicia Summers, and Shawn C. Marsh bring insight from their analytical backgrounds coupled with their experience offering training to suggest methods for evaluating this kind of work.

The final two chapters return to judges and to reflection. In Chapter 14, "Combating Bias through Judicial Leadership," Judge Sophia H. Hall, Presiding Judge of the Circuit Court of Cook County, Illinois, describes her journey learning and teaching about bias. The chapter is certainly aptly titled; her convening power and leadership are extraordinary. Also inspirational is Chapter 15, "On Being Mindful," Judge Jeremy Fogel's thoughtful—and dare I say mindful— essay on the value of mindfulness in the judicial arena. Judge Fogel gives us a chance to reflect, and well we should.

If we are to ever eradicate the "colour-line," that DuBois spoke of over 100 years ago, each of us must be mindful; each of us must cast a critical eye inward and examine our attitudes far more carefully than will be comfortable. This book provides an excellent starting point for explaining the need for this introspection as well as for developing strategies and mechanisms that will hopefully, one day, allow each of us to "stop discriminating" so that we can more honestly and intelligently move toward a judicial system that is truly based on impartiality and fairness and is recognized as such.

ABOUT THE AUTHOR

Judge **Theodore McKee** recently stepped down from the position of Chief Judge of the U.S. Court of Appeals for the Third Circuit. He was appointed to that court in 1994 by President Clinton after having served 11 years as a state trial judge and after serving as an Assistant U.S. Attorney and a Deputy City Solicitor. During his tenure on the court, he co-chaired a task force on racial bias within the Third Circuit and made implicit bias a focal point of his tenure as chief judge.

ENDNOTES

1. PETER FRYER, STAYING POWER: THE HISTORY OF BLACK PEOPLE IN BRITAIN 285 (1984).
2. *See* C. VANN WOODWARD, THE STRANGE CAREER OF JIM CROW (2002); *see also* MICHELLE ALEXANDER, THE NEW JIM CROW: MASS INCARCERATION IN THE AGE OF COLORBLINDNESS (2010).
3. See, e.g., Chapter 2, "Framing the Discussion," and Chapter 4, "Manifestations of Implicit Bias in the Courts" (discussing the manifestation of bias in the criminal justice system and elsewhere).
4. The U.S. Department of Education has collected data from which it has concluded that Black children represent only 19 percent of preschool enrollment but account for 47 percent of preschool children receiving out-of-school suspensions. The report concluded that racial disparities in suspensions are also apparent in K-12 schools. U.S. DEP'T EDUC., OFFICE FOR CIVIL RIGHTS, 2013–2014 CIVIL RIGHTS DATA COLLECTION: A FIRST LOOK 3 (2016), *available at* http://www2.ed.gov/about/offices/list/ocr/docs/2013-14-first-look.pdf.
5. Phillip Atiba Goff, *A Measure of Justice: What Policing Racial Bias Research Reveals, in* BEYOND DISCRIMINATION: RACIAL INEQUALITY IN A POST-RACIST ERA 157, 173 (Fredrick C. Harris & Robert C. Lieberman eds., 2013).
6. Daniel Gilbert, Op-Ed., *I'm O.K., You're Biased*, N.Y. TIMES, Apr. 16, 2006, http://www.nytimes.com/2006/04/16/opinion/im-ok-youre-biased.html.
7. 551 U.S. 701, 748 (2007).
8. Harry T. Edwards, *The Role of a Judge in Modern Society: Some Reflections on Current Practice in Federal Appellate Adjudication*, 32 CLEV. ST. L. REV. 385, 409–10 (1983–84).
9. *Id.*
10. *See* Jane W. Gibson-Carpenter & James E. Carpenter, *Race, Poverty, and Justice: Looking Where the Streetlight Shines*, 3–SPG KAN. J.L. & PUB. POL'Y 99, 101 (1994) ("Police officers who have worked in many types of neighborhoods acknowledge that they call home to middle-class parents more readily. Between suburban and urban departments, the difference can be even more striking. A department of college-educated officers in a suburb of Minneapolis in the 1970s went so far as to invite parents and children into the station to discuss their problems confidentially, with virtual immunity from formal handling."). The discrepancy in arrests rates based on race and socioeconomic factors has also been borne out by a 2013 report by the Sentencing Project, which pointed to a wide body of scholarship indicating that socioeconomic factors influence disparities in arrest rates. *See generally* THE SENTENCING PROJECT, REPORT OF THE SENTENCING PROJECT TO THE UNITED NATIONS HUMAN RIGHTS COMMITTEE (2013), *available at* http://sentencingproject.org/wp-content/uploads/2015/12/Race-and-Justice-Shadow-Report-ICCPR.pdf.
11. *See generally* MAHZARIN R. BANAJI & ANTHONY G. GREENWALD, BLINDSPOT: HIDDEN BIASES OF GOOD PEOPLE (2013).
12. Jeffrey J. Rachlinski et al., *Does Unconscious Racial Bias Affect Trial Judges?*, 84 NOTRE DAME L. REV. 3 (2009). Researchers studied judicial attitudes using questionnaires that had been completed by a random sample of 167 federal magistrate judges. Relying on that study, as well as others, the researchers concluded that judges harbor implicit bias like

others and the biases can affect judicial decision making when we are unaware of the need to monitor our decisions for racial bias. *Id.* The good news is that researchers also concluded that when judges are aware of a need to suppress implicit bias, it appears that we are willing and able to do so.

13. Shankar Vedantum, *The Bias Test,* WASHINGTON POST MAGAZINE, Jan. 23, 2005, at 42, *available at* http://www.washingtonpost.com/wp-dyn/articles/A27067-2005Jan21_4.html.

14. *See generally* PAMELA M. CASEY ET AL., NAT'L CENTER FOR STATE COURTS, HELPING COURTS ADDRESS IMPLICIT BIAS: RESOURCES FOR EDUCATION (2012), *available at* www.ncsc.org/~/media/Files /PDF/Topics/Gender%20and%20Racial%20Fairness/IB_report_033012.ashx.

15. Personal interview with Judge Fogel, reprinted with his permission.

Chapter 1

Decision Making, Implicit Bias, and Judges
Is This Blindfold Really Working?

Judge Chad Schmucker (ret.) and
Joseph Sawyer, the National Judicial College

Chapter Highlight

- The leading judicial educators offer their perspective on implicit bias and a pre-test to capture your interest.

At the National Judicial College, we have long worked to teach judges to make impartial decisions. Over the past decade, we have been leaders in talking with our participants about the emerging science concerning implicit bias. This chapter offers a brief introduction from our perspective at the college. While later chapters provide more in-depth information and analysis on implicit bias, we offer something of a pre-test to spark thinking on the subject and to spur interest in learning more.

We begin by asking whether all human beings have implicit bias, even judges. And we answer in the affirmative. Since they are implicit, we are unaware of these biases and their impact on judicial decision making. But we need to be aware of their potential impact. Also referred to as heuristics, mental shortcuts, cognitive blind spots, schemas, mental associations, and implicit associations, implicit biases allow the human brain to operate more efficiently. But unfortunately, the increase in efficiency can come at a price with a human toll. What are we to make of the claim of implicit bias in judges? Is it real? Is there something that can be done about it? Does it apply to you as a judge?

At the National Judicial College, we know many of us are active learners who learn the most not from reading but from interaction—such as answering questions or participating in a discussion. In this context, think about and answer the questions that follow. Write your answers down on a separate piece of paper and review them after you finish this book.

How Much Do You Know?

For questions 1–6, answer A (agree), D (disagree), or DK (don't know).

_____   1. Fairness is a core value of judges and courts.

_____   2. Decisions influenced by implicit bias are unfair.

_____   3. If a judge is trying to be fair and is listening to the argument or evidence, it doesn't matter if the judge has an implicit bias.

_____   4. Using common sense will avoid the effects of implicit bias.

_____   5. Most judges who have an implicit bias already know they have it.

_____   6. Implicit bias is a process that works unconsciously in our brain.

For questions 7–21, answer T (true) or F (false).

_____   7. Judges are different from human resources managers, large law firm partners, college professors and doctors so we shouldn't expect any implicit bias in judges.

_____   8. Judges are regularly given feedback on their decisions or courtroom behavior which would highlight the need for implicit bias training.

_____   9. The appellate process is effective in preventing decisions based on implicit bias.

_____   10. The judicial discipline process is effective in preventing decisions based on implicit bias.

We are assuming you have some idea of what is meant by implicit bias, but just in case you don't, here is what we mean: implicit bias is the bias that you have that you are unaware of. Although you can have an implicit bias relating to gender, race, national origin, religion, ethnicity, age, size, sexual orientation, and many other characteristics, for this quiz, let us assume we are talking about an implicit racial bias.

How do you think you did on the pre-test? From those of us who come to this book with little knowledge to those who come with much, there is no doubt still much to be learned. And why should we be paying attention? The science-based research on implicit bias is significant. Writing a decade ago, researchers observed, "As disturbing as this evidence is, there is too much of it to be ignored."[1] By 2015, the annual national review of evidence on implicit bias concluded, "As convincing research evidence accumulates, it becomes difficult to understate the importance of considering the role of implicit racial biases when analyzing societal inequities."[2] Indeed, by 2016 that same review observed, "It is hardly exaggeration to say that at times 2015 felt like the year that the term

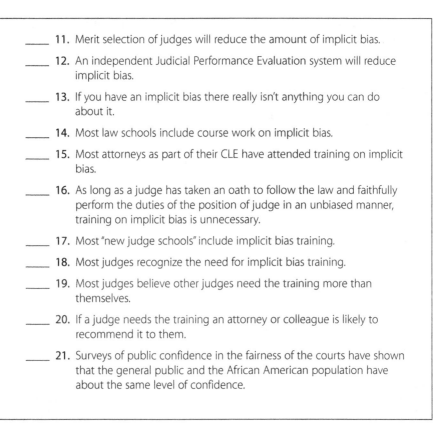

_____ 11. Merit selection of judges will reduce the amount of implicit bias.

_____ 12. An independent Judicial Performance Evaluation system will reduce implicit bias.

_____ 13. If you have an implicit bias there really isn't anything you can do about it.

_____ 14. Most law schools include course work on implicit bias.

_____ 15. Most attorneys as part of their CLE have attended training on implicit bias.

_____ 16. As long as a judge has taken an oath to follow the law and faithfully perform the duties of the position of judge in an unbiased manner, training on implicit bias is unnecessary.

_____ 17. Most "new judge schools" include implicit bias training.

_____ 18. Most judges recognize the need for implicit bias training.

_____ 19. Most judges believe other judges need the training more than themselves.

_____ 20. If a judge needs the training an attorney or colleague is likely to recommend it to them.

_____ 21. Surveys of public confidence in the fairness of the courts have shown that the general public and the African American population have about the same level of confidence.

'implicit bias' truly permeated society in ways that had previously been beyond compare."[3] This cumulated research demonstrates that implicit bias is found across multiple areas of society—in medical care, in employment, in education, in housing, in criminal justice. So too emerging research continues to demonstrate the significance of ingroup and outgroup status where the structure of the human brain compels each of us to think in terms of "us and them."[4]

If the emerging science and our own perspective at the National Judicial College are correct, then what does this all mean? Can we deny that many of our decisions are probably affected by implicit bias? If fairness is a core value, then can we accept this as an unavoidable influence on decisions? Is periodic implicit bias education essential for the judiciary? As a judicial officer, when attending your next training event, will you sign up for the latest update on evidence or choose a session on implicit bias? Which subject matter, evidence or implicit bias, will most improve the administration of justice?

We expect these questions have started you thinking about the importance of regular judicial education on implicit bias for all judges. We trust that you will continue on with the other chapters in this book, which offer answers to most of the questions we posed; after completing this book, review your original quiz and see if your answers change.

So You'd Like to Know More

- ABA, Hidden Injustice: Bias on the Bench, http://www.americanbar.org/diversity-portal /diversity-inclusion-360-commission/implicit-bias.html

- ABA, Implicit Bias & Judges: How Innate Attitudes Shape Behavior, Even on the Bench, http://www.americanbar.org/diversity-portal/diversity-inclusion-360-commission /implicit-bias.html

- ABA, *The Science and Implications of Implicit Bias*, http://www.americanbar.org/groups /litigation/initiatives/task-force-implicit-bias/implicit-bias-videos.html

- Mahzarin R. Banaji & Anthony G. Greenwald, *Blindspot: Hidden Biases of Good People* (2013)

About the Authors

Judge Chad C. Schmucker is president of the National Judicial College. He has been a lawyer, judge, and state court administrator. He is a graduate of the University of Michigan and Wayne State Law School. The National Judicial College has been teaching judges about bias since its inception over 50 years ago and incorporates implicit bias training into many of its courses.

Joseph Sawyer has been a member of the National Judicial College's staff since 1986 and is the Distance Learning and Educational Technology Director. He is a former president of the National Association of State Judicial Educators and serves on the association's diversity committee. He was a lecturer at the Russian Academy of Justice in Moscow during the summer of 2004, the James A.A. Pierre Judicial Center in Liberia in 2009 and 2011, and in Bosnia in 2011 for the Organization for Security and Cooperation in Europe. Mr. Sawyer is a graduate of the Leadership Institute for Judicial Education. Within the United States, he has taught more than 200 educational workshops for judges and judicial branch staff in 22 states and the District of Columbia on behalf of the National Judicial College, the U.S. Department of Justice, the Executive Office of Immigration Review, the U.S. Department of Labor, the American Bar Association Rule of Law Initiative, the Occupational Health and Safety Hearing Commission, and the Administrative Office of the Courts of various states.

Endnotes

1. Jerry Kang & Mahzarin Banaji, *Fair Measures: A Behavioral Realist Revision of Affirmative Action*, 94 Calif. L. Rev. 1063 (2006).
2. Cheryl Staats et al., *State of the Science: Implicit Bias Review* 61, Kirwan Institute 2015, *available at* http://kirwaninstitute.osu.edu/wp-content/uploads/2015/05/2015 -kirwan-implicit-bias.pdf.
3. Cheryl Staats et al., *State of the Science: Implicit Bias Review* 11, Kirwan Institute 2016, *available at* http://kirwaninstitute.osu.edu/wp-content/uploads/2016/07/implicit-bias -2016.pdf.
4. Mahzarin R. Banaji & Anthony G. Greenwald, Blindspot: Hidden Biases of Good People 69 (2013).

Chapter 2

Framing the Discussion[1]

Judge Bernice B. Donald
and Sarah E. Redfield

Chapter Contents

Chapter Highlights

- Frameworks are provided that form scaffolding upon which later chapters build.

- Three related areas of implicit response are outlined: implicit bias, group dynamics, and micromessaging.

- Stories from the authors give a personal view of the start, growth, and significance of the interest in implicit bias.

I. Introduction from the Judge and the Professor

A. Judge Donald

I begin with the universal truth that all people observe and experience things through the lens of their own personal experience. At the same time, we are shaped by our environment, and our norms and mores are formed on the basis of these societal constructs.

For much of my life, I have experienced explicit and implicit bias, both of which were directed at me and which I observed from the bench. For many years, I struggled to understand how so much bias could endure when so many (though of course far from all) were people of good will and intention. Disproportionalities, the differences between a group's representation in the population at large and its over- or under-representation in specific areas,[2] have been known and have persisted for so long as to defy explanation.

As an African-American female growing up in the segregated South, I quickly learned how to navigate society within the constraints of racial norms. I learned that laws and edicts were imprecise in their interpretation and inconsistent in their application. I learned that the blanket of equal opportunity, equal protection, and equal justice was not wide enough to cover all people, and more often than not, people who looked like me were left exposed and vulnerable. I learned that strong, eloquent, and majestic laws were magnificent in the abstract but deficient in application and enforcement. I also learned that laws are not self-executing, and that racial hierarchy and a racial hegemony are often realities from which many disparities flow.

How did I learn these unwritten lessons? Through experience and observation.

I was born three years before the Supreme Court handed down its seminal 1954 decision in *Brown v. Board of Education*,[3] striking down the "separate but equal" doctrine that had allowed states to maintain a racial caste structure in their systems of education. The Supreme Court held that "separate but equal is inherently unequal"[4] and that states were required to dismantle and desegregate their de facto segregated, unequal systems "with all deliberate speed."[5]

When I began school in 1957, public education was still defiantly segregated, and Mississippi showed no visible signs of being aware of the Supreme Court's *Brown* mandate. At age six, I enrolled in the Union School, a two-room cinderblock structure with the first and second grades in Room 1 and the third grade in Room 2. African-American students arrived daily with tin pails or worn paper bags containing a lunch of whatever their parents could scrape together. Ours, the school for "negroes," had no running water, no indoor plumbing, no cafeteria, no central heating or cooling, and an impossible number of students for even our supremely dedicated teachers. Our books were well-worn and frayed, and they contained the Eurocentric names of people foreign to us (ten years later, I would meet some of those people). Our school's physical plant, in contrast to that of our White counterparts, sent an unmistakable message of inferiority, low expectations, and lack of merit. In other words, racial caste circumscribed our situation.

In 1967, after further intervention by the federal government, Mississippi implemented the School Choice Plan. The School Choice Plan was a remedy that purported to give each student the unrestricted right to attend any school in the district, barring overcrowding or some other extraordinary circumstance.[6] I enrolled, along with four other African-American girls, in the all-White Olive Branch High School. While each of us experienced explicit bias and overt discrimination, there were actions, attitudes, and behaviors that I now understand were deeply rooted in implicit bias—"mental associations that are so well established as to operate without awareness, or without intention, or without control."[7] These biases manifested themselves in the low expectations for African-American students that obviated any need to provide them with information or counseling regarding college, and in a perception of the young men as predators that led to an extreme reluctance to allow African-American males to be around White females.

After my school experiences, I continued to witness and experience further bias, both explicit and implicit, in employment, housing, retail, and travel. The following example is illustrative. While phoning to inquire about an apartment, I was taken aback at the brazenness with which the rental agent, who had not discerned my race, cautioned me that I did not want to live in that particular community because "only n—s (racial epithet) lived in that part of town." Another housing encounter led to my filing a housing discrimination lawsuit because the landlord, having learned my race only after having contractually agreed to rent an apartment to me, revoked the agreement. I provide these stark examples to give those who view life through different lenses a chance to understand and appreciate the different realities that often exist for people of color.

In the 1980s, as a judge of the General Sessions Criminal Court, I noted the startling racial disparities in persons arrested, prosecuted, and sentenced. Alongside my colleagues, I tried to administer justice fairly and impartially, free from bias, and without regard to race, ethnicity, socioeconomic status, or any other arbitrary characteristic. Having reflected upon the administration of justice and considered the judicial process in light of what I now understand about implicit bias, I am left with the haunting realization that implicit biases likely infected decisions and actions of our court and the entire justice process.[8] For the six years I operated in the high-volume General Sessions court environment, I observed constant reinforcing of stereotypes and few counter stereotypes.

In the late 1980s and early 1990s, as a U.S. bankruptcy judge, I again observed racial disparities in the judicial process. While I personally have no causative empirical research, I observed that African-American debtors, more often than not, entered into Chapter 13 bankruptcies where they undertook a repayment plan to pay back a percentage of their debts, while their White counterparts more frequently filed Chapter 7 bankruptcies where they received a quick discharge and the fresh start contemplated by the Bankruptcy Code. Scholars have pointed out the probability of this bias in the system. Professor Bernard has observed,

A survey conducted as part of [the] research found that bankruptcy lawyers were much more likely to steer black debtors into a Chapter 13 than white filers even when they had identical financial situations. The lawyers, the survey found, were also more likely to view blacks as having "good values" when they expressed a preference for Chapter 13. . . . Results from the second part of the study, which illustrated the lawyer's influence in determining which bankruptcy chapter to choose, came from a survey sent to lawyers asking them questions based on fictitious couples who were seeking bankruptcy protection. When the couple was named "Reggie and Latisha," who attended an African Methodist Episcopal Church—as opposed to a white couple, "Todd and Allison," who were members of a United Methodist Church—the lawyers were more likely to recommend a Chapter 13, even though the two couples' financial circumstances were identical.[9]

As a U.S. District Court judge for 15 years, I have observed implicit bias at every stage of the process—in arrests, adjudications, plea bargains, and sentencings. One striking contrast occurred on a single day in my courtroom. During the morning session of court, an African-American male pled guilty to an eight-count indictment charging violations of 18 U.S.C. § 922(g), felon in possession of a firearm. The defendant pled guilty to each count of the indictment. In the afternoon session, a young White male pled guilty to a two-count indictment; the first count charged a violation of 18 U.S.C. § 922(j) (eight stolen weapons), while the second count charged a violation of 18 U.S.C. § 922(g), felon in possession of a firearm (eight weapons). While the prosecutors argued that no racial disparity resulted from the disparate charging decisions, the African-American male "stereotype of dangerousness" was perpetuated by a conviction on eight counts of being a felon in possession of a firearm, while the conviction of his White counterpart on a single count of the same activity reinforced a less dangerous stereotype—even though each possessed the same number of weapons. As several of our coauthors discuss further, situations like the preceding may help explain why African-Americans and Latinos feel that the weight of the law and the unfairness of outcomes fall disparately on them, and why distrust of the system tends to be so pronounced among those groups.

Nevertheless, having considered these varied foundational experiences, some readers will rightly observe that a number of the examples are from many years ago, from a less enlightened, less pluralistic, and less inclusive era. The readers may contend that we have moved far beyond that. It is true that we have made extraordinary progress—but, unfortunately, the sorts of concerns raised here have not been consigned to the distant past.

Far too much disproportional and disparate treatment continues to fit the old narrative. As my personal observations would suggest, the entire criminal justice system clearly provides one such manifestation, a manifestation on such a vast scale and so long enduring that fatigue has set in for those of us working for change in this arena. We have needed to seek new ways to think about the problem. Writing in 2014, my colleague Professor Levinson, one of the authors of Chapter 3, offered one possibility:

> Criminal law scholars have employed implicit bias-based analyses to help explain racial discrepancies in police stop-and-frisk rates, arrest rates, prosecutorial charging and bargaining, sentencing, and other areas where disparities persist. These scholars have demonstrated, project by project, that implicit negative stereotypes of black Americans pervade the American psyche. For example, Americans rate ambiguous pieces of evidence to be more probative of guilt when a suspect is dark-skinned and display a stronger implicit connection between "black" and the concept "guilty" than they do between "white" and "guilty." The overriding theme in this work is that implicit negative stereotypes of black Americans as hostile, violent, and prone to criminality create a lens through which criminal justice actors automatically perpetuate inequality.[10]

Other scholars have joined Professor Levinson in this observation.[11]

While Professor Levinson focuses on differences between Black and White, as does my personal experience, implicit bias against and for particular groups cuts across all groups and affects every part of our legal system and society. More recently, as I've been watching the news, I've been reading some of the research about media and reflecting on the origins and reach of implicit bias. Professor Redfield and I often use two pictures from the days after Hurricane Katrina in our trainings. One photograph, showing a young African-American man, offers this caption: "A young man walks through chest deep flood water after *looting* a grocery store in New Orleans on Tuesday." The second photo depicts a young White couple; its caption reads: "Two residents wade through chest-deep water after *finding* bread and soda from a local grocery store in New Orleans, Louisiana."[12] These photos, with their captions, so starkly convey the issue that they are almost iconic.[13] We have no doubt that the publishers *did not intend* to be racist.[14]

Those who study news media have long recognized such different treatment in television news—"the rise of the black perpetrator and the white hero or victim"—where the police officers and victims shown are more often and disproportionately White and the perpetrators Black.[15] Researchers have shown that this coverage "activates racialized stereotypes" and that "heavy news viewing perpetuates fear of Black perpetrators."[16] When researchers showed heavy news consumers images of race-unidentified subjects, study participants cast these race-unidentified persons into the stereotypical race and related roles. That is, as the social scientists would describe it, the Black image served as a stimulus or prime of "a concept in memory that is then given increased weight in subsequent judgment tasks" and is "accessible so that it can be readily used in evaluating related objects."[17] Put more simply, when we bring a concept to mind, we also bring to mind other concepts that are closely associated with it—for example, doctor/nurse[18] or, in this example, Black/criminal.[19] This research is generally well known. What is perhaps less often considered is how this might directly influence aspects of the criminal justice system where a prime of *Black* has a significant implicit association with *guilt*.[20] Consider what it means, in general and for the potential juror pool, that the image of the Black perpetrator was "more accessible" to those who follow the news regularly.[21]

Today, many of us are more attuned to Internet and digital news sources than to television; and, here too the research shows the same kind of stereotyping and stereotype activation. While research on the impact of viewing news via social media is relatively recent, it seems that this approach to media may be even more problematic. For television news, there are producers and editors; in social media, what is seen or heard is often self-selected, easily repackaged, and subject to "self-reinforcing search behaviors and closed social networks."[22] The information may even be deliberately false.[23] It is easy to see how this kind of media will perpetuate stereotypes that the user may already hold, implicit or explicit. The ways in which the conclusions about media and explicit/implicit bias parallel the work of Professor Levinson are significant: "This [racial stereotyping] reaction was found even among respondents who condemned explicit racism, meaning that independent of one's prior racial attitudes, seeing Black men depicted as criminals in the news is positively correlated with negative racial thoughts about all African Americans."[24]

My own introduction to the science of implicit bias came several years before Professor Levinson's article, primarily through my work with the American Bar Association (ABA) Section of Litigation. Following the work of several notable scholars, including Professors Levinson (coauthor of Chapter 3), Professor Plaut (coauthor of Chapter 10), Professors Kang and Eberhardt, and many others cited throughout the book, the section was an early leader in identifying the significance of this topic.[25] I credit them and the Criminal Justice Section[26] with much of the initial and ongoing effort at the ABA and beyond to understand the negative impacts of implicit bias throughout the legal system. Their attention to the issue sparked the interest that has led to this book and other publications and videos released by the ABA 360 Commission to help educate the profession.[27]

All stakeholders in the civil and criminal justice systems must work diligently to enhance fairness by reducing bias. Through the resource you hold in your hands or see on your screen, we define the issue, frame the discussion, and offer strategies and solutions.

B. Professor Redfield

As this book is being written, the discussion of implicit bias is very present in American society. The director of the FBI is calling it a hard lesson for policing;[28] the Civil Rights Division of the U.S. Department of Justice is citing it as a cause of St. Louis's overwhelming racial disparities in juvenile justice;[29] the

Justice Department is requiring its personnel to be trained;[30] leading corporations are doing likewise;[31] and the courts have been and remain seriously involved, both in defining and training on the issue[32] and to some extent in their opinions.[33] One might not have predicted this when Professor Jerry Kang's *Primer* on implicit bias, was written in 2009 for the National Center for State Courts. But the *Primer* reflected earlier work on the topic, considered the emerging social science,[34] and certainly presaged an explosion of attention to the topic among legal scholars and the legal community writ large. Reflecting on the growth and endurance of this attention to implicit bias, I think of my own introduction to the terminology and its implications. Like Judge Donald, my initial involvement came by way of a request from colleagues in the Section of Litigation at the ABA to serve on their early Implicit Bias Task Force. At that point, I'd been long engaged in research examining why the pipeline to law school and the profession remained so White despite the extensive attention the issue had received for so many years.[35] As I looked at the pipeline data, I did not doubt the good intentions and commitment of my colleagues to change this picture, but I was frankly depressed by the lack of progress. As I studied the implicit bias literature, I saw a glimmer of an explanation. Individual judges and lawyers (and law professors!) did not intend to maintain the diversity numbers as they were, but perhaps their *unintentional implicit* responses at various decision points were contributing to the cumulative White result. While the manifestation and results for the pipeline to law school and the profession of course remained troubling, the human possibility of unintentional bias offered some explanation.

My other area of research and scholarship is education law. There too the numbers have long been deeply concerning.[36] Differences are evident as early as preschool and kindergarten, and continue on through grade school and high school, where students of color and students with disabilities read at lower grade levels.[37] And if you can't read well, your likelihood of academic success is limited. As Judge Donald notes, differences in expectations are well-documented and powerful all along the pipeline.[38] We know that "no one rises to low expectations,"[39] nor is it likely we rise to biased expectations.[40] These factors are the roots of many other concerns including differences in rates for dropping out, high school graduation, and pursuit of higher education. They are also the roots of the so-called school-to-prison pipeline. All of these points show glaring disproportionalities, all have been long identified, and all seem intransigent.

Still, the educators I knew, just as my colleagues in the legal profession, were people of good will. They were people who would not intentionally discriminate against a child of color, a child with disabilities, an LGBT youth, or one who practiced an "other" religion. Perhaps, though, their unintentional implicit responses, read cumulatively, were part of the cause. While these two areas of work are in the forefront of my thinking, there are, so many other areas where the numbers appear equally intransigent and defy ready explanation, including the criminal justice arena about which Judge Donald writes.

On a more personal note, as the second woman to work for the Maine Attorney General, I often found myself the first woman in many Maine courts. Other early career experiences were also as the only woman in my professional circles. I was not treated as my male colleagues were treated in large and small ways. I suppose to this day I am not sure how much of this was explicit gender bias, but at that time, I did not even have the vocabulary to consider how much of this might be implicit and unintended. I had no theoretical basis to understand how small but negative micromessages would accumulate and influence and hurt my work and my career. Had I known then what I know now, my professional life no doubt would have been different. The idea of *unintended* response or treatment casts a different light than what I perceived at the time to be negative, intentional, personal treatment.[41] Knowing that there may be a difference allows for a different response.

My sense is that others felt and feel the same way. In the research about implicit bias and related concepts surrounding intentionality, many colleagues have also found a partial answer to the societal disconnects and intransigent disproportionalities we all recognize. Psychologist Philip Atiba Goff puts it in a more sophisticated and thoughtful way:

> How does one explain persistent racial inequality in the face of declining racial prejudice? This riddle, which I call the "attitude-inequality mismatch" question . . . is the fundamental problem facing contemporary scholars of race in the United States. . . . A related and equally provocative question, however, is this: Why have we not answered this question yet?[42]

Professor Goff considers implicit bias as part of the answer.[43] Perhaps thinking of Professor Goff's riddle, some of our coauthors have put it this way: "Implicit bias research has been compelling for a range of reasons—perhaps chiefly among them that individual implicit biases often diverge from people's egalitarian self-concepts."[44] This divergence offers both explanation and hope for change and for convergence, making us eager to learn more about the science that is behind this new understanding. I see the work of this book to be exactly that.

C. And from Them Both

This book is a collaborative work. Our coauthors are legal and social science scholars, researchers, and practitioners. They are lawyers, judges, academics, and on-the-ground trainers. The book is enriched by the diversity of their perspectives and experience. Together, the authors offer readers the opportunity to become familiar with the so-called manifestation data, which suggests why implicit bias is a relevant concern, and with the science, which offers a basis for understanding implicit bias and ameliorating its impact.

As we have each discussed, the manifestation data shows ongoing dispro-portionalities based on race and other group status that otherwise defy expla-nation in a society where most decision makers make their decisions in good faith not based on group status or similar attributes. Together, from various experiences and perspectives, the authors offer insight into what this work on implicit bias and its manifestations may mean going forward. Of course, there is much work still to be done on the topic. The science here is relatively young; its implications for the legal system are also young.[45] Even younger is the evalu-ative data on what impact we can expect from focusing and training on implicit bias.[46] These are issues discussed in almost all chapters of this book, particularly those by our social science colleagues. Indeed, it may well be that given the com-plex and layered nature of our legal system, we may never identify an appro-priate opportunity for a study that shows long-term impact from training on implicit bias.

Still, we have been involved individually and together in training many of our colleagues in the legal and education worlds on the topics in this book. We have ourselves changed in the learning, and we know others have also changed. We are of the view that becoming aware of implicit biases, allowing for the time and opportunity to be more deliberate—be more mindful, as Judge Fogel puts it—can only be to the good.[47] To this end, we are honored to have had the opportunities to work with so many scholars and practitioners both before and during the writing of this book. We look forward to a continued collaboration with them and to hearing from and working further with our readers.

II. Defining the Concepts and Considering Their Convergence

A. Defining and Finding Implicit and Explicit Bias

As the title of Professor Kang's *Implicit Bias: A Primer for Courts*[48] suggests, early work on the topic of implicit bias focused on that very terminology and its implications. As we look back and reflect on the response we sometimes hear when participants are invited to participate in implicit *bias* training, it might have been preferable to use the somewhat broader and more neutral term *implicit association*.[49] Be that as it may, the *bias*[50] terminology has become preva-lent as we consider our implicit attitudes[51] and stereotypes.[52] As more research has emerged, additional concepts have made their way into the discussion of and training on implicit bias, including a focus on group preference and related implicit communication, particularly micromessaging. What these three topics have in common is their implicit nature. Each involves responses to people and situations that may well not be what the responder would consciously intend or acknowledge. Each of these topics is discussed briefly here to form a scaffold for some of the other chapters in this book.

Explicit bias is a preference deliberately generated and consciously experienced as one's own; implicit bias is an association or preference that is not consciously generated and is experienced without awareness.[53] Implicit biases may well be dissociated from what we actively and honestly believe.[54] When Miami police officers circulated a "Black Monopoly" board with every square labeled *Go to Jail*, they revealed their explicit bias.[55] When the data on police stops shows that persons of color are stopped far more often than their representation in the population might support, this is likely a reflection of implicit bias.[56] When Jennifer Mendoza made baseball history as the first woman to call a nationally televised game and a fan tweeted that "[n]o one wants to hear a women [sic] in the booth . . . I will not listen or watch those games she is on," that fan expressed an explicit bias.[57] When an employer who has consistently and sincerely expressed his commitment to hire more qualified women selects men over women (based on names or pictures making gender clear), even where the women applicants have the same[58] or better[59] credentials, that employer is likely responding with implicit bias. Similarly, when an employer evaluates candidates of color differently[60] or provides harsher review when work is labeled as from an African-American associate, that employer is likely responding to a racial prime and acting with implicit bias.[61]

It used to be the case that if we wanted to know a person's bias, we asked.[62] Asking measured explicit bias. Not surprisingly, the answers, particularly in socially sensitive situations,[63] were often less than accurate. We likely report less than accurately because we believe we are not biased, because we do not want those around us to know we think we may be biased, or because we do not know ourselves.[64]

Now, in addition to asking, we can measure bias in indirect ways where automatic associations or implicit biases can be reliably tested at an unconscious level.[65] The underlying theory in the indirect approach to ascertaining bias is that we will respond more accurately and quickly when the response is consistent with our preformed mental templates or schemas. For example, we are more comfortable with, and likely respond more quickly to, the name *Greg* paired with *male* and the name *Emily* paired with *female*, as compared to a match of *male* with *Emily*. To test implicit bias, we measure implicit reaction time (called response latency) to paired stimuli. In these tests, researchers measure our response time to certain *primes*,[66] where exposure to the prime prompts certain responses without our conscious awareness.[67] For example, in one experiment, study participants who were primed with the words *gray*, *Florida*, and *retired* walked more slowly as they headed toward the elevator than those not so primed.[68] In another example, when primed with words related to *helpfulness*, participants were more helpful in picking up belongings "accidentally" dropped by the experimenter than those who were not so primed (though this prime could be interrupted by other factors— for example, if the participants were late for their next appointment).[69] These are implicit automatic associations and responses, and they exist in many domains,[70] from early education[71] to communicating with clients[72] to appellate review.[73]

The Implicit Association Test (IAT)[74] is a computerized priming test that measures these associations[75] using pictures and words (see Figure 2.1).

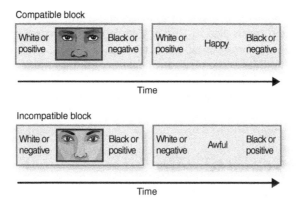

FIGURE 2.1   During "compatible" trials, White faces and positive words are categorized using one key, whereas Black faces and negative words are categorized with a different key. During "incompatible" trials, categories are rearranged: White faces and negative words are categorized with one key, and Black faces and positive words with the other key. A tendency to respond more quickly on compatible than incompatible blocks is taken to indicate an anti-Black and/or pro-White attitude.[76]

While race is the most commonly discussed, there are many variations of the IAT available online including fat/thin, elderly/young, Native American/foreign, and skin color.[77] Another variation of this approach measures implicit associations between race and weapons.[78] Emerging physical neuroscience also supports this kind of implicit bias analysis.[79]

As Judge Bennett discusses in Chapter 5 about his own experience with the IAT, IAT results can be surprising and disturbing.[80] This is perhaps particularly so for those who consider themselves egalitarian but whose IAT results show the typical American preferences—for example, White over Black,[81] women with families over working women,[82] the abled over the disabled.[83] As one might predict, as these results accumulated and the use of the IAT and related assessments increased,[84] there was an explosion of research and attention to IAT results and implications in a wide range of contexts,[85] including the legal system.[86] From this research, a wealth of literature, including meta-analyses, supports

"On the one hand, biases are helpful and adaptive. Biases help us use previous knowledge to inform new decisions, a kind of cognitive shorthand, as we do not have the cognitive resources to make every decision fresh. However, many of our biases can also be unhelpful. Biases can blind us to new information, or inhibit us from considering a broad range of options when making an important decision and choosing our path carefully. . . . In a hyperconnected world where poor decisions can multiply like a chain reaction, breaking free of unhelpful bias has never been more urgent or important."[87]

the science behind the IAT as a measure of implicit bias.[88] Surprising or not, there is now too much data to ignore.[89] While not all researchers agree,[90] IAT findings have been shown to be connected with real-world responses:[91] "Notably, implicit attitudes show predicative validity; the magnitude of preference exhibited on the test predicts a host of discriminatory behaviors, from nonverbal avoidance to evaluating an individual's work."[92] For those of us who pride ourselves on our fairness, this potential for an unintended implicit bias playing out in our decisions is indeed too much to ignore and needs to give us pause.

B. Implicitly Biased Responses

The following bullets summarize in skeletal form the basic concepts of implicit bias research, providing a backdrop for more detailed and nuanced discussion in later chapters:

- Acquired at an early age, implicit bias is part of being human.[93]

- Scientists can now measure implicit biases using the IAT and other measures.[94]

- After decades of administering the IAT, researchers have concluded that implicit biases are "pervasive."[95]

"Even those who consciously renounce prejudice have been shown to have implicit or automatic biases that conflict with their nonprejudiced values that may disadvantage the targets of these biases."[100]

- Our thinking has been described in two systems: System 1, which is intuitive and quick, and System 2, which is more deliberative and reflective.[96]

- Responding with implicit bias is System 1—it is fast and reflexive, it feels good,[97] and it takes less cognitive energy.[98] (And we do tend to be cognitive misers.)[99]

- These systems are not completely distinct.[101] We need both kinds of thinking, but we also need to know when to call on one or the other. Not all decisions call for a stare rather than a blink, but some do.[102]

- Implicit biases are often different from what we self-report.[103]

- Implicit biases may "become activated automatically, without a person's awareness or intention, and can meaningfully influence people's evaluations and judgments."[104]

- Such biases are often predictive of explicit action or decisions.[105]

- Implicit biases are more prevalent in ambiguous situations,[106] where we are more likely to fall back on mental shortcuts and implicit response.[107] For example, study participants will more likely interpret a "shove" as violent if the "shover" is Black.[108]

- Implicit biases can cause anxiety, which can exacerbate a biased situation and cause other problems.[109]

- Implicit bias is connected to misremembering.[110] For example, research done by Professor Levinson (one of the coauthors of Chapter 3) and his colleagues has shown that participants recalled facts as less aggressive and more mitigating when associated with a typically White name.[111]

- Situations that call for the exercise of discretion are fertile ground for implicit bias.

- "[E]ven high cognitive ability does not protect someone from the effects of bias."[112]

> "We need to accept that intelligence, expertise, and education simply do not reduce bias in a meaningful way."[113]

- Judges are not immune; they "hold implicit biases" that can "influence their judgment."[114] As Professor Rachlinski and Judge Wistrich (coauthors of Chapter 6) concluded in their study, "First, judges, like the rest of us, carry implicit biases concerning race. Second, these implicit biases can affect judges' judgment, at least in contexts where judges are unaware of a need to monitor their decisions for racial bias."[115]

- Judges also are likely to succumb to the "overconfidence effect," where "we believe that we are better than average in a whole host of different ways" including being less biased.[116] As Professor Rachlinski and Judge Wistrich reported, "Our research demonstrates that judges are inclined to make the same sorts of favorable assumptions about their own abilities that non-judges do."[117]

- Ameliorating implicit bias is possible, and several debiasing approaches are discussed in the debiasing section of this overview and in almost all other chapters of this book.

C. Ingroup and Outgroup Response

The findings on implicit bias are related to, and often overlap with, a second area of social science research that considers group identities.[118] We all are part of cultural groups defined by traits such as race, ethnicity, religion, gender, sexual orientation, national origin, family, or social or professional status.[119] Such group identities are one of the major categorization mechanisms that all humans use to process information,[120] and they link to our decision making.[121]

The following bullets summarize, in a general way, the concepts of group-oriented research to provide a backdrop for more detailed and nuanced discussion in later chapters:

- We tend to recognize members of our ingroup more quickly and more accurately.[122]

- As Professors Greenwald and Pettigrew note in their article "With Malice Toward None and Charity for Some: Ingroup Favoritism Enables Discrimination" (reproduced in Chapter 7), our automatic group identification is significant.

"[M]ere classification of people into social groups allows people to understand others with regard to one or a few main characteristics, such as their age, gender, social role, physical appearance, or relation to the self. One should not confuse the process of categorization, which facilitates the ability to think clearly, with the 'cultural baggage' associated with these categories."[123]

- Perhaps more significant than our negative response to outgroups is our positive response to ingroups.[124]

- Our response to others is influenced by our self-concept, which transfers to others like us. Without conscious attention, we start with this assumption: if I am *good* and I am *blue*, then *blue* is *good* . . . and if you are *blue*, then you are also *good*.[125]

- We make connections (or not) when someone appears a certain way—based on age, sex, or race, for example[126]—or is labeled a certain way—for example, American[127] or poor.[128]

- We tend to prefer our own, no matter how we define our own,[129] even if the group is defined "by flimsy and unimportant" characteristics[130] or by no similarities.[131] Indeed, even if we know the group to have been randomly constituted, these loyalties can appear.[132]

- But status tempers ingroup favoritism so that children[133] and adults from groups viewed as higher status show strong implicit bias for their ingroup, while those from other groups may not, favoring, instead, the outgroup—for example, the old favoring the young.[134]

- Differences between groups tend to be exaggerated. We associate positive traits with our ingroup[135] and negative with outgroups.[136]

- We consider those in our ingroup to be more competent, cooperative, confident, independent, intelligent, warm, affirming, tolerant, good-natured, sincere, and concerned with group goals.[137]

- For the ingroup, especially a high-status ingroup, individualistic tendencies or the "propensity to emphasize personal distinctiveness and uniqueness" are more likely to be maintained.[138]

- We treat ingroup members more favorably, and we think it is "fair" that we do so.[139]

- As Professors Greenwald and Pettigrew write in Chapter 7, it's not so much that we are hostile to outgroup members, it's just the "nonoccurrence of a helpful act,"[140] whether because, from our ingroup perspective, we do not perceive there is a problem or whether we do not see that is our responsibility to act.[141]

- Group status also implicitly influences how we think about behavior as in or out of character.[142]

- For outgroup members, we assign blame for someone's poor actions as internal to that person—for example, the person lacks morals. For ingroup members, we attribute poor behavior to something in the external situation—for example, just bad luck.[143]

- This assignment of blame has been described as the "ultimate attribution error,"[144] and it is easy to see the implications in a litigation context.[145]

- As discussed in the implicit bias section above, these group-related tendencies also implicitly influence memory, so that, for example, we are apt to remember the outgroup as more aggressive[146] or to implicitly favor the ingroup and inhibit memory of stereotype-inconsistent aggression for them.[147]

> "These errors are related not to consciously racist attitudes or preferences but to participants "systematically and implicitly mak[ing] stereotype-driven memory errors."[148]

- Attitudes held by the group influence an individual group member's attitudes. For example, if we know our colleagues have an association regarding certain groups—a dislike of Jews for example—then we will likely follow suit.[149]

- While group identities influence our behavior toward others, they also turn inward in what researchers have labeled stereotype threat or boost, where one feels that one is being judged in terms of a stereotype about one's group and where one's performance is influenced by that perception.[150]

- A common example of stereotype threat is girls who internalize the message that girls are not good at math;[151] another example is police officers working under the stereotype threat of being thought racist because they are police officers.[152]

- Working under stereotype threat may cause anxiety, decreased performance, or withdrawal from the enterprise.[153]

- This kind of group dynamic and self-perception can have life-directing consequences.[154]

D. Micromessaging

The effects of implicit biases and group dynamics are reinforced by micromessaging. Micromessages are small messages—calling the male attorneys "mister" and the female attorneys by their first names is a simple example.[156] Another example is the demonstrated tendency to interrupt women more often than men[157] or to credit men more often than women.[158]

Mary Rowe, defining these messages based on her work at Massachusetts Institute of Technology in the early 1970s, described them as Saturn's rings: each dust particle is small, but cumulatively they obscure the planet.[159]

The following bullets summarize micromessaging and provide some context for later chapters of the book:

> "I was born a woman. Thirteen years ago, at the age of 40, I decided to change my sex. I did this not to gain any male advantage, but rather, because of a lifelong gender identity confusion. . . . [B]y far, the biggest difference I have noticed is that people who do not know that I was a woman treat me with far more respect. I can even complete a whole sentence without being interrupted by a man."
>
> —Ben Barres, PhD, Professor of Neurobiology and Chair of the Department of Neurobiology, Stanford University School of Medicine[155]

- Like implicit bias and group dynamics, micromessages often involve implicit assumptions and communications.[160]

- Micromessages can be verbal or nonverbal—what you say or do not say, who you sit next to,[161] what messages[162] or pictures are displayed in your office or courthouse.[163]

- Micromessages can be affirming, conveying inclusion and respect—for example, having your contribution to the meeting meaningfully acknowledged. Or these messages can be negative—for example, not having your work acknowledged when others are acknowledged, or not being noticed when you volunteer for a particular committee assignment (and committee assignments do count!).[164]

- If you are in the ingroup, you are more likely to be the recipient of microaffirmations than microinequities or microaggressions.[165] (This is sometimes called the *Matthew Effect,* from the biblical quotation, "For whomsoever hath, to him shall be given, and he shall have more abundance; but whomsoever hath not, from him shall be taken away even that he hath.")[166]

- Once received, positive or negative, micromessages accumulate[167] and influence engagement, behaviors, and outcomes.[168]

- These messages can have power for the recipient and others. For example, when a person with higher status—a judge for example—acknowledges someone, that acknowledgement influences others to also think better of the acknowledged person—a defendant who has not yet been tried as an innocent person, to use Judge Bennett's example in Chapter 5. The reverse is also true. If a person in authority or power does not acknowledge someone, others are likely to also ignore that person.[169]

- While each message may seem trivial or even meaningless, to the recipient and often to other observers they are not, and they gain intensity as they accumulate.[170]

E. Debiasing

As many other chapters review, research continues to mount as to what may (or may not) prove effective to interrupt and suppress implicit responses in appropriate situations—a process called debiasing.[171] Within this book, our coauthors vary in their perspectives,[173] but all suggest that some interventions can bring about change to break the habit of prejudice.[174] As Drs. Devine and Forscher describe it in Chapter 12, to ameliorate or cause a break in the path of bias calls for *a more reflective* approach, one that is more *mindful* as Judge Fogel describes it in Chapter 15. It is certainly not enough just to tell someone not to be biased.[175] New training[176] and tools[177] are called for—*not* your mother's diversity training[178] (which has not proven all that successful).[179]

"However, the path from implicit bias to discriminatory action is not inevitable. People's awareness of potential bias, their motivation and opportunity to control it, and sometimes their consciously held beliefs can determine whether biases in the mind will manifest in action."[172]

We add one cautionary note before the outline for this section: because implicit biases are human nature, it may be easy to dismiss them as something for which we do not carry individual responsibility. But this cannot be the case; once aware, we need to be mindful and adopt approaches that may help minimize negative or inequitable results that might flow from such biases. In this context, the following bullets outline some points about debiasing, which are amplified in many other chapters:

- Although the evidence is still developing, and with some caution,[180] as discussed from different perspectives in most other chapters, we know it is possible to break habits and ameliorate some of the effects of implicit responses.[181]

- While the exact mechanisms for change continue to be researched,[182] we know that implicit biases are malleable.[183]

- Motivation to be less biased makes a difference.[184] For example, for judges, Professor Rachlinski and Judge Wistrich's research concluded that "when judges are aware of a need to monitor their own responses for the influence of implicit racial biases, and are motivated to suppress that bias, they appear able to do so."[185]

- While research is still emerging, existing research supports initiatives that train us to become aware of our implicit biases—for example, by taking the Implicit Association Test (IAT)[186]—and that educate us as to the manifestation of disparities and impacts of implicit bias in society.[187]

- Such awareness and education, while likely insufficient on their own,[188] provide the underpinning for further training in specific practices that can reduce the impacts of implicit bias[189] at critical decision points.[190]

- Training is likely to work best where it is fashioned with the particular circumstances of judges in mind[191] and where it is longer and more intensive than just an introduction or overview.[192]

- Some implicit responses can be interrupted by adopting new patterns of behavior such as by doing the following:
  o Increasing exposure to positive exemplars[193]
  o Increasing positive contact[194] with counter-typical groups[195] or behavior[196]

- Some implicit responses can be interrupted by attending to the particulars of a situation, such as by doing the following:
  o Individualizing attention (individuating) to consider the individual's characteristics as apart from group stereotypes—thinking about the attributes of this particular person that distinguish him or her from his or her group[197]
  o Considering the individual apart from a given context[198]
  o Slowing down enough to *not* just see what is expected[199]
  o The reverse, considering what we *do* see—it's worthwhile to review the images in your courtroom[200]

- Some implicit biases can be interrupted by adopting certain techniques to brake your thinking and reduce the easy accessibility of stereotypic knowledge and stereotypic response by doing the following:
  o Considering the opposite[201] or plausible alternative(s)—for example, if the facts were applied to the father instead of the mother[202]
  o Taking another's perspective or imagining yourself in the other person's situation—for example, if I found myself unemployed[203]

o Using if-then exercises, where goals are specifically set to be triggered at a certain event; for example, *if* I am deciding to detain a young person, *then* I will consider a set (given number) of options[204]

o Using specific preventive steps such as checklists,[205] bench cards,[206] or decision guides[207]

"In rough terms, if we have a negative attitude toward some group, we need exposure to members of that group to whom we would have a positive attitude. If we have a particular stereotype about some group, we need exposure to members of that group that do not feature those particular attributes."[208]

III. The Concepts Read Together

Implicit bias, group dynamics, and micromessaging have obvious implications for all decision makers. Consider the decision makers who play a role in deciding and judging all along the educational pipeline starting in preschool. These decision makers are part of the process that determines whether that pipeline ends in prison or not.

Consider the actions of these decision makers in the context of implicit bias, group dynamics, and micromessaging.[209] Consider a teacher who decides that a student's name is too hard to learn to pronounce and so calls that student "Frank" to the amusement of the rest of the class.[210] Consider the principal who assumes when her White student is disruptive it's because the student is overtired and calls that student's parents, but who views similar behavior by "Frank" as insubordinate and threatening and suspends him or calls in law enforcement to deal with him.[211] Consider the school resource officer who chats with a White student about an argument that got out of hand in the school cafeteria and then calls that student's parents, but who takes the student of color engaged in that same behavior to police headquarters.[212] Consider how teachers and school administrators then perceive a second infraction by the same student of color, now labeled as troubling, compared with a second offense by the White student.[213] Consider the juvenile justice workers and judges who refer, formally process, and detain these students of color out of proportion to their numbers in the population.[214] Consider the student of color who is charged as an adult and harshly sentenced.[215] This chain is an obvious example of how negatives accumulate—the young person suspended from school is far more likely to find him- or herself in the juvenile justice system than are those who stay in school[216]—and, as might be predicted, these patterns then are paralleled in the adult system.[217]

At each step, the decision makers described here are each most likely acting in good faith, believing themselves to be making objective decisions.[218] Still, when those decisions are read cumulatively, if each is indeed acting in good faith and objectively, it is hard to understand the disproportionate results.[219] These decisions cannot be read as ones that serve to build trust and collective responsibility,[220] nor do they serve to make our schools or institutions safer.[221] Scenarios like these led the National Research Council to observe the following: "Because bias (whether conscious or unconscious) also plays some role, albeit of unknown magnitude, juvenile justice officials should embrace activities designed to increase awareness of unconscious biases and to counteract them, as well as to detect and respond to overt instances of discrimination."[222] We think this advice is applicable to all justice officials; when implicit bias and its correlates in group dynamics and messaging are considered as against what we know about the enduring disproportionalities, new avenues for change become available.

So You'd Like to Know More

Here we include a few old and a few new resources, plus video clips, some of which are definitely entertaining:

- Adam Davidson, *The Lunch Date*, http://www.youtube.com/watch?v=epuTZigxUY8

- ABA, *Hidden Injustice: Bias on the Bench*, http://www.americanbar.org/diversity-portal/diversity-inclusion-360-commission/implicit-bias.html

- Mahzarin R. Banaji & Anthony G. Greenwald, *Blindspot: Hidden Biases of Good People* (2013)

- Pamela M. Casey et al., Nat'l Center for State Courts, *Helping Courts Address Implicit Bias: Resources for Education*, www.ncsc.org/~/media/Files/PDF/Topics/Gender%20and%20Racial%20Fairness/IB_report_033012.ashx

- Daniel Kahneman, *Thinking Fast and Slow* (2011)

- Rosabeth Moss Kanter, *A Tale of O Video on Diversity*, https://www.youtube.com/watch?v=p56b6nzslaU

- Cheryl Staats et al., *State of the Science: Implicit Bias Review*, Kirwan Institute 2016, http://kirwaninstitute.osu.edu/wp-content/uploads/2016/07/implicit-bias-2016.pdf; Kirwan Institute 2015, http://kirwaninstitute.osu.edu/wp-content/uploads/2015/05/2015-kirwan-implicit-bias.pdf; Kirwan Institute 2014, http://kirwaninstitute.osu.edu/wp-content/uploads/2014/03/2014-implicit-bias.pdf; Kirwan Institute 2013, http://kirwaninstitute.osu.edu/docs/SOTS-Implicit_Bias.pdf

About the Authors

Judge Bernice Donald is a judge on the U.S. Court of Appeals for the Sixth Circuit. She has previously served on the U.S. District Court, as the first African-American woman judge of U.S. Bankruptcy Court, and as the first African-American woman judge in the history of the State of Tennessee. She is active in the American, Tennessee, and Memphis Bar Associations, serving most recently as the Chair of the ABA Criminal Justice Section. She has spoken to a large variety of audiences on issues of race and bias, both implicit and explicit.

Professor Sarah Redfield is a law professor at the University of New Hampshire. She is an expert in education law, including special education law, and has written widely on issues of the education pipeline from preschool to the profession, including the school-to-prison pipeline—all areas where implicit bias manifests itself. She has written and spoken widely on the role of implicit bias in education and in the legal profession.

Individually and together, Judge Donald and Professor Redfield are widely respected and experienced presenters on issues of implicit bias for educators and the bench and bar.

ENDNOTES

1. Some of this chapter is taken directly from the authors' previous work on the American Bar Association's project *Achieving an Impartial Jury,* http://www.americanbar.org /groups/criminal_justice/voir_dire.html; from their work with Professor Jason Nance on the American Bar Association's Preliminary Report on the School-to-Prison Pipeline, https://www.americanbar.org/content/dam/aba/administrative/diversity_pipeline/stp _preliminary_report_final.authcheckdam.pdf; Sarah E. Redfield & Jason N. Nance, *Reversing the School to Prison Pipeline,* 47 U. MEMPHIS L. REV. 1 (2016); and from their various presentations and trainings. *See, e.g.,* Sarah E. Redfield, Presentation to the Nebraska State Bar Association: Understanding Implicit Bias to Gain Justice & Equal Opportunity (Oct. 8, 2015); Bernice B. Donald & Sarah E. Redfield, Presentation to the Committee on the Federal Judiciary: Implicit Bias Training (July 31, 2015); Sarah E. Redfield & Jason Nance, Presentation to the Warren County Department of Human Services: Implicit Bias & the School-to-Prison Pipeline (May 29, 2015).
2. For example, African-American students comprised only 16 percent of the student population, but they represented 27 percent of the students who were referred to law enforcement and 31 percent of students who were subject to a school-based arrest. U.S. Dep't of Educ., Office for Civil Rights, Civil Rights Data Collection, *Data Snapshot: School Discipline* 6 (2014), http://ocrdata.ed.gov/Downloads/CRDC-School -Discipline-Snapshot.pdf. These disproportionalities cannot be explained based on bad or worse behavior of students in these groups. U.S. Dep't of Justice & U.S. Dep't of Educ., *Dear Colleague Letter on the Nondiscriminatory Administration of School Discipline* 4 (2014).
3. Brown v. Board of Education, 347 U.S. 483, 495 (1954).
4. *Id.*
5. Brown v. Board of Education II, 349 U.S. 294, 301 (1955).
6. Richard W. Brown, *Freedom of Choice in the South: A Constitutional Perspective,* 28 LA. L. REV. 455 (1968).
7. *Project Implicit,* https://implicit.harvard.edu/implicit/demo/background/faqs.html# faq22 (last visited Nov. 29, 2016).
8. Jerry Kang et al., *Implicit Bias in the Courtroom,* 59 UCLA L. REV. 1124 (2012).
9. Tara Siegel Bernard, *Blacks Face Bias in Bankruptcy, Study Suggests,* N.Y. TIMES, Jan. 20, 2012, http://www.nytimes.com/2012/01/21/business/blacks-face-bias-in-bankruptcy -study-suggests.html (citing Jean Braucher, Dov Cohen & Robert M Lawless, *Race, Attorney Influence, and Bankruptcy Chapter Choice,* 9 J. EMPIRICAL LEGAL STUD. 393 (2012)).
10. Robert J. Smith, Justin D. Levinson & Zoe Robinson, *Implicit White Favoritism in the Criminal Justice System,* 66 ALA. L. REV. 871, 873–74 (2014) (internal citations omitted); *see also* MICHELLE ALEXANDER, THE NEW JIM CROW: MASS INCARCERATION IN THE AGE OF COLORBLINDNESS (2010); Chapters 3 and 13, but see Chapter 12 (questioning cause relationship).
11. Many chapters in the book discuss this, including Chapters 2, 3, 4, 5, 12, and 14; *see also, e.g.,* Professor Goff quoted *infra* at note 42; Emily L. Fisher & Eugene Borgida, *Intergroup Disparities and Implicit Bias: A Commentary,* 68 J. SOC. ISSUES 385, 398 (2012)

(noting "a strong body of evidence in support of the claim that implicit biases are contributing to an understanding of ongoing real-world disparities" and concluding "[a]s such, we believe that implicit bias research will continue to play a crucial role in understanding and hopefully reducing these aggregate-level disparities as they surface in employment, legal, and health care domains").

12. Tania Ralli, *Who's a Looter? In Storm's Aftermath, Pictures Kick Up a Different Kind of Tempest*, N.Y. TIMES, Sept. 5, 2005, http://www.nytimes.com/2005/09/05/business /whos-a-looter-in-storms-aftermath-pictures-kick-up-a-different.html?_r=0 (emphasis added).

13. Interestingly, most of the copies of these images seem to have disappeared from the Web, but they can still be seen here: http://web.archive.org/web/20070115110858 /http://cache.gawker.com:80/news/lootfind.jpg.

14. Several other chapters in the book discuss the media; see particularly Chapters 6 and 8.

15. Travis L. Dixon, *Understanding How the Internet and Social Media Accelerate Racial Stereotyping and Social Division, in* RACE AND GENDER IN ELECTRONIC MEDIA: CONTENT, CONTEXT, CULTURE 216 (Rebecca Lind ed., 2016).

16. *Id.* at 220.

17. *Priming, in* ENCYCLOPEDIA OF SURVEY RESEARCH METHODS 612 (Paul J. Lavrakas ed. 2011); see further discussion *infra* starting at note 66 and accompanying text. This concept is discussed in several other chapters, including, in particular, Chapters 3, 4, and 5.

18. Philip Atiba Goff et al., *Protecting Equity: The Consortium for Police Leadership in Equity Report on the San Jose Police Department* 2 (2016) (cited with permission of the Consortium).

19. *See* R. Richard Banks, Jennifer L. Eberhardt & Leet Ross, *Discrimination and Implicit Bias in a Racially Unequal Society*, 94 CAL. L. REV. 1169, 1170, 1173–76 (2006) (citing Eberhardt et al., *infra* at note 78).

20. Justin D. Levinson, Huajian Cai & Danielle Young, *Guilty by Implicit Bias: The Guilty-Not Guilty Implicit Association Test*, 8 OHIO ST. J. CRIM. L. 187, 190 (2010).

21. Dixon, *supra* note 15, at 220; *see also* Justin D. Levinson, *Suppressing the Expression of Community Values in Jurors: How "Legal Priming" Systematically Alters the Way People Think*, 73 U. CIN. L. REV. 1059 (2005) (finding that just placing a person on a (mock) jury triggers harsher decisions against the outgroup).

22. Dixon, *supra* note 15, at 223.

23. *See* Laura Sydell, *We Tracked Down A Fake-News Creator in the Suburbs. Here's What We Learned, available at* http://www.npr.org/sections/alltechconsidered/2016/11 /23/503146770/npr-finds-the-head-of-a-covert-fake-news-operation-in-the-suburbs (reporting that the story "FBI Agent Suspected in Hillary Email Leaks Found Dead in Apparent Murder-Suicide" was a "totally false story shared half a million times").

24. Dixon, *supra* note 15, at 221.

25. ABA, Section of Litig. *Implicit Bias Toolbox*, ABA http://www.americanbar.org/groups /litigation/initiatives/task-force-implicit-bias/implicit-bias-toolbox.html.

26. ABA Criminal Justice Section, *Building Community Trust Model Curriculum and Instruction Manual*, ABA (2010), http://www.americanbar.org/groups/criminal_justice/pages /buildingcommunity.html.

27. *See generally* ABA, *Diversity & Inclusion 360 Commission*, ABA, https://www.americanbar .org/diversity-portal/diversity-inclusion-360-commission.html.

28. James B. Comey, Dir., Fed. Bureau of Investigation, Remarks at Georgetown University (Feb. 12, 2015), *available at* https://www.fbi.gov/news/speeches/hard-truths -law-enforcement-and-race.

29. Richard Pérez-Peña, *St. Louis County Biased Against Black Juveniles, Justice Department Finds*, N.Y. TIMES, July 31, 2015, http://www.nytimes.com/2015/08/01/us/st-louis -county-biased-against-black-juveniles-justice-department-finds.html?_r=0.

30. Press Release, U.S. Dep't of Justice, Department of Justice Announces New Department-Wide Implicit Bias Training for Personnel (June 27, 2016), *available at* https://www.justice.gov/opa/pr/department-justice-announces-new-department-wide-implicit-bias-training-personnel.

31. *E.g.*, Facebook, *Managing Unconscious Bias* (2016), *available at* https://managingbias.fb.com/ (Facebook training); Google, *Unbiasing* (2016), *available at* https://rework.withgoogle.com/subjects/unbiasing/ (Google's training and resources).

32. *See, e.g.*, Pamela M. Casey et al., Nat'l Center for State Courts, *Helping Courts Address Implicit Bias: Resources for Education*, www.ncsc.org/~/media/Files/PDF/Topics/Gender%20and%20Racial%20Fairness/IB_report_033012.ashx.

33. *See, e.g.*, Texas Dep't of Hous. & Cmty. Affairs v. Inclusive Cmtys. Project, Inc., 135 S. Ct. 2507, 2511–12 (2015) ("Recognition of disparate-impact liability under the [Fair Housing Act] plays an important role in *uncovering discriminatory* intent: it permits plaintiffs to counteract *unconscious prejudices* and disguised animus that escape easy classification as disparate treatment.") (emphasis added); *see also* Karlo v. Pittsburgh Glass Works, LLC, 2017 U.S. App. LEXIS 406, *45 (3d Cir. Pa. Jan. 10, 2017) (referring to potential testimony of Dr. Greenwald, coauthor of Ch. 7: "That is not to say, however, that implicit-bias testimony is never admissible. Courts may, in their discretion, determine that such testimony elucidates the kind of headwind disparate-impact liability is meant to redress. We are simply unable here to conclude that the District Court abused its discretion in excluding this evidence."); Commonwealth v. Warren, 475 Mass. 530 (2016) (observing that Black men may have legitimate reason to run from police and courts should consider findings of a report documenting disproportionate encounters); Washington v. Saintcalle, 309 P.3d 326, 336 (discussing *Batson* and stating "discrimination in this day and age is frequently unconscious and less often consciously purposeful. That does not make it any less pernicious. Problematically, people are rarely aware of the actual reasons for their discrimination and will genuinely believe the race-neutral reason they create to mask it.").

34. Jerry Kang, Nat'l Ctr. for State Courts, *Implicit Bias: A Primer for Courts* 1 (2009), http://www.americanbar.org/content/dam/aba/migrated/sections/criminaljustice/PublicDocuments/unit_3_kang.authcheckdam.pdf.

35. *See, e.g.*, ABA, *Diversity in the Legal Profession: The Next Steps* 9 (Apr. 2010), http://www.americanbar.org/content/dam/aba/administrative/diversity/next_steps_2011.authcheckdam.pdf; *see also* Jason Nance & Paul E. Madsen, *An Empirical Analysis of Diversity in the Legal Profession*, 47 CONN. L. REV. 271, 279 (2014); SARAH E. REDFIELD, DIVERSITY REALIZED: PUTTING THE WALK WITH THE TALK FOR DIVERSITY IN THE LEGAL PROFESSION (2009).

36. *See, e.g.*, Redfield & Nance, *supra* note 1; Sarah E. Redfield & Theresa Kraft, *What Color Is Special Education?*, 41 J.L. & EDUC. 129 (2012), http://ssrn.com/author=723634; Sarah E. Redfield, *Hispanics and the Pipeline to the Legal Profession*, HISPANIC NAT'L BAR ASS'N J.L. & POL'Y (2011).

37. For further citations for data described here, see Nance & Redfield, Preliminary Report, *supra* note 1 *at* 24–54.

38. *E.g.*, Elizabeth R. Peterson et al., *Teachers' Explicit Expectations and Implicit Prejudiced Attitudes to Educational Achievement: Relations with Student Achievement and the Ethnic Achievement Gap*, 42 LEARNING & INSTRUCTION 123, 123 (2016) (concluding that "mathematics achievement scores were largely unrelated to teachers' explicit expectations and that teachers' implicit prejudiced attitudes predicted student performance").

39. Kevin Carey, *No One Rises to Low Expectations*, CHRON. HIGHER EDUC., Nov. 28, 2008, http://www.chronicle.com/article/No-One-Rises-to-Low/7128.

40. Dylan Glover et al., *Discrimination as a Self-Fulfilling Prophecy: Evidence from French Grocery Stores*, Working Paper (2015), http://perso.uclouvain.be/william.pariente/documents/Discrimination%20as%20a%20Self-Fulfilling%20Prophecy.pdf (finding

in a different context, employees working for biased managers work less hard, are absent more, etc.).

41. Sarah E. Redfield, *The Courage to Pay Heed: Knowing and Responding to Implicit Bias*, 17 Woman Advocate (online), *available at* http://apps.americanbar.org/litigation /committees/womanadvocate/articles/summer2012-0812-courage-pay-heed-knowing -responding-implicit-bias.html.

42. Phillip Atiba Goff, *A Measure of Justice: What Policing Racial Bias Research Reveals, in* Beyond Discrimination: Racial Inequality in a Post-Racist Era 157, 173 (Fredrick C. Harris & Robert C. Lieberman eds., 2013).

43. *Id.* at 172–73.

44. Justin D. Levinson, Mark Bennett & Koichi Hioki, *Judging Implicit Bias: A National Empirical Study of Judicial Stereotypes Beyond Black and White*, 69 Fl. L. Rev. __ (forthcoming 2017).

45. *See generally Implicit Bias, in* Stanford Encyclopedia of Philosophy, http://plato.stanford .edu/entries/implicit-bias/#IndMeaAtt; Anthony G. Greenwald et al., *Measuring Individual Differences in Implicit Cognition: The Implicit Association Test*, 74 J. Personality & Soc. Psychol. 1464 (1998).

46. This concept is discussed in several other chapters, including Chapters 10, 12, and 14.

47. See Chapter 15.

48. Kang, *supra* note 34.

49. We use the implicit bias vocabulary here, but the vocabulary describing the brain's dual response mechanisms does vary. *See, e.g.*, Matthew D. Lieberman, *Reflective and Reflexive Judgment Processes: A Social Cognitive Neuroscience Approach, in* Social Judgments: Implicit and Explicit Processes 44 (Joseph P. Forgas et al. eds., 2003) (using reflexive/reflective or x/c); Daniel Kahneman, Thinking Fast and Slow (2011) (using fast/ slow and System 1/System 2); *see generally* Pam Casey, Kevin Burke & Steve Leben, Am. Judges Ass'n, *Minding the Court: Enhancing the Decision-Making Process* (2012), http:// aja.ncsc.dni.us/pdfs/Minding-the-Court.pdf (discussing terminology and approach).

50. *See* Matthew D. Lieberman et al., *Breaking Bias*, 5 Neuroleadership 1–17 (2013), *available at* http://www.scn.ucla.edu/pdf/Lieberman(2014)NLI.pdf (providing an extensive list of biases that may influence our responses/decisions often without our awareness).

51. Attitudes are our evaluations of some concept (person, place, thing, or idea). *Frequently Asked Questions*, Project Implicit, https://implicit.harvard.edu/implicit/faqs.html (last visited Nov. 16, 2016).

52. Stereotypes are our beliefs that most members of a group have a particular characteristic. *Id.*

53. *See* Kang, *supra* note 34, at 1.

54. *See, e.g.*, Patricia G. Devine, *Stereotypes and Prejudice: Their Automatic and Controlled Components*, 56 J. Personality & Soc. Psychol. 5, 5–6, 15 (1989); Brian A. Nosek & Rachel G. Riskind, *Policy Implications of Implicit Social Cognition*, 6 Soc. Issues & Pol'y Rev. 113 (2012).

55. Kyle Munzenrieder, *Miami Beach Police Caught Sending Hundreds of Racist and Sexist E-Mails*, Miami New Times, May 14, 2015, http://www.miaminewtimes.com/news /miami-beach-police-caught-sending-hundreds-of-racist-and-sexist-e-mails-7615984.

56. Am. Civil Liberties Union, *Black, Brown and Targeted: A Report on Boston Police Department Street Encounters from 2007–2010* at 1–2 (2014), https://aclum.org/sites/all/files /images/education/stopandfrisk/black_brown_and_targeted_online.pdf (discussing differences in "Field Interrogation, Observation, Frisk and/or Search").

57. Dominique Mosberger, *Jessica Mendoza Makes Baseball History, Prompting Sexist Backlash*, Huffington Post, Oct. 17, 2015, http://www.huffingtonpost.com/entry /jessica-mendoza-playoffs_5614d906e4b0cf9984d7a353.

58. Rhea E. Steinpreis et al., *The Impact of Gender on the Review of the Curricula Vitae of Job Applicants and Tenure Candidates: A National Empirical Study*, 41 Sex Roles 509, 509

(1999) (demonstrating that men get more votes to hire even where their records are identical to women's).

59. Ernesto Reuben, Paola Sapienza & Luigi Zingales, *How Stereotypes Impair Women's Careers in Science*, 111 Proc. Nat'l. Acad. Sci. 4403, 4404–05 (2014) (showing that employers will choose a male employee over a female employee for a job requiring arithmetic skills even where actual task results show the female with better test scores).

60. Arin N. Reeves, *Colored by Race: Bias in the Evaluation of Candidates of Color by Law Firm Hiring Committees: The 2015 Update & Summary of Data from 2005* (2015), http://www .nextions.com/wp-content/files_mf/14479367492015111 5ColoredbyRaceYPS.pdf ("Racial/ethnic minority candidates are also more likely to receive negative comments about their names, the lack of 'polish' in their overall appearance, and their 'comfort levels' in talking with people in the firm.").

61. Arin N. Reeves, *Written in Black & White: Exploring Confirmation Bias in Racialized Perceptions of Writing Skills* (2014), http://www.nextions.com/wp-content/files_mf/144 68226472014040114WritteninBlackandWhiteYPS.pdf (demonstrating empirically significant evaluation differences when law firm reviewing partners were provided with an associate's work with race/ethnicity designation as Caucasian or African-American on identical writing samples).

62. *See, e.g.*, John B. McConahay, *Modern Racism, Ambivalence, and the Modern Racism Scale*, *in* Prejudice, Discrimination, and Racism 91 (John Dovidio et al. eds., 1986); Smith, *supra* note 10, at 878.

63. *See* David M. Amodio & Patricia G. Devine, *On the Interpersonal Functions of Implicit Stereotyping and Evaluative Race Bias: Insights from Social Neuroscience*, *in* Attitudes: Insights from the New Implicit Measures 193 (Richard E. Petty et al. eds., 2008).

64. Willhem Hofmann et al., *A Meta-Analysis on the Correlation between the Implicit Association Test and Explicit Self-Report Measures*, 31 Personality & Soc. Psychol. Bull. 1369, 1370 (2005); Brian A. Nosek et al., *The Implicit Association Test at Age 7: A Methodological and Conceptual Review*, *in* Social Psychology and the Unconscious: The Automaticity of Higher Mental Processes 265 (John A. Bargh ed., 2007).

65. *See* Anthony G. Greenwald et al., *Understanding and Using the Implicit Association Test: III. Meta-analysis of Predictive Validity*, 97 J. Personality & Soc. Psychol. 17 (2009); Cheryl Staats et al., Kirwin Inst. for the Study of Race and Ethnicity, *State of the Science: Implicit Bias Review* 26 (2013) (summarizing review of reliability and validity).

66. *Priming*, Psychol. Today, https://www.psychologytoday.com/basics/priming (last visited Nov. 16, 2016).

67. Daniel T. Gilbert & J. Gregory Hixon, *The Trouble of Thinking: Activation and Application of Stereotypic Beliefs*, 60 J. Personality & Soc. Psychol. 509, 510–11 (1991) (revealing that a prime presented by an Asian research assistant as compared to a Caucasian assistant activated ethnic stereotypes of Asians such that those primed completed more stereotypic words (for example, RICE, POLITE) than those not primed).

68. John A. Bargh et al., *Automaticity of Social Behavior: Direct Effects of Trait Construct and Stereotype Activation on Action*, 71 J. Personality & Soc. Psychol. 230, 236 (1996).

69. Neil Macrae & Lucy Johnston, *Help, I Need Somebody: Automatic Action and Inaction*, 16 Soc. Cognition 400, 413 (1998).

70. Jerry Kang, Nilanjana Dasgupta, Kumar Yogesswarn & Gary Blasi, *Are Ideal Litigators White? Measuring the Myth of Colorblindness*, 7 J. Empirical Legal Stud. 886, 912 (2010) (discussing a client's preference for a White lawyer); *see also* Chapter 4 (elaborating further on these relationships).

71. *See, e.g.*, Walter S. Gilliam et al., *Do Early Educators' Implicit Biases Regarding Sex and Race Relate to Behavior Expectations and Recommendations of Preschool Expulsions and Suspensions?* (2016), *available at* http://ziglercenter.yale.edu/publications/Preschool%20 Implicit%20Bias%20Policy%20Brief_final_9_26_276766_5379.pdf.

72. L. Song Richardson & Phillip A. Goff, *Implicit Racial Bias in Public Defender Triage*, 122 YALE L.J. 2626, 2636–37 (2013) (discussing public defender relationship with clients).

73. Maya Sen, *Is Justice Really Blind? Race and Appellate Review in U.S. Courts*, 44 J. LEG. STUD-IES 187, 187, 192, 194–95 (2015), *available at* http://j.mp/SnB591 ("[B]lack federal district judges are consistently overturned on appeal more often than white district judges, a gap in reversal of up to ten percentage points. This gap is robust and persists after taking into account previous professional and judicial experience, educational backgrounds, qualification ratings assigned by the American Bar Association, and differences in appellate panel composition.").

74. The workings of the IAT are discussed in many chapters of the book, including Chapters 3, 4, and 5; *see also About the IAT*, Project Implicit, https://implicit.harvard.edu /implicit/iatdetails.html (last visited Nov. 16, 2016).

75. David M. Amodio, *The Neuroscience of Prejudice and Stereotyping*, 15 NATURE REV. NEURO-SCI. 640, 640 (2014); *see also, e.g.,* Anthony G. Greenwald & Linda Hamilton Krieger, *Implicit Bias: Scientific Foundations*, 94 CALIF. L. REV. 945, 948 (2006); Cheryl Staats et al., *supra* note 65, at 26–34 (providing an overview of method).

76. Illustration from Amodio, *supra* note 75, at 674.

77. *About the IAT*, Project Implicit, https://implicit.harvard.edu/implicit/iatdetails.html (last visited Nov. 16, 2016).

78. *See* Jennifer L. Eberhardt, Phillip Atiba Goff, Valerie J. Purdie & Paul G. Davies, *Seeing Black: Race, Crime, and Visual Processing*, 87 J. PERSONALITY & SOC. PSYCHOL. 876, 891 (2004) (showing a quicker connection between Black faces and crime-related objects); *see also* Joshua Correll et al., *Across the Thin Blue Line: Police Officers and Racial Bias in the Decision to Shoot*, 92 J. PERSONALITY & SOC. PSYCHOL. 1006 (2007); *but see* Lois James, Stephen M. James & Bryan J. Vile, *The Reverse Racism Effect: Are Cops More Hesitant to Shoot Black than White Suspects?*, 15 CRIMINOLOGY & PUB. POL'Y 457, 457, 460–61, 469–71 (2016) (reporting that in deadly force simulations, Blacks are less likely to be shot); Chapter 3.

79. *See, e.g.,* Amodio, *supra* note 75, at 674; Jennifer T. Kubota, Mahzarin R. Banaji & Elizabeth A. Phelps, *The Neuroscience of Race*, 15 NATURE NEUROSCI. 940, 942, 944 (2012) (reviewing and cumulating the research).

80. Chapters 3 and 5; *see also, e.g.,* Theodore Eisenberg & Sheri Lynn Johnson, *Implicit Racial Attitudes of Death Penalty Lawyers*, 53 DEPAUL L. REV. 1539, 1542 (2004) (finding, in early use of the IAT, that capital defense lawyers showed implicit biases against Blacks).

81. Seventy percent of the sample show a pro-White implicit preference and twelve percent pro-Black. *Black-White IAT Results: Feedback*, Project Implicit, https://implicit .harvard.edu/implicit/takeatest.html (last visited Jan. 25, 2016) (testing available that shows one's implicit biases on race relative to others, with the statistics cited). The remaining percent score shows preference in neither direction. The bias is more dominant in White test takers, but some Blacks also show pro-White results, though in a more nuanced way. Project Implicit reports, "Data collected from this website consistently reveal approximately even numbers of Black respondents showing a pro-White bias as show a pro-Black bias. Part of this might be understood as Black respondents experiencing the similar negative associations about their group from experience in their cultural environments, and also experiencing competing positive associations about their group based on their own group membership and that of close relations."

82. IAT results show that women are more strongly associated with family and men are more strongly associated with careers. Seventy-six percent of the sample show women-family preference, 6.3 percent women-career preference. *Gender-Career IAT Results: Feedback*, Project Implicit, https://implicit.harvard.edu/implicit/takeatest.html (last visited Jan. 25, 2016) (testing available that shows one's implicit biases on gender

relative to others, with the statistics cited); Justin D. Levinson & Danielle Young, *Implicit Gender Bias in the Legal Profession: An Empirical Study*, 18 Duke J. Gender L. & Pol'y 1, 3–4 (2010) (finding that law students more readily associate men with judges and women with paralegals).

83. IAT results show 76 percent of the sample show a pro-abled implicit preference, in contrast to 9 percent pro-disabled *See Disability IAT Results: Feedback*, Project Implicit, https://implicit.harvard.edu/implicit/takeatest.html (last visited Jan. 25, 2016) (testing available that shows one's implicit biases on disability relative to others).

84. *See, e.g.*, Patricia G. Devine, *Implicit Prejudice and Stereotyping: How Automatic Are They? Introduction to the Special Section*, 81 J. Personality & Soc. Psychol. 757, 757 (2001) (summarizing development and interest in the IAT).

85. *See* Nancy Hopkins, Amgen, Inc. Professor of Biology at MIT, Baccalaureate Address at Boston University, *Invisible Barriers and Social Change* (May 18, 2014), *available at* http://www.bu.edu/news/2014/05/19/boston-universitys-141st-commencement -baccalaureate-address-nancy-hopkins/ (describing discovery of unconscious bias as one of greatest scientific discoveries of the past 50 years).

86. Robert J. Smith & Justin D. Levinson, *The Impact of Implicit Racial Bias on the Exercise of Prosecutorial Discretion*, 35 Seattle U. L. Rev. 795, 797–98 (2012) (noting this interest and cumulating references); *see also, generally, e.g.*, Casey, *supra* note 32; Jerry Kang, Judge Mark Bennett, Devon Carbado, Pam Casey, Nilanjana Dasgupta, David Faigman, Rachel Godsil, Anthony G. Greenwald, Justin Levinson & Jennifer Mnookin, *Implicit Bias in the Courtroom*, 59 UCLA L. Rev. 1124 (2012).

87. Lieberman et al., *supra* note 50, at 1–2.

88. *See, e.g.*, Mahzarin R. Banaji & Anthony G. Greenwald, Blindspot: Hidden Biases of Good People 49–52 (2013); Anthony G. Greenwald, *IAT Studies Showing Validity with "Real-World" Subject Populations* (2012), http://faculty.washington.edu/agg/pdf/Real-world _samples.pdf; Nosek et al., *supra* note 64, at 265; Anthony G. Greenwald, Mahzarin R. Banaji & Brian A. Nosek, *Statistically Small Effects of the Implicit Association Test Can Have Societally Large Effects*, 108 J. Personality & Soc. Psychol. 553, 557–58 (2015) (discussing how effects are predictable from IATs either where a small number has widespread application or where the number cumulates to affect one or a few persons many times).

89. *E.g.*, John T. Jost, Laurie A. Rudman, Irene V. Blair, Dana R. Carney, Nilanjana Dasgupta, Jack Glaser & Curtis D. Hardin, *The Existence of Implicit Bias Is Beyond Reasonable Doubt: A Refutation of Ideological and Methodological Objections and Executive Summary of Ten Studies that No Manager Should Ignore*, 29 Org. Behav. 39, 39 (2009) (summarizing ten studies finding that "students, nurses, doctors, police officers, employment recruiters, and many others exhibit implicit biases with respect to race, ethnicity, nationality, gender, social status, and other distinctions" and concluding that "participants' implicit associations do predict socially and organizationally significant behaviors, including employment, medical, and voting decisions made by working adults"); Kang & Banaji, *Fair Measures: A Behavioral Realist Revision of Affirmative Action*, 94 Calif. L. Rev. 1063, 1074–75 (2006).

90. *See, e.g.*, Frederick L. Oswald et al., *Predicting Ethnic and Racial Discrimination: A Meta-Analysis of IAT Criterion Studies*, 105 J. Personality & Soc. Psychol. 170, 171 (2013) ("IATs were poor predictors of every criterion category other than brain activity, and the IATs performed no better than simple explicit measures."); *see generally* Justine E. Tinkler, *Controversies in Implicit Race Bias Research*, 6 Soc. Compass 987, 992–93 (2012) (providing overview).

91. Fisher & Borgida, *supra* note 11, at 392 (summarizing criticism and concluding that "[r]egardless of any debate over IAT validity, the broader point that is often lost amidst the methodological and ideological cacophony is that considerable implicit

bias research goes beyond the IAT and uses methods that have been regarded with less criticism . . . using these types of techniques also finds that implicit bias predicts a variety of behavioral outcomes in intergroup domains").

92. Kubota, *supra* note 79, at 942; *see also* Allen R. McConnell & Jill M. Liebold, *Relations Among the Implicit Association Test, Discriminatory Behavior, and Explicit Measures of Attitudes*, 37 J. EXPERIMENTAL SOC. PSYCHOL. 435, 440 (2001) (concluding that "researchers can be confident that attitudes assessed by the IAT do relate to intergroup behavior"); Greenwald, Banaji & Nosek, *supra* note 88, at 553–54.

93. Sarah E. Hailey & Kristina R. Olson, *A Social Psychologist's Guide to the Development of Racial Attitudes*, SOC. & PERSONALITY PSYCHOL. COMPASS 457, 459–60, 462–63 (2013) (explaining that infants can distinguish faces based on race as early as three months, though it is not clear what they prefer at that age, and that by preschool, their preferences are remarkably like adults' preferences for ingroup/status, are evident and appear to remain stable).

94. See discussion *supra* at notes 74–76.

95. *Id;* Brian Nosek et al., *Pervasiveness and Correlates of Implicit Attitudes and Stereotypes*, 18 EUROPEAN REV. SOC. PSYCHOL. 36 (2007), *available at* http://projectimplicit.net/nosek /stimuli/.

96. *E.g.*, Kahneman, *supra* note 49, at 26; see also Chapters 5, 6, and 15.

97. Matthew D. Lieberman, *Research*, Soc. Cognitive Neuroscience Lab., http://www.scn .ucla.edu/research.html (last visited Nov. 16, 2016).

98. DAVID ROCK & HEIDI GRANT HALVORSON, BREAKING WORKPLACE BIAS AT THE SOURCE 13–14 (2015), https://neuroleadership.com/wp-content/uploads/2015/03/Breaking-Workplace -Bias-at-its-Source_Rock_17Mar15.pdf (describing "biases of expedience," which include availability bias, confirmation bias, and the halo effect).

99. GORDON ALLPORT, THE NATURE OF PREJUDICE 20–21 (1954) ("We like to solve problems easily. We can do so best if we can fit them rapidly into a satisfactory category and use this category as a means of prejudging the solution. . . . So long as we can get away with coarse overgeneralizations we tend to do so. Why? Well, it takes less effort, and effort, except in the area of our most intense interests, is disagreeable.").

100. *E.g.*, Devine, *supra* note 84, at 757.

101. Philip N. Meyer, *Psychological Shortcuts: A Behavioral Economist's Work Offers Lessons for Legal Storytellers about Judgment and Decision-Making*, 102 ABA J. 26 (Jan. 2016) ("Strategic exposure to what is seemingly 'irrelevant' matters profoundly."); see also Chapters 5 (describing the division into two systems as an "imperfect fiction") and 6.

102. Donald & Redfield, *supra* note 1.

103. See discussion and references *supra* note 64.

104. Mason D. Burns, Laura Ruth M. Parker & Margo J. Monteith, *Self-Regulation Strategies for Combatting Prejudice*, in THE CAMBRIDGE HANDBOOK OF THE PSYCHOLOGY OF PREJUDICE 3 (Chris G. Sibley & Fiona Kate Barlow eds., 2016), *available at* www.psych.purdue .edu/~mmonteit/assets/burns,-parker,---monteith-(in-press).docx (last visited Nov. 15, 2016).

105. See discussion and references *supra* note 78; *see also, e.g.*, Brian A. Nosek, *Implicit Social Cognition: From Measures to Mechanisms*, 15 TRENDS COGNITIVE SCI. 152, 152 (2011); Jeffery J. Rachlinski, Sheri Lynn Johnson, Andrew J. Wistrich & Chris Guthrie, *Does Racial Bias Affect Trial Judges?*, 84 NOTRE DAME L. REV. 1195, 1196 (2009); *but see* James et al., *supra* note 78, at 457 (finding that "despite clear evidence of implicit bias against Black suspects, officers were slower to shoot armed Black suspects than armed White suspects, and they were less likely to shoot unarmed Black suspects than unarmed White suspects" and concluding that these "findings challenge the assumption that implicit racial bias affects police behavior in deadly encounters with Black suspects.").

106. *See* Gordon Hodson, John F. Dovidio & Samuel L. Gaertner, *Processes in Racial Discrimination: Differential Weighting of Conflicting Information*, 28 Personality & Soc. Psychol. Bull. 460, 460 (2002) (finding that when a candidate is clearly great or clearly poor, race doesn't seem to matter, but where not so clear, race becomes (unconscious) factor).

107. *See* Kurt Hugenberg & Galen V. Bodenhausen, *Facing Prejudice: Implicit Prejudice and the Perception of Facial Threat*, 14 Psychol. Sci. 640, 640 (2003) (showing White observers are quicker to observe anger in ambiguously hostile African-American faces than in White); *see also* Justin D. Levinson & Danielle Young, *Different Shades of Bias: Skin Tone, Implicit Racial Bias, and Judgments of Ambiguous Evidence*, 112 W. Va. L. Rev. 307 (2010).

108. *See* Birt L. Duncan, *Differential Social Perception and Attribution of Intergroup Violence: Testing the Lower Limits of Stereotyping of Blacks*, 34 J. Personality & Soc. Psychol. 590, 596–97 (1976) (describing research involving viewing a video of an ambiguous shove where White observers were much quicker to call the shove violent where performed by a Black than by a White participant).

109. *See, e.g.*, Jennifer A Richeson & J. Nicole Shelton, *When Prejudice Does Not Pay: Effects of Interracial Contact on Executive Function*, 14 Psychol. Sci. 287, 287 (2003) ("Research suggests, however, that intergroup interaction is often a source of anxiety and distress for members of dominant groups" and may impair subsequent cognitive function).

110. *See generally* Danny Osborne & Paul G. Davies, *Crime Type, Perceived Stereotypicality, and Memory Biases: A Contextual Model of Eyewitness Identification*, 28 Appl. Cognit. Psychol. 392, 394 (2014) (describing that "the type of crime committed systematically affects whom eyewitnesses mistakenly identify"); Mark W. Bennett, *Unspringing the Witness Memory and Demeanor Trap: What Every Judge and Juror Needs to Know About Cognitive Psychology and Witness Credibility*, 64 Notre Dame L. Rev. 1331, 1335 (2015).

111. Justin D. Levinson, *Forgotten Racial Equality: Implicit Bias, Decisionmaking, and Misremembering*, 57 Duke L.J. 345, 394, 399–401 (2007) (finding that when participants read two short stories, with some participants assigned to the story with the protagonist with a typically Black name, Tyronne; some to stories with a typically Hawaiian name, Kawika; and some to stories with typically White name, William, they recalled facts from the stories such that Tyronne and Kawika were more aggressive with fewer mitigating factors than William).

112. Lieberman, *supra* note 50, at 4.

113. *Id.* at 6. Indeed, there is research that suggests that when a person believes he or she is objective, that gives license to be less so. Kang et al., *supra* note 86, at 1173.

114. Rachlinski, *supra* note 105, at 1197; Levinson, *supra* note 44, at 18 (summarizing the research and while noting most research to date has focused on Black and White, finding thus for Asians and Jews).

115. Rachlinski, *supra* note 105, at 1221; *see also* Adam N. Glynn & Maya Sen, *Identifying Judicial Empathy: Does Having Daughters Cause Judges to Rule for Women's Issues?* 59 Am. J. Pol. Sci. 37 (2015).

116. Lieberman, *supra* note 50, at 9; Rachlinski, *supra* note 105, at 1225 (finding that 97 percent of judges in the study believed they were in the top quartile of judges in "avoiding racial prejudice in decisionmaking").

117. Rachlinski, *supra* note 105, at 1228 (observing that "while education regarding implicit bias as a general matter might be useful, specific training revealing the vulnerabilities of the judges being trained would be more useful").

118. Chapter 7; Rock & Halvorson, *supra* note 98, at 12 (describing these responses as biases of similarity).

119. *See* ABA Criminal Justice Section, *Building Community Trust Model Curriculum and Instruction Manual*, ABA (2010), http://www.americanbar.org/groups/criminal_justice /pages/buildingcommunity.html.http://www.americanbar.org/content/dam/aba /migrated/sections/criminaljustice/PublicDocuments/bctext.authcheckdam.pdf. Culture is also described as shared meanings and shared language or representational communications. *Id.*

120. Galen V. Bodenhausen, Sonia K. Kang & Destiny Peery, *Social Categorization and the Perception of Social Groups*, *in* SAGE HANDBOOK OF SOCIAL COGNITION 311 (Susan T. Fiske & C. Neil Macrae eds., 2012).

121. Merlin Donald, *How Culture and Brain Mechanisms Interact in Decision Making*, *in* BETTER THAN CONSCIOUS? DECISION MAKING, THE HUMAN MIND, AND IMPLICATIONS FOR INSTITUTIONS 191 (Christoph Engel & Wolf Singer eds., 2008) (e-book) ("The human brain does not acquire language, symbolic skills, or any form of symbolic cognition without the pedagogical guidance of culture and, as a result, most decisions made in modern society engage learned algorithms of thought that are imported from culture.").

122. Michael J. Bernstein et al., *The Cross-Category Effect: Mere Social Categorization Is Sufficient to Elicit an Own-Group Bias in Face Recognition*, 18 PSYCHOL. SCI., 706, 706, 710 (2007).

123. CONFRONTING RACISM: THE PROBLEM AND THE RESPONSE 40 (Jennifer Lynn Eberhardt & Susan T. Fiske eds., 1998).

124. *See* Anthony G. Greenwald & Thomas F. Pettigrew, *With Malice toward None and Charity for Some: Ingroup Favoritism Enables Discrimination*, 69 AM. PSYCHOL. 669, 670 (2014), reproduced *infra* at Chapter 7 ("this article builds a case for understanding ingroup favoritism as not just *a* cause but as the *prime* cause of American discrimination"); Charles W. Perdue et al., *Us and Them: Social Categorization and the Process of Intergroup Bias*, 59 J. PERSONALITY & SOC. PSYCHOL. 475, 478–79, 482–84 (1990); *see also* Smith, *supra* note 10, at *passim*.

125. *See* Bertram Gawronski et al., *I Like It, Because I Like Myself: Associative Self-Anchoring and Post-Decisional Change of Implicit Attitudes*, 43 J. EXPERIMENTAL SOC. PSYCHOL. 221 (2007); Laurie A. Rudman, *Social Justice in Our Minds, Homes, and Society: The Nature, Causes, and Consequences of Implicit Bias*, 17 SOC. JUSTICE RES. 129, 137 (2004); Laurie A. Rudman, *Sources of Implicit Attitudes*, 13 CURRENT DIRECTIONS PSYCHOL. SCI. 79, 79 (2004); Casey, *supra* note 32, at B3 (describing as "self anchoring").

126. *See* Nilanjana Dasgupta, *Implicit Ingroup Favoritism, Outgroup Favoritism, and Their Behavioral Manifestations*, 17 SOC. JUST. RES. 143 (2004) (summarizing the research); Nayeli Y. Chavez-Dueña et al., *Skin-Color Prejudice and Within-Group Racial Discrimination: Historical and Current Impact on Latino/a Populations*, 36 HISP. J. BEHAV. SCI. 3 (2014); Jennifer A. Richeson & Samuel R. Sommers, *Toward a Social Psychology of Race and Race Relations for the Twenty-First Century*, 67 ANN. REV. PSYCHOL. 439, 441–43 (discussing how even the categorization by race can be a malleable category and noting relationship between stereotypes and malleability).

127. *See, e.g.*, Thierry Devos & Mahzarin Banaji, *American = White?*, 88 J. PERSONALITY & SOC. PSYCHOL. 447 (2005).

128. John M. Darley & Paget H. Gross, *A Hypothesis-Confirming Bias in Labeling Effects*, 44 J. PERSONALITY & SOC. PSYCHOL. 20, 20 (1983) (showing that after witnessing the same video of nine-year-old Hannah taking a test, "those who had information that the child came from a high SES rated her abilities well above grade level, whereas those for whom the child was identified as coming from a lower-class background rated her abilities as below grade level").

129. Hailey, *supra* note 93, at 457 (summarizing research data that adults' strong tendency is to favor their own groups, with race as a key indicator of group identity, that adults show "a surprisingly strong consensus in their assessment of the relative status of

different groups," and that group status influences their responses to others). See also Chapter 6. Appearance is not the only basis for defining a group. We also sometimes define "our own" based on similar attitudes. *See* Donn Byrne, *Interpersonal Attraction and Attitude Similarity*, 62 J. ABNORMAL & SOC. PSYCHOL. 713, 713–15.

130. Henri Tajfel, *Experiments in Intergroup Discrimination*, 223 SCI. AM. 96, 101 (1970) (counting dots and choosing an abstract artist).

131. Michael Billig & Henri Tajfel, *Social Categorization and Similarity in Intergroup Behaviour*, 3 EUROPEAN J. SOC. PSYCHOL. 27, 47–48 (1973).

132. Greenwald & Pettigrew, *supra* note 124, at 671 (summarizing research and describing this "minimal group paradigm").

133. *See, e.g.*, Claude M. Steele, *Race and the Schooling of Black Americans*, THE ATLANTIC (April 1992) (observing that "because these images are conditioned in all of us, collectively held, they can spawn racial devaluation in all of us, not just in the strongly prejudiced" and that these images "can do this even in blacks themselves: a majority of black children recently tested said they like and prefer to play with white rather than black dolls—almost fifty years after Kenneth and Mamie Clark, conducting similar experiments, documented identical findings"); Anna-Kaisa Newheiser & Kristina R. Olson, *White and Black American Children's Implicit Intergroup Bias*, 48 J. EXPERIMENTAL SOC. PSYCHOL. 264, 264 (2012).

134. Dasgupta, *supra* note 126, at 143, 147, 149; *see also* Greenwald & Pettigrew, *supra* note 124, at 674 (explaining how extending favoritism to an already advantaged outgroup works to "exacerbate the relative disadvantage of lower status groups").

135. Perdue et al., *supra* note 124, at 476–80.

136. *See* Bodenhausen, Kang & Peery, *supra* note 120, at 317; Bernadette Park & Myron Rothbart, *Perception of Out-Group Homogeneity and Levels of Social Categorization: Memory for the Subordinate Attributes of In-Group and Out-Group Members*, 42 J. PERSONALITY & SOC. PSYCHOL. 1051 (1982); *see also* Yael Granot et al., *Justice Is Not Blind: Visual Attention Exaggerates Effects of Group Identification on Legal Punishment*, 143 J. EXPERIMENTAL PSYCHOL. 2196 (2014).

137. *See* Perdue et al., *supra* note 123, at 476–84; *see also* Marilyn B. Brewer, *The Psychology of Prejudice: Ingroup Love or Outgroup Hate?*, 55 J. SOC. ISSUES 429, 438 (1999) (observing that "the absence of overt antagonism toward outgroups, is not benign" and that research shows that the "essence of 'subtle racism' is not the presence of strong negative attitudes toward minority outgroups but the absence of positive sentiments toward those groups").

138. Vincenzo Iacoviello & Fabio Lorenzi-Cioldi, *Individualistic Tendencies: When Group Status Makes the Difference*, 18 GROUP PROCESSES & INTERGROUP REL. 540, 540–41 (2015); Jennifer G. Boldry, Lowell Gaertner & Jeff Quinn, *Measuring the Measures: A Meta-Analytic Investigation of the Measures of Outgroup Homogeneity*, 10 GROUP PROCESSES & INTERGROUP REL. 157, 164, 172 (2007) (reviewing the literature and noting that the general rule of perceived outgroup homogeneity may be moderated by status).

139. Greenwald & Pettigrew, *supra* note 124, at 675.

140. *Id.* at 673.

141. See Chapter 10 (discussing the literature on "helping" behavior).

142. Brenda L. Russell & Linda S. Melillo, *Attitudes toward Battered Women Who Kill: Defendant Typicality and Judgments of Culpability*, 33 CRIM. JUSTICE & BEHAVIOR 219, 223–29 (2006) (discussing in another context how jurors view a "battered woman defense" and suggesting the defense is found more believable if "out of character"); see further discussion of this in Chapter 13.

143. *See* Thomas Pettigrew, *The Ultimate Attribution Error*, 5 PERSONALITY & SOC. PSYCHOL. BULL. 461, 461 (1979).

144. *See id.*

145. Assessing guilt readily falls within this paradigm. *Id.* ("(1) when prejudiced people perceive what they regard as a negative act by an outgroup member, they will more than others attribute it dispositionally, often as genetically determined, in comparison to the same act by an ingroup member: (2) when prejudiced people perceive what they regard as a positive act by an outgroup member, they will more than others attribute it in comparison to the same act by an ingroup member to one or more of the following: (a) 'the exceptional case,' (b) luck or special advantage, (c) high motivation and effort, and (d) manipulable situational context").

146. Levinson, *supra* note 111, at 348–49.

147. Smith, *supra* note 10, at 901.

148. Levinson, *supra* note 111, at 389–90.

149. *See* Reeves, *supra* note 60, at 3–4; *see also* Reeves, *supra* note 61, at 44; *see generally* Ap Dijksterhuis & John A. Bargh, *The Perception-Behavior Expressway: Automatic Effects of Social Perception on Social Behavior*, 33 ADV. EXPERIMENTAL PSYCHOL. 1, 32 (2001) (discussing imitation and noting that imitation can be inhibited if some other process intervenes).

150. *See* Smith, *supra* note 10, at 894–95; Claude M. Steele, *A Threat in the Air: How Stereotypes Shape Intellectual Identity and Performance*, 52 AM. PSYCHOL. 613, 614 (1997); Claude M. Steele, *Stereotyping and Its Threat Are Real*, 53 AM. PSYCHOL. 680, 680–81 (1998); CLAUDE M. STEELE, WHISTLING VIVALDI AND OTHER CLUES TO HOW STEREOTYPES AFFECT US (2010); see also Chapter 3.

151. Margaret J. Shih et al., *Stereotype Susceptibility: Identity Salience and Shifts in Quantitative Performance*, 10 PSYCHOL. SCI. 80, 82 (1999) (observing that when Asian-American women are primed with primes for both Asian stereotypes and gender stereotypes, the former boosts their performance but the latter reduces it).

152. *See* Goff, *supra* note 18, at 5.

153. *See generally Should I Be "Shipley" or "Flores Collazo" Today? The Racialization of the Law Student and Legal Workplace Candidate*, 31 BERKELEY J. GENDER L. & JUST. 183 (providing an overview of ways stereotype threat and microaggressions impact Latino/a law students); Goff, *supra* note 18, at 11 (discussing levels of stereotype threat and use of force ratios).

154. *See* Shih, *supra* note 151, at 82 (describing "the powerful influence of sociocultural stereotypes on individual performance" as triggered not explicitly but when identity is "made salient at an implicit level" to enhance performance, or not); *see also, e.g.,* Brian A. Nosek, Mahzarin R. Banaji & Anthony Greenwald, *Math = Male, Me = Female, Therefore Math ≠ Me*, 83 J. PERSONALITY & SOC. PSYCHOL. 44, 44 (explaining that because they associate math with males, even females who had chosen math-intensive majors couldn't easily associate math with themselves); *see generally* Dasgupta, *supra* note 126, at 163 (noting that new research "suggests that implicit biases exhibited by individuals who belong to socially disadvantaged groups towards their own group may have unintended behavioral consequences that are harmful to their ingroup and themselves"); Russell G. Pearce et al., *Difference Blindness vs. Bias Awareness: Why Law Firms with the Best of Intentions Have Failed to Create Diverse Partnerships*, 83 FORDHAM L. REV. 2407 (2015).

155. Ben Barres, *Does Gender Matter?*, 442 NATURE 133, 135 (2006).

156. Sarah E. Redfield, Presentation to the University of New Hampshire Faculty Chairs: Advancing Women in STEM Fields (May 15, 2016).

157. Arin N. Reeves, *Mansplaining, Manterrupting & Bropropriating: Gender Bias and the Pervasive Interruption of Women* 7 (2015), http://www.nextions.com/wp-content/files_mf /14285084452015041 5ManterruptionsBropropriationandMansplaining2YPS.pdf?utm _source=Nextions+Impact&utm_campaign=2752202dd8-April_2015_Impact4_8_2015 &utm_medium=email&utm_term=0_5cb2ba7743-2752202dd8-334161021.

158. The *Punch* cartoon is an easily grasped example. First published in 1985, it remains relevant. The chairman of the board says to the only woman at the table, "That's an excellent suggestion Ms. Triggs. Perhaps one of the men here would like to make it." Riana Duncan, Punch (1985), *available at* http://punch.photoshelter.com/gallery /Riana-Duncan-Cartoons/G0000Bx1FqQLTU1M/.

159. Mary Rowe, *The Saturn's Rings Phenomenon*, 50 Harv. Med. Alumni Bull. 14 (1975).

160. While some writers describe some of these messages as intentional, we focus here on the unintentional aspects. Derald Wing Sue, Microaggressions in Everyday Life: Race, Gender, and Sexual Orientation 29 (2010) (outlining various forms of micromessages, most unintentional).

161. *See* Dasgupta, *supra* note 126, at 155–60 (2004) (discussing implicit-nonverbal behavior); *see also* Chapter 8.

162. Chapter 9 (discussing fairness pledge posted by Alaska state courts).

163. Consider, for example, female law students' view when every picture in the law school lobby is a portrait of a White male; there is no intent here, as all former deans were White males. *See generally* Nilanjana Dasgupta & Anthony G. Greenwald, *On the Malleability of Automatic Attitudes: Combating Automatic Prejudice with Images of Admired and Disliked Individuals*, 81 J. Personality & Soc. Psychol. 800, 800 (2001).

164. *See generally* ABA Presidential Task Force on Gender Equity and the Commission on Women in the Profession, *Gender Pay Equity in Law Firm Partner Compensation*, http://www .americanbar.org/content/dam/aba/administrative/women/closing_the_gap.authcheckdam .pdf (reporting that law firms with no women on management committees promoted "significantly fewer women" than did those firms with a "'critical mass' of three or more women" on those committees); Arturo Casadevall & Jo Handelsman, *The Presence of Female Conveners Correlates with a Higher Proportion of Female Speakers at Scientific Symposia*, 5 mBIO (2014), http://mbio.asm.org/content/5/1/e00846-13.full; *see also* Jennifer L. Peresie, Note, *Female Judges Matter: Gender and Collegial Decisionmaking in the Federal Appellate Courts*, 144 Yale L.J. 1759, 1778 (2005).

165. *See* JoAnn Moody, *Rising Above Cognitive Errors: Improving Searches, Evaluations, and Decision-Making* (2010), *available at* http://www.ccas.net/files/ADVANCE/Moody%20 Rising%20above%20Cognitive%20Errors%20List.pdf; Mary P. Rowe, *Barriers to Equality: The Power of Subtle Discrimination to Maintain Unequal Opportunity*, 3 Emp. Resp. & Rts. J. 153 (1990); Mary Rowe, *Micro-affirmations & Micro-inequities*, 1 J. Int'l Ombudsman Ass'n 45 (2008).

166. Robert K. Merton, *The Matthew Effect in Science*, 159 Sci. 56, 63; *see generally* Stephen Young, Micromessaging: Why Great Leadership Is Beyond Words (2006); Brianne Dávila, *Critical Race Theory, Disability Microaggressions and Latina/o Student Experiences in Special Education*, in Race Ethnicity & Educ. 443, 458 (2015) (describing "disregard" as a microaggression).

167. *See* Sue, *supra* note 160, at 6–7.

168. *See, e.g.*, Virginia Valian, Why So Slow? The Advancement of Women 4 (1999); Caroline E. Simpson, *Nibbled to Death by Ducks: The Accumulation of Disadvantage*, Am. Astronomical Soc. Meeting Abstracts, 216 (2010); Redfield, *supra* note 156.

169. *See* Valian, *supra* note 168, at 4. Some bias research describes this as "contagious." Max Weisbuch & Kristin Pauker, *The Nonverbal Transmission of Intergroup Bias: A Model of Bias Contagion with Implications for Social Policy*, 5 Soc. Issues & Policy Rev. 257 (2011).

170. Shipley, nee Flores Collazo, *supra* note 153, at 202.

171. *See, e.g.*, Lieberman, *supra* note 50, at 14; Kerry Kawakami, John F. Dovidio & Simone van Kamp, *The Impact of Counterstereotypic Training and Related Correction Processes on the Application of Stereotypes*, 10 Group Processes & Intergroup Rel. 139, 139 (2007) (finding that "correction is a deliberate and calibrated process that people use strategically to compensate for undesired external influence").

172. Dasgupta, *supra* note 126, at 143.

173. See, e.g., Chapters 3, 4, 5, 9, 10, 12, and 14.

174. See, e.g., Chapters 11 and 12; Patricia G. Devine et al., *Long-Term Reduction in Implicit Bias: A Prejudice Habit-Breaking Intervention*, 48 J. EXPERIMENTAL Soc. PSYCHOL. 1267, 1268 (2012).

175. *See generally* C. Neil Macrae, Galen V. Bodenhausen, Alan B. Milne & Jolanda Jetten, *Out of Mind but Back in Sight: Stereotypes on the Rebound*, 67 J. PERSONALITY & Soc. PSYCHOL. 808, 815 (1994) ("As a consequence of post suppression rebound effects, formerly unwanted stereotypic thoughts were shown to return and impact on perceivers' treatment of a stereotyped target."); Chapter 13.

176. *See, e.g.*, Jessi L. Smith et al., *Now Hiring! Empirically Testing a Three-Step Intervention to Increase Faculty Gender Diversity in STEM*, 65 BIOSCIENCE 1084, 1086 (2015) (describing successful training regarding faculty STEM hiring); National Council of Juvenile and Family Court Judges, *Courts Catalyzing Change, Preliminary Protective Hearing Benchcard Study Report: Report Testing a Tool for Judicial Decision-Making*, http://www.ncjfcj.org /sites/default/files/CCC%20Benchcard%20Study%20Report.pdf (describing successful training for the National Council for Juvenile and Family Court Judges); *see generally* Burns, *supra* note 104; Devine, *supra* note 174 (describing successful training); but see Chapter 12 (raising some questions).

177. See Chapters 10 and 12.

178. So described in a Fair and Impartial Policing training Professor Redfield observed; *see also Fair & Impartial Policing*, http://www.fairimpartialpolicing.com/ (last visited Nov. 17, 2016).

179. *E.g.*, Frank Dobbin & Alexandra Kalev, *Why Diversity Programs Fail*, HARV. BUS. REV., July–Aug. 2016, at 52–60, *available at* https://hbr.org/2016/07/why-diversity-programs-fail.

180. *See, e.g.*, Calvin K. Lai et al., *Reducing Implicit Racial Preferences: II. Intervention Effectiveness Across Time*, 145 J. EXPERIMENTAL PSYCHOL. 1001, 1002 (2016) (questioning effectiveness over time); Calvin K. Lai et al., *Reducing Implicit Racial Preferences: I. A Comparative Investigation of 17 Interventions*, 143 J. EXPERIMENTAL PSYCHOL.: GENERAL 1765 (2014) (reporting on results of a competition to find effective methods for changing implicit bias). But see Alex Madva, *Biased Against Debiasing: On the Role of (Institutionally Sponsored) Self-Transformation in the Struggle Against Prejudice* (forthcoming Ergo) (asking why other writers and reviewers are so reluctant to accept the value of such training to change implicit biases and raising the question of whether the "absence of evidence is evidence of absence" in terms of the ongoing worry about "relearning" bias and of demonstrating lasting effects of certain debiasing training).

181. *See, e.g.*, Devine, *supra* note 54, at 5–6, 15 (1989); Rachlinski, *supra* note 105, at 1197. As with measurement of implicit bias generally, scientists have found that certain regions of the brain are activated when we are "braking" against too quick a response. Lieberman, *supra* note 50, at 5.

182. Thomas C. Mann & Melissa J. Ferguson, *Can We Undo Our First Impressions? The Role of Reinterpretation in Reversing Implicit Evaluations*, 108 J. PERSONALITY & Soc. PSYCHOL. 823, 824 (2015) (reporting positively on a "heretofore little-examined possibility: that . . . when new information forces a reinterpretation of the prior impression, reversal of implicit evaluations may be possible"); Nilanjana Dasgupta, Presentation to the Mind Science Conference: Debiasing Implicit Attitudes (Apr. 26, 2013).

183. *E.g.*, Dasgupta, *supra* note 126, at 158–59 (2004); *but see generally* Lai I and II, *supra* note 180.

184. Katherine T. Bartlett, *Making Good on Good Intentions: The Critical Role of Motivation in Reducing Implicit Workplace Discrimination*, 95 VA L. REV. 1893 (2009); Dasgupta, *supra* note 126, at 158 (2004); Devine et al., *supra* note 174, at 1267; Patricia G. Devine et al., *The Regulation of Explicit and Implicit Race Bias: The Role of Motivations to Respond*

without Prejudice, 82 J. PERSONALITY & SOC. PSYCHOL. 835 (2002); Margo J. Monteith, Jill E. Lybarger & Anna Woodcock, *Schooling the Cognitive Monster: The Role of Motivation in the Regulation and Control of Prejudice*, 3 SOC. & PERSONALITY PSYCHOL. COMPASS 211 (2009).

185. Rachlinski, *supra* note 105, at 1221; *see also* Chapter 5; Joyce Ehrlinger et al., *Peering into the Bias Blind Spot: People's Assessments of Bias in Themselves and Others*, 31 PERSONALITY & SOC. PSYCHOL. BULL. 680, 690–91 (2005); Joyce Ehrlinger, Ainsley L. Mitchum & Carol S. Dweck, *Understanding Overconfidence: Theories of Intelligence, Preferential Attention, and Distorted Self-Assessment*, 63 J. EXPERIMENTAL SOC. PSYCHOL. 94, 99 (2016) (outlining strategies to address overconfidence).

186. *See* Alexander R. Green et al., *Implicit Bias among Physicians and Its Prediction of Thrombolysis Decisions for Black and White Patients*, 22 J. GEN. INTERNAL MED. 1231, 1237 (2007) ("These findings support the IAT's value as an educational tool."); *see also* Jennifer K. Elek & Paula Hannaford-Agor, *First, Do No Harm: On Addressing the Problem of Implicit Bias in Juror Decision Making*, 49 CT. REV. 190 (2013) (suggesting that although mock jurors who were given the implicit bias instruction responded to it in "subtle ways," the instruction did not produce any backfire or harmful effect); *but see* Jacquie D. Vorauer, *Completing the Implicit Association Test Reduces Positive Intergroup Interaction Behavior*, 23 PSYCHOL. SCI. 1168 (2012) (finding that White participants' taking race-based IAT led to their non-White (Aboriginal) partners feeling less well regarded than after a non-race-based IAT).

187. See Chapters 8, 12, and 13.

188. *Id.*; see also Chapters 6, 10, and 11.

189. See Chapter 12; *see also, e.g.*, Smith et al., *supra* note 176, at 1086; Tom R. Tyler, Phillip Attiba Goff & Robert J. MacCoun, *The Impact of Psychological Science on Policing in the United States: Procedural Justice, Legitimacy, and Effective Law Enforcement*, 16 PSYCHOL. SCI. PUB. INT. 75 (2015); Lorie Fridell & Sandra Brown, *Fair and Impartial Policing: A Science Based Approach*, POLICE CHIEF, June 2015, at 20–25, *available at* http://www.policechiefmagazine.org/fair-and-impartial-policing-a-science-based-approach/.

190. *See generally* Casey, *supra* note 32, at 6–7; Sarah E. Redfield & Jason Nance, Presentation to Clark County Diversity Leaders: Understanding Implicit Bias (Dec. 10, 2015); Nance & Redfield, *supra* note 1.

191. Rachlinski, *supra* note 105, at 1228; Ehrlinger et al., *supra* note 185.

192. See Chapters 8 and 12; *see also* Lai II, *supra* note 180, at 1013.

193. *See* Corey Columb & E. Ashby Plant, *The Obama Effect Six Years Later: The Effect of Exposure to Obama on Implicit Anti-Black Evaluative Bias and Implicit Racial Stereotyping*, 34 SOC. COGNITION 523, 526, 538 (2016) (cumulating references and finding that research shows that exposure to exemplars can change implicit attitudes regarding the exemplars' social group but not necessarily explicit attitudes); *but see* Kathleen Schmidt & Jordan R. Axt, *Implicit and Explicit Attitudes toward African Americans and Barack Obama Did Not Substantively Change During Obama's Presidency*, 34 SOC. COGNITION 559, 559 (2016).

194. *See, e.g.*, Nilanjana Dasgupta & Luis M. Rivera, *When Social Context Matters: The Influence of Long-Term Contact and Short-Term Exposure to Admired Outgroup Members on Implicit Attitudes and Behavioral Intentions*, 26 SOC. COGNITION 112, 115 (2008) (finding that prior experience with the outgroup is significant in predicting "implicit attitudes toward gays and lesbians and their willingness to vote for equal rights for this group," but so did brief positive intervention).

195. Bertram Gawronski et al., *When "Just Say No" Is Not Enough: Affirmation versus Negation Training and the Reduction of Automatic Stereotype Activation*, 44 J. EXPERIMENTAL SOC. PSYCHOL. 370 (2008) (showing the influence of training on selecting women for employment); Thomas F. Pettigrew, *Intergroup Contact Theory*, 49 ANN. REV. PSYCHOL. 65 (1998); Thomas F. Pettigrew & Linda R. Tropp, *A Meta-Analytic Test of Intergroup*

Contact Theory, 90 J. PERSONALITY & SOC. PSYCHOL. 751 (2006); *see also* Lai I, *supra* note 180, at 1778; Chapter 12.

196. Shaki Asgari, Nilanjana Dasgupta & Nicole Gilbert Cote, *When Does Contact with Successful Ingroup Members Change Self-Stereotypes? A Longitudinal Study Comparing the Effect of Quantity vs. Quality of Contact with Successful Individuals*, 41 SOC. PSYCHOL. 203, 203 (2010) ("Frequent contact with ingroup members predicted stronger implicit self-conceptions of leadership and more career ambitions, but only when contact experiences were of high quality rather than superficial. Quality and quantity of contact independently predicted assertive behavior."); Lai I and II, *supra* note 180 (discussing vivid counterstereotypes).

197. *See, e.g.*, Markus Brauer et al., *Describing a Group in Positive Terms Reduces Prejudice Less Effectively than Describing It in Positive and Negative Terms*, 48 J. EXPERIMENTAL SOC. PSYCHOL. 757, 757-58 (2012); *see also* Irene V. Blair, *The Malleability of Automatic Stereotypes and Prejudice*, 6 PERSONALITY & SOC. PSYCHOL. REV. 242, 255 (2002); *but see* Greenwald & Pettigrew, *supra* note 124, at 675 (suggesting stereotypes may well "insinuate themselves subtly" into individuated judgments).

198. Bernd Wittenbrink, Charles M. Judd & Bernadette Park, *Spontaneous Prejudice in Context: Variability in Automatically Activated Attitudes*, 81 J. PERSONALITY & SOC. PSYCHOL. 815, 815 (2001) (showing that when study participants saw a video with a positive stereotypic context (church or family barbecue), there was significantly less "spontaneous prejudice bias" than when the video had a negative stereotypic context (street corner or gang-related incident)).

199. Matthew Riccio, Shana Cole & Emily Balcetis, *Seeing the Expected, the Desired, and the Feared: Influences on Perceptual Interpretation and Directed Attention*, 7 SOC. & PERSONALITY PSYCHOL. COMPASS 401, 402, 404 (2013).

200. *See, e.g.*, Cecelia Trenticosta & William C. Collins, *Death and Dixie: How the Courthouse Confederate Flag Influences Capital Cases in Louisiana*, 27 HARV. J. RACIAL & ETHNIC JUST. 125, 144, 149 (2011); Robert J. Smith & Bidish J. Sarma, *How and Why Race Continues to Influence the Administration of Criminal Justice in Louisiana*, 72 LA. L. REV.361 (2012); Kerry Kawakami, Curtis E. Phills, Jennifer R. Steele & John F. Dovidio, *(Close) Distance Makes the Heart Grow Fonder: Improving Implicit Racial Attitudes and Interracial Interactions through Approach Behaviors*, 92 J. PERSONALITY & SOC. PSYCHOL. 957 (2007).

201. *See* Charles G. Lord et al., *Considering the Opposite: A Corrective Strategy for Social Judgment*, 47 J. PERSONALITY & SOC. PSYCHOL. 1231, 1239 (1984) (reporting that participants "induced to consider the opposite" either by direct instructions or by making the opposite "more salient" showed "greater corrective effect than more demand-laden alternative instructions to be as fair and unbiased as possible"); see also, e.g., Chapters 5 and 10.

202. *See* Edward R. Hirt & Keith D. Markman, *Multiple Explanation: A Consider-an-Alternative Strategy for Debiasing Judgments*, 69 J. PERSONALITY & SOC. PSYCHOL. 1069, 1069 (1995) (reporting that "debiasing occurred in all multiple explanation conditions, including those that did not involve the opposite outcome" and noting that the "perceived plausibility" of the alternative was important).

203. Example from Chapter 14; *see* Adam D. Galinsky & Gordon B. Moskowitz, *Perspective-Taking: Decreasing Stereotype Expression, Stereotype Accessibility, and In-Group Favoritism*, 78 J. PERSONALITY & SOC. PSYCHOL. 708, 709 (2000); Andrew R. Todd, Galen V. Bodenhausen, Jennifer A. Richeson & Adam D. Galinsky, *Perspective Taking Combats Automatic Expressions of Racial Bias*, 100 J. PERSONALITY & SOC. PSYCHOL. 1027, 1027 (2011) (explaining that perspective taking prompts "more favorable automatic interracial evaluations" and "does not blind perceivers to the realities of interracial disparities").

204. Peter M. Gollwitzer, *Weakness of the Will: Is a Quick Fix Possible?*, 38 MOTIVATION & EMOTION 305, 308 (2014) (reporting "vast empirical evidence that if–then planners

act more quickly, deal more effectively with cognitive demands . . . and do not need to consciously intend to act in the critical moment"); *see also* Macrae & Johnston, *supra* note 69, at 400 (observing that if "inhibitory cues" such as a competing goal were present, then "automatic behavioral priming effects were eliminated").

205. Atul Gawande, The Checklist Manifesto: How to Get Things Right (2009).

206. *See* National Council of Juvenile and Family Court Judges, *supra* note 176.

207. Pamela M. Casey et al., Nat'l Ctr. for State Courts, *Strategies to Reduce the Influence of Implicit Bias* 12, http://www.ncsc.org/~/media/Files/PDF/Topics/Gender%20and%20 Racial%20Fairness/IB_Strategies_033012.ashx; Geoffrey Beattie, Doron Cohen & Laura McGuire, *An Exploration of Possible Unconscious Ethnic Biases in Higher Education: The Role of Implicit Attitudes on Selection for University Posts*, 197 Semiotica 171 (2013); see also Chapter 13.

208. Kang et al., *supra* note 86, at 1170.

209. See background and additional references for this section in Nance & Redfield, *supra* note 1 (delineating disproportionality at virtually every decision-making point in the juvenile justice system); *see also* Daniel J. Losen & Jonathan Gillespie, Opportunities Suspended: The Disparate Impact of Disciplinary Exclusion From School 35–37 (2012), http://civilrightsproject.ucla.edu/resources/projects/center-for-civil-rights -remedies/school-to-prison-folder/federal-reports/upcoming-ccrr-research/losen -gillespie-opportunity-suspended-2012.pdf.

210. Rita Kohlia & Daniel G. Solórzano, *Teachers, Please Learn Our Names!: Racial Microaggressions and the K-12 Classroom*, 15 Race Ethnicity & Educ. 441, 451 (2012).

211. U.S. Dep't of Educ. Office for Civil Rights, Civil Rights Data Collection, *Data Snapshot: School Discipline* 6 (2014). The CRDC also shows that African-American students (16 percent of the population reported in the CRDC sample) are 27 percent of students referred to law enforcement and 31 percent of students subject to school-related arrest. American Indian-Alaskan Native (AIAN) numbers are also out of proportion. Although AIAN students amount to 1 percent of the student population, they are 3 percent of students referred to law enforcement and 2 percent of students subject to school-related arrest. For White students, only 41 percent are referred to law enforcement and 39 percent are subject to school-related arrest, both lower than their 51 percent of the population. *Id.*

212. *See id.; see generally* Linnea Nelson; Victor Leung & Jessica Cobb, *The Right to Remain a Student: How California School Policies Fail to Protect and Serve* (2016), https://www.aclunc .org/sites/default/files/20161019-the_right_to_remain_a_student-aclu_california_0.pdf.

213. Jason A. Okonofua & Jennifer L. Eberhardt, *Two Strikes: Race and the Disciplining of Young Students*, 26 Psychol. Sci. 617, 617, 622 (2015) (describing "Black escalation" where students of color are more harshly perceived and punished over time).

214. National Council on Crime and Delinquency, And Justice for Some: Differential Treatment of Youth of Color in the Justice System 1–2 (2007) (describing differences at each step of the process), *available at* http://www.nccdglobal.org/sites/default/files /publication_pdf/justice-for-some.pdf (last visited Nov. 15, 2016).

215. *See* Aneeta A. Rattan et al., *Race and the Fragility of the Legal Distinction between Juveniles and Adults*, 5 PloS one e36680, Abstract (2012) (concluding that priming with Black led participants "to view juveniles in general as significantly more similar to adults in their inherent culpability and to express more support for severe sentencing" and that the results "highlight the fragility of protections for juveniles when race is in play").

216. *See* Jason P. Nance, *Dismantling the School-to-Prison Pipeline: Tools for Change*, 48 Ariz. St. L.J. 313, 324 (2016) (reporting for example that "with each subsequent exclusionary punishment the student received, the odds of involvement with the juvenile justice system further increased").

217. *E.g.*, Marc Mauer, *Addressing Racial Disparities in Incarceration*, 91 Prison J. 875 *passim*, file:///C:/Users/Sarah%20Thinkpad/Downloads/Addressing-Racial-Disparities-in -Incarceration.pdf.

218. *See* Eric Luis Uhlmann & Geoffrey L. Cohen, *"I Think It, Therefore It's True": Effects of Self-Perceived Objectivity on Hiring Discrimination*, 104 Org. Behavior & Hum. Decision Processes 207 (2007); *see also* Laurie T. O'Brien et al., *But I'm No Bigot: How Prejudiced White Americans Maintain Unprejudiced Self-Images*, 40 J. Applied Soc. Psychol. 917 (2010).

219. National Center for Youth Law, *Implicit Bias and Juvenile Justice: A Review of the Literature, passim* (Michael Harris & Hannah Benton eds., 2014) (reviewing research on all these points).

220. Jason P. Nance, *Students, Police, and the School-to-Prison Pipeline*, 93 Wash. U. L. Rev. 919, 927; Chapters 8 and 9.

221. Daniel J. Losen & Russell Skiba, Suspended Education: Urban Middle Schools in Crisis 2 (2010), http://www.splcenter.org/sites/default/files/downloads/publication /Suspended_Education.pdf (concluding that there is no evidence that frequent reliance on removing misbehaving students improves school safety or student behavior).

222. Comm. on Assessing Juvenile Justice Reform, Nat'l Research Council, *Reforming Juvenile Justice: A Developmental Approach* 7 (Richard J. Bonnie et al. eds., 2013), http://www.nap.edu/download.php?record_id=14685#.

Chapter 3

Implicit Bias

A Social Science Overview[1]

Justin D. Levinson, Danielle M. Young,
and Laurie A. Rudman

Chapter Contents

Chapter Highlights

- Research on implicit bias suggests that when implicit stereotypes are activated, the human mind is prone to making critical mistakes.

- The Implicit Association Test (IAT) has been shown to predict discriminatory decision making and behavior in a broad range of contexts.

- In light of the evidence linking implicit bias to a variety of discriminatory outcomes, legal scholars and empiricists must consider deeply the various ways in which implicit bias may affect all areas of the law in which disparities appear.

Introduction

At approximately 3:30 p.m. on November 22, 2014, Cleveland patrol officers Timothy Loehmann and Frank Garmback arrived at a local park after a police dispatcher received a report of a Black male, "probably a juvenile," sitting on a park swing and pointing a "probably fake" handgun at people.[2] As Garmback drove the car to a rapid stop less than ten feet away from 12-year old Tamir Rice, who had been playing alone with an Airsoft toy gun,[3] Loehmann leaped out of the stopping vehicle and rapidly fired two shots, one of which hit Rice in the abdomen. Although Rice was critically injured by the officer's bullet, neither Loehmann nor Garmback provided medical assistance. Rice died from the gunshot wound the next day.

Despite the recommendations by a Cleveland judge that probable cause existed to charge both officers with crimes, including Loehmann with various forms of homicide, a grand jury declined to prosecute either officer for the shooting.[4] This decision not to indict indicates that the grand jury likely believed two key pieces of information: first, that Loehmann thought Rice was not a child playing at a park with a toy but rather a criminal; and second, that Loehmann and Garmback thought that the boy was preparing imminently to shoot either them—the police—or civilians. How could trained officers possibly perceive a playing 12-year-old as a gun-toting threat worthy of immediate and lethal force?

Research on implicit bias suggests that when implicit stereotypes are activated, the human mind is prone to making critical mistakes, such as turning a playing 12-year-old into a gun-toting aggressor. When researchers describe implicit bias, they are referring to "attitudes or stereotypes that affect our understanding, decision making, and behavior, without our even realizing it."[5] For more than a decade, researchers have explored how implicit bias (as contrasted with self-reported, or explicit, bias) contributes to systematic racial discrimination. One fundamental aspect of the implicit attitudes uncovered by implicit social cognition research is that they frequently differ from people's self-reported (often egalitarian) racial attitudes. Because of the automatic nature of these biases, people are often unaware of them or how they affect their judgments.

> Research on implicit bias suggests that when implicit stereotypes are activated, the human mind is prone to making critical mistakes, such as turning a playing 12-year-old into a gun-toting aggressor.

In this chapter, we lay the foundation for studying implicit bias in the law by examining examples from over two decades of research on unconscious and automatic activation of stereotypes. This examination includes a discussion of the ease with which racial stereotypes are activated (particularly through the phenomenon known as priming), a consideration of how social scientists measure implicit bias (including the Implicit Association Test and the shooter bias video game), and an exploration of the relationship between implicit bias and real-world behaviors and decision making. The chapter concludes by describing empirical studies of implicit bias in the legal system.

I. Racial Priming: The Unconscious Activation of Stereotypes

Cognitive psychologists coined the term *priming* to describe an associative process whereby a stimulus exposure has an effect on a subsequent task. Psychologists have defined it as "the incidental activation of knowledge structures, such as trait concepts and stereotypes, by the current situational context."[6] Simply put, priming studies show how causing someone to think about a particular domain can trigger associative networks related to that domain.[7] Activating these associative networks, which can include stereotypes, can affect people's decision making and behavior, often without their conscious awareness.

A. Ease of Activation

Racial and ethnic stereotypes can be primed with ease. In one simple and elegant study, participants watched a video in which a research assistant held cue cards containing word fragments.[8] All participants watched identical videos, except the ethnicity of the research assistant was changed for each group. Half of the participants saw a video in which the research assistant was Asian; the other half saw a video in which the research assistant was White. In the video, the assistant held cue cards containing incomplete words, including words that were potentially stereotypic of Asians, such as "RI_E," "POLI_E," "S_ORT," and "S_Y." Participants were asked to generate as many word completions as possible for each card during a 15-second period. Results of the study showed that simply seeing an Asian research assistant was enough to activate ethnic stereotypes of Asians. Participants who watched the video with the Asian assistant completed more stereotypic words (RICE, POLITE, SHORT, and SHY) than participants who watched the video with the White assistant.

The cue card study demonstrated that even simple visual cues (seeing an Asian person) can prime a person's racial and ethnic stereotypes. Laurie Rudman and Matthew Lee tested whether auditory, rather than visual, cues could similarly prime participants' racial stereotypes.[9] Participants in their study listened to either rap or pop music for 13 minutes.[10] As they hypothesized, Rudman and Lee found that rap music indeed activated participants' racial stereotypes, including stereotypes associating Black Americans with attributes such as hostile, violent, and dangerous. Furthermore, participants whose racial stereotypes were activated subsequently rated a Black (but not a White) person's behavior as less intelligent and more hostile. Finally, participants' self-reported (explicit) prejudice levels did not predict their judgments of a Black person, indicating that automatic biases can leak into people's decision making without their endorsement or awareness. This study demonstrates that auditory primes (such as hearing music) can automatically activate a network of associated implicit racial stereotypes.

Research has also shown that racial categories can be activated by stereotype-related primes. Black Americans are often stereotypically associated with crime. Jennifer Eberhardt and her colleagues primed some participants with crime-related images,[11] such as a police badge, a fingerprint, and guns, as part of a "dot-probe" task that measures attention by seeing how quickly participants can find a dot on a screen. This dot was presented on a computer screen near either a White male or a Black male face. The results demonstrated that participants who were primed with crime-related images were faster to find the dot near Black faces compared to participants who were not primed, suggesting a high degree of cognitive association between the concepts *crime* and *Black male*. The researchers found similar results by priming participants with basketball-related words, a positively valenced Black stereotype. Participants who had been primed with basketball-related words found the dot faster near Black faces than participants who were not primed.

B. Decision Making and Behavioral Consequences of Priming

Racial stereotypes are not only primed easily in a variety of situations, but their activation can also promote bias in decision making and behavior. Keith Payne examined how merely showing participants a photograph of a White or Black face for 200 milliseconds could affect the speed at which they could subsequently identify weapons.[12] In the study, participants saw photos of Black or White faces followed immediately by photos of objects. The participants' only task, Payne told them, was to quickly identify the objects when they appeared on the screen.[13] Payne also told them that the flashing photographs of faces served only to signal the participant that a photograph of an object was about to appear. The study found that when participants saw photos of Black faces immediately before photos of guns, they were significantly faster at identifying the guns. Similarly, when participants saw photos of White faces immediately before photos of tools, they were significantly faster at identifying the tools. Payne's study shows that racial associations can be elicited automatically in a fraction of a second, and that these stereotypes can affect the speed and accuracy of meaningful object classification tasks.

In addition to affecting object recognition, priming can also affect people's judgments of others' behavior. Patricia Devine had participants watch flashing category words that were associated with African-Americans, such as

> Racial stereotypes are not only primed easily in a variety of situations, but their activation can also promote bias in decision making and behavior.

"Blacks" and "Negroes," and stereotype words that were associated with African-Americans, such as "poor" and "athletic."[14] After the priming was accomplished, participants read a story about a man engaging in behaviors that might be interpreted one way or another—such as withholding rent until the landlord made repairs—and were asked to make judgments about the person engaging in these ambiguous behaviors. Participants who were primed with more stereotyped words judged the actor's ambiguous behavior as more hostile than participants who were primed with fewer stereotyped words. As Devine summarized, "The automatic activation of the racial stereotype affects the encoding and interpretation of ambiguously hostile behaviors for both high- and low-prejudice subjects."[15] Although traits such as "poor" and "athletic" are unrelated to the trait of "hostile," the stereotype congruence between the primed social category (Blacks) and the trait of hostility made participants more likely to judge a behavior as hostile.

Another study of priming's effects on impression formation was conducted by James Johnson and Sophie Trawalter, who, like Rudman and Lee, used rap music to prime negative Black stereotypes. In their study, Johnson and Trawalter primed participants by playing segments of either a violent or nonviolent rap song.[16] Participants later read supposedly unrelated stories of violent behavior (e.g., breaking car windows) on the part of either a Black or White man upset about a romantic breakup and were asked to make judgments about the cause of his actions. Those who heard the violent rap music, compared to other participants, judged a Black male's, but not a White male's, aggressive behavior as caused by dispositional factors (e.g., a violent personality) rather than situational factors (e.g., alcohol or stress related to the breakup). In addition, participants who heard the violent rap music were more likely to judge a different man, described as an applicant for a job requiring intelligence, as unqualified if he was Black rather than White. This study shows that racial stereotype primes (here, rap music) can influence seemingly unrelated judgments (here, job qualification) so long as they are both stereotypes of African-Americans. When people make such dispositional attributions for antisocial behavior, it has implications for the legal system because criminal punishments and tort awards, for example, often take into account whether transgressions are judged as due to "character" (a stable cause) rather than due to "situation" (an unstable cause).

C. Priming and the Self: Stereotype Threat

Thus far, the priming research we have reviewed shows that in legal contexts scholars and triers-of-fact should be on the lookout for racial stereotype priming as they make their observations and decisions. But the concern extends further because priming can also unconsciously affect the self. Some of the most famous priming experiments have studied the effect of racial, ethnic, and gender stereotypes on students' test-taking performance. In contrast to the foregoing priming studies, the primes in these studies affect a person's performance based on his or her own stereotyped identity.

Claude Steele and Joshua Aronson first identified this concept of "stereotype threat" by priming college students in verbal GRE test-taking situations.[17] They directly primed half of their sample of White and Black college students by asking them to identify their race just before they took a test. The researchers found that merely identifying their race reduced African-Americans' (but not Whites') test performance. After adjusting for initial skill level, African-American participants took longer to answer questions and achieved lower overall scores relative to White participants, but only when their race was primed. Thus, Steele and Aronson argue that reporting racial identity likely primed negative stereotypes about African-Americans' academic ability, which led to anxiety and stress about confirming the stereotype when taking the test. This anxiety reduces working memory, thus impairing task performance.[18]

In a second study, Steele and Aronson also found that stereotype threat could be primed in another way. In this study, participants did not report their race. Instead, half of the sample was told that the test was diagnostic of intelligence; the other half was assured that it was not diagnostic. After adjusting for initial skill level, researchers found results similar to those obtained when they primed race directly: African-American students in the diagnostic condition performed worse than White students in the same condition, whereas African-American and White students performed similarly in the non-diagnostic condition. This study demonstrates the ease and influence of indirect racial priming. Simply priming a non-explicit but related stereotype, even without mentioning race, can cause profound effects. Although it would not be intuitive to many that race-neutral concepts (here, test instructions) can elicit powerful racial stereotypes, social cognition research shows that priming can occur as long as historical, cultural, or popular associations connect the concept with a racial stereotype. In the case of stereotype threat, evaluation instructions activated stereotypes relating to African-Americans and intellectual ability in Black students. As a result, their anxiety (fear of confirming the stereotype) diminished their performance.[19]

Follow-up studies of stereotype threat have also shown that it can be elicited even by using more indirect primes. Margaret Shih and colleagues used an indirect method of priming student-participants' ethnic identity but

> Simply priming a non-explicit but related stereotype, even without mentioning race, can cause profound effects. Although it would not be intuitive to many that race-neutral concepts . . . can elicit powerful racial stereotypes, social cognition research shows that priming can occur as long as historical, cultural, or popular associations connect the concept with a racial stereotype.

found similarly powerful results.[20] In that study, the researchers asked Asian-American female participants to fill out questionnaires prior to taking a math test. Some of these questionnaires asked the participants about their roommate and dormitory living situations. This condition was designed to prime female gender identity, which has negative stereotypes about math performance. Others received questionnaires asking them about their family, including asking what languages were spoken at home and how many generations of their family had lived in the United States. This condition was designed to prime Asian ethnic identity, which has positive stereotypes about math performance. Results of the study showed that this method of indirect priming significantly affected the participants' test performance. Participants who had their Asian identity primed performed best on the test, while participants who had their female identity primed performed worst on the test. Considered together, these studies on stereotype threat show the dangers of subtly priming people's negative stereotypes about their own groups.[21]

In the legal system, stereotype threat research has led to reconsidering what it means to have a merit-based college admissions system in the context of affirmative action. Building on the research by Steele and Aronson, it has been argued that admissions officers should take stereotype threat into account when deciding whether to admit minority students despite lower SAT scores, on average, compared with Whites.[22] In other words, because stereotype threat diminishes minority students' ability to perform well on standardized tests for reasons external to their ability, properly implemented countermeasures are needed to ensure a meritorious selection policy.

II. Defining the Implicit—Reaction Times, Shooter Bias, and the IAT

This chapter has explained how easily racial stereotypes can be primed and how they can affect impression formation, decision making, and behavior in troubling ways: for example, in object recognition tasks, when making judgments about others' behaviors, and in academic test performance. Each of the reviewed studies shows the dynamic nature of implicit cognitive processes—processes that are important components of human decision making. This chapter now turns to unique ways social scientists have used to measure implicit bias and specifically examines two established methods that use reaction times to measure implicit bias: shooter bias studies and the IAT.

A. Quick Trigger Finger: The Shooter Bias

In the aftermath of the killing of Tamir Rice, as had happened with the killing of unarmed Black boys and men before and after him, observers wondered whether officer Loehmann would have grabbed his gun and pulled the trigger if Rice had been a 12-year-old White child. Faced with this question after each instance in which police have shot unarmed Black men, beginning with the 1999 shooting of Amadou Diallo by New York police officers, social scientists developed a measure of "shooter bias." Shooter bias studies use simulated video games to examine race-based differences in reactions to potentially threatening individuals.[23] Bias can be tested when participants play a video game that instructs them to shoot perpetrators (who are holding guns) as fast as they can but not to shoot innocent bystanders (who are unarmed but holding a non-gun object, such as a cell phone). The "shooter bias" refers to the consistent results of these studies: participants tend to shoot Black perpetrators more quickly and more frequently than White perpetrators and to decide not to shoot White bystanders more quickly and frequently than Black bystanders.

Once shooter bias became an established phenomenon in non-police officer participants, researchers wondered whether actual police officers would display this bias. After all, unlike non-police citizens, police officers receive extensive handgun training and exercise visual discrimination tasks (such as detecting a gun) as a regular part of their job. Perhaps then, police officers can resist or overcome the bias shown by other citizens. Joshua Correll and his colleagues tested this question by using both a community sample and a sample of police officers.[24] They found that although police officers were generally faster and more accurate than the community sample, their reaction times followed the same pattern as that of community members.[25] Police officers were faster to "shoot" armed Black perpetrators than armed White perpetrators and took longer to make "don't shoot" decisions for unarmed Black targets than unarmed White targets.[26]

Researchers have investigated the cognitive roots of shooter bias, hypothesizing that it may manifest in brain processes that moderate responses to fear. To that end, Correll and his colleagues observed fluctuations in participants' electrical brain activity (known as "event-related brain potentials") while the participants played the shooter bias video game.[27] Measuring event-related brain potentials can identify when people detect threats and when they have a desire to control a behavioral response. The results of the study showed that as participants played the video game, racial discrepancies manifested in the electrical activity of their brains. That is, participants' brain activity showed more threat-related brain activity for Black actors than White actors (even for Black actors without guns) and more control response activity for White actors compared to Black actors. These brain responses then correlated with the participants' performance—the more biased brain activity they displayed, the more shooter bias they exhibited.

B. The Implicit Association Test

Shooter bias studies are not the only social science measure that use reaction times and accuracy rates to measure potential racial bias. Within legal discourse, for example, the most frequently discussed measure of implicit social cognition is the Implicit Association Test (IAT). The IAT pairs an attitude object (such as a racial group) with an evaluative dimension (good or bad) and tests how response speed indicates implicit and automatic attitudes and stereotypes. Participants sit at a computer and are asked to pair an attitude object (for example, Black or White, men or women, fat or thin) with either an evaluative dimension (for example, good or bad) or an attribute dimension (for example, home or career, science or arts) by pressing a response key as quickly as they can. The Black/White test is illustrative. Here, participants are told to quickly pair together pictures of Black American faces with positive words from the evaluative dimension. In a second task, participants are asked to pair Black American faces with negative words. The difference in the speed at which the participants can perform the two tasks is interpreted as the strength of the attitude (or in the case of attributes, the strength of the stereotype). For example, if participants perform the first task faster than the second task, they are showing implicitly positive attitudes toward Black Americans. In a similar example, if they are faster to perform tasks that categorize women with home than tasks that pair women with career, they are showing implicit sex stereotyping.

Nilanjana Dasgupta and Anthony Greenwald succinctly summarize the cognitive heuristic underlying the IAT: "When highly associated targets and attributes share the same response key, participants tend to classify them quickly and easily, whereas when weakly associated targets and attributes share the same response key, participants tend to classify them more slowly and with greater difficulty."[28] Laurie Rudman and Richard Ashmore add, "The ingeniously simple concept underlying the IAT is that tasks are performed well when they rely on well-practiced associations between objects and attributes."[29]

Scores of studies have found that people harbor implicit associations that are biased against stereotyped group members.[30] According to Brian Nosek and his colleagues, who reviewed hundreds of thousands of IATs taken on the Web and elsewhere, the IAT has consistently shown that a majority of test takers exhibit implicit racial bias—and other, non-racial biases—on a variety of measures.[31] For example, 68 percent of participants demonstrated an implicit preference for "White people" versus "Black people" (or "light skin" versus "dark skin"), 75 percent of participants showed an implicit preference for "abled people" versus "disabled people," and 69 percent of participants showed an implicit preference for "thin people" versus "fat people." Similar to other community members, law students have also been shown to harbor implicit biases, such as showing an implicit association between men and judges (and women and paralegals).[32]

One particularly interesting characteristic of IAT results, as well as the results of other implicit measures, is that they frequently diverge from self-reported (explicit) attitudes. That is, people who display strong implicit biases are often not the same people who claim to have strong explicit biases.[33] According to

Devine, "Even those who consciously renounce prejudice have been shown to have implicit or automatic biases that conflict with their nonprejudiced values."[34] For example, in the context of shooter bias, explicit measures of racial preferences do not correlate with results for the video game. That is, people who exhibit greater amounts of shooter bias are not necessarily the same ones who endorsed more racially unequal preferences.[35] For example, both male and female law students have been shown to display implicit gender stereotypes that are sometimes negative toward women.[36] Similarly, Nosek and his colleagues reported that even older people show an implicit preference for young over old.[37]

Despite its consistent results, the IAT has not been without critique.[38] One question regarding the IAT is whether it measures something entirely unconscious or only partially unconscious. Russell Fazio and Michael Olson explored this question and argued that that it is difficult, if not impossible, to know if these associations are in fact completely unknown to the participant. In fact, in many non-sensitive domains, the IAT has been shown to correlate well with explicit measures (such as voter intention).[39] It is important to acknowledge that while the entirely unconscious nature of the attitudes tested by the IAT may be legitimately questioned, support for the IAT tapping into automatic associations is supported because results are based on swift reaction times. This automaticity assertion is bolstered by research demonstrating that incentives to fake the IAT are ineffective.[40]

C. The IAT as Predictor of Real-World Behaviors

Social scientists have also been captivated by the question of whether the IAT has predictive utility, the ability to predict real-life behaviors. One of the most pressing questions surrounding any psychological assessment technique is whether it illuminates human behavior. If a person possesses an implicit dislike of snakes but shows no signs of bias against snakes in the real world, what does that person's implicit bias actually mean? And is that measure something useful? Predictive utility research establishes the validity of an implicit measure (such as the IAT) by determining its relationship with a behavioral measure. The IAT has been shown to predict discriminatory decision making and behavior in a broad range of contexts. Here, we review five particularly compelling studies of the IAT's predictive validity in economics, health care, and employment, and then discuss a meta-analysis that was conducted on over 100 IAT studies.

Rudman and Ashmore tested whether the IAT predicted economic discrimination.[41] Student participants first took a series of IATs, including those testing negative stereotypes related to minority groups. Ostensibly for a separate study, the same participants then completed a survey designed to test economic discrimination. Participants were told that their input was needed in order to implement a mandatory 20 percent budget cut to university student organizations. They were then provided a list of current student organizations along with funding levels and were asked to allocate the new budget across the various groups. The researchers then compared the student participants' IAT scores with their recommended budget cuts and found that scores on the stereotype IAT predicted economic discrimination. Specifically, "people who associated minority group members with negative attributes and majority group members with positive attributes were also likely to recommend budget cuts for the target minority group's student organization."[42] Rudman and Ashmore's study demonstrates a meaningful connection between implicit racial bias and monetary discrimination.

Alexander Green and his colleagues tested whether doctors held implicit racial bias against African-Americans and whether this bias predicted their decisions to treat patients.[43] Nearly 300 emergency room and internal medicine doctors in Boston and Atlanta participated in the study. Doctors were presented with a vignette in which a patient, who was described as either Black or White, arrives at an emergency room suffering from acute coronary syndrome. The doctors were asked to recommend a course of treatment for the patient and were then asked to complete three IATs testing their implicit racial biases. The study showed not only that doctors implicitly preferred White patients to Black patients, but also that their implicit racial biases predicted whether or not they would recommend state-of-art clot busting (thrombolysis) treatment to a White or Black patient suffering from myocardial infarction. The more the doctors implicitly preferred the White patients, the more likely they were to recommend thrombolysis treatment to White but not Black patients. No similar predictive validity was found by asking doctors about their explicit racial preferences. On average, doctors self-reported no racial preferences at all.

Lisa Cooper and colleagues, in a separate study of implicit bias in health care outcomes, measured the relationship between physician implicit bias levels and the quality of care given to patients.[44] In that study, researchers gathered and analyzed actual doctor-patient audio communications from a separate medical study (which allowed them to code and measure, for example, length and quality of doctor-patient interactions). They also collected patients' post-appointment reports of the interactions with their physicians and separately measured physicians' implicit bias levels. The researchers found that doctors' negative implicit racial biases (relating to both implicit racial attitudes and racial stereotypes) were associated not only with patients' reports of their care, but also with objective markers of doctor-patient interactions, such as whether a doctor dominated a conversation with a patient. For example, the study found that higher levels of doctors' implicit bias predicted Black patients' perceptions of the care they received as well as the amount of doctor-dominated dialogue; the higher the level the doctors' implicit bias, the less satisfied their Black patients were with their care and the more the doctors dominated the conversation.

Dan-Olof Rooth examined whether human resources officers at corporations harbored implicit bias that affected their choices of which candidates to interview for vacant positions.[45] In the first stage of his study, Rooth responded to over 1,500 job postings in Sweden for a variety of jobs, ranging from computer professionals to motor vehicle operators. For each job posting, Rooth sent two equal resumes, with the only difference being whether the applicant's name appeared to be Swedish or Arabic/Muslim. He then measured whether the fictitious candidates were summoned for interviews. Once this first interview stage was complete, Rooth tracked down the human resources officers responsible for the hiring decision and invited them to participate in his study (these participants were unaware of the bias-related purpose of the study). Rooth provided an IAT testing of implicit racial stereotypes of Swedes and Arab/Muslims and evaluated whether the IAT predicted the human resources officers' previous decision of whether or not to interview the applicants. The results of the study found that the human resources officers' implicit racial stereotypes of Arabs predicted whether those employers would call Arab job candidates for interviews. Human resources officers that held implicit stereotypes relating to Arabs were less likely to interview candidates with Arab-sounding names.[46] Rooth's study supports the connection between implicit bias and hiring decisions. Other studies have confirmed the link. For example, a study by Kumar Yogeeswaran and Nilanjana Dasgupta found that American study participants who more strongly associated White with American and Asian with foreign on an IAT were less likely to recommend hiring American job applicants with Chinese-sounding names for national security jobs as compared to applicants with White-sounding names.[47]

A meta-analysis confirms the predictive validity of the IAT, particularly when it is employed in socially sensitive domains such as racial attitudes. Greenwald and colleagues analyzed 122 studies that mapped IAT scores onto various predictors, such as behaviors, judgments, or physiological measures.[48] They included in their analyses a comprehensive list of IAT studies (spanning beyond those on race) that tested a range of implicit attitudes, stereotypes, self-concepts, and self-esteem.[49] The researchers coded each study on a number of items including social sensitivity (a study of implicit racial bias, for example, was coded as being highly socially sensitive). Results showed that the IAT's relationship to behavioral measures was heterogeneous, ranging from low to high. Overall, explicit measures had a larger relationship with the response criterion. However, when dealing with socially sensitive issues such as racial attitudes, the relationship between explicit measures and the response criterion was diminished, whereas the relationship between the IAT and response criterion was not. In fact, when looking specifically at interracial (or other intergroup) topics, IATs performed better than explicit measures at predicting behaviors, judgments, and physiological responses. This result confirms that implicit

IATs performed better than explicit measures at predicting behaviors, judgments, and physiological responses. This result confirms that implicit biases, particularly in the context of race, are meaningful.

biases, particularly in the context of race, are meaningful. It would be advisable, then, if scholars concerned with racial bias in the legal system systematically examined implicit racial bias across the law.

III. Implicit Bias Research in the Legal Setting

Although the vast majority of empirical studies on implicit bias have been conducted outside of the legal setting, a limited number of studies have used priming procedures, IATs, or both to measure bias in the law. As the following review demonstrates, significant progress has been made in empirically examining implicit racial bias in a few narrow domains, such as the criminal justice area, but most other legal areas have yet to be studied empirically.

The first empirical use of the IAT in the legal setting occurred when Theodore Eisenberg and Sheri Lynn Johnson tested whether capital defense attorneys harbor implicit racial bias.[50] The researchers found that defense attorney participants, a group one might expect to resist bias, harbored strong implicit biases against African-Americans. Eisenberg and Johnson, however, did not test whether the defense attorneys' implicit biases predicted anything about their behavior or decisions. Nonetheless, this study documented implicit bias among a particularly noteworthy participant population and opened the door for future research.

An early empirical examination of priming in the legal setting was conducted by Justin Levinson in 2005.[51] Levinson hypothesized that simply placing citizens on juries activates implicit and explicit knowledge structures that change the way people make decisions. He provided study participants the facts of a crime and asked half of the participants to imagine that they were jurors in the criminal trial. The other half of the participants were informed that they were simply reading newspaper accounts of the crime. The results of the study showed that mock juror participants were significantly harsher when making judgments of criminal intentionality than participants making lay judgments about the same facts. In addition, when the defendant was portrayed as an outgroup member, participants in the legal prime condition became even harsher in their decisions.

In a law-focused study that employed the IAT, Jeffrey Rachlinski, Sheri Lynn Johnson, and their colleagues examined whether judges harbored implicit bias by having them complete a Black/White racial bias IAT.[52] The researchers found that judges displayed an implicit preference for Whites over Blacks. A 2016 study of federal and state judges by Levinson, Judge Mark Bennett, and Koichi Hioki also tested implicit stereotypes of sitting judges.[53] In that study, the researchers found that judges held negative implicit stereotypes (e.g., liar, controlling, and greedy, as compared to positive stereotypes, such as honest, trustworthy, and charitable) of Asian-Americans compared to White Americans and also more negative stereotypes of Jews compared to Christians.

Levinson and Danielle Young tested how priming mock jurors with the image of a dark-skinned perpetrator might alter judgments about the probative value of evidence.[54] Levinson and Young provided all jurors with the story of an armed robbery. After reading the story, participants were shown five crime scene photos for four seconds each. All participants saw the same five photos, except that in the third photo, half of the participants saw a dark-skinned perpetrator and the other half saw a lighter-skinned perpetrator.[55] The researchers then presented participants with various pieces of evidence that were described as trial testimony and instructed them to rate each piece of evidence based upon its probative value. As hypothesized, Levinson and Young found that participants who had seen a photo of a darker-skinned perpetrator were more likely to evaluate the evidence as tending to indicate guilt.

A field study conducted by psychologists Rebecca Hetey and Jennifer Eberhardt examined whether visually depicting prisons as either more or less "Black" (based on the percentage of Black inmates) affected citizens' willingness to take action against punitive criminal justice policies. In that study, California residents viewed photographs depicting over-incarceration in the context of considering the state's controversial "three strikes law." The researchers found that residents were more willing to sign a petition urging the repeal of the three strikes law when the prison population was depicted in photographs as relatively White.[56] When the prison population was depicted as more Black, residents were significantly less likely to sign the petition.

Levinson, Cai, and Young also created an IAT specifically for the criminal law context.[57] Notably, the researchers designed a guilty/not guilty IAT that they expected might be a meaningful measure in the legal context. As predicted, Levinson, Cai, and Young found that participants held a significant implicit association between Blacks and guilty compared to Whites and guilty.

In another project tailored specifically for the legal setting, Jerry Kang and his colleagues created an IAT designed to test whether people rely on implicit ethnic biases when evaluating the performance of litigators.[58] Specifically, the researchers tested implicit anti-Asian bias and related it to evaluations for Asian male litigators compared to White male litigators. The researchers predicted that participants would implicitly associate White males, relative to Asian males, with characteristics frequently associated with successful litigators as opposed to successful scientists. As the results of the study showed, participants did in fact implicitly associate White males with successful litigators compared to Asian males. In addition, these implicit associations showed predictive validity. The IAT scores predicted participants' judgments of White and Asian litigators' performance in a mock trial.

A study by Young, Levinson, and Sinnett used priming to follow up Levinson and colleagues' guilty/not guilty IAT, which raised the issue that the presumption of innocence may have a different implicit meaning for White and Black defendants.[59] The researchers hypothesized that the presumption of innocence itself would actually prime participants to think about guilty African-Americans, a counterintuitive result that might call into question the racial fairness of the presumption of innocence. Participants watched a video recording of a U.S. District Court judge reading a series of jury instructions. Half of the participants received instructions that included a presumption of innocence instruction, and the other half received an alternative matched-length instruction. Participants then completed a computer-based dot-probe task to assess if participants' attention was primed for Black faces. Participants who were given the presumption of innocence instruction were faster to find a dot when it appeared on the same side of the screen as Black faces than when it appeared on the same side of the screen as White faces. Participants who did not receive the presumption of innocence instructions displayed a similar response time for faces regardless of race. These results demonstrate that presumption of innocence instructions prime vigilance for Black faces.

A 2014 study of implicit bias in the context of the death penalty raises questions about the ways in which unique jury selection rules may inadvertently increase racial biases in trials involving capital punishment.[60] Levinson, Smith, and Young studied jury-eligible citizens in six death penalty states using an IAT that asked participants to categorize Black and White faces with concepts of value or worthlessness. The researchers found that study participants implicitly devalued the lives of Black Americans compared to White Americans; that is, participants automatically associated White with worth and Black with worthless on the IAT. The researchers also found that citizens who would be considered death-qualified jurors—those who would be allowed to sit on a death penalty jury—held larger implicit and explicit racial biases than those who would be excluded because of their death penalty opposition. Statistical analysis further revealed that the dehumanization bias gap between death-qualified and non-death-qualified jurors was explained by the disproportionate removal of non-White citizens from the jury pool through the process of death qualification. In other words, death qualification, supposedly a race-neutral process integral to capital trials, might itself lead to "Whiter" juries disproportionately likely to dehumanize Black defendants.

A later study conducted by Smith, Levinson, and Hioki followed up on the possible connection between implicit racial biases and punishment, both inside and outside the death penalty context.[61] The researchers tested whether one of the core theoretical supports for punishment—the concept of retribution—may be cognitively associated with racial categories. To do this, researchers surveyed jury-eligible citizens across the United States and measured, on an IAT, whether participants associated retribution (e.g., payback, avenge, retaliate) or leniency (e.g., mercy, redemption, forgive) with Black or White faces. Results of the study showed that participants more easily associated Black with retribution-related words and White with mercy-related words, and that these associations predicted greater overall support for retributive theories of punishment. Furthermore, the results of the study matched Levinson and colleagues' 2014 findings (and with a different IAT) that death-qualified jurors held higher levels of implicit racial bias as compared to those who would be excluded due to their death penalty opposition.

The foregoing studies show progress made in empirically testing implicit bias in the legal domain. Yet, the summaries also underscore the limited nature of these studies. Future research should continue to empirically investigate implicit bias in the legal setting.

Conclusion

In light of the evidence linking implicit bias to a variety of discriminatory outcomes, legal scholars and empiricists must deeply consider the various ways in which implicit bias may affect all areas of the law in which disparities appear. The killing of Tamir Rice, which reopened old wounds for many Americans clinging to the prospect of a future with equal justice, serves as a stark reminder of the powerful role that racial stereotypes can exert, even in a society that espouses racial equality. Although significant research has begun to point the way for progress in the legal system, researchers must continue paving a path to justice.

ABOUT THE AUTHORS

Justin Levinson is professor of law at the University of Hawaii, a leader in the field of implicit bias and the law, and an expert in psychological decision making in the legal system. His scholarship, which regularly employs experimental social science methodology, has appeared in the *NYU Law Review*, *UCLA Law Review*, and *Duke Law Journal*, among others, and has been cited by the U.S. Supreme Court. Professor Levinson served as lead editor of *Implicit Racial Bias Across the Law*, a volume that was published by Cambridge University Press in 2012 (coedited by Robert J. Smith).

Danielle M. Young completed her doctoral work at the University of Hawaii at Manoa and her postdoctoral work at Rutgers University. She is an assistant professor at Manhattan College (which is in the Bronx). Her collaborative work on implicit bias and death-qualified jurors has been published in journals including *New York University Law Review* and *PlosOne*.

Laurie A. Rudman is a professor of psychology at Rutgers University–New Brunswick. Her research examines how implicit biases deter gender and racial equality. The author of over 70 peer-reviewed publications and four books, including *Implicit Measures for Social and Personality Psychology*. Dr. Rudman has also served as an expert witness in several employment discrimination cases.

ENDNOTES

1. An earlier version of this chapter appeared as Chapter 1 in Implicit Racial Bias Across the Law (Justin D. Levinson & Robert J. Smith eds. 2012).
2. The facts we present are largely based on media accounts, including *Tamir Rice Shooting: No Charges for Officers*, CNN, Dec. 29, 2015, and Tessa Berenson, *Cleveland Police Officers Will Not Face Charges in Death of Tamir Rice*, Time.com, *available at* http://time.com/4162457/tamir-rice-shooting-grand-jury-no-indictment/. For a video of the shooting, see https://www.youtube.com/watch?v=sdAYPQd1H1A (last visited July 18, 2016).
3. Unlike other toy guns, the toy that Rice was playing with did not have an orange cap.
4. David A. Graham, *"Probable Cause" in the Killing of Tamir Rice*, The Atlantic, June 2016, *available at* http://www.theatlantic.com/politics/archive/2015/06/tamir-rice-case-cleveland/395420/.
5. Jerry Kang et al., *Implicit Bias in the Courtroom*, 59 UCLA L. Rev. 1124 (2012).

6. John A. Bargh et al., *Automaticity of Social Behavior: Direct Effects of Trait Construct and Stereotype Activation on Action*, 71 J. PERSONALITY & SOC. PSYCHOL. 230, 230 (1996).

7. Several of the descriptions we provide of priming and the Implicit Association Test are based, sometimes verbatim, upon the descriptions given in Justin Levinson, *Forgotten Racial Equality: Implicit Bias, Decisionmaking, and Misremembering*, 57 DUKE L.J. 345 (2007), and Justin D. Levinson, *Race, Death and the Complicitous Mind*, 58 DEPAUL L. REV. 599 (2009).

8. Daniel T. Gilbert & J. Gregory Hixon, *The Trouble of Thinking: Activation and Application of Stereotypic Beliefs*, 60 J. PERSONALITY & SOC. PSYCHOL. 509 (1991).

9. Laurie A. Rudman & Matthew R. Lee, *Implicit and Explicit Consequences of Exposure to Violent and Misogynous Rap Music*, 5 GROUP PROCESSES & INTERGROUP REL. 133, 138–39 (2002).

10. Participants were led to believe that they were participating in a marketing study.

11. Jennifer L. Eberhardt et al., *Seeing Black: Race, Crime, and Visual Processing*, 87 J. PERSONALITY & SOC. PSYCHOL. 876 (2004).

12. B. Keith Payne, *Prejudice and Perception: The Role of Automatic and Controlled Processes in Misperceiving a Weapon*, 81 J. PERSONALITY & SOC. PSYCHOL. 181, 185–86 (2001).

13. *Id.* The objects consisted of guns and non-gun objects (the non-gun objects were hand tools, such as a socket wrench and an electric drill).

14. Patricia G. Devine, *Stereotypes and Prejudice: Their Automatic and Controlled Components*, 56 J. PERSONALITY & SOC. PSYCHOL. 5, 9 (1989) (citing J.C. Brigham, *Ethnic Stereotypes*, 76 PSYCHOL. BULL. 15 (1971)).

15. *Id.* at 11.

16. James D. Johnson & Sophie Trawalter, *Converging Interracial Consequences of Exposure to Violent Rap Music on Stereotypical Attributions of Blacks*, 36 J. EXPERIMENTAL SOC. PSYCHOL. 233, 239 (2000).

17. Claude M. Steele & Joshua Aronson, *Stereotype Threat and the Intellectual Test Performance of African-Americans*, 69 J. PERSONALITY & SOC. PSYCHOL. 797 (1995).

18. For a review of stereotype threat literature, see Toni Schmader et al., *An Integrated Process Model of Stereotype Threat Effects on Performance*, 115 PSYCHOL. REV. 336 (2008).

19. While Steele and Aronson's work focused initially on Black stereotypes, research has shown that stereotype threat is equally relevant for other group identities, such as girls and math, and Whites and athletics. *See, e.g.*, CLAUDE M. STEELE, WHISTLING VIVALDI AND OTHER CLUES TO HOW STEREOTYPES AFFECT US (2010).

20. Margaret Shih et al., *Stereotype Susceptibility: Identity Salience and Shifts in Quantitative Performance*, 10 PSYCHOL. SCI. 80 (1999).

21. This kind of internalizing of stereotypes also can work to "boost" or "lift" performance in ways consistent with positive stereotypes. Robert J. Smith, Justin D. Levinson & Zoe Robinson, *Implicit White Favoritism in the Criminal Justice System*, 66 ALA. L. REV. 871, 891–94 (2014).

22. Amicus Brief of Experimental Psychologists, filed in support of respondents, Fisher v. University of Texas, Writ of Cert to the Fifth Circuit Court of Appeals.

23. Joshua Correll et al., *The Police Officer's Dilemma: Using Ethnicity to Disambiguate Potentially Threatening Individuals*, 83 J. PERSONALITY & SOC. PSYCHOL. 1314 (2002).

24. Joshua Correll et al., *Across the Thin Blue Line: Police Officers and Racial Bias in the Decision to Shoot*, 92 J. PERSONALITY & SOC. PSYCHOL. 1006 (2007). The study looked at two measures of shooter bias: response times and accuracy. This chapter reports the results for the reaction time study in the text. The study of accuracy demonstrated that police officers were generally more accurate in their decisions to shoot than the community sample.

25. *Id.*; *see also* LORIE FRIDELL, PRODUCING BIAS-FREE POLICING: A SCIENCE BASED APPROACH (2016) (discussing the need for vigilance in both directions).

26. Recent research efforts have begun to test shooter bias theory in a more realistic context. A 2016 experimental study of 80 Spokane, Washington, police officers, conducted by Lois James and colleagues, found that, when presented with a series of realistic threat and non-threat simulations akin to normal police trainings, those officers were less, not more, likely to shoot unarmed Black suspects than White suspects, and were slower, not faster, in shooting armed Black suspects compared to White suspects. Lois James et al., *The Reverse Racism Effect: Are Cops More Hesitant to Shoot Black Than White Suspects?*, 15 CRIMINOLOGY & PUB. POL'Y 457 (2016).
27. Joshua Correll et al., *Event-Related Potentials and the Decision to Shoot: The Role of Threat Perception and Cognitive Control*, 42 J. EXPERIMENTAL SOC. PSYCHOL. 120, 122 (2006).
28. Nilanjana Dasgupta & Anthony G. Greenwald, *On the Malleability of Automatic Attitudes: Combating Automatic Prejudice with Images of Admired and Disliked Individuals*, 81 J. PERSONALITY & SOC. PSYCHOL. 800 (2001).
29. Laurie A. Rudman & Richard D. Ashmore, *Discrimination and the Implicit Association Test*, 10 GROUP PROCESSES & INTERGROUP REL. 359 (2007).
30. *See* Anthony Greenwald et al., *Understanding and Using the Implicit Association Test: III: Meta Analysis of Predictive Validity*, 97 J. PERSONALITY & SOC. PSYCHOL. 17 (2009).
31. Brian Nosek et al., *Pervasiveness and Correlates of Implicit Attitudes and Stereotypes*, 18 EUR. REV. SOC. PSYCHOL. 36 (2008).
32. Justin D. Levinson & Danielle Young, *Implicit Gender Bias in the Legal Profession: An Empirical Study*, 18 DUKE J. GENDER L. & POL'Y 1 (2010).
33. *See* Patricia G. Devine, *Implicit Prejudice and Stereotyping: How Automatic Are They? Introduction to the Special Section*, 81 J. PERSONALITY & SOC. PSYCHOL. 757, 757 (2001).
34. *Id.*
35. *Id.* Not all studies show no relationship between implicit and explicit attitudes. Some studies reveal at least a weak correlation between the two. *See, e.g.*, Russell H. Fazio & Michael A. Olson, *Implicit Measures in Social Cognition Research: Their Meanings and Use*, 54 ANN. REV. PSYCHOL. 297, 304 (2003) (observing that there is "no simple answer" to the issue of whether and how implicit and explicit attitudes are related, but nonetheless suggesting that both are predictive of behavior in different ways); Wilhelm Hofmann et al., *A Meta-Analysis on the Correlation between the Implicit Association Test and Explicit Self-Report Measures*, 31 PERSONALITY & SOC. PSYCHOL. BULL. 1369, 1382 (2005) (finding a relationship between implicit and explicit attitudes).
36. Levinson & Young, *supra* note 32.
37. Nosek, *supra* note 31.
38. Within legal scholarship, a few scholars have cautioned against embracing the results of the IAT as a measure of bias to be considered in lawmaking. *See, e.g.*, Gregory Mitchell & Philip E. Tetlock, *Antidiscrimination Law and the Perils of Mindreading*, 67 OHIO ST. L.J. 1023 (2006). Most psychologists and legal scholars, however, have argued that the IAT has been sufficiently validated as a measure. *See, e.g.*, Samuel R. Bagenstos, *Implicit Bias, "Science," and Antidiscrimination Law*, 1 HARV. L. & POL'Y REV. 477 (2007); John T. Jost et al., *The Existence of Implicit Bias Is Beyond Reasonable Doubt: A Refutation of Ideological and Methodological Objections and Executive Summary of Ten Studies That No Manager Should Ignore*, 29 RES. ORG. BEHAV. 39 (2009).
39. *See* Greenwald et al., *supra* note 30.
40. Do-Yeong Kim, *Voluntary Controllability of the Implicit Association Test (IAT)*, 66 SOC. PSYCHOL. Q. 83 (2003); Rainer Banse et al., *Implicit Attitudes Toward Homosexuality: Reliability, Validity, and Controllability of the IAT*, 48 ZEITSCHRIFT FUR EXPERIMENTELLE PSYCHOLOGIE 145 (2001).
41. Rudman & Ashmore, *supra* note 29.
42. *Id.* at 367.
43. Alexander R. Green et al., *Implicit Bias among Physicians and Its Prediction of Thrombolysis Decisions for Black and White Patients*, 22 J. GEN. INTERNAL MED. 1231 (2007).

44. Lisa A. Cooper et al., *The Associations of Clinicians' Implicit Attitudes about Race with Medical Visit Communication and Patient Ratings of Interpersonal Care*, 102 Am. J. Pub. Health 979 (2012).

45. Dan-Olof Rooth, *Automatic Associations and Discrimination in Hiring: Real World Evidence*, 17 Labour Econ. 523 (2010).

46. Another study, conducted in the United States and the Netherlands, found that Dutch participants with higher implicit prejudice scores were more likely to negatively rate resumes with Arab names and affiliations. Eva Derous et al., *Hiring Discrimination against Arab Minorities, Interactions between Prejudice and Job Characteristics*, 22 Human Performance 297 (2009).

47. Kumar Yogeeswaran & Nilanjana Dasgupta, *Will the "Real" American Please Stand Up? The Effect of Implicit National Prototypes on Discriminatory Behavior and Judgments*, 36 Personality & Soc. Psychol. Bull. 1332 (2010). Interestingly, the researchers found that this association did not predict hiring for a corporate context in which national loyalty was not relevant, a finding that underscores the connection between the content of the implicit stereotype (foreignness) and the decision task (loyalty to country).

48. Greenwald et al., *supra* note 30.

49. The resulting studies included a range of areas of research that dealt with topics from smoking to racial equality.

50. *See* Theodore Eisenberg & Sheri Lynn Johnson, *Implicit Racial Attitudes of Death Penalty Lawyers*, 53 DePaul L. Rev. 1539, 1542 (2004).

51. Justin D. Levinson, *Suppressing the Expression of Community Values in Jurors: How "Legal Priming" Systematically Alters the Way People Think*, 73 U. Cin. L. Rev. 1059 (2005). Levinson's study was conducted both in the United States and in China. The results presented are for American participants only.

52. *See* Jeffrey J. Rachlinski et al., *Does Unconscious Bias Affect Trial Judges?*, 84 Notre Dame L. Rev. 1195 (2009).

53. Justin D. Levinson, Mark Bennett & Koichi Hioki, *Judging Implicit Bias: A National Empirical Study of Judicial Stereotypes beyond Black and White*, Florida L. Rev. ___ (forthcoming, 2017).

54. Justin D. Levinson & Danielle Young, *Different Shades of Bias: Skin Tone, Implicit Racial Bias, and Judgments of Ambiguous Evidence*, 112 W. Va. L. Rev. 307 (2010).

55. None of the other photos showed the perpetrator.

56. Rebecca Hetey & Jennifer Eberhardt, *Cops and Criminals: The Interplay of Animalistic and Mechanistic Dehumanization in the Criminal Justice System, in* Humanness and Dehumanization (Paul G. Bain et al. eds., 2013).

57. Justin D. Levinson, Huajian Cai & Danielle Young, *Guilty by Implicit Bias: The Guilty-Not Guilty Implicit Association Test*, 8 Ohio St. J. Crim. L. 187 (2010).

58. Jerry Kang et al., *Are Ideal Litigators White? Measuring the Myth of Colorblindness*, 7 J. Empirical Leg. Stud. 886 (2010). Although we do not describe it in the text, another 2010 study employed the IAT to test whether law students possess implicit gender biases related to women in the legal profession. *See* Levinson & Young, *supra* note 32 (finding, for example, that law students associate men with judges and women with paralegals).

59. Danielle Young, Justin D. Levinson & Scott Sinnett, Presumption of Innocence: Biasing Racial Cues (2011) (unpublished manuscript) (on file with authors).

60. *See* Justin D. Levinson, Robert J. Smith & Danielle M. Young, *Devaluing Death: An Empirical Study of Implicit Racial Bias on Jury-Eligible Citizens in Six Death Penalty States*, 89 N.Y.U. L. Rev. 513, 513, 556 (2014).

61. Robert J. Smith et al., The Racial Architecture of Retribution (2016) (unpublished manuscript) (on file with authors).

Chapter 4
Manifestations of Implicit Bias in the Courts

Judge Mark W. Bennett

Chapter Contents

Chapter Highlights

- One judge provides a personal introduction to implicit bias and his unique approach to implicit bias and the presumption of innocence.

- Implicit biases affect a client's choice of lawyers.

- Unique caseload pressures, combined with implicit biases, may result in initial evaluations by lawyers, such as public defenders, which impact future case decisions in significant and potentially undesirable ways.

- Implicit biases unknown to prosecutors may dramatically affect prosecutorial discretion in undesirable ways.

- Implicit biases affect lawyers' evaluations of judges.

- Implicit bias affects jurors' memories, their interpretation of ambiguous evidence, and the presumption of innocence in ways often averse to minorities.

Introduction

> If you asked me to name the greatest discoveries of the past 50 years, alongside things like the internet and the Higgs particle, I would include the discovery of unconscious biases and the extent to which stereotypes about gender, race, sexual orientation, socioeconomic status, and age deprive people of equal opportunity in the workplace and equal justice in society.[1]

> And we knew . . . that even the good cops with the best of intentions—including, by the way, African American police officers—might have unconscious biases, as we all do.[2]

This chapter addresses several ways in which implicit bias manifests itself in the civil and criminal justice systems. Implicit bias and judges' decision making has its own chapter, Chapter 5, "Implicit Bias in Judicial Decision Making: How It Affects Judgment and What Judges Can Do About It," and is ably addressed there by two of the leading scholars in the country on the subject, Professor Jeffery J. Rachlinski and Judge Andrew J. Wistrich.

Social scientists, academics, lawyers, judges, and court administrators have recently demonstrated an increased and heightened interest in and knowledge of implicit bias. Despite Professor Nancy Hopkins's claim in the opening quote of this chapter, the concept that unconscious bias affects decision making in the civil and criminal justice system is not new. One of my personal heroes, Lena Olive Smith, the first Black female member of the Minnesota bar and a renowned civil rights lawyer of her time in Minnesota, wrote the following in a 1928 motion for new trial in a state court prosecution of a Black man for raping a White woman, before an all-White jury:

The court fully realizes I am sure, that the very fact that the defendant was a colored boy and the prosecutrix a white woman, and the entire panel composed of white men—there was a delicate situation to begin with, and counsel for the State took advantage of this delicate situation. . . . [P]erhaps [the jurors] were, with a few exceptions, conscientious in their expressions [of no race prejudice]; yet it is common knowledge a feeling can be so dormant and subjected to one's sub-consciousness, that one is wholly ignorant of its existence. But if the proper stimulus is applied, it comes to the front, and more often than not one is deceived in believing that it is justice speaking to him; when in fact it is prejudice, blinding him to all justice and fairness.[3]

Lena Olive Smith understood more than eight decades ago what scientists, through implicit social cognition (ISC), now understand—that is, that implicit biases "can function automatically, including in ways that the person would not endorse as appropriate if he or she did have conscious awareness."[4] While Lena Olive Smith intuitively understood this from her own personal history, Professor Nancy Hopkins is correct that the discovery of the extent to which implicit biases infect so many discretionary decisions and impact human behavior is truly an astounding revelation. What aspects of today's civil and criminal justice systems might be implicated and affected by participants' implicit biases? Everything and everybody. Before turning to the next section of this chapter, I share a personal narrative of how I became involved with the study of and concerned with the implications of implicit bias both in my courtroom and in my life.

> What aspects of today's civil and criminal justice systems might be implicated and affected by participants' implicit biases? Everything and everybody.

My unexpected and sudden introduction to my own implicit biases was unnerving. Before I was a federal trial judge, I was a civil rights lawyer in one of the first racially integrated law firms at the partner level in Iowa. For many years I had been teaching Advanced Employment Discrimination at the Drake University Law School along with then Associate Dean Russ Lovell (also a former civil rights lawyer). A little more than a decade ago, Lovell explained and suggested I take the race Implicit Association Test (IAT), which I had never heard of. I was eager to take my first IAT and confident, as a former civil rights lawyer and sitting federal judge with a lifelong commitment to egalitarian values, I would "pass" with flying colors. I didn't. I retook the test. Same results. I then did what any self-respecting trial lawyer or trial judge would do—I assumed the IAT was invalid and proceeded to read everything I could about the IAT to prove it. After weeks of intense research, I came to the conclusion, by at least clear and convincing evidence if not beyond a reasonable doubt, that the IAT was a valid measure of my own racial implicit biases and those of the millions of others who had taken the test. My epiphany was reflected in the cartoon character Pogo's statement: "We have met the enemy and

> I was eager to take my first IAT and confident, as a former civil rights lawyer and sitting federal judge with a lifelong commitment to egalitarian values, that I would "pass" with flying colors. I didn't.

he is us."[5] Once judges, lawyers, and court staff members learn about their own implicit biases and those of others, there should be a call to action to attempt to reduce the negative and serious effects of implicit bias in the court system.

I. Overview: First Principles of Implicit Bias

Lawyers, judges, litigants, jurors, and court personnel interact with each other in various ways and often in complex combinations. Very few of these relationships have been studied in the context of implicit biases. However, there are some first principles of implicit bias that are uncontroversial and worthy of repeating. First, no one is likely free of implicit biases. While some of us may not have implicit biases in some areas, implicit bias against Muslims, for example, if we look at sex, disabilities, sexual orientation, age, national origin, skin tone, obesity, slenderness, political affiliation, religion, large firm and small firm lawyers, bowtie wearers, and so on, it is highly likely that all of us would have some implicit biases. But like snowflakes, fingerprints, and DNA, it is also likely that none of us would have the identical implicit bias profile. Second, there is no reason to believe that lawyers, judges, and court personnel have any fewer or less potent implicit biases than members of the general public do. Indeed, in the only two empirical studies to date on implicit bias and judges, both found judges are either equal to members of the general public or have greater implicit biases.[6] Third, researchers have repeatedly found and determined that not only are people unaware of their specific implicit biases, but also these biases often conflict with self-reported egalitarian values.[7] Fourth, all vertebrates have a *scomata* (the Greek word for darkness) in each eye.[8] It is where the optic nerve exits the retina. It's our blind spot, "where light arriving at that spot has no path to the visual areas of the brain."[9] Here, we are not concerned with this visual blind spot except as a metaphor for the cognitive blind spot of recognizing biases in others while not being able to see or recognize them in ourselves.[10] This blind spot and our tendency to attribute it to others and not ourselves is not attenuated by how smart we are![11] In one study, Professor Jeffery Rachlinski and coauthors found that 97 percent of state court administrative law judges attending an educational conference rated their ability "to avoid racial prejudice in decisionmaking" in the top half of other judges at the conference.[12] Of course, that is mathematically impossible. The authors worried that "this result means that judges are overconfident about their ability to avoid the influence of race."[13] In my recent national empirical study, I found that 92 percent of senior federal district judges, 87 percent of non-senior federal district judges, 72 percent of U.S. magistrate judges, 77 percent of federal bankruptcy judges, and 96 percent of federal probation and pre-trial services officers ranked themselves in the top 25 percent of respective colleagues in their ability to make decisions free from racial bias.[14] Again, that is mathematically impossible. Justice Anthony Kennedy recently penned an excellent definition of the cognitive blind spot bias in judges, without naming it, when he wrote about the unconstitutional failure of a state supreme court justice to recuse himself in a criminal case: "Bias is easy to attribute to others and difficult to discern in oneself."[15] Because of this very strong cognitive blind spot bias, judges and other courtroom actors are unlikely to question whether their decisions and actions are influenced by either explicit or implicit biases.

Last, and perhaps most important, social scientists are beginning to understand that much of implicit bias is due to ingroup favoritism rather than outgroup hostility.[16] Thus, for example, judges, lawyers, jurors, or court staff can make decisions affected by implicit bias without a hostility toward another race, religion, gender, or so on, but based on their ingroup favoritism, favoring folks who are more like them and with whom they have more in common. These group dynamics of implicit responses are discussed further in Chapters 7 and 8.

II. The Participants

A. Lawyers: Client Choice of a Lawyer

The only empirical study of explicit and implicit biases in the hypothetical selection of a lawyer for a civil matter reveals that both explicit and implicit biases of potential clients affect the choice of a lawyer.[17] In this study, the authors created a customized IAT to measure the degree to which White American men versus Asian-American men are associated with traits that embody the ideal litigator.[18] A second IAT was also administered to measure the degree to which the participants favored White American men over Asian-American men—a measure of the participants' implicit racial attitudes.[19] Concerning explicit biases, the authors measured "the degree to which participants personally endorsed" personality and societal stereotypes linking an ideal litigator to Asian-Americans or White Americans.[20] The participants listened to two audio depositions involving an auto accident and a slip-and-fall accident, which were selected because they are typical civil cases.[21] Before listening to each deposition, the participants were shown the deposing (male) litigator's picture and name for five seconds.[22] The race and name of the litigator were manipulated by varying the name and photograph "to be prototypically White (William Cole) or Asian (Sung Chang)."[23] After viewing the depositions, the participants rated the litigator's competence on six items, warmth on six items, and whether they would retain the litigator or recommend him to family and friends.[24]

- No *Explicit* Bias in Selecting Asian or White Litigator. On the measure of explicit bias, the authors found no statistically significant difference on the self-reported measure of whether the participants "viewed Whites as more the ideal litigator as compared to Asian Americans."[25] However, statistically significant differences were found on the cultural stereotype measure.[26] While the participants did not self-report any explicit biases of their own regarding the ideal litigator, "they thought 'most Americans'" think Asian-American litigators "possess fewer characteristics necessary to be a successful litigator."[27]

- *Implicit* Bias Favored White Litigators over Asian Litigators. Now for the "dissociation" between explicit and implicit stereotypes. As in other implicit bias empirical studies, here, on average, participants personally disavowed litigator stereotypes while actually holding moderate implicit stereotypes (although they did report that "most Americans" possessed them). When examining whether implicit and explicit stereotypes predicted evaluations of the litigator, the researchers once again found an interesting difference. Participants' implicit stereotypes in favor of White litigators were correlated with their evaluations of the White litigator (outcome variables): how much they liked him, how competent they thought he was, and their willingness to hire him and recommend him to friends and family.[28] In contrast, evaluations of the Asian litigator were significantly correlated to the participants' explicit stereotypes.[29] Thus, the authors found that explicit stereotypes that an ideal litigator was White predicted "out group derogation" while implicit stereotypes predicted preferential evaluation of the White litigator demonstrating "in group favoritism."[30] At bottom, the authors concluded, "Our study demonstrates that explicit and implicit stereotypes about litigators and Whiteness alter how we evaluate identical lawyering, simply because of the race of the litigator."[31]

B. Public Defenders

Turning the tables from potential implicit bias of clients toward lawyers is an examination of the ways in which implicit biases affect attorney interaction with clients. A prime example, drawn from the criminal context, is the way public defenders perform triage, much like an ER, because of overwhelmingly large caseloads. Professors L. Song Richardson and Phillip A. Goff explore this phenomenon in their article "Implicit Racial Bias in Public Defender Triage."[32] They start by noting the recent fiftieth anniversary of the Supreme Court's landmark decision in *Gideon v. Wainright*, which promised those accused of felonies "the guiding hand of counsel."[33] Burgeoning caseloads and a crisis in lack of resources "make it virtually impossible to provide zealous and effective representation to every client."[34] Instead, Richardson and Goff describe what they see as public defender triage this way:

> In an ideal world, defenders would have unlimited opportunities to interview and investigate all of the state's witnesses, canvass

the neighborhood where the crime occurred, and otherwise thoroughly investigate the case. Furthermore, defenders could conduct legal research, file motions, request funds for expert assistance, and engage in extensive plea negotiations. They also would have the time to develop relationships with clients, which is critical because clients have important information that can aid attorneys in their trial preparation and their arguments for pretrial release, better plea offers, and reduced sentences. However, most PDs do not work in an ideal environment. They cannot realistically provide each client with zealous and effective advocacy. PDs are forced by circumstances to engage in triage, i.e., determining which clients merit attention and which do not. As one defender put it, "The present M.A.S.H. style operating procedure requires public defenders to divvy effective legal assistance to a narrowing group of clients, [forcing them] to choose among clients as to who will receive effective legal assistance."[35]

In this context, Professors Richardson and Goff identify three areas where implicit racial bias may adversely influence public defenders' judgments: biased evaluation of evidence, biased interactions with clients, and biased acceptance of punishments.[36]

1. Biased Evaluation

First, like all lawyers, public defenders begin evaluating cases upon the initial assignment. However, because of their unique caseload pressures, their initial evaluations likely impact their future case decisions in more significant and potentially undesirable ways than in other practices. Professors Richardson and Goff described this as follows:

> Their initial evaluations will affect a variety of subsequent decisions important to the ultimate resolution of the case. For instance, after reviewing the discovery, they may decide that expending resources to conduct a fact investigation would be a waste of time because the state's evidence is strong. On the other hand, if attorneys determine that the state's case has weaknesses they can exploit, they may expend more resources to defend the client, including investigating the case and engaging in vigorous plea bargaining. Thus, early appraisals of cases can become self-fulfilling prophecies. While attorneys must evaluate a case's merits, the problem is that IB's [implicit biases] may influence these judgments.[37]

2. Client Interaction

Second, implicit biases may have a dramatic impact on crucial interactions with clients. This is especially true with clients associated with negative stereotypes.[38] Studies demonstrate that this can involve "interpreting clients' ambiguous behaviors and facial expressions," including viewing behavior as more aggressive, ending contact with the client earlier, believing their clients to be less truthful, developing earlier perception of guilt, and "the attorney's unconscious negative expectations may produce perceptions and attributions consistent with them."[39]

3. Acceptance of Punishment

Third, implicit racial biases "may result in defenders unconsciously being more accepting of harsher sentences for some clients than others."[40] Professors Richardson and Goff cite studies that raise serious concerns that public defenders may accept harsher punishment for Black versus White offenders.[41] This may lead to less aggressive negotiations for lower sentences or failing to conduct more thorough mitigation investigations that could lead to lower sentences.[42]

Professors Richardson and Goff have five recommendations for curtailing the "pernicious effects" of implicit biases on public defender decision making: (1) transforming office culture, (2) developing objective triage standards, (3) implementing accountability mechanisms; (4) increasing awareness of implicit biases and how they affect attorney behavior, and (5) developing intentional goals for situations where implicit biases are likely activated.[43] A fuller discussion of strategies for reducing the effects of implicit bias is contained in later chapters.

In addition to Richardson and Goff's work, there is a study of implicit bias of habeas and death penalty defense lawyers.[44] In this study, Professors Theodore Eisenberg and Sheri Lynn Johnson note that criminal defense lawyers are notoriously skeptical of prosecutors' decisions to seek the death penalty based on the race of the defendant (Black) and the race of the victim (White).[45] There is also skepticism as to jurors' racial attitudes when the death penalty is imposed on Black defendants.[46] Yet, the study found, based on IAT scores, that capital defense lawyers demonstrate essentially the same types and degrees of racial implicit biases as law students, trial lawyers, and the general public.[47] The study concludes by suggesting that "introspection" about racial stereotypes by capital defense lawyers and "vigilance concerning those effects on others is necessary."[48]

While this subsection focused on criminal defense lawyers, specifically public defenders and death penalty defense lawyers, the importance of the principles discussed here obviously has much wider applications.

C. Prosecutors

With the possible exception of police officers, it is unassailable that prosecutors in state and federal courts possess greater and broader unreviewable discretion than any other actor in the criminal justice system.[49] Award-winning author Michelle Alexander, although not the first, recognized that numerous studies established that prosecutors interpret and respond to identical criminal activity differently based on the offenders' race.[50] In their breakthrough article *The Impact of Implicit Racial Bias on the Exercise of Prosecutorial Discretion*, Professors Robert Smith and Justin Levinson explore how implicit racial biases may unknowingly affect prosecutors and the myriad discretionary decisions they daily encounter.[51] The authors focus on three primary areas: charging decisions, pretrial strategy, and trial strategy.[52]

1. Charging Decisions

The most important decision prosecutors make is the fundamental decision of whether or not to charge a suspect with a crime, if their jurisdiction allows them to do that or, alternatively, to seek a grand jury indictment if that is required. Professors Smith and Levinson's discussion of this "charge or release" dilemma used several examples, including a hypothetical but realistic forcible rape case.[53]

Here are the facts:

> According to the suspect, after a romantic dinner and a movie, the complaining witness invited him back to her house. They entered her bedroom. The complaining witness grabbed his crotch area and started kissing him. He directed her onto the bed and began taking off her (and then his) clothes and began having intercourse. After roughly one minute, she slapped his face. Taking this as a sign of sexual play, he slapped her back. After roughly another minute, he saw tears rolling down her face, immediately stopped having intercourse and asked her, "What's wrong?"
>
> The witness tells a different story. She contends that the suspect closed the door after they entered the bedroom. He approached her quickly as though he was going to shove her against the door. She put up her hand in a defensive posture and struck him in the crotch area. He began kissing her. At first she tried to pull away, but then she "just sort of stopped resisting." He shoved her onto the bed and began taking off her (and then his) clothes. She said it "all happened so quickly" that she didn't know what was happening and felt like she was in "shock." She slapped his face as hard as she could muster. He then slapped her across the face with such force that she thought "my jaw had shattered." She began to sob. After a pause, he asked her, "What is wrong?" and then rolled off from on top of her. She began to sob very loudly.[54]

A prosecutor who reads these conflicting witness and suspect reports, and sees the mug shot photo of the suspect, a Black male, might implicitly and subconsciously associate aggressiveness, insatiability, and even rape with the suspect.[55] Indeed, as Professors Smith and Levinson discuss, research indicates people associate Black perpetrators with the crime of rape.[56] It's important to note that Professors Smith and Levinson are not suggesting that a prosecutor intentionally makes these associations. Rather, due to the insidious nature of how implicit biases work, these associations are automatic and not "consciously linked to race."[57] Of course, this is just one example of how unconscious implicit bias may affect the prosecutorial charging decision.

2. Pretrial Strategy

Once the charging decision is made, there are numerous pretrial decisions that prosecutors routinely make: to agree to or oppose pretrial release; the amount of bail or personal bond, if any, to request; what conditions of pretrial release to ask for; to engage in formal or informal discovery with the other side; what potential evidence is exculpatory or inculpatory and what should be turned over to the defense; what types of scientific evidence should be obtained; what motions to file; whether to allow the defendant to cooperate, and if so, what benefits to provide the defendant at sentencing; the numerous factors that go into plea bargaining decisions, including the seriousness of the crime and the accused's remorse; the race and views of the victim; and the value of cooperation, if any, just to mention just a few.

At each of the pretrial stages, it is likely that implicit biases to some degree will affect these important discretionary prosecutorial decisions. With regard to minority defendants, Professors Smith and Levinson argue that a plethora of social science research suggests "that a majority of Americans . . . harbor negative implicit attitudes toward blacks and other disadvantaged groups."[58] Social science studies "repeatedly demonstrate black Americans are stereotyped as being less intelligent, lazier, and less trustworthy than white Americans."[59] Thus, it is likely that "stereotypes that black citizens are violent, hostile and prone to criminality" adversely impact pretrial prosecutorial decisions.

3. Trial Strategy

With respect to trial strategy, two areas are discussed: jury selection and closing arguments. As all lawyers and judges in the criminal justice system know, the "prohibition against race-based strikes is clear, but policing the rule is far murkier."[60] The prohibition is clear because of the 30-year precedent established in *Batson v. Kentucky*,[61] which held the Equal Protection Clause of the 14th Amendment precludes removing potential jurors based on their race. It did not take long for Batson to be criticized. Indeed, Justice Powell wrote in his majority opinion in *Batson* that "peremptory challenges constitute a jury selection practice that permits 'those to discriminate who are of a mind to discriminate.'"[62] Even more compelling and prophetic was Justice Marshall's concurring opinion in *Batson*:

> A prosecutor's own conscious or unconscious racism may lead him easily to the conclusion that a prospective black juror is "sullen," or "distant," a characterization that would not have come to his mind

if a white juror had acted identically. A judge's own conscious or unconscious racism may lead him to accept such an explanation as well supported. . . . Even if all parties approach the Court's mandate with the best of conscious intentions, that mandate requires them to confront and overcome their own racism on all levels—a challenge I doubt all of them can meet.[63]

I have previously observed that one of the many problems with *Batson* is that a judge must essentially call a prosecutor a liar when disbelieving their alleged proffered non-discriminatory reason to sustain a challenge.[64] The problem of implicit bias in jury selection is even more insidious considering the exceptionally lame excuses that trial and appellate courts have accepted as non-discriminatory.[65] This includes, for example, potential jurors excluded because "Hindus tend . . . to have feelings a good bit different from us and the prosecutor preferred an American juror," or where a Black juror was struck "for dying her hair blond."[66] Examples like these led one court to conclude, "Any neutral reason, no matter how implausible or fantastic, even if it is silly or superstitious, is sufficient to rebut a prima facie case of discrimination."[67] In sum, implicit bias helps explain why even egalitarian prosecutors strike minority jurors disproportionately.[68]

D. Closing Argument

Professors Smith and Levinson also discuss the potential effects on jurors of closing arguments infused with implicit biases.[69] They focus on closing arguments that cast defendants as animals using language laced with animal imagery.[70] They cite a case where the prosecution referred to the defendant in closing argument as an "animal" and said that the jurors needed to "send a message to the jungle" by convicting the defendant.[71] Their article then discusses a social science study that people, even those who claim to have never heard of the stereotype, link Blacks with apes.[72] In a related study, the researchers found animalistic references in the press referring to Black defendants, but not White defendants, correlated with receiving the harshest punishments available.[73]

E. Judicial Evaluations

Does implicit bias affect lawyers' evaluations of judges—especially concerning judges of color, other minority judges, and women judges? In many states, judicial performance evaluations (JPEs) "are a critical part of selecting judges, especially in states using merit-based selection systems."[74] These evaluations can also apply in states with retention voting by the public where the constituents are simply voting a sitting judge up or down. Do female judges get penalized in their JPEs based on unconscious perceptions and implicit biases? Are they, like other women in the profession, in a "double bind" because they may be penalized in their performance evaluations both in legal jobs and as judges "for being too masculine and for not fitting the masculine stereotype of the position"?[75]

Professor Rebecca Gill's article raises probing questions about how and the likelihood that implicit bias disadvantages minority and women judges in JPEs.[76] She states,

> Unfortunately, the results presented here suggest that there is significant cause for concern about JPE attorney surveys. The sex and race disparities in the Judging the Judges survey act as a thumb on the scales, systematically disadvantaging groups that have been traditionally underrepresented on the bench. There is not a single category of questions that escapes this problem; the effects of judge sex and race are significant, large, and consistent across all of the dimensions of judicial performance evaluated by the Judging the Judges survey.[77]

It appears the evidence is not yet fully developed to reach any firm conclusions. However, the issues raised by Professor Gill should be of great concern to the legal profession. Further, critical study is imperative to ensure that implicit biases are not affecting judgments about the merits of selecting or retaining judges.[78]

F. Jurors

1. Implicit Bias Affecting Jurors' Memories

There has been little empirical study or analysis about the role of implicit bias in jury decision making. In fact, one is hard pressed to find any study involving actual trial jurors. However, there are a few studies involving mock jurors that reveal important insights into how implicit bias likely affects jurors in very significant ways. In this section, I examine the role of implicit bias in jurors misremembering important facts in racially biased ways, in evaluating ambiguous evidence in racially biased ways, and in devaluing the presumption of innocence in racially biased ways. It also shows how implicit bias likely impacts the administration of the death penalty in America.

The first study of mock jurors and implicit bias was done by Professor Justin D. Levinson in 2007 and involved the relationship between implicit bias and mock jurors misremembering case facts in racially biased ways.[79] Before turning to this study, it is important to realize that "the arc of thinking and writing about human memory reaches back at least 2,000 years to Aristotle's treatise on the nature of living things, *On the Soul*.[80] For many centuries, Aristotle's memory theory compared memory to wax impressions.[81] Other memory metaphors developed comparing memory to retrieving information from a file cabinet or a video recording.[82] We now know that the way memory works cannot be accurately described by wax impressions, file cabinets, or video cameras.[83] We now know that the memories of witnesses and jurors are not as accurate as most people think they are. Instead, the accuracy of memories is affected by a host of external and internal factors. Thus, our brains "recreate or reconstruct our experiences rather than retrieve copies of them."[84] As long as we think of human memory as a video recording, we greatly overvalue its reliability.

In Professor Levinson's study, 153 participants from wide-ranging ethnic backgrounds read two unrelated stories. Seventy-two percent of the respondents indicated they were from mixed racial backgrounds.[85] One story involved a fist-fight after two males accidentally bumped elbows in a crowded bar. The other involved the termination from employment of a marketing clerk.[86] The race of the protagonist in the stories provided the independent variable. For the fight story, participants read about William, a White; Tyronne, a Black; or Kawika, a Hawaiian—all males. In the employment termination story, participants read about Brenda, a White; Keisha, a Black; or Ka'olu, a Hawaiian—all females. Participants were randomly assigned the race and names of the protagonist. Other than that, the stories were identical.[87]

After a ten-minute distraction exercise, participants were asked to respond to 16 questions designed to test their memory of the salient facts in the stories.[88] The details of this study are fascinating, but only the general results are recounted here. As to the fight story, aggressive facts were recalled in racially biased ways. Aggressive facts were much more likely to be recalled when Tyronne was the protagonist. For example, when asked "[William/Kawika/Tyronne punched James (White) from behind]," 59 percent correctly remembered this fact when it was Tyronne; 43 percent when it was William, and 35 percent when it was Kawika.[89] Participants also misremembered important facts in racially biased ways that favored William (White).[90]

As to the employment termination story, the rate of false memories was lower. There was only a 15.2 percent false memory rate for the employment story, yet it was 34 percent for the fight story. Participants who read about Brenda (White) falsely remembered she was the employee of the month 17 percent of the time; for Keisha (Black), it was 10 percent, and for Ka'olu only 2 percent.

This study and others establish "compelling evidence linking false memory generation to stereotypes."[91] Professor Levinson, in part based on the research of other scholars, suggests that allowing jurors to take notes and ask questions of witnesses *may* reduce the effects of juror implicit memory bias and increase overall juror accuracy.[92] This is because it helps jurors focus on actual evidence, and "active juror" reforms improve the ways jurors process information.

2. Implicit Bias and Evaluation of Ambiguous Evidence

In another empirical study, Professor Levinson and Professor Danielle Young examined the effect of implicit bias on mock jurors' evaluations of ambiguous evidence in a robbery scenario.[93] This study examined the effect of altering skin tone on the arm of a perpetrator in a security camera photo of a robbery of a Quick Stop Mini Mart.[94] After participants read a paragraph about the robbery, they were shown a series of five photographs each for four seconds. The third photo was the subject of the experimental manipulation. It contained an image of the robber wearing a ski mask and holding a gun. Only the skin on the fore-arm was visible. Participants received a photo of either light- or dark-skinned forearms—everything else in the photos was identical.[95] After viewing the photos, participants were informed a suspect had been arrested. They were then asked to individually evaluate 20 items of ambiguous evidence. Here are a few examples:

The defendant used to be addicted to drugs.

The defendant has been served with a notice of eviction from his apartment.

The defendant is left-handed.

The defendant was a youth Golden Gloves boxing champ in 2006.

The defendant is a member of an anti-violence organization.

The defendant does not have a driver's license or car.[96]

The ambiguous evidence was designed so that some items tended to suggest guilt, some were neutral, and some tended to indicate innocence. After reading each piece of evidence, participants evaluated on the following 1–7 Likert Scale:

1 = very strongly tending to indicate Not Guilty

2 = strongly tending to indicate Not Guilty

3 = somewhat indicating Not Guilty

4 = neutral evidence

5 = somewhat tending to indicate Guilty

6 = strongly tending to indicate Guilty

7 = very strongly tending to indicate Guilty[97]

After completing the evidence evaluation task, participants completed sev-eral other tasks measuring explicit racial bias (the Modern Racism Scale), a task to measure how guilty or not guilty the defendant was ("On a scale of 0 [defi-nitely not guilty] to 100 [definitely guilty], how guilty is the defendant?"), and two IATs designed to measure concepts of race and guilt.[98]

Here are the key results:

- **Skin Tone Affects Judgments of Ambiguous Evidence.** The perpe-trator's forearm skin tone in the photo meaningfully affected mock jurors' judgments of the evidence. Participants who saw the photo of the darker-skinned forearm judged ambiguous evidence significantly more probative of guilt than those who viewed the lighter-skinned forearm.[99]

- **Skin Tone Affects Judgments of "How Guilty Is the Defendant?"** The perpetrator's forearm skin tone in the photo meaningfully affected how guilty the defendant was perceived to be. Participants who viewed the photo with the darker-skinned forearm judged the defendant guiltier than those who viewed the lighter-skinned forearm. Thus, simply being primed with darker skin tone not only affected judgments about ambiguous evidence, but also led participants to view the defendant as more guilty.[100]

- **Evidence Judgments Unrelated to Explicit Biases.** Scores on the two measures of explicit bias had no predictable effect on the participants' views of ambiguous evidence or on their guilty/not guilty decisions.[101]

- **The Judgments and Implicit Bias.** At the end of the study, participants were asked if they could remember the race of the perpetrator in the security camera photo. Many participants, regardless of the skin tone they viewed, could simply not recall. This result suggests that skin tone of the perpetrator was not consciously considered by participants in the judgments they made. This was reinforced by the IAT results that predicted evidence judgments, thus strengthening the conclusion that the judgments made in the study were implicit in nature.[102]

III. Implicit Bias and Effect on the Presumption of Innocence

A. In General

Over a century ago, the U.S. Supreme Court declared that the enforcement of the presumption of innocence is the foundation of our nation's criminal law.[103] But is it? Again, drawing insights from another study by Professor Levinson, the question of whether implicit racial bias calls into question the fair administration of the bedrock principle of the presumption of innocence is examined.[104] Professor Levinson found the following:

- **Racial Implicit Bias Reduced the Benefit of the Presumption of Innocence.** Participants in the study were jury-eligible students. The study further refined the data from the Quick Stop Mini Mart robbery study, and results showed that "when it comes to racial equality and the presumption of innocence, there is reason for concern."[105] The study established that there is implicit racial bias in being able to give Black defendants the same benefit of the presumption of innocence that White defendants receive. Specifically, study participants held implicit associations between Black and guilty as compared with White and not guilty.[106]

- **Warm Feeling Toward Blacks Correlated with Guilty Implicit Bias.** There was one very interesting twist that reinforces the pernicious effects of implicit bias in the courtroom. Participants who reported warmer feelings toward Blacks on an *explicit* bias test were *more* likely to show implicit guilty bias toward Blacks.[107] Thus, they were less likely to be able to give Black defendants the full benefit of the presumption of innocence.

The bottom line is that if judges, defense lawyers, and prosecutors want to ensure that jurors give minority defendants the full benefit of the presumption of innocence available to White defendants, more has to be done in the jury selection and trial process. Allowing broader questioning into potential biases and more time in jury selection to explore such biases is one potential modification to current practice.[108] As one defense lawyer put it,

> It is not that I believe that racial or demographic stereotypes are an accurate proxy for the attitudes and life experience of all prospective jurors. I do not. It is that, absent a meaningful exploration of the latter, I am stuck with the former, and it would be foolhardy or worse not to at least consider the generalizations on which the stereotypes are based.[109]

While this helps with explicit biases, it does not help with implicit biases. Also, judges could be more open to allowing questioning about bias because "it is precisely when race is not an obvious issue that white juror bias is particularly likely."[110]

B. One Judge's Approach to Implicit Bias and the Presumption of Innocence

In an attempt to increase the likelihood that jurors give defendants the full benefit of the presumption of innocence, I have taken some unusual and unconventional measures in jury selection.[111] This is important, because the research discussed above clearly indicates that jurors have a more difficult time giving minorities the full benefit of the presumption of innocence due to stereotypes of those minorities engaging in greater criminality.

I have nothing but a wellspring of admiration for my federal and state court colleagues on the trial bench. They are the bedrock of the best system for delivering justice known to humankind. As a group, however, we, along with defense counsel and prosecutors, have woefully failed to assist potential jurors in internalizing the meaning of the presumption of innocence. The hope of all judges, defense lawyers, and prosecutors should be that each juror selected will be committed to giving the accused the full benefit of the presumption of innocence. Unless we collectively and dramatically improve our efforts to explain the presumption, that hope will not be realized.

As a new trial court judge in 1994, I quickly realized that jurors lacked the information necessary to give the accused the full benefit of the presumption of innocence. In one of my first criminal jury trials, after giving what I thought was an outstanding explanation of the presumption, I discovered how little the potential jurors actually understood. I decided to ask a question I had asked in my first criminal trial, in July 1975, when I was a newly minted member of the bar. I picked a prospective juror at random and stated, "Please take a very good look at defendant Tyronne Williams." I paused and then asked, "Does he look guilty or not guilty?" The juror responded, as thousands have since, "I have no idea, I haven't heard any of the evidence yet." I proceeded to ask six or so prospective jurors the same question. Their responses were all eerily similar. I instantly knew I had been completely wrong in assuming that the potential jurors actually understood the presumption. Experience teaches that simply defining the presumption of innocence or sprinkling a few platitudes about its importance is nowhere near enough.

So what do I do? I start, like most of my colleagues, by explaining some important elements of the presumption of innocence. I explain that the presumption is so important that it applies in every criminal case from Maine to California and Hawaii to Florida. It applies in all 94 federal district courts and all state courts. The presumption, and "reasonable doubt" (which I also explain in great detail), are, for my money, the two most important concepts in the American judicial system. It is because of these two bedrock principles that our system of justice is envied around the world.

In visual terms, I explain that the presumption is like a steel curtain that surrounds the accused—except it is transparent, so we cannot actually see it. I tell potential jurors that the presumption surrounds the accused throughout the entire trial. I explain that the only way the presumption can be overcome is if the prosecution can produce enough evidence, beyond all jurors' reasonable doubts, to completely chip away the steel curtain.

I explain that the presumption may, all by itself, be sufficient to find the accused not guilty. Using my hands as the scales of justice, I explain that in civil cases the parties start even and the party filing the suit has to prove its case by just a slight movement of the scales—as if a feather has been placed on one. I then move my hands very far apart to demonstrate that the presumption requires that the scales start very far apart. So far, so good—but I assume (and hope) that most judges do this and more.

Here comes the innovative part. It happens immediately after my "trick" question when I tell potential jurors to take a good look at the accused and ask several prospective jurors if the accused looks guilty. I stand up, leave the bench, make my way into the well of the courtroom, walk directly over to the defendant, shake the accused's hand, instantly spin around, and walk up within a few feet of the front row of the prospective jurors. I assure you, there is shock and awe in the courtroom. The potential jurors are wide-eyed, and several mouths are gaping. I then state as confidently as I can, "I just shook hands with an accused that is absolutely not guilty. I believe this to my core and each of you must believe it, too, or you cannot sit on this jury." I remind them that the accused is absolutely not guilty "unless and until" the prosecution can establish guilt beyond a reasonable doubt. As my words sink in, I walk slowly back to the bench.

> The potential jurors are wide-eyed and several mouths are gaping. I then state as confidently as I can, "I just shook hands with an accused that is absolutely not guilty. I believe this to my core and each of you must believe it, too, or you cannot sit on this jury."

After taking my seat, I say, "Here is your free pass off jury duty. If any of you cannot give the accused the full benefit of the presumption of innocence, you can stand up and walk out the courtroom doors because you are free to leave. You serve your country just as well as those that are selected because you are being honest about your inability to give the accused the full benefit of the presumption of innocence."

Then I go into scenarios about the defense lawyer not doing anything and the accused not testifying. I ask the potential jurors if this would affect their ability to give the accused the full benefit of the presumption of innocence. Next, I ask this question: "If you were charged with a crime and believed you were not guilty, would you want to testify?" There are many reasons a particular defendant would not want to testify. I explore these reasons. I ask the prospective jurors, especially if they said they would want to testify, if, in the event the accused does not testify, they can promise not to hold it against the accused and not to discuss it with their fellow jurors during deliberations. Then, to re-emphasize how serious I am about the presumption, I repeat, "As I said, any of you are free to leave if, for whatever reason, you are unable to give the accused the full benefit of the presumption."

Potential jurors hear about my father, a World War II veteran who fought in the Pacific for our enduring freedoms. I tell them that, shortly after I was confirmed as a judge, my father came and watched an early criminal trial. After the trial, my father told me that he was proud of me for going out of my way to make sure the parties got a fair trial because that was one of the precious freedoms for which he and others had fought. I ask the potential jurors if they have loved ones who have served in the military or alternative service. I close this portion of the voir dire by asking if they agree that, by giving the accused the full benefit of the presumption of innocence, they honor all who have served and are serving our country. I then move on to reasonable doubt and a colorful reasonable doubt chart that I display in my PowerPoint voir dire.

IV. Summary and Expanding What We Have Learned

Memories are not like a video recorder or file cabinet but are affected by many internal and external factors. Jurors' memories of actual case facts and the creation of false memories are significantly affected by implicit biases. The darkness or lightness of the skin tone of a defendant can dramatically influence how jurors view ambiguous evidence and how convinced they are of a defendant's guilt. Jurors are less likely to give defendants with a darker skin tone the benefit of the presumption of innocence.[112] However, these things can be overcome. One judge's effort to inculcate in potential jurors a belief in the importance of giving every defendant the full benefit of the presumption of innocence and what it means can be replicated across the country.

It is my belief that judges and lawyers will be more interested in, and proactive in learning and experimenting with, strategies to reduce implicit bias in their courtrooms by understanding and comprehending the pernicious effects of implicit bias discussed in this chapter. Because most implicit bias research is in areas unrelated to the legal system, much needs to be explored.[113] Here are just a few areas of potential future inquiry: Does implicit bias result in jurors giving minority witnesses' testimony less weight, giving minority jurors' opinions less weight, or finding minority lawyers' arguments less credible? The answers to these and other probing questions await further empirical research. Later chapters discuss many of the debiasing strategies and interventions to reduce the impact of implicit bias. Thankfully, cognitive social scientists are rapidly expanding research on debiasing techniques.[114]

Conclusion

This chapter examined ways in which implicit bias manifests in the players in the criminal and civil justice systems. Implicit bias impacts a plethora of discretionary decision makers in virtually unlimited ways.

Near the end of their book, *Blindspot*, the authors (two of the three social scientists who invented the IAT), Drs. Banaji and Greenwald, indicated that we need to be concerned, not only about large consequential outcomes, but also about repeated small effects. They give as one example of a consequential outcome sending an innocent person to prison.[115] However, they observe that repeated small effects, even those so small they cannot be accurately measured, can still have enormous consequences. As an example, they use an athlete who improves 1/100th of 1 percent a day, too small an effect to be measured in a few day or even a few weeks. The improvement in a world-class 100-meter sprinter would be 1/1,000th of a second—the time to run one centimeter.[116] But, over 200 days, that is enough impact to improve .2ths of a second, which is "enough to be the difference between holding a world record and being an unnoticed also-ran."[117]

Small impacts of implicit bias have huge consequences in the larger scheme of our civil and criminal justice systems. As Martin Luther King Jr. so often reminded us, "The arc of the moral universe is long, but it bends towards justice."[118] As history has taught us, it does not bend on its own. Each of us must do more to overcome the insidious effects of implicit bias.

So You'd Like to Know More

- Jerry Kang et al., *Implicit Bias in the Courtroom*, 59 U.C.L.A LAW REVIEW 1124 (2012)

- L. Song Richardson & Phillip A. Goff, *Implicit Racial Bias in Public Defender Triage*, 122 YALE LAW JOURNAL 2626 (2013)

- Robert J. Smith & Justin D. Levinson, *The Impact of Implicit Racial Bias on the Exercise of Prosecutorial Discretion*, 35 SEATTLE UNIVERSITY LAW REVIEW 795 (2012)

- Justin D. Levinson & Danielle Young, *Different Shades of Bias: Skin Tone, Implicit Bias, and Judgments of Ambiguous Evidence*, 112 WEST VIRGINIA LAW REVIEW 307 (2010)

- Jeffery J. Rachlinski et al., *Does Racial Bias Affect Trial Judges?*, 84 NOTRE DAME LAW REVIEW 1195 (2009)

- ABA, Criminal Justice Section, Achieving and Impartial Jury, http://www.americanbar.org/groups/criminal_justice/voir_dire.html

About the Authors

Mark W. Bennett is in his 23rd year as a federal district judge in the northern district of Iowa. Judge Bennett has written, conducted empirical studies, and lectured on implicit bias across the country and trained more than 1,500 state and federal court judges on the subject. He was also the first judge in the country to both extensively discuss implicit bias with potential jurors in jury selection and provide jurors with specialized implicit bias instructions.

Endnotes

1. Dr. Nancy Hopkins, Amgen, Inc., Professor of Biology, MIT, Boston University's 141st Commencement Baccalaureate Address: Invisible Barriers and Social Change (May 18, 2014).
2. President Barack H. Obama, Remarks by the President at Howard University Commencement Ceremony (May 7, 2016).
3. Defendant's Motion for New Trial at 7–8, State of Minn. v. Haywood (4th Dist. Ct. 1928) (No. 26241) (filed June 18, 1928).
4. Jerry Kang, Mark Bennett et al., *Implicit Bias in the Courtroom*, 59 UCLA L. REV. 1124, 1129 (2012). ISC "is a field of psychology that examines the mental processes that affect social judgment but operate without conscious awareness or conscious control." *Id.* at 1129 n.10; *see generally* Kristin A. Lane, Jerry Kang & Mahzarin R. Banaji, *Implicit Social Cognition and Law*, 3 ANN. REV. L. & SOC. SCI. 427 (2007).
5. The Pogo quote, originally appearing on an Earth Day poster in 1970, has been attributed to American Navy Commodore Oliver Hazard Perry, who uttered the words on September 10, 1813, after defeating a British naval squadron on Lake Erie during the War of 1812, THIS DAY IN QUOTES (Apr. 22, 2015), http://www.thisdayinquotes.com/2011/04/we-have-met-enemy-and-he-is-us.html.
6. Jeffery J. Rachlinski et al., *Does Racial Bias Affect Trial Judges*, 84 NOTRE DAME L. REV. 1195, 1210–11 (2009) (On race implicit bias, the authors "found that the black judges

produced IAT scores comparable to those observed in the sample of black subjects obtained on the Internet. The white judges, on the other hand, demonstrated a statistically significantly stronger white preference than that observed among a sample of white subjects obtained on the Internet.") (footnotes omitted); Justin D. Levinson, Mark W. Bennett & Koichi Hioki, *Judging Implicit Bias: A National Empirical Study of Judicial Stereotypes Beyond Black and White*, 69 Fl. L. Rev. (forthcoming 2017) (authors found that federal and state trial judges demonstrated moderate to strong implicit bias against Asians and Jews on IAT tests).

7. Robert J. Smith & Justin D. Levinson, *The Impact of Implicit Racial Bias on the Exercise of Prosecutorial Discretion*, 35 Seattle U. L. Rev. 795, 798 (2012).

8. Mahzarin R. Banaji & Anthony G. Greenwald, Blindspot xi (2013).

9. *See id.* at viii–xii (for a discussion how this blind spot works).

10. Mark W. Bennett, *Confronting Cognitive "Anchoring Effect" and "Blind Spot" Biases in Federal Sentencing: A Modest Solution for Reforming a Fundamental Flaw*, 104 J. Crim. L. & Criminology 489, 491 (2014) ("This psychological blind spot prevents us from seeing our own cognitive biases, yet allows us to see them in others.") (footnote omitted); *see also* Joyce Ehrlinger et al., *Peering into the Bias Blind Spot: People's Assessments of Bias in Themselves and Others*, 31 Personality & Soc. Psychol. Bull. 680, 681–82 (2005); Emily Pronin & Matthew B. Kugler, *Valuing Thoughts, Ignoring Behavior: The Introspection Illusion as a Source of the Bias Blind Spot*, 43 J. Experimental Soc. Psychol. 565 (2007).

11. Richard West, Russell J. Meserve & Keith E. Stanovich, *Cognitive Sophistication Does Not Attenuate the Bias Blind Spot*, 103 J. Personality & Soc. Psychol.506, 513, 514 (2012) (discussing cognitive blind spots and concluding, "We found that none of these bias blind spot effects displayed a negative correlation with measures of cognitive ability (SAT total, CRT) or with measures of thinking dispositions (need for cognition, actively open-minded thinking). If anything, the correlations went in the other direction.").

12. Rachlinski et al., *supra note 6, at* 1225–26.

13. *Id.* at 1226.

14. Mark W. Bennett, *Implicit Racial Bias in Sentencing: The Next Frontier*, 126 Yale L.J. Forum ___ (forthcoming 2017) (manuscript at 8–9) (on file with the author). The data for this study and a series of spreadsheets analyzing the data are on file with the author.

15. Williams v. Pennsylvania, 136 S. Ct.1899, 1905 (2016).

16. *See infra* note 30.

17. Jerry Kang, Nilanjana Dasgupta, Kumar Yogesswarn & Gary Blasi, *Are Ideal Litigators White? Measuring the Myth of Colorblindness*, 7 J. Empirical Legal Stud. 886 (2010).

18. *Id.* at 892–93.

19. *Id.* at 895.

20. *Id.* at 899.

21. *Id.* at 896.

22. *Id.* at 897, 912.

23. *Id.* at 897.

24. *Id.* at 898.

25. *Id.* at 899.

26. *Id.*

27. *Id.*

28. *Id.* at 901.

29. *Id.*

30. *Id.* at 886. For detailed discussions of the role of both ingroup favoritism and outgroup derogation, *see* Anthony G. Greenwald & Thomas F. Pettigrew, *With Malice towards None and Charity for Some—Ingroup Favoritism Enables Discrimination*, Am. Psychol. 669, 680 (2014) ("Our strong conclusion is that, in present-day America, discrimination results

more from helping ingroup members than from harming outgroup members."); Robert J. Smith, Justin D. Levinson & Zoe Robinson, *Implicit White Favoritism in the Criminal Justice System*, 66 Ala. L. Rev. 871, 923 (2015) ("Yet, the picture created by the implicit racial bias as out-group derogation model is necessarily an incomplete one. To provide a more behaviorally rich portrait, as well as to contribute to understanding of racial disparities to which the out-group derogation model cannot speak, this Article provided the first systemic account of implicit favoritism and its role in perpetuating disparities in the criminal justice system. We explained the multiple ways in which implicit favoritism operates (e.g., through priming, through bias in explaining why an event occurred, through enhanced in-group empathy) to give the reader a sense that implicit favoritism is an umbrella term that applies to a variety of mechanisms—all of which operate without conscious intention. We then illustrated how implicit favoritism can operate in the criminal justice system by focusing on how it can impact the discretionary decisions of legislators, police officers, jurors, and legal professionals. This importation of implicit favoritism into the legal literature on racial disparities in criminal justice means that we now have a more behaviorally accurate understanding of how racial disparities are perpetuated, a better sense of the magnitude of the problem, and an understanding that scholars will need to address how we might curb favoritism—as well as derogation—if we hope to achieve a racially fair criminal justice system.").

31. Kang et al., *supra* note 5, at 912.
32. L. Song Richardson & Phillip A. Goff, *Implicit Racial Bias in Public Defender Triage*, 122 Yale L.J. 2626 (2013).
33. *Id.* at 2628.
34. *Id.* at 2631. *See also* Jonathan A. Rapping, *Implicitly Unjust: How Defenders Can Affect Systemic Racist Assumptions*, 16 N.Y.U. J. Legis. & Pub. Pol'y 999, 1007 (2013) ("Having a lawyer without the time and resources to adequately prepare only exacerbates this disparity."); Rebecca Marcus, *Racism in Our Courts: The Underfunding of Public Defenders and Its Disproportionate Impact on Racial Minorities*, 22 Hastings Const. L.Q. 219 (1994).
35. Richardson & Goff, *supra* note 32, at 2635 (footnote omitted).
36. *Id.* at 2634–40.
37. *Id.* at 2635.
38. *Id.* at 2636–37.
39. *Id.* at 2637–38.
40. *Id.* at 2641.
41. *Id.* at 2640.
42. *Id.*
43. *Id.* at 2641–48.
44. Theodore Eisenberg & Sherri Lynn Johnson, *Implicit Racial Attitudes of Death Penalty Lawyers*, 53 DePaul L. Rev. 1539 (2004).
45. *Id.* at 1539.
46. *Id.*
47. *Id.* at 1542, 1553, 1556.
48. *Id.* at 1556.
49. Smith & Levinson, *supra* note 8, at 805. *See also* Stephanos Bibas, *Prosecutorial Regulation Versus Prosecutorial Accountability*, 157 U. Pa. L. Rev. 959, 960 (2009).
50. Michelle Alexander, The New Jim Crow 115 (2010).
51. Smith & Levinson, *supra* note 8, at 805–22.
52. *Id.* at 805.
53. *Id.* at 808–10.
54. *Id.* at 808–09.
55. *Id.* at 809.
56. *Id.*
57. *Id.* at 809–10.

58. *Id.* at 797.
59. *Id.* at 814.
60. *Id.* at 818.
61. 476 U.S. 79 (1986).
62. Smith & Levinson, *supra* note 8 at 818, citing Batson v. Kentucky, 476 U.S. 79, 96 (1986) (quoting Avery v. Georgia, 345 U.S. 559, 562 (1953)).
63. *Batson*, 476 U.S. at 106 (1986) (Marshall, J., concurring).
64. Mark W. Bennett, *Unraveling the Gordian Knot of Implicit Bias in Jury Selection: The Problems of Judge-Dominated Voir Dire, the Failed Promise of Batson, and Proposed Solutions*, 4 Harv. L. & Pol'y Rev. 149, 162 (2010).
65. *Id.* at 162–65.
66. *Id.*
67. *Id.* at 163, citing Pruitt v. McAdory, 337 F.3d 921, 928 (7th Cir. 2003) (internal quotation marks and citations omitted).
68. Anthony Page, *Batson's Blind-Spot: Unconscious Stereotyping and the Peremptory Challenge*, 85 B.U. L. Rev. 155 (2005).
69. Smith & Levinson, *supra* note 8, at 819–20.
70. *Id.*
71. *Id.* at 820.
72. *Id.*
73. *Id.*
74. Rebecca D. Gill, *Implicit Bias in Judicial Performance Evaluations: We Must Do Better than This*, Justice Sys. J. 1 (2014).
75. *Id.* at 6–7.
76. *Id.* at 19–20.
77. *Id.* at 19.
78. In a different but related context, a recent study found that implicit bias was a likely factor in Black federal district judges being reversed more often than their White colleagues after taking into account factors such as education, qualifications, and experience. Maya Sen, *Is Justice Really Blind? Race and Reversal in U.S. Courts*, 44 J. Legal Stud. 187, 221 (2015).
79. Justin D. Levinson, *Forgotten Racial Equality: Implicit Bias, Decisionmaking, and Misremembering*, 57 Duke L.J. 345 (2007).
80. Mark W. Bennett, *Unspringing the Witness Memory and Demeanor Trap: What Every Judge and Juror Needs to Know about Cognitive Psychology and Witness Credibility*, 64 Notre Dame L. Rev. 1331, 1340 (2015) (footnote omitted).
81. *Id.*
82. *Id.* at 1335–36.
83. *Id.*
84. *Id.* at 1336, citing Daniel L. Schacter, The Seven Sins of Memory: How the Mind Forgets and Remembers 9 (2001).
85. Levinson, *supra* note 79, at 390.
86. *Id.* at 392, 423.
87. *Id.* at 394–95.
88. *Id.* at 393–94.
89. *Id.* at 400–01.
90. *Id.*
91. *Id.* at 408.
92. *Id.* at 400–11. For a comprehensive empirical study of lawyers and judges' perceptions of allowing jurors to ask questions of witnesses, see Thomas D. Waterman, Mark W. Bennett & David C. Waterman, *A Fresh Look at Jurors Questioning Witnesses: A Review of Eighth Circuit and Iowa Appellate Precedents and an Empirical Analysis of Federal and State Trial Judges and Trial Lawyers*, 64 Drake L. Rev. 485 (2016).

93. Justin D. Levinson & Danielle Young, *Different Shades of Bias: Skin Tone, Implicit Bias, and Judgments of Ambiguous Evidence*, 112 W. VA. L. REV. 307 (2010).

94. *Id.* at 331–32.

95. *Id.* at 332. The skin tone manipulation in this study was what social scientists call a between-subjects independent variable.

96. *Id.* at 333.

97. *Id.*

98. *Id.* at 334.

99. *Id.* at 337. This result was obtained using a MANCOVA (a multivariate analysis of a variance test) statistical model. *Id.* at 336.

100. *Id.* at 337. A MANCOVA statistical model was also used to determine how guilty the suspect was perceived to be with the addition of a logical regression analysis to determine these two variables on the decision of guilty or not guilty. *Id.* at 336–337.

101. *Id.* at 338. This was also true when adding the explicit bias results to the regression analysis. *Id.*

102. *Id.*

103. Coffin v. United States, 156 U.S. 432, 453 (1895) ("The presumption of innocence in favor of the accused is undoubted law, axiomatic and elementary, and its enforcement lies at the foundation of the administration of our criminal law.").

104. Justin D. Levinson, Huajian Cai & Danielle Young, *Guilty by Implicit Bias: The Guilty/Not Guilty Implicit Association Test*, 8 OHIO ST. J. CRIM. L. 187 (2010).

105. *Id.* at 207.

106. *Id.* at 204.

107. *Id.* at 205.

108. *See* Anna Roberts, *(Re)Forming the Jury: Detection and Disinfection of Implicit Juror Bias*, 44 CONN. L. REV. 827, 843–44 (2012).

109. Abbe Smith, *"Nice Work If You Can Get It": "Ethical" Jury Selection in Criminal Defense*, 67 FORDHAM L. REV. 523, 530–31 (1998).

110. Roberts, *supra* note 108, at 846.

111. Mark W. Bennett, *The Presumption of Innocence and Trial Court Judges: Our Greatest Failing*, THE CHAMPION 18–20 (May 2015).

112. In a well-known and often-cited study, researchers found that the extent to which a Black defendant in a capital case with a White victim is perceived by the jury to have stronger Afrocentric features, the more likely that defendant will be sentenced to death. Jennifer L. Eberhardt et al., *Looking Deathworthy, Perceived Stereotypicality of Black Defendants Predicts Capital-Sentencing Outcomes*, 17 PSYCHOL. SCIENCE 383 (2006); *see also* Jill Viglione et al., *The Impact of Light Skin on Prison Time for Black Female Offenders*, 48 SOC. SCIENCE J. 250 (2011) (collecting studies on lighter skin tone and shorter sentences).

113. Mike Morrison et al., *Stacking the Jury: Legal Professionals' Preemptory Challenges Reflect Jurors' Levels of Implicit Bias*, 42 PERSONALITY & SOC. PSYCHOL. BULL. 1129, 1130 (2016) ("[C]ompared to the exponentially growing body of research in the area of implicit social cognition empirical data . . . in legal decision-making it is still scarce.").

114. *See, e.g.*, Calvin K. Lai et al., *Reducing Implicit Racial Preferences: A Comparative Investigation of 17 Interventions*, 143 J. EXPERIMENTAL PSYCHOL. 1765 (2014).

115. MAHZARIN R. BANAJI & ANTHONY G. GREENWALD, BLINDSPOT 202 (2013).

116. *Id.* at 205.

117. *Id. But see* Frederick L. Oswald et al., *Using the IAT to Predict Ethnic and Racial Discrimination: Small Effect Sizes of Unknown Societal Significance*, 108 J. PERSONALITY & SOC. PSYCHOL. 562 (2015) (disputing the extent of Banaji & Greenwald's repeated small effects claim of implicit bias being a predictor of discriminatory behavior).

118. *See* TAYLOR BRANCH, PARTING THE WATERS: AMERICA IN THE KING YEARS, 1954–63, 197 (1988) ("[O]ne of King's favorite lines, from the abolitionist preacher Theodore Parker, [was] 'The arc of the moral universe is long, but it bends toward justice.'").

Chapter 5

Implicit Bias in Judicial Decision Making
How It Affects Judgment and What Judges Can Do About It

Judge Andrew J. Wistrich and Jeffrey J. Rachlinski

Chapter Contents

Chapter Highlights

- Empirical research indicates that—like jurors, lawyers, and other non-judges—judges possess implicit biases.

- Evidence of implicit bias in judges includes judges' scores on the Implicit Association Test, experimental results, and archival analysis of litigation outcomes.

- Research on judges shows that judges are good decision makers, but like most people, they tend to rely too heavily on their intuition.

- Implicit bias and overreliance on emotion and intuition can lead judges to make predictable errors in judgment and can exacerbate the influence of ingroup preferences and implicit biases.

- Judges and others can take practical steps to reduce the risk that implicit biases might taint judges' decisions.

Introduction

Perhaps no more disturbing allegation can be leveled against a judge than that of bias. Impartiality undergirds the judicial role. Biases arising from the race or gender of a party are especially pernicious. The mere suspicion that a judge has acted on such bias inspires protest. Consider that over one million people have signed a petition calling for the removal of California judge Aaron Persky, after he sentenced a White Stanford undergraduate to six months for sexual assault yet also sentenced a Mexican immigrant to three years for a similar crime a few weeks later.[1] And consider the fierce reaction to then-candidate Donald Trump's charge that the judge assigned to a case involving one of his businesses could not be fair because the judge was of Mexican heritage.[2] We rightly expect our judges to produce decisions free of racial and gender bias and react strongly when we fear that they do not.

Virtually all contemporary judges embrace egalitarian norms, but suspicion that the legal system retains substantial biases persists. A majority of White Americans state that they believe the criminal justice system is fair, but most African-Americans disagree. A recent survey by the Pew Research Center, for example, shows that although only 43 percent of White

Americans think that racial bias influences outcomes in court, 75 percent of African-Americans believe that "blacks are treated less fairly in the courts."[3] A 2015 survey by the National Center for State Courts concludes that "there is a massive racial gap on most measures [of trust in the courts], with African Americans much more distrustful of the courts and the broader justice system."[4]

Concerns about bias in the justice system have some justification. African-Americans comprise roughly 40 percent of the prison population in the United States, even though they constitute only 13 percent of the overall population.[5] To be sure, some of this disparity arises from other structural aspects of society, including disparities in poverty and access to educational opportunities. Careful studies of the criminal justice system that control for the background of offenders, however, still reveal pervasive racial disparities. African-American suspects are more likely to be arrested, more likely to be indicted when they are arrested, more likely to be convicted when they are indicted, and serve longer sentences on average than their White counterparts.[6] Studies of "departures" in the federal system (in which a judge deviates from the sentencing guidelines) show that downward departures are much more common for White defendants than for Black defendants—even for identical crimes.[7]

Results like these are a puzzle. In an era in which judges embrace egalitarian norms, why do we continue to observe large disparities in outcomes between Black and White parties in court? On rare occasions, judges do still make questionable statements that seem tinged with latent racism. Judge James Gosnell, the presiding judge in the case of accused mass murderer and White supremacist Dylann Roof, for example, once stated from the bench that he believed that the world contained "white people, black people, red necks and n---rs,"[8] prompting obvious concerns for his impartiality. Periodic utterances such as this (repugnant though they are) are now a rarity—and represent a far cry from the racist rhetoric and thinking that once pervaded our judicial system. We seriously doubt that many judges harbor the kind of open racial animus and bigotry that once plagued the courts and society at large. But if nearly all judges are color-blind egalitarians, then why do racial minorities still obtain less favorable outcomes in the courtroom?

Outside of the judicial context, evidence continues to mount that unconscious bias taints how people think about others.[9] Even people committed to egalitarian norms commonly harbor invidious unconscious associations. Most adults more easily associate African-Americans than Whites with violent imagery and more closely associate women with domestic, rather than career-oriented, imagery. These associations can influence how people think, even though they might not be aware of it. Most people believe that accepting a consciously race-neutral outlook is enough to eliminate the role race plays in decision making, but the research on implicit bias suggests that it is not. Consequently, most people have a blind spot in which unconscious associations can still influence their judgment.[10]

Does unconscious bias affect judges in the courtroom? And if so, what can be done about it? This chapter presents evidence that judges rely too heavily on cognitive processes that can allow bias to creep unwittingly into their decisions. It also discusses ways in which judges can reduce these influences.

I. Does Unconscious Bias Influence Judges?

In this section, we present evidence that hidden factors can influence how judges think. We explain the role that intuitive cognitive processes play in judicial decision making and show how the same processes can (and do) produce undesirable influences on judicial decision making.

A. Unconscious Influences on Judgment: Intuitive Reactions Can Trump Careful Deliberation

Identifying how unconscious biases can influence the judgment of well-meaning judges requires taking a step back and assessing how human judgment functions more generally. An increasing body of research indicates that people have two distinctive styles of decision making: intuitive and deliberative.[11] Intuitive decision making consists of relying on one's first instinct. Intuition is emotional. It relies on close associations and rapid, shallow cognitive processing. Intuitively, if a choice sounds right and feels right, then it is the right choice. Psychologists sometimes refer to this style of decision making as System 1 reasoning. System 1 produces rapid, effortless, confident judgments and operates outside conscious awareness. When we go with our gut, we decide quickly and feel that we are right.

But human beings did not develop advanced civilizations with System 1. Human beings, of course, have an enormous capacity for higher-order deliberative reasoning. Mathematics, deductive logic, and analogical reasoning require much more than simple intuition. Psychologists sometimes refer to higher-order reasoning as System 2. System 2 is slower and conscious. It requires effort, and if we are distracted, rushed, or tired, we use System 2 less. Oddly, when the two conflict, people have less faith in System 2 than in System 1.[12] But System 2 is where logic—and hence most legal reasoning—lies.

The concept that we make decisions with intuition or with deliberation is an imperfect fiction, of course. First impressions sometimes guide deliberation—so System 1 can bleed over into System 2. Also, some cognitive processes start out requiring System 2 reasoning but can become System 1 processes over time. Mathematics works this way in grade-school children. At first, 3 + 5 requires effort (sometimes fingers). But most adults process 3 + 5 as 8 with no effort; with repetition, it has become intuitive. But for all except mathematical savants, 137 + 285 requires effort. The conversion of assessments that once required System 2 into System 1 underlies many kinds of expertise.

Some mental processes are also hard to classify as System 1 or System 2. And neuroscientists can identify dozens of different neurological structures that are engaged (or not) in various reasoning tasks. But on the whole, the distinction between quick, intuitive reactions and slow, deliberative reasoning has been a useful construct for understanding human reasoning—and it can help explain much of the problem of unconscious race and gender bias.

System 1 seems like the chief source of unwanted influences on judging. The temptation is to think that suppressing or ignoring System 1 would produce egalitarian assessments. We cannot truly suppress System 1, however. Doing so would be unwise, even if it were possible. Intuition is the engine that drives judgment in many circumstances. Consider the research on people who have poorly developed affective systems.[13] One might think they are excellent decision makers, since they are free from irrational emotional reactions. In fact, they are terrible decision makers. System 1 is an unavoidable and essential part of human judgment. It is actually crucial in emergencies and facilitates good judgment in many settings.[14] But it can be a source of error.

Consider the following problem:[15]

A bat and a ball together cost $1.10. The bat cost $1.00 more than the ball. How much does the ball cost?

The combination of seeing the $1.10 and the $1.00 triggers the intuitive response of 10 cents in most people. But if the ball costs 10 cents, then the bat would cost $1.10, and together they would sum to $1.20—which is not right. The correct answer is five cents. If the ball costs five cents, then the bat costs a dollar more, or $1.05, and together they sum to $1.10. Calculating the correct answer is not difficult, but most well-educated adults get it wrong. Ironically, altering the problem to make it more difficult produces more correct answers. For example, consider this variation:

A banana and a bagel together cost 37 cents. The bagel costs 13 cents more than the banana. How much does the banana cost?

Although the math is more complicated, more people get this problem correct (12 cents). Intuition suggests no obvious answer, and so only some math will solve the problem. In the case of the bat and the ball, however, 10 cents simply seems like the right answer.

The bat-and-ball problem creates a powerful illusion of judgment and shows how System 1 can create a blind spot that makes decision makers vulnerable to error. System 1 produces an excess of confidence, which can be seen in how people react to the problem. People who get the problem wrong by choosing the intuitive answer think the problem is easier than those who get it right. Also, offering a reward for getting the correct answer does not improve accuracy;

people paid to be correct feel more strongly that they must go with their gut. So powerful is the intuition that a majority of undergraduates still choose 10 cents as the answer even after the following statement is added underneath the problem: "Hint, it's not 10 cents."[16] Confidence in the intuitive answer overshadows the barest hint that another answer is even possible, creating the intuitive blind spot.

But much of this research relies on undergraduates as subjects. What about professionals such as judges? Some types of professionals—notably engineers—learn that they should distrust their intuition and perform the calculations. Judges must constantly disentangle competing arguments to see which logical structure best fits a set of legal rules and precedent. All of this is System 2 work. Maybe by proclivity or through experience, judges, like engineers, simply know they need to do the math.

Not so. Studies of judges indicate that they are not, by nature, System 2 thinkers—at least on problems of this sort.[17] For example, judges, like most adults, get questions like the bat-and-ball question wrong. In one study, Florida trial judges answered the bat-and-ball question, along with two similar questions (which together comprise the Cognitive Reflection Test, or CRT), and answered an average of only 1.23 (out of three) questions correctly.[18] In another study, a group of administrative law judges did a little better, getting 1.33 correct, but still got most wrong. Thousands of judges have now taken the CRT with similar results. Judges follow their intuition, even though it is wrong. Intuition creates a blind spot on the CRT questions.

Insight can be domain specific, however. Perhaps judges find it easier to set aside their intuitive reactions in judicial settings. Dozens of studies on precisely this subject have been conducted. As we discuss below, although judges sometimes avoid common errors that intuition can produce, judges more frequently rely on misleading intuitive reactions, even when doing so leads to erroneous or otherwise indefensible judgments.[19]

B. Intuition in Judicial Settings: The Example of Anchoring

In assessing whether judges rely on misleading intuitions in legal settings, research has focused on intuitive processes that psychologists have found to be common sources of mistaken judgments. One such process that we believe influences judges is "anchoring." Anchoring refers to an excessive reliance on numeric reference points when making numeric judgments.[20] Numeric reference points (or "anchors") create a powerful intuition that the correct answer lies somewhere near the starting point. In many circumstances, this is a helpful intuition. When you are determining how much you will pay for a new car, for example, the sticker price provides a useful anchor. Car buyers generally negotiate down from that initial number, but buyers know that they will not pay $10,000 for a car with a sticker price of $36,998. Numeric reference points are generally useful, which is why most decision makers, including judges, rely on them.

The problem with anchors is that they create powerful intuitions even when they are meaningless. In one study, researchers asked undergraduates to write down the last three digits of their phone number, add 400 to that result, and then assess first whether Attila the Hun was born before or after that year and then when Attila the Hun was actually born.[21] The students obviously knew that Attila the Hun has nothing to do with their phone numbers, but their estimates of Attila's birth year correlated with their phone numbers nonetheless. In a similar demonstration, business school students actually altered their bids on bottles of fine wine when asked to first assess whether their reservation prices were greater or less than the last two digits of their Social Security number.[22] In the actual auction, the wine almost invariably sold to those who had a Social Security number with an 8 or a 9 as the penultimate digit.

Anchors also affect judges. A series of studies have shown that numeric anchors influence how judges determine appropriate damage awards, criminal sentences, and fines.[23] In one such study, for example, a group of administrative law judges were asked to determine an appropriate damage award for a civil rights complaint filed by a secretary.[24] The secretary had been fired for complaining about a new supervisor who had ridiculed her ancestry at work (she was described as Mexican-American). Although the facts make out an easy case for recovery, the secretary secured a position in another company immediately after being fired, so her damages were limited to "mental anguish" over the firing. The materials described the anguish in some detail and requested a damage award. For half of the judges, the materials also stated that the plaintiff testified that "she recently saw a case similar to hers on a 'court television show' where the plaintiff received a compensatory damage award for mental anguish." The other half of the judges received the same testimony, except that the plaintiff also stated the amount of the award she had seen on television—namely $415,300. Without this number present, the median award to the plaintiff was $6,250; with the number present, it was $50,000. The reference to $415,300 had a huge effect on how the judges thought about the case.

In this study, the judges were certainly aware that the plaintiff's reference to $415,300 was irrelevant. In a separate session, a group of appellate judges were asked whether the testimony (containing the number) was admissible. All agreed it was not. Nearly all of them (87 percent) also stated admitting this testimony in a bench trial would have been a "harmless error." The anchor clearly created a blind spot for the judges. They believed the number to be harmless when in fact it increased the median award dramatically.

In many other settings, research shows that irrelevant anchors influence how judges assess cases. These include statutory damage caps that vastly exceed the expected award, the jurisdictional minimum in federal court (even in a case that obviously exceeded the minimum), prior criminal sentences in unrelated cases, and extreme (and inadmissible) settlement offers.[25] In one study, judges imposed a higher fine on a nightclub for a noise ordinance violation when the club was identified as "Club 11,866" (after its street address) than when it was identified as "Club 58." Judges also imposed a shorter sentence on a criminal defendant when asked to do so in months as opposed to years; in that study, a nine-year sentence seemed appropriate to the judges sentencing in years, but 63 months seemed appropriate to the judges sentencing in months. Research also shows that judges sitting in actual cases rely on misleading recommendations in imposing sentences and that altering the scale (in this instance from months to days) influences sentences.[26]

C. Instructing Judges to Ignore Intuition: The Example of Inadmissible Evidence

Beyond numeric estimates, judges face many sources of potentially misleading intuition when deciding cases. Chief among these might be the influence of inadmissible evidence. All factfinders—judge or jury—must found their decisions on the record and only on the record. Inadmissible evidence must be set aside and cannot be the basis for a legitimate decision.

Setting aside what we know is extremely difficult. Ignoring known information is not something the human brain is designed to accomplish. "Man's great misfortune is that he has no organ, no kind of eyelid or brake, to mask or block a thought, or all thought, when he wants to."[27] Part of what makes intuition a powerful force is that the brain quickly absorbs new information and updates our beliefs. Indeed, when people try to ignore known information, they actually pay more attention to it.[28] Efforts to disregard inadmissible evidence in legal settings are no different. Dozens of mock jury studies show that no reliable mechanism exists to expunge the inadmissible evidence from jurors' minds.[29] Some studies find that jurors pay more attention to evidence they are instructed to disregard; others show that jurors sometimes ignore inadmissible evidence; and still others show that they can overreact to instructions to ignore. The best option is to ensure that jurors never hear the inadmissible evidence in the first place.

Judges, however, cannot shield themselves from inadmissible evidence. They are both the gatekeepers of evidence and the decision makers. Debate persists as to whether judges are any different than jurors. Some scholars have argued that "[n]ature does not furnish a jurist's brain with thought-tight compartments to suit the convenience of legal theory, and convincing evidence does leave its mark."[30] Others contend that "[i]t is realistic to suppose that judges can do better than juries in relying on what is admissible and ignoring what is not."[31] We believe that although judges understand better than jurors why some evidence must be excluded, they are unlikely to have developed any meaningful ability to compartmentalize it. Relevant but inadmissible evidence can create an intuitive sense of how a case should be resolved, and that intuitive sense likely influences how judges decide.

In a series of studies that compared decisions in hypothetical cases made by judges who were exposed to inadmissible information and by those who were not, judges found it difficult to ignore inadmissible information.[32] In most of these studies, judges first determined whether the information was admissible and then had to ignore it if they suppressed it. If judges can ignore inadmissible information, then those judges who suppressed the inadmissible evidence should have made roughly the same decisions as those judges who never saw the inadmissible evidence. With a notable exception, however, judges were unable to ignore the inadmissible evidence.

As one example of the difficulties that judges had ignoring inadmissible evidence, a group of trial judges in Arizona were asked to assess a criminal case involving sexual assault.[33] They were presented with a case in which a college co-ed accused a fellow student of sexual assault during a fraternity party. The complainant admitted to having intercourse with the defendant but denied that she had given consent. The facts indicated that the complainant immediately contacted police after the incident and had bruising consistent with a sexual assault. For half of the judges, the materials stated that the defendant had attempted to introduce testimony concerning the complainant's sexual history. The testimony consisted of the complainant's roommate's assertions that the complainant "liked to loosen her inhibitions with a few beers too many and have rough sex with the first guy she saw." Such testimony is inadmissible under Arizona's rape-shield statute,[34] and most of the judges ruled the testimony inadmissible. Even though they suppressed the evidence, the conviction rate plummeted from 49 percent among the judges who did not see this testimony to 20 percent among judges who saw the testimony and suppressed it. The conviction rates of those judges who suppressed the testimony and those who admitted it (8 percent) were similar. In effect, it made no difference whether the judges who read the inadmissible evidence excluded or admitted it; regardless of their rulings, they relied on it.

Other studies have found a similar inability to disregard inadmissible evidence in other contexts. Judges could not ignore; a discussion protected by attorney-client privilege in a civil case; the past criminal conviction of a civil defendant; discussions that occurred during a settlement conference; and statements made by a criminal defendant that a prosecutor had agreed not to use as part of a plea agreement.[35] Although these studies uncovered some evidence that judges were able to ignore criminal confessions, subsequent research revealed that judges actually did pay attention to criminal confessions but suppressed their influence so as to penalize the police who had violated the constitutional rights of criminal suspects.[36]

The one area in which judges clearly ignored inadmissible evidence was in making probable cause determinations. In a series of studies, judges assessing whether to grant warrants in hypothetical cases made roughly the same assessments as judges who had to determine whether a search conducted pursuant to an exception to the warrant requirement was supported by the requisite probable cause.[37] The latter determination required a judge to ignore the fact that the search turned up incriminating evidence. Surprisingly, most judges were able to do this. We believe that in this intricate area of law judges focus on the relevant precedent, which requires them to engage in a deliberative analysis that nudges judges to look beyond their intuitive reactions.

On the whole, however, knowing too much is a problem for judges. They cannot really mentally sequester the inadmissible evidence. In the sexual assault case we studied, learning that the complainant had engaged in consensual conduct similar to that which formed the basis of her complaint undermined the judges' assessments of her credibility. Judges were unable to factor it out of their calculus. In most of our examples, the bulk of the evidence supported one conclusion, but the inadmissible evidence made it seem that the bulk of the evidence was simply wrong. This intuition then tainted how the judges ultimately viewed the materials.

D. Emotional Decision Making in Judges

The intuitive reactions to anchors and inadmissible evidence are both understandable and maybe defensible. Numeric anchors are usually informative, so asking judges to disregard them is a tall order. In some cases, judges can defend a reliance on an anchor as a sensible approach. The research on anchoring thus shows that judges find it difficult to identify when their intuition is misleading them (just as we found with the cognitive reflection test). The research on ignoring inadmissible evidence goes a little further. These results suggest that judges find it difficult to confine their decisions to the facts in the record. Their reliance on the inadmissible evidence shows that judges cannot easily avoid relying on their extraneous knowledge and beliefs. This concern led us to hypothesize that judges might also have emotional reactions to cases (or litigants) that could shape or guide their legal judgments.

Judges usually deny that emotion influences their decisions. In her confirmation hearings, for example, Justice Sotomayor stated, "[I]t's not the heart that compels conclusions in cases, it's the law."[38] Her statement reflected an effort to distance herself from some of her own earlier statements as well as from President Obama's assertions that he wanted to appoint empathetic judges. Justice Kagan similarly navigated the same waters when asked if she agreed that "law is only 25 miles of the marathon and emotion is the last mile"; she rejected the assertion outright by claiming, "it is law all the way down."[39] Judges seem to understand that our society wants them to reject emotion as a source of guidance.[40]

We doubt that emotional influences vanish when judges put on their robes. Emotion is a powerful source of intuition, and its influence on decision making is robust and even useful.[41] People react negatively to horrific criminal acts, and disgust should perhaps guide sentencing. Defendants who have behaved horribly in the past might sensibly be thought to lack credibility. Attending to emotional cues is thus potentially desirable, and it might be impossible to avoid doing so in any event. Justice Robert Jackson, in fact, likened dispassionate judges to "Uncle Sam, Santa Clause, the Easter Bunny, and other fictional characters."[42]

> We are skeptical that emotional influences vanish when judges put on their robes. Emotion is a powerful source of intuition, and its influence on decision making is broad and robust. Like most intuitions, emotion often provides useful guidance.

Emotional reactions can have an undesirable influence on judges, however. Invidious reactions based on race and gender commonly manifest as emotional reactions that are hard to ignore. Emotional reactions to people can also be erratic and might possess little or no relevance to case outcomes. For example, Dan Simon and his coauthors showed that emotions can influence how lay people view the development of a legal theory, even when the emotion is transparently irrelevant to the legal issue.[43] In their study, they varied the social desirability of a litigant making a novel legal argument. Their variation not only influenced how their subjects reacted to the litigant, but also influenced how they viewed that litigant's argument in a subsequent case involving unrelated parties. The emotional reaction to the initial litigant tainted people's reaction to a more general legal issue. If spillovers like this are common, then the concerns first raised by Jeremy Bentham that the path of the law can follow a chaotic course dictated by the characteristics of an early case might be valid.[44]

Research has shown that irrelevant emotions influence judges.[45] In one study, judges were asked to evaluate a (hypothetical) statute meant to shield the use of medical marijuana from prosecution.[46] The statute provided that a defendant may not be prosecuted for marijuana possession if "a physician has stated in an affidavit or otherwise under oath" that the defendant has a medical need for marijuana. The materials described a defendant who did not have such an affidavit at the time of his arrest but obtained one afterward and then moved to dismiss the prosecution. Ruling on the motion required the judges to determine if the phrase "has stated" can include a post-arrest affidavit. This determination is an exercise of statutory construction that does not depend on characteristics of the defendant making the motion. The defendant's characteristics mattered enormously, however. Judges were far less inclined to rule favorably for a defendant described as a 19-year-old taking the drug to combat seizures than for a defendant described as a 55-year-old who was dying of bone cancer. One can understand being more sympathetic to the 55-year-old, but the materials requested a ruling on the meaning of a statute of general applicability, which should not depend on the characteristics of any individual defendant. Judges were nevertheless unable to put aside their sympathies to make an abstract judgment.

In other research, sympathetic litigants induced judges to make more favorable rulings in a range of cases.[47] Judges were more inclined to bend the law to favor an undocumented immigrant who had entered the United States to earn money for a sick daughter than one who was tracking down a rogue member of a drug cartel. They were more likely to rule a city jail's blanket strip-search policy was per se unconstitutional when the lead plaintiff was a co-ed protestor than a male armed robber. Bankruptcy judges treated a debtor who ran up debt to help an ailing parent more favorably than one who ran up debt to go on vacation, even though the relevant law does not authorize disparate treatment based on the source of the debt. Judges were more inclined to declare a search of an employee's locker constitutionally acceptable when the search uncovered a large quantity of heroin than when it uncovered only two marijuana cigarettes. Notwithstanding Justice Kagan's assertions, emotion seems to be some portion of the marathon.

E. Judicial Intuition Favoring Ingroups

Because invidious influences often arise as emotional reactions, the influence that emotion has on judges has the potential to undermine judges' egalitarian commitments. Research suggests that judges do not easily set aside their intuitions, even when their intuitions are misleading and even when doing so is essential to being impartial. Judges are highly motivated to set aside "invidious" preconceptions and prejudices, however, so they might avoid some of the common prejudices that social scientists find to be widespread in ordinary adults.

The tendency to favor ingroups is perhaps one of the most widespread findings in social science. As William Graham Sumner put it over a century ago,

> [Ethnocentrism is] the view of things in which one's own group is the center of everything and all others are scaled and rated with reference to it. . . . Each group nourishes its own pride and vanity, boasts itself superior, exalts its own divinities, and looks with contempt on outsiders.[48]

A seemingly endless set of studies indicate that even the most minimal, most meaningless distinctions between people facilitate ingroup favoritism.[49] Classic social psychology experiments in which researchers divided children in obviously random ways produced enormous discrimination between the groups.[50]

> Research suggests that judges do not easily set aside their intuitions, even when that intuition is misleading and even when doing so is essential to being impartial. But judges are so highly motivated to set aside "invidious" preconceptions and prejudices that maybe they manage to avoid some of the common prejudices that social scientists find to be widespread in ordinary adults.

Geographic favoritism among sports fans is also notoriously potent but largely harmless.

Geographic favoritism in the judicial process, however, is hardly benign. Diversity jurisdiction owes its existence to the concern that litigants cannot get equal justice when pursuing or defending claims outside of their home states.[51] Although one might think that such parochialism has faded since the founding of the Republic, lawyers still believe it persists.[52] But do judges also express home-team favoritism in litigation? Consider the following quote from the former chief justice of the West Virginia Supreme Court, Justice Richard Neely:

> [A]s long as I am allowed to redistribute wealth from out-of-state companies to injured in-state plaintiffs, I shall continue to do so. Not only is my sleep enhanced when I give someone else's money away, but so is my job security, because the in-state plaintiffs, their families, and their friends will re-elect me.[53]

Most judges would reject such an overt bias—just as they would overtly reject other invidious biases. But the role that we have found that intuition and emotion play in judicial decision making suggests that ingroup bias might still influence their judgment, even if they reject the overt bias Judge Neely expresses.

In a test for this influence in judges, over 100 Minnesota judges were asked to assess a hypothetical case involving a business that began dumping hazardous chemicals in a nearby lake on private land so as to avoid the cost of proper disposal.[54] This activity injured the landowner after he went swimming in the lake just after the business owner dumped some dangerous chemicals. The materials indicated that the parties had settled on an amount for compensatory damages, but the injured plaintiff was seeking punitive damages. The materials asked the judges whether they would award punitive damages (most did) and if so, how much. For half of the judges, the materials indicated that both the plaintiff and defendant were in-state residents. For the other half, the plaintiff was a Minnesotan, but the defendant was from Wisconsin. The judges expressed a large in-state bias. The median award against the Minnesota defendant was $1,000,000, but the median award against the Wisconsin defendant was $1,750,000. We found similar, albeit smaller, effects in New Jersey (with Pennsylvania as the foreign jurisdiction) and Ohio (with Michigan as the foreign jurisdiction). The results are similar to those of an archival study of judicial decisions in tort cases.[55]

F. Implicit Racial Bias in Judges

Ingroup, racial, and gender biases can arise from similar processes to those that produced the results we report above. Many social psychologists even assert that racial bias is simply one form of ingroup bias. Just as judges reject the idea that they should redistribute wealth in the way Judge Neely suggests, judges also reject the influence of race and gender. But explicit rejection of ingroup bias was not enough to insulate judges from its influence.

One recent study, in fact, shows an interesting ingroup effect on federal appellate judges that interacts in an odd way with gender biases. Researchers found that decisions federal appellate judges made in cases involving gender discrimination claims changed after judges fathered a daughter.[56] Male judges became more solicitous of female claims of gender discrimination after they had daughters. Judges who had sons did not show such an effect. Most of the effect occurred among Republican appointees, who were generally less favorably disposed toward gender discrimination claims than Democratic appointees. Another study also found results suggesting ingroup favoritism. It concluded that "White judges are far more likely to dispose of any employment discrimination case at the summary judgment phase than are minority judges."[57]

Research on implicit bias shows that people who embrace egalitarian norms nevertheless harbor invidious implicit associations. Most White adults more easily associate African-Americans with negative imagery and White Americans with positive imagery.[58] And most adults, male and female, more easily associate women with domestic concepts and men with career concepts. What is more, these associations can influence judgment. Several studies identify settings in which divergent treatment of African-Americans in particular occurs largely among individuals who have strong negative implicit associations with African-Americans.[59] That said, people who are highly motivated to avoid making prejudiced judgments can avoid some of these influences. Judges, who take oaths to avoid racial prejudice in decision making, are surely so motivated. But do they avoid reliance on implicit biases in judgment?

The research on invidious implicit biases in judges paints a complex portrait.[60] Judges harbor the same measure of implicit biases concerning African-Americans as most lay adults. In our study, we used the most widely studied measure of implicit biases—the Implicit Association Test (IAT).[61] The IAT measures how quickly people can sort categories, such as White and Black faces and positive and negative words. The IAT pairs categories together in a computer task, so that the research participant must evaluate whether a word or face appearing in the center of a computer screen is either a White or Black face, or a positive or negative word. At the outset of the task, the participant typically presses a designated key on the left-hand side of the keyboard (the "E" key) if the target stimuli is either a White face or a positive word, and presses a key on the right-hand side of the keyboard (the "I" key) if the target is either a Black face or a negative word. The computer times each response, down to the millisecond. After a few rounds, the computer switches the pairings, so that the subject must press the "E" key if the target is a White face or a negative word and the "I" key if the target is a Black face or a positive word. (Sometimes the order of the tasks is reversed, and several practice rounds are given but not scored, so as to reduce order effects.) Most White adults find the White-positive/

Black-negative pairing easier to sort than the White-negative/Black-positive pair-ing. Faster progress on the sorting task suggests that people associate the con-cepts easily. When most White adults assess the White-positive/Black-negative pairing, they are effectively making only one judgment (good or bad). The opposite pairing thus requires two judgments for most White adults (face or name and then on which side does it belong) and hence slows response rates.

The results show that judges resemble most adults on the IAT.[62] That is, 85 percent of the White judges sorted the White-positive/Black-negative pair-ing faster than the opposite pairing. On average, the judges performed roughly one-fifth of a second slower on the White-negative/Black-positive pairing. These results are similar to those found in the general population. African-Ameri-can judges were more split. Only 45 percent of the African-American judges performed faster on the White-positive/Black-negative pairing. Overall, they showed great variation and no distinct tendency. This is also similar to results found in the general population. Therefore, judges express the same pattern of implicit biases as lay adults.

This same study also tested whether these implicit biases influenced judges' judgment. The same judges who took the IAT also took two tests of whether they would act on their biases, one in which the materials explicitly identi-fied the race of the parties and one in which the materials manipulated race implicitly. In the explicit identification experiment, the materials asked the judges to decide a criminal case.[63] The case involved a fight in a high school basketball locker room. One student pushed another hard into a bank of lockers, sending the victim to the emergency room. The perpetrator was then charged with battery and claimed that he felt threatened in an effort to sub-stantiate a self-defense claim. The materials asked the judges to assume the case was a bench trial and determine whether the defendant was guilty or not guilty by reason of self-defense. For half of the judges, the materials identi-fied the defendant as African-American, and for the other half, the materials identified the defendant as Caucasian-American. The materials also identi-fied the victim as the opposite race. Using the same materials, Sommers and Ellsworth found that White lay adults were more likely to convict the Black defendant than the White defendant (90 percent to 70 percent).[64] White judges, however, expressed no difference—roughly 80 percent convicted regardless of race.[65]

More critical to understanding the role of implicit bias, we found that the judges' individual results on the IAT did not predict how they reacted to the materials. If implicit biases constitute an important influence on judg-ment, we would have expected those judges with strong White-positive and Black-negative associations to treat the Black and White defendants differently. Other researchers have uncovered this pattern of results in medical doctors and human resources managers.[66] In the study discussed above, judges expressed no such tendencies. Even though they harbored strong negative associations with African-Americans, these associations had no effect on their judgment.

In contrast to the explicit racial identification experiment, a second experiment also manipulated the race of litigants in a subtle way.[67] The materials asked the judges to assign one of seven dispositions to two juvenile cases: a shoplifter and an armed robber. The disposition options ranged from dismissal, probation, detention in a juvenile facility, or transfer to an adult court. Before reading each case, we asked the judges to engage in an odd-looking computer task. The task consisted of identifying in which quadrant of the computer screen a string of 16 letters appeared. In reality, the string of letters masked words that appeared for about one-sixth of a second, making it impossible to detect consciously. For half of the judges, the words were closely associated with African-Americans (jerricurl, Harlem, Oprah), and for the other half, the words had no distinct racial content. In effect, we were priming half of the judges to think unconsciously about African-Americans right before we asked them to assign a disposition to the juvenile defendants. In a previous version of this study, police officers given this task recommended more severe sentences after being primed with the African-American words.[68] Manipulating race in an implicit way, we supposed, might more closely track a situation in which judges are not thinking about the race of the litigant.

> More critical to understanding the role of implicit bias, we found that the judges' individual results on the IAT did not predict how they reacted to the materials. If implicit biases constitute an important influence on judgment, we would have expected that those judges who held strong White-positive and Black-negative influences to treat the Black and White defendants differently. Other researchers have uncovered this pattern of results in medical doctors and human resources managers.

The results were troubling. Overall, the judges did not treat the defendants differently. The average disposition for the shoplifter divided between an adjournment in contemplation of dismissal and six months on probation, and for the armed robber it was between a lengthy probation and confinement in a juvenile facility for six months. Race did influence judges, however. Those judges who harbored strong White-positive/Black-negative associations on the IAT assigned more severe dispositions to the juvenile after being primed with African-American words than when primed with race-neutral words. In turn, judges who harbored White-negative/Black-positive associations on the IAT treated the juvenile less harshly after being primed with African-American words. The differences were small but noteworthy. For the shoplifter, the priming effect tended to shift the disposition from an adjournment to probation, and for the armed robber it often meant the difference between probation and detention.

What do the results mean? Although the pattern of results is intricate, we take a clear message from it. When the materials explicitly identified the defendants' race, judges were on guard. In effect, the explicit references to race triggered their System 2 thinking. They focused on the elements of self-defense and worked out whether it was an appropriate defense in the case presented—very much a System 2 process. When the materials did not explicitly identify the defendant's race but merely suggested it unconsciously, implicit associations influenced the judges. The lesson is fairly straightforward—thinking about race explicitly is a better approach than trying to ignore it. Judges are highly sensitive to charges of racism and will try to avoid it. But they still harbor the kinds of invidious associations that can influence their judgment if they are not making conscious efforts to avoid that distortion. Racial influences thus operate much like the influence of emotion and other intuitive processes in judges.

To be sure, this only reflects one study of judges, and one that involves a hypothetical setting. Other studies, including several

> Racial influences operate much like the influence of emotion and other intuitive processes in judges. Unchecked, they can influence judgment, but an effort to engage System 2 thinking can reduce or eliminate the undesirable intuitive influences.

using actual courtroom outcomes, support our conclusions. Using similar methods, Levinson and Bennett,[69] for example, have found that federal judges harbor invidious biases concerning Jewish, Christian, and Asian litigants. They also did not find conclusive evidence that these influences altered the judges' decision making when the race of the litigants was explicitly identified, although implicit biases influenced the judges' perceptions of the litigants.

Studies of behavior in the courtroom show that judges treat White and Black litigants differently in bail hearings,[70] exhibit modest racial disparities in criminal sentences favoring defendants of their own race,[71] impose harsher sentences on dark-skinned defendants,[72] and are more likely to deviate favorably from sentencing guidelines for White than for Black defendants.[73] The size of the effects observed in these studies cannot account for the sizeable racial disparities in the criminal justice system as a whole but support the idea that in some circumstances, implicit biases influence judges.

Although few studies of gender bias in judges exist, some studies suggest that invidious associations influence how judges assess male and female litigants. As-yet unpublished studies we have conducted showed that judges award more in compensatory damages for lost wages for a deceased male than a deceased female in a wrongful death hypothetical, treat male and female parents differently in divorce cases, and impose shorter sentences on female than male defendants convicted of identical crimes (and with identical backgrounds). Studies of actual sentences in drug cases dovetail with the latter finding.[74] Women convicted of drug offenses in federal court appear to draw shorter sentences than their male counterparts do, even when researchers control for background characteristics of the litigants.[75] As with race, widely held implicit associations that women are better caretakers, less deserving of punishment, and less career-minded seem to influence judges.

In sum, research on judges supports a few key points. First, judges are good decision makers, but like most adults, they tend to rely too heavily on their intuition. Second, this over-reliance can lead them to make predictable errors in judgment that can arise from simple mental shortcuts such as anchoring. Third, an excessive reliance on intuition opens the door for emotional reactions in judges that can influence how judges decide cases. Fourth, these emotional reactions facilitate the influence of more pernicious influences, such as ingroup preferences and invidious biases. Finally, it is clear that more careful System 2 thinking can (and often does) lead judges to avoid unwanted reliance on intuitive cognitive processes. In the next section, we discuss ways judges can facilitate a more deliberative approach that would avoid unwanted influences on their judgment.

> In sum, research on judges supports a couple of key points. First, judges are good decision makers, but like most adults, they tend to rely too heavily on their intuition. Second, this over-reliance can lead them to make predictable errors in judgment that can arise from simple mental shortcuts such as anchoring.

II. What Can Judges Do to Avoid Unconscious Bias?

Eliminating—or even merely mitigating—the undesirable influence of over-reliance on intuition is not easy. There is no "smart pill" that judges can take or failsafe protocol that judges can follow to inoculate themselves against implicit biases. Implicit bias is present even in children,[76] and the sources of implicit bias accumulate over a lifetime. It would be unrealistic to expect that implicit bias could be erased overnight.

Before discussing possible countermeasures, some caveats should be kept in mind. One of the special challenges of devising reforms to minimize the impact of implicit bias on judicial decisions is that judges likely already benefit from factors that tend to reduce implicit bias. For example, most judges are relatively well-educated, thoroughly trained, experienced at making important decisions, vetted by appointment or election, explicitly directed to avoid bias, highly motivated to be fair, and so on. Judges are also accountable for their decisions: they are subject to appellate review (although that is rare, and many interstitial rulings are effectively immune); they make their decisions publicly (either on the record in open court or in written opinions); many are subject to intense scrutiny when re-election or re-appointment is approaching; and the definition of their role imposes upon them a sense of public responsibility. Although these forms of accountability seem insufficient to eradicate judicial implicit bias as reflected in our experiments and in archival data regarding sentencing, countermeasures that merely duplicate the bias-reducing factors already at play should be avoided.

Unique aspects of the judicial role also rule out obvious countermeasures shown to be effective in other situations. Theoretically, hiding the identity of parties could prevent judges from learning the race or gender of litigants. The prototypical example of this is the audition screen, which increased the hiring of women and racial minority musicians by orchestras when implemented in the 1970s.[77] Hiding identities in the justice system, however, would be challenging if not impossible. Our norm is for judges to see witnesses, parties, jurors, and lawyers. Even though justice is supposed to be blind to persons, hiding them from the factfinder might seem unfair. People also assume—perhaps incorrectly—that the appearance and demeanor of parties and witnesses is diagnostic. Finally, information such as race or gender that could be misused might also possess some probative value that category masking would foreclose. In any event, race, gender, and the like can often be readily inferred from other characteristics

> Solutions must focus on both parts of the equation: the individual decision maker *and* the environment in which the individual makes decisions.

that would be difficult to conceal—such as name, neighborhood, job, and so on. As we observed in our research, it might be better for a judge to consciously know a litigant's race than to be subconsciously aware of it.

Solutions must focus on both parts of the equation: the individual decision maker *and* the environment in which the individual makes decisions. To minimize the risk that unconscious or implicit bias might distort decisions in court, judges and others could take the steps listed below, among others. Taking these steps would tend to reduce implicit bias and encourage judges to compensate for any bias that may persist. We divide our suggestions into two categories: those that target implicit bias directly, and those that target it indirectly by minimizing judicial reliance on intuition.

A. Combatting Implicit Bias Directly

1. Exposure to Stereotype-Incongruent Models

Several scholars have suggested that society might try to reduce the presence of unconscious biases by exposing decision makers to stereotype-incongruent models.[78] For example, posting a portrait of former President Barack Obama alongside the parade of mostly White male judges in many courthouses would be an inexpensive, laudable intervention.

Evidence concerning the effectiveness of this technique appears to be "quite mixed."[79] Although some have found it to be effective, our results, for example, also raise questions about its effectiveness. The White judges in our study exhibited a strong implicit bias, even though one of the jurisdictions we studied consisted of roughly half White judges and half Black judges.[80] Exposure to a group of esteemed Black colleagues apparently was not enough to counteract the social influences that produce implicit negative associations regarding African-Americans.

Consciously attempting to change implicit associations might be too difficult for judges. Most judges have little control over their dockets, which tend to include an over-representation of Black criminal defendants.[81] Frequent exposure to Black criminal defendants is apt to perpetuate negative associations with Black Americans. This exposure perhaps explains why capital defense attorneys harbor negative associations with Blacks,[82] and might explain why we found slightly greater negative associations among the White judges than are found among the population as a whole (although as we have noted, the latter finding might have other causes).[83] To reduce this risk, courts might consider rotating judges among specialist assignments so that implicit negative attitudes formed while deciding criminal cases will not take root.

2. Testing and Training

The criminal justice system might test candidates for judicial office using the IAT or other devices to determine whether they harbor implicit biases. We do not suggest, however, that people who display a strong White preference on the IAT should be barred from serving as judges, nor do we support using the IAT as a measure of qualification to serve on the bench.[84] The direct link between IAT score and decision making is still too tenuous, and our data—and the data of others—suggest that judges can overcome implicit biases at least to some extent and under some circumstances. Rather, knowing a judge's IAT score might serve two other purposes. First, it might help newly elected or appointed judges understand the extent to which they have implicit biases and alert them to the need to correct for those biases on the job.[85] Because judges take their responsibility to do justice seriously, becoming aware of the problem will motivate them to attempt to correct it. Second, knowledge of a judge's implicit biases would make it possible to provide targeted training about bias to new judges.

Training for experienced judges is also important. Continuing judicial education is common, but one shortcoming is that it is seldom accompanied by any testing of the individual judge's susceptibility to implicit bias, or by any analysis of the judge's own decisions. As a consequence, judges are less likely to appreciate their personal susceptibility to implicit bias.[86] As researchers have observed, "people's default response is to assume that their judgements are uncontaminated."[87] Moreover, because people are prone to egocentric bias, they readily assume that they are better than average, or that factors that might induce others to make poor or biased decisions would not affect their own decisions. This is true of judges as well. Our research demonstrates that judges are inclined to make the same sorts of favorable assumptions about their own abilities that non-judges do. For example, 97.2 percent (35 out of 36) of one group of judges we tested ranked themselves above the median judge with respect to "avoiding racial bias in making decisions."[88] This result suggests that specific training revealing the vulnerabilities of the particular judges would be more helpful than general education regarding implicit bias.[89] Further, to ensure that what judges encounter on the job does not inadvertently reinforce biased stereotypes and undo any benefit of general counter stereotypical training, such training should be repeated.

> Although general education regarding implicit bias is useful, specific training revealing the vulnerabilities of the particular judges being trained would be more helpful. Further, to ensure that what judges encounter on the job does not inadvertently reinforce biased stereotypes and undo any benefit of general counter stereotypical training, such training should be repeated.

Some types of implicit bias are highly salient and embarrassing, such as implicit racial bias. Judges seem to be on guard against these. Thus, the greater risk may be factors other than race or gender—such as beauty, age, obesity, religion, ethnicity, skin tone, and so on—that are not likely to be as salient or worrisome to judges.[90] Training regarding less obvious or non-hot-button sources of implicit bias would help to reduce this risk.

Another shortcoming of training is that although insight into the direction of an implicit bias frequently can be gained, insight into the magnitude of that bias cannot. How is one to know whether correction is warranted, and if so, how much? There is a risk of insufficient correction, unnecessary correction, or even overcorrection, resulting in a decision that is distorted as a result of the adjustment but simply in the opposite direction.[91] Testing might mitigate this problem by helping judges understand how much compensation or correction is needed to improve *their* decision making.

Using training to promote conscious self-correction, however, might result in unintended consequences. Conscious suppression or self-correction of implicit bias ties up or depletes cognitive resources.[92] This might make judges more susceptible to other types of cognitive error. In addition, consciously trying to correct for implicit bias may distract judges from devoting their full attention to the relevant facts and law. Finally, self-correction might also have the ironic effect of strengthening implicit bias.[93] On the other hand, some research suggests that telling mock jurors about implicit bias and instructing them to avoid it might be effective, and there is evidence that training people about implicit bias can reduce it.[94]

> Some types of implicit bias are highly salient and embarrassing, such as implicit racial bias. Judges seem to be on guard against these. Thus, the greater risk may be factors other than race or gender—such as beauty, age, obesity, religion, ethnicity, skin tone, and so on—that are not likely to be as salient or worrisome to judges. Training regarding less obvious or non-hot-button sources of implicit bias would help to reduce this risk.

Training for non-judges is also important. Judges accept inputs from repeat players such as police, prosecutors, pretrial services officers, probation officers, and the like. The recommendations of prosecutors and probation officers have been shown to be especially influential.[95] Judges rely on these professionals, but they are also vulnerable to implicit bias.[96] If inputs from other actors are biased, then the outputs of judges may be tainted, even if judges succeed in freeing themselves from implicit bias. Training legal actors other than judges would perhaps reduce the risk that their implicit bias might impact judges' decisions.

3. Auditing

There is a great deal of aggregate data about how litigant race, gender, and other demographic characteristics influence pretrial detention, sentencing, motions for summary judgment, trial outcomes (whether judge or jury), and so on. There is also aggregate data about how judges' demographic characteristics influence their decisions. What we have less of is data about what individual judges are doing that might enable them to better calibrate their decisions. This makes it easier for individual judges to deny that *they* are part of the problem, and our research suggests that they are strongly inclined to do so.

Quite a bit of data concerning individual judges might already be available. Pretrial services and probation offices already collect some data that can be sorted by judge, although concerns over the possible misuse of such data may inhibit them from making it available. Legal research services such as Westlaw, Bloomberg, and Lex Machina can report data by judge, although the quality and completeness of their data is unclear. Westlaw Judicial Reports, for example, contains judge-level data on reversal, caseload, and rulings on motions, primarily for federal judges. Finally, public online court dockets can be mined by researchers with the time and resources to do so.[97]

Apart from what already exists or can be gleaned, the justice system could implement an auditing program to evaluate the decisions of individual judges in order to determine whether they appear to be influenced by implicit bias. For example, judges' discretionary determinations, such as bail-setting, sentencing, or child-custody allocation, could be audited periodically to determine whether they exhibit patterns indicative of implicit bias. Similar proposals were advanced as correctives for umpires in Major League Baseball and referees in the National Basketball Association after both groups displayed evidence of racial bias in their judgments.[98]

Auditing could provide a couple of benefits. First, it would increase the available data regarding the extent to which bias affects judicial decision making. Second, it could enhance the accountability of judicial decision making. Unfortunately, judges operate in an institutional context that provides little prompt and useful feedback. Existing forms of accountability, such as appellate review, public scrutiny immediately prior to retention elections or reappointment, or online evaluations, even when timely and accurate,[99] primarily focus on a judge's performance in a particular case, not on the systematic study of long-term patterns within a judge's performance that might reveal implicit bias.[100]

Accountability mechanisms, including auditing, can also be effective at promoting cognitively complex thinking and self-awareness.[101] Auditing can motivate judges to be more vigilant and thorough in deliberations, lessening their reliance on low-effort mental shortcuts that are often susceptible to unconscious biases.[102] Auditing can also encourage judges to predict counter arguments while making decisions, thus helping them to identify flaws in their informational processing.[103] Awareness of flaws can reduce overconfidence bias—a common tendency to overemphasize belief-affirming information—thus providing the added benefit of improving judges' self-assessment abilities.[104]

Auditing could be implemented in several different ways. First, individual judges could self-audit by recording data such as sentence length, defendant's race, victim's race, and so on and periodically reviewing it for consistency.[105] Although some heroic judges report doing this on their own, not every judge will have the time or motivation to undertake this arduous task.

A second option would be to create committees composed of a small group of judges who meet periodically to discuss sentencing decisions and associated issues.[106] The prospect of explaining their decision making to esteemed colleagues may motivate judges to engage in high-effort deliberation. The effectiveness of these roundtables in reducing implicit bias would be bolstered by ensuring that the participants are diverse. Not only would diversity enrich the discussion by including a variety of perspectives, but the goal-oriented collaboration among members of different races and genders that such committees would foster itself tend to reduce implicit biases.[107]

A third option would be to create a peer review board to conduct periodic informal evaluations of judges' opinions and provide feedback. Such a board would focus on assessing the impartiality and consistency of sentencing both across an individual judge's cases and across judges within a particular jurisdiction.

Increased self-critical, complex thinking is most likely to result when judges do not know the views of the evaluator.[108] Knowing the views of an evaluator can result in cognitively lazy thinking, or decisions that simply conform to the opinions thought to be favored by that evaluator. For this reason, it may be best to cycle judges through different peer committees or to enlist review board members from other jurisdictions to limit familiarity.

Another condition that maximizes the effectiveness of auditing is review subject anonymity. Under conditions that do not create anonymity, evaluators might exhibit implicit bias in their reviews, potentially discounting the performance of female and racial minority judges.[109] One option is a blind review format in which evaluators are assigned a sample of decisions without knowing the identity and characteristics of the judge who made them.

Unless carefully implemented, there might be danger inherent in implicit bias remedies, like auditing, that can be perceived as placing external pressure on individuals to reduce their implicit biases. In a recent study, participants were primed with autonomous motivations such as, "I can freely decide to be a non-prejudiced person" or controlling motivations such as "I would feel guilty if I were prejudiced" before taking an IAT.[110] Exposure to the controlling motivational statements increased the implicit bias reflected in the participants' IAT scores. This result suggests the need for caution in the implementation of auditing regimes, so as to avoid triggering paradoxical results.

We recognize that judges are apt to be reluctant to implement auditing procedures. They might worry that auditing might reveal variation or inconsistency that looks like bias but for which an innocent explanation exists, thereby exposing them to unfair criticism. That said, the widespread availability of courtroom data has inspired some news services to conduct their own audits of judges to search for perceived biases.[111] Judges unwilling to engage in self-auditing might find such audits imposed on them by the media.

4. Altering Courtroom Practices

The justice system could be modified to minimize the untoward impact of unconscious bias. For example, the justice system could expand the use of three-judge trial courts.[112] Creating diversity for trial judges poses a challenge. We know how to create diversity on appellate panels—appoint more female and minority (race, ethnicity, sexual orientation, and so on) judges. Research reveals that improving the diversity of appellate court panels can affect outcomes. One study found that "adding a female judge to the panel more than doubled the probability that a male judge ruled for the plaintiff in sexual harassment case . . . and nearly tripled this probability in sex discrimination cases."[113] In trial courts, judges typically decide alone, so adopting this mechanism would require major structural changes. Although convening a three-judge trial court was once required by statute when the constitutionality of a state's statute was at issue,[114] and was occasionally used or suggested in other contexts,[115] three-judge trial courts are virtually nonexistent today.[116] The inefficiency of having three judges decide cases that one judge might be able to decide nearly as well led to their demise, and this measure might simply be too costly to resurrect.

Trial judges could attempt to create their own diversity in their chambers by hiring a diverse staff and discussing cases with them.[117] A non-White law clerk or judicial assistant might react very differently to particular facts or arguments than a White judge, and vice versa. But there is a risk that the views of others—especially those expressed off the record and not subject to testing in the cauldron of the adversary process—might be overly influential.[118] Increasing the information available to judges off the record raises fairness or ethical concerns similar to those posed by judges' private Internet research. Accordingly, this technique should be implemented with caution.

The more people learn about an individual who belongs to a group, the less likely they are to make stereotyped judgments about him or her based on his or her membership in that group. Judges might spend a few extra minutes getting to know defendants when taking guilty pleas and sentencing. They also might put efficiency concerns aside for a few moments and allow lawyers more latitude to humanize their clients during direct examination.

The form in which law is expressed also might be examined. Reducing discrimination by requiring judges to apply rules rather than standards leaves less room in which implicit bias can operate.[119] Rules, mandatory minimum sentences, or damages schedules eliminate part of the potential for bias (but not all of it, because it is unlikely that credibility determination, child custody allocation, and so on could ever be reduced to a rule), and sentencing guidelines or damages ranges confine and check it. Of course, judges must be able to individualize and to tailor outcomes to achieve justice and equity. Only in this way can law evolve and outcomes be viewed by society as fair. But there is a tradeoff: the more discretion, the more risk of bias.

Strengthening the adversary system might help. For example, if public defenders are well-compensated and well-resourced, and if there are a sufficient number of them, that will increase the odds that the diverse perspectives of racial minority or low socioeconomic status defendants will be adequately presented in court. Reducing over-detention of criminal defendants prior to trial will help ensure that all defendants—especially over-represented racial minorities—will have their viewpoints effectively expressed.[120] Pretrial detention constricts defendants' ability to meet with their counsel and to assist in investigation and trial preparation.

Some courts routinely issue tentative rulings.[121] Tentative rulings might help combat implicit bias by requiring writing (and thereby enhancing deliberation); by masking the race or gender of clients and lawyers (but not knowing may not be an advantage if judges are subconsciously primed by names or background information); and most importantly by allowing specific, concrete, pre-decision feedback or pushback from counsel or pro se litigants that can help to ensure that perspectives that might not spontaneously occur to the judge are taken into account.

Another possibility would be to increase the depth of appellate scrutiny, such as by employing de novo review rather than clear error review, in cases in which particular trial court findings of fact might be tainted by implicit bias. For example, some evidence suggests that male judges may be less receptive to sex discrimination claims than they ought to be.[122] If that bias does exist, less deferential appellate review by a diverse panel might offer a partial solution.

5. Mindfulness Meditation

The criminal justice system might also reduce implicit bias by offering training in mindfulness meditation. Mindfulness is a form of meditation in which the individual focuses on the present moment by slowing down his or her mental processes.[123] Instruction often involves developing awareness of one's breathing, the contents of one's mind (i.e., thoughts and emotions), and awareness itself.[124]

Mindfulness targets implicit bias by reducing automatic associations with outgroup members, or with individuals outside of the race or ethnicity one identifies as, with negative concepts.[125] Recent scholarship has found that after exposure to a short audiotape instructing listeners to be aware of their current thoughts and feelings, White participants' IAT results showed a significant reduction of bias against African-Americans, attributable at least in part to reduced automatic associations.[126] This suggests that through the practice of meditation, judges can limit their reliance on these knee-jerk reactions, allowing for fairer decision making.

Research also suggests that mindfulness meditation increases compassionate feelings toward others. A 2013 study revealed that participants who engaged in mindfulness meditation training were five times more likely than a control group to give up their seat to a person on crutches and in visible and audible pain.[127] If these results extend to scenarios in which the target is not someone in pain but rather someone of a different race, then the compassion generated by mindfulness may mediate implicit bias toward those disadvantaged by race, gender, or low socioeconomic status.

Mindfulness meditation may also help to control conditions that increase the magnitude of implicit bias, such as mood. For example, when people are in a heightened emotional state—be it from stress, anger, or even happiness—implicit bias manifests more strongly in their decisions.[128] Practicing mindfulness meditation can enhance emotional regulation.[129] In a recent study, participants were exposed to emotion-evoking images before and after an eight-week course in mindfulness.[130] After the course, individuals exhibited a reduced activation of the amygdala, the area of the brain that appraises and responds to emotional stimuli.[131] If mindfulness meditation improves emotional regulation, then it may allow judges to better maintain the mental state most suited to unbiased decision making.

6. Consider-the-Opposite

Consider-the-opposite, or consider-the-alternative, is a technique that requires an individual to imagine and explain the basis for alternate outcomes, specifically those that conflict with the opinion the individual holds.[132] Consider-the-opposite has proven to be effective at combating various biases including hindsight, anchoring, and overconfidence.[133] The effectiveness of consider-the-opposite may be attributable to its ability to reengage an individual's reasoning processes. Generally, once people generate a plausible explanation of events, they stop considering new possibilities. Considering-the-opposite forces an interruption of this single-direction processing, thus allowing for a more comprehensive analysis.[134]

A judge who believes that a defendant is liable or guilty, or that a particular damage award or sentence is warranted, could implement this technique by considering a counterfactual in which the victim and defendant were of opposite, or swapped, gender or race. If, upon reconsideration, the judge realizes that the outcome might be different in the alternate scenario, then he or she could attempt to remedy the bias by considering the possibility of adjusting the outcome accordingly.

Suppose, for example, that a judge is sentencing a female defendant. After determining the sentence, the judge could ask himself or herself: What if this defendant were male?[135] How would that alter my assessment of the defendant, the crime, and the other sentencing factors? Would my sentence for the male defendant be the same? Why or why not? Not only would this process promote deliberation, but it also would prompt the judge to consider the role (if any) played by gender (a forbidden factor)[136] in determining the sentence. If a judge experiences difficulty in implementing this technique, it may be more effective to formalize and externalize it by designating a law clerk or other member of chambers staff to serve as a devil's advocate.[137]

7. Perspective Taking

Perspective taking consists of adopting the viewpoint of other individuals and examining the scenario at issue through the lens of their life experience.[138] Perspective taking may be effective in reducing bias because of its ability to increase altruism or to reduce egocentric tendencies. The altruistic theory posits that perspective taking increases compassion and empathy toward an individual or group, which mediates existing bias against that individual or group.[139] The egocentric theory is based on the concept that ingroup preference stems from a perception that those of the same race are inherently like us, so we attribute our own positive self-conceptions to them.[140] The theory suggests that by perspective taking, we can increase the overlap between our favorable self-concept and our conception of outgroup members.[141] Through this active consideration of shared similarities, we may increase mental reliance on our self-concept, rather than implicit stereotypes, when making character determinations.[142]

Judges could implement this technique by attempting to imagine themselves in the shoes of the party before them. Alternately, the court system could approach the issue more broadly by including perspective taking exercises as part of a training course in implicit bias. Some research suggests that improvements in outgroup evaluations did not require an individual-targeted perspective-taking exercise.[143] Even abstract perspective taking directed toward a fictional target can improve outgroup perceptions. The inclusion of abstract perspective taking in judicial training might reduce implicit bias without requiring case-by-case perspective taking.

The inclusion of perspective taking in training courses may also bolster other efforts to combat implicit bias. One study revealed that when individuals take the perspective of Black or Latino subjects, they become more open to the possibility of intergroup racial discrimination.[144] Because motivation to remedy implicit racial bias is often a prerequisite for effective solutions, helping judges to appreciate that there may be discrimination is an important first step.[145]

Another approach would be to encourage a more literal form of perspective taking in which judges expose themselves to the experiences faced by many minorities who pass through their courtrooms. Exposure to other's experiences can increase a judge's probability of instinctual perspective taking, thus reducing their implicit biases. One study demonstrated that when able-bodied persons experienced wheelchair travel for an hour, their sensitivity toward people with disabilities increased.[146] This effect was significant, lasting at least four months. Though actual role playing may be impractical in the legal context, the study also revealed that participants who vicariously experienced perspective taking through observation showed similar results.

Perspective taking might have a downside. One concern may be that the positive feelings generated will overcompensate for implicit bias, increasing partiality toward the persons whose perspective was taken and impeding fair judgment. Research on juror decision making has shown that when laypeople are instructed to take the perspective of a defendant, they perceive the defendant to be less culpable than those given no instruction.[147] Furthermore, those instructed to take the victim's perspective found the defendant more culpable than the control group. Given that the facts of the cases remained constant for all participants, the results reveal that perspective taking can increase partiality toward the target. Considering the perspective of both victims and defendants may help to mitigate any imbalance.

Another worry is that perspective taking might actually increase a judge's reliance on implicit stereotypes. In a case where stereotype-congruent facts are present, judges may rely on stereotypes in envisioning the defendant's perspective, thus making implicit bias more salient. Skorinko and Sinclair provide an apt illustration: "[Y]oung people who take the perspective of a clearly stereotypic elderly man, such as an ailing one sitting in a hospital bed, may be struck by his age and frailty and be more apt to assume that his other characteristics and experiences coincide with stereotypes of his group."[148] Accordingly, judges should exercise caution when perspective taking, particularly in stereotype-congruent cases.

Recently, a variety of forces have combined to reduce the number of settlement conferences over which judges preside. Private alternative dispute resolution, attorney settlement panels, retired judges, and so on have diminished this particular burden on judges. This welcome development, however, may have a hidden disadvantage. Settlement conferences are an occasion in which judges can interact relatively informally with litigants, some of whom possess characteristics or backgrounds unlike those of most judges. This opportunity to engage with divergent perspectives may be withering away.

8. Foster Diversity in Private Life

Trial judges could create more diversity for themselves outside the courthouse. This would enhance the effectiveness of other debiasing steps such as exposure to stereotype-incongruent models and perspective taking. For example, White judges could choose to live in racially and socioeconomically diverse neighborhoods rather than in wealthy, mostly White enclaves, at least temporarily, and Black judges could do the opposite. They could send their children to public schools where they—and their children—will encounter a more diverse mix of students, parents, and teachers than they would in an exclusive private school.[149] A judge inclined to teach a law course at a local predominantly White law school might elect to teach it at a historically Black college instead—not just to help ensure that minority students benefited from the course, but more importantly to allow the judge to learn from the students. Similarly, a judge who is White and male could take a course (online or at a community college) in Black history, gender discrimination, or the like.

9. Creating a Constructive Courtroom Environment

Courthouse art and architecture should be attractive, but they might also be instrumental. The impact of environment on choice can be powerful and ought not to be overlooked. Displaying photographs in the courthouse of respected women judges, inspiring civil rights leaders, and so on in the courthouse could expose judges to counter stereotypic role models on a daily basis[150] and also create a feeling of responsibility to live up to the great judges of the past. Although this may seem superficial, it is not. It works.[151] And, it is relatively inexpensive. Although what South Africa did in designing a new constitutional court rich with symbolic meaning is admirable,[152] court architects need not necessarily go that far to achieve the desired effect.

10. Reminders of Professional Norms

Most judges probably keep their professional obligation of impartiality firmly in mind, but occasional reminders might help to ensure their vigilance against bias. If such reminders can help students resist cheating, maybe they can help judges guard against making biased decisions as well.

In one experiment, college students were given a test and provided an opportunity to obtain a reward by cheating in reporting their results.[153] They were divided into two groups. One group was asked to recall ten books they had read during high school. They cheated in order to obtain a higher reward for test performance. A second group, who were asked instead to recall as many of the Ten Commandments as they could, did not cheat. Similar results were obtained in a different study in which one-half of the college student subjects were asked to acknowledge that they would be bound by an honor code (which did not even exist) before they were given an opportunity to cheat. In both of these experiments, reminding the students of ethical norms resulted in a greater level of ethical behavior.

While such reminders or acknowledgments might have to be repeated, and might reach a point of diminishing returns (or have a smaller effect on judges than on others for whom the ethical dimension of their role is less inherently salient), this technique might still be worth trying. For example, judges could be required to retake their oath periodically, perhaps at the beginning of each year in a formal ceremony in which all members of the court would be encouraged to participate. A periodic public reaffirmation of key professional norms—such as avoiding implicit bias—might not only remind the judges of those norms but also deepen their commitment to them.[154] If married couples find it valuable to renew their vows, perhaps judges would too. Alternatively, professional norms, inspirational quotations, slogans, and the like could be etched into courthouse walls and doors, especially in places where judges, not merely lawyers and the public, can see them.[155] This is reminiscent of constant reminders to physicians and nurses to wash their hands, a campaign that has dramatically reduced the incidence of infection.[156]

B. Combatting Implicit Bias Indirectly

In Part I, we argued that intuitive reasoning is the primary way that bias influences judges. Mechanisms to facilitate deliberative reasoning should therefore play a critical role in reducing the influence of these biases. This poses a dilemma for busy judges. Judges with heavy caseloads might have little choice but to rely on rapid, intuitive judgments to manage their dockets. Nevertheless, if judges need to take care to slow down and deliberate so as to override their intuitive biases, then the justice system should encourage that process. Of course, features of the existing justice system exist for many reasons, and efforts to encourage deliberation might undercut other policy goals, such as cost reduction. Our objective here is simply to identify steps that the justice system could take to facilitate deliberation, while recognizing that reforms would have to balance the benefits associated with these reforms against any costs they might impose.

1. Reduce Time Pressure

The justice system might expand the amount of time judges have to make decisions. Judges facing cognitive overload due to heavy dockets, case complexity, or other on-the-job constraints are more likely to make intuitive rather than deliberative decisions because the former are speedier and easier.[157] Furthermore, being cognitively "busy" induces judges to rely on intuitive judgment.[158] As many of the judges we have studied candidly admit, time pressures present an enormous challenge, often diminish motivation, and induce less-than-optimal decision making. Stress and burnout can result in heightened implicit bias.[159]

No easy cure for time pressure exists, but the justice system could employ a few strategies to mitigate it. Most obviously, legislatures could expand the number of authorized judgeships in their jurisdictions, particularly in those courts with the heaviest dockets, thereby enabling judges to spend more time per case and per decision. Short of that, legislatures could ensure that all judges have law clerks.

Minimizing the number of spur-of-the-moment decisions that judges are expected to make might also help. Decisions made during pretrial conferences, settlement conferences, motion hearings, and so forth are more likely to be intuitive and impressionistic than deliberative and well-reasoned. Likewise, evidentiary rulings made during hearings or trials are apt to be more prone to error than if they were made based on written briefs and with time for the judge to research and reflect. When ruling on the admissibility of evidence at trial, judges often have little choice but to think intuitively. Our model suggests that judges should not make difficult or important evidentiary rulings in such a setting. To be sure, pretrial motions in limine sometimes deprive the judge of the full context in which the evidence will be heard. Accordingly, judges might require parties to file important evidentiary motions before trial, but delay ruling on them until the issues arise during the trial, and even then pause for a recess to allow an opportunity to study the papers and deliberate.

Occasionally, the mere passage of time may help. If judges are susceptible to the "beauty bias," for example, they might unwittingly evaluate an attractive witness's credibility too positively and an unattractive witness's credibility too negatively if they make a hasty judgment in the courtroom.[160] A reflective determination made in chambers after the impact of the witness's appearance has worn off might be more accurate.

2. Opinion Writing

The justice system also might require judges to write opinions more often.[161] Arguably, judges already explain the reasons for their decisions more frequently and completely than any other public official. And this prescription conflicts with the previous recommendation because opinion writing takes extra time, which judges might not have. Despite this cost, writing opinions could induce deliberation that otherwise would not occur. Rather than serving merely to describe an allegedly deliberative process that has already occurred (as the formalists might argue) or to rationalize an intuitive decision already made (as the realists might argue), the discipline of opinion writing might enable well-meaning judges to overcome their intuitive, impressionistic reactions. The process of writing challenges the judge to assess a decision more carefully, logically, and deductively. Some have encouraged the preparation of written opinions for exactly this reason.[162]

Preparing a written opinion is sometimes too inconvenient or simply infeasible. In such situations, perhaps judges should be required to articulate the basis for the decision before announcing the conclusion. Though there is little opportunity for reflection in the midst of hearings or trials, simply stating the reasons for the decision before the ruling is announced may encourage the judge to be more deliberative.

The psychological literature on the effects of requiring decision makers to give reasons is mixed. Providing reasons for one's decision induces deliberation,[163] but it does not always produce better decisions. In one of our experiments, providing a written explanation for a decision did not insulate judges from the powerful anchoring heuristic.[164] Explaining can also impair performance on tasks that benefit from intuition.[165] Some studies suggest that deliberation can sometimes produce results that are inferior to results produced by intuition, particularly where a task involves aesthetic judgement.[166] We suspect, however, that most of the judgments that judges make are not the sort that are impaired by deliberation.

3. Training and Feedback

Training could help judges understand the extent of their reliance on intuition and identify when such reliance is risky—the necessary first steps in self-correction. Judges could learn to interrupt their intuition, thereby allowing deliberation to intervene and modify behavior, if not actually altering underlying prejudices or attitudes.[167]

Likewise, jurisdictions could adopt peer-review processes to provide judges with feedback. For example, every two years, three experienced judges from other jurisdictions could visit a target court. They could select a few cases recently decided by each target court judge, read all of the rulings and transcripts, and then provide the judges with feedback on their performance and constructive suggestions for improvement. This would give judges an opportunity to obtain feedback on issues that typically escape appellate review. When aggregated, the results of such a process might also identify structural problems that amendments to rules or statutes should remedy. Such a procedure also would increase judicial accountability by subjecting decisions that usually escape appellate review to a different form of peer review. Research has shown that accountability of this sort can improve decision-making performance.[168] If a peer review process is not feasible, courts could, at a minimum, record and provide judges with outcome data on relevant decisions—for example, whether a defendant released on bail actually appeared for trial. Armed with this feedback, judges might be better able to learn what they are doing well and what they are doing poorly.

Of course, most judges are generalists, which might impede their efforts to learn good decision-making skills and to apply knowledge gained from training and peer-review processes. With the exception of the tasks judges perform repeatedly, it might take a long time for judges to acquire sufficient experience in handling a particular issue to accumulate enough feedback to avoid errors. It is as if a professional tennis player divided his or her time among tennis, volleyball, softball, soccer, and golf rather than concentrating on tennis—the player's opportunity to develop "tennis intuition" would be diminished. Although we have concluded elsewhere that specialization may not insulate judges from cognitive illusions such as anchoring,[169] it might mitigate such biases by maximizing the opportunity to benefit from a large quantity of relevant feedback. Moreover, because the benefit of experiential learning on the job is limited, training may be necessary to compensate for deficiencies in the learning environment.[170]

4. Scripts, Checklists, and Multifactor Tests

Scripts and checklists can free judges from reliance on their memories and encourage them to proceed methodically, thereby ensuring that they touch all of the deliberative bases relevant to a decision. A judge who reviews a script or checklist at each step in the decision-making process is less likely to rely on intuition when doing so is inadvisable.

In some respects, the justice system already takes this approach. Judges receive "scripts" for some tasks after they are appointed or elected. Judges also develop their own scripts and checklists for various tasks and share them with one another. Multifactor or balancing tests are another device for structuring decision making and promoting deliberation.

Multifactor tests can help ensure that judges consider all relevant factors and can remind them of their responsibility to base decisions on more than mere intuition.[171] A system that forces judges to weigh each of the factors expressly also might help reduce judges' reliance on intuition. Similar reminder systems have reduced medical diagnostic error.[172]

Although multifactor tests are ubiquitous, they are imperfect. Some multifactor tests are poorly designed. They also may be indeterminate, and applying or weighing some of the factors within the test may require intuition. Moreover, if judges rely excessively on multifactor tests, scripts or checklists, there is a risk of mechanical jurisprudence that might discourage judges from tailoring their analysis to the case. Finally, judges sometimes employ heuristics to circumvent the multifactor analysis by relying on just a few of the factors in making their decision, thereby diminishing the value of the test as a corrective device.[173]

Nevertheless, such tests possess the potential for mitigating cognitive error by nudging judges toward more deliberative processes. This could explain why some appellate courts require administrative agencies or lower courts to expressly consider or weigh each of the factors in a multifactor test, sometimes in a particular sequence.[174] In their more extreme forms, such techniques are known as "forcing functions," which are exemplified by computer systems that force the user to complete step two before moving to step three.[175]

Conclusion

Empirical research suggests the likely presence of implicit racial bias in judges. We have identified several suggestions and reforms designed to prevent implicit biases from influencing outcomes in the courtroom. To render justice blind to persons, as it is supposed to be, these and other reforms should be considered.

So You'd Like to Know More

- Jeffrey J. Rachlinski, Sheri Lynn Johnson, Andrew J. Wistrich & Chris Guthrie, *Does Unconscious Racial Bias Affect Trial Judges?*, 84 Notre Dame Law Review 1195 (2009)

- Chris Guthrie, Jeffrey J. Rachlinski & Andrew J. Wistrich, *Blinking on the Bench: How Judges Decide Cases*, 93 Cornell Law Review 1 (2007)

- Kirwan Institute for the Study of Race and Ethnicity, *State of the Science: Implicit Bias Review* (2016)

- Jerry Kang et al., *Implicit Bias in the Courtroom*, 59 UCLA Law Review 1124 (2012)

- Pamela Casey et al., *Minding the Court: Enhancing the Decision-Making Process*, 49 Court Review 76 (2013)

About the Authors

The Honorable Andrew J. Wistrich is a magistrate judge of the U.S. District Court for the Central District of California. He holds A.B. degrees in philosophy and political science from the University of California at Berkeley and a J.D. from the University of Chicago. Judge Wistrich is the author or coauthor of more than a dozen articles and book chapters regarding judicial decision making.

Jeffrey Rachlinski holds a B.A. and an M.A. in psychology from the Johns Hopkins University, a J.D. from Stanford Law School, and a Ph.D. in Psychology from Stanford. In 1994, Dr. Rachlinski joined the faculty at Cornell Law School and is now the Henry Allen Mark Professor of Law. He has also served as visiting professor at the University of Chicago, the University of Virginia, the University of Pennsylvania, Yale, and Harvard. Dr. Rachlinski's research interests primarily involve the application of cognitive and social psychology to law with special attention to judicial decision making.

Endnotes

1. *See* Alexandra Klausner, *Judge in Stanford Swimmer Trial under Fire for New Sex Assault Case*, N.Y. Post, June 27, 2016, http://nypost.com/2016/06/27/judge-in-stanford-sex -assault-case-gives-immigrant-harsher-sentence/.
2. *See* Alan Rappeport, *Donald Trump Says His Remarks on Judge Were "Misconstrued,"* N.Y. Times, June 7, 2016, http://www.nytimes.com/2016/06/08/us/politics/trump -university-judge.html?_r=0.
3. Pew Research Center, *On Views of Race and Inequality, Blacks and Whites Are Worlds Apart* (June 27, 2016), http://www.pewsocialtrends.org/files/2016/06/ST_2016.06.27_Race -Inequality-Final.pdf.

4. National Center for State Courts, *Analysis of Survey of Registered Voters* (Nov. 17, 2015), http://www.ncsc.org/~/media/Files/PDF/Topics/Public%20Trust%20and%20Confi dence/SoSC_2015_Survey%20Analysis.ashx.

5. *See* Bureau of Justice Statistics, U.S. Dep't of Justice, *Felony Defendants in Large Urban Counties, 2004*, at 1 (2004), http://www.ojp.usdoj.gov/bjs/pub/pdf/fdluc04.pdf.

6. *See* The Sentencing Project, *Issues: Racial Disparity*, http://www.sentencingproject.org /issues/racial-disparity/.

7. *See* David B. Mustard, *Racial, Ethnic, and Gender Disparities in Sentencing: Evidence from the U.S. Federal Courts*, 44 J.L. & Econ. 285, 286–88 (2001).

8. *See* Michael Daly, *Racist Talk from Dylann Roof's Judge*, The Daily Beast, June 19, 2015, http://www.thedailybeast.com/articles/2015/06/19/racist-talk-from-dylann-roof-s -judge.html.

9. For reviews, *see* Anthony G. Greenwald & Linda Hamilton Kreiger, *Implicit Bias: Scientific Foundations*, 94 Cal. L. Rev. 945 (2006); Kirstin A. Lane, Jerry Kang & Mahzarin R. Banaji, *Implicit Social Cognition and Law*, 3 Ann Rev. L. & Soc. Sci. 427 (2007).

10. *See* Mahzarin R. Banaji & Anthony G. Greenwald, Blindspot: Hidden Biases of Good People (2013).

11. *See* Danial Kahneman, Thinking Fast and Slow (2011).

12. *See* Veronika Denes-Raj & Seymour Epstein, *Conflict Between Intuitive and Rational Processing: When People Behave Against Their Better Judgment*, 66 J. Personality & Soc. Psychol. 819 (1994).

13. *See* Antonio Damasio, Descartes Error: Emotion, Reason and the Human Brain (1995).

14. *See* Malcolm Gladwell, Blink: The Power of Thinking Without Thinking (2005).

15. This problem is taken from Shane Frederick, *Cognitive Reflection and Decision Making*, 19 J. Econ. Persp. 25, 26 (2005).

16. Andrew Meyer, Bob Spunt & Shane Frederick, The Bat and Ball Problem (2013) (unpublished manuscript).

17. Chris Guthrie, Jeffrey J. Rachlinski & Andrew J. Wistrich, *Blinking on the Bench: How Judges Decide Cases*, 93 Cornell L. Rev. 1 (2007).

18. *See id.*

19. *See* Chris Guthrie, Jeffrey J. Rachlinski & Andrew J. Wistrich, *Inside the Judicial Mind*, 86 Cornell L. Rev. 777 (2001).

20. *See* Amos Tversky & Daniel Kahneman, *Judgment under Uncertainty: Heuristics and Biases*, 185 Sci. 1124, 1128 (1974).

21. J. Edward Russo & Paul J.H. Schoemaker, Decision Traps 90 (1989).

22. Dan Ariely, Predictably Irrational: The Hidden Forces that Shape Our Decisions 28–38 (rev. & expanded ed., 2009).

23. Jeffrey J. Rachlinski, Andrew J. Wistrich & Chris Guthrie, *Can Judges Make Reliable Numeric Judgments? Distorted Damages and Skewed Sentences*, 90 Ind. L.J. 695 (2015).

24. Chris Guthrie, Jeffrey J. Rachlinski & Andrew J. Wistrich, *The "Hidden Judiciary": An Empirical Examination of Executive Branch Justice*, 58 Duke L.J. 1477, 1518–20, 1525–26 (2009).

25. Rachlinski et al., *supra* note 23.

26. *See* Tapio Lappi-Seppälä, *Sentencing and Punishment in Finland: The Decline of the Repressive Ideal, in* Sentencing and Sanctions in Western Countries 92, 113–14 (M. Tonry & R. Frase eds., 2001) (reporting results of legal reforms in Finland that altered a sentencing system to use days instead of months); Shawn D. Bushway, Emily Greene Owens & Anne Morrison Piehl, *Sentencing Guidelines and Judicial Discretion: Quasi-Experimental Evidence from Human Calculation Errors* 1, 5–6 (NBER Working Paper No. w169611, 2011) (reporting an analysis of misleading sentencing recommendations in Maryland); *see also* Denise Leifer & Lisa L. Sample, *Do Judges Follow Sentencing Recommendations, or Do Recommendations Simply Reflect What They Want to Hear?, An*

Examination of One State Court, 33 J. CRIME & JUSTICE 127, 145 (2010) (finding "a strong association between sentence recommendations and sentence outcomes").

27. PAUL VALERY, COLLECTED WORKS OF PAUL VALERY, VOLUME 14: ANALECTS 329 (Stuart Gilbert trans. 2015).

28. *See* Daniel M. Wegner, David J. Schneider, Samuel R. Carter III & Teri L. White, *Paradoxical Effects of Thought Suppression*, 53 J. PERSONALITY & SOC. PSYCHOL. 5 (1987).

29. For a review, *see* Andrew J. Wistrich, Chris Guthrie & Jeffrey J. Rachlinski, *Can Jurors Ignore Inadmissible Information: The Difficulty of Deliberately Disregarding*, 153 U. PENN L. REV. 1251, 1270–76 (2005).

30. John MacArthur Maguire & Charles S.S. Epstein, *Rules of Evidence in Preliminary Controversies as to Admissibility*, 36 YALE L.J. 1101, 1116–17 (1927).

31. CHRISTOPHER B. MUELLER & LAIRD C. KIRKPATRICK, FEDERAL EVIDENCE § 3, at 10 (2d ed. 1994).

32. *See* Wistrich et al., *supra* note 29.

33. *Id.* at 1298–1303.

34. ARIZ. REV. STAT. ANN. § 13-1421 (West 2003).

35. *See* Wistrich et al., *supra* note 29, at 1308–11.

36. Jeffrey J. Rachlinski, Andrew J. Wistrich & Chris Guthrie, *Altering Attention in Adjudication*, 60 UCLA L. REV. 1586, 1609–15 (2013).

37. Jeffrey J. Rachlinski, Andrew J. Wistrich & Chris Guthrie, *Probability, Probable Cause, and the Hindsight Bias*, 8 J. EMPIRICAL LEGAL STUD. 72 (2011).

38. *Confirmation Hearing on the Nomination of Hon. Sonia Sotomayor to Be an Associate Justice of the Supreme Court of the United States: Hearing before the Senate Committee on the Judiciary*, 111th Cong. 121, at 120 (2009).

39. *Confirmation Hearing on the Nomination of Elena Kagan to Be an Associate Justice of the Supreme Court of the United States: Hearing before the Senate Committee on the Judiciary*, 111th Cong. 103 (2010).

40. For a thorough discussion of judges and emotions, *see* Terry A. Maroney, *The Persistent Cultural Script of Judicial Dispassion*, 99 CAL. L. REV. 629 (2011).

41. *See* ROBERT H. FRANK, PASSIONS WITHIN REASON: THE STRATEGIC ROLE OF EMOTION (1988).

42. United States v. Ballard, 322 U.S. 78, 93–94 (1944) (Jackson, J., dissenting).

43. Dan Simon, *A Third View of the Black Box: Cognitive Coherence in Legal Decision Making*, 71 U. CHI. L. REV. 511, 523–44 (2004) (describing this research).

44. For a discussion of Bentham's views, *see* Dean Alfange, Jr., *Jeremy Bentham and the Codification of Law*, 55 CORNELL L. REV. 58 (1969).

45. Andrew J. Wistrich, Jeffrey J. Rachlinski & Chris Guthrie, *Heart versus Head: Do Judges Follow the Law or Follow Their Feelings*, 93 TEX. L. REV. 855 (2015).

46. *Id.* at 880–83.

47. *Id.*

48. WILLIAM GRAHAM SUMNER, FOLKWAYS: A STUDY OF THE SOCIOLOGICAL IMPORTANCE OF USAGES, MANNERS, CUSTOMS, MORES AND MORALS 12–13 (1906).

49. *See* Henri Tajfel & John C. Turner, *An Integrative Theory of Intergroup Conflict*, in THE SOCIAL PSYCHOLOGY OF INTERGROUP RELATIONS 33, 38 (Stephen Worchel & William Austin eds., 1979) ("[T]he mere perception of belonging to two district groups—that is, social categorization per se—is sufficient to trigger intergroup discrimination favoring the in-group. In other words, the mere awareness of the presence of an out-group is sufficient to provoke intergroup competitive or discriminatory responses on the part of the in-group.").

50. *See* MUZAFIR SHERIF, IN COMMON PREDICAMENT: SOCIAL PSYCHOLOGY OF INTERGROUP CONFLICT AND COOPERATION (1966).

51. *See* ERWIN CHEMERINSKY, FEDERAL JURISDICTION 296 (5th ed. 2007) ("The traditional theory is that diversity jurisdiction was intended to protect out-of-state residents from the bias that they might experience, or at least fear that they might face, in state courts.").

52. *See* Jerry Goldman & Kenneth Mark, *Diversity Jurisdiction and Local Bias: A Preliminary Empirical Inquiry*, 9 J. LEGAL STUD. 93, 97–99 (1980) (40 percent of attorneys cited "bias against an out-of-state resident" as a reason for choosing a federal forum).

53. Joani Nelson-Horschler, *Lobby the Courts, State Judges Says, But Critics Balk*, IND. WK. 36 (Nov. 7, 1988); Michael Rustad & Thomas Koenig, *The Supreme Court and Junk Social Science: Selective Distortion in Amicus Briefs*, 72 N.C. L. REV. 91 n.248 (1993).

54. Wistrich et al., *supra* note 45, at 893–98.

55. Eric Helland & Alexander Tabarrock, *The Effect of Electoral Institutions on Tort Awards*, 4 AM. L & ECON. REV. 341 (2002).

56. Adam N. Glynn & Maya Sen, *Identifying Judicial Empathy: Does Having Daughters Cause Judges to Rule for Women's Issues?*, 59 AM. J. POL. SCI. 37 (2015).

57. Jill D. Weinberg & Laura Beth Nielsen, *Examining Empathy: Discrimination, Experience, and Judicial Decisionmaking*, 85 S. CAL. L. REV. 513, 346 (2012).

58. *See* Kirstin A. Lane et al., *Implicit Social Cognition and Law*, 3 ANN. REV. L. & SOC. SCI. 427, 433 (2007) (calling implicit social cognitions "robust" and "pervasive").

59. *See* Greenwald & Krieger, *supra* note 9, at 961 ("[E]vidence that implicit attitudes produce discriminatory behavior is already substantial and will continue to accumulate." (footnote omitted)).

60. Jeffrey J. Rachlinski, Sheri Lynn Johnson, Andrew J. Wistrich & Chris Guthrie, *Does Unconscious Racial Bias Affect Trial Judges?*, 84 NOTRE DAME L. REV. 1195 (2009).

61. *Id.* at 1207–08 (describing our methods).

62. *Id.* at 1210.

63. *Id.* at 1217–21.

64. Samuel R. Sommers & Phoebe C. Ellsworth, *White Juror Bias: An Investigation of Prejudice against Black Defendants in the American Courtroom*, 7 PSYCHOL. PUB. POL'Y & L. 201 (2001).

65. Rachlinski et al., *supra* note 60, at 1218. African-American judges expressed a large difference in conviction rates: 92 percent convicted the White defendant as compared to 50 percent for the African-American defendant. *Id.*

66. Jens Agerström & Dan-Olof Rooth, *Implicit Prejudice and Ethnic Minorities: Arab-Muslims in Sweden*, 30 INT'L J. MANPOWER 43 (2009) (human resources managers); Alexander R. Green et al., *Implicit Bias among Physicians and Its Prediction of Thrombolysis Decisions for Black and White Patients*, 22 J. GEN. INTERNAL MED. 1231 (2007) (doctors).

67. Rachlinski et al., *supra* note 60, at 1212–17.

68. Sandra Graham & Brian S. Lowery, *Priming Unconscious Racial Stereotypes About Adolescent Offenders*, 28 LAW & HUM. BEHAV. 483 (2004).

69. Justin D. Levinson, Mark W. Bennett & Koichi Hioki, *Judging Implicit Bias: A National Empirical Study of Judicial Stereotypes Beyond Black and White*, 69 FLA. L. REV. (forthcoming 2017).

70. Ian Ayres & Joel Waldfogel, *A Market Test for Race Discrimination in Bail Setting*, 46 STAN. L. REV. 987, 992 (1994) (Black defendants were forced to post 35 percent higher bail to obtain pretrial release than similar White defendants).

71. David S. Abrams, Marianne Bertrand & Sendhil Mullainathan, *Do Judges Vary in Their Treatment of Race?* 41 J. LEGAL STUD. 347 (2012).

72. Traci Burch, *Skin Color and the Criminal Justice System: Beyond Black and White Disparities in Sentencing*, 12 J. EMPIRICAL LEGAL STUD. 395 (2015).

73. *See* Mustard, *supra* note 7.

74. Cassia Spohn, *The Effects of the Offender's Race, Ethnicity, and Sex on Federal Sentencing Outcomes in the Guidelines Era*, 76 L. & CONTEMP. PROBS. 75 (2013).

75. *See* Mustard, *supra* note 7.

76. *See* Anna-Kaisa Newheiser & Kristina R. Olson, *White and Black American Children's Implicit Intergroup Bias*, 48 J. EXPERIMENTAL SOC. PSYCHOL. 264 (2012); Schubert Center for

Clinical Studies, *Play, Implicit Bias, and Discrimination in Early Childhood* (Nov. 2014) (collecting sources).

77. Claudia Goldin & Cecilia Rouse, *Orchestrating Impartiality: The Impact of "Blind" Auditions on Female Musicians*, 90 Am. Econ. Rev. 715 (2000).

78. See Christine Jolls & Cass R. Sunstein, *The Law of Implicit Bias*, 94 Cal. L. Rev. 969, 988–90 (2006).

79. See Kirwin Institute for the Study of Race and Ethnicity, *Implicit Bias: The State of the Science* 43 (2015).

80. See Rachlinski et al., *supra* note 60, at 1210.

81. See Bureau of Justice Statistics, U.S. Dept. of Justice *supra* note 5.

82. See Theodore Eisenberg & Sheri Lynn Johnson, *Implicit Racial Attitudes of Death Penalty Lawyers*, 53 DePaul L. Rev. 1539, 1546–48 (2004).

83. See Rachlinski et al., *supra* note 60, at 1210.

84. Others have tentatively suggested that the IAT be used as a screening device for certain professions. See, e.g., Ian Ayres, Pervasive Prejudice? 424 (2001) ("Implicit attitude testing might also itself be used as a criterion for hiring both governmental and nongovernmental actors.").

85. Green et al., *supra* note 66, at 1237 ("These findings support the IAT's value as an educational tool.").

86. See Siri Carpenter, *Buried Prejudice: The Bigot in Your Brain*, 27 Sci. Am. Mind 32, 32 (May 2008).

87. Timothy D. Wilson et al., *Mental Contamination and the Debiasing Problem, in* Heuristics and Biases 184, 190 (Thomas Gilovich et al. eds., 2002).

88. Guthrie et al., *supra* note 24, at 1525–26.

89. For suggestions regarding how such training may be conducted most effectively, see Chapter 10.

90. See, e.g., A. Chris Downs & Phillip M. Lyons, *Natural Observations of the Links between Attractiveness and Initial Legal Judgments*, 17 Personality & Soc. Psychol. Bull. 541, 544–45 (1991) (reporting that judges required higher bail from unattractive defendants than from attractive defendants); John E. Stewart, *Defendant's Attractiveness as a Factor in the Outcome of Criminal Trials: An Observational Study*, 10 App. Soc. Psychol. 348, 358 (1980) (reporting that unattractive defendants received longer sentences than attractive defendants).

91. See Anthony Page, Batson's *Blind-Spot: Unconscious Stereotyping and the Preemptory Challenge*, 85 Q. 155, 239–40 (2005) ("One major problem for any correction strategy is determining the magnitude of the correction required. Unfortunately, people are not very good at this determination. Some research suggests that among those who are very motivated to avoid discrimination, overcorrection is a common problem.").

92. *Id.* at 241–42 ("[T]o consciously and willfully regulate one's own . . . evaluations [and] decisions . . . requires a limited resource that is quickly used up, so conscious self-regulatory acts can only occur sparingly and for a short time." (omissions in original) (quoting John A. Bargh & Tanya L. Chartrand, *The Unbearable Automaticity of Being*, 54 Am. Psychol. 462, 476 (1999)).

93. See Wistrich et al., *supra* note 30, at 1262–64.

94. See Mark W. Bennett, *Unraveling the Gordian Knot of Implicit Bias in Jury Selection: The Problems of Judge-Dominated Voir Dire, the Failed Promise of Batson, and Proposed Solutions*, 4 Harv. L. & Pol'y Rev. 149 (2010); Elizabeth Ingriselli, *Mitigating Jurors' Racial Biases: The Effects of Content and Timing of Jury Instructions*, 124 Yale L.J. 1690, 1729 (2015). But see Jennifer K. Elek & Paula Hannaford-Agor, Can Explicit Instructions Reduce Expressions of Implicit Bias? New Questions Following a Test of a Specialized Jury Instruction (2014) (finding no significant benefit from giving such an anti-bias instruction and counseling caution because such an instruction might backfire).

95. *See, e.g.*, Leifer & Sample, *supra* note 26, at 145.
96. *See, e.g.*, National Center for Youth Law, Implicit Bias and Juvenile Justice: A Review of the Literature 18–26 (Michael Harris & Hannah Benton eds., 2014).
97. David Hoffman et al., *Docketology, District Courts, and Doctrine*, 85 Wash. U.L. Rev. 681 (2007).
98. *See* Christopher A. Parsons et al., *Strike Three: Umpires' Demand for Discrimination*, 101 Am. Econ. Rev. 1410 (2011); Joseph Price & Justin Wolfers, *Racial Discrimination among NBA Referees*, 125 Q.J. Econ. 1859 (2010).
99. *See* Thomas Miles, *Do Attorney Surveys Measure Judicial Performance or Respondent Ideology? Evidence from Online Evaluations*, 44 J. Legal Stud. S231 (2015) (reporting that online evaluations do not accurately reflect judges' performance).
100. *See, e.g.*, Jean E. Dubofsky, *Judicial Performance Review: A Balance between Judicial Independence and Public Accountability*, 34 Fordham Urb. L.J. 315, 320–22 (2007) (explaining that judicial performance review system in Colorado focuses only on a judge's performance in a particular case).
101. *See* Philip E. Tetlock & Jae I. Kim, *Accountability and Judgment Processes in a Personality Prediction Task*, 52 J. Pers. & Soc. Psychol. 700, 700 (1987).
102. *See id.* ("Social pressure for accountability can, under certain conditions, motivate people to become more vigilant, thorough, and self-critical information processors.").
103. *See id.* at 702; Philip E. Tetlock, *Accountability and Complexity of Thought*, 45 J. Pers. & Soc. Psychol. 74, 81 (1983).
104. *See* Tetlock & Kim, *supra* note 102, at 701–02.
105. Robert E. Beach, *The Value of Keeping Sentence Statistics*, 11 Judges J. 57, 57 (1972).
106. *See* Nat'l Ctr. for State Courts, Strategies to Reduce the Influence of Implicit Bias 18, http://www.ncsc.org/~/media/Files/PDF/Topics/Gender%20and%20Racial%20Fairness/IB_ Strategies_033012.
107. *See* Gordon W. Allport, The Nature of Prejudice 281 (1954); Thomas F. Pettigrew & Linda R. Tropp, *A Meta-Analytic Test of Intergroup Contact Theory*, 90 J. Personality & Soc. Psychol. 751, 766 (2006).
108. *See* Tetlock, *supra* note 102, at 81.
109. *See* Rebecca Gill, Sylvia R. Lazos & Mallory M. Waters, *Are Judicial Performance Evaluations Fair to Women and Minorities? A Cautionary Tale from Clark County, Nevada*, 45 Law & Soc'y Rev. 731, 749 (2011) ("[J]udicial performance evaluation surveys may carry with them unexamined and unconscious gender and race biases"); *see also* Maya Sen, *Is Justice Really Blind? Race and Reversal in U.S. Courts*, 44 J. Legal Stud. S187 (2015) (presenting evidence that African-American trial judges are more apt to be reversed by White appellate judges than are White trial judges).
110. *See* Lisa Legault, Jennifer N. Gutsell, and Michael Inzlicht, *Ironic Effects of Antiprejudice Messages: How Motivational Interventions Can Reduce (But Also Increase) Prejudice*, 22 Psychol. Sci. 1472, 1475 (2011).
111. Josh Salman and Emily Le Coz, *Race and Politics Influence Judicial Decisions*, Sarasota Herald-Tribune, available at http://projects.heraldtribune.com/bias/politics/
112. *See* Michael E. Solimine, *Congress, Ex Parte Young, and the Fate of the Three-Judge District Court*, 70 U. Pitt. L. Rev. 101, 128–34 (2008).
113. Jennifer L. Peresie, Note, *Female Judges Matter: Gender and Collegial Decisionmaking in the Federal Appellate Courts*, 114 Yale L.J. 1759, 1778 (2005). The effects may be more complicated and less predictable than they seem. *See* Rebecca D. Gill, Michael Kagan & Fatma Marouf, Chivalry, Masculinity, and the Importance of Maleness to Judicial Decision Making 13 (2015) (finding that female litigants fare better than male litigants with all male appellate panels than with mixed gender appellate panels). Similar effects have been observed with appellate panels of different races. *See* Charles Cameron & Craig Cummings, Diversity and Judicial Decision Making: Evidence from Affirmative Action Cases

IN THE FEDERAL COURTS OF APPEALS, 1971–1999, presented at the Crafting and Operating Institutions Conference, Yale University (2003).

114. *See* Note, *Judicial Limitation of Three-Judge Court Jurisdiction*, 85 YALE L.J. 564, 564 (1976).

115. *See* William R. Bayes, C.J. *Criminal Cases Tried to a Bench of Three Judges*, 24 J. AM. JUD. SOC. 182 (1940–41); *Support Given of Idea of Three-Judge Trial Bench*, 22 J. AM. JUD. SOC. 167 (1938–39); *The Trial Bench of Three Judges*, 12 J. AM. JUD. SOC. 185 (1928–29).

116. *See* Arthur D. Hellman, *Legal Problems of Dividing a State Between Federal Judicial Circuits*, 122 U. PA. L. REV. 1188, 1225 (1974).

117. *See* Jerry Kang et al., *Implicit Bias in the Courtroom*, 59 UCLA L. REV. 1124, 1170 (2012) (recommending that judges hire a diverse staff).

118. *See* ROBERT CIALDINI, INFLUENCE: SCIENCE AND PRACTICE 98–141 (2001).

119. *See* Erik J. Girvan, *Wise Restraints? Learning Legal Rules, Not Standards, Reduces the Effect of Stereotypes in Legal Decision-Making*, 22 PSYCHOL. PUB. POL'Y & L. 31, 42 (2016) (reporting that outcomes in hypothetical cases were 1.5 times as likely to be stereotype consistent when subjects applied a standard than when they applied a rule, and concluding that "rules have a comparative advantage over standards in reducing the impact of bias on legal decisions").

120. *See* Samuel R. Wiseman, *Fixing Bail*, 84 GEO. WASH. L. REV. 417, 419 (2016) ("[D]efendants jailed pretrial . . . are more likely to be convicted and to receive longer sentences").

121. *See* Alexander J. Konick, *Tentative Rules in California Trial Courts: A Natural Experiment*, 47 COLUM. J. L. & SOC. PROBS 324 (2014) (describing the use of tentative rulings in California state trial courts). For a similar but more far-reaching proposal, which would allow the public as well as the litigants to comment on tentative rulings, *see also* Michael Abramowicz & Thomas B. Colby, *Notice-And-Comment Judicial Decisionmaking*, 76 U. CHI. L. REV. 965, 967–68 (2009).

122. *See* Peresie, *supra* note 114, at 1778.

123. *See* JEREMY D. FOGEL, MINDFULNESS AND JUDGING 2 (2016) ("In essence it involves slowing down one's mental processes enough to allow one to notice as much as possible about a given moment or situation.").

124. *See* Gaëlle Desbordes et al., *Effects of Mindful Attention and Compassion Meditation Training on Amygdala Response to Emotional Stimuli in an Ordinary, Non-Meditative State*, 6 FRONT. HUM. NEUROSCI. 1, 3 (2012).

125. *See* Adam Lueke & Bryan Gibson, *Mindfulness Meditation Reduces Implicit Age and Race Bias: The Role of Reduced Automaticity of Responding*, 6 SOC. PSYCHOL. & PERSONALITY SCI. 284, 285 (2015).

126. *Id.* at 288.

127. Paul Condon et al., *Meditation Increases Compassionate Responses to Suffering*, 24 PSYCHOL. SCI. 2125, 2126–27 (2013) ("As predicted, meditation directly enhanced compassionate responding.").

128. *See* Kang et al., *supra* note 118, at 1177 (2012) ("There is also evidence that elevated emotional states, either positive or negative, can prompt more biased decisionmaking.").

129. *See* Yi-Yuan Tang & Leslie D. Leve, *A Translational Neuroscience Perspective on Mindfulness Meditation as a Prevention Strategy*, 63 TRANSLATIONAL BEHAV. MED. 63, 64 (2015).

130. *See* Desbordes et al., *supra* note 125, at 6–7.

131. *See id.* at 10 ("We found a longitudinal decrease in right amygdala activation in response to positive images, and in response to images of all valences overall."). *See generally* Adrienne A. Taren et al., *Mindfulness Meditation Training Alters Stress-Related Amygdala Resting State Functional Connectivity: A Randomized Controlled Trial*, 10 SOC. COGN. AFFECT. NEUROSCI. 1758 (2015).

132. *See* Charles G. Lord et al., *Considering the Opposite: A Corrective Strategy for Social Judgment*, 47 J. Personality & Soc. Psychol. 1231, 1231–32 (1984).

133. *See* Hal R. Arkes, David Faust, Thomas Guilemette & Kathleen Hart, *Eliminating the Hindsight Bias*, 73 J. Applied Psychol. 305, 305–07 (1988); Asher Koriat, Sarah Lichtenstein & Baruch Fischhoff, *Reasons for Confidence*, 6 J. Experimental Psychol.: Hum. Learning & Memory 107, 107–18 (1980); Thomas Mussweiler, Fritz Strack & Tim Pfeiffer, *Overcoming the Inevitable Anchoring Effect: Considering the Opposite Compensates for Selective Accessibility*, 26 Personality & Soc. Psychol. Bull. 1142, 1142–50 (2000).

134. *See* Edward R. Hirt & Keith D. Markman, *Multiple Explanation: A Consider-an-Alternative Strategy for Debiasing Judgments*, 69 J. Personality & Soc. Psychol. 1069, 1084 (1995) ("As a result, it appears that the counterexplanation task breaks participants' inertia with regard to the focal hypothesis and leads to a more thorough and comprehensive consideration of the likely outcome of the event.").

135. *See* Wistrich et al., *supra* note 45, at 910 (suggesting this technique to help judges avoid favoring sympathetic litigants over unsympathetic ones).

136. U.S. Sentencing Guidelines Manual § 5H1.10.

137. *See* Elizabeth J. Reese, *Techniques for Mitigating Cognitive Biases in Fingerprint Identification*, 59 UCLA L. Rev. 1252, 1286 (2012) ("The devil's advocate technique is somewhat similar to the consider-an-alternative technique; however, the devil's advocate technique formalizes the dissent process by bringing in a second person to question the decisionmaker's conclusion.").

138. Adam D. Galinsky & Gillian Ku, *The Effects of Perspective-Taking on Prejudice: The Moderating Role of Self-Evaluation*, 30 Personality & Soc. Psychol. Bull. 594, 596 (2004) ("[P]erspective-taking entails the active consideration of another's point of view, imagining what the person's life and situation are like, walking a mile in the person's shoes.").

139. *See* Adam D. Galinsky & Gordon B. Moskowitz, *Perspective-Taking: Decreasing Stereotype Expression, Stereotype Accessibility, and In-Group Favoritism*, 78 J. Personality & Soc. Psychol. 708, 720 (2000) (referencing the "on-going debate over whether increased helping after perspective-taking is truly altruistic of egoistically motivated.").

140. *See* Galinsky & Ku, *supra* note 139, at 596.

141. *See* Galinsky & Moskowitz, *supra* note 140, at 709 (reporting experiments that "suggest that perspective-taking increased the evaluations of the out-group through the creation of a cognitive representation of the out-group that now overlaps with the participants' own self representation.").

142. *See id.* at 709 ("The increased accessibility of the self-concept after perspective-taking might result in the use of the self-concept over the stereotypic construct when categorizing and evaluating a member of a stereotyped group.").

143. *See id.* at 719 ("The results demonstrate the success of perspective-taking at alleviating intergroup bias, even when there is no known content of the stereotype of the out-group or a specific target individual whose perspective one has taken").

144. Andrew R. Todd, Galen V. Bodenhausen & Adam D. Galinsky, *Perspective Taking Combats the Denial of Intergroup Discrimination*, 48 J. Experimental Soc. Psychol. 738, 743 (2012).

145. *See* Legault, *supra* note 111, at 1476 (finding that autonomous motivations are more effective than controlling motivations in reducing implicit bias).

146. Gerald L. Clore & Katherine M. Jeffery, *Emotional Role Playing, Attitude Change, and Attraction Toward a Disabled Person*, 23 J. Personality & Soc. Psychol. 105, 115–16 (1972).

147. Jeanine L. Skorinko et al., *Effects of Perspective Taking on Courtroom Decisions*, 44 J. Applied. Soc. Psychol. 303 (2014).

148. Jeanine L. Skorinko & Stacey A. Sinclair, *Perspective Taking Can Increase Stereotyping: The Role of Apparent Stereotype Confirmation*, 49 J. Experimental Soc. Psychol. 10, 11 (2013).

149. *Cf.* Robert J. Smith & Justin D. Levinson, *The Impact of Implicit Racial Bias on the Exercise of Prosecutorial Discretion*, 35 Seattle U.L. Rev. 795, 826 (2012) (suggesting that prosecutors live in high-crime neighborhoods).

150. *See* Kang et al., *supra* note 118, at 1171.

151. *See* Melissa Bateson, Daniel Nettle & Gilbert Roberts, *Cues of Being Watched Enhance Cooperation in a Real-World Setting*, 2 Biol. Lett. 412, 412 (2006) (finding that office workers contributed more money to a coffee honor box when being "watched" by a photograph of eyes than by a photograph of flowers).

152. *See* Bronwyn Law-Viljoen, Art and Justice: The Art of the Constitutional Court of South Africa (2008).

153. Ariely, *supra* note 22, at 282–84.

154. *See* Cialdini, *supra* note 119, at 92 ("Once we make a choice or take a stand, we will encounter personal and interpersonal pressures to behave consistently with that commitment. . . . Commitments are most effective when they are active, public, effortful, and viewed as internally motivated (uncoerced)." (emphasis omitted).

155. Although some courthouses already possess this feature, such exhortations or symbols often are more visible to the public than to judges, who may enter the courthouse through a secure garage and private elevators and corridors, rather than through the public lobby and corridors where inspirational statements are typically are displayed.

156. *See* The Joint Commission, Measuring Hand Hygiene Adherence: Overcoming the Challenges (2009).

157. *See* Melissa L. Finucane, Ali Alhakami, Paul Slovic & Stephen M. Johnson, *The Affect Heuristic in Judgments of Risks and Benefits*, 13 J. Behav. Decision Making 1, 8 (2000) (finding that subjects were more likely to rely on intuitive, heuristic-driven decision making rather than on deliberate decision making when operating under time pressure).

158. *See* Daniel T. Gilbert, *Inferential Correction, in* Heuristics and Biases: The Psychology of Intuitive Judgment 167, 179 (Thomas Gilovich et al. eds., 2002) ("The busyness-induced undercorrection of dispositional inferences is now a well-established and widely replicated phenomenon.").

159. *See* Fatma Marouf, *Implicit Bias and Immigration Courts*, 45 New Eng. L. Rev. 435, 435–37 (2011).

160. *See* Judith H. Langlois et al., *Maxims or Myths of Beauty? A Meta-Analytic and Theoretical Review*, 126 Psychol. Bull. 390, 399–401 (2000).

161. Judges generally disclose the reasons behind their actions, and they are often required to do so. *See, e.g.*, Fed. R. Civ. P. 52(a) (requiring findings of fact after a bench trial).

162. Robert A. Leflar, *Some Observations Concerning Judicial Opinions*, 61 Colum. L. Rev. 810, 810 (1961) ("[T]he necessity for preparing a formal opinion assures some measure of thoughtful review of the facts in a case and of the law's bearing upon them. Snap judgments and lazy preferences for armchair theorizing . . . are somewhat minimized."). *But see* Chad M. Oldfather, *Writing, Cognition, and the Nature of the Judicial Function*, 96 Geo. L.J. 1283 (2008) (arguing that verbalization does not always enhance understanding or decision making, particularly when important factors are not readily susceptible to verbalization).

163. *See* Robin Hogarth, Educating Intuition 263 (2006) ("Verbalization . . . forces people to act in [a] deliberate mode and cuts off access to tacit processes.").

164. Guthrie et al., *supra* note 24, at 1501–06.

165. *See* Johon McMakin & Paul Slovic, *When Does Explicit Justification Impair Decision Making?*, 14 Applied Cognitive Psychol. 527, 535–39 (2000) (finding that asking subjects

to provide reasons adversely affected their performance on intuitive tasks, such as indicating which advertisement people would prefer, but improved their performance on analytical tasks, such as estimating the length of the *Amazon River); Timothy D. Wilson & Jonathan W. Schooler, Thinking Too Much: Introspection Can Reduce the Quality of Preferences and Decisions,* 60 J. PERSONALITY & SOC. PSYCHOL. 181, 181 (1991) (finding that subjects' preferred choices of strawberry jam were less likely to correspond with experts' preferred choices if the subjects were required to give reasons for their choices).

166. *See* Timothy D. Wilson et al., *Introspecting about Reasons Can Reduce Post-Choice Satisfaction,* 19 PERSONALITY & SOC. PSYCHOL. BULL. 331, 337 (1993).

167. *See* Hogarth, *supra* note 164, at 209 ("Just as we cannot avoid tacitly forming prejudices, we cannot avoid forming a good first impression of con men. But we can learn not to act uncritically on the basis of that first impression.").

168. *See* Jennifer S. Lerner & Philip E. Tetlock, *Accounting for the Effects of Accountability,* 125 PSYCHOL. BULL. 255, 256–59 (1999). The authors explain that decision makers are more likely to engage in self-critical thinking if they learn prior to making their decisions that they will be accountable to an audience whose views are unknown, who is well-informed, and who has a legitimate reason for evaluating the decision makers' judges. *See id.* at 259.

169. Guthrie et al., *supra* note 24, at 1236–37.

170. *See* Baruch Fischoff, *Heuristics and Biases in Application, in* HEURISTICS AND BIASES: THE PSYCHOLOGY OF INTUITIVE JUDGMENT 730, 731 (Thomas Gilovich et al. eds., 2002) ("Training provides feedback that everyday life typically lacks, allowing people to test and refine judgment skills.").

171. *See* Chip Heath, Richard L. Larrick & Joshua Klayman, *Cognitive Repairs: How Organizational Practices Can Compensate for Individual Shortcomings,* 20 RES. ORG. BEHAV. 1, 15 (1998) ("[I]ndividuals attend to and process information more comprehensively when they have a mental *schema* that tells them what information is needed in a given situation and where to find it.").

172. *See* Paul R. Dexter et al., *A Computerized Reminder System to Increase the Use of Prevention Care of Hospitalized Patients,* 345 NEW ENG. J. MED. 965, 965 (2001) (reporting positive results from use of a computerized reminder system to remind physicians to deliver preventive care to hospital patients); Padmanabham Ramnarayan et al., *Diagnostic Omission Errors in Acute Pediatric Practice: Impact of a Reminder System on Decision-Making,* 6 BMC MED. INFORMATICS & DECISION MAKING 37, 37–38 (2006) (reporting that physicians' use of an Internet-based diagnostic reminder system improved diagnostic workups and reduced diagnostic omission errors; the reminder system reduced unsafe diagnostic workups from 45.2 percent to 32.7 percent).

173. *See* Barton Beebe, *An Empirical Study of the Multifactor Tests for Trademark Infringement,* 94 CAL. L. REV. 1581, 1581–82 (2006).

174. *See, e.g.,* Ng v. I.N.S., 804 F.2d 534, 538 (9th Cir. 1986) ("[W]e require that the BIA state its reasons and show proper consideration of all factors when weighing equities. . . . [T]his court cannot assume that the BIA considered factors that it failed to mention in its decision."); Education Credit Mgmt. Corp. v. Pope, 308 B.R. 55, 59 (N.D. Cal. 2004) ("[T]he Ninth Circuit adopted a three-part undue hardship test. . . . [C]ourts must consider each element [of the test] in turn and, where one of the three elements is not met, the court must stop there with a finding of no dischargability."); Frankel v. Frankel, 886 A.2d 136, 154 (Md. App. 2005) ("A trial judge must consider each factor listed . . . when determining the amount of monetary award.").

175. *See* Mads Soegaard, *Forcing Functions,* https://www.interaction-design.org/literature/book/the-glossary-of-human-computer-interaction/forcing-functions ("A forcing

function is an aspect of a design that prevents the user from taking an action with-out *consciously* considering information relevant to that action. It *forces* conscious attention something . . . and thus deliberately disrupts the efficient or automatized [sic] performance of a task. . . . It is . . . in situations where the behavior of the user is *skilled,* as in performing routine or well-known tasks. Execution of this type of task [] is often partly or wholly automatized, requiring few or no attentional resources . . . , and it can thus be necessary to 'wake the user up' by deliberately disrupting the performance of the task.").

Chapter 6
When Myths Become Beliefs
Implicit Socioeconomic Bias in American Courtrooms

Michele Benedetto Neitz

Chapter Contents

Chapter Highlights

- Our society's myths about socioeconomic status, perpetuated by media stereotypes, can become ingrained as beliefs and contribute to biases.

- Judicial bias based on socioeconomic status is not discussed often in caselaw or legal academic literature, and it tends to be a more hidden and implicit type of bias.

- Implicit socioeconomic bias on the part of judges can have severe detrimental effects on vulnerable populations.
- Judges can combat implicit socioeconomic bias with simple techniques.

Introduction

Can a judge's socioeconomic status involuntarily affect his or her decision-making processes? Ninth Circuit Judge Alex Kozinski believes the answer is yes. Dissenting in a Fourth Amendment search and seizure case in 2010, Judge Kozinski rebuked his judicial colleagues for failing to recognize how their decision in the case would have a more detrimental effect on poor people than wealthy people.[1] Judge Kozinski proposed that judges did not deliberately act in a biased manner against poor people, but "the every day problems of people who live in poverty are not close to our hearts and minds because that's not how we and our friends live."[2] Judge Kozinski, who was the Ninth Circuit chief judge at the time he wrote the dissent, correctly acknowledged that judges' beliefs about low-income populations are often not based on personal experience. Consequently, judges may inadvertently hold mistaken beliefs about poor people that influence their judicial opinions.

This chapter examines the causes and effects of implicit socioeconomic bias on the part of judges. Part II explains why particular myths about socioeconomic status, particularly regarding low-income populations, are commonplace in modern American discourse. Drawing from the research of Daniel Kahneman, winner of the Nobel Prize in Economics, this section explains how those myths become implicit beliefs that can motivate behavior—even for individuals who profess to have no explicit prejudices. Part III verifies the persistence of implicit socioeconomic bias on the part of judges. Using cases as evidence, this part details how the manifestation of a judge's implicit socioeconomic biases can have severe detrimental effects on judicial decisions and litigants in courtrooms. Part IV addresses the prohibition of socioeconomic bias in the ABA Model Code of Judicial Conduct. Although this type of bias is specifically referenced in the ABA Code, not all states have actually adopted an explicit ban on socioeconomic bias. This section considers the impact of this omission. The Conclusion proposes practical ways for judges to reduce implicit socioeconomic bias in their courtrooms. These recommendations include raising awareness of this unique type of bias, increasing judges' familiarity with low-income populations, modifying courtroom conditions, and minimizing judicial burnout. Even a few simple changes in this area can have long-term positive effects on judicial decision-making processes.

I. How Myths Become Beliefs: The Effects of Media Stories about Low-Income Populations

A. *What Is a Myth?*

Every society holds collective myths about its populations. Myths are actually stories that serve "to unfold part of the world view of a people or explain a practice, belief or natural phenomenon."[3] Myths are not truths but instead are popular beliefs or traditions intended to "embod[y] the ideals and institutions of a society or a segment of society."[4]

In modern American society, our collective myths are mostly perpetrated through the media. Indeed, "[n]ews coverage influences the public by 'priming' certain perceptions through its coverage of an issue."[5] These myths can be quite influential; for example, media portrayals of crime can promote increased punitiveness in actual criminal justice practice, as well as increased "misperceptions of crime, higher perceptions of crime risk; fear of crime; and fear of poor, minority males."[6] It is no surprise, therefore, that American media stories about poor people have contributed to our shared myths about this population.

B. *Media Portrayals of Low-Income Populations*

The media has an outsized influence in the lives of everyday Americans. Readers of newspapers, magazines, and blogs or viewers of television who lack "direct personal experience or specific background knowledge of an issue" are not able to properly "evaluate the accuracy of the stories they read or the images they view."[7] Moreover, given the fact that a few large corporations control most mainstream media outlets, "highly politicized issues are likely to be defined by and to reflect the interest of dominant social groups."[8] As a result, "less powerful groups (e.g., the poor, people of color, women) are at risk of being devalued and stereotyped in the media."[9]

Moreover, the majority of American adults now receive their news updates from social media websites, such as Facebook and Twitter.[10] In May 2016, the Pew Research Center found that 62 percent of Americans obtain their news from social media sites.[11] While social media certainly can be useful, studies show that consumers of news on social media generally operate "within clusters of users known as 'echo chambers'—polarized communities that tend to consume the same types of information."[12] Thus, individuals on social media websites tend to gravitate toward communities that already share their opinions and beliefs.[13] This can result in "confirmation bias," enabling people to "pay attention to or believe information that confirms the personal values and beliefs they already hold," instead of challenging those beliefs with new information.[14]

Of course, some traditional news outlets have been slanted toward one political viewpoint or another for many years.[15] But confirmation bias is especially problematic in the context of social media because of the high level of

> Judges who receive most of their news updates in the echo chamber of social media may be less able to distinguish between truth and falsehoods. In addition, personal confirmation biases might prevent judges from seeking alternative viewpoints or new information.

inaccurate information and falsehoods prevalent on the Internet. In fact, a recent study published in the Proceedings of the National Academy of Sciences found that "massive digital misinformation" is "pervasive in online social media," with the Web serving as "a fruitful environment for the massive diffusion of unverified rumors."[16] Judges who receive most of their news updates in the echo chamber of social media may be less able to distinguish between truth and falsehoods. In addition, personal confirmation biases might prevent judges from seeking alternative viewpoints or new information.

These factors contribute to ongoing myths about socioeconomic status. Social scientists studying the media have repeatedly found that stereotypes about the behavior of the poor are pervasive.[17] For example, women receiving welfare assistance are portrayed in the media as "lazy, disinterested in education, and promiscuous."[18] An illustrative case is the 1980s image of the "welfare queen" who would rather receive public assistance than work.[19]

News stories about poverty are also heavily racialized; poor people are presented disproportionately as African-Americans.[20] In fact, public opposition to welfare recipients can be explained, in part, by the media-influenced "perception that welfare primarily benefits African Americans, combined with stereotypes that African Americans lack a work ethic and thus do not deserve assistance."[21] These depictions reinforce the concept of poor people as "deserving" of their plights. After all, if poverty is caused by laziness or promiscuity, persons with lower socioeconomic status can be viewed as personally responsible for their poverty. Furthermore, if poor individuals themselves are to blame, society's burden of responsibility for any structural causes of poverty can be alleviated.

This viewpoint is particularly evident in the public statements of American politicians. When House Budget Chairman (now Speaker of the House) Paul Ryan discussed upcoming legislative proposals related to poverty during a television appearance, he blamed poverty on a "tailspin of culture, in our inner cities in particular, of men not working and just generations of men not even thinking about working or learning the value and the culture of work, and so there is a real culture problem here that has to be dealt with."[22] To support his claim, Representative Ryan cited Charles Murray, a conservative social scientist noted for believing that poverty is a problem because "a lot of poor people are born lazy."[23]

Republican presidential nominee Mitt Romney notoriously endorsed a similar point during the 2012 presidential election. Romney was secretly recorded at a fundraising event stating that 47 percent of the public are people who "are dependent upon government, who believe that they are vic-tims, who believe the government has a responsibility to care for them, who believe that they are entitled to health care, to food, to housing, you name it."[24] Romney added that "[m]y job is not to worry about those people. I'll never convince them they should take personal responsibility and care for their lives."[25]

Similar themes echoed through the 2016 presidential election. In 2015, Republican presidential candidate Mike Huckabee suggested that the criminal justice system should deal with poor people convicted of nonviolent criminal behavior by selling them into slavery to work off their debts.[26] Republican nom-inee Donald Trump attempted to reach African-American voters by stating, "You live in your poverty, your schools are no good, you have no jobs, 58 percent of your youth is unemployed. What the hell do you have to lose [by voting for Trump]?"[27] In fact, most African-Americans do not live in poverty.[28] Reflecting on this, President Barack Obama complained that conservative news outlet Fox News consistently portrays poor people as unwilling to work: "They will find folks who make me mad. . . . I don't know where they find them. They're like, 'I don't want to work, I just want a free Obamaphone,' or whatever, and that becomes an entire narrative."[29]

President Obama accurately noted that statements correlating poor people with laziness, like other stereotypes, have become an ongoing narrative. Ulti-mately, these narratives about socioeconomic class are embedded in American culture as myths. These myths are powerful: "Even very young children learn value-based, biased messages about socioeconomic class both directly (for example, comments from family members or educators) and indirectly (for example, media invisibility or bias)."[30] These types of messages influence chil-dren's "ideas and feelings about where and how they live, what they own or do not own, how they speak and behave, and what they eat and wear."[31] For adults as well as children, these myths can eventually become implicit personal beliefs about specific populations.

C. How Myths Turn into Biases

How can media stories and cultural myths affect the way we think about a particular issue? Nobel Prize-winning economist Daniel Kahneman explains that the answer lies in the way our brains process information. Most peo-ple "tend to assess the relative importance of issues by the ease with which they are retrieved from memory—and this is largely determined by the extent of coverage in the media. Frequently mentioned topics populate the mind even as others slip away from awareness."[32] Thus, repeated exposure to the types of media stories described above can leave people (including judges) thinking about poor people in a stereotyped way. Judges themselves may not even be consciously aware of how these thoughts came about or why they think this way. But if the stereotypes are not challenged, they may ultimately become cognitive beliefs. This occurs through the interaction of two thought processes in our minds, described by Kahneman as "System 1" and "System 2."[33] System 1 is the intuitive part of the mind, operating "automatically and quickly, with little or no effort and no sense of voluntary control."[34] System 1 represents our autopilot, our "fast, intuitive, and typically story-based decision making and judgmental process."[35] This is the part of our mind that can detect the distance of objects and drive our car (seemingly automatically) down an empty road.[36]

In contrast, System 2 is the analytical mind, constructing "thoughts in an orderly series of steps" and requiring attention devoted to "effortful mental activities."[37] Examples of System 2 include telling a person your phone number and counting the number of times the letter "A" appears on a page.[38]

These two systems operate concurrently. System 1 creates recommendations for System 2 in the form of "impressions, intuitions, intentions, and feelings."[39] If System 2 accepts these recommendations, which happens most of the time, "impressions and intuitions turn into beliefs, and impulses turn into voluntary actions."[40] Kahneman's research suggests that most judgments and decisions are made in this intuitive manner proposed by System 1, not from the analytical process of System 2 as many of us would like to believe.[41]

This two-step process in our mind has clear advantages. As Kahneman recognizes, "You generally believe your impressions and act on your desires, and that is fine—usually."[42] For example, if you are about to walk in front of a car, System 1 will react intuitively to lead you out of the road to safety. If you need to complete a technical mathematics problem, System 2 will enable you to bypass your intuition to focus intensely to accomplish the proper steps.

But the process is problematic when it comes to the type of cognitive decision making we require of judges. System 1 is an automatic process; consequently, "errors of intuitive thought are often difficult to prevent."[43] System 2 may recognize the intuitive error, but it requires a great deal of effort to override our instincts.[44] In fact, it is unreasonable to expect any person to expend the effort required to second-guess every intuitive decision throughout the day.[45] Even if judges try to rethink decisions made during a workday, "[a]s the cognitive energy needed to exercise System 2 is depleted, problems of bias and inadequate motivation may arise."[46]

This explains why "individuals are notoriously poor at recognizing and controlling their own biases—in fact, our brains are wired to promote fast, efficient information processing."[47] If a bias is explicit, such as a professed prejudice vocalized against a particular group of people, it is much easier to identify and remedy. But if a bias stems from System 1's impression or feeling, such as a reaction to a news story, an *individual may not even be aware of how that impression affects his or her cognitive decision making.*

Given that System 2 usually accepts System 1's suggestions, it not surprising that "researchers have provided convincing evidence that implicit biases exist, are pervasive, are large in magnitude, and have real-world effects."[48] This is a special concern for judges, since the presence of these implicit biases can have a detrimental effect on the impartiality of their opinions.

II. Implicit Socioeconomic Bias in the Courtroom

A. Do Judges Hold Socioeconomic Biases?

Most experts believe that judges, like all humans, are not free from bias.[49] But judges themselves have a skewed view of the level of neutrality in their decisions. For example, one study found that 97 percent of judges believed that they were in the top quartile of judges able to avoid "racial prejudice in decision-making"—a number that is "mathematically impossible."[50]

In fact, like all of us, judges have System 1 and System 2 processes working simultaneously. They are therefore subject to implicit biases in the way that all people experience. As a result, judges should be aware that "strategic exposure to what is seemingly 'irrelevant' matters profoundly."[51] A judge's decision may be influenced by something the judge him- or herself may not recognize.

Indeed, judges have access to the same media outlets and websites that lawyers and litigants in their courtrooms do. Accordingly, they can hear the same messages about poverty and low-income populations that average Americans receive. If media messages translate into negative System 1 impressions about poor people, the result can be implicit socioeconomic bias.

The word "socioeconomic" is defined as "of, relating to, or involving a combination of social and economic factors."[52] A classic example of socioeconomic bias can be found in a 1983 experiment by John Darley and Paget Gross in which participants were asked to view a 12-minute videotape of a young girl answering questions.[53] As Professor Jerry Kang and his coauthors detailed in a *UCLA Law Review* article in 2012, when the participants did not have any economic information about the girl, they did not recognize a relationship between her intelligence and her economic class.[54] However, if participants believed the girl was rich, they viewed the video as confirmation that she was "smart."[55] Those participants who were told the girl was poor "interpreted the same video as confirmation that she was not so bright."[56] Later studies defined this bias as "social judgeability" and confirmed its effects.[57]

The issue of socioeconomic bias in courtrooms recently made headlines in England, when Lord Neuberger, President of the Supreme Court, admonished judges to be "sensitive" to the fact that they usually come from a "more privileged sector of society" than the parties appearing in their courtrooms.[58] Lord Neuberger added that judges should understand the "different cultural and social habits" of litigants[59] and further noted that judges and lawyers "often failed to recognize how 'artificial and intimidating' courts could be for ordinary people."[60] Lord Neuberger correctly identified the potential for implicit socioeconomic bias in English courts. As demonstrated in the case study below, the same potential exists in American courtrooms.

B. *Case Study 1:* Wisconsin Judicial Commission v. Michelson

In 1998, the Honorable Robert Michelson was a municipal judge in the city of Racine, Wisconsin.[61] On January 5 of that year, a woman named Lynn Marchant appeared before Judge Michelson and stated that she would not be able to pay a court fine because she was the caretaker for two young children of her daughter, who was ill and receiving chemotherapy.[62] Judge Michelson stated that he could not accept that "excuse" because the woman had "no legal obligation to support her daughter's children."[63] He asked why the children's father would not support them, and the woman responded that the father of one child could not be found and the identity of another child's father was not established.[64]

Judge Michelson became angry at that response, stating, "I suppose it was too much to ask that your daughter keep her pants on and not behave like a slut."[65] He also stated that the daughter "should not have brought into the world children she was not in a position to support."[66] Judge Michelson then ordered a monthly payment plan for the fine.[67]

Ms. Marchant was angered by Judge Michelson's comments and discussed them with her high-school-age daughter. Ms. Marchant's daughter wrote a letter demanding an apology from Judge Michelson. In response, Judge Michelson sent a letter to Ms. Marchant's daughter stating,

> I will clearly state that my remarks are what I personally believe— that people should not bear children out of a marriage relationship; that it is immoral, and often means that a child will grow up both without a father and in poverty. With the planet already overcrowded, my personal belief is that a young woman who finds herself unmarried and pregnant should get an abortion.[68]

Judge Michelson also noted in the letter that he recognized that it is "not appropriate" for a judge to express personal beliefs "from the bench because the judge is in a position of power at that moment and the person being spoken to cannot talk back."[69]

The Wisconsin Judicial Commission instituted judicial disciplinary proceedings against Judge Michelson for his conduct on the bench, as well as his apology letter. In April 1999, the Wisconsin Supreme Court agreed with a three-judge panel of the Court of Appeals recommending the reprimand of Judge Michelson for violating the Wisconsin Code of Judicial Conduct.[70] Specifically, the Supreme Court noted that Judge Michelson's comments were "intemperate, discourteous and undignified," and his words "manifested a bias based on a person's socioeconomic status."[71] The court stated that Judge Michelson's letter demonstrated "a lack of sensitivity to the socioeconomic differences in society."[72] The court also agreed with the panel's suggestion that "Judge Michelson [should] participate in anger management and diversity training to assist him in conforming his conduct to the appropriate standards of judicial behavior."[73]

If this were the end of the case, it would appear that Judge Michelson manifested *explicit*, not implicit, socioeconomic bias. But in fact, Judge Michelson later denied that he acted in a biased way.[74] In a news article written after the Wisconsin Supreme Court ordered a reprimand, Judge Michelson argued, "I've been a judge for 25 years. One outburst in what might be a quarter of a million cases doesn't make a case that I am a monster."[75] Judge Michelson said most people he had spoken with "were glad he spoke his mind about children being born out of wedlock."[76] Moreover, given the "outrageous" things judges must "hear in court," Judge Michelson found it "remarkable [that] most of us haven't exploded more often."[77] Finally, Judge Michelson declared that he would not participate in the anger management and diversity training recommended (but not ordered) by the Wisconsin Supreme Court.[78]

Judge Michelson truly believed that his actions were not based on socioeconomic bias. Even after the Wisconsin Supreme Court reprimanded him for violating the Code of Judicial Conduct provisions related to such bias, Judge Michelson protested that his actions were reasonable. In effect, Judge Michelson's System 1 impressions about single mothers and poverty overrode his System 2 analytical mind, which (with effort) could have limited his personal beliefs from interfering with the case at hand.

It is worth noting that Judge Michelson's outburst occurred soon after a national debate on welfare reform, in which single mothers were particularly demonized. Just a few years before Judge Michelson's outburst, the 1996 welfare reform law stated that "[m]arriage is the foundation of a successful society" and "[p]romotion of responsible fatherhood and motherhood is integral to successful child rearing and the well-being of children."[79] Judge Michelson appeared to have believed the myth, perpetuated extensively in media and politics during the 1980s and 1990s, that single mothers were (in his words) "immoral" and responsible for their own poverty. Unfortunately for the litigants in his courtroom, Judge Michelson's implicit socioeconomic bias detrimentally influenced his decision-making process in the courtroom.

C. *Case Study 2:* In the Matter of Marvin Wayne Wiggins

On September 17, 2015, Judge Marvin Wiggins was presiding over the "pay-due" docket in the Fourth Judicial Circuit of Alabama.[80] The purpose of the docket was to collect court-ordered fees and fines owed by criminal defendants, and the defendants had been told that attorneys were not required to be present.[81]

During the proceeding, Judge Wiggins addressed the defendants from the bench. He stated,

> For your consideration, there's a blood drive outside and if you do not have any money and you don't want to go to jail, as an option to pay it, you can give blood today. If you do not have any money,

> go out there and give blood and bring in a receipt indicating that you gave blood. Consider that as a discount rather than putting you in jail, if you do not have any money. So, if you do not have any money and you don't want to go to jail, consider giving blood today and bring your receipt back or the sheriff has enough handcuffs for those who do not have money.[82]

Consequently, defendants from Judge Wiggins' courtroom gave 41 of the 47 blood donations made at the mobile blood bank that day.

The Southern Poverty Law Center filed an ethics complaint against Judge Wiggins, alleging that he violated the "bodily integrity" of the defendants.[83] Moreover, the complaint asserted that the U.S. Constitution and the Alabama Constitution do not permit "indigent persons to be jailed because they cannot pay" court-ordered fines.[84] The complaint also alleged numerous violations of the Alabama Canons of Judicial Ethics.[85]

The Judicial Inquiry Commission agreed with the complaint and filed its own complaint against Judge Wiggins. The Commission declared that Judge Wiggins' instruction to "either donate blood or go to jail" violated multiple canons of judicial ethics, including the following:

- Canon 1's requirements to "uphold the integrity and independence of the judiciary" and establish "high standards of conduct"[86]

- Canon 2's obligation to "avoid impropriety and the appearance of impropriety"[87]

- Canon 2A's provision mandating judges to behave "in a manner that promotes public confidence in the integrity and impartiality of the judiciary"[88]

- Canon 2B's provision requiring judges to "avoid conduct prejudicial to the administration of justice which brings the judicial office into disrepute"[89]

The Commission notably did not allege violations based on the judge's showing of socioeconomic bias, even though Judge Wiggins' actions—ordering poor people to give blood to avoid incarceration—would clearly constitute such a bias. The reason for this omission is that Alabama's Canons of Judicial Ethics do not expressly prohibit bias on the basis of socioeconomic status.[90] As discussed in Part IV, below, the Canons' failure to delineate particular types of bias precluded the Judicial Inquiry Commission from charging Judge Wiggins with a violation of socioeconomic bias. Instead, the Commission's complaint was based on general and vague canons relating to integrity, impropriety, and (the perennial catch-all) "conduct prejudicial to the administration of justice."[91] The complaint might have had a more instructive effect on other judges if it had specifically addressed the issue of socioeconomic bias.

After the Judicial Inquiry Commission filed its Complaint, Judge Wiggins was suspended from the bench.[92] In January 2016, the Court of the Judiciary of Alabama censured Judge Wiggins for "violating the Canons of Judicial Ethics."[93] Notwithstanding this censure, he will remain on the bench.[94]

Like Judge Michelson, Judge Wiggins did not initially believe his actions rose to the level of judicial misconduct. In an interview with the Alabama News Network in October 2015, Judge Wiggins defended his controversial "blood for fines" order.[95] Judge Wiggins stated that "[w]e're trying to find creative ways to help people pay their fees and expense."[96] Additionally, he said, "[b]ecause of our area, we know that the people don't have the kind of income, the salaries to pay the fines and we have to collect them. So, as an option sometimes to paying the fine you may allow them to do community services."[97]

Judge Wiggins clearly believed that his "blood for fines" order enabled "community service," and he would undoubtedly have protested if he had been accused of socioeconomic bias. However, as indigent defendants who could not pay their fines, Judge Wiggins' litigants did not believe they had any choice to avoid jail time unless they donated blood.[98] Judge Wiggins did not recognize that, in the words of medical ethics expert Arthur L. Caplan, "What happened is wrong in about 3,000 ways. . . .You're basically sentencing someone to an invasive procedure that doesn't benefit them and isn't protecting the public health."[99]

In this way, Judge Wiggins' order was an example of *implicit* socioeconomic bias. Judge Wiggins did not recognize that he was placing the poor defendants in his courtroom in an unreasonable position—one that any defendant who could afford to pay the fines would not have to experience. In fact, Judge Wiggins' decision to issue the order was made instinctively that morning when he noticed the mobile blood bank was parked outside the courthouse.[100] Judge Wiggins likely made the determination to give the order using his "fast, intuitive" System 1 part of the brain, without fully analyzing the decision with his System 2 reasoning.[101]

Two months later, after Judge Wiggins' order and the ensuing disciplinary proceedings made national headlines, the judge acknowledged through his attorney that he had "used very poor language in encouraging people to donate blood as a 'community service' for which they would receive credit against what they owed."[102] In its decision to censure Judge Wiggins instead of issuing more serious punishment, the Alabama Court of the Judiciary noted that Judge Wiggins had admitted the "wrongfulness" of his order, and "has before this Court acknowledged such misconduct."[103] Thus, upon reflection, it appears that Judge Wiggins ultimately recognized the unethical (and unconstitutional) nature of his order.

Judge Wiggins' case illustrates that implicit bias can be minimized upon reflection. Had he been able to take the time to consider the ethical implications of his "blood for fines" order, Judge Wiggins may have pursued a different course. Instead, with an overly crowded docket and dozens of defendants waiting, Judge Wiggins instinctively chose that morning to issue a biased order. As we seek to reduce implicit socioeconomic bias in American courtrooms, this case demonstrates the need for the recommendations in the Conclusion below.

The disciplinary proceedings in this case also highlight the lack of specificity regarding bias in the *Alabama Canons of Judicial Ethics*. As discussed in the next section, the *ABA Model Code of Judicial Conduct*'s provisions regarding bias have not been adopted by every state, and the result is an uneven disciplinary framework with regard to socioeconomic bias.

III. Socioeconomic Bias in Judicial Codes of Conduct

The *ABA Model Code of Judicial Conduct* prohibits judges from manifesting "bias or prejudice," including but not limited to bias based on "race, sex, gender, religion, national origin, ethnicity, disability, age, sexual orientation, marital status, socioeconomic status, or political affiliation."[104] The ABA added the specific prohibition of socioeconomic bias in 1990, when the committee revising the rules determined "that a specific listing of examples of prohibited bias or prejudice would provide needed strength to the rule."[105] Like all provisions of the *Model Code*, states can choose to adopt this prohibition in its entirety, with modifications, or not at all.

As of March 2016, 40 states had chosen to adopt the ABA's language prohibiting bias or prejudice against specific classes *including* "socioeconomic" or "economic" status.[106] Six states specify some classes or groups but *do not* include language related to socioeconomic or economic status.[107] Four states do not prohibit bias against *any* specific class or group, and instead list general prohibitions against bias or prejudice.[108] Notably, Judge Wiggins' home state of Alabama is among the four states without any mention of socioeconomic bias in its judicial ethics rules.[109]

What difference does it make if a state fails to elucidate socioeconomic status as a specific form of prohibited bias? The answer lies in the distinctive character of socioeconomic bias. As discussed above, judges are much more likely to learn about poor people through the negative stereotypes of the media than through personal experience or formal (and objective) judicial trainings. Unlike race or gender discrimination, there is no constitutional right to be free from discrimination on the basis of economic status.[110] Consequently, judicial bias based on socioeconomic status is not discussed often in caselaw or legal academic literature, and it tends to be a more hidden and implicit type of bias.[111]

Including socioeconomic status in the list of prohibited biases in a

[J]udges are much more likely to learn about poor people through the negative stereotypes of the media than through personal experience or formal (and objective) judicial trainings. Unlike race or gender discrimination, there is no constitutional right to be free from discrimination on the basis of economic status.

state's judicial code of conduct "brings judicial attention to the fact that this type of bias exists."[112] The ten states that do not currently include socioeconomic status as a specific form of prohibited bias should revise their codes of conduct to include this prohibition. While such revisions would not entire remedy the problem of socioeconomic bias on the bench, they would send the message that judges should be more conscious of the potential for this type of bias to influence their decisions.

IV. Recommendations

A. *Increase Judicial Awareness of Implicit Socioeconomic Bias*

Most people, including judges, do not want to believe they harbor biases. It is enjoyable to feel right in our decisions and judgments, and it is unpleasant to feel that we are wrong.[113] As a result, individuals make decisions "based on what feels right, even though what feels right may be based on information that is irrelevant, faulty, or just plain wrong."[114] In fact, "even high cognitive ability does not protect someone from the effects of bias."[115]

How, then, can judges fight against implicit bias? One part of the answer lies in awareness. As more judges learn about the causes and effects of implicit bias, the potential for unconscious decision making will decrease. Judicial trainings about implicit bias are critical to developing judges' recognition of the ways in which their cognitive processes are subject to influences, such as the myths perpetrated in media stories. Once recognized, these influences can be challenged and laid aside.

These trainings are already taking place in some jurisdictions. The National Center for State Courts organized pilot projects for three-day trainings in California, Minnesota, and North Dakota.[116] The goal of such trainings is "to persuade judges, on the merits, to recognize implicit bias as a potential problem, which in turn should increase motivation to adopt sensible countermeasures."[117] Professor Jerry Kang recommends that such trainings occur early in a judge's tenure, such as during new-judge orientation, and should include the potential for judges to measure their own implicit bias through the Implicit Association Test or other measurements.[118]

Judges can also take advantage of the growing interest in mindfulness in the legal profession.[119] A rising number of law schools, including my employer, Golden Gate University School of Law, now offer mindfulness classes to law students and faculty. As a participant in a "Mindful Lawyering" class, I can attest to the impact of learning about the way our brains unconsciously embrace implicit messages. Indeed, neuroscience studies conclusively prove that "mindfulness training enhances self-awareness and reduces susceptibility to unconscious bias and emotional reactivity."[120] Thus, in addition to educating judges about the science of implicit bias, mindfulness training may also serve to reduce bias in the courtroom.

B. Increase Familiarity with Challenges Facing Low-Income Populations

While the trainings described above can effectively mitigate implicit bias generally, reducing socioeconomic bias may be more complicated. In light of the negative media portrayals of poor people described in Part II above, judges seeking to minimize implicit socioeconomic bias face an uphill climb. This is especially true because most judges do not come from socioeconomically disadvantaged backgrounds. In his dissenting opinion in *Pineda-Moreno*, Chief Judge Kozinski noted that "[n]o truly poor people are appointed as federal judges, or as state judges for that matter. Judges, regardless of race, ethnicity or sex, are selected from the class of people who don't live in trailers or urban ghettoes."[121] Judges graduate from law schools, particularly elite law schools. The nine justices of the 2014 Supreme Court, for example, all attended either Harvard or Yale law schools, leading one reporter to describe them as *An Ivy League Clan Disconnected from Reality*.[122] Once on the bench, judges earn substantially more than the average American. Federal district judges, who also enjoy life appointments, earned $199,100 in 2014,[123] while the median income in the United States was $53,657.[124] Consequently, "[t]his discrepancy creates an economic imbalance in courtrooms that may result in socioeconomic bias."[125] Hence, many judges simply do not know the challenges facing low-income populations on a daily basis.

Two ways for judges to remedy this lack of knowledge about lives lived with fewer resources than their own are (1) visiting the communities judges serve and (2) priming.

1. Community Visits

The daily work life of a judge often consists of similar routines: arriving in chambers, quickly reviewing cases before commencing the morning calendar, and then spending most of the day on the bench. Judges do leave their courtrooms for meetings, lunch dates, or other obligations, but most of a typical day is spent inside a judge's courtroom.

As a result, judges often do not get a chance to witness the complexities of life in low-income communities firsthand. For most judges, encounters with low-income populations occur inside the courtroom. By leaving their courtrooms to visit poor communities and "trying to look at [themselves and their] message through other people's eyes," judges could use field trips as an effective way to mitigate bias.[126] One study showed that "actively contemplating others' psychological experiences weakens the expression of racial biases."[127] The same would hold true for socioeconomic bias.

Metaphorically walking in the shoes of the poor people who appear before them would allow judges to engage in "perspective shifting."[128] This could change the impressions held by the System 1 parts of their minds about particular populations. For example, a housing court judge could visit the low-income neighborhoods in which evictions are common to appreciate housing shortages and the potential habitability problems in the homes at issue in his or her courtroom. Moreover, a judge who recognized the potential difficulties in transportation from a certain neighborhood to the courthouse would be more understanding of litigants who arrived late to a hearing. For instance, perhaps it was not disrespect for the court that caused a litigant to be late but instead having to take three buses (one of which ran late) to arrive at the courthouse. Some judges already experience these types of field trips. As part of their orientations, federal judges visit federal prisons to "view firsthand the conditions that defendants they sentence will confront."[129] Exposure to the struggles and strengths of low-income people would assist judges in combatting the negative myths depicted in the media.

> Exposure to the struggles and strengths of low-income people would assist judges in combatting the negative myths depicted in the media.

2. Priming

Community visits are certainly beneficial, but "de-biasing exposures would have to compete against the other daily real-life exposures in the courtroom that rebias."[130] Priming is one way to consistently remind judges that their impressions and beliefs about low-income populations may not be accurate.

According to Daniel Kahneman, exposure to a particular word causes "immediate and measurable changes in the ease with which many related words can be evoked."[131] If you are thinking of eating, for example, you are more likely "to recognize the word SOUP when it is spoken in a whisper or presented in a blurry font."[132] This effect is not limited to words, since "your actions and your emotions can be primed by events of which you are not even aware."[133] In one experiment, experienced German judges reviewed a description of a woman caught shoplifting.[134] The judges then rolled a pair of dice, which were fixed to result in either a three or a nine for every roll.[135] When the dice stopped, the judges were asked for the number of months they would sentence the shoplifter.[136] The judges who had rolled the number nine on the dice stated they would sentence the shoplifter, on average, to eight months.[137] The judges who rolled the number three gave an average sentence of five months.[138] The experiment showed that "the sentences were adjusted in relation to the priming numbers."[139]

The priming effect supports the idea that repeated positive images of poor people can oppose negative beliefs a judge may (even inadvertently) hold. In fact, implicit biases can be minimized through the use of videos or photographs "juxtaposing ordinary people with counter-typical settings."[140] Professor Jerry Kang suggests that court administrators and judges could create "photographs, posters, screen savers, pamphlets, and decorations" in chambers and court-rooms that "bring to mind countertypical exemplars or associations for participants in the trial process."[141] For example, the Honorable Mark W. Bennett, a federal judge in the Northern District of Iowa and a coauthor of this book, placed photographs of immigrants becoming new citizens in the jury assembly room of his courthouse.[142] The images remind potential jurors of the power of the law to create social change, and they reinforce the importance of citizen-ship and civic duty. Even if these strategies seem merely "cosmetic," they could compete with the myths judges are consistently "bombarded" with from the media.[143] Since we know the priming effect is real, why not prime the System 1 part of a judge's brain with positive images about low-income populations?

C. Modify Daily Courtroom Conditions to Allow Time and Attention

Any type of bias will be more common if people are overloaded or "are cog-nitively depleted."[144] Judges, like all people, can decide matters more clearly if they are able to engage in deep thinking.[145] Thus, one of the most effective ways for a judge to override a System 1 bias is through the use of a System 2 analyti-cal response. However, it requires "effort and acts of self-control" to overcome the "intuitions and impulses of System 1."[146] Courts with overcrowded dockets, like Judge Wiggins' court described in Part III above, limit judges' capacities to access the System 2 parts of their brains to countermand the impressions of System 1. Without time to reflect on the specific circumstances of each case, judges cannot be expected to deeply consider—and reconsider—their decisions. These are precisely the conditions in which implicit biases can have the most detrimental effects on the decision-making processes of judges. Many of the overcrowded courts in this country serve low-income populations, including criminal courts,[147] housing courts,[148] and immigration courts.[149]

Given the significant impact of relying too heavily on System 1 thinking, judges who work in courts with overloaded dockets "need to be especially on guard against their biases."[150] Properly staffing such courts with enough judges and court staff would lengthen the time judges have for each case, enabling judges to reflect more deliberately to minimize implicit bias. Small changes can make a difference. For example, does a judge's docket have enough breaks dur-ing the day? Is it realistic for a judge to be able to take those breaks? Does a judge have enough time in chambers to reason through decisions?

In some courtrooms, judges are not able to make staffing, scheduling, or other changes themselves. All parties who control courtroom environments, including judges, court administrators, and legislators, must therefore commit to affirmatively creating atmospheres that diminish implicit bias. Working collaboratively to ease the caseloads of judges, particularly judges who work with low-income populations, would have a significant impact on the ability of judges to combat their implicit socioeconomic biases on a daily basis.

D. Minimize Long-Term Burnout

Like many professionals, including physicians, judges are susceptible to burnout. The term "burnout" can be defined as "loss of enthusiasm for work, depersonalization, and a low sense of personal accomplishment."[151] The term is now coded in the tenth edition of the *International Classification of Diseases* (ICD-10) "as a 'state of vital exhaustion.'"[152]

Since courts with high numbers of low-income litigants tend to have overcrowded dockets,[153] judges in these courts may be especially prone to burnout. For example, in 2007, 96 immigration judges who were tested using the Copenhagen Burnout Index "reported more burnout than any other group of professionals to whom the CBI had been administered, including prison wardens and physicians in busy hospitals."[154]

The possibility of burnout raises additional concerns about biases on the bench, since individuals experiencing professional burnout may also be more inclined to hold biases. Indeed, a recent survey of physicians found that those individuals who reported burnout were more likely to report that they held explicit biases toward their patients.[155] Given the hidden nature of implicit bias, it can be difficult to quantify a connection between burnout and implicit bias. However, it is reasonable to believe that a judge in a state of burnout may be unable to follow some of the recommendations described above to prevent implicit bias, including mindfulness and increased reflection time.

While this has not been conclusively determined in the context of judges, it might be that one way to mitigate burnout, and potentially the manifestation of implicit biases, is to enable judges to periodically rotate their roles. For example, housing court judges could spend time in family court, and criminal judges could serve on the civil court bench. A housing court judge might be surprised to learn how the impact of an eviction can affect a child custody hearing. Moving to another bench within the same courthouse, or even moving to another court entirely, could prevent judicial burnout and allow judges to keep fresh perspectives about the litigants in their courtrooms.[156] In this way, judges would also be able to recognize the challenges faced by poor litigants throughout the various parts of the judicial system.

Conclusion

Judges enjoy a powerful role in our justice system. But with this power comes an obligation to ensure their decisions are made in an unbiased and neutral manner. This is not an easy task in the age of mass media, as judges are repeatedly exposed to myths regarding low-income populations. But judges do have the ability to prevent these cultural myths about poor people from becoming implicit beliefs that affect their judgments on the bench.

Social scientists and neuroscientists are now able to explain how implicit biases can be created and minimized. Understanding Daniel Kahneman's framework, which explains how the System 1 and System 2 parts of our brains work, can be a useful step toward lessening the impact of our intuitions and impressions on our actions.

> Judges do not have to give up their personal wealth to be fair adjudicators. But in the words of the Honorable Jonathan Lippman, Chief Judge of the New York Court of Appeals, "Meeting our responsibilities to the most disadvantaged in society is not a luxury and it isn't a choice—it is a simple matter of justice."

There is increasing interest in the areas of implicit racial and gender bias, but more focused attention should be paid to the reduction of socioeconomic bias. States should ensure their judicial codes of conduct specifically prohibit this type of bias. In addition, judges themselves can take concrete measures to combat implicit socioeconomic bias, including learning more about this type of bias, leaving their courtrooms to experience the challenges of low-income communities firsthand, and advocating for courtroom conditions that encourage reflection and minimize burnout. Judges do not have to give up their personal wealth to be fair adjudicators. But in the words of the Honorable Jonathan Lippman, Chief Judge of the New York Court of Appeals, "Meeting our responsibilities to the most disadvantaged in society is not a luxury and it isn't a choice—it is a simple matter of justice."[157]

So You'd Like to Know More

- Daniel Kahneman, THINKING, FAST AND SLOW (2011)

- Jerry Kang et al., *Implicit Bias in the Courtroom*, 59 UCLA LAW REVIEW 1124 (2012).

- Michele Benedetto Neitz, *Socioeconomic Bias in the Judiciary*, 61 CLEVELAND STATE LAW REVIEW 137 (2013)

About the Author

Michele Benedetto Neitz joined the Golden Gate University School of Law faculty in 2006. Prior to joining GGU, she worked as a law clerk in the Southern District of California and served as an Equal Justice Works Fellow at the Legal Aid Society of San Diego. She also worked an associate in the San Diego office of Morrison & Foerster, LLP, specializing in corporate labor and employment matters. Professor Neitz researches, publishes, and lectures in the areas of implicit bias and judicial ethics, professional responsibility, and corporate law. In 2013, she published the first article in legal academia focused on implicit socioeconomic bias on the part of judges. Her publications include law review articles in *Georgetown Journal of Legal Ethics, The Southern Methodist University Law Review,* and *Brooklyn Law Review,* as well as smaller articles in *San Francisco Business Times, San Francisco Attorney Magazine,* and the online Legal Ethics Forum. Professor Neitz currently teaches poverty law, business associations, and professional responsibility.

ENDNOTES

1. United States v. Pineda-Moreno, 617 F.3d 1120 (2010).
2. *Id.* at 1123.
3. Matthew Robinson & Marian Williams, *The Myth of a Fair Criminal Justice System,* 6 JUSTICE POL'Y J. 1, 1 (Spring 2009), citing MERRIAM-WEBSTER'S DICTIONARY (2009).
4. *Id.*
5. TONY THOMPSON, RELEASING PRISONERS, REDEEMING COMMUNITIES 41 (2009).
6. Robinson & Williams, *supra* note 3, at 33.
7. Heather E. Bullock et al., *Media Images of the Poor,* 57 J. SOC. ISSUES 2, 229–30 (2001).
8. *Id.* at 230; *see also id.* at 243 ("for the most part, economic inequality, social class, and poverty are presented superficially or are rendered invisible by the mainstream media").
9. *Id.* at 230.
10. Jeffrey Gottfried & Elisa Shearer, *News Use across Social Media Platforms 2016* (May 26, 2016), http://www.journalism.org/2016/05/26/news-use-across-social-media -platforms-2016/.
11. *Id.*
12. *Id.*
13. Chelsea Harvey, *Here's How Scientific Misinformation, Such as Climate Doubt, Spreads through Social Media,* WASH. POST, Jan. 4, 2016, *available at* https://www.washingtonpost.com /news/energy-environment/wp/2016/01/04/heres-how-scientific-misinformation-such -as-climate-doubt-spreads-through-social-media/?utm_term=.1d401a5b61ee/.
14. *Id.*
15. For an interesting assessment of the influence of "slanted news," *see* Gregory J. Martin & Ali Yurukoglu, *Bias in Cable News: Persuasion and Polarization,* May 27, 2016, http:// web.stanford.edu/~ayurukog/cable_news.pdf.
16. Michela Del Vicario et al., *The Spreading of Misinformation Online,* 113 PROC. NAT'L ACAD. OF SCI. 554–59 (2015), *available at* http://www.pnas.org/content/113/3/554.full.
17. *Id.; see also* Martin Gilens, *Race and Poverty in America: Misconceptions and the American News Media,* 60 PUB. OPINION Q. 515 (1996); Bas W. van Doorn, *Media Portrayals of Poverty and Race in Pre-and Post-Welfare Reform America,* 43 POL. & POL'Y 142 (2015).
18. Bullock et al., *supra* note 7, at 229–30 ("By portraying poor women as promiscuous and neglectful mothers and welfare recipients as uneducated, lazy 'freeloaders,' media images fail to contextualize the reality of poverty or the structural factors that perpetuate inequality.").
19. *Id.* at 230.
20. van Doorn, *supra* note 17, at 156–57; *see also* Gilens, *supra* note 17, at 536 ("If 560 people were selected at random from America's poor, we would expect 162 to be black. But of the 560 poor people of determinable race pictured in news magazines between 1988 and 1992, 345 were African American. In reality, two out of three poor Americans are nonblack, but the reader of these magazines would likely come to exactly the opposite conclusions.").
21. van Doorn, *supra* note 17, at 144.
22. Igor Volsky, *Paul Ryan Blames Poverty on Lazy "Inner City" Men,* THINK PROGRESS, Mar. 12, 2014, http://thinkprogress.org/economy/2014/03/12/3394871/ryan-poverty -inner-city/.

23. *Id.*
24. Michelle Singletary, *The Moocher Class,* WASH. POST, Sep. 30, 2012, *available at* https://www.washingtonpost.com/business/economy/the-moocher-class/2012/09/20/a8a7658a-029d-11e2-8102-ebee9c66e190_story.html.
25. *Id.*
26. Scott Eric Kaufman, *Mike Huckabee Just Endorsed "Biblical" Slavery over the Modern Prison System* (Oct. 15, 2015), http://www.salon.com/2015/10/15/mike_huckabee_just_endorsed_biblical_slavery_over_the_modern_prison_system/.
27. Philip Bump, *It's Hard to Imagine a Much Worse Pitch Donald Trump Could Have Made for the Black Vote,* WASH. POST, Aug. 20, 2016, https://www.washingtonpost.com/news/the-fix/wp/2016/08/20/its-hard-to-imagine-a-much-worse-pitch-donald-trump-could-have-made-for-the-black-vote/.
28. *Id.*, noting that approximately one-quarter of the African-American population lives in poverty.
29. Hunter Schwartz, *Obama Said Fox News Vilifies the Poor. Jon Stewart Presses His Point,* WASH. POST, May 14, 2015, *available at* https://www.washingtonpost.com/news/the-fix/wp/2015/05/14/obama-said-fox-news-vilifies-the-poor-jon-stewart-presses-his-point/.
30. Louise Derman-Sparks, National Association for the Education of Young Children, *Children—Socioeconomic Class and Equity* (May 2009), https://www.naeyc.org/files/yc/file/200905/BTJOnOurMinds.pdf.
31. *Id.*
32. DANIEL KAHNEMAN, THINKING, FAST AND SLOW 8 (2011).
33. *Id.* at 20.
34. *Id.* at 8.
35. Philip N. Meyer, *Psychological Shortcuts,* 102 ABA J. 26 (Jan. 2016).
36. Kahneman, *supra* note 32, at 21.
37. *Id.*
38. *Id.* at 22.
39. *Id.* at 24.
40. *Id.* at 24.
41. Meyer, *supra* note 35, at 26.
42. Kahneman, *supra* note 32, at 24.
43. *Id.*
44. *Id.; see also* Chris Guthrie, Jeffrey J. Rachlinski & Andrew J. Wistrich, *Blinking on the Bench: How Judges Decide Cases,* 93 CORNELL L. REV. 1 (2007).
45. Kahneman, *supra* note 32, at 278.
46. John Beshears & Francesca Gino, *Leaders as Decision Architects,* HARV. BUS. REV. 54 (May 2015).
47. Matthew D. Lieberman et al., *Breaking Bias,* 5 NEUROLEADERSHIP J. 1, Abstract (May 2014).
48. Jerry Kang et al., *Implicit Bias in the Courtroom,* 59 UCLA L. REV. 1124, 1126 (2012).
49. *Id.* at 1146 ("There is no inherent reason to think that judges are immune from implicit biases. The extant empirical evidence supports this assumption.").
50. *Id.* at 1172 (citing Jeffrey J. Rachlinski, Sheri Lynn Johnson, Andrew J. Wistrich & Chris Guthrie, *Does Unconscious Racial Bias Affect Trial Judges,* 84 NOTRE DAME L. REV. 1195, 1225 (2009)).
51. Meyer, *supra* note 35, at 27.
52. MERRIAM-WEBSTER'S COLLEGIATE DICTIONARY (11th ed. 2014).
53. Kang et al., *supra* note 48, at 1161.
54. *Id.*
55. *Id.*
56. *Id.*

57. *Id.*
58. Harriet Sime, *Let Muslim Women Wear a Full-Face Veil in Court, Says Head of Supreme Court as He Warns Over Bias Against Poor and Foreign Defendants*, DAILY MAIL.COM, Apr. 16, 2015, http://www.dailymail.co.uk/news/article-3042922/Judges-warned-beware -subconscious-bias-against-poor-foreign-defendants-head-Supreme-Court.html.
59. *Id.*
60. *Id.*
61. Judge Michelson passed away in 2007. His obituary is available at http://www.legacy .com/obituaries/stltoday/obituary.aspx?n=robert-michelson&pid=86876304
62. Wisconsin Judicial Commission v. Michelson (*In re* Michelson), 225 Wis. 2d. 221, 224 (1999); *see also* Joe Buttweiler, *Mother's Pain Over Judge's Remarks Won't Go Away*, JOURNAL TIMES, May 6, 1999, http://journaltimes.com/news/local/mother-s-pain-over -judge-s-remarks-won-t-go/article_baf72ff2-90c2-5aa1-983f-164b313db185.html.
63. *Wisconsin Judicial Commission*, 225 Wis. 2d. at 224.
64. *Id.*
65. *Id.*
66. *Id.*
67. *Id.*
68. *Id.*
69. *Id.*
70. *Id.* For more on the state Codes of Judicial Conduct, see *infra* Part IV.
71. *Id.* at 225.
72. *Id.* at 226.
73. *Id.* at 223.
74. Buttweiler, *supra* note 62.
75. *Id.*
76. *Id.*
77. *Id.*
78. *Id.*
79. Personal Responsibility and Work Opportunity Reconciliation Act § 101, 42 U.S.C. § 601 (1996).
80. In the Matter of Marvin Wayne Wiggins, Alabama Court of the Judiciary, Case No. 45 at 3 (Jan. 8, 2016).
81. *Id.*
82. *Id.*
83. Complaint Against Judge Marvin Wiggins, Before the Judicial Inquiry Commission of Alabama (Oct. 19, 2015) at 3, *available at* http://www.scribd.com/doc/286079426 /Judge-Wiggins-Complaint. One of the defendants, Carl Crocker, "grew even more uncomfortable . . . after he recognized the blood bank, LifeSouth Community Blood Centers, which had recently lost a $4 million judgment for an H.I.V.-tainted blood transfusion." Campbell Robertson, *For Offenders Who Can't Pay, It's a Pint of Blood or Jail Time*, N.Y. TIMES, Oct. 19, 2015, *available at* http://www.nytimes.com/2015/10/20 /us/for-offenders-who-cant-pay-its-a-pint-of-blood-or-jail-time.html?_r=0.
84. Complaint, *supra* note 83.
85. *Id.* at 3–6.
86. *Id.* at 4–5.
87. *Id.* at 4.
88. *Id.* at 6.
89. *Id.* at 6.
90. The Canons only mention personal or issue-related bias in the context of disqualification. *See* Alabama Canon 3(C)(1)(a) (2016), http://judicial.alabama.gov/library /rules/can3.pdf.

91. Complaint, *supra* note 83, at 6.
92. Andrew J. Yawn, *"Give Blood or Go to Jail" Judge Marvin Wiggins Censured*, MONT-GOMERY ADVERTISER, Jan. 21, 2016, http://www.montgomeryadvertiser.com/story/news /2016/01/21/blood-seeking-judge-censured/79128074/.
93. *Id.*
94. *Id.*
95. Jeremy Grey, *Alabama Judge Defends Blood for Fines Plan* (Oct. 26, 2015), http://www .al.com/news/index.ssf/2015/10/alabama_judge_defends_blood_fo.html.
96. *Id.*
97. *Id.*
98. Robertson, *supra* note 83. Defendant Traci Green "said he had offered to pay as much as he could but had been led to believe that he had to give blood anyway. '[Judge Wiggins] told us we got to go there and give some blood or we go to jail'." *Id.*
99. *Id.*
100. Judge Wiggins' attorney stated that "Judge Wiggins did not know about the blood drive until he came to Court that morning and was trying to find alternatives for those unable to make a payment." Kent Faulk, *Judge Who Demanded Blood from Defendants Charged, Suspended*, Jan. 16, 2016, http://www.al.com/news/birmingham/index .ssf/2016/01/alabama_blood_or_jail_judge_su.html.
101. Meyer, *supra* note 35, at 26.
102. Faulk, *supra* note 100.
103. Adam Ganucheau, *Judge Who Demanded Blood from Defendants Censured after Suspension* (Jan. 21, 2016), http://www.al.com/news/index.ssf/2016/01/judge_who _demanded_blood_from.html.
104. MODEL CODE OF JUDICIAL CONDUCT R. 2.3(B) (2011).
105. LISA L. MILORD, THE DEVELOPMENT OF THE ABA JUDICIAL CODE 18 (1992). The ABA code is not perfect; it does not define the terms "socioeconomic" or "bias" in its "Terminology" section. Michele Benedetto Neitz, *Socioeconomic Bias in the Judiciary*, 61 CLEV. ST. L. REV. 137, 145 (2013).
106. A research list of states and corresponding ethics codes, compiled by the author's research assistant Christopher Chang, is on file with author.
107. These six states are Arkansas, Delaware, Idaho, Missouri, South Carolina, and South Dakota. *Id.*
108. These four states are Alabama, Louisiana, Michigan, and North Carolina. *Id.*
109. Alabama Canon 3, *supra* note 90.
110. Poverty is not a classification deserving strict or intermediate scrutiny in constitutional law analysis. *See* Mario L. Barnes & Erwin Chemerinsky, *The Disparate Treatment of Race and Class in Constitutional Jurisprudence*, 72 LAW & CONTEMP. PROBS. 109, 111 (2009); *see also* Neitz, *supra* note 105, at 146–49 (discussing the "unique nature of socioeconomic bias.").
111. To date, I am the author of the only law review article focusing on implicit socioeconomic bias on the part of judges. *See* Neitz, *supra* note 105.
112. *Id.* at 145.
113. Lieberman et al., *supra* note 47, at 4.
114. *Id.* at 5.
115. *Id.* at 4.
116. Kang et al., *supra* note 48, at 1175. The National Center for State Courts posted resources used in implicit bias trainings on its website. *See* National Center for State Courts, *Helping Courts Address Implicit Bias: Resources for Education*, http://www.ncsc .org/ibeducation (last visited Mar. 22, 2016).
117. Kang et al., *supra* note 48, at 1175.
118. *Id.* at 1176–77. For more on the Implicit Association Test, *see* Neitz, *supra* note 105, at 150–52.

119. For an examination of the growing mindfulness movement in law, *see* Jeena Cho, *Why Every Lawyer Should Be Practicing Mindfulness (Part 1)*, Above the Law.com (Apr. 20, 2015), http://abovethelaw.com/2015/04/why-every-lawyer-should-be-practicing -mindfulness-part-i/; *see also* Michele Benedetto Neitz, *How to Create a Less Stressful Workplace*, San Francisco Bus. Times, July 17, 2015, http://www.bizjournals.com /sanfrancisco/feature/how-to-create-a-less-stressful-workplace.html.

120. Lieberman et al., *supra* note 47, at 15.

121. Pineda-Moreno, *supra* note 1, at 1123.

122. Dahlia Lithwick, *The 2014 Supreme Court: An Ivy League Clan Disconnected From Reality*, New Republic, Nov. 13, 2014, *available at* https://newrepublic.com/article/120173/2014 -supreme-court-ivy-league-clan-disconnected-reality; *see also* Ian Millhiser, *What Do You Need to Do to Be a Justice?*, N.Y. Times, Mar. 18, 2016, at SR3 ("elite credentials cannot teach a judge what it means to seek shelter in the law, or how it feels to be a victim of discrimination").

123. United States Courts, *Judicial Compensation*, *available at* http://www.uscourts.gov /judges-judgeships/judicial-compensation (last visited Mar. 22, 2016).

124. Carmen DeNavas-Walt & Bernadette D. Proctor, *Income and Poverty in the United States: 2014*, Sept. 2015, at 5, *available at* https://www.census.gov/content/dam /Census/library/publications/2015/demo/p60-252.pdf.

125. Neitz, *supra* note 105, at 143.

126. Lieberman et al., *supra* note 47, at 4.

127. Kang et al., *supra* note 48, at 1185.

128. *Id.*

129. The Hon. Barbara Rothstein, *The Federal Judicial Training Center Offers Training and Research*, Federal Lawyer, Oct. 2009, at 36–37, *available at* http://www.fjc.gov/public /pdf.nsf/lookup/FedL1009.pdf/$file/FedL1009.pdf.

130. Kang et al., *supra* note 48, at 1170.

131. Kahneman, *supra* note 32, at 52.

132. *Id.* at 53.

133. *Id.*

134. *Id.* at 125.

135. *Id.*

136. *Id.* at 125–26.

137. *Id.* at 126.

138. *Id.*

139. Meyer, *supra* note 35, at 27.

140. Kang et al., *supra* note 48, at 1171.

141. *Id.*

142. Interview with the Honorable Mark W. Bennett (2016).

143. Kang et al., *supra* note 48, at 1172.

144. Lieberman et al., *supra* note 47, at 12.

145. *Id.*

146. Kahneman, *supra* note 32, at 31.

147. Mike Gallagher, *Dysfunctional Court System Fuels Overcrowding*, Albuquerque J., Sept. 21, 2014, *available at* http://www.abqjournal.com/465872/news/court-system-fuels -jail-overcrowding.html.

148. Michael Diller, *Fixing New York City's Broken Housing Courts*, Sept. 30, 2015, http:// www.huffingtonpost.com/michael-diller-/new-york-citys-broken-hou_b_8116710. html (describing the "frantic environment" of New York City's housing courts).

149. Eli Saslow, *In a Crowded Immigration Court, Seven Minutes to Decide a Family's Future*, Wash. Post, Feb. 2, 2014, https://www.washingtonpost.com/national/in-a-crowded -immigration-court-seven-minutes-to-decide-a-familys-future/2014/02/02/518c3e3e -8798-11e3-a5bd-844629433ba3_story.html. One immigration court judge testified

to Congress that his job was "[l]ike doing death-penalty cases in a traffic-court setting." *Id.* The stress on immigration court judges is particularly high. *See* Michele Benedetto Neitz, *Crisis on the Immigration Bench: An Ethical Perspective*, 73 Brook. L. Rev. 467 (2008).

150. Kang et al., *supra* note 48, at 1177.

151. Carol Peckham, *Bias and Burnout: Evil Twins*, Medscape, Jan. 12, 2016, *available at* http://www.medscape.com/viewarticle/856814_1.

152. *Id.*, citing World Health Organization, The ICD-10 Classification of Mental and Behavioural Disorders: Clinical Descriptions and Diagnostic Guidelines (1992).

153. See *supra* Section V.C and notes 147–49.

154. Stuart L. Lustig et al., *Inside the Judges' Chambers: Narrative Responses from the National Association of Immigration Judges Stress and Burnout Survey*, 23 Geo. Imm. L.J. 57, 60 (2008).

155. Peckham, *supra* note 151.

156. The American Management Association suggests that employees rotate roles because "[p]erformance usually improves when you move people to another physical location. Also, the change in job location may bring a change in responsibilities, which provides people with new challenges and goals." American Management Association, *How to Prevent Burnout and Improve Productivity*, Feb. 15, 2006, http://www.amanet .org/training/articles/How-to-Prevent-Burnout-and-Improve-Productivity.aspx.

157. Hon. Jonathan Lippman, *Closing the Justice Gap for Low-Income New Yorkers*, Mar. 5, 2015, http://talkpoverty.org/2015/03/05/closing-justice-gap-low-income-new-yorkers/.

Chapter 7

With Malice toward None and Charity for Some
Ingroup Favoritism Enables Discrimination

Anthony G. Greenwald and Thomas F. Pettigrew

> **Editor's Note:** *This chapter begins a reprint of an article of the same title as the chapter written by Professors Greenwald and Pettigrew in 2014. The text of the article is followed by an interview that Professor Greenwald recently did with Peter Koelling, Director Chief Counsel, Judicial Division American Bar Association.*
>
> *This article is reprinted with the generous permission of the American Psychological Association.*[1]

Chapter Contents

Imagine: You are a well-positioned manager in a large business. You supervise several other managers who also have substantial responsibility. One of your subordinate managers, Sylvia, mentions that her daughter, Kate, who is a school classmate of your daughter, was just sent home from school with the flu. You encourage Sylvia to take time off until Kate can return to school. When it later becomes time for you to conduct Sylvia's annual performance review you have a problem because her above-average performance falls just between levels that could justify your giving her an overall judgment of "meets expectations" or "exceeds expectations." You opt for "exceeds expectations," which ultimately helps Sylvia to qualify for a promotion and a salary raise. Another employee, Robert, is equally above average. Robert's records show that he too missed several days of work, but you do not know him as well and do not know why he missed work. You give Robert a "meets expectations" evaluation, and he gets a smaller raise and no promotion.

It is not difficult to understand why you, in your managerial role, would resolve doubt more favorably for a supervisee with whom your daughter provides a personal connection. Theories to explain effects of such personal connections on social judgment have existed at least since Heider's (1958) analysis of interpersonal relations. Related explanations appear in more recent theoretical analyses of social identity (e.g., Brewer, 1999; Gaertner et al., 1997; Greenwald et al., 2002; Tajfel & Turner, 1979).

If your favorable judgment of Sylvia's work performance is understandable, then it is also understandable that many other types of connections between people—including ones due to shared race, ethnicity, age, religion, or perhaps even just a shared birthday (Finch & Cialdini, 1989)—can likewise result in tipping the balance toward a favorable judgment, giving "the benefit of the doubt." This role of ingroup connections in shaping favorable feelings, judgments, and actions underlies this article's thesis that ingroup-directed favoritism is, in the United States, a more potent engine for discriminatory impact than is outgroup-directed hostility.

Quite often ingroup favoritism is hidden even from those who practice it. Consider the way much job recruitment occurs. Good workers are asked frequently to seek out others for job openings. Because of extensive racial segregation in residences, schools, and workplaces, this practice often leads White workers, drawing on virtually all-White acquaintanceship networks, to seek out only other Whites for job vacancies (Reskin, 1998; Rivera, 2012). By drawing heavily on ingroup ties, this unremarkable process can sustain or exacerbate racial or other imbalances, entirely without involvement of hostility toward minorities. In qualitative studies of White workers, DiTomaso (2012) showed how such ingroup-enabled networking affords increased access to job openings.

I. Prejudice, Hostility, Discrimination, and Ingroup Favoritism

The *Oxford English Dictionary* defines prejudice as "dislike, hostility, or unjust behaviour deriving from preconceived and unfounded opinions."[2] This definition, which links prejudice to both hostile intergroup attitude and discriminatory behavior, fits well with scholarly scientific analyses. To confirm that this understanding of "prejudice" was not merely our own caricature of scientific treatments, we searched for authoritative definitions in published research on prejudice and also in well-regarded past and current social psychology texts that we found on our bookshelves (see the Appendix). We retrieved 24 definitions, 18 of which explicitly connected prejudice to negative attitude or negative evaluation; four others identified prejudice with *either* positive or negative attitudes; the remaining two identified prejudice with emotional reactions without specifying the emotions' affective character.

Only two of the 24 definitions we retrieved included "discrimination" as part of the definition of prejudice. Following Gordon Allport's (1954) lead, social psychologists have long held that the connection of prejudicial attitude to discriminatory behavior is not something to be assumed but, rather, something that requires empirical demonstration. Complementing this scientific understanding that the link between prejudicial attitude and discrimination is not obligatory, legislators have likewise treated them as separable. With the exception of a few references to "hostile work environments," America's civil rights laws interpret discrimination in nonemotional terms, making it illegal to treat people unequally "because of" race, skin color, sex, religion, national origin, age, or disability status. Civil rights laws do not take either hostility or negative prejudicial attitude to be a necessary feature of discrimination. Likewise, in this article, we hold that discrimination does not require hostility. Unequal treatment can be produced as readily (or, as we will conclude, more readily) by helping members of an advantaged group as by harming members of a disadvantaged group.

The scientific study of prejudice has been pursued uninterruptedly since the introduction of the first measures of intergroup attitudes by Bogardus (1925) and Thurstone (1928). In this (now) massive body of scientific work, one is unlikely to encounter completely new ideas. True to that expectation, this article's central thesis—that ingroup favoritism is a prime cause of discrimination—is not new. The importance of ingroup favoritism in discrimination was described especially clearly by both S. L. Gaertner et al. (1997) and Brewer (1999). S. L. Gaertner et al. (1997) wrote that "racial bias, particularly in its contemporary manifestations, may reflect a prowhite, not simply [the] antiblack sentiment that many traditional theories and measures have implied" (p. 175). Brewer (1999) wrote, "Ultimately, many forms of discrimination and bias may develop not because outgroups are hated, but because positive emotions such as admiration, sympathy, and trust are reserved for the ingroup and withheld from outgroups" (p. 438). In a review article, Hewstone, Rubin, and Willis (2002) carefully considered the interplay of ingroup favoritism and outgroup hostility as components of intergroup bias, in the process presaging several topics central to this article. More recently, Dixon, Levine, Reicher, and Durrheim (2012) asked, "Has the time come to challenge the assumption that negative evaluations are inevitably the cognitive and affective hallmarks of discrimination?" (p. 411). We proceed further in this direction, concluding that, at least in the United States, ingroup favoritism is the *prime* mechanism of discrimination.[3]

Perhaps because the most dramatic forms of discrimination contain no hint of ingroup favoritism, statements such as those by S. L. Gaertner et al. (1997) and Brewer (1999) have not displaced the view that outgroup hostility is discrimination's primary antecedent. Studies collected for two meta-analyses confirm this observation. Among 1,351 individual tests of effects of intergroup contact on intergroup relations (Pettigrew & Tropp, 2006, 2011), not even one employed a measure of ingroup favorability as a dependent variable. Likewise, among 370 tests analyzed by H. J. Smith, Pettigrew, Pippen, and Bialosiewicz (2012) to determine the effects of group relative deprivation on prejudice, only two used ingroup favorability as a dependent variable (Amiot, Terry & Callan, 2007; Terry & O'Brien, 2001). The only ingroup-related measures—used in a small minority of tests in these two meta-analyses—were measures of collective self-esteem and ingroup identification.

Consider, too, the *Journal of Social Issues* special issue in 2012 that focused on discrimination (Nier & Gaertner, 2012b). Several authors in that issue acknowledged that hostility is not a necessary precondition for discrimination. For example, Nier and Gaertner (2012a, p. 218) wrote, "In many cases

. . . discrimination is likely to be subtle and difficult to detect, and in some instances, may be unintentional." Nevertheless, throughout the special issue the dominant assumption was that, in most instances, hostile prejudice is the well-spring of discrimination. And common throughout the research literature are studies that show how hostile prejudice is linked to discriminatory intentions without regard for ingroup favorability (e.g., Wagner, Christ & Pettigrew, 2008).

In three steps, the remainder of this article builds a case for understanding ingroup favoritism as not just *a* cause but the *prime* cause of American discrimination. First, we review findings supporting the two phenomena that are merged in this article's main thesis: the existence of strong positive dispositions toward ingroup members (i.e., ingroup favoritism) and evidence that discrimination occurs more often as differential favoring than as differential harming. Although both of these phenomena are thoroughly established empirically, the connection between them has received very little recognition. Second, we consider theories that explain the psychological antecedents of favoritism. Third, we review research methods that have been used in studies of discrimination to understand why there are so few available direct tests of the link between ingroup favoritism and discrimination. In the concluding discussion, we reflect on implications of this article's ingroup favoritism thesis.

II. Findings: Favoring Ingroup Members

A. Similarity and Attraction

Byrne (1961) introduced a method for investigating attraction as a function of *attitude similarity*. In an initial session, experimenters obtained subjects' responses to 26 attitude questions. Two weeks later, the same subjects were asked to evaluate an otherwise unknown person for whom the only available information consisted of that person's responses to the same 26 questions. Unknown to subjects, the attitude responses of these "strangers" had been filled out by researchers so as to vary systematically, in four levels, ranging from exactly agreeing with all of the subjects' own responses to exactly disagreeing with all of them. Byrne's finding, which proved to be robustly replicable, was that liking and attraction toward the strangers were strongly a function of attitude similarity. In Byrne's (1961) report, across six dependent measures, effect sizes for the greater positivity of evaluations for most versus least similar strangers averaged a Cohen's d of 3.40, constituting a *very* large effect. As a reference point, Cohen (1977) described a d of 0.80 as a *large* effect. Subsequent studies showed that Byrne's similarity–attraction principle was not limited to effects of attitude similarities; it occurred equally for similarities in personality traits and similarities in behavior (e.g., Byrne, Ervin & Lamberth, 1970).

Furthering Byrne's contentions, Rokeach proposed that the perception of conflicting beliefs and values triggers race prejudice more than does race itself (Rokeach, 1960; Rokeach & Mezei, 1966). This is plausible if, as Rokeach supposed, outgroup members are typically assumed to harbor beliefs and values conflicting with those of the ingroup. Rokeach's position was initially controversial (see Stein, Hardyck & Smith, 1965; Triandis, 1961; Triandis & Davis, 1965), but the controversy gradually disappeared. And, as already mentioned, by 1970 the similarity–attraction principle had been extended beyond attitudes to other characteristics (Byrne et al., 1970). Nevertheless, the effect of (especially) race similarity on interpersonal attitudes has continued to be of interest.

In work settings, evaluations have often been shown to be more favorable when the evaluator and evaluatee (e.g., a hiring manager and a job applicant) are similar, rather than different, in race or gender (e.g., Riordan, 2000). Interpretation of this *demographic similarity* effect as a form of discriminatory bias has been made plausible by reports that the effect can be minimized or eliminated when highly structured interview methods are used (e.g., McCarthy, Van Iddekinge & Campion, 2010; Sacco, Scheu, Ryan & Schmitt, 2003). Highly structured interviews are understood to minimize discriminatory effects because they leave little to the interviewer's subjectivity or discretion (e.g., Heilman & Haynes, 2008). The interesting question as to whether effects of demographic similarity in the workplace are due to ingroup favoritism or outgroup hostility has not been directly addressed in most of the available research. However, the (earlier mentioned) studies by DiTomaso (2012), Reskin (1998), and Rivera (2012) are supportive of a favoritism interpretation. In sum, the similarity–attraction principle is consistent with an expectation that attitudes toward members of one's own group (ingroup) will typically be more positive than attitudes toward members of other groups (outgroups).

B. The Minimal Group Paradigm (MGP)

More than 40 years after the discovery of *minimal group paradigm* (MGP) effects, the original report of that finding by Tajfel, Billig, Bundy, and Flament (1971; see also Tajfel, 1970) continues to shape research and theory on intergroup relations. Tajfel et al. found that even when subjects were assigned arbitrarily to groups in a laboratory study, they preferentially allocated resources to members of their own group rather than to those in another group. Later studies found that this occurred even when subjects knew that the basis for assignment was random. It also occurred when subjects did not know which of the other subjects who were present were members of their own group and which were members of the other group (Billig & Tajfel, 1973). Platow and Van Knippenberg (2001), using the MGP, showed that subjects expect and believe it is fair for an ingroup member to treat all ingroup members fairly. But they also tend to expect and believe it to be fair for an ingroup member to favor another ingroup member over an outgroup member. Not surprisingly, ingroup members cannot be expected to identify their ingroup favoritism as discrimination when they see their behavior as legitimate, normative, and even procedurally fair.

A further study by L. Gaertner and Insko (2001) showed that distributions of monetary payments in the MGP are partly constrained by equity norms—which prescribe giving equal rewards to all. Nevertheless, these investigators also observed ingroup favoritism when the monetary distributions were described as bonus payments (making equity irrelevant) and when subjects were asked to describe their feelings toward unspecified members of each group. Their article also introduced a new dependent measure format ("multiple alternative matrices") that avoided a strict inverse relationship between outcomes of ingroup and outgroup members. This measure allowed the conclusion that, on average, subjects were more motivated by ingroup favoritism (higher payments to ingroup members) than by outgroup hostility (lower payments to outgroup members). In the context of similarity–attraction research, MGP research indicates that similarity that is solely due to membership in the same group suffices to provide a basis for both attraction and favoritism, even when no specific attributes are known to be shared with members of that (minimal) ingroup.

C. Ingroup and Outgroup Are Differentiated More as Targets of Positive Than of Negative Feelings

If negative outgroup attitudes are expressed primarily in hostile form, we can expect that negative emotions should be more readily expressed toward outgroups than ingroups—a phenomenon that is indeed observed (cf. E. R. Smith, 1993; E. R. Smith & Mackie, 2005). A rarely addressed empirical question (but cf. Dovidio, Mann & Gaertner, 1989; Gaertner & McLaughlin, 1983) is how ingroup–outgroup differences in negative feelings compare to ingroup–outgroup differences in positive feelings.

A study of racial attitudes in the 2012 American presidential election (Ziegler, Kirby, Xu & Greenwald, 2013) included data from more than 45,000 volunteers who responded to (among other measures) two measures of emotional responses to Black and White persons. One of these was a standard feeling thermometer, which instructed, "Please rate how warm or cold you feel toward White [or Black] people." We conducted a secondary analysis of these data, limited to Whites who expressed strong White preference and Blacks who expressed strong Black preference, to ensure a focus on Whites and Blacks who clearly perceived their own racial groups as "ingroups." For these participants, thermometer responses of strong warmth toward the ingroup exceeded expressions of strong cold feelings toward the outgroup by a ratio of approximately 4:1 for Whites and more than 50:1 for Blacks. That is, expressions of warmth toward the ingroup greatly exceeded expressions of coldness toward the outgroup.

The second emotion measure used by Ziegler et al. (2013) was an adaptation of Pettigrew and Meertens's (1995) measure of subtle racism. It consisted of two items asking "How often have you felt _____ for African Americans who grew up in slums and poverty?" The blank was replaced by "sympathy" or "admiration" in the two items. The same items were also used to ask about "Americans" in place of "African-Americans." Subjects of both races whose Likert-item responses stated *very strong* racial ingroup preference were more disposed to feel positively toward impoverished members of their own racial group than toward comparable members of the outgroup.[4]

Pettigrew; Meertens & Pettigrew, 1997) found in seven independent samples from France, Germany, Great Britain, and the Netherlands that these items correlated highly with other measures of prejudice. Although the sympathy and admiration items are typically *not* seen by Europeans as reflecting prejudice, they nevertheless predicted pro-discrimination beliefs. For example, those who reported that they rarely or never felt sympathy or admiration for immigrants were significantly more likely to support expelling immigrants who have committed crimes or who have no immigration papers. These survey respondents are more appropriately described as withholding positive emotions (sympathy and admiration) from immigrants than as expressing hostile feelings toward immigrants.

III. Findings: Discrimination Often Occurs as Differential Favoring

Studies of intergroup behavior in field settings have examined the extent to which significant discriminatory effects result from differential helping or favoring. There are limitations on conclusions from these studies that we will mention later. Nevertheless they are quite consistent in showing the potential for discrimination to result from differential favoring.

A. Helping Behavior

Experiments on unobtrusively observed helping of ingroup and outgroup members began with an ingenious study using a "wrong number" method devised by S. L. Gaertner and Bickman (1971). Researchers, speaking with accents that were racially identifiable as Black or White, placed telephone calls in which they claimed to be stranded drivers calling an automobile mechanic and urgently needing help for their disabled cars. Because of strong residential segregation in the Brooklyn, New York, neighborhoods to which those calls were directed, researchers could know whether the call recipients were racially White or Black. Claiming to have used his last coin in a pay phone, the caller asked the recipient to help by calling the mechanic to relay the emergency request for road service. The key finding: White call recipients discriminated by race—they were less likely to help Black callers (53%) than White callers (65%). Three later repetitions of the experiment replicated Gaertner and Bickman's finding (see Crosby, Bromley & Saxe, 1980; Saucier, Miller & Doucet, 2005).

A crucial element of S. L. Gaertner and Bickman's (1971) wrong-number method was that potential helpers could not know that their helping or non-helping was being monitored. Dozens of later experiments in the 1970s used similar unobtrusive measures to compare the amount of help that Black and White help seekers would receive from White potential helpers. In reviewing the accumulated collection of more than 30 such studies, Crosby et al. (1980) concluded, "Discriminatory behavior is more prevalent in the . . . ; unobtrusive studies than we might expect on the basis of survey data" (p. 557).

Similar results have more recently been found in studies of tipping behavior. Obtaining the cooperation of taxi drivers in New Haven, Connecticut, Ayres, Vars, and Zakariya (2005) asked the drivers to keep records of fares and tips. White drivers received tips that were 51% larger than those received by Black drivers, a ratio that was even greater when computed as a percentage of fare. A study of restaurant tipping behavior by Lynn et al. (2006, 2008) likewise revealed a race difference—White waiters received tips that, on average, were 22% larger than those received by Black waiters.

B. Hiring and Housing Audits

Many field experiments using *audit* methods have assessed discrimination in employment and housing. The standard audit method uses paired testers who differ in race or ethnicity while being matched in relevant qualifications such as (for housing audits) income, assets, debt levels, family circumstances, employment history, credit record, and neatness of appearance. Randomizing which of the two members of each pair arrives first, the two testers apply for work or housing to each of a large sample of hiring managers or real estate agents. This method almost invariably reveals discrimination against Blacks and Hispanics in access to jobs (reviewed by Bendick, 2004) and housing (e.g., Turner, Ross, Galster & Yinger, 2002).

Results obtained from field audit experiments strongly suggest that significant acts of discrimination in housing and employment can often occur without expression of hostility toward the people who are disadvantaged by those acts. Some of the individual hiring managers or real estate agents might have been hostile in their denials of consideration for job interviews or housing. However, the great majority of declinations of hiring and housing applications involve simply the *nonoccurrence of a helpful act*—either the act of inviting the job seeker for an interview or the act of escorting the housing seeker to view an apartment or home. The greater nonoccurrence of those helpful actions when applicants are Black or Hispanic than when they are White can effectively cause substantial discrimination in housing or hiring.[5] Recently, Bendick (2007) and colleagues (Bendick, Rodriguez & Jayaraman, 2010), using a method of *situation testing* in hiring studies, have shown that discrimination in hiring interactions is linked more to occurrences of favorable than of hostile actions.

C. Policing

Large bodies of data on discrimination in policing have been accumulated in studies of *profiling* by police in their interactions with pedestrians or with drivers who have been stopped for driving violations or for vehicle maintenance infractions. Discrimination is evident when there is a greater probability of searching or issuing a citation when the driver is Black or Hispanic rather than White and when there is a greater probability of subjecting Black or Hispanic pedestrians to search (Lamberth, 1994; Spitzer, 1999; Verniero & Zoubek, 1999; Weiss & Rosenbaum, 2009).

In summarizing available profiling data, The Leadership Conference on Civil and Human Rights (2011) concluded that (a) Blacks and Hispanics were stopped more frequently than Whites; (b) among those stopped, higher proportions of Blacks and Hispanics than Whites received citations; (c) among those stopped, higher proportions of Blacks and Hispanics than Whites were subjected to searches; and (d) among those searched, a *smaller* proportion of the searches of Blacks and Hispanics than of Whites yielded contraband (e.g., drugs or weapons). The lower yields of contraband from searches of Blacks and Hispanics establishes that the greater searching of Blacks and Hispanics is not justified by greater criminal activity of Blacks and Hispanics than of Whites among those who are stopped. The greater rate of discovering contraband from searches of vehicles driven by Whites suggests that White drivers are being stopped and searched at inappropriately low rates. This is consistent with the proposition that discrimination reflected in profiling data is in part—perhaps large part—due to favorable acts of either not stopping White drivers or (as the data show) not searching their vehicles after they are stopped.

D. Public Opinion Surveys

Surveys of White Americans' racial attitudes over the past 50 years show that Whites have steadily increased their support for policies that provide educational or housing opportunities for African-Americans. (The finding just mentioned and the other findings described in this paragraph are documented in Schuman, Steeh, Bobo & Krysan, 1997.) Surveys also have revealed White Americans' increasing support for racial intermarriage, for equal opportunity in employment, and for the acceptability of an African-American candidate for U.S. president. At the same time, White Americans' levels of support for policies that provide governmental help to minorities have been largely unchanged during the past half century. In particular, majorities of White Americans have steadily opposed financial assistance to minorities, social services to minorities, and affirmative action to benefit minorities in hiring or college admissions. Put differently, national American surveys across the past five decades have found that most White Americans accept basic principles of equal opportunity while, at the same time, resisting the implementation of policies that would increase equality directly by helping outgroups (see also DiTomaso, 2012; Pettigrew, 1979).

In combination, these evidences of White Americans' current high levels of opposition to both antiminority segregation policies and prominority assistance policies suggest that the preferred policies of White Americans amount to a generalized antidiscrimination stance. That is, they favor neither segregation policies that could potentially harm Black Americans nor assistance policies that could potentially favor impoverished Black Americans more than other impoverished Americans. At the same time, there are some government assistance programs that many White Americans *do* support. As was documented by political opinion polling during the American presidential campaign of 2012, White Americans (more than other demographic categories) supported tax laws that assist very wealthy Americans. Because America's Black and Hispanic minorities are underrepresented at high income levels, benefits received via tax laws necessarily help Whites more than racial minorities. At the same time, many White Americans are more likely to oppose laws that would disproportionately benefit relatively impoverished minorities than ones that disproportionately benefit relatively wealthy Whites. Although some of Whites' support for benefits via tax laws can be attributed to economic self-interest, the supported laws often include benefits (such as low income tax rates on the extremely wealthy) that directly affect only Americans much wealthier than many of those laws' supporters.

IV. Theories: Roots of Favoritism

A variety of theories explain conditions that promote and sustain favoritism—not limited to ingroup favoritism. This section describes theoretical accounts of favoritism stated at four levels of psychosocial analysis: intrapersonal, interpersonal, intergroup, and societal.

A. Balance Theory and Balanced Identity Theory

In explaining the powerful similarity–attraction phenomenon revealed in his research, Byrne (1961) proposed that "any time that another person offers us validation by indicating that his percepts and concepts are congruent with ours, it constitutes a rewarding interaction and, hence, one element in forming a positive relationship" (p. 713). Byrne advanced this reward theory toward the end of an era in which learning–reinforcement theories were psychology's dominant theories. By the 1960s, however, those reinforcement theories were in decline. At that same time, affective–cognitive consistency theories—especially Heider's (1958) balance theory, Osgood and Tannenbaum's (1955) congruity theory, and Festinger's (1957) dissonance theory—were on the ascent in social psychology (see Abelson et al., 1968).

Although consistency theories themselves declined in the 1970s, they have recently experienced a resurgence (cf. Gawronski & Strack, 2012). The recent "balanced identity" theory (BIT), which was developed as an extension of Heider's balance theory (Greenwald et al., 2002), offers a cognitive consistency interpretation of similarity attraction. BIT's *balance–congruity principle* holds that two concepts that are both associated with the same third concept will become associated with each other. When a newly encountered person (P) is an ingroup member, both *self* and P are associated with the ingroup (a third concept) that they share. BIT's balance–congruity principle therefore predicts that the association between *self* and P will strengthen. The same principle then extends to the combination of the new (*self–P*) association and the pervasive association of *self* with *positive valence* (i.e., self-esteem). When P and *positive valence* are thus both associated with *self* (third concept), the association between P and *positive valence* should itself strengthen, theoretically explaining attraction to the ingroup member (P).

B. Social Identity Theory

Social identity theory (SIT) was developed by Tajfel and Turner (1979) in part to account for Tajfel et al.'s (1971) findings of intergroup discrimination in the minimal group paradigm (MPG). In contrast to BIT's association-formation interpretation of the relation between self-esteem and ingroup favoritism, SIT offers a motivational interpretation rooted in understanding self-esteem as a motive with the goals of achieving and sustaining positive self-regard. SIT links intergroup discrimination in the MGP to increased self-esteem in two ways: Either (1) a self-esteem increase is achieved as a *consequence* of perceiving one's own group as superior to the other in the MGP, or (2) approximately the reverse—the motive to elevate self-esteem is the *cause* of perceiving one's group as superior to the other (Abrams & Hogg, 1988, pp. 320–321). Hewstone et al. (2002) summarized SIT's *self-esteem hypothesis* this way: "(1) [S]uccessful intergroup bias enhances self-esteem and (2) depressed or threatened self-esteem motivates intergroup bias" (p. 41). However, Hewstone et al. also concluded that the evidence for this SIT theorization is at best mixed.

C. System Justification Theory

If ingroup favoritism is practiced equally by all, then the greatest benefits will necessarily flow to members of a society's more powerful groups. Their greater power, along with their (typically) greater numbers, translates to their being better positioned to benefit from ingroup helpers. System justification theory (SJT; Jost & Banaji, 1994) explains how a complementary form of favoritism, rooted in existing status, adds to the benefits accruing to high-status groups.

Jost and Banaji (1994) defined system justification as a "process by which existing social arrangements are legitimized, even at the expense of personal and group interest" (p. 2). There has been substantial empirical support for this theorized reversal of ingroup favoritism for low-status groups, including the prediction that "[a]s system justification tendencies increase . . . ; members of low-status groups will exhibit increased *outgroup* [emphasis added] favoritism" (Jost, Banaji & Nosek, 2004, p. 901).

In their review of ten years of SJT research, Jost et al. (2004) cited substantial evidence for SJT's outgroup favoritism hypothesis. This evidence took the form of finding outgroup-favoring attitudes among members in low-status minorities, sometimes assessed with unobtrusive behavioral indicators (Jost, Pelham & Carvallo, 2002). Behavioral evidence for outgroup favoritism was also obtained in some of the unobtrusive-measure studies of helping in the 1970s and in the more recent studies of tipping behavior. Although the first of the unobtrusive helping studies (S. L. Gaertner & Bickman, 1971) found (non-significantly) that Blacks helped Whites more than they helped fellow Blacks, subsequent replications did not show that pattern. On the other hand, the two tipping studies—by Ayres et al. (2005) with taxi passengers and by Lynn et al. (2006, 2008) with restaurant patrons—both found, consistent with SJT's expectations, that Black customers gave larger tip percentages to White than to Black service providers.

When, as theorized in SJT, favoritism thus extends to an advantaged outgroup, the consequence is to exacerbate the relative disadvantage of lower status groups. SJT thus explains an additional source of favoritism that may disproportionately benefit a society's highest status groups. For a high-status group that constitutes a societal minority, this additional source of favoritism might exceed ingroup favoritism as a basis for sustaining the group's advantage.

D. Unrecognized Discrimination and Illusory Individuation

Learning about a person's distinctive characteristics—"individuating" that person—is widely understood as a means of overcoming the disadvantaging effects of stereotypes (Fiske & Neuberg, 1990; Kunda & Thagard, 1996; Locksley, Borgida, Brekke & Hepburn, 1980). An unfamiliar person whose distinctive characteristics are unknown may be judged, unthinkingly, by applying stereotypes. Logically, knowing specific (individuating) characteristics of a person should preempt this use of stereotypes. This plausible theory notwithstanding, a series of studies conducted over the last 30 years has demonstrated that the expected reduction of stereotyping by individuation is rather easily thrown off track. Instead, stereotypes can insinuate themselves subtly into apparently individuated judgments that can prove disadvantageous to outgroup members.

Darley and Gross (1983) found that their college-student subjects resisted applying stereotypes to judge the academic skills of a 9-year-old child (Hannah) for whom the only available information made clear that her upbringing had been in either an impoverished or a well-to-do family environment. Perhaps the research setting put these subjects on alert not to let their knowledge of

Hannah's socioeconomic status influence their judgment of her academic skills. In two further conditions, subjects additionally observed a twelve-minute videotape of Hannah's responses to twenty-five "achievement-test" questions. Her performance on these—showing Hannah giving a mixture of correct and incorrect responses—gave no clear impression of Hannah's ability. Nevertheless, findings showed that, in these two *individuated* conditions, subjects interpreted the added information by applying social class stereotypes. They credited the well-to-do Hannah with having abilities at a higher grade level than the working-class Hannah. Exposure to the extra (presumably individuating) information apparently licensed subjects to apply stereotypes that they resisted applying when they had no opportunity to observe Hannah's test performances. The process afforded by the videotape plausibly left subjects unaware that their knowledge of Hannah's socioeconomic status had in any way affected their judgment.

Yzerbyt, Schadron, Leyens, and Rocher (1994) conducted two experiments inspired by Darley and Gross's (1983) finding. Remarkably, they found similarly that stereotype-confirming effects occurred even when subjects received no actual individuating information. Instead, they had merely been told that relevant information had been presented to one of their ears, outside of conscious awareness, in a selective listening ("shadowing") task that required repeating an audible message presented to the other ear.

Hodson, Dovidio, and Gaertner (2002) constructed a further variation on the use of illusory individuating information. They observed White subjects' evaluations of two presumed college applicants, one White and one Black, whose qualifications differed. Although the two applicants were otherwise matched, one applicant was higher in high school grades and the other was higher on a standardized aptitude test. The two applicants therefore deserved, objectively, to be treated as approximately equally qualified. Hodson et al.'s noteworthy finding was that, in comparing the White and Black applicants, subjects who scored relatively high on a measure of prejudice attributed greater predictive weight to the measure on which the White applicant was superior. Again, this result reveals discrimination in the presence of actually uninformative, but presumably individuating, information. This discriminatory use of the information was apparent to the experimenters, who could compare the data from different conditions, but the subjects themselves had no basis for suspecting that stereotypes had influenced their judgments.

Stronger biased-processing findings of the type obtained by Hodson et al. (2002) were obtained in subsequent studies by Norton, Vandello, and Darley (2004) and by Uhlmann and Cohen (2005). The biased processing observed in these studies was labeled variously as *hypothesis-confirming bias* (Darley & Gross, 1983), *social judgeability bias* (Yzerbyt et al., 1994), *differential weighting* (Hodson et al., 2002), *casuistry* (Norton et al., 2004), and *constructed criteria* (Uhlmann & Cohen, 2005). These variations in labels notwithstanding, the several studies support each other in demonstrating the readiness with which people "engage in biased behavior while retaining a view of the self as objective" (Norton et al., 2004, p. 828). In each case the bias started with exposure to information that presumably afforded a basis for objective, individuated judgment but was nevertheless used in a biased fashion. These illusory individuation phenomena relate to this article's main point in showing a subtle form of favoritism that can give the benefit of the doubt to an ingroup member.[6]

E. Conformity to Social Norms

Sociologists stress the importance of societal structures in producing intergroup discrimination (DiTomaso, 2012; Pettigrew, 1975; Pettigrew & Taylor, 2002). An important form of this theory is that historical realities such as past slavery and immigrant poverty are inevitably associated with differences in employment and wealth and consequently with residential segregation. The resulting limitations of intergroup contact in turn provide a breeding ground for perceived differences that can take the form of stereotypes, intergroup threat, and wariness, if not outright dislike, of the outgroup (Pettigrew & Tropp, 2011). Just-world reasoning (Lerner, 1980) or "blaming the victim" (Ryan, 1976) can lead to perceiving the impoverished as deserving of their low status, as, in effect, having brought their disadvantages on themselves. In this way, the residue of past discrimination can sustain and even exacerbate discrimination in a "vicious circle" (Myrdal, 1944).

Sociologists appeal to *norms*, which are widely shared understandings of what constitutes acceptable social behavior. Both formal norms (e.g., a posted 65-miles-per-hour [mph] automobile speed limit) and informal norms (keeping to the right if driving below the speed limit) powerfully guide behavior (Pettigrew, 1991, 2011). Also important are rewards and punishments that may independently shape the norms (e.g., an enforced 75-mph limit on a highway with a posted 65-mph limit). Norms shape intergroup interaction and provide a common meaning to all participants in the interaction.

Moreover, discriminatory norms are typically cumulative. That is, discriminatory norms build on themselves and tend to reinforce each other across societal realms. Thus, America's extreme residential segregation by race shaped and continues to maintain racial discrimination in employment, schools, home mortgages, and civic services generally (Pettigrew, 1975; Pettigrew & Taylor, 2002). Norms are also self-perpetuating. They come in time to be unquestioned, to be accepted simply because "that's just the way things are done" (Pettigrew, 1991, 1998).

The persistence of norms means that their discriminatory effects can outlive the initiating past causes of discriminatory practices. Those who initiated the norms may have been motivated by hostile prejudice, but later generations can adhere to norms that benefit their ingroup without harboring the animosity felt by the norms' creators. The result is that norms are likely to remain unchanged even while attitudes are shifting markedly. At present, in the midst of rapid formal change in intergroup relations in Northern Ireland, South Africa, and the southern United States, old norms are slowly receding while new equalitarian norms have yet to develop fully. In all three societies, reticence and awkwardness characterize intergroup interaction, often accompanied by intergroup avoidance and informal discrimination that occurs without hostile intent (see especially Dovidio and Gaertner's analyses of aversive racism—e.g., Dovidio & Gaertner, 2004; also Pettigrew, 1991, 2011).

Norms can be so unquestioned that people think and behave in conflicting ways in different social contexts while remaining unaware of the inconsistency. At an Indiana steel mill in the 1950s, Blacks and Whites were members of the same racially desegregated union and worked well together (Reitzes, 1953; for a similar example, see Minard, 1952). Only 12% of the White workers reported low acceptance of African-Americans on the job. Those most involved in the union were the strongest supporters of the union's pro-desegregation norms. Yet these same White workers also lived in racially segregated, all-White neighborhoods, and many belonged to activist pro-segregation neighborhood groups. Indeed, 84% of those who accepted African-Americans at work were highly resistant to Blacks living in their neighborhoods. Those most involved with their neighborhoods were the most resistant to having Blacks as neighbors. The behavior in each setting favored the setting's prominent ingroup—union solidarity at work, racial solidarity at home.

Allport (1954) considered conformity an essential concept for understanding prejudice, devoting a full chapter of his classic volume to the subject. In a later article, Allport (1962) wrote, "Conformity is the missing link that explains why and how societal forces eventuate into patterns of acceptance or discrimination" (p. 132). Thus, conformity research also supports our thesis. Relatively unprejudiced Americans typically follow their ingroup's norms. If, as is typical, these norms demand preferential treatment of the ingroup, most people—like the Indiana steel workers—will conform without personal animus toward the outgroup.

V. Method Limitations

Discrimination has been investigated with a wide range of measures, including behavioral interactions (overt and nonverbal), behavioral intentions, interpersonal judgments, self-reported attitudes, and implicit attitudes—all of which we consider in this section. We will explain why most research procedures used in studies of prejudice are inadequate to distinguish ingroup favoritism from outgroup hostility as mechanisms of discrimination. The consequence is that relatively few studies provide data optimal for evaluating the role of ingroup favoritism in discrimination.

To distinguish ingroup favoritism from outgroup hostility as a cause of discrimination, a study must meet two requirements. First, the study's measures must distinguish favorableness from hostility in thoughts, feelings, or behavior toward others. To do this, a measure must have an unambiguous neutral point—a value that is neither favorable nor hostile. Second, the study must use a design that permits comparison between behavior toward ingroup members and behavior toward outgroup members. The first requirement is needed to distinguish favorable from hostile behavior. The second requirement is needed to assess whether discrimination has occurred. Only a small fraction of the many existing studies of intergroup behavior meet even one of these two criteria, and many lack both. Most of this section analyzes methods regarding the first requirement. Shortcomings regarding the second requirement are more easily and briefly described at the end of this section.

A. Overt Behavior Measures

Numerous experiments have investigated discrimination by using unobtrusive assessments of overt helping behavior (see the reviews by Crosby et al., 1980, and Saucier et al., 2005). These studies succeeded in unambiguously identifying favorable behavior by scoring subjects simply as helping or as not helping (inaction). Inaction is neutral behavior, and helping is positive. The studies have no hostile behavior option.

Given the widespread understanding of prejudice as hostile behavior, one might expect that there must be many studies in which discrimination has been observed in the form of overtly hostile behavior toward members of an outgroup. In searching, we could find just seven laboratory studies in which discrimination was assessed using measures that appeared unambiguously to involve outgroup-directed hostile behavior. The behaviors were electric shock administration in six (Baron, 1979; Donnerstein, Donnerstein, Simon & Ditrichs, 1972; Genthner & Taylor, 1973; Griffin & Rogers, 1977; Prentice-Dunn & Rogers, 1980; Rogers & Prentice-Dunn, 1981; Wilson & Rogers, 1975) and aversive noise administration in the seventh (Mummendey et al., 1992). The shock administration studies incorporated electric shock either as an outcome to be administered to another player in a competitive game or as an experimental stimulus to be presented for the ostensible purpose of increasing another subject's heart rate. In most conditions of these studies, White subjects administered more shocks to Whites (i.e., to presumed ingroup members) than to Blacks.[7] Experimenters interpreted this in terms of egalitarian norms and concerns about appearing prejudiced. In only one condition of one of these experiments did White subjects administer more shocks to another presumed subject who was Black than to one who was White. Contrary to researchers' expectations, both in experiments with aversive shock and experiments with aversive noise stimuli, fairness (i.e., ingroup and outgroup receiving the same outcomes) prevailed in distributing the aversive outcomes.

Accordingly, no evidence of outgroup hostility has been reported in experiments using unambiguously aversive stimuli.

A famous early field experiment on prejudice also found no evidence for discrimination in a situation in which had discrimination occurred, it would have had to take an overtly hostile form. LaPiere (1934) and two Chinese traveling companions toured the southwestern United States, seeking housing and dining accommodations at 251 establishments. Face-to-face denial of service to potential customers is undeniably a hostile act. LaPiere and the Chinese couple were refused service only once in their 251 requests. This result was in stark contrast with the finding that, in response to a subsequent mailed questionnaire, more than 90% of these same establishments reported that they would not accommodate "members of the Chinese race."

B. Nonverbal Behavior Measures

One might expect that nonverbal measures, such as facial expressions, body orientation, and voice tone, can easily be classified into positive and negative categories. However, nonverbal measures rarely afford a clear neutral point. As one example, when the subject can position his or her chair at variable distances from a fellow participant, even though smaller distance translates unambiguously to greater positivity toward the other participant (cf. Amodio & Devine, 2006), it is not possible to identify a specific distance that can be scored as "neutral." Measures of speaking time are similarly unambiguous in direction (more conversation is more favorable) but equally lack specifiable neutral values. Likewise, when measures of facial affect are being obtained (cf. McConnell & Leibold, 2001), it is difficult to score them so as to identify a neutral point. Problems come in combining multiple responses for a subject. Clearly, smiles cannot all be counted as equally positive nor frowns as equally negative, and some of each might even be intended to convey the opposite.[8]

C. Behavioral Intention Measures

The procedure introduced by Tajfel et al. (1971) identifies an unambiguous neutral point when the measures involve distribution of payments to others. Neutral behavior takes the form of allocating a payment equal to the per-person average of available points or funds. Favoring (positive) and disfavoring (negative) behavior then takes the form of payment that falls, respectively, above or below that average level. LaPiere's (1934) mailed questionnaire provides another illustration of a behavioral intention measure—willingness or refusal to accept Chinese guests—that could be scored unambiguously as positive or negative.[9]

D. Interpersonal Judgment Measures

Consider the judgment task of recommending a jail sentence for a convicted defendant for whom the available evidence indicates both guilt and mitigating circumstances. If the permissible sentence range is from a low of 6 months to a high of 5 years, it is clear that the shortest sentence is favorable and the longest sentence is unfavorable. But how can one identify an intermediate sentence term that is neutral—neither favorable nor hostile to the defendant? Furthermore, if the dependent measure is obtained as (say) a 7-point Likert-format judgment of endorsement of the maximum sentence, what level of agreement can be assumed to be neither favorable nor unfavorable to the defendant? This limitation can be overcome by providing the subject with information about an average sentence for the defendant's circumstances, then requesting endorsement of either a shorter, equal, or longer sentence.

E. Self-Report Attitude Measures

Self-report attitude measures are easily constructed with neutral points, as with thermometer scales that have end anchors of *warm* (positive) and *cold* (negative) and a middle anchor of *neutral*. A useful alternative recommended by S. L. Gaertner et al. (1997) is to have separate rating scales for positive and negative traits, with the low anchor indicating absence of the trait. Using this method, S. L. Gaertner and McLaughlin (1983) and Dovidio et al. (1989) found that White subjects did not discriminate against Blacks on negative-trait scales; they rated Whites and Blacks equally on these. In contrast, they did discriminate on positive-trait scales (rating Whites higher than Blacks). This strong finding (subsequently replicated in several Western European countries by Pettigrew & Meertens, 1995, and Meertens & Pettigrew, 1997) reveals discriminatory judgment in the form of favoring the ingroup rather than disfavoring the outgroup.

F. Implicit Attitude Measures

For the most widely used implicit attitude measures, subjects make rapid classification responses to both valenced word stimuli and to images, words, or names that represent two contrasted categories, which can be an ingroup and outgroup, such as White and Black. These implicit measures generate relative-attitude scores that index greater favorability to one group than to the other (e.g., Fazio, Sanbonmatsu, Powell & Kardes, 1986; Greenwald, McGhee & Schwartz, 1998). These measures often reveal evaluative separation between the two groups, but they do not unambiguously locate either group relative to a neutral point (i.e., a score that indicates neither positive nor negative evaluation). Some implicit measures may do a better job than others in distinguishing favorability from unfavorability in an absolute sense (e.g., Nosek & Banaji, 2001; Sriram & Greenwald, 2009), but even these measures are not established as having neutral zero points. Their zero points more confidently indicate indifference between the groups, which could mean that both groups are regarded equally positively or that they are regarded equally negatively.

G. The "Second Requirement"

Our analysis of method has to this point considered only the first require-ment that we stated, which is to use measures of behavior or judgment that have an unambiguous neutral point. The second requirement is that the study must demonstrate discrimination by comparing behavior or judgments toward ingroup members versus outgroup members. To meet the second requirement at the individual-subject level requires a within-subjects design in which each subject provides a measure for both ingroup and outgroup. Designs in which ingroup versus outgroup is a between-subjects factor also permit assessment of discrimination, but not for individual subjects. For either type of design, deter-mination of whether discrimination takes the form of ingroup favoritism or outgroup hostility is possible only if the first requirement (neutral point of dependent measure) is also met. The minimal group paradigm and studies that use unobtrusive measures of helping are the rare paradigms for which more than an occasional study meets both the neutral-point requirement and the ingroup–outgroup comparison requirement.

VI. Three Conclusions about Methods

A. Methods Used in Most Studies of Discrimination Have Limited Capabilities

Few studies in the voluminous research literature on prejudice and discrimi-nation have used methods that can distinguish the relative roles of ingroup-favorable and outgroup-hostile behavior in producing discrimination. This could well be a consequence of the widespread (but, to us, incorrect) belief that discrimination most often occurs in the form of outgroup-directed hostility. When one makes this assumption, it might well appear unnecessary to inves-tigate relative contributions of favoritism and hostility to discrimination. Most studies of discrimination address one of two other questions: (1) determining whether various experimental manipulations increase or reduce discrimination or (2) determining whether various individual-difference measures of prejudice successfully predict individual differences in discriminatory behavior. These aims do not require either of the two criteria for determining whether observed discrimination has resulted from ingroup favoritism or outgroup hostility.

It is remarkable that relatively few studies have used dependent measures that assessed unequivocally hostile behavior. This paucity cannot be explained simply in terms of experimenters' benevolence, because a paradigm involving aggression via (presumed) administration of electric shocks was widely used in the 1960s and 1970s (cf. Buss & Brock, 1963). The use of this well-known method in only six studies of race discrimination, during the same era in which more than 30 studies had investigated race discrimination in unobtrusive helping (Crosby et al. 1980), suggests that it may be much easier to observe discrimination in studies using unobtrusive measures of helping behavior than in studies that observe shock administration or other unequivocally hostile behavior.

B. Balance of Findings with Existing Methods

More studies have demonstrated discrimination resulting from ingroup favoritism than from outgroup hostility—an unexpected observation in light of the prevailing wisdom that discrimination typically occurs in the form of hostility directed toward outgroups. For whatever reason, it is apparently easier to demonstrate discrimination in the form of differential favoritism than in the form of differential hostility. The most parsimonious and plausible explanation is that, indeed, discrimination more often takes the form of ingroup favoritism than outgroup hostility. However, some portion of this imbalance in findings may also be due to the greater ease of meeting ethical research standards in laboratory studies that use measures of benign behavior than in ones investigating hostile behavior.

C. New Methods Are Needed

Prejudice researchers need to add methods to their toolboxes—methods that (1) distinguish ingroup-favorable from outgroup-hostile subject behavior, (2) provide a comparison of outcomes to ingroup and outgroup members, and (3) are easy to administer in standardized form. Among existing laboratory methods, L. Gaertner and Insko's (2001) multiple alternative matrices procedure for the minimal group paradigm comes closest to meeting this combination of requirements but is not adapted to investigating face-to-face intergroup interactions. The most important method recommendation is to use measures—whether nonverbal, behavioral, self-report, or implicit—that have unambiguous neutral points that enable distinguishing between favoring and hostile responses.

VII. Discussion

We conclude that ingroup favoritism is currently more potent than outgroup hostility as a cause of intergroup discrimination in the United States. The support for this conclusion comes from multiple, well-established empirical paradigms, including laboratory studies of minimal group and similarity–attraction paradigms, field experiments using unobtrusive observations of helping behavior, and field audit studies of police profiling and of treatment accorded to potential job seekers, apartment renters, and home buyers.

Two caveats to our conclusion are necessitated by the available research literature. First, many of the studies we cited involved race. It is conceivable that outgroup hostility may play a greater role in nonracial discrimination than in racial discrimination. Second, most of the studies we reviewed were conducted in the United States. Although conclusions based on these studies may also hold in other nations, it is premature to assume that the same will be found elsewhere—especially in locations such as Northern Ireland and South Africa, which have centuries-old histories of intergroup hostility and discrimination. Tests of the ingroup favoritism thesis in those countries should be highly informative. Pending broader investigations in other countries and with other forms of discrimination, our conclusion that ingroup favoritism enables discrimination should be regarded as most strongly established for Black–White racial discrimination in the United States.

A. The Nature of the Evidence

An obvious question prompted by our main conclusion is: Why is the "ingroup favoritism enables discrimination" thesis not already generally accepted as a prime explanation of discrimination? If the evidence is so extensive and most of it has been available for at least a few decades, why have students of prejudice and discrimination not previously arrived at this conclusion? The answer has two parts. The more important part is that, throughout the history of prejudice's scientific study, most researchers have defined and understood prejudice as an affectively negative outgroup-directed attitude that they expect to result in hostile acts of discrimination. That view was justified for a long time but is now questionable given the societal transformations that have cumulatively produced dramatic reductions in both endorsements of negative attitudes toward minority groups and in hostile forms of discrimination. The second part is that—as explained in this article's analysis of research methods—very few empirical studies of discrimination have used methods that can evaluate the relative contributions of ingroup favoritism and outgroup hostility to observed discrimination.

Our conclusion about limitations of research methods raises a second question: If methods to evaluate relative contributions of ingroup favoritism and outgroup hostility are so inadequate, how can we reach a strong conclusion about those relative contributions? Our strategy in this article was to build our case by establishing three points. First, ingroup-directed positivity is pervasive, and there is no comparable evidence for an equivalent pervasiveness of outgroup-directed negativity. Second, discrimination frequently occurs in the form of differential favoring, and there is no comparable evidence for discrimination occurring so frequently in the form of differential harming. Third, established theories offer multiple bases for understanding the development of positive regard for others—a point to which we next turn.

B. Multiplicity of Explanations for Ingroup Favoritism

Societal factors . . . ; are distal causal factors in group relations . . . . ; At the same time, the intervening factor of personality is ever the proximal cause of human conduct . . . . ; There are no good reasons for professional rivalry and backbiting among social scientists preferring one approach or the other. They can and should be blended in our outlook. (Allport, 1962, p. 132)

This review has sought to establish that multiple theories, at both individual and societal levels, can explain the strength of ingroup favoritism. Allport's (1962) observation about the synergy of theories applies not only to theories that fall on different sides of the disciplinary boundary between psychology and sociology but equally to the sets of theories within each of those disciplines. Furthermore, the various theories most often do not conflict in their explanations. Rather, they offer multiple, complementary theoretical routes to the goal of understanding ingroup favoritism. Our focus on ingroup favoritism therefore affords a *rapprochement* among social psychology's person-centered explanations and the other social sciences' social-structure-centered explanations.

We do not claim that hostile prejudice plays no role in discrimination. However, we do claim that much discrimination occurs without hostile intent; it occurs either as a consequence of social structures (such as the self-sustaining properties of segregation in schools, homes, workplaces, and institutional discrimination) or as a consequence of mental processes that lack animus (such as norms, similarity attraction, and the judgment processes that we labeled illusory individuation).

A common denominator in these discrimination-producing societal and mental processes is that, without engaging outgroup-directed hostility, they all tend to result in favoring already advantaged groups. In this way, discriminatory outcomes will often occur without the intergroup animus that, traditionally, has been a defining feature of prejudice. We do not suggest that prejudice should therefore be reconceived without reference to hostility. That would be too radical a conclusion from our observations, especially because we are not inclined to claim that it has always been thus. The important, and perhaps no less radical, conclusion is that in contemporary American society intergroup discrimination has a potent life that now can occur without intergroup hostility.

C. Has There Been a Decline of Malice?

Although much societally significant discrimination continues to occur in hostile forms, it is even more apparent that hostile acts of race discrimination in the United States have steadily declined during the past century. Perhaps the most dramatic indication of decline is evident in data concerning lynchings. Lynchings—which were group killings of (mostly) Black Americans—declined from an average of 150 per year in the late 19th century to their disappearance in the 1950s ("4,733 Mob Action Victims Since '82, Tuskegee Reports", 1962). A second compelling source of evidence is much more recent: In 1996, the Federal Bureau of Investigation (FBI) started compiling data on hate crimes.[10] Hate crimes targeting Black victims declined steadily from an average of 4,071 per year in 1996–1998 to 2,762 per year in 2009–2011. As percentages of the U.S. Black population in 2000 and 2010, the percentages of Blacks who were victims of hate crimes had declined (between 1999–2001 and 2009–2011) by a third, from 0.030% to 0.020%.

VIII. Implications

Our strong conclusion is that, in present-day America, discrimination results more from helping ingroup members than from harming outgroup members. This conclusion has substantial implications for the conduct of research on discrimination, for teaching about prejudice and discrimination, and for the design of programs to reduce discrimination. Because the implications for research and teaching both follow from the potential importance of the conclusion for practical application, this section focuses on the implications for practice.

Our conclusion adds force to the approach of S. L. Gaertner and Dovidio (2000), who emphasized the possible discrimination-reducing impact of forming "superordinate" identities, which extend ingroup boundaries and thereby increase the diversity of others who are encompassed within the ingroup fold. Our conclusion also suggests a quite different approach to discrimination reduction: adopting policies of targeted outgroup helping, in effect seeking to level the ingroup-favoritism playing field. This suggestion fits with affirmative action strategies that aim to increase benefits for disadvantaged minorities or for groups regarded as underrepresented in workplaces and selective educational institutions. Relatedly, DiTomaso (2012) observed that resistance to affirmative action programs has at least a partial explanation in affirmative action's disruption of routine forms of ingroup favoritism, which include seeking friends to fill job vacancies and admitting "legacy" applicants to elite educational institutions.

In regard to employment discrimination, the courts provide opportunities for discrimination reduction that depend not on intergroup attitudes and behavior but on judges' interpretations of law. It is therefore relevant to ask whether establishment of the potency of ingroup favoritism as a source of discrimination might affect efforts to reduce discrimination via litigation. Krieger (1998) pointed out that federal courts' interpretations of Title VII of the Civil Rights Act of 1964 largely disallowed the argument that plaintiff employees in protected classes were adversely impacted by ingroup favoritism that benefited others.

By way of contrast with the situation when Krieger was writing in 1998, a 2012 federal court decision allowed a case to proceed, based on an ingroup favoritism theory of discrimination. If the 2012 decision presages a future legal environment in which discrimination suits appealing to ingroup favoritism will generally be allowed to proceed, this article's conclusions may prove useful to the courts deciding those cases.[11]

A provocative recent article by Dixon et al. (2012) started, as we did, by observing that current conceptions may incorrectly link discrimination primarily to negative intergroup attitudes. Dixon et al. proceeded to conclude that collective political action by historically disadvantaged groups might be more efficacious in ending discrimination than efforts directed at increasing positivity toward outgroups.[12]

In closing, we must counter any impression that we regard favoritism as the *only* cause of discrimination worthy of scholarly attention. Although hostile forms of discrimination have declined steadily during the period in which prejudice has been studied scientifically, hostile discrimination nevertheless continues to exist in many forms, including racial and ethnic slurs, hostile work environments, hate crimes, and terrorism. At the same time, legal, ethical, and normative constraints against hostile discrimination now widely prevail in the United States, and there are few parallel constraints against the multiple forms of favoritism that can generate discrimination. As ethnic and racial minorities become increasingly represented in American work settings, it is even plausible that opportunities for favoritism to produce significant discrimination are increasing.

References

"4,733 mob action victims since '82, Tuskegee reports." (1962). In R. Ginzburg, *100 years of lynchings* (p. 244). New York, NY: Lancer Books. (Reprinted from *The Montgomery Advertiser*, April 26, 1959)

Abelson, R. P., Aronson, E., McGuire, W. J., Newcomb, T. M., Rosenberg, M. J. & Tannenbaum, P. (Eds.). (1968). *Theories of cognitive consistency: A sourcebook*. Chicago, IL: Rand-McNally.

Abrams, D. & Hogg, M. A. (1988). Comments on the motivational status of self-esteem in social identity and intergroup discrimination. *European Journal of Social Psychology, 18*, 317–334. doi:10.1002/ejsp.2420180403

Allport, G. W. (1954). *The nature of prejudice*. Reading, MA: Addison-Wesley.

Allport, G. W. (1962). Prejudice: Is it societal or personal? *Journal of Social Issues, 18*, 120–134. doi:10.1111/j.1540-4560.1962.tb02205.x

Amiot, C. E., Terry, D. J. & Callan, V. J. (2007). Status, equity and social identification during an intergroup merger: A longitudinal study. *British Journal of Social Psychology, 46*, 557–577. doi:10.1348/014466606X146015

Amodio, D. M. & Devine, P. G. (2006). Stereotyping and evaluation in implicit race bias: Evidence for independent constructs and unique effects on behavior. *Journal of Personality and Social Psychology, 91*, 652–661. doi:10.1037/0022-3514.91.4.652

Aronson, E. (1988). *The social animal* (5th ed.). New York, NY: Freeman.

Aronson, E., Wilson, T. D. & Akert, R. M. (2012). *Social psychology* (8th ed.). Old Tappan, NJ: Pearson.

Ayres, I., Vars, F. E. & Zakariya, N. (2005). To insure prejudice: Racial disparities in taxicab tipping. *Yale Law Journal, 114*, 1613–1674.

Baron, R. A. (1979). Effects of victim's pain cues, victim's race, and level of prior instigation upon physical aggression. *Journal of Applied Social Psychology, 9*, 103–114. doi:10.1111/j.1559-1816.1979.tb00797.x

Baron, R. A. & Byrne, D. (1974). *Social psychology* (7th ed.). Boston, MA: Allyn & Bacon.

Baron, R. M. & Graziano, W. G. (1991). *Social psychology*. Fort Worth, TX: Holt, Rinehart & Winston.

Bendick, M. (2004, June). *Using paired-comparison testing to develop a social psychology of civil rights*. Paper presented at the biennial conference of the Society for the Psychological Study of Social Issues, Washington, DC.

Bendick, M. (2007). Situation testing for employment discrimination in the United States of America. *Horizons Stratégiques*, 5, 17–39.

Bendick, M., Rodriguez, R. E. & Jayaraman, S. (2010). Employment discrimination in upscale restaurants: Evidence from matched pair testing. *The Social Science Journal*, 47, 802–818. doi:10.1016/j.soscij.2010.04.001

Billig, M. & Tajfel, H. (1973). Social categorization and similarity in intergroup behaviour. *European Journal of Social Psychology*, 3, 27–52. doi:10.1002/ejsp.2420030103

Bogardus, E. S. (1925). Measuring social distance. *Journal of Applied Sociology*, 9, 299–308.

Brewer, M. B. (1999). The psychology of prejudice: Ingroup love or outgroup hate? *Journal of Social Issues*, 55, 429–444. doi:10.1111/0022-4537.00126

Brewer, M. B. & Crano, W. D. (1994). *Social psychology*. Minneapolis, MN: West Group.

Brigham, J. C. (1991). *Social psychology* (2nd ed.). New York, NY: HarperCollins.

Brown, R. (1995). *Prejudice: Its social psychology*. Oxford, England: Blackwell.

Buss, A. H. & Brock, T. C. (1963). Repression and guilt in relation to aggression. *The Journal of Abnormal and Social Psychology*, 66, 345–350. doi:10.1037/h0043707

Byrne, D. (1961). Interpersonal attraction and attitude similarity. *The Journal of Abnormal and Social Psychology*, 62, 713–715. doi:10.1037/h0044721

Byrne, D., Ervin, C. R. & Lamberth, J. (1970). Continuity between the experimental study of attraction and real-life computer dating. *Journal of Personality and Social Psychology*, 16, 157–165. doi:10.1037/h0029836

Cohen, J. (1977). *Statistical power analysis for the behavioral sciences* (rev. ed.). New York, NY: Academic Press.

Crosby, F., Bromley, S. & Saxe, L. (1980). Recent unobtrusive studies of Black and White discrimination and prejudice: A literature review. *Psychological Bulletin*, 87, 546–563. doi:10.1037/0033-2909.87.3.546

Darley, J. M. & Gross, P. H. (1983). A hypothesis-confirming bias in labeling effects. *Journal of Personality and Social Psychology*, 44, 20–33. doi:10.1037/0022-3514.44.1.20

DiTomaso, N. (2012). *The American non-dilemma: Racial inequality without racism*. New York, NY: Russell Sage Foundation.

Dixon, J., Levine, M., Reicher, S. & Durrheim, K. (2012). Beyond prejudice: Are negative evaluations the problem and is getting us to like one another more the solution? *Behavioral and Brain Sciences*, 35, 411–425. doi:10.1017/S0140525X11002214

Dollard, J., Doob, L., Miller, N. E., Mowrer, O. H. & Sears, R. R. (1939). *Frustration and aggression*. New Haven, CT: Yale University Press.

Donnerstein, E., Donnerstein, M., Simon, S. & Ditrichs, R. (1972). Variables in interracial aggression: Anonymity, expected retaliation, and a riot. *Journal of Personality and Social Psychology*, 22, 236–245. doi:10.1037/h0032597

Dovidio, J. F. & Gaertner, S. L. (2004). Aversive racism. In M. P. Zanna (Ed.), *Advances in experimental social psychology* (Vol. 36, pp. 1–52). San Diego, CA: Academic Press.

Dovidio, J. F., Mann, J. & Gaertner, S. L. (1989). Resistance to affirmative action: The implications of aversive racism. In F. Blanchard & F. Crosby (Eds.), *Affirmative action in perspective* (pp. 83–103). New York, NY: Springer-Verlag. doi:10.1007/978-1-4613-9639-0_7

Eagly, A. H. & Dickman, A. B. (2005). What is the problem? Prejudice as an attitude-in-context. In J. F. Dovidio, P. Glick & L. A. Rudman (Eds.), *On the nature of prejudice: Fifty years after Allport* (pp. 17–35). Oxford, England: Blackwell. doi:10.1002/9780470773963.ch2

E.E.O.C. v. Consolidated Service Systems, 989 F.2d 233 (7th Cir. 1993).

Fazio, R. H., Sanbonmatsu, D. M., Powell, M. C. & Kardes, F. R. (1986). On the automatic activation of attitudes. *Journal of Personality and Social Psychology*, 50, 229–238. doi:10.1037/0022-3514.50.2.229

Feagin, J. R. & Feagin, C. B. (1996). *Racial and ethnic relations* (5th ed.). Upper Saddle River, NJ: Prentice Hall.

Festinger, L. (1957). *A theory of cognitive dissonance*. Palo Alto, CA: Stanford University Press.

Finch, J. F. & Cialdini, R. B. (1989). Another indirect tactic of (self-) image management: Boosting. *Personality and Social Psychology Bulletin, 15,* 222–232. doi:10.1177/0146167289152009

Fiske, S. T. & Neuberg, S. L. (1990). A continuum model of impression formation from category-based to individuating processes: Influences of information and motivation on attention and interpretation. In M. P. Zanna (Ed.), *Advances in Experimental Social Psychology* (Vol. 23, pp. 1–74). San Diego, CA: Academic Press.

Franzoi, S. L. (1996). *Social psychology.* Madison, WI: Brown & Benchmark.

Gaertner, L. & Insko, C. A. (2001). On the measurement of social orientations in the minimal group paradigm: Norms as moderators of the expression of intergroup bias. *European Journal of Social Psychology, 31,* 143–154. doi:10.1002/ejsp.28

Gaertner, S. L. & Bickman, L. (1971). Effects of race on the elicitation of helping behavior: The wrong number technique. *Journal of Personality and Social Psychology, 20,* 218–222. doi:10.1037/h0031681

Gaertner, S. L. & Dovidio, J. F. (2000). *Reducing intergroup bias: The common ingroup identity model.* Philadelphia, PA: Psychology Press. doi:10.4135/9781446218617.n9

Gaertner, S. L., Dovidio, J. F., Banker, B. S., Rust, M. C., Nier, J. A., Mottola, G. R. & Ward, C. M. (1997). Does racism necessarily mean anti-Blackness? Aversive racism and pro-Whiteness. In M. Fine, L. Powell, L. Weis & M. Wong (Eds.), *Off white: Readings on race, power, and society* (pp. 167–178). London, England: Routledge.

Gaertner, S. L. & McLaughlin, J. P. (1983). Racial stereotypes: Associations and ascriptions of positive and negative characteristics. *Social Psychology Quarterly, 46,* 23–30. doi:10.2307/3033657

Gawronski, B. & Strack, F. (Eds.). (2012). *Cognitive consistency: A fundamental principle in social cognition.* New York, NY: Guilford Press.

Genthner, R. W. & Taylor, S. P. (1973). Physical aggression as a function of racial prejudice and the race of the target. *Journal of Personality and Social Psychology, 27,* 207–210. doi:10.1037/h0034776

Greenwald, A. G., Banaji, M. R., Rudman, L. A., Farnham, S. D., Nosek, B. A. & Mellott, D. S. (2002). A unified theory of implicit attitudes, stereotypes, self-esteem, and self-concept. *Psychological Review, 109,* 3–25. doi:10.1037/0033-295X.109.1.3

Greenwald, A. G., McGhee, D. E. & Schwartz, J. K. L. (1998). Measuring individual differences in implicit cognition: The Implicit Association Test. *Journal of Personality and Social Psychology, 74,* 1464–1480. doi:10.1037/0022-3514.74.6.1464

Griffin, B. Q. & Rogers, R. W. (1977). Reducing interracial aggression: Inhibiting effects of victim's suffering and power to retaliate. *Journal of Psychology: Interdisciplinary and Applied, 95,* 151–157. doi:10.1080/00223980.1977.9915872

Hebl, M. R., Foster, J. B., Mannix, L. M. & Dovidio, J. F. (2002). Formal and interpersonal discrimination: A field study of bias toward homosexual applications. *Personality and Social Psychology Bulletin, 28,* 815–825. doi:10.1177/0146167202289010

Heider, F. (1958). *The psychology of interpersonal relations.* New York, NY: Wiley.

Heilman, M. E. & Haynes, M. C. (2008). Subjectivity in the appraisal process: A facilitator of gender bias in work settings. In E. Borgida & S. T. Fiske (Eds.), *Beyond common sense: Psychological science in the courtroom* (pp. 127–155). Oxford, England: Blackwell.

Hewstone, M., Rubin, M. & Willis, H. (2002). Intergroup bias. *Annual Review of Psychology, 53,* 575–604. doi:10.1146/annurev.psych.53.100901.135109

Hodson, G., Dovidio, J. F. & Gaertner, S. L. (2002). Processes in racial discrimination: Differential weighting of conflicting information. *Personality and Social Psychology Bulletin, 28,* 460–471. doi:10.1177/0146167202287004

Jost, J. T. & Banaji, M. R. (1994). The role of stereotyping in system-justification and the production of false consciousness. *British Journal of Social Psychology, 33,* 1–27. doi:10.1111/j.2044-8309.1994.tb01008.x

Jost, J. T., Banaji, M. R. & Nosek, B. A. (2004). A decade of system justification theory: Accumulated evidence of conscious and unconscious bolstering of the status quo. *Political Psychology, 25*, 881–919. doi:10.1111/j.1467-9221.2004.00402.x

Jost, J. T., Pelham, B. W. & Carvallo, M. R. (2002). Non-conscious forms of system justification: Implicit and behavioral preferences for higher status groups. *Journal of Experimental Social Psychology, 38*, 586–602. doi:10.1016/S0022-1031(02)00505-X

King, E. B., Spiro, J. R., Hebl, M. R., Singletary, S. L. & Turner, S. (2006). The stigma of obesity in customer service: A mechanism for remediation and bottom-line consequences of interpersonal discrimination. *Journal of Applied Psychology, 91*, 579–593. doi:10.1037/0021-9010.91.3.579

Krieger, L. H. (1998). Civil rights Perestroika: Intergroup relations after affirmative action. *California Law Review, 86*, 1251–1333. doi:10.2307/3481107

Kunda, Z. & Thagard, P. (1996). Forming impressions from stereotypes, traits and behaviors: A parallel-constraint satisfaction theory. *Psychological Review, 103*, 284–308. doi:10.1037/0033-295X.103.2.284

Lamberth, J. (1994). *Revised statistical analysis of the incidence of police stops and arrests of Black drivers/travelers on the New Jersey Turnpike between Exits or Interchanges 1 and 3 from the years 1988 through 1991.* Unpublished report, Temple University.

LaPiere, R. (1934). Attitudes versus actions. *Social Forces, 13*, 230–237. doi:10.2307/2570339

The Leadership Conference on Civil and Human Rights. (2011). *Restoring a national consensus: The need to end racial profiling in America.* Washington, DC: Author.

Lerner, M. J. (1980). *The belief in a just world: A fundamental delusion.* New York, NY: Plenum. doi:10.1007/978-1-4899-0448-5

Lippa, R. A. (1994). *Introduction to social psychology* (2nd ed.). Pacific Grove, CA: Brooks/Cole.

Locksley, A., Borgida, E., Brekke, N. & Hepburn, C. (1980). Sex stereotypes and social judgment. *Journal of Personality and Social Psychology, 39*, 821–831. doi:10.1037/0022-3514.39.5.821

Lynn, M., Sturman, M., Ganley, C., Adams, E., Douglas, M. & McNeil, J. (2006). *Consumer racial discrimination in tipping: A replication and extension.* Unpublished manuscript, Cornell University.

Lynn, M., Sturman, M., Ganley, C., Adams, E., Douglas, M. & McNeil, J. (2008). Consumer racial discrimination in tipping: A replication and extension. *Journal of Applied Social Psychology, 38*, 1045–1060. doi:10.1111/j.1559-1816.2008.00338.x

McCarthy, J. M., Van Iddekinge, C. H. & Campion, M. A. (2010). Are highly structured job interviews resistant to demographic similarity effects? *Personnel Psychology, 63*, 325–359. doi:10.1111/j.1744-6570.2010.01172.x

McConnell, A. R. & Leibold, J. M. (2001). Relations among the Implicit Association Test, discriminatory behavior, and explicit measures of racial attitudes. *Journal of Experimental Social Psychology, 37*, 435–442. doi:10.1006/jesp.2000.1470

McReynolds v. Merrill Lynch, 672 F.3d 482 (7th Cir. 2012).

Meertens, R. & Pettigrew, T. F. (1997). Is subtle prejudice really prejudice? *Public Opinion Quarterly, 61*, 54–71. doi:10.1086/297786

Minard, R. D. (1952). Race relations in the Pocahontas coal field. *Journal of Social Issues, 8*, 29–44. doi:10.1111/j.1540-4560.1952.tb01592.x

Mummendey, A., Simon, B., Dietze, C., Gmnert, M., Haeger. G., Kessler, S., . . . Schaferhoff, S. (1992). Categorization is not enough: Intergroup discrimination in negative outcome allocation. *Journal of Experimental Social Psychology, 28*, 125–144. doi:10.1016/0022-1031(92)90035-I

Myers, D. G. (1995). *Psychology* (4th ed.). New York: NY Worth.

Myrdal, G. (1944). *An American dilemma.* New York, NY: Harper & Row.

Nelson, T. D. (2002). *The psychology of prejudice.* Boston, MA: Allyn & Bacon.

Nier, J. A. & Gaertner, S. L. (2012a). The challenge of detecting contemporary forms of discrimination. *Journal of Social Issues, 68*, 207–220. doi:10.1111/j.1540-4560.2012.01745.x

Nier, J. A. & Gaertner, S. L. (Eds.). (2012b). The reality of contemporary discrimination in the United States: The consequences of hidden bias in real world contexts [Special issue]. *Journal of Social Issues, 68*(2).

Norton, M. I., Vandello, J. A. & Darley, J. M. (2004). Casuistry and social category bias. *Journal of Personality and Social Psychology, 87*, 817–831. doi:10.1037/0022-3514.87.6.817

Nosek, B. A. & Banaji, M. R. (2001). The go/no-go association task. *Social Cognition, 19*, 625–666. doi:10.1521/soco.19.6.625.20886

Osgood, C. E. & Tannenbaum, P. H. (1955). The principle of congruity in the prediction of attitude change. *Psychological Review, 62*, 42–55. doi:10.1037/h0048153

Pettigrew, T. F. (Ed.). (1975). *Racial discrimination in the United States.* New York, NY: Harper & Row.

Pettigrew, T. F. (1979). Racial change and social policy. *Annals of the American Academy of Political and Social Science, 441*, 114–131. doi:10.1177/000271627944100109

Pettigrew, T. F. (1991). Normative theory in intergroup relations: Explaining both harmony and conflict. *Psychology and Developing Societies, 3*, 3–16. doi:10.1177/097133369100300102

Pettigrew, T. F. (1998). Prejudice and discrimination on the college campus. In J. L. Eberhardt & S. T. Fiske (Eds.), *Confronting racism: The problem and the response* (pp. 263–279). Thousand Oaks, CA: Sage. (Reprinted from the *Higher Education Extension Service Review*, 1994, *6*(1), 1–9).

Pettigrew, T. F. (2011). Toward sustainable psychological interventions for change. *Peace and Conflict: Journal of Peace Psychology, 17*, 179–192. doi:10.1080/10781919.2010.536758

Pettigrew, T. F. & Meertens, R. (1995). Subtle and blatant prejudice in Western Europe. *European Journal of Social Psychology, 25*, 57–75. doi:10.1002/ejsp.2420250106

Pettigrew, T. F. & Taylor, M. C. (2002). Discrimination. In N. J. Smelser & P. B. Baltes (Eds.), *International encyclopedia for the social and behavioral sciences* (pp. 3762–3766). Oxford, England: Pergamon.

Pettigrew, T. F. & Tropp, L. (2006). A meta-analytic test of intergroup contact theory. *Journal of Personality and Social Psychology, 90*, 751–783. doi:10.1037/0022-3514.90.5.751

Pettigrew, T. F. & Tropp, L. R. (2011). *When groups meet: The dynamics of intergroup contact.* New York, NY: Psychology Press.

Platow, M. J. & Van Knippenberg, D. (2001). A social identity analysis of leadership endorsement: The effects of leader ingroup prototypicality and distributive intergroup fairness. *Personality and Social Psychology Bulletin, 27*, 1508–1519. doi:10.1177/01461672012711011

Prentice-Dunn, S. & Rogers, R. W. (1980). Effects of deindividuating situational cues and aggressive models on subjective deindividuation and aggression. *Journal of Personality and Social Psychology, 39*, 104–113. doi:10.1037/0022-3514.39.1.104

Reitzes, D. C. (1953). The role of organizational structures: Union versus neighborhood in a tension situation. *Journal of Social Issues, 9*, 37–44. doi:10.1111/j.1540-4560.1953.tb01259.x

Reskin, B. F. (1998). *The realities of affirmative action in employment.* Washington, DC: American Sociological Association.

Riordan, C. M. (2000). Relational demography within groups: Past developments, contradictions, and new directions. In G. R. Ferris (Ed.), *Research in personnel and human resources management* (Vol. 19, pp. 131–173). Greenwich, CT: JAI Press.

Rivera, L. A. (2012). Hiring as cultural matching: The case of elite professional service firms. *American Sociological Review, 77*, 999–1022. doi:10.1177/0003122412463213

Rogers, R. W. & Prentice-Dunn, S. (1981). Deindividuation and anger-mediated interracial aggression: Unmasking regressive racism. *Journal of Personality and Social Psychology, 41*, 63–73. doi:10.1037/0022-3514.41.1.63

Rokeach, M. (Ed.). (1960). *The open and closed mind*. New York, NY: Basic Books.

Rokeach, M. & Mezei, L. (1966). Race and shared belief as factors in social choice. *Science, 151*, 167–172. doi:10.1126/science.151.3707.167

Ryan, W. (1976). *Blaming the victim*. New York, NY: Vintage Books.

Sacco, J. M., Scheu, C. R., Ryan, A. M. & Schmitt, N. (2003). An investigation of race and sex similarity effects in interviews: A multilevel approach to relational demography. *Journal of Applied Psychology, 88*, 852–865. doi:10.1037/0021-9010.88.5.852

Saucier, D. A., Miller, C. T. & Doucet, N. (2005). Differences in helping Whites and Blacks: A meta-analysis. *Personality and Social Psychology Review, 9*, 2–16. doi:10.1207/s15327957pspr0901_1

Schuman, H., Steeh, C., Bobo, L. & Krysan, M. (1997). *Racial attitudes in America*. Cambridge, MA: Harvard University Press.

Secord, P. F. & Backman, C. W. (1964). *Social psychology*. New York, NY: McGraw-Hill.

Simpson, G. E. & Yinger, J. M. (1985). *Racial and cultural minorities* (5th ed.). New York, NY: Plenum.

Smith, E. R. (1993). Social identity and social emotions: Toward new conceptions of prejudice. In D. M. Mackie & D. L. Hamilton (Eds.), *Affect, cognition, and stereotyping* (pp. 297–315). San Diego, CA: Academic Press.

Smith, E. R. & Mackie, D. M. (1995). *Social psychology*. New York, NY: Worth.

Smith, E. R. & Mackie, D. M. (2005). Aggression, hatred, and other emotions. In J. F. Dovidio, P. Glick & L. A. Rudman (Eds.), *On the nature of prejudice: Fifty years after Allport* (pp. 361–376). Malden, MA: Blackwell.

Smith, H. J., Pettigrew, T. F., Pippin, G. & Bialosiewicz, S. (2012). Relative deprivation: A theoretical and meta-analytic critique. *Personality and Social Psychology Review, 16*(3), 203–232. doi:10.1177/1088868311430825

Spitzer, E. (1999). *The New York City Police Department's "stop & frisk" practices: A report to the people of the State of New York from the Office of the Attorney General*. New York, NY: New York State Attorney General's Office, Civil Rights Bureau.

Sriram, N. & Greenwald, A. G. (2009). The Brief Implicit Association Test. *Experimental Psychology, 56*, 283–294. doi:10.1027/1618-3169.56.4.283

Stangor, C. (Ed.). (2000). *Stereotypes and prejudice: Essential readings*. Philadelphia, PA: Psychology Press.

Stein, D. D., Hardyck, J. A. & Smith, M. B. (1965). Race and belief: An open and shut case. *Journal of Personality and Social Psychology, 1*, 281–289. doi:10.1037/h0021870

Stephan, W. G. & Stephan, C. W. (1993). *Improving intergroup relations*. Thousand Oaks, CA: Sage.

Tajfel, H. (1970). Experiments in intergroup discrimination. *Scientific American, 223*, 96–102. doi:10.1038/scientificamerican1170-96

Tajfel, H. (1982). Social psychology of intergroup relations. *Annual Review of Psychology, 33*, 1–39. doi:10.1146/annurev.ps.33.020182.000245

Tajfel, H., Billig, M. G., Bundy, R. P. & Flament, C. (1971). Social categorization and intergroup behaviour. *European Journal of Social Psychology, 1*, 149–178. doi:10.1002/ejsp.2420010202

Tajfel, H. & Turner, J. C. (1979). An integrative theory of intergroup conflict. In S.Worchel & W. G.Austin (Eds.), *The social psychology of intergroup relations* (pp. 33–47). Monterey, CA: Brooks/Cole.

Taylor, S. E., Peplau, L. A. & Sears, D. O. (1994). *Social psychology* (8th ed.). Englewood Cliffs, NJ: Prentice Hall.

Terry, D. J. & O'Brien, A. T. (2001). Status, legitimacy, and ingroup bias in the context of an organizational merger. *Group Processes & Intergroup Relations, 4*, 271–289. doi:10.1177/1368430201004003007

Thurstone, L. L. (1928). An experimental study of nationality preferences. *Journal of General Psychology, 1*, 405–425. doi:10.1080/00221309.1928.9918018

Triandis, H. C. (1961). A note on Rokeach's theory of prejudice. *The Journal of Abnormal and Social Psychology, 62*, 184–186. doi:10.1037/h0043114

Triandis, H. C. & Davis, E. E. (1965). Race and belief as determinants of behavioral intentions. *Journal of Personality and Social Psychology, 2*, 715–725. doi:10.1037/h0022719

Turner, M. A., Ross, S. L., Galster, G. C. & Yinger, J. (2002). *Discrimination in metropolitan housing markets: National results from Phase I HDS 2000.* Washington, DC: Urban Institute. doi:10.1037/e717912011-001

Uhlmann, E. L. & Cohen, G. L. (2005). Constructed criteria: Redefining merit to justify discrimination. *Psychological Science, 16*, 474–480. doi:10.1111/j.0956-7976.2005.01559.x

Verniero, P. & Zoubek, P. H. (1999). *Interim report of the state police review team regarding allegations of racial profiling.* Paper presented at the Race, Police and the Community Conference sponsored by the Criminal Justice Institute of Harvard Law School, December 7–9, 2000, Cambridge, MA. Retrieved from http://www.state.nj.us/lps/intm_419.pdf

Wagner, U., Christ, O. & Pettigrew, T. F. (2008). Prejudice and group-related behavior in Germany. *Journal of Social Issues, 64*(2), 403–416. doi:10.1111/j.1540-4560.2008.00568.x

Weiss, A. & Rosenbaum, D. P. (2009). *Illinois traffic stops statistics study: 2008 annual report.* Chicago, IL: Center for Research in Law and Justice, University of Illinois. Retrieved from http://www.dot.state.il.us/travelstats/ITSS2008 Annual Report.pdf

Wilson, L. & Rogers, R. W. (1975). The fire this time: Effects of race of target, insult, and potential retaliation on Black aggression. *Journal of Personality and Social Psychology, 1975, 32*, 857–864. doi:10.1037/0022-3514.32.5.857

Worchel, S., Cooper, J. & Goethals, G. R. (1988). *Understanding social psychology.* Chicago, IL: Dorsey.

Yzerbyt, V. Y., Schadron, G., Leyens, J.-P. & Rocher, S. (1994). Social judgeability: The impact of meta-informational cues on the use of stereotypes. *Journal of Personality and Social Psychology, 66*, 48–55. doi:10.1037/0022-3514.66.1.48

Ziegler, S. A., Kirby, T. A., Xu, K. & Greenwald, A. G. (2013, January). *Implicit race attitudes predict vote in the 2012 presidential election.* Poster presented at the Political Psychology Preconference of the Annual Meeting of the Society for Personality and Social Psychology, New Orleans, LA.

APPENDIX A
Definitions of Prejudice

Citation	Definition
Dollard, Doob, Miller, Mowrer & Sears (1939, p. 152)	"Race prejudice, according to the present view, is a form of aggression"
Allport (1954, p. 9)	"an antipathy based upon a faulty and inflexible generalization"
Secord & Backman (1964, p. 413)	"an attitude that predisposes a person to think, perceive, feel, and act in favorable or unfavorable ways toward a group or its individual members"
Baron & Byrne (1974, p. 218)	"Prejudice refers to a special type of attitude—generally a negative one—toward the members of some social group"

(continued)

Citation	Definition
Tajfel (1982, p. 3)	"a favorable or unfavorable predisposition toward any member of the category in question"
Simpson & Yinger (1985, p. 21)	"an emotional, rigid attitude (a predisposition to respond to a certain stimulus in a certain way) toward a group of people"
Aronson (1988, p. 231)	"a hostile or negative attitude toward a distinguishable group based on generalizations derived from faulty or incomplete information"
Worchel, Cooper & Goethals (1988, p. 49)	"an unjustified negative attitude towards an individual based solely on that individual's membership in a group"
Baron & Graziano (1991, p. 526)	"negative attitudes toward members of social groups"
Brigham (1991, p. 459)	"a negative attitude that is considered to be unjustified by an observer"
E. R. Smith (1993, p. 304)	"a social emotion experienced with respect to one's social identity as a group member, with an outgroup as a target"
Stephan & Stephan (1993, p. 125)	"negative evaluations of social groups"
Brewer & Crano (1994, p. 464)	"negative affect directed toward all members of a specific social category"
Taylor, Peplau & Sears (1994, p. 216)	"negative evaluations toward the outgroup"
Lippa (1994, p. 272)	"negative attitude that is based on another person's membership in a social group"
Brown (1995, p. 8)	"the holding of derogatory social attitudes or cognitive beliefs, the expression of negative affect or the display of hostile or discriminatory behaviour towards members of a group on account of their membership of that group"
Myers (1995, p. G–10)	"an unjustifiable (and usually negative) attitude toward a group and its members [involving] stereotyped beliefs, negative feelings, and a predisposition to discriminatory action"
E. R. Smith & Mackie (1995, p. 170)	"a positive or negative evaluation of a social group and its members"
Feagin & Feagin (1996, p. 504)	"an antipathy, felt or expressed, based upon a faulty generalization and directed toward a group as a whole or toward individual members of a group"
Franzoi (1996, p. 386)	"a negative attitude directed toward people simply because they are members of a specific social group"

Citation	Definition
Stangor (2000, p. 1)	"a negative feeling or attitude toward the members of a group"
Nelson (2002, p. 11)	"an evaluation (positive or negative) [and] a biased perception of a group . . . ; based on the real or imagined characteristics of the group"
Eagly & Dickman (2005, p. 31)	"the relative devaluation in specific role contexts of members of a particular group compared to equivalent members of other groups"
Aronson, Wilson & Akert (2012, p. 362)	"a hostile or negative attitude toward people in a distinguishable group, based solely on their membership in that group"

Professor Greenwald Interview

PETER KOELLING: Professor Greenwald would you start out by giving a little bit of your background and how you became interested in this field, in this question of implicit bias?

TONY GREENWALD: I was trained as a social psychologist. I got my Ph.D. at Harvard quite a while ago. At Harvard, I worked with Gordon Allport, who was one of the major figures in the study of prejudice. I wasn't interested in that at the time, I was interested in another of his topics, the study of attitudes, a traditional topic of social psychology that was also one of his central interests.

I studied mainly attitudes and persuasion until the 1980s, when my work both in social and cognitive psychology shifted towards trying to understand processes that happen, as were then called, "automatically," which was just a way of referring to unconscious processes. This was at a time when the word "unconscious" was informally taboo in academic psychology. That eventually led me to where I am now, focusing on implicit bias. When I created the Implicit Association Test in the mid-1990s, it was clear not only to me but to the collaborators I persuaded to work with me, Mahzarin Banaji who is now at Harvard and Brian Nosek who is now at University of Virginia—persuaded them to help develop the Implicit Association Test to study stereotypes and attitudes, and we soon started calling what the IAT measured "implicit" attitudes and "implicit" stereotypes. The rest is increasingly public knowledge because that work received a lot of public attention, as well as the attention of other researchers.

PETER KOELLING: Yes, it only took two decades for it to make its way to the courts because we are a conservative institution after all.

Tony Greenwald: Well, you're faster than some other institutions, I must say.

Peter Koelling: What is implicit bias? How would you define it?

Tony Greenwald: There's a nice definition of implicit bias that was stated by Jerry Kang who's a law professor at UCLA and also a very sharp social psychologist even though he never formally studied psychology. Jerry defines implicit bias as attitudes and stereotypes that operate automatically and influence our decision making and judgment without our even realizing that influence. Implicit bias is a generic name that encompasses attitudes and stereotypes.

Peter Koelling: The key to it is that we're not aware of these influences, correct?

Tony Greenwald: Yes, and the relationship between the word "implicit" and the word unconscious is interesting. I resist talking about implicit biases as unconscious biases mainly because 'unconscious' would imply that people are not aware what they are doing when implicit biases are operating. People are acting consciously and they are experiencing the biases. What makes biases implicit is that the influence of past learning shaping their judgments and perceptions is not recognized. People often have the impression that they are operating objectively and rationally, rather than on the basis of attitudes and stereotypes.

Peter Koelling: That is the ideal that most judges strive for; they want to think that they are making rational and objective decisions without bias. Even if they are striving for that, can they be influenced by these biases?

Tony Greenwald: They can be influenced by a wide variety of influences including biases that are triggered by demographic characteristics of the people that that they deal with. These are biases based on race, ethnicity, age, socioeconomic status, disability status, gender, and combinations of those things. One cannot hope to understand how these biases operate automatically. Most people are not even aware that these implicit attitudes and stereotypes are present in their minds. It wasn't until the Implicit Association Test came along to provide a new window into the mind that many became aware of possessing hidden biases that could affect judgment in ways that they could not previously recognize.

Peter Koelling: When you took the IAT yourself, were you surprised by some of the results?

Tony Greenwald: Yes, very definitely. The first version of the IAT that I took was one in which the concepts being compared were flowers and insects, and they were being associated with pleasant and unpleasant. I was not surprised that I showed an association more of flowers with pleasant than insects with pleasant, but I was actually surprised by the magnitude with which it was indicated by the speed differences I had in the two parts of the IAT.

And that encouraged me to try it with other things. It was just a matter of months after creating the first version of the IAT with flowers and insects that I tried it with first names that were recognizably categorizable as African-American or European by almost all Americans and found that it produced in me a rather large effect. It showed that I had a much easier time associating White American names with positive valence or pleasantness than I did for Black Americans. This is what we now refer to as, automatic white preference. It was a large one and I was very surprised to find it in myself. It was something I did not know I had. I was both pleasantly surprised and unpleasantly surprised at the same time. Unpleasantly surprised to discover that I had it at all, pleasantly surprised that the procedure, the IAT, picked this up so strongly. It was amazing and it was what encouraged me to prompt my colleagues to start doing research. Fortunately, Mahzarin Banaji and Brian Nosek picked it up right away and helped with the research that would tell us how the test was working and how best to use it.

PETER KOELLING: Are there other kind of forms of bias that we are unaware of that might influence the decision making process in the courts that we should be concerned about?

TONY GREENWALD: Yes, there are. For example, in the area of criminal justice the first IAT measured was a race attitude IAT involving associating racial groups with pleasant and unpleasant. One that came along not too much longer after that was one that associated the racial groups with weapons versus harmless objects, which was of interest for obvious reasons. That turned out to be quite a strong stereotype.

Another one that was of great interest was one that associated male and female gender with career versus family. This turned out to be very important in the workplace because stereotypes that associate women with family and home rather than career and office are often influences that operate outside awareness to influence managerial judgments about what kind of work should be assigned to women and what their potential is for leadership. There is also a stereotype that associates male gender more than female gender with leadership. All these things have IAT measures now.

PETER KOELLING: What is in-group associations or in group favoritism?

TONY GREENWALD: In-group favoritism is the term that is used in associating in-group with pleasantness more than out-group and so these are associations that can be measured with the IAT. In-group favoritism is plausibly also an implicit bias, but there hasn't yet been much research specifically investigating that. But it seems very likely that in-group favoritism influences judgments and decisions outside our awareness

PETER KOELLING: Within the criminal justice system, there are a number of discretionary decisions that are made by different entities, starting with the police, then with the district attorney or the prosecutor with regard to the decision of whether or not to prosecute. The public defender makes decisions in terms of the vigorousness with which they want to defend. In court, you have the judge and you might have a jury. It seems that all of these actors can be impacted by their own biases. Does that have a cumulative effect on the impact?

TONY GREENWALD: Yes, it certainly does have a cumulative effect. The criminal justice system and most court systems, perhaps less in the civil system than in criminal justice, is a long series of opportunities for this. Actors at various levels, ranging from the police interacting with citizens at the front end—and perhaps even earlier authorities in schools dealing with young children—and going all the way through to the various stages of court processing, including bail setting, determining guilt or innocence, sentencing and then later possibilities of probation and parole by lawyers, by judges, by juries, and by other court administrators all cumulate. I don't even know how to count the number of cumulative steps. At each, it is possible for some level of bias to enter, possibly implicit bias, possibly biases that are built into the procedures of the institutions. Some of these biases are better called institutional biases and, although they don't operate in the same way that implicit biases do, they operate with similar effect to produce disparities, and these all cumulate. It seems a certainty that these biases cumulate to produce huge disparities of in rates of incarceration for African-Americans relative to Whites.

PETER KOELLING: The focus of this book is on what judges can do. Can you train yourself to eliminate your implicit biases?

TONY GREENWALD: There is widespread belief—unfortunately it is not scientifically based belief—that by thinking carefully, by acting slowly, by trying to be wise and to be objective, and to be deliberate, one can remove implicit biases from the realm of operation. There are two reasons to question that. One is that there's no evidence for it. The other is that the theoretical understanding of these processes suggest that it should not be possible because it requires that one understands how implicit biases are working, what they are, and what effect they have on judgment. These biases by definition operate outside of awareness. Knowing intellectually that such bias exists, knowing that one may possess such biases, does not tell you how and when they are working, and what they are doing. There is no satisfactory basis for believing that conscious thought, or mindfulness as it is sometimes called, can overcome their effect. It is an idea that has been around for quite a while. It is interesting that there is no evidence now for it because one would think, with an idea that is so interesting and so compelling as a way to control implicit bias, that people would be trying to demonstrate that yes, mindfulness helps. But, at this point, that research evidence doesn't exist.

I have learned, functioning as a scientist for quite a few decades, that when an interesting question has been asked and has been around for a long time, and an answer doesn't exist to it, that doesn't mean that no one has studied it. It means that people who have studied it have not found answers. And I think that is the circumstance here.

PETER KOELLING: Are there steps that judges can take though that can have an impact? Or are we just kind of doomed to our system?

TONY GREENWALD: I advise, not just in courts but in almost any circumstances, such as my own university, anytime where we are talking about judgments made, the hiring or promotion process in corporations or healthcare decisions in hospitals, I advise looking at the data, discovering whether decisions that are being made by key actors actually produce racial disparities. So, in answer to the question about judges, it would be the same as for others. It would be to keep track of the data.

Are your decisions producing racial disparities? If you are a judge in a court that is making bail decisions, are you assigning bail equally to different racial socioeconomic groups strictly in terms of the specifics of the offence? It is not always easy to look at those data. I know that courts don't always keep records in a form that makes it easy to do this.

Judges can play a role in seeing that it does get done; keep the data on these things in a form in which these questions can be answered. Is race and ethnicity recorded for all persons coming before the court? Are the judgments recorded in a way that will allow them to be related to race and ethnicity and socioeconomic status so it can be observed whether there are disparities? There are probably some high-volume courts in which individual judges are producing enough data so that they can actually have the potential to do this on their own. That would be a good place to start, just as I recommended to the police departments with the traffic stops and pedestrian stops that they are doing; these are high-volume things that are being done many times by more police officers. These are the easiest pieces of data to keep track of to look at race disparities.

It is interesting that a lot of police departments have these data and have never analyzed them for race disparities. When they have been analyzed for race disparities, it is generally found that in most large cities that Blacks and Hispanics are being stopped as pedestrians and drivers at a higher rate than others. They are being searched at a higher rate than others, and they are being found to have contraband, drugs or weapons, at a lower rate than others, particularly whites. These traffic-stop or pedestrian-stop data, like in the New York stop-and-frisk study, generally show disparities—racial and ethnic disparities. They indicate that Whites are not being stopped and searched at a comparable rate to blacks and Hispanics, which is why when Whites show up—when they are stopped, they are found more often to have contraband.

PETER KOELLING: If a judge is setting bail, and we've done the data analysis and we know that we are setting higher bail for African-Americans, for example, can we consciously apply that information to make sure that we're trying to keep it equitable?

TONY GREENWALD: Yes, there are two possibilities for applying the information. One is if judges keep these data on themselves—that is not required, although there is absolutely nothing wrong with it. And I think if I were a judge, I would probably want to see these data for myself. But the courts should have a system for being able to track this. I am virtually certain that if these data were being tracked, one would find that it is not a uniform phenomenon across all courts and all judges, but actually you'll find some types of courts, some types of decisions in which this is happening more than others. Until you have done that kind of data analysis, you may be aware that an overall disparity exists, but you may not be able to locate where it is happening in the system. The data analysis is really necessary to locate where it is happening in the overall system. If enough data are tracked, these disparities will be identified and located at multiple points in the system.

PETER KOELLING: Recently the ABA modified its principles for juries and jury trials and added a component that said that the court should instruct the jury on implicit bias and how such bias may impact the decision making process without the juror being aware of it. How can judges do that? Would it be an effective tool?

TONY GREENWALD: Yes, the principle I think is a great one. I think the jury situation is an excellent opportunity to try to do something like this. I've been interested for a few years now in the possibility of developing implicit bias jury instructions, and I know there are several judges who have been trying to do this. The problem is that we don't know what form of implicit bias instruction will achieve the desired goal.

The first few efforts to produce such instructions are probably not successes mainly because they make the assumption—which I mentioned earlier—they make the assumption that understanding the concept of implicit bias, knowing that one may have implicit biases that can produce disparities, and wanting not to produce those disparities, is sufficient to undo the effects of implicit biases. But there is no indication that this is an effective method. I don't want to abandon the idea of judges finding ways to instruct juries, but the effort to do that should make more use of social psychological understanding of how juries operate, how the mind operates and what kinds of things can control implicit biases. I have ideas about this but they are far from being tested, so I am not ready to state them publicly.

PETER KOELLING: I think that we would like them as soon as possible. The people reading this book are going to be those that are interested in creating these kinds of instructions.

TONY GREENWALD: I can tell you that I see a key part of the problem is the notion of accountability of jurors. By tradition we have jury systems in which jurors have large amounts of discretion. They are entitled to form their opinion of the case and vote for a verdict without having to convince others that they are perfectly rational in doing this. That sounds very good in principle. On the other hand, it is a characteristic of the jury system that makes it difficult to control implicit biases because discretion in making any judgment is actually the component of a decision process that opens the door for biases to enter. Discretion can be used in any number of ways; the problem is that when implicit biases exist, one of the ways that discretion is going to operate is allowing implicit biases to enter unrecognized into influencing decisions. Merely instructing jurors that this is possible doesn't actually allow them to recognize when this might be happening.

PETER KOELLING: One of the issues that we struggle with is the use of smaller juries, just as a cost savings issue. With a smaller jury there is a lower probability of having a more representative group of citizens. Do you think having a broader representation, people from different communities, helps in the communal decision-making process?

TONY GREENWALD: There has been some research on this. The most active researcher is Samuel Sommers at Tufts University. He has been favoring a principle which I think I can agree with, and he's been fairly persuasive about it, that diverse juries may do a better job of looking at the evidence from all angles.

An interesting question is, does this mean that during the jury deliberation process jurors are actually considering more and different things and the diverse jurors are actually bringing up different things, or does it mean—and this is where my preferences lean, and I know Sam Sommers thinks this is a possibility also—that when the jury is diverse, the jurors enter the jury situation with a more open mind as to what range of opposing opinions they may be exposed to. That in itself, independent of arguments that are actually made during the deliberation, can be a useful force. Diversity in juries is almost certainly a good thing, even if we don't understand entirely how it operates.

This also goes back to a question that we were talking about earlier, which is what can judges do, what can courts do in terms of data tracking? One thing is to keep track of peremptory jury challenges because when this has been looked at by legal scholars, it is often found that in cases in which race may be an issue that prosecutors use peremptory challenges to dismiss African-American jurors from the pool. That is a perfect example of data that can be useful in tracking where disparities are occurring. It may turn out that some prosecutorial offices are using far more peremptory challenges against African-Americans relative to the jury population than others are. This would not be difficult to track, but I do know that in some jurisdictions, the race of jurors who are dismissed from the jury pool is not tracked.

PETER KOELLING: I think it is important to understand the concept that in any individual case the decision to dismiss a juror may be made for cause. But if we can look at this at a macro level or a wider level that is where you are going to see these patterns and how bias influences the use of preemptory challenges from a systemic stand point.

TONY GREENWALD: That is a very good point. The larger the aggregate you can look at, the more likely you are to notice disparities that may not be huge in individual courts or by individual judges. Even though they might not even be noticeable in individual judges, when they are aggregated they can show up statistically in a way that cannot be dismissed. Standing back to look at the big picture for things like this requires keeping track of data and it is much to be recommended.

PETER KOELLING: Courts have been slow to develop and use performance measures based on their own effectiveness and efficiency. So, I can see why we are slow to develop these measures that might indicate our less than stellar processes. Keeping these records requires two kinds of things that many court systems don't have. One is a system for actually recording the data that keeps the data available in a useable form. The other is expertise in data analysis, which may not be present in most court systems. Is there any advice you can give to judges as they go through their daily work, how to be better at what they do?

TONY GREENWALD: I have two main categories of recommendations. One is a don't, a big don't, don't assume that your good intentions, your understanding of the concept of implicit bias and your desire to shed the effect of implicit bias from decisions are anywhere near enough to actually achieve that effect. So, that is the don't.

The do, is find ways to keep track of operations, to make it easy to find where in the system disparities are occurring. In a complex system where disparities are occurring in multiple places and they accumulate to huge impact. It is really important not only to know that you've got a disparity that shows up in the end of the line such as in incarceration disparity, but to know at which stage the greatest contributions to those disparities are being made.

I guess there is just one more message. These changes, such as the development of a jury instruction, are things that really have to be initiated or supported at the very top level of any system. In a city, the mayor should be behind these things. In a state, the attorney general should be behind these things. The highest levels in the courts, the state supreme court, should be behind these things and taking the initiative on the assumption that, while it is fine for other judges to do things and try out things, institutional changes that are going to affect the system, really have to motivated from the top. If the people at the top are not motivated to make changes, it will be very difficult for the system to change.

PETER KOELLING: Thank you so much for your time. Thank you for contributing the article as well.

About the Authors

Anthony G. Greenwald was elected a member of the American Academy of Arts and Sciences in 2007. He is presently Professor of Psychology at University of Washington (1986–present) and was previously at Ohio State University (1965–86). Greenwald received his B.A. from Yale (1959) and Ph.D. from Harvard (1963). He has published over 180 scholarly articles, served on editorial boards of 13 psychological journals, and received three major research career awards—the Donald T. Campbell Award from the Society of Personality and Social Psychology (1995), the Distinguished Scientist Award from the Society of Experimental Social Psychology (2006), and the William James Fellow Lifetime Achievement Award from the Association for Psychological Science (2013). In 1995 Greenwald invented the Implicit Association Test (IAT), which rapidly became a standard for assessing individual differences in implicit social cognition. The IAT method has provided the basis for three patent applications and numerous applications in clinical psychology, education, marketing, and diversity management.

Thomas Pettigrew is Professor Emeritus of Social Psychology at the University of California, Santa Cruz. Professor Pettigrew earned his Ph.D. in Social Psychology from Harvard University. With more than 450 publications, Professor Pettigrew has been at the forefront of research on racial prejudice for a half-century.

Endnotes

1. Anthony G. Greenwald & Thomas F. Pettigrew, *With Malice Toward None and Charity for Some: Ingroup Favoritism Enables Discrimination*, 69 Am. Psychologist 669 (2014).
2. Retrieved from http://www.oxfordreference.com.prxy4.ursus.maine.edu.
3. At about the same time that it began to appear in the psychological literature, the proposition that workplace discrimination could occur importantly as ingroup favoritism also began to appear in legal scholarship (see Krieger, 1998).
4. Note that the researchers assumed that "Americans" would be interpreted as White Americans. This is presumably a valid assumption, but we are not aware of direct empirical tests.
5. A necessary qualification in regard to ingroup favoritism follows from audit studies' lack of systematic report of effects due to variations in race or ethnicity of real estate agents and hiring managers. Although it is a near certainty that the majority of agents and managers in all of the published audit studies were White, it remains unknown whether ingroup favoritism occurred equally across variations in agent or manager race and ethnicity. This same qualification applies to the following section on policing.
6. Norton et al.'s (2004) Studies 3–6 found that the majority of simulated college admissions choices by their (mostly White) subjects favored Black over White applicants. These decisions were clearly not ingroup-favoring. Nevertheless, Norton et al.'s findings agreed with the other studies in this collection by revealing that subjects were highly flexible in their weighting of qualification criteria, with this flexibility serving to justify outgroup-favoring biased decisions based on knowledge of applicants' racial categories. In nonlaboratory settings in which those who make judgments do not expect that their judgments will be monitored by others, illusory individuated judgments may more consistently favor ingroup members.
7. Although the Black subjects of the Wilson and Rogers (1975) experiment chose higher intensity shocks to administer to (outgroup) White than to (ingroup) Black confederates, the product of intensity and shock duration measures revealed that they had chosen somewhat greater shocks for Black (ingroup) confederates.

8. The difficulty of characterizing nonverbal intergroup behavior unambiguously as positive or negative can be seen in some innovative studies in field settings that have demonstrated discrimination based on sexual orientation (Hebl, Foster, Mannix & Dovidio, 2002) and obesity (King, Spiro, Hebl, Singletary & Turner, 2006).

9. In the context of assessing favoritism, behavioral intention measures compare interestingly with overt behavior measures. Crosby et al. (1980) found that outgroup-directed helping was greater when White potential helpers were in face-to-face interactions with Black potential help recipients, compared to "remote" situations in which the two were not face to face. Whites' opposition to helping minorities, expressed on surveys, may be an analog of the low rate of helping found in the remote conditions of the unobtrusive-measure-helping studies reviewed by Crosby et al.

10. Annual counts of multiple categories of hate crimes for 1996 through 2011 are available at http://www.fbi.gov.prxy4.ursus.maine.edu/about-us/cjis/ucr/hate-crime.

11. The contrast of two federal court opinions in 1993 and 2012 signals a change of direction regarding ingroup favoritism. The 1993 opinion, in the case of *E.E.O.C. v. Consolidated Service Systems*, declared that if a hiring policy "produce[s] a work force whose racial or religious or ethnic or nation-origin or gender composition pleases the employer, this is not intentional discrimination. The motive is not a discriminatory one." The 2012 opinion, in the case of *McReynolds v. Merrill Lynch*, concluded that the defendant company might have discriminated by allowing a form of company-wide ingroup favoritism involving teams of brokers who could choose to exclude African-American brokers: "The teams . . . ; are little fraternities [in which] the brokers choose as team members people who are like themselves. If they are white, they, or some of them anyway, are more comfortable teaming with other white brokers." Especially noteworthy regarding the contrast between these two opinions is that they were written by the same federal judge.

12. See Chapter 11 of Pettigrew and Tropp (2011) for an additional view on the conclusions reached by Dixon et al. (2012).

Chapter 8

Hearing All Voices
Challenges of Cultural Competence and Opportunities for Community Outreach

Judge Karen Arnold-Burger, Jean Mavrelis,
and Phyllis B. Pickett

Chapter Contents

Chapter Highlights

- Social and cultural underpinnings of unconscious bias are described.

- Public perceptions of justice are linked to levels of confidence in
  the judicial system. Based on several national surveys, a majority of
  Americans believe that the justice system treats minority groups and
  the poor less favorably than Whites and other groups.

- Deeply learned cultural norms and biases are programmed within
  the early years of life. Each individual implicitly carries with him or
  her expectations on how a social transaction or encounter is likely to

unfold. Learned norms and biases influence how individuals interpret and evaluate their own behaviors and the behaviors of others. A
judge is no different than the average person when it comes to these
learned cultural norms and biases.

- The recognition that others do not view the world the same way, do
  not have the same experiences that the judge has had, and will not
  necessarily behave as the judge might under identical circumstances
  will help a judge to recognize cultural differences and implicit biases,
  thereby increasing a judge's cultural competence.

- Cultural competence offers a skill set that will aid judges in their
  efforts to improve perceptions of justice. By sponsoring judicial outreach programs and events, judges can encourage awareness, interaction, and communication in a manner that strengthens the justice
  system, with the potential to improve perceptions of justice.

- Training for judges and court staff can make a difference, but to
  move individuals from an ethnocentric stage of multicultural development to an ethnorelative stage of appreciating and accepting our
  differences is not a quick process accomplished fully by a two-hour
  diversity training program. The training must be long enough to
  move people through their own stages of cultural understanding.

Introduction

> We are a country bound together by our magnificent Constitution. It
> guarantees the promise that our country will be a country based on
> the rule of law. . . . There is not one law for one color or another.
> There is not one law for rich and a different one for poor. There is
> only one law. And, Judge, I remember so well when you sat in my
> office, and you said that "ultimately and completely" a judge has to
> follow the law, no matter what their upbringing has been. That is the
> kind of fair and impartial judging the American people expect.[1]

Judges strive to hold fair hearings and to analyze evidence and arguments logically and impartially before rendering well-considered opinions. Like everyone
else, a judge's world view, personal experiences, and cultural background come
into play when a judge interprets the words and actions of others. Nor does
the deliberative process occur in a vacuum. The public's interactions with the
justice system will shape a community's perceptions of justice.

In order to "hear all voices" and move toward true understanding, it is
important to appreciate how the public currently views our justice system, how

judges may have contributed to that perception, and what actions judges can take to change those perceptions. This chapter employs a four-part approach. First, it examines current perceptions as measured in several national studies. Next, it examines how something as simple as cultural communication style may trigger different implicit biases or intuitive reactions in judges and litigants, leaving court users with a sense they were not treated fairly. Becoming aware of these differences may alert judges to think carefully

> Judges strive to hold fair hearings and to analyze evidence and arguments logically and impartially before rendering well-considered opinions. Like everyone else, a judge's world view, personal experiences, and cultural background come into play when a judge interprets the words and actions of others. Nor does the deliberative process occur in a vacuum. The public's interactions with the justice system will shape a community's perceptions of justice.

(or "slowly," as described by Daniel Kahneman in his book *Thinking, Fast and Slow*)[2] about the behavior they are observing or the communicative interaction in which they are involved during any one proceeding. Third, this chapter provides proactive suggestions for judicial outreach to assist judges in planning events that open local dialogues about community perceptions of justice. Only when such discussions take place can we hope to improve the perceptions of fairness. Finally, an approach to training is presented that has proven successful in effecting long-term changes in behavior.

I. Perceptions of the Justice System

When an individual goes before a judge, that person brings along his or her existing perceptions of the justice system. Over the years, several attempts have been made to gauge these perceptions and determine how the public as a whole views the American justice system. In preparation for a national symposium in 1999, the American Bar Association (ABA) released a report titled "Perceptions of the U.S. Justice System," which was a comprehensive nationwide survey of the general public's views of the legal system.[3] The survey was conducted by an independent research firm using telephone interviews. Consisting of 1,000 respondents ages 18 and over, the sample closely matched the profile

> When an individual goes before a judge, that person brings along his or her existing perceptions of the justice system.

of the U.S. population and was tantamount to a "report card for justice" in America.[4] Eighty percent of the respondents reported that they considered the American justice system the best in the world. But two other key findings from this survey are important to our understanding of implicit bias in the court system.

Those individuals with more knowledge of the justice system had more confidence in it. Likewise, and unsurprisingly, those who had more positive court experiences tended to have more confidence in the system, and males, people of higher income, and people with a higher level of education were more confident than other demographic groups were. Substantial numbers of people believed that the justice system treats different groups of people unequally. Only about half of the respondents agreed that men and women were treated equally, and even fewer believed that treatment was equal among differing racial and ethnic groups or between different socioeconomic classes.[5] In fact, 47 percent of respondents disagreed with the statement "In most cases the courts treat all ethnic and racial groups the same," while only 39 percent of respondents agreed.[6]

The National Center for State Courts (NCSC) conducted a more extensive survey in 2003 called "Perceptions of the Courts in Your Community: The Influence of Experience, Race, and Ethnicity."[7] That study found that 62 percent of White respondents who had experience in the court system believed that African-Americans are sometimes, often, or always treated worse than other groups are. Eighty-seven percent of African-Americans and seventy-two percent of Latinos surveyed agreed. As for Latinos' treatment by the court, 60 percent of Whites who had experience in the court system believed that Latinos are sometimes, often, or always treated worse by the court than other groups. Eighty-four percent of African-Americans and seventy percent of Latinos with experience in the courts agreed.[8] Similar results were found among each of the three groups when the question related to whether non-English speakers were treated worse than other groups. There was also broad agreement among each group when the question was whether people with low incomes are treated worse.[9] Finally, the three factors across racial lines that impacted how favorably a person viewed his or her local court were fairness of the outcome, fairness of the procedures, and efficiency.[10] The report concluded with a call to counter negative images by providing more education and collaboration between the court and community.[11]

Another source of information about perceptions of the justice system and implicit bias is the Perceptions of Justice (POJ) project conducted by the Lawyers Conference of the ABA Judicial Division. This POJ initiative started in 2008 under the leadership of Judge Michael B. Hyman of Chicago. The Lawyers Conference held POJ programs in cities such as Boston, Dallas, Chicago, San Francisco, Atlanta, and New Orleans over a four-year period to offer an open forum for dialogue between judges, lawyers, law enforcement, prosecutors, and local citizens about perceptions of and personal experiences with the justice system. A modified town hall format was used for some of the programs, and expert panels and audience participation were used for others. These were all considered "community voice" events in which participants expressed varied personal perceptions of the justice system in their local communities. Anecdotal accounts enhanced an understanding of how engagement with the legal system forms the basis of community perception. These events both identified areas of general concern and also allowed the participants to develop common goals.[12] Several suggestions on how to improve minority perceptions of the justice system materialized as part of the POJ initiative, with a recurring theme of promoting more discussions and interactions between judges and members of the community.[13]

In 2013, under the leadership of Judge William Missouri of Maryland, the Judicial Division followed up by holding the POJ Summit, a two-day national event in Chicago that focused on perceptions of bias and fairness in the justice system. The POJ Summit started from the premise that both implicit and explicit bias exist in the justice system and that recognizing the realities of such biases lies at the core of improving the impartiality and fairness of the justice system. Fifteen judges were in attendance, including administrative, trial, and appellate judges from both the state and federal levels. Other participants represented judicial organizations, national bar associations, public defenders and prosecutors, public interest organizations, and ABA sections and committees.[14]

Most recently, in 2015, the National Center for State Courts (NCSC) commissioned another survey of public perception of the courts and found that a majority of people still believe that African-Americans and the poor are treated worse than other groups by the justice system.[15] On a positive note, the study found that a majority of people surveyed who had direct experience with the court believe the system was fair to them. But there was still racial disparity in the level of satisfaction, with African-Americans reporting a 52 percent satisfaction rate, whereas the rate for all Americans was 70 percent.[16]

This data manifests a kind of intransigence that other chapters

> Unfortunately, as evidenced by these studies, public perception has changed very little over the last 20 years.

have described across the judicial system.[17] The data certainly leads to the conclusion that we still have work to do in making sure our courts are both actually fair and perceived as fair to all groups. Unfortunately, as evidenced by these studies, public perception has changed very little over the last 20 years.

II. Bias Awareness and Cultural Competence Scenarios

> There is in each of us a stream of tendency whether you choose to call it philosophy or not, which gives coherence and direction to thought and action. Judges cannot escape that current any more than other mortals. All their lives, forces which they do not recognize and cannot name, have been tugging at them—inherited instincts, traditional beliefs, acquired convictions.
>
> —Benjamin N. Cardozo, *The Nature of the Judicial Process*[18]

Those forces that Justice Cardozo spoke of 100 years ago—inherited instincts, traditional beliefs, and acquired convictions—can also be described as our cultural or implicit biases as we use those terms today. Cardozo also described it as the difference between a judge's conscious and unconscious decision making. He wrote that, while "[w]e [as judges] may try to see things as objectively as we please . . . we can never see them with any eyes except our own."[19] In other words, when litigants, witnesses, and the judge all come from varying cultural backgrounds, each participant interprets the interaction through his or her own cultural lens. We don't just observe behavior; we apply a cultural meaning to it and then respond to the cultural meaning we assign. Cardozo went on to point out, "It is often through these subconscious forces that judges are kept consistent with themselves, and inconsistent with one another."[20]

To help judges achieve greater awareness of bias arising from cultural differences, this section offers several communicative interaction scenarios to illustrate the issue. All the scenarios are actual situations submitted by judges and gleaned from the POJ community voice events held across the nation. The scenarios are straightforward, but we know our cultural biases are often multilayered. Many of us are multicultural with several group identities—consider an African-American lesbian woman who "belongs to at least three cultural groups, each with its own unique cultural content and distinct manifestations in the woman's life."[21] While recognizing these overlapping identities, we have intentionally chosen a single-layer approach for ease of explanation.

Comments from three different perspectives will follow each scenario with an emphasis on what culturally based issues may be involved in the interaction. These scenarios also include suggestions for ways people can attempt to minimize or neutralize their implicit bias reactions. The commentators are Jean Mavrelis, commenting from the perspective of a cultural anthropologist; Phyllis B. Pickett, commenting from a perspective informed by her participation in the POJ initiative and other community outreach efforts; and Judge Karen Arnold-Burger, commenting from a judicial perspective.

Analysis of the courtroom scenarios begins with background information from Jean Mavrelis on archetypes and their use in this chapter.

Mavrelis:

Archetypes are cultural values, attitudes, and patterns of behavior that insiders consider authentic and representative of many, if not all, members of their group. Archetypes differ from stereotypes in that they reflect the views of insiders of the culture, while stereotypes are what outsiders of the group think.

Archetypal values and attitudes not only motivate and explain behavior but also shape cultural perspectives and style. They also implicitly carry with them expectations on how a social transaction or encounter is likely to unfold, and they influence how individuals interpret and judge the behaviors of themselves and others. This pattern lends itself to implicit or unconscious bias as individuals don't simply observe behavior but rather assign a meaning to it and then react to the meaning they assign. Obviously, misunderstandings can and do occur with individuals from the same culture. When individuals from different cultures interact, the likelihood of misunderstanding increases exponentially.

Deeply learned cultural norms and biases are programmed within the early years of life. If a U.S. mainstream[22] couple adopts an infant from China, that infant will learn the values of the parents who raise the child. On the other hand, a child raised in China until age 12 and then adopted by U.S. mainstream parents and moved to the United States will learn English and acquire U.S. mainstream behaviors, but he or she will likely continue to react to others' behavior based on his or her early cultural experiences in China. For this 12-year-old, behaviors will change before the more deeply held cultural values about how people "should" behave will change. In other words, the 12-year-old is *acculturated* into U.S. mainstream society while the infant is *assimilated* into U.S. mainstream culture.

> Deeply learned cultural norms and biases are programmed within the early years of life.

The following scenarios illuminate the unconscious culturally based biases of both judges and litigants from different cultural perspectives. All scenarios are presented from the perspective of a judge from the U.S. mainstream culture.

A. Scenario One: Taking Personal Responsibility for Criminal Offenses

> When faced with a plea or sentencing to a criminal offense, accepting personal responsibility for one's crime is very important. In fact, it is often taken into consideration in the plea bargains that are offered or the sentences imposed.
>
> I expect defendants to speak for themselves. Unless an attorney is representing the person, I do not allow friends or family members to speak for the individual. When defendants try to have others speak for them, I assume they are not taking responsibility and are trying to hide behind others. I will often sternly remind the defendant of my expectations when confronted with such behavior, and I think it might have an effect on the sentence I impose.

Mavrelis:

This scenario reveals implicit bias of the judge based on U.S. mainstream cultural values: individual accountability ("standing up for oneself," "God helps those who help themselves"), self-reliance ("taking the initiative"), and egalitarianism as well as Christian values (of forgiveness based on accepting responsibility and being truly sorry). These values fly in the face of the values and experiences of people from hierarchical, collectivistic cultures in which the patron, boss, father, tribal leader, or dictator has the power. Collectivistic, community-based cultures such as Asian, Latino, or Middle Eastern often prize what other people say about you more than what you say about yourself. It is common for members of these cultures to rely on brokers and mediators, especially when dealing with authority. In Latin America, for example, saying someone is *ambicioso* or ambitious is an insult. It implies the person is only out for him- or herself. Such individuals would "toot their own horns" about achievements and making changes, but those statements would not be trusted as much as what others said about the individual. For that reason, traditional, hierarchically programmed individuals may assume that the judge will be more impressed by what others say about them. They may also find it hard to believe that the judge won't be offended if they speak up on their own behalf. They believe that if no one is willing to speak for them, it suggests that they are not to be trusted.

If the person is represented by an attorney, the attorney should make it clear to his or her client that the judge will only allow an attorney or the defendant to speak in the courtroom. But this does not negate the fact that the defendant may personally find this to be very uncomfortable. Nervousness may become apparent. But even though the nervousness is related to the defendant's fear that he or she may not be viewed as trustworthy by speaking on his or her own behalf, the judge may view his or her reluctance as evidence of guilt.

Similarly, in addition to expectations of speaking on your own behalf, the judge also assumes that admitting guilt is an important part of showing remorse and accepting responsibility. Christian values of forgiveness require accepting responsibility and being truly sorry. In other traditional shame-based cultures such as those in Russia and both East and South Asia, the rule is not "learn from your mistakes" as it is in U.S. mainstream culture but is instead "don't make mistakes." Russians, for example, go to great extremes to avoid admitting guilt, because admission is not the first sign of remorse or seeking forgiveness but the first sign that you can expect to be punished or fired. An example of Russian avoidance of admission of error at a high level was the Chernobyl incident where radioactive material was released into the environment. There was no report of what happened the first few days after the explosion when the wind was blowing to the east, solely over Russian territory. Nothing would have been reported if the wind hadn't shifted and blown the radioactive material over Europe.

Pickett:

This scenario raises several issues related to cultural competence. First, people from minority groups often display meekness and are silent when in a confrontation with those they perceive to be in authority or to have power over them. Then, add that to a situation where the defendant's parent or other familial or cultural authority figure is present and feels publicly humiliated by the judge for trying to assist the defendant. A judge may not always be aware of the level of embarrassment and/or timidity felt by someone from another cultural background.

Second, in some cultures, silence is a way of showing respect and contrition, but speaking up directly to the authority figure is considered disrespectful. Having someone else speak for you may be the best way to be heard in matters of importance. The relative who speaks up on a defendant's behalf may be in fact that defendant's advocate, but in a way that the judge may not recognize.

Finally, in some cultures, self-revelation and showing emotion publicly are contrary to good manners. The same behaviors in other cultures might be considered candid and forthcoming, therefore making the person seem more credible to those who share the same cultural background.

Arnold-Burger:

This scenario also raises the question of whether there is a difference between having an advocate based on one's cultural communication preferences and practicing law without a license. Judges are very concerned about allowing someone who is not an attorney to represent a party in an action. A judge can be confident that an attorney will properly advise a litigant of his or her rights and responsibilities before the court. The same confidence is not present when dealing with a friend or family member who may be equally as unfamiliar with the legal system as the litigant. That said, allowing a nonlawyer to assist is not unheard of around the country. For example, courts often allow a comfort person to sit next to a child witness during trial.[23] Judges will simply want to make sure that the person is not a paid representative and is only there to help the litigant or witness navigate the system, not provide legal advice.

B. Scenario Two: Sharing Personal Information

When someone is unable to afford an attorney in a criminal case in which they face a jail term, the court is required to appoint an attorney for him or her. I require defendants to fill out a state-approved financial affidavit, which I review after completion to determine if the person qualifies as indigent and may receive an attorney at taxpayer expense. I am often confronted with people who simply put a name and address at the top of the form and sign the bottom without filling in any of the personal financial information. The instructions on the form are clear, and I have confirmed that the defendant is able to read. I have noticed that African-Americans are the primary offenders of this rule. I often become very frustrated when I am presented with an incomplete form. It usually takes two or three trips to the bench to get the form fully completed, ending with me meticulously going over each question with the defendant because I interpret the behavior as trying to game the system or hide something. My frustration becomes visible. I have a busy docket, and devoting so much time to get information from someone that should have given it the first time makes me question the person's veracity from that point forward.

Mavrelis:

African-Americans share personal information when there is a demonstrated need to know it.[24] Giving out information such as address, phone number, place of work, and even name, marital status, and number of children is considered personal to African-Americans, while it is often considered standard information for U.S. mainstream culture. There are both social and cultural reasons why African-Americans do not share this kind of information. The social issues are vulnerability, safety, and status: "Who else is going to get this information?" "Will they use it to hurt me or my family?" "Am I being qualified as worthy of consideration?" Concerns about safety are also present for immigrants from totalitarian countries or anyone who might have undocumented relatives staying in his or her home.

For example, at a domestic violence shelter, protocol required that women had to fill out a form with their address, number of children, income, health, and other personal information before being admitted. One African-American victim of domestic violence reported that when she arrived at the shelter, there sat a little white lady, and she thought, "Oh my god, she'll ask everything under the sun." While completing the intake procedure, the African-American woman said, "I'll get that information later." Upon arriving at a shelter, a woman needs to feel safe, and immediately sharing such personal information does not seem like a safe thing to do at such a vulnerable time. No trust had been established, and no one had provided her with any reason why the information was needed or how it would be used. Later, the intake worker told her, "If we don't get the information, we won't get funding." This statement did provide more information, although not much. In order to obtain personal information from people or cultures that are reluctant to share it, those asking for the information must build some level of initial trust and rapport, explain the reason that personal information is required and how it will be used, and demonstrate a clear need to know the information requested.

In another example that we learned from one of our corporate clients, patients at a health clinic were repeatedly giving false addresses and phone numbers. Administrators were dumbfounded as to why anyone would be reluctant to provide what they considered to be such basic information. But after becoming aware of cultural differences in information sharing, the intake staff started telling all patients the reason the information was needed—namely, so the clinic could contact the patient with test results. The clinic immediately discovered that when it provided a reason for the request, patients shared accurate information.

For African-Americans and many other cultures, there is another reason for keeping personal information private in addition to social vulnerability. Even among friends and relatives, it is simply considered inappropriate to ask for personal information. It is up to an individual to decide when, where, and with whom he or she will share information. On the other hand, many African-Americans are great conversationalists about anything public. They may even start a conversation in a public space and expect others to chime in as long as it is about what is going on publicly. By comparison, for many U.S. mainstream women, sharing information is quite different. They often build relationships by asking and sharing marital status, where they live, how many children they have, and even personal struggles; African-American women often find these kinds of questions "nosy."

Cultures also have different boundaries as to what is considered personal. For example, some Asian cultures may not hesitate to ask, "How much did you pay for that?"[25] But, in U.S. mainstream culture, that is considered a personal information violation, in part because of our egalitarian values that seek to avoid what might be invidious comparisons and in part out of fear of criticism around Puritan values of thrift.

If judges or court personnel explain at the outset of the proceeding why the information is needed and how it will be used, they can minimize the vulnerability felt by the individual navigating the system. But it still does not deal with the cultural norm that where you live, how much money you make, and even how many children you have is considered personal. So not only should the reason information is required and how it will and will not be used be explained at the outset, but also it must be relevant and necessary to the proceedings.

Pickett:

The issue with completing forms may have to do with literacy issues. Many members of foreign minority groups have difficulty with reading and writing in English, as do some people educated in U.S. public schools, including disadvantaged African-Americans and Latinos, and persons of modest means educated in low-performing schools. Also, gauging one's financial self-worth may not be something that low-income people do routinely. And they may view their possessions and assets differently than people of the judge's background or income group do.

Stereotype threat may also be in play here. Stereotype threat occurs when people of a particular group recognize the stereotypes that accompany their membership in that group and fear that anything they do that fits the stereotype could be taken as confirming it. Once the stereotype is confirmed, the person fears that he or she will be judged and treated accordingly.[26] When a minority person is asked about his or her educational level or required to take tests or possibly even fill out forms, he or she may feel that this information may be used to confirm a negative stereotype. If so, that person would likely experience more difficulty in filling out the form.

Clearly, from the judge's perspective, the pressure to handle court cases quickly makes it easier to get frustrated by delay. But if the forms are getting done eventually with help, maybe needed assistance could be built in at a timely stage or in a timely manner—that is, in a way that lessens both the delay and the judge's frustration. Moreover, although it is not the judge's intent, the display of frustration may look like bias to the defendant and/or others in the courtroom. Nor is it the judge's intent to embarrass the defendant. Building the skill of frustration tolerance is an important part of maintaining demeanor. Acknowledging frustration openly with an explanation of the importance of the form, an offer of assistance by court personnel, or a statement about respecting everyone's time might help others' perception of the situation. More information and candidness are often appreciated so that the wrong impression or assumption is not made.

Finally, emotions such as anger can color a judge's perceptions and make it more difficult for the judge to be fair and objective. Learning techniques to control anger should be a priority if anger is affecting judicial performance either consciously or unconsciously.

Arnold-Burger:

This scenario really highlights the need to fully explain court procedures to all participants in the system as suggested by Judges Leben and Burke in Chapter 9. Many people are hesitant to give out personal information. A simple explanation of the necessity for and use of that information will save both the judge and the defendant a lot of frustration. A judge should start with the assumption that court users have no information about how the court system works when they walk into the courtroom. The judge can then take on the role of educator to demystify the process. I really like Phyllis Pickett's idea of having someone on staff help with completion of forms, particularly in high-volume courtrooms. Additionally, many courts now use technology to explain the process to people as they wait in the courtroom or before they get to court. It may be in the form of a slideshow (with audio for those who cannot read) or a video (close-captioned for those who cannot hear) that can be provided in multiple languages. These are very inexpensive to produce and can often be created by a local high school media class or at a local college. Lately, a few courts are using some engaging avatar programs to provide information both in the courtroom and on the court website.[27]

C. Scenario Three: Driving while Black

An African-American male appears in court, very angry and loud. He is convinced that the police stopped him solely because he was Black, a clear incident of racial profiling. After the officer stopped him, she forced him to get out of the car and asked him if there were any drugs or guns in the car. As much as I tried to speak calmly and explain that because he admitted he had an expired tag, the police clearly had a legitimate basis to stop him, he continued to interrupt me. He wanted to know how many White people were stopped for expired tags in the city and how many were pulled out of their cars and asked about drug use. The conversation escalated as I asked him to be quiet and let me speak. When he continually refused and argued, I firmly told him he could either plead not guilty and take his case to trial or plead guilty and pay the fine. He said it was clear I had already made my decision, and he would not get a fair hearing. He said he would just pay the fine and stormed out of the courtroom.

Mavrelis:

There are both societal and ethnic cultural issues at play here.

The societal issues embedded in this scenario are in the media every day. African-Americans are much more likely to be victims of racial profiling and often use the phrase "driving while Black" to describe the reason for their stop. While a White person may be stopped for having an expired tag, he or she is much less likely to be asked to get out of the car, to have the car searched, or to be asked if there are drugs in the vehicle.

The ethnic cultural issue at play here is communication style. While African-American culture is hierarchical and children are taught to respect elders, they are also taught to defend and protect themselves when circumstances require it. In the face of perceived injustice, it is expected that a person of integrity will speak his or her truth and do it passionately, taking into consideration the risk involved.

Another communication style difference between U.S. mainstream culture and African-American culture is relevant to this scenario: specifically, the point at which one is supposed to calm down. For a member of the U.S. mainstream culture, it is expected that one should calm down before speaking so that what is said will not be affected by the speaker's emotional state. An emotional discourse is less credible than a calm, reasoned one in which people take turns in speaking. But a request to calm down when speaking about something one feels strongly about seems bizarre to individuals from cultures that promote "passionate advocacy" (e.g., African-American, Russian, and Middle Eastern cultures). They believe that emotion communicates that they are sincere in their convictions. In African-American culture, for example, if the speaker were to calm down, it would suggest that he or she doesn't care enough about the person or the issue to show the requisite emotion. Only after emotion is shared and registered and there is indication that something will be done about a situation is there reason to calm down. Calming down before having a legitimate reason to do so—such as a successful resolution of the case—is illogical, especially when that individual feels he or she has justice on his or her side. In these cultures, a lack of emotion actually suggests insincerity.

If the judge had listened to the man, shared his concern about racial profiling, and registered that the court shared that concern, the man would likely have left with the same outcome in terms of paying a fine for his lapsed tag but would have had a sense that the judge and the court shared his concern and were fair. The judge would have been less agitated in terms of the disrespect she experienced. This man started believing that the police were racially biased, and, as he stormed out, he implicitly accused the judge and court of being the same. He certainly left with his initial perception intact.

Pickett:

Managing angry people and de-escalating situations is a skill that judges must have in the context of criminal law, family law, business law disputes, and many other areas. Here, the judge was confronted by the defendant's apparent anger and bias toward the judge. Overgeneralization and assumptions can affect both judges and litigants. What would have happened if the judge acknowledged that there is such a thing as racial profiling? After such an acknowledgment, the judge could have added, "There is no way we can even get to the facts in your case unless we can talk more calmly about these proceedings. If you choose not to do so, here are your options."

Communication is a two-way street. The responsibility is on the defendant to be heard while the judge is there to hear. But suppose the defendant had been offered the opportunity to have the case continued for him to hire counsel if he was unable to participate without such anger? Or if the judge had offered even a 15-minute delay for the defendant to get himself together so he could be heard? Cooling-off periods, if appropriate, can go a long way. But no court can tolerate blatantly disrespectful behavior.

Arnold-Burger:

I have yet to see data collected from any area of this country that does not show that African-Americans and Latinos are stopped, searched, arrested, and incarcerated at several times the rate of Caucasians. The reality of racial profiling and disproportionate confinement simply cannot be denied.

> Studies have consistently documented that officers employ "greater force, including lethal force, with minority suspects than with White suspects." Forty percent of felony defendants are black, and a black male is over five times more likely to serve time in prison during his lifetime than a white male. Blacks also receive significantly higher bail amounts, are given longer sentences, and are more likely to be sentenced to death than their white counterparts.

The reality of racial profiling and disproportionate confinement simply cannot be denied.

In fact, the more stereotypically black your features are, the more likely you are to receive the death penalty. . . . [I]n one study of Ohio court records, blacks were found to be "about twice as likely to get [traffic] tickets as those who are not black." And, since twenty-one percent of black households do not have an automobile, the impact is actually starker. Other studies suggest that similar disparities exist around the United States.[28]

Recently, a Department of Justice investigation into the policing practices in Ferguson, Missouri, found that African-Americans drivers were not only more likely to be stopped, cited, and arrested than White drivers were, but they also were more likely to receive multiple citations out of a single incident, more likely to be targets of unreasonable force by police, and more likely—by 100 percent—to be involved in a police canine-bite incident.[29] The Supreme Court of Massachusetts took a bold step recently to recognize that a judge should not ignore the reality of racial profiling in analyzing the interaction between minorities and the police. In addressing the conclusions of other courts that "flight" from police by an individual may give the police a reasonable suspicion to stop the individual, the realities of police encounters with Black males may change that calculus. The court took note of studies conducted by the Boston Police Department and held,

> black males in Boston are disproportionately and repeatedly targeted for [Field Interrogation and Observation] encounters [and this] suggests a reason for flight totally unrelated to consciousness of guilt. Such an individual, when approached by the police, might just as easily be motivated by the desire to avoid the recurring indignity of being racially profiled as by the desire to hide criminal activity. Given this reality for black males in the city of Boston, a judge should, in appropriate cases, consider the report's findings in weighing flight as a factor in the reasonable suspicion calculus.[30]

In light of this reality in the daily life experiences of African-Americans, is it any wonder that the young man in this scenario is agitated? He starts by viewing the judge as a neutral person in power who will clearly see the injustice that has been done to him. He depends on the judge to make sure the system is fair. But in U.S. mainstream culture, we distrust people who we believe are letting their emotions rule their conduct. Even outside the courtroom environment, members of U.S. mainstream culture "prefer calm, reasoned discourse and are uneasy when the discussion gets too heated."[31] But "[f]or many black Americans, a sense of feeling and conviction is required to convince listeners you are telling the truth and care about what you are saying."[32] As Jean Mavrelis has explained to me before, U.S. mainstream culture values peace before truth, whereas African-American and some other cultures value truth before peace. This man wanted to tell his truth, and the judge just wanted peace. Clearly, a judge must ensure that a certain level of decorum is observed in the courtroom, and the judge had the right to demand the appropriate level of respect be demonstrated; but if the judge had first acknowledged the man's concern about how he was treated before outlining the way to get those issues properly before the court, it may have allowed the man to leave the courtroom with a feeling that he had at least been heard and treated fairly.

D. Scenario Four: Eye Contact

> While telling his or her story, if a witness will not look me or the questioning attorney in the eye, I inherently doubt the veracity of the story being told, and I think jurors do too.

Mavrelis:

Nonverbal behavior is critical here. If reprimanded by authority, people from hierarchical cultures will look down not out of a sense of guilt but out of respect, fear, or both. Conversely, looking someone in the eye in these cultures is seen as an act of defiance. On the other hand, in U.S. mainstream culture, looking down or away in the face of authority is often interpreted as evasion ("You look me in the eye when I'm talking to you!") or a sign of guilt.

In hierarchical cultures, it is important to respect the dignity of authority and to avoid anything that might be perceived as confrontational. If asked in the face of authority whether there are any questions, persons from a hierarchical culture (e.g., Asians, Latinos) are likely to say no because to have a question would imply that the authority did not do a good job of explaining. Rather, if they didn't understand, they will ask someone they trust to explain what happened after the fact.

Identifying the implicit cultural values of the judge or jury based on deeply held unconscious beliefs is unlikely to produce different behavior on the part of the defendant. However, it would be helpful for the judge to keep these differences in mind and to give instructions to the jury to keep in mind that eye contact, speaking on your own behalf, and even admitting guilt may be unlikely for individuals who come from another cultural system.

Pickett:

Eye contact is a sensitive matter across cultures. In some cultures, looking away while someone is talking shows good manners, while in others, the opposite is true. In some cultures, keeping the eyes diverted when talking to someone is not viewed as a sign of untrustworthiness; in others, it is again the opposite.

Failure to make eye contact can also indicate paranoia, anxiety, and/or fear. The courtroom is a very stressful environment. It is well established that child witnesses and sexual assault victims should not be perceived as less credible because of avoidance of eye contact and displays of timidity. Defendants and litigants may be uneasy and show feelings of distress by similar behaviors.

Arnold-Burger:

In his insightful article "Unspringing the Witness Memory and Demeanor Trap: What Every Judge and Juror Needs to Know about Cognitive Psychology and Witness Credibility," Federal District Judge Mark Bennett points out,

> Few legal principles in contemporary American jurisprudence are more entrenched than the notion that demeanor evidence is important in deciding witness credibility. . . . Yet, cognitive psychological studies have consistently established that the typical cultural cues that jurors rely on, including averting eye contact, a furrowed brow, a trembling hand, and stammering speech, for example, have little or nothing to do with a witness's truthfulness.[33]

Jury instructions in virtually every state authorize jurors' use of demeanor evidence to detect evasiveness.[34] Similarly, pattern jury instructions in virtually every state authorize jurors' use of demeanor evidence to detect evasiveness. The preferred pattern instruction directs jurors that they may consider the manner of the witness while testifying.[35] A knowledge of cultural differences immediately informs a judge that some cues he or she relies on to detect truthfulness may have a completely different meaning outside of the judge's culture.

E. Scenario Five: Allegations of Bias or Racism

> A local reporter asked to speak to me in my chambers. She advised that her group had been studying the amount of bonds and the likelihood of release on a signature bond (also known as a personal recognizance bond) between White defendants and African-American and Latino defendants in my courtroom. She said she had the data to show that I was much more likely to release Whites than African-Americans or Latinos and on a lower bond. She wanted to know why I was discriminating against these groups.
>
> I was very offended by her suggestion. I had not, nor had I ever, intended to discriminate against anyone. In fact, I have a long professional history of not being biased. She insisted that the numbers don't lie. Regardless of whether I intended it or not, it was happening. I thought this was an unfair attack on my character.

Mavrelis:

It is a brave judge indeed who will investigate disparate impact in terms of bond decisions. Many judges will even say, "I've been doing this a long time. I know when someone's guilty and when he or she is a flight risk."

In this scenario, the judge was shocked that her moral character would be called into question. Her first cultural reaction was to defend that moral character by explaining that she did not and had never intended to discriminate against anybody. U.S. mainstream culture grew out of Protestant underpinnings where your intent stood for your moral character and established you as a good, God-fearing person. When called into question, moral character becomes the "elephant in the room," taking precedence over everything else. For other cultures, such as those in the Middle East, you cannot violate honor. For African-Americans, it's respect, and for Latinos, it's *dignidad* and *respeto*.

The key point of these examples is that once a violation of whatever each culture considers sacred occurs, nothing else can be considered until that matter is addressed and remedied.

The key point of these examples is that once a violation of whatever each culture considers sacred occurs, nothing else can be considered until that matter is addressed and remedied.

U.S. mainstream culture treats intent (state of mind or what was meant) separately from what was said and done. But in the absence of trust or any ongoing relationship, African-Americans work backward, inferring intent from what was said or done ("If you didn't mean it, you would have found a different way to do it."). How it looks is how it is! The catalyst that generally triggers a charge of racism for African-Americans is inconsistent or disparate actual treatment (such as being singled out or treated differently), not what was intended or meant.

In fairness, the judge is now also aware and concerned about disparate impact. However, until her moral character is recognized and validated by the journalist, it will be very difficult for the judge to consider the factual basis because she will be preoccupied with defending her character. Furthermore, she may feel that the journalist is out of line and disrespectful and therefore doesn't deserve the dignity of a response. But a response that will be accepted by the community impacted by the judge's decisions requires a judge who is willing to consider her unconscious bias.

So how did this well-intentioned judge come to set higher bonds and longer sentencing for minorities? The reasons are societal, procedural, cultural, and even political. As discussed throughout this book, unconscious societal or social bias grows out of different assumptions based on stereotypes. For example, characterizations in the media contribute to these biases. Crimes by White individuals are "unmarked" for race, meaning that we read or hear about a minority committing a crime but when a perpetrator is White, race is not mentioned. Our prisons contain a disproportionate number of our nation's minorities. Deep-seated unconscious bias, both negative bias against Blacks and positive favoritism toward Whites, is unavoidable in a country with a legacy of slavery and discrimination.

Procedural issues are often more subtle. For example, an African-American judge recently reported—in a meeting related to implicit bias—her shock when she was faced with a White defendant who was charged with two gun possession offenses for possession of eight guns followed by the case of an African-American defendant who was charged with eight separate gun possession offenses, one charge for each of his eight guns.

A trickier bias to uncover is based upon how different cultures read and communicate guilt or innocence based upon their level of protestation. U.S. mainstream judges (and others) have in mind a sense of how a person should protest and look when he or she is innocent, and how he or she should protest, verbally and nonverbally, when he or she is not. Innocence within U.S. mainstream culture, like a firm handshake, is shown through strength of conviction. Protests of innocence are expected to show both force and righteous indignation. But not all cultures view how an innocent person should behave the same way. African-Americans, for example, assert their innocence more as a matter of fact than as righteous protestation, often causing U.S. mainstream individuals to question whether they really are innocent. Conversely, were African-Americans to assert their innocence more forcefully—showing moral indignation—approximating more closely what is normative within U.S. mainstream culture, they risk coming across as guilty to themselves and other African-Americans.

This different assignment of guilt and innocence to the same behavior often occurs and is most apparent when accusations are being leveled by members of one group against the other. U.S. mainstream individuals who feel falsely accused become righteously indignant, which to themselves and other Whites present communicates innocence. African-Americans see that level of protestation as a sign of guilt; it is not a righteous defense of moral character but a sign that a chord has been struck that wouldn't have been struck if the person had been truly innocent. The African-American saying that goes along with this view is, "If you throw a stone in a pack of dogs, the one that yelps is the one that got hit."

This matter is further complicated in that U.S. mainstream and African-American cultures differ on who is ultimately responsible for the "hit." U.S. mainstream culture places responsibility for having hit one or another target on the one making the accusation. African-American culture places responsibility for the accusation on the one who "yelps," the cultural logic being—this applies to general accusations where no specific individual is being targeted—that receivers are the ones who ultimately determine whether the accusation applies to them or not. The African-American adage that supports this view is, "If the shoe fits, wear it." In Barbados, the saying is, "Whoever the cap fit, pull the string."

Finally, what is also culturally different are how group generalizations are seen and heard. For the U.S. mainstream culture, group generalizations are categorical, including all members of the group. For African-Americans, group generalizations do not include all. Add to the mix who the different cultures hold ultimately responsible for the targets that are hit, and you get the following scenario: In the case of White police officers, for example, if African-Americans say something about White "cops," individual officers may well protest and say, "I'm not like that," while African-Americans will hear that as "It most have struck a chord or you wouldn't be protesting." When African-Americans hear a general characterization about African-Americans, they do not necessarily feel included, don't hear it as "all," and are more likely to claim personal exemption by saying, "I know you're not talking to me."

There is also politically driven bias. When judges are elected rather than appointed, they may crack down during certain cycles so as not to appear "soft" on crime.[36] State's attorneys, too, may encourage their deputies to get more convictions in an election year. They then encourage prosecuting attorneys to "win" more cases. Police also get points for arrests and closures as part of their performance measures. Despite this, judges who consider social, cultural, procedural, and political biases when determining bond opportunities will maximize just outcomes.

Pickett:

Regardless of whether the judge accepts or rejects the reporter's contention, if the story is printed, it will become a matter of public concern. What good might happen after publication of the story?

Could the story serve as a catalyst for community interaction? Suppose the judge held an open house or community forum where the judge could discuss how she makes bail and sentencing decisions as well as hear the concerns of the community? Would the court system be diminished in anyway by such an event? Or, might there be an opportunity for positive interaction and greater understanding that stretches to and from the courthouse?

Could the encounter with the reporter be a catalyst for more training, of the judge and court personnel, on how to handle such personal and professional challenges with the potential to improve communication with the community they all serve?

In 1992, New Jersey Chief Supreme Court Justice Robert N. Wilentz said succinctly, "[We] have long known that the same bias that has affected all of society for so long exists in all of its institutions, including the Judiciary."[37] Bias is a natural part of life. Bias can be positive or negative, helpful or hurtful. Developing mindfulness and becoming aware of one's own negative biases is not easy. Not only is it an effort worth making, but also it is an effort that is required in order to be fair and impartial. The reporter's question certainly should become a teachable moment for the judge and, indeed, for the community.

Arnold-Burger:

I have never met a judge who did not believe that he or she was fair and impartial. But how does a judge know if his or her practices are having a disparate impact on a particular community or culture? Should you wait for the knock on the door from the reporter to learn that information?[38] I submit that as judges, we have a responsibility to examine the impact of our decisions.

As Jean Mavrelis points out, much of our legal system, which is based on U.S. mainstream culture, incorporates what we now know to be a culturally based belief that the level of intent corresponds to the level of culpability. If a person does not intend his or her actions to cause harm, he or she is less culpable than one who did intend such a result. Accordingly, it is easy to downplay the serious consequences of racial bias by simply claiming lack of intent. On the other hand, other cultures believe that the proof is in the results; in other words, if you are going to talk the talk, you better walk the walk.

This cultural view of culpability, which was also deeply imbedded in our justice system, started to change with the growth of the civil rights movement and the subsequent adoption of the Civil Rights Act of 1964.[39] There, the legal theory

> I have never met a judge who did not believe that he or she was fair and impartial. But how does a judge know if his or her practices are having a disparate impact on a particular community or culture?

of disparate impact started to take form. The U.S. Supreme Court took the position that by adopting the Civil Rights Act, Congress "proscribe[d] not only overt discrimination but also practices that are fair in form, but discriminatory in operation."[40] In these cases, when determining whether practices are discriminatory, the courts look first to the impact. Motivation is irrelevant in determining whether the plaintiff has made a prima facie case. As such, these cases usually focus on statistical and quantitative analysis.

By 1986, the need to focus on the impact of the behavior became clear in criminal cases when examining racial challenges to jury selection in criminal cases.[41] In *Batson v. Kentucky*, the Supreme Court held that "the Equal Protection Clause forbids the prosecutor to challenge potential jurors solely on the basis of race or on the assumption that black jurors as a group will be unable impartially to consider the State's case against a black defendant."[42] In these challenges, the court first looks to whether that defendant has made a prima facie showing that the prosecutor has exercised peremptory challenges to jurors on the basis of race. Intent is irrelevant at this stage. And again, this initial review is primarily based on a quantitative analysis regarding the number of jurors removed of a particular race. In both criminal and civil cases, once a prima facie case is made, the burden shifts to the other side to show a race-neutral reason for the disparity.[43]

So back to the judge in this scenario: Why not examine our own court practices the same way? Do you in fact give higher bonds for minority populations? Maybe you don't intend that to be the result, but wouldn't the quantitative analysis give you an idea of whether there might be implicit biases at work that you should examine more carefully? Maybe the systems we have in place need to be examined if they are creating an unintended negative consequence to a whole section of the community. Do this before the reporter knocks on your door to tell you something you should have known already.

I also strongly encourage community involvement, a topic that is discussed more thoroughly in the next section of this chapter. As Jean Mavrelis noted, it does takes a brave judge to request assistance from the minority community when he or she has discovered disparate impact related to court policies, procedures, or decisions. But I suggest that is exactly what a judge should do. Engage the community in the solution. Ask for their assistance in identifying problems you may not be able to recognize. I appreciate that there is a fear that if impacted groups are advised of statistical proof of disparate impact, the information will be used against the judge and he or she will be labeled a racist. But that has not been my experience. Instead, my personal experience has been that minority groups recognize the courage needed to come forward and are encouraged by a judge's desire to correct any problems that exist. It promotes a sense of legitimacy in the system. The alternatives are to ignore the problem altogether or address the problem without this valuable input and perhaps devise a solution that ends up worsening the problem. Both alternatives breed distrust in the communities impacted.

> [M]y personal experience has been that minority groups recognize the courage needed to come forward and are encouraged by a judge's desire to correct any problems that exist. It promotes a sense of legitimacy in the system. The alternatives are to ignore the problem altogether or address the problem without this valuable input and perhaps devise a solution that ends up worsening the problem. Both alternatives breed distrust in the communities impacted.

F. Scenario Six: Latino Hospitality

I had a case where two Latino families lived next to each other and were very friendly. One day, Alejandro went to Diego's house and just walked in, unannounced. But it turns out Diego wasn't there. Instead, Charlie, who had recently become a co-owner of the house and roommate of Diego's, was there with his friends. Alejandro did not know Charlie, and Charlie did not know Alejandro. When Charlie told Alejandro to get out of his house, Alejandro (who was intoxicated) said, "I am here to see Diego." Charlie's friends surrounded Alejandro. He felt threatened, and a fight ensued where people were injured. Alejandro was convicted of battery.

The issue was which defense would prevail: "defense of home" for Charlie or "defense of self" for Alejandro. On appeal, the case came down to whether Alejandro could have assumed it was okay for him to enter Diego's home without an invitation. The court found that because everyone agreed Alejandro walked in the back door without an invitation, he was an intruder. Because he was an uninvited guest, he could not claim self-defense. Should the defense attorney have called a witness about the meaning of hospitality in a Latino home?

Mavrelis:

One of the standing rules for Latinos in matters of hospitality is *mi casa es su casa* (my house is your house). Also, Latinos and U.S. mainstream culture view presence and availability differently. U.S. mainstream culture conflates presence and availability, meaning that if a U.S. mainstream host cannot be exclusively available at that moment, he or she denies presence ("I can't see you right now. I'm busy packing for a trip"). For Latinos, it is rude to deny presence simply because you can't be available. Thus, a Latino host would say, "Come on in. You can help me pack for my trip," or, "Come on in and make yourself a cold drink while I pack my bag."

From a Latino cultural perspective then, it would not necessarily be seen as a violation that Alejandro would come and make himself at home even if his friend Diego was not there. This would have been confirmed if no one else had been there (no Charlie or his friends) and Diego found Alejandro there when he got home. Testimony regarding this difference in understanding may have helped the judge or jury understand why Alejandro thought it was acceptable to enter his friend's house without an invitation.

Pickett:

Before asking if the lawyer acted appropriately, consider whether there may have been a different outcome if the persons involved in the brawl had used communication rather than force to deal with the conflict. Or if they all, both Latino and non-Latino, had greater cultural awareness and competence about people different from themselves culturally. What was the cultural competence level of the responding law enforcement officers?

Judges, lawyers, and police officers—like all people—rely on their own life experiences when they interpret what is going on in a situation. If one has limited experiences with members of a group, there may be deficits in understanding how members of that group may or may not react in certain instances. A recurring theme that emerged from the POJ town hall meetings was that sensitivity and diversity training for law enforcement, judges, and court personnel would improve court administration and perceptions of justice. Such training may have alerted law enforcement and the judge to the fact that it would not have been outside the cultural norm for Alejandro to walk into Diego's home uninvited.

Arnold-Burger:

People act pursuant to their culturally based communication styles and norms. If the judge or jury members evaluate the litigant's actions based on their own cultural norms or lens, important details may be lost, and justice might not be served. Courts around the country have allowed testimony from cultural anthropologists or other experts in cultural norms to assist the trier of fact.[44] Some courts have even taken cultural norms into account in determining the sentence.[45] The recognition that everyone does not view the world the same way, have the same experiences that the judge has had, or behave as the judge might under identical circumstances will help the judge recognize cultural differences and implicit biases.

> Our U.S. mainstream system of justice often uses a "reasonable person" standard in evaluating conduct, but that reasonable person is generally modeled off the behaviors and social norms of the U.S. mainstream culture.

Our U.S. mainstream system of justice often uses a "reasonable person" standard in evaluating conduct, but that reasonable person is generally modeled off the behaviors and social norms of the U.S. mainstream culture. And U.S. mainstream culture may no longer represent the vast majority of Americans it once did.

> Cross-cultural jurisprudence is a vital subject in the twenty-first century. With increased migration, regional integration, and tourism, individuals cross borders more frequently. As a consequence, opportunities for cultural misunderstandings are greater, and legal systems must be prepared to consider cultural arguments.[46]

In fact, some courts have held that the Sixth Amendment right to effective assistance of counsel is implicated when an attorney fails to present evidence of cultural pressures as a mitigating factor.[47] Other courts have held that the exclusion of cultural evidence is a reversible error.[48] Certainly, people in this country should be required to comply with the laws of this country, and the use of testimony regarding different cultural norms as a means to excuse illegal behavior is subject to much controversy.[49] But the point I make here is that culture does influence behavior, and simply recognizing that not all people behave the same way the judge would under the same circumstances is an important step in recognizing implicit biases.

III. Judicial Outreach and Community Voice

One of the country's leading researchers in the field of procedural justice, Dr. Tom R. Tyler, has found that *how* people and their problems are managed by the court has more influence than the actual outcome of their case on their willingness to accept and abide by the court's decision.[50] Similarly, the six-year ABA POJ initiative was founded on the proposition that a minority community's perception of justice matters because the perception of fairness is a fundamental requirement of an effective and legitimate judicial system. If these groups lack confidence in the courts, something must be done to improve their confidence. One demonstrated way to enhance understanding and confidence in the justice system and to develop strategies to improve the way people and cases are managed in the system is by community engagement, such as the POJ community voice events held by the ABA Judicial Division Lawyer's Conference. Each POJ community voice event held around the country was much more than just a forum for "venting" about the justice system. Importantly, the events produced suggestions for change that form a model and firm foundation for building judicial outreach efforts.

Why should your court engage in judicial outreach to hear community voice? Because a local community voice event will provide a dedicated time for community members, judges, lawyers, and other stakeholders to consider how court users in your area perceive the justice system. These events can afford positive interaction across cultures and become catalysts for change. For example, the voices heard at previous POJ programs produced the following suggestions for judicial outreach and positive change:

- Promote more discussions and interaction between judges and members of the community.

- Recognize that perceptions run all ways: Judges, court personnel, attorneys, and litigants all make assumptions about the people they see.

- Enhance civics and law-related education because educating the community about the legal system will promote more positive views of the system.

- Require mandatory sensitivity and diversity training for law enforcement, judges, and court personnel.

- Increase the number of persons of color working in the justice system; court users have a greater perception that the system is fair the more it "looks" like them.

- Promote training for judges and court personnel that leads to consistent answers on procedure for litigants.

- Provide greater resources to the justice system.

- Consider sentencing that is less punitive as well as substantive law changes offering more creative and fair sentencing.

Judges have great convening power, and they can help shape the format of a community event to reflect that community style and preference. Outreach events can range from town hall-style meetings to panel discussions that might include court personnel, local residents, and even researchers, professors, or other experts in the field of procedural justice. These do not have to be large events. They can be small meetings with a few judicial and local community leaders to simply begin the dialog and outline future discourse. Whatever the approach, the ABA's toolkit for planning these events offers resources.[51]

One such meeting that Judge Arnold-Burger participated in proved to be the impetus for several more to follow. Police and court personnel met with leaders of the local National Association for the Advancement of Colored People, League of United Latin American Citizens, and Jewish Community Relations Board. The meetings resulted in the development of a computer program tracking police stops identified by race and opened a dialog about the way complaints against the police and court were handled. Members of these groups were encouraged to court watch and give feedback about the process. The relationships have continued as police have embarked on community policing strategies.

Small group discussions can facilitate interactions and openness, and any of these options can provide an opportunity for robust interactions. The topics for discussion could be as complex as procedural justice and fairness issues or as simple as exploring the actual experiences and questions of local residents. As the Lawyers Conference POJ toolkit notes,

> One way to identify positive and negative experiences is to discuss, in chronological order, what a court user experiences from the minute he receives a notice to appear in court, to the time he enters the parking garage at the courthouse, to the minute he leaves. How were his interactions with court personnel prior to, during, and after court proceedings? What signage and policies in the courtroom contributed to the user's experience? Did the judge directly address the litigant? Did the litigant have an opportunity to be heard? Did the litigant leave with questions unanswered?[52]

Moreover, the format could directly address questions of bias head on through a frank discussion of instances when court users felt they were treated unfairly. The information and insights gleaned from this kind of judicial outreach will inform a judge's perspective and give voice to the community.

IV. Training for Change

Jean Mavrelis, with a team of social scientists, linguists, and anthropologists, has been conducting training for individuals and corporations in the area of culturally based bias for over 30 years. She has agreed to share her thoughts regarding whether we can ever truly change our culturally based behavior and resulting implicit biases based upon training. She specifically addresses the method she has personally found to be most effective for long-term change. Admittedly, her statements here are based on her experience and are primarily anecdotal in nature. By including this discussion, the authors do not intend for this to serve as a recommendation for Jean's specific training program. It is presented only as one example. In writing this book, the editors have attempted to elicit other examples throughout the country; to the extent examples have been provided, they are included in the appropriate chapters.

Mavrelis:

Chapter 10, "Considering Audience Psychology in the Design of Implicit Bias Education," does a nice job of identifying factors that increase the likelihood of effective implicit bias training: minimize reactiveness, maximize relevance, encourage active participation (respect for expertise of presenters is important here), and set expectations. Judges, lawyers, court staff, translators, police officers, and jurors will be at many different stages of intercultural understanding. So, what is realistic here in terms of implicit bias training? Plaut and Carbone identify research that suggests simply talking about bias already raises people's awareness to watch for their own prejudice. The problem is, prejudice is different than cultural awareness. Very well-intentioned people who do not understand cultural differences will evaluate others through their own filter in terms of deeply learned cultural values and beliefs that range from the meaning of eye contact, to signs of guilt and innocence, to when it is appropriate to trust people or institutions.

To address the impact of one's own cultural filtering and true understanding of cultural differences, Dr. Mitchell R. Hammer, President of IDI, LLC, developed a cross-culturally valid assessment of where people are on a continuum of multicultural development called the Intercultural Development Inventory (IDI).[53] The tool was developed based on Dr. Milton Bennett's research model of intercultural sensitivity[54] and revised based on IDI research (Intercultural Development Continuum).[55] The IDC identifies several orientations of multicultural development that range from more monocultural mind-sets (Denial, Polarization) to the transitional orientation of Minimization to intercultural mind-sets (Acceptance, Adaptation). So how does one move through Hammer's continuum?

"There are five stages of multicultural development: Denial of Differences, Polarization, Minimization, Acceptance and Adaptation." People new to the concept that culture is real and impacts how we interact with others may be in Orientation 1: Denial of Differences. With this orientation, people deny that culture matters because they see themselves as colorblind and firmly believe that they treat everyone as an individual. In Orientation 2: Polarization, individuals begin to recognize that our cultures are different but judge cultural patterns as right or wrong. In other words, there is one "right" way of believing and interacting, and it is usually the individual's cultural view that is the right one. The first two orientations (Denial and Polarization) are monocultural because the individual is focused on the belief that there is one "right" way of viewing the world that we all share and it is "my" view. At Orientation 3: Minimization, people say, "OK, I get this about culture, but it's not really a big deal—we all are human and we all do 'that.'" Minimization is a "transitional" orientation between the more monocultural orientations and the intercultural orientations of Acceptance and Adaptation. Next comes movement into the intercultural mind-/skillset of Acceptance of differences, where individuals

realize the significance of understanding culture but have yet to develop expertise. They recognize that there are viable alternatives to their own worldview.
They no longer see cultures as threatening, inferior, or wrong. Next, is the stage
of Adaptation to differences and the
ability to shift the individual's frame
of reference and understand and be
understood across cultural boundaries. People at this stage have a strong
desire to research and understand
different cultures. Differences are
seen as positive. Hammer suggests
that it takes 30–40 hours of immer-
sion to move from one stage to another.[56] In my experience with training at my
company, KMA,[57] we have found that to be true.

> "There are five stages of multicultural development: Denial of Differences, Polarization, Minimization, Acceptance and Adaptation." . . . [I]t takes 30–40 hours of immersion to move from one stage to another.

When we do a 40-hour weeklong immersion training where our colleagues
from many different cultures get up and present on their culture, the number
one comment we hear is, "That was life-changing." When we do one-day or
half-day trainings, people tend to react based on where they are developmen-
tally in the process of developing multicultural expertise. Our sessions are a
little different from most implicit bias trainings, which make the case we all
have bias. As social scientists, linguists, and anthropologists, we say, "People tell
you to respect differences, but they don't tell you what the differences are that
you should respect." We do that in our training and find that people at all levels
of intercultural development are nodding their heads and "get it."

We often tell people in these shorter training sessions that our expectation is not that they become cultural anthropologists but simply that the next
time they are making a decision, they ask themselves, "I wonder if something
cultural is going on here?" That's a reasonable expectation. The other goal and
way we measure the effectiveness of training is by asking: "Can people have different conversations than they could have otherwise had?" We want people to
be able to share a language, and to "spill the milk," make mistakes, but learn
from them. This kind of training is very different from compliance training,
which often intimidates by informing, "Don't do these 15 things or else." We
tell people, "OK, don't do those 15 things, but since there are plenty of other
mistakes to be made, let's create an environment where we can learn and talk
about them."

> I firmly believe that training can result in change, because I have seen it. But it is not a quick and easy process.

At KMA, we have e-learning
modules that carefully examine
several different cultures, starting
with the culture of U.S. mainstream
White men. Anybody who wants to
start the journey of multicultural learning should know that recognizing we all
have been programmed with implicit bias by our parents, families, communities, and institutions is just the first step, but it's a big one. I firmly believe that

training can result in change, because I have seen it. But it is not a quick and easy process. A one- or two-hour training on diversity is not sufficient to move individuals through Hammer's stages of intercultural development.

Conclusion

> Have a bias toward action—let's see something happen now.
> You can break that big plan into small steps and take the first step right away.
>
> —Indira Gandhi[58]

Bias in our judicial system, whether implicit or explicit, threatens the promise of justice for all. This chapter has provided the reader a few examples out of the many that could have been presented highlighting cultural differences in communication styles and behavior. A judge may not realize that his or her reactions to litigants and evaluation of testimony are seen through his or her own cultural frame of reference. These cultural norms are so ingrained in every fiber of a judge's being that it is often impossible for that same judge to realize their effect on his or her interpretations of communications and behaviors in the courtroom. But there are actions that judges can take to mitigate bias. By recognizing that there are litigants and court users evaluating judicial behavior through a different cultural lens and experiencing different intuitive reactions regarding judicial fairness than the judge is experiencing, a judge can take the first step toward an all-inclusive approach to justice. And a judge can take a second step to increase cultural competence and improve perceptions of justice by sponsoring judicial outreach events that encourage awareness, interaction, and communication. Finally, the notion of having a "bias for action" helps us understand that each step that a judge takes toward self-awareness and understanding the community will help bring about justice for all.

So You'd Like to Know More

- Thomas Kochman & Jean Mavrelis, Corporate Tribalism: White Men/White Women and Cultural Diversity at Work (2009); see also http://www.kmadiversity.com

- Thomas Kochman, Black and White Styles in Conflict (1981)

- David Cole, No Equal Justice: Race and Class in the American Criminal Justice System (1999)

- David A. Harris, Profiles in Injustice: Why Racial Profiling Cannot Work (2002)

- Jim Myers, Afraid of the Dark (2000)

- Masua Sagiv, *Cultural Bias in Judicial Decision Making*, 35 Boston College Journal of Law and Social Justice 29 (2015), http://lawdigitalcommons.bc.edu/jlsj/vol35/iss2/3

- Adam Benforado, Unfair: The New Science of Criminal Injustice (2015)

ABOUT THE AUTHORS

Judge Karen Arnold-Burger has been on the bench for over 25 years at both the appellate and trial court levels and has taught at the National Judicial College for 15 years. She currently serves as Chief Judge of the Kansas Court of Appeals. Judge Arnold-Burger has presented numerous programs for the ABA, including sessions on implicit bias, racial profiling, and disproportionate minority confinement.

Jean Mavrelis is Chief Executive Officer of Kochman Mavrelis Associates and coauthor of *Corporate Tribalism: White Men, White Women and Cultural Diversity at Work.*[59] She has been consulting in the field of cultural diversity for over 25 years and is considered an expert in the field of cross-cultural communication.

Phyllis B. Pickett is an attorney and mediator with over 30 years of legal experience. Ms. Pickett began her career as a federal Legal Services Corporation litigator representing low-income citizens in coastal North Carolina and then practiced privately before serving as an Assistant Wake County Attorney in Raleigh. She is currently a Principal Legislative Analyst with the North Carolina General Assembly and an active participant in the Task Force on Perceptions of Justice.

ENDNOTES

1. *Confirmation Hearing on the Nomination of Hon. Sonia Sotomayor, to Be an Associate Justice of the Supreme Court of the United States: Hearing Before the S. Comm. on the Judiciary*, 111th Cong. 1 (2009) (statement of Sen. Patrick J. Leahy, Chairman, S. Comm. on the Judiciary).
2. DANIEL KAHNEMAN, THINKING, FAST AND SLOW 8 (2011).
3. Symposium, *American Bar Association Symposium II: Public Understanding and Perceptions of the American Justice System*, 62 ALB. L. REV. 1307 (1999) [hereinafter *Symposium II*]. The statistics presented in this symposium originated from a November 1998 survey that is available online at http://www.Americanbar.org/content/dam/aba/publishing /abanews/1269460858_20_1_1_7_upload_file.authcheckdam.pdf.
4. Phillip S. Anderson, *President's Message: Justice and Inequality Don't Mix*, ABA J. 6 (May 1999).
5. *Symposium II, supra* note 4, at 1317.
6. *Id.* at 1343. Fourteen percent of the respondents expressed no opinion.
7. David B. Rottman, Randall Hansen, Nicole Mott & Lynn Grimes, *Perceptions of the Courts in Your Community: The Influence of Experience, Race and Ethnicity*, Nat'l Ctr. for State Courts at 41 (2003), https://www.ncjrs.gov/pdffiles1/nij/grants/201302.pdf.
8. *Id.* at 41.
9. *Id.* at 42.
10. *Id.* at 53–54.
11. *Id.* at 93.
12. ABA Judicial Div. Lawyers Conference, *Perceptions of Justice: A Dialogue on Race, Ethnicity, and the Courts* (2011), *available at* http://www.americanbar.org/content/dam/aba /administrative/lawyers_conference/2011_poj_writtenreport.authcheckdam.pdf.
13. *Id.* at 5.
14. ABA Judicial Div., *Perceptions of Justice Summit Report* 2 (2013), http://www.americanbar .org/content/dam/aba/administrative/judicial/poj_summit_report.authcheckdam.pdf.
15. Nat'l Cntr. for State Courts, *National Survey 2015* 4 (2015), http://www.ncsc.org /~/media/Files/PDF/Topics/Public%20Trust%20and%20Confidence/SoSC_2015_ Survey%20Analysis.ashx.
16. *Id.*
17. *See also, e.g.*, IMPLICIT RACIAL BIAS ACROSS THE LAW (Justin D. Levinson & Robert J. Smith eds., 2012).
18. BENJAMIN CARDOZO, THE NATURE OF THE JUDICIAL PROCESS 12 (1921).
19. *Id.* at 13.
20. *Id.* at 12.

21. Masua Sagiv, *Cultural Bias in Judicial Decision Making*, 35 B.C.J.L. & Soc. Just. 229 (2015), http://lawdigitalcommons.bc.edu/jlsj/vol35/iss2/3.

22. When we discuss cultural communication styles in this chapter, we will often refer to the culture of the "U.S. mainstream." It is a term Dr. Thomas Kochman and Jean Mavrelis have coined to mean a cultural style based upon values, beliefs, and behaviors of the White Anglo-Saxon Protestant men who were the first to enter corporate America. As such, most of our long-standing American institutions, including our court system, are based on this cultural model. Some refer to it as an "Anglo" or "majority" cultural model, but because many cultures have begun to assimilate to this model over time, the term "U.S. mainstream" seems to be the best way to describe it.

23. *See, e.g.*, Baxter v. State, 522 N.E.2d 362, 365 (Ind. 1988) (mother); State v. Rochelle, 298 P.3d 293, 298 (Kan. 2013) (school counselor); State v. T.E., 775 A.2d 686 (N.J. Super. Ct. App. Div. 2001) (therapist).

24. Thomas Kochman, Black and White Styles in Conflict 97–99 (1981).

25. Bob Davis, *Right or Rude? An Expat's Etiquette Guide to China*, Wall St. J., Jan. 20, 2015, http://blogs.wsj.com/expat/2015/01/20/why-expats-think-chinese-are-rude-and-what -chinese-think-about-rude-americans/.

26. Claude Steele, Whistling Vivaldi and Other Clues to How Stereotypes Affect Us 5 (2010); *see also* Jonathan Feingold, *Racing Toward Color-Blindness: Stereotype Threat and the Myth of Meritocracy*, 3 Geo. J.L. & Mod. Critical Race Persp. 231, 233 (2011).

27. For an example of one such program, visit http://www.sitepal.com/.

28. Adam Benforado, *Frames of Injustice: The Bias We Overlook*, 85 Ind. L.J. 1333, 1367 (2010).

29. U.S. Dep't of Justice, Investigation of the Ferguson Police Department 4–5 (2015), https://www.justice.gov/sites/default/files/opa/press-releases/attachments/2015/03/04 /ferguson_police_department_report.pdf.

30. Commonwealth v. Warren, 475 Mass. 530, 58 N.E.3d 333, 342 (Mass. 2016).

31. Jim Myers, Afraid of the Dark 167 (2000).

32. *Id.* at 166; *see also* Kochman, *supra* note 25, at 29–30.

33. Mark W. Bennett, *Unspringing the Witness Memory and Demeanor Trap: What Every Judge and Juror Needs to Know about Cognitive Psychology and Witness Credibility*, 64 Notre Dame L. Rev. 1331, 1331 (2015).

34. Renée McDonald Hutchins, *You Can't Handle the Truth! Trial Juries and Credibility*, 44 Seton Hall L. Rev. 505, 521 n.68 (2014).

35. Bennett, *supra* note 34, at 1350.

36. Kate Berry, *How Judicial Elections Impact Criminal Cases*, Brennan Center for Justice (Dec. 5, 2015).

37. John F. Sullivan, *Bias Found Widespread in the Courts*, N.Y. Times, Aug. 7. 1992, http:// www.nytimes.com/1992/08/07/nyregion/bias-found-widespread-in-the-courts.html.

38. Such tactics by reporters are not out of the realm of possibility. *See* Ian Ayres & Joel Wald-fogel, *A Market Test for Race Discrimination in Bail Setting*, 46 Stan. L. Rev. 987, 991 (1994).

39. Civil Rights Act of 1964, Pub. L. 88-352, 78 Stat. 241 (codified as amended in 42 U.S.C. §§ 1981–2000h (2012)).

40. Griggs v. Duke Power, 401 U.S. 424, 431 (1971).

41. 476 U.S. 79 (1986).

42. *Id.* at 89.

43. *But see* Washington v. Saintcalle, 309 P.3d 326, 336 (Wash. 2013), where the Supreme Court of Washington opines that the *Batson* analysis is woefully inadequate. "But discrimination in this day and age is frequently unconscious and less often consciously purposeful. That does not make it any less pernicious. Problematically, people are rarely aware of the actual reasons for their discrimination and will genuinely believe the race-neutral reason they create to mask it. . . . More troubling for *Batson* is research showing that people will act on unconscious bias far more often if reasons exist giving plausible deniability (e.g., an opportunity to present a race-neutral reason.)." *Id.* The court goes on to express its frustration with the needed showing in the later stages of the *Batson* challenge of purposeful discrimination in order to ultimately prevail. "The main problem is that *Batson's* third

step requires a finding of 'purposeful discrimination,' which trial courts may often interpret to require conscious discrimination. This is problematic because discrimination is often unconscious. A requirement of conscious discrimination is especially disconcerting because it seemingly requires judges to accuse attorneys of deceit and racism in order to sustain a *Batson* challenge. Imagine how difficult it must be for a judge to look a member of the bar in the eye and level an accusation of deceit or racism. And if the judge chooses not to do so despite misgivings about possible race bias, the problem is compounded by the fact that we defer heavily to the judge's findings on appeal. . . . A strict 'purposeful discrimination' requirement thus blunts *Batson's* effectiveness and blinds its analysis to unconscious racism." (citations omitted). *Id.; see also* Mark W. Bennett, *Unraveling the Gordian Knot of Implicit Bias in Jury Selection: The Problems of Judge-Dominated Voir Dire, the Failed Promise of Batson, and Proposed Solutions,* 4 Harv. L. & Pol'y Rev. 149, 162 (2010).

44. *E.g., Vang v. Toyed,* 944 F.2d 476, 481 (9th Cir. 1991) (upholding decision in civil trial to allow epidemiologist to testify about women in the Hmong culture); People v. Aphaylath, 502 N.E.2d 998, 999 (N.Y. 1986) (reversing order excluding expert testimony on the stress encountered by Laotian refugees); *see also* Douangpangna v. Knowles, No. CIV S-01-0764 GEB JFM P, 2007 WL 1040967 (E.D. Cal. 2007) (cultural anthropologist allowed to testify at trial on Laotian belief in black magic); People v. Keichler, 29 Cal. Rptr. 3d 120 (Cal. Ct. App. 2005) (allowing restitution for traditional Hmong healing ceremony for victim of battery following testimony from experts on the Hmong cultural traditions). *But see* People v. Poddar, 103 Cal. Rptr. 84, 88 (Cal. Ct. App. 1972), *rev'd on other grounds,* 111 Cal. Rptr. 910 (1974) (holding that testimony relating to defendant's culture properly excluded as to issue of diminished capacity); State v. Girmay, 652 A.2d 150, 152 (N.H. 1994) (holding that testimony of expert in Ethiopian culture not relied on by defendant's psychiatric expert in murder case involving Ethiopian defendant was irrelevant and properly excluded).

45. Guy Ben-David, *Cultural Background as a Mitigating Factor in Sentencing in the Federal Law of the United States,* 47 Crim. L. Bull., no. 4 at 1 (2011).

46. Alison Dundes Renteln & Rene Valladares, *The Importance of Culture for the Justice System,* 92 Judicature 194 (Mar.–Apr. 2009).

47. *Loza v. Mitchell,* 705 F. Supp. 773, 812 (S.D. Ohio 2010); *Mak v. Blodgett,* 754 F. Supp. 1490 (W.D. Wash, 1991), *aff'd* 970 F.2d 614 (9th Cir. 1992), *cert. denied* 507 U.S. 951 (1993).

48. *See, e.g., Aphaylath,* 476 U.S. 79.

49. Cynthia Lee, *Cultural Convergence: Interest Convergence Theory Meets the Cultural Defense,* 49 Ariz. L. Rev. 911, 916 (2007); Doriane Lambelet Coleman, *Individualizing Justice through Multiculturalism: The Liberals' Dilemma,* 96 Colum. L. Rev. 1093 (1996).

50. Tom R. Tyler, *Procedural Justice and the Courts,* 44 Ct. Rev. 26, 26 (2007–08).

51. ABA Judicial Div. Lawyers Conference, *Perceptions of Justice Toolkit: A How-to Guide for Planning a Local Event to Discuss Perceptions of Justice in Your Community,* Judicial Division Record, at 15 (2013).

52. *Id.* at 15.

53. A wealth of information about the Intercultural Development Inventory can be found at the company's official website, https://idiinventory.com/.

54. Milton J. Bennett, *Towards Ethnorelativism: A Developmental Model of Intercultural Sensitivity, in* Education for the Intercultural Experience (R. Michael Page ed., 1993).

55. Mitchell R. Hammer, *Additional Cross-Cultural Validity Testing of the Intercultural Development Inventory,* 35 Internat'l J. Intercultural Rel. 474–87 (2011); Mitchell R. Hammer, *The Intercultural Development Inventory: A New Frontier in Assessment and Development of Intercultural Competence, in* Student Learning Abroad 115–36 (Michael Vande Berg et al. eds., 2012).

56. Letter from Mitchell R. Hammer, Ph.D., President of IDI, LLC to Jean Mavrelis (Nov. 7, 2016) (on file with author).

57. For more information about the company, please visit http://kmadiversity.com/.

58. Joan McMahan Flatt, Powerful Political Women: Stirring Biographies of Some of History's Most Powerful Women 190 (2012).

59. Thomas Kochman & Jean Mavrelis, Corporate Tribalism: White Men/White Women and Cultural Diversity at Work (2009).

Chapter 9
Procedural Fairness

Judge Kevin Burke and Judge Steve Leben

Chapter Contents

Chapter Highlights

- Research shows that public attitudes toward courts are driven more by how people are treated than by case outcomes.

- When judges and court personnel implement four basic concepts of procedural fairness, participants in court proceedings have higher levels of overall satisfaction with the courts and a greater likelihood of voluntarily complying with court orders.

- The key elements of procedural fairness are voice (or the opportunity for participation), neutrality, respect, and trust (or trustworthy authorities).

- The positive response of court participants to procedural fairness applies equally to majority and minority populations.

- Focusing on procedural-fairness principles may help to lessen the effects of implicit bias.

Introduction

In the past few years, procedural fairness—also known as procedural justice—has emerged as a dominant theme when considering how courts should function in the United States. Indeed, researcher David Rottman of the National Center for State Courts has called procedural fairness "the organizing theory for which 21st-century court reform has been waiting."[1]

Procedural-fairness concepts by themselves don't form a complete checklist of what judges or a justice system must do; in addition to using fair procedures, we still need to get the outcome right. And we need to process cases expeditiously, which is not an explicit procedural-fairness construct. But there's substantial evidence that procedural-fairness concepts best match what the public looks for from its justice system and that adherence to procedural-fairness principles improves public acceptance of the courts and compliance with court orders.

In this chapter, we will provide an overview of the commonly accepted elements of procedural fairness as well as some of the research about how adherence to these principles affects public and litigant perceptions. We will then discuss some of the ways these principles may be applied in trial and appellate courts. We will close with a discussion about how a focus on procedural fairness may help to lessen perceptions—and perhaps even the reality—of implicit bias.

I. An Overview of Procedural-Fairness Concepts[2]

In 2006, we began to draft a white paper on procedural fairness for the American Judges Association. Before that, Kevin Burke had served several terms as chief judge of the 62-judge Minneapolis trial court, where he worked to incorporate procedural-fairness principles throughout his court. Our paper was based on the extensive research work of law and psychology professor Tom Tyler and other social scientists who have demonstrated that how disputes are handled has an important influence on people's evaluations of their experience in the court system. In fact, these researchers have convincingly shown that people's views of the justice system are driven more by how they are treated by the courts than by whether they win or lose their particular case.[3]

The American Judges Association approved the procedural-fairness white paper in 2007, and the Conference of State Court Administrators (representing the administrative leaders of the American judiciary) formally endorsed the AJA's white paper in early 2008.[4] Since 2007, we have had a chance to present these concepts to many state and national judicial conferences, and others have been doing so as well.

Many courts have made strong moves to incorporate these principles into their daily work. In 2013, the Alaska state courts posted a fairness pledge near the entrance to every courthouse, telling all who visit the Alaska courts that its judges and court staff will listen to them, will treat them with respect, and will respond to their questions about court procedure.[5] By creating the poster (written in the six languages most used in Alaska), then-Alaska Chief Justice Dana Fabe emphasized that procedural-justice principles were at the center of the court's mission and made a permanent statement about fairness in Alaska's courts. In Utah, the state courts have for many years surveyed court users at courthouses throughout the state with statements like, "I was treated with courtesy and respect," and "The judge listened to all sides."[6] When these regular surveys show a drop in satisfaction at a particular courthouse, court officials work to determine what may have changed. And in New York, researchers concluded that the highly acclaimed Red Hook Community Justice Center had achieved reductions in crime and recidivism primarily from adherence throughout that courthouse to procedural-justice principles.[7] So there is growing acceptance in both academia and the justice system that courts must pay attention to procedural-fairness principles.

Tyler has identified four basic concepts that comprise procedural fairness and drive public opinion about the courts:

1. *Voice (or the opportunity for participation)*: Litigants are able to participate in their case by expressing their viewpoint
2. *Neutrality*: Legal principles are applied consistently, decision makers are unbiased, and the decision-making process is transparent
3. *Respect*: Individuals are treated with dignity, and their rights are explicitly protected
4. *Trust*: Authorities are benevolent, caring, and sincerely trying to help the litigants; trust is garnered by listening to individuals, openly protecting litigants' rights, and explaining or justifying decisions that address the litigants' needs[8]

People view fair procedures as a way to produce fair outcomes.

The California state court system was an early leader in implementing procedural-fairness principles in its courts. An extensive 2005 study in California found that perceptions of procedural fairness were "the strongest predictor by far" of public confidence in the California court system—if litigants or members of the public perceived that the court provided fair treatment in the aspects

Tyler identified, their overall opinion of the court system was much more positive.[9] Significantly, the elements of procedural fairness dominate people's reactions to the legal system across ethnic groups, across gender, and across income and educational levels.[10]

While the public focuses on the fairness of the process, judges and lawyers tend to focus on fair outcomes, often at the expense of meeting the criteria of procedural fairness that are critical to public perceptions of the courts.[11]

> Significantly, the elements of procedural fairness dominate people's reactions to the legal system across ethnic groups, across gender, and across income and educational levels.

Figure 9.1, a chart provided in the report of California's separate surveys of attorneys and the general public, aptly demonstrates the different ways in which these two groups look at the importance of procedural fairness and outcome fairness. For attorneys, overall approval of the court was tied most closely to whether the court got the outcome right; for the public, overall approval of the court was tied most closely to whether the court applied fair procedures in deciding the case.

We can only speculate about the reasons for this. Traditional law-school education focuses on outcomes; first-year students learn the holding of each case and then take those legal rules and make them into outlines of the key legal principles of substantive courses. In addition, attorneys are more familiar than others are with a court's typical procedures and thus do not feel as lost during the process.[12]

But whatever the cause for these differences in the views of the public and those of the law-trained community of attorneys and judges, the justice system depends upon public trust. That trust is enhanced when those in the justice system focus on making sure that all who pass through it feel that they were treated fairly.

All of this must be considered in the context of diminished public trust in almost all institutions. As of a June 2016 Gallup survey, the percentage of

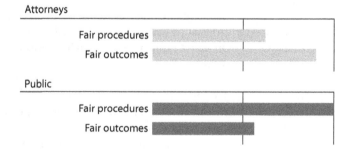

FIGURE 9.1   Relative Importance of Significant Factors on Overall Court Approval[13]

people with a "great deal" of confidence had fallen to only 3 percent of people for the U.S. Congress, 16 percent for the U.S. president, 15 percent for the U.S. Supreme Court, 9 percent for the criminal justice system, and 25 percent for the police. Even if we add those who had "quite a lot" of confidence, the totals rise only to 9 percent for Congress, 36 percent for the president, 36 percent for the Supreme Court, 23 percent for the criminal justice system, and 56 percent for the police. The police were one of only two government institutions—the other being the military—to have more than 50 percent of respondents express overall confidence. For the criminal justice system, 40 percent had only "some" confidence, 34 percent had "very little" confidence, and 2 percent had no confidence.[14] Given the general lack of trust in public institutions, we must pay special attention to anything we can do to maintain or improve the public's trust in its justice system.

In addition to improving the public's overall opinion of the court system, procedural fairness plays an important role in improving compliance with court orders. A substantial body of evidence suggests that when litigants perceive that they've been treated fairly, they are more likely to comply with the court orders that follow.[15]

For trial judges, then, if more procedural fairness results in greater compliance with court orders, mastering the principles of procedural fairness is doubly important. Procedural fairness can both help to improve public opinion about the courts and help judges reduce caseload pressures without increasing court staff or resources. Even a small decrease in the number of hearings required for violations of bonds, probation conditions, or domestic-violence orders could be quite helpful.

II. Putting Concepts into Practice

A. Areas of Trial Work Implicating These Concepts

For most trial judges, the majority of their work takes place in the open—on the bench in a courtroom open to the public. For many, the day is primarily spent sitting at the bench. People in the courtroom will form impressions of the judge based on verbal and nonverbal cues, the substance of what the judge says and does, and the actions of the judge's staff. Let's consider each of these separately.

1. Verbal and Nonverbal Cues

Once a judge begins to consider the world from a procedural-fairness viewpoint, he or she may realize that what once seemed normal behavior for a judge may actually be counterproductive. For example, most trial judges we've met have at some time signed a stack of orders on the bench. We've done it too—without giving a thought to what the parties in the case then proceeding in front of us were thinking. Putting computers on the bench may eliminate the visible signing of orders in now-paperless courts, but the computer is a potential distractor, too. Just as divided attention for drivers is a bigger problem now that computers are available in smartphones and car consoles, divided attention on the bench is a bigger problem now that computers are omnipresent. A lot of research is showing that a person can't really sufficiently do a task with divided attention.[16] Judges are no different.

When you think about on-the-bench activities from a procedural-fairness standpoint, doing anything other than paying attention to the case and parties in front of you while presiding over a hearing is indefensible. You could not explain to the editorial board of your local newspaper that the parties in court proceedings in front of you are only entitled to 50 percent—or less—of your attention. Nor could you explain that directly to the attorneys and parties in front of you. But they can *see* whether or not you are giving them your undivided attention.

One of the film clips we have used in training judges about procedural fairness came from the courtroom of a well-regarded and experienced New Hampshire judge. He was hearing arguments by the attorneys about whether to change the bail conditions pending trial in a domestic violence case. The main issue was whether to lift the no-contact order. The defendant was the primary breadwinner for the family, but he had no car. Since the no-contact order went into place, the woman he had been living with was unable to provide rides for him to and from work, and the family's income had dried up. Whether you think the no-contact order should have been lifted or kept in place, all judges would surely agree that this family had no more important issue to be decided by a court than whether this no-contact order was to remain in place for another three months or more pending trial. But during most of the argument, the judge was flipping through and processing a stack of routine documents requiring his signature. When the victim's turn to speak came, she started telling the judge that the defendant "never really hit me that night," and the prosecutor objected. Before the judge looked up and reacted, the victim had in effect sustained the objection by moving on to something else. The judge had lost control of his own courtroom, his attention sufficiently divided that he could not react as quickly as the prosecutor or the lay victim did.

That video clip provided an example both of divided attention and of a situation in which the parties in court might well perceive that the judge didn't give his full attention and appropriate concern to their case. More broadly, videotapes can be a great way to assess the various verbal and nonverbal cues a judge gives from the bench.

In New Hampshire, six trial judges volunteered to be filmed for half a day each, and we've used portions of these videos in judicial-training programs. In addition, though, part of what we wanted to do was to see what a judge could learn on his or her own simply by watching such a videotape. In Appendix A, you can read the comments made by these New Hampshire judges after watching their tapes. In all likelihood, many of the comments of the New Hampshire judges would apply to most judges across the United States.

Doing a video self-assessment this way is not difficult. For the New Hampshire project, each judge advised those in attendance that a film was being made solely for judicial-training purposes and that only the judge was being filmed. The camera, set up to the side of the courtroom, was turned on and generally ran for about half a day. While the audio in such a setup is not ideal, it's certainly adequate for this limited purpose. If a judge wants to go beyond self-assessment, the tape could be viewed by someone else who could give feedback—the judge's spouse, another judge, a communications professor or student, or someone else whose opinion the judge would respect.

2. What the Judge Says and Does

Paying attention to procedural-fairness concepts doesn't mean that people no longer care about outcomes; it's still important for a judge to get the outcome right. But what the judge says and does along the way, including the judge's explanation of the ruling, goes a long way in determining whether litigants and others will accept that decision.

Many judges are great at outcomes but weak on explanations. The research we've cited shows that the explanation is critical to decision acceptance. But to a judge, it is also a useful "self-check": If you cannot provide a reasonable explanation, maybe you got the outcome wrong.

For those trial judges who issue written opinions or rule frequently on written motions, the suggestions contained in the next section for appellate judges may be equally applicable to you. For the many rulings that are made from the bench, however, procedural-fairness concepts still remain in play. Most rulings should be understandable not only to attorneys but also to parties and courtroom observers. If the parties and observers don't understand what has happened, they can't tell whether the judge was trying to be fair or not. Explaining decisions in clear language, while showing that the decision was made based on neutral principles (such as a statute that might govern a landlord-tenant dispute), is important in showing neutrality and trustworthiness.

In addition to actual rulings, our trial-judge author found another way to use a written document in family court that was consistent with procedural-justice principles. In cases with contested child-custody issues, Kevin sent the parties a "Judicial Suggestion," noting up front that while judges usually send orders, he was making a suggestion—that the parties try as hard as they could to resolve the case. In doing so, Kevin personalized the order—and showed he had listened to the parties at their initial scheduling conference—by noting some of what they had said there. He provided suggestions for additional resources they might consult and gave them a compelling letter he had received in another case from a 16-year-old girl who had been involved for too long in a custody battle between her parents. Through this Judicial Suggestion, Kevin suggested resolution of the case in a forum (negotiation) in which the parties' voices are maximized, showed he had listened at his initial meeting with them, and expressed a sincere interest in a positive outcome for them. (The full order is attached as Appendix C to this chapter.)

Listening skills are another key ingredient for a trial judge who wants to master procedural fairness. The voice aspect requires both that parties have a chance to be heard and that they perceive they were understood, even if the court ultimately rules against them. Unless the judge correctly understands what has been said and gives an indication of that understanding, parties can go away without having their need for voice in the proceedings met.

Despite their importance, listening skills are rarely taught in either legal or judicial education. Reading and writing are a focus, but listening is not. Some useful training programs are available, and judges and other court personnel might be able to work together to develop listening-skills training at their courts. For a judge who wants to work on this individually, a useful online evaluation test and booklet about how to improve listening skills is available from a company called HRDQ.[17] Such a course can help a judge think through topics such as how to maintain attention during a lengthy hearing, how to focus, and how to help speakers (such as attorneys and witnesses) communicate with the listener (here, the judge).

3.   Actions of the Judge's Staff

Courtroom personnel also give verbal and nonverbal cues suggesting who and what is important in the courtroom and courthouse. Moreover, their behavior may be different depending on whether the judge is present. Ultimately, judges are responsible for those who work in our courts, and we should try to bring the staff on board in meeting the procedural-fairness expectations of the public. Court employees will never fully embrace procedural fairness in the courthouse if the management style of court leaders does not embrace procedural-fairness principles in dealing with those employees.

B.   Areas of Appellate Work Implicating These Concepts

To date, procedural-fairness research has concentrated on trial courts, not appellate ones. But there are obviously procedural-fairness perceptions at work at the appellate level as well. Let's review some of the settings in which procedural-fairness concepts might play out at the appellate level.

1.   Motions

Appellate courts get lots of motions. The Kansas Court of Appeals, where Steve sits as a judge, gets about 10,000 each year. Obviously you can't issue detailed written orders that show you've carefully considered each of 10,000 motions and still keep up with the rest of the work. After all, an appellate court's main task is deciding the cases based on briefing and argument, not figuring out all those motions.

But sometimes lawyers and litigants may rightly wonder whether appellate judges are paying any attention at all to the substance of the motions they've filed. In the Kansas Court of Appeals, motion rulings were traditionally handled by a single judge, who would write something like, "Accepted," "Denied," or "Denied on present showing" on the first page of the motion. And that was all the court said. If you received such an order, how confident would you be that the court understood what you had requested, respected your right to ask, cared about your rights, and applied neutral principles in its decision?

Perhaps judges sometimes hide behind a generally heavy workload; with overall numbers showing 10,000 motions a year, it's tempting to conclude that providing more appropriate orders could be impossible. But when you look behind the 10,000-motion number, you find that replies were filed in less than 5 percent of those motions. Thus, even if we assume that all motions with replies are opposed (while in fact some replies tell us that the other party has no objection), that means that fewer than 5 percent of the court's motions are contested. Now we're down to only 40 motions per month.

It's likely that only a few of the 40 or fewer contested motions per month need something more than the traditional terse handwritten order. In recent years, the Kansas court's motions judges have been preparing explanatory written orders on a regular basis as they've deemed it appropriate. Whether explicitly focused on procedural fairness or not, the increased use of written orders has undoubtedly helped in public perceptions of procedural fairness in the court's handling of motions. But, to the extent appellate courts throughout the country are not yet doing so, they should start thinking more carefully about perceptions of procedural fairness when ruling on motions. What *do* lay people think when their attorney tells them that their motion has been "denied on present showing"?

2. Oral Argument

The way a judge acts during oral argument can leave an impression about whether the judge genuinely seems to want to hear the litigant's position, acts in a respectful manner to the parties and their attorneys, and seems sincerely interested in a fair resolution. Judges can certainly argue about whether those are the primary purposes of oral argument. But if the public is viewing our work through a procedural-fairness lens, then a failure by appellate judges to consider this perspective when conducting oral argument risks alienating the public we serve.

Let's consider the views of one litigant who attended an argument in the U.S. Supreme Court. Senator John McCain attended oral argument in *Citizens United v. Federal Election Commission*.[18] After the decision came out, McCain said that he wasn't surprised by it: "I went over to observe the oral arguments. It was clear that Justice[s] Roberts, Alito, and Scalia, by their very skeptical and even sarcastic comments, were very much opposed to [it]."[19] McCain was left with the impression that these justices, who McCain noted had no experience in the political arena, weren't really interested in understanding the perspectives of others, including the majority of both houses of Congress. Leaving impressions like that is not healthy for the court system.

Now, one may say that this was an unusual case because, most of the time, few if any members of the public come to watch appellate arguments. But public access to appellate courtrooms is changing. Many state supreme courts offer streaming audio or video coverage, and a simple Google search for a judge's name can lead to a blog or other nontraditional account of someone's experience with the courts.

Moreover, judges generally don't know who the people in the gallery are. Was the crime victim present when a judge made a cavalier comment? Did the judge seem to care about the case as much as how much time was left for oral argument? Did the judge seem to pay attention at all? It's easy to think of many situations in which judges might give attendees a bad impression of the court system—one that could stick with them for a very long time.

3. Opinions

Our opinions say a lot from a procedural-fairness vantage point as well. Opinions that skip over any recognition of the concerns of the parties may leave the impression that the court didn't care about them, especially if the case ended up being decided on something that seems like a legal technicality, such as the statute of limitations. Opinions written in anything other than plain terms understandable to a lay reader imply that the court's intended audience is lawyers, not litigants or members of the public.

Judges have certainly differed over whether opinions should be written for a lay audience or for lawyers. But from a procedural-fairness viewpoint, the answer is clear: Opinions must be written for a lay audience. Can a litigant who finds that she cannot understand portions of the opinion really feel that the judge cares about her? Will a litigant who does not understand the explanation of the legal principles involved feel that his case has been decided on neutral principles rather than judicial bias disguised in gobbledygook?

We must recognize that the audience for judicial opinions has changed dramatically with Web access. When most of today's appellate judges went to law school, appellate opinions were mostly read by—and understandably were written for—lawyers. But that's not the state of things today. By 2009, the Minnesota court system's website had been visited 4.75 million times by nearly 2 million different individuals.[20] Those visitors generated more than 100,000 separate viewings of Minnesota Supreme Court opinions that year. Published Minnesota Court of Appeals opinions were viewed about 74,000 times on the website, and even that court's *unpublished* opinions were viewed 139,000 separate times.[21] With ease of access, litigants and the public are reading the opinions of appellate courts. Unless appellate opinions are written for lay readers, citizens cannot be expected to understand what the appellate courts are doing.

Here's one example from Steve's appellate-court work. His court had a case in which a man who now lives in Africa had filed a court case to set aside the adoption of his biological son. This wasn't his first visit to the Kansas court system, and his new claim was barred by res judicata. But the district court had already told him that, and he had appealed, listing 21 different reasons he said the district court had erred in a 45-page initial brief and a 12-page reply brief. The appellate court's majority opinion told him that he had "fail[ed] to present a single reason why the district court erred in denying his motion as res judicata," but it neither addressed his separate claims nor explained the concepts beyond res judicata rules.[22] The opinion was undoubtedly typical, though, of how most courts in the United States would resolve such a case: It provided the basic factual background, and it told the litigants that the father's attempt to reopen the adoption more than four years after it had been court-approved was too late and barred by the doctrine of res judicata.

Steve wrote a six-paragraph concurring opinion (one that with minor revision could have served as the court's opinion). We include it here because it provides one example of how appellate courts might tailor an opinion to focus on procedural-fairness concepts through plain English and an explanation of the concepts at issue:

> The history of N.M.'s sporadic appearances in the Kansas court system to reassert claims that he previously had abandoned suggests that he may not understand some of the overriding legal principles we must follow. I offer this concurring opinion in the hope that he may yet understand them. See Ronner, Therapeutic Jurisprudence on Appeal, 37 Ct. Rev. 64 (Spring 2000).
>
> The American court system works hard to ensure that court proceedings involving children are resolved in as short a time frame as possible. We recognize that children deserve an answer to the most basic questions about their lives—like, who are my parents? Where will I live?—within a time frame that is reasonable as judged from a child's viewpoint.
>
> The ultimate need for legal disputes to be resolved, so that people may get on with their lives and business affairs, is also the driving force behind the legal doctrine called res judicata. Under res judicata, when a dispute has been decided in a final court judgment, the same issues may not be relitigated in a later suit. That allows parties to go on about their business based on the court's final judgment without worrying that some later court action might yet revisit the same issues.
>
> The court's opinion has correctly held that res judicata applies here. N.M.'s parental rights were terminated by the district court in its January 2003 ruling. N.M. appealed, but when he dismissed that appeal, the district court's ruling terminating his parental rights became a final judgment. And after that, the proposed adoptive parents proceeded with their adoption of B.M.J.F. based upon the final

judgment, which terminated N.M.'s parental rights. So res judicata prevents further litigation over the matter.

Even if some exception to the res judicata rule were available— and I am not aware of one—this is exactly the sort of case in which we would be reluctant to apply it. This child has lived with the adoptive family from a few days after his birth in 2002 until now. From the time the adoption was finalized in October 2004 until N.M. filed pleadings in April 2009 seeking to reopen the case, the child's family knew that there was a final judgment terminating N.M.'s parental rights and an order of adoption in place. When we look at this situation from the standpoint of the child, he has had only one home and one family. He and his family have a right to rely upon the finality of the 2003 ruling terminating N.M.'s parental rights, a judgment that became final when N.M. voluntarily dismissed his appeal in 2004.

N.M.'s continued interest in his biological son is understandable, perhaps even laudable. But no matter its sincerity, it is no longer an interest that Kansas law can force this 8-year-old boy's adoptive parents to respond to.[23]

Obviously, at least at the time that case was decided in 2010, not all judges on the Kansas Court of Appeals had been convinced to apply procedural-fairness tactics (such as writing in plain English and clearly explaining legal concepts) in every case; after all, the opinion we reprinted here was a concurrence, not the court's opinion. We do recognize that an intermediate state appellate court has a very busy docket, and the judges simply can't take the time to write every opinion as if they were sitting on the U.S. Supreme Court. Compromises often must be made between the dual goals of timeliness and thoroughness.

But, aside from the additional time it may take, we see no downside to writing for the lay audience. Doing so will often expose flaws in legal reasoning that were hidden when the underlying concepts weren't explained. Sometimes a judge will find that the result that at first seemed appropriate really makes little sense. It's a rare case—if one exists—that a judge would not be able to explain to a high-school student, a family member, or any other nonlawyer if the judge really made that a goal for every opinion.

C. Placing the Court's Role in Context[24]

Sometimes both trial and appellate courts can help litigants and the public better understand that a case has been handled fairly by clearly explaining the role of the courts.[25] The court's role often is more limited than the public in general—and the litigants in particular—realize. For example, when citizens appeal government action in the courts, they rarely think in advance about the standard of review the court will use to judge that governmental action.

Rather, having lost in round one, they seek a second round to press their case on the merits. Although judges often recite the standard of review in their written opinions, they often write this section in legalese rather than using it to explain, in plain language, whatever limits there may be on the court's role.

Zoning appeals are a good example of the type of case where the court's role is more limited than the appellants may realize. (One might wonder how often lawyers take the time to explain to their clients what role the court will play in resolving these disputes.) As a trial judge, Steve handled the appeal of a city's approval of a large auto mall in a Kansas City suburb. The appeal was filed by neighboring property owners and their homeowners' association, each of which had opposed the rezoning before the city commission. In a 15-page written opinion, Steve noted that he had reviewed the full 2,600-page administrative record and devoted a full page of the opinion to a discussion of the role of a court in zoning matters, which began by noting that elected officials had made the decision:

> We live in a democracy in which many of the important decisions to be made that affect our lives are rightly to be made by our elected officials. Although the consideration by a city council of a rezoning request is deemed a quasi-judicial proceeding, the initial decision is to be made by elected officials, not judges. It is in the making of that initial decision that a great deal of discretion exists. In a given case, it might well be a reasonable decision either to grant or to deny the requested rezoning, and the decision would depend upon the elected body's preferences for its city's development.[26]

That introduction set the stage for further discussion of the court's formal standard of review, under which the elected body makes a decision that must be upheld unless it is well beyond the range of potentially reasonable decisions.

A similar explanation may have been helpful in *Kelo v. City of New London*,[27] a U.S. Supreme Court decision upholding a city's eminent-domain power and one of the Court's most unpopular decisions in recent decades. Historically, public approval of the U.S. Supreme Court has been at about 60 percent—but approval in the Gallup Poll's regular surveys dipped to 42 percent in the immediate aftermath of the *Kelo* decision, which was not well explained for a lay audience. It returned to 56 percent in the next survey, only three months later, and to 60 percent by the following year. (More recently, perhaps related to general dissatisfaction with all branches of government, approval of the Supreme Court has dipped back down to 42 percent in the July 2016 survey.)[28] When one looks at the *Kelo* opinion, it reads like a typical legal discussion of relatively abstract concepts. Perhaps had it been written more for the lay reader—and emphasized the leeway that a court must give to elected officials—the negative public reaction might have been lessened.[29]

III. Procedural Fairness and Implicit Bias

Few studies, if any, specifically test whether the application of procedural-fairness principles can be effective to lessen the impact of implicit bias in court.[30] But there is enough research to make some conclusions that are relevant to that question.

[A]lthough studies often find that racial and ethnic minorities have less trust in the judicial system than Whites do,[31] procedural-fairness research consistently shows that the positive effects of procedural fairness apply equally to majority and minority populations.[32] Accordingly, it certainly appears that adherence to procedural-fairness principles lessens the *appearance* of bias.

Second, a judge who focuses on procedural-justice principles essentially has a checklist that should help to lessen the impact of bias. To give voice, the judge concentrates both on listening to what's presented and summarizing the key points back to the parties. To show neutrality, the judge carefully explains the ruling—a process that may move step by step through the analysis rather than skipping over a missing connection as a result of bias. To show respect, the judge consciously thinks of each person before him or her as an individual. Collectively, these things may lessen the impact of bias. In addition, since people who are acting emotionally or have depleted cognitive resources are more likely to lack empathy and to act reflexively,[33] forcing the judge to be more deliberative and reflective through this focus on each element of procedural fairness may also lessen the impact of bias. Andrew Wistrich, Jeff Rachlinski, Sheri Lynn Johnson, and Chris Guthrie have shown that judges generally do better in overcoming implicit bias when they focus on the need to do so,[34] a subject discussed in more detail in Chapter 5. Focusing on procedural-fairness principles may be helpful as well.

Third, to the extent that more than one person—such as judges, clerks, and probation officers—has contact with those who come through the court system, it's reasonable to believe that following procedural-justice principles in the supervision of those judges, clerks, and probation officers may lessen the chance that those who are being supervised will be unfair with others, including in racially disparate ways. At least two studies of large police departments showed better job performance by officers when those officers reported a perception that procedural-fairness principles guided their supervision.[35] In particular, a study of officers in Las Vegas concluded that "the more officers feel they are treated well in the department, the less we observe racially disparate patterns of force use."[36]

> [A]lthough studies often find that racial and ethnic minorities have less trust in the judicial system than Whites do, procedural-fairness research consistently shows that the positive effects of procedural fairness apply equally to majority and minority populations.

We should also note that implicit bias in the courtroom is likely a two-edged sword—judges are not the only ones who come to court with implicit bias. So even if the judge works hard to limit the effects of his or her own biases, the judge must also keep in mind that those listening and observing may have biases too. By providing an understandable explanation of procedures and decisions as well as showing an empathetic and caring attitude, the judge may help cut through the bias of others. A judge who clings to neutrality so strongly as to mask signs that the judge is caring and empathetic may not be able to overcome implicit biases, leaving some observers feeling that the decision lacks legitimacy even though the judge—internally and out of the public eye—has tried hard to be fair.

From our vantage point, relatively recent events in both racial relations and public trust in institutions call for increased attention to procedural fairness. Highlighted by events in Ferguson, Missouri; Dallas, Texas; and other cities, the country has been roiled by police shootings of African-Americans, demonstrations, and shootings targeted at police. A 2016 survey of more than 500 criminal defendants in Hennepin County, Minnesota, state court showed that Blacks there consistently scored the court lower than Whites did on procedural-fairness questions, such as whether they felt listened to in court, whether the judge made sure they understood the decision, and whether the judge treated the defense attorney the same as the prosecutor.[37] The scores were lower than they had been a decade earlier, suggesting either that the court's performance had declined or perhaps that outside pressures on opinions of court fairness had become greater.

We have no doubt that courts that are open to measuring their procedural-fairness performance, like those in Utah and in Hennepin County, can improve their performance. Moreover, improved performance in this key area will result in better scores among Whites and Blacks, even if the appraisals of fairness by Black respondents remain somewhat lower than those of Whites. It will also achieve the other benefits that have now been documented for decades in the use of procedural-fairness principles in court.

Conclusion

Procedural-fairness effects in court and in law enforcement have been carefully studied by social scientists for more than three decades. Their research shows that public attitudes toward the courts are driven more by how people are treated than by case outcomes—and implementing the four basic principles of procedural fairness throughout the courthouse leads to greater satisfaction with the courts and greater compliance with court orders. Moreover, this positive response has been shown to occur for both majority and minority populations, suggesting that practicing procedural fairness may help to lessen the impacts of implicit bias.

APPENDIX A
New Hampshire Video Study

A few years ago, six New Hampshire trial-court judges agreed to let themselves be videotaped while presiding on the bench for several hours, and then let us use excerpts from those tapes in training other judges about procedural-fairness practices. Another part of the exercise was that each of the judges had to watch his or her own tape and then answer a couple of questions about what he or she had learned. Their answers are probably typical of what most judges could learn from such an exercise, so we have included them in this appendix. Our thanks to the New Hampshire trial judges—Gerry Boyle, Sue Carbon, Ned Gordon, James Leary, Deborah Kane Rein, and Mike Ryan—for their valuable contributions.

Question 1: Please give two observations of things you noted when watching the tapes that you may not have been aware of or paid sufficient attention to before.

A. Time seems to go faster when you are sitting on the bench than when you are watching the hearing. Parties from other cases who are waiting to be heard are probably bored stiff and must feel that the Court has wasted their time.

B. An enormous amount of time is taken up in completing forms while on the bench, particularly in criminal matters. This diverts the judge's focus away from the litigants and may make it appear like the judge is not paying attention to what is being said.

C. I was reading and sometimes even writing while defendants were speaking. I was flipping complaints and other paperwork over and reading them while the defendant is presenting his position on bail conditions. Pretty rude.

D. [There] is an appearance of impatience. I say appearance because I believe I am patient but, when presented with dozens of files to get through in a restricted time period, I have a sense of urgency that appears to me to come across as impatience. Rush, rush, rush.

E. I have a tendency to look angry.

F. I nod my head a lot—on the tape it's annoying. Perhaps in person it's not as bad (I hope!).

G. I had no idea how much I nod during the course of a presentation. I am not sure whether this is good (because it shows I am affirming that I am listening) or whether it seems that I am agreeing with what they are saying, which can cause some problems.

H. I was already aware of how slow I speak (not just on the bench but generally), but I was not aware of the number of large gaps in time that occur when I am thinking and how much of an opportunity it provides for a litigant/lawyer to fill the gap with unnecessary talk.

I. The first behavior I noted was it appeared as though I was constantly looking down. I have found that in marital cases, the taking of good notes is very important so I look down to write more often than I would in other type[s of] cases. I think participants could find my inconsistent eye contact as meaning I was not paying attention.

J. A second behavior was to ask counsel questions before asking the pro se litigant. I do not know how this is perceived by the pro se litigant. I do it only because counsel usually has a better handle on what the issues are.

Question 2: Please list two items on which you believe you might be able to improve your on-the-bench performance after viewing the tapes.

A. Don't call a hearing and then spend 10 minutes trying to figure out the background of the case on the bench. I should read the file in advance or take a recess if necessary in order to appear informed when the hearing begins.

B. I show my emotions easily. I tend to show more warmth toward attorneys I know and respect. I could perhaps be more stoic in that regard, particularly when the other party is pro se.

C. I plan to put the paperwork down and make eye contact with the defendant when s/he is speaking. This change may well further exasperate the issue of time constraints, but I was truly struck by my putting my head down and doing busy work while someone was speaking to me.

D. I plan to have the courtroom clerk separate those files with multiple or more complex charges so I can review them before the hearing. With such preparation, I will have a better idea of the charges when I address the defendant and not have to read everything for the first time with him/her standing there.

E. It would be helpful to smile and make a more welcoming greeting at the beginning of the case. I always thought I did, but at least from this angle, it seemed very curt.

F. I should try to sound and look more even-tempered. Even though I am questioning the litigant (and suspicious of what he was telling me), it is nonetheless important to appear open-minded and even-tempered.

G. I realized that I need to smile more to make people feel more at ease in the courtroom.

H. I would like to decrease the number of pauses I create. In addition to the problem expressed above, I wonder if it makes people feel that I lack confidence, which in turn may make them less confident in me. I am not sure how to do this since it is the way I speak in general, but I might be able to come up with some helpful technique.

I. If I were looking at this tape, I might think that I have all the time in the world to hear these cases because each hearing was longer than probably necessary. It was just an unusual day (generally we are swamped), but each case stayed within the time allowed on the docket (and the last one with the prisoner was just marking time until the plaintiff[']s (wife and daughter) appeared, which they did right after Gina turned off the camera). I am sure, however, that I am wont to allow people to go on longer than needed. I am not sure that this related to procedural fairness, but it does effect the court calendar. So, I could work on being more efficient while still giving everyone a full opportunity to speak.

J. The first thing I need to work on is to be better prepared before the hearing so that it does not appear that I am unprepared by going through the file to look at the Motion when introducing the case. I try to read the pleadings the morning of the hearings but sometimes when I get to a hearing, I have forgotten what the issues were.

K. The second thing is to remember to explain legal terms to the pro se litigants. I sometimes forget that not everyone speaks legalese.

APPENDIX B
Utah Judicial Performance Evaluation Commission Courtroom Observation Report Form*

Judges can alleviate much of the public dissatisfaction with the judicial branch by paying critical attention to the key elements of procedural fairness: voice, neutrality, respectful treatment, and engendering trust in authorities. Judges must be aware of the dissonance that exists between how they view the legal process and how the public before them view it. While judges should definitely continue to pay attention to creating fair outcomes, they should also tailor their actions, language, and responses to the public's expectations of procedural fairness. By doing so, these judges will establish themselves as legitimate authorities; substantial research suggests that increased compliance with court orders and decreased recidivism by criminal offenders will result. Procedural fairness also will lessen the difference in how minority populations perceive and react to the courts.

> —Hon. Kevin Burke, Minnesota District Court, Hennepin County, and Hon. Steve Leben, Kansas Court of Appeals, "Procedural Fairness: A Key Ingredient in Public Satisfaction," Court Review

This observation report has two parts. Part I is based on the principles of procedural justice. Please describe

1) the behaviors that you observe; and
2) your personal reaction to those behaviors.

Be as detailed as you can in describing the judge's behaviors as well as your reaction to them. Do not expect to see all of the listed sample behaviors each time you observe.

Part II asks additional, more general questions and provides an opportunity to comment on other aspects of your courtroom experience not covered in Part I.

Judge Name:

Date(s) of observation:

Type(s) of proceedings observed:

*We reprint here the Courtroom Observation Report used by the Utah Judicial Performance Evaluation Commission. This form is given to citizen volunteers who then sit in court and observe a judge's work on the bench. The form could be used by judges anywhere to have someone evaluate how well that judge is adhering to procedural-fairness principles, which were explicitly adopted as the standard for observers by the Utah commission.

Was the judge aware of this observation?   Yes   No   DK (Don't Know)

Any additional comments can be made in Part II of the report

Part I

Neutrality

People bring their disputes to the court because they view judges as neutral, principled decision makers who make decisions based upon rules and not personal opinions, and who apply legal rules consistently across people and over cases.

—Tom Tyler, "Procedural Justice and the Courts," Court Review

Consider, for example, whether the judge

- displayed judicial fairness and impartiality toward all parties;

- acted in the interests of the parties without regard to personal prejudices;

- listened carefully and impartially;

- applied rules consistently across people and over cases;

- maintained a neutral demeanor or expression while in court;

- was open, clear, and transparent about how the rules of law were applied and how decisions were being made;

- consistently treated participants equally and displayed behavior appropriate for the situation;

- was unhurried, patient, and careful.

1. How would you describe this judge's ability to be neutral, principled, and consistent?

Observer comments:

Respect

Respect includes treating people well, that is, with courtesy and politeness, and showing respect for people's rights.

Providing people with information about what to do, where to go, and when to appear, all demonstrate respect for both those people and their right to have their problems handled fairly by the courts.

—Tom Tyler, "Procedural Justice and the Courts," Court Review

Consider, for example, whether the judge

- provided participants with specific information about what to do, where to go, and when to appear;
- treated everyone with courtesy, dignity, and respect;
- maintained appropriate courtroom tone and atmosphere;
- demonstrated appropriate consideration for the rights of all persons in the court;
- demonstrated an intention to do what is right for everyone involved;
- helped interested parties understand decisions and what parties must do as a result;
- used clear language when speaking to jurors, litigants, witnesses, and attorneys;
- demonstrated respect for people's time and acknowledged their patience as needed;
- demonstrated interest in the needs, problems, and concerns of participants;
- seemed prepared for the proceedings;
- demonstrated appropriate body language (e.g., eye contact, facial expressions, posture, attire);
- demonstrated respectful voice quality (e.g., pitch, volume, tone);
- clearly articulated awareness of the practical impact on the parties of the judge's rulings, including the effect of delay and increased litigation expense;
- clearly explained the reasons for his/her decisions when appropriate.

2. How would you describe this judge's respect for people and their rights?

Observer Comments:

Voice

People want to have the opportunity to tell their side of the story in their own words before decisions are made about how to handle the dispute or problem. Having an opportunity to voice their perspective has a positive effect upon people's experience with the legal system

irrespective of their outcome, as long as they feel that the authority sincerely considered their arguments before making their decisions.
—Tom Tyler, "Procedural Justice and the Courts," *Court Review*

Consider, for example, whether the judge

- allowed participants to voice their perspectives/arguments;

- demonstrated to the parties that their story or perspective had been heard;

- behaved in a manner that showed the judge had fully considered the case as presented through witnesses, arguments, and documents before the court;

- attended, where appropriate, to the participants' comprehension of the proceedings.

3. How would you describe this judge's skill at providing the participants a voice in the proceedings?

Observer Comments:

Part II

A: Understanding that the Judicial Performance Evaluation Commission will ultimately recommend that the voters retain a judge or not, is there anything else you would like the commission to know about your courtroom observation experience?
   Consider, for example,

- the organization, administrative efficiency and/or timeliness of this judge's court;

- whether the judge earned your trust and/or seemed to earn the trust of others in the courtroom;

- the overall strengths and weaknesses of this judge's performance; and

- anything else particularly notable about your courtroom observation experience, not already covered in the report.

Observer Comments:

B: If you were to appear before this judge as a litigant, would you have confidence that this judge would treat you fairly? Why or why not?

APPENDIX C
Judicial Suggestion

STATE OF MINNESOTA   FOURTH JUDICIAL DISTRICT COURT
COUNTY OF HENNEPIN   FAMILY DIVISION

In Re the Marriage of: Court File No. 27-FA-13-0000

Ms. Petitioner,

         Petitioner,

and   **JUDICIAL SUGGESTION**

Mr. Respondent,

         Respondent.

At its best, a contested custody case can be painful. At its worst, a contested custody case can be very painful, very acrimonious, and very expensive. Judges typically issue orders. This is a suggestion.

Experienced trial lawyers will tell you to be cautious about reading too much into a judge's reaction during a court trial or, in this case, an initial case management conference. Sometimes a judge may probe an attorney or witness to confirm a tentative position the judge has arrived at. Sometimes a judge really has reached an immovable position. And sometimes reading anything into the reaction of a judge is useless. The bottom line is neither party nor their attorney should presently believe that they know what this Court might ultimately decide in this case and clearly cannot safely predict what the Court of Appeals might do if the aggrieved party decides to appeal. Clearly neither party can accurately predict whether or not the Minnesota Supreme Court might have an interest in the legal issues they are litigating.

The question to Mr. Respondent is this: Do you want to engage in a legal battle that could last several years with Ms. Petitioner or do you want to be focused on the quality of your relationship and bonding with your child?

For Ms. Petitioner there is a similar question: Do you want to engage in a legal battle that could last several years with Mr. Respondent or do you want to focus on ensuring your child has the benefit of the love from their entire family and the experience of having both a mother and a father in their life?

The impression that this Court left the initial case management conference with is that Mr. Respondent and Ms. Petitioner are nice people, have a nice child, and have the potential to embark on a very expensive and high-conflict dissolution. Ms. Petitioner's position as articulated by her attorney, that parenting time for the parties should be driven by the child support and maintenance issues, is an invitation to disaster. When judges are confronted with motions by deadbeat dads to increase parenting time simply to avoid child support, the motions are denied. Loving and caring moms whose position is that they need the child support and maintenance and that need drives their thinking about an appropriate parenting time schedule may fare better in court than a deadbeat dad, but they invite conflict that is destructive. That is precisely why the Court advised the parties to decide the parenting time issue first and not to combine them as Ms. Santana advocated on behalf of Ms. Petitioner.

Closure is needed for both parties. More importantly, closure is needed for your child. Although I would like to think that I am wise, I am more realistic than wise. A District Court order is not going to bring closure to this case. This Court has seen parties litigate throughout their child's entire childhood. This is clearly not in the best interest of any child. It may be difficult to see now, but at some point, your child will become an adult. Maybe easier to see is that very soon, she will no longer be a child. There is a brief window of opportunity for both parents to enjoy the phases of your child's life that will not come again. The question for both parents then is: Do either of you want to risk the impact that protracted litigation will have on those years and those relationships?

There is no better fair warning to the parties of what is at stake for your child than a letter the Court received recently from a 16-year-old girl. It read:

> Dear Judge,
>
> I am sixteen years old and am self-reliant. I have a job that I have been working at since September, but have been employed in some way for nearly a year. I have been emotionally and psychologically damaged from the events surrounding and the aftermath of my parents' divorce.
>
> Although I believe I am healed (not fully of course) there is an excess of emotional trauma I have to cope with on a daily basis. **I have night terrors, anxiety, paranoia, depression, insomnia and have trouble paying attention in school.** These symptoms have all built up on each other since I was in sixth grade. Now I deal with pent-up repressed emotions. . . . **I have been a pawn in this ridiculous legal battle between my parents** and I am ready to voice my opinion and wishes.
>
> I would like to be emancipated, gaining full rights to myself. . . .
>
> Sincerely,
>
> *[Name Withheld]* (emphasis added)

My "Judicial Suggestion" is this: I suggest that the parties sit down with their attorneys, listen to their advice, but commit to finding a compromise that is in your child's best interest. Look at the material the Court provided on parenting options. Go to the Social Early Neutral Evaluation with an open mind but a commitment to finding a solution. If your child is to avoid the fate of the 16 year old who wrote to this Court, the parties must spend the rest of their lives cooperating in parenting. The sooner they can reach agreements on their own, the better for your child. Neither side will get the "deal" they want, even though they likely believe that their proposal is the best choice for your child. Because they love their child so much and because of their character, they can do this.

I do not want a reaction from either party or the attorneys to this suggestion. Trial lawyers can at times become so embroiled in the battle that they fear that suggesting a return to negotiation is a sign of weakness on their part as opposed to wisdom. In this case, a negotiated agreement may be the most wise suggestion that a very good family lawyer can make to their client. Perhaps Ms. Petitioner and Mr. Respondent feel that they or the other party has become so entrenched in their positions that compromise is not possible. I have enough wisdom to know that this is not true. Ms. Petitioner and Mr. Respondent, no matter what their faults, are smart people. Smart people intuitively understand that controlling your own destiny is far preferable than letting other people dictate it.

BY THE COURT:

/s/
Kevin S. Burke
Judge of District Court

So You'd Like to Know More

Browse:

- Procedural Fairness website (www.proceduralfairness.org)
- Center for Court Innovation: Procedural Justice Materials (http://www.courtinnovation .org/topic/procedural-justice)

Read:

- Kevin Burke & Steve Leben, *Procedural Fairness: A Key Ingredient in Public Satisfaction,* 44 Court Review 4 (2008), *available at* http://goo.gl/afCYT
- Tom R. Tyler, *Procedural Justice and the Courts,* 44 Court Review 26 (2008), *available at* http://goo.gl/UFDT2g
- Terry A. Maroney, *The Emotionally Intelligent Judge: A New (and Realistic) Ideal,* 49 Court Review 100 (2013), *available at* http://goo.gl/NrQyiT
- Paula Lustbader, *Listening from the Bench Fosters Civility and Promotes Justice,* 13 Seattle Journal of Social Justice 903 (2015), *available at* http://digitalcommons.law.seattleu .edu/sjsj/vol13/iss3/13/

Practice:

- If you're on a multi-judge court, talk to a colleague who is also interested in procedural fairness and agree to observe each other on the bench. The form in Appendix B suggests what to look for.
- Videotape yourself on the bench and review your own tape.

About the Authors

Kevin Burke is a District Judge in Hennepin County, Minnesota. He is the coauthor of two American Judges Association white papers, "Procedural Fairness: A Key Ingredient in Public Satisfaction" and "Minding the Court: Enhancing the Decision-Making Process." Judge Burke has been named one of the 100 most influential lawyers in the history of Minnesota by *Law & Politics* magazine. He is the recipient of the 2003 National Center for State Court's William H. Rehnquist Award for Judicial Excellence. The Rehnquist Award is presented annually to a state judge who exemplifies the highest level of judicial excellence, integrity, fairness, and professional ethics.

Steve Leben is a judge on the Kansas Court of Appeals, where he has served since 2007. Before that, he was a general-jurisdiction trial judge in Kansas for nearly 14 years. He and chapter coauthor Kevin Burke wrote a white paper for the American Judges Association in 2007 on how to improve perceptions of fairness in court. The two have provided educational programs for state and federal judges on this topic throughout the United States and beyond since 2007. In 2014, the National Center for State Courts gave Leben its highest honor for a judge, the William H. Rehnquist Award for Judicial Excellence, largely for this work; Judge Burke won the same award in 2003.

Endnotes

1. David B. Rottman, *Procedural Fairness as a Court Reform Agenda*, 44 Ct. Rev. 32, 32 (2008).
2. For this section, we have drawn liberally on two prior articles we coauthored: Kevin Burke & Steve Leben, *Procedural Fairness: A Key Ingredient in Public Satisfaction*, 44 Ct. Rev. 4 (2008), *available at* http://goo.gl/afCYT/ [hereinafter *Procedural Fairess*]; and Kevin Burke & Steve Leben, *The Evolution of the Trial Judge from Counting Case Dispositions to a Commitment to Fairness*, 18 Widener L. Rev. 397 (2009).
3. *See, e.g.*, David B. Rottman, *Adhere to Procedural Fairness in the Justice System*, 6 Criminology & Pub. Pol'y 835 (2007); Tom R. Tyler et al., Social Justice in a Diverse Society 75 (1997); Jonathan D. Casper et al., *Procedural Justice in Felony Cases*, 22 Law & Soc'y Rev. 483, 483, 486–87, 504 (1988); Jason Sunshine & Tom R. Tyler, *The Role of Procedural Justice and Legitimacy in Shaping Public Support for Policing*, 37 Law & Soc'y Rev. 513, 514–15 (2003); John Thibaut & Laurens Walker, Procedural Justice: A Psychological Analysis 67–96 (1975).
4. Conference of State Court Administrators, Resolution 6, *In Support of AJA White Paper on Procedural Fairness* (July 30, 2008), *reprinted in* 44 Ct. Rev. 48 (2008).
5. Steve Leben, *The Procedural-Fairness Movement Comes of Age, in* National Center for State Courts, Trends in State Courts 2014 at 59–60 (2014), *available at* http://goo.gl /bmDPGQ (last visited Aug. 1, 2016).
   The Alaska Pledge of Fairness states the following:
   > The fundamental mission of the Alaska Court system is to provide a fair and impartial forum for the resolution of disputes according to the rule of law. Fairness includes the opportunity to be heard, the chance to have the court process explained, and the right to be treated with respect. The judges and staff of the Alaska Court System therefore make the following pledge to each litigant, defendant, victim, witness, juror, and person involved in a court proceeding:
   > We will LISTEN to you.
   > We will respond to your QUESTIONS about court procedure.
   > We will treat you with RESPECT.
   Id. at 60.

6. *Id.* at 60–61.
7. *Id.* at 61–62; *see* Cynthia G. Lee et al., *A Community Court Grows in Brooklyn: A Comprehensive Evaluation of the Red Hook Community Justice Center, Final Report* 177–78 (2013), *available at* http://goo.gl/ODNyDB (last visited Aug. 1, 2016).
8. David B. Rottman & Tom R. Tyler, *Thinking About Judges and Judicial Performance: Perspective of the Public and Court Users*, 4 Oñati Socio-Legal Series 1046, 1049–50 (2014); Tom R. Tyler, *Procedural Justice and the Courts*, 44 Ct. Rev. 26, 30–31 (2008).
9. David B. Rottman, *Trust and Confidence in the California Courts: A Survey of the Public and Attorneys* 19–20, 24 (2005), *available at* http://www.courts.ca.gov/5275.htm.
10. Burke & Leben, *Procedural Fairness, supra* note 2, at 7; Tyler, *supra* note 8, at 28.
11. *See* Larry Heuer, *What's Just About the Criminal Justice System?: A Psychological Perspective*, 13 J.L. & Pol'y 209, 215–17 (2005).
12. *See* Rottman, *supra* note 9, at 11, 18; Rottman & Tyler, *supra* note 8, at 1051–57.
13. Reprinted from Rottman, *supra* note 9, at 25.
14. These results were from a Gallup survey taken June 1–5, 2016. Gallup has tracked most of these measures at least annually since 1973. *See Confidence in Institutions*, Gallup, http://www.gallup.com/poll/1597/confidence-institutions.aspx (last visited Aug. 1, 2016).
15. *See, e.g.*, Tom R. Tyler, Why People Obey the Law 8, 172 (1990); Tom R. Tyler, *Legitimacy and Legitimation*, 57 Ann. Rev. Psychol. 375 (2006); Tom R. Tyler, *Procedural Justice, Legitimacy, and the Effective Rule of Law*, 30 Crime & Just. 283, 286 (2003); Burke & Leben, *Procedural Fairness, supra* note 2, at 7; Tyler, *supra* note 8, at 28; Tom R. Tyler et al., *Reintegrative Shaming, Procedural Justice, and Recidivism: The Engagement of Offenders' Psychological Mechanisms in the Canberra Rise Drinking-and-Driving Experiment*, 41 Law & Soc'y Rev. 553, 570–78 (2007); Rottman & Tyler, *supra* note 8, at 1050; Kevin S. Burke, *Just What Made Drug Courts Successful?*, 36 N.E.J. Crim. & Civ. Confinement 39, 56–58 (2010); Allison Redlich, *Voluntary, But Knowing and Intelligent?*, 11 Psychol. Pub. Pol'y & L. 605, 610 (2005); Deborah A. Eckberg & Marcy R. Podkopacz, Family Court Fairness Study 3, 29, 32–33, 34–35, 38 (Fourth Judicial Dist. [Minn.] Research Division 2004), *available at* http://www.mncourts.gov/Documents/4/Public/Research/Family_Court_Fairness_Report_Final (2004).pdf (last visited Aug. 1, 2016); Katherine M. Kitzmann & Robert E. Emery, *Procedural Justice and Parents' Satisfaction in a Field Study of Child Custody Dispute Resolution*, 17 Law & Hum. Behav. 553, 554 (1993); Lee et al., *supra* note 7, at 177–78; Tom R. Tyler & Justin Sevier, *How Do Courts Create Popular Legitimacy?: The Role of Establishing the Truth, Punishing Justly, and/or Acting Through Just Procedures*, 77 Albany L. Rev. 1095, 1101–02, 1104–05 (2013/2014).
16. *See generally* Pamela Casey, Kevin Burke & Steve Leben, *Minding the Court: Enhancing the Decision-Making Process*, 49 Ct. Rev. 76, 89–90 (2013); M.H. Sam Jacobson, *Paying Attention or Fatally Distracted? Concentration, Memory, and Multi-Tasking in a Multi-Media World*, 16 J. Leg. Writing Inst. 419 (2010); David Glenn, *Divided Attention: In an Age of Classroom Multitasking, Scholars Probe the Nature of Learning and Memory*, Chron. Higher Ed., Feb. 28, 2010, *available at* http://chronicle.com/article/Scholars-Turn-Their-Attention/63746/ (last visited Aug. 1, 2016). The U.S. Department of Transportation has a separate website providing information about distracted driving at www.distraction.gov.
17. Their program guide and assessment test, called "Learning to Listen," can be accessed online at http://www.hrdqstore.com/Learning-To-Listen-Online-Participant-Guide.html (last visited Aug. 1, 2016). At present, the test and guidebook cost $45 when purchased online.
18. 130 S. Ct. 876 (2010).
19. Transcript, *Face the Nation*, Jan. 24, 2010, *available at* 2010 WLNR 1538117 (Westlaw).
20. *Id.*

21. E-mail correspondence with John Kostouros, Minnesota Court Information Office, Jan. 29, 2010 (on file with the author).

22. *In re* Adoption of B.M.J.F., No. 104,008, 2010 WL 3665154, at *2 (Kan. App. Sept. 10, 2010).

23. *Id.* at *2–3 (Leben, J., concurring). Professor David Wexler reprinted this concurring opinion in a law-review article to show an example of an appellate opinion designed to make sure the losing litigant knew that his or her voice had been heard. David B. Wexler, *Elevating Therapeutic Jurisprudence: Structural Suggestions for Promoting a Therapeutic Jurisprudence Perspective in the Appellate Courts*, 5 Phoenix L. Rev. 777, 782–85 (2012).

24. Parts of this section are adapted from Steve Leben, *Thoughts on Some Potential Appellate and Trial Court Applications of Therapeutic Jurisprudence*, 24 Seattle U.L. Rev. 467 (2000).

25. *See generally* Deanell Reece Tacha, *Renewing Our Civic Commitment: Lawyers and Judges as Painters of the "Big Picture,"* 41 Kan. L. Rev. 481 (1993).

26. Lancaster Homes Ass'n v. City of Overland Park, No. 99C10769, slip op. at 1 (Johnson Co., Kan., Dist. Ct. Jan. 6, 2000). A longer excerpt from the opinion is found at Leben, *supra* note 24, at 468–69.

27. 545 U.S. 469 (2005).

28. Gallup Poll data regarding its surveys of public approval of the U.S. Supreme Court is reported on Gallup's website at http://www.gallup. com/poll/4732/Supreme-Court .aspx (last visited Aug. 1, 2016). The data reported are from Gallup surveys from June 24–26, 2005 (42 percent); September 12–15, 2005 (56 percent); September 7–10, 2006 (60 percent); and July 13–17, 2016 (42 percent). The *Kelo* decision was issued June 23, 2005.

29. For suggestions on dealing with high-profile cases, see Robert Alsdorf, *High-Profile Cases: Are They More Than a Wrinkle in the Daily Routine?*, 47 Ct. Rev. 32 (2011).

30. In fact, at a recent symposium at which experts identified questions needing further research, one of the questions identified was, "[D]oes acting with procedural justice lessen the likelihood of expressing bias?" Report, National Initiative for Building Community Trust & Justice: *Research Roundtable* [hereinafter Research Roundtable Report] 26 (Nov. 19–20, 2015), *available at* https://uploads.trustandjustice.org/misc/NI_Round _Table_Final_Report.pdf (last visited Aug. 1, 2016).

31. *See, e.g.*, Robert V. Wolf, *Race, Bias & Problem-Solving Courts*, 21 Nat'l Black L.J. 27, 32–33 (2009); Jon Hurwitz & Mark Peffley, *Explaining the Great Racial Divide: Perceptions of Fairness in the U.S. Criminal Justice System*, 67 J. Politics 762 (2005).

32. Rottman, *supra* note 3, at 835; Tom R. Tyler & Yuen J. Huo, Trust in the Law: Encouraging Public Cooperation with the Police and Courts 160–64, 207 (2002); Tom R. Tyler, *Public Trust and Confidence in Legal Authorities: What Do Majority and Minority Group Members Want from Law and Legal Institutions*, 19 Behav. Sci. & L. 215, 233–34 (2001); Rick Trinkner & Phillip Atiba Goff, *The Color of Safety: The Psychology of Race & Policing, in* The SAGE Handbook of Global Policing (B. Bradford, B. Jauregui, I. Loader & J. Steinberg eds.) (in press), *available at* https://www.researchgate.net/publication/301492464_The _Color_of_Safety_The_Psychology_of_Race_Policing (last visited Aug. 1, 2016).

33. Research Roundtable Report, *supra* note 30, at 15–16.

34. Jeffrey J. Rachlinski, Sheri Lynn Johnson, Andrew J. Wistrich & Chris Guthrie, *Does Unconscious Racial Bias Affect Trial Judges?*, 84 Notre Dame L. Rev. 1195, 1225–26 (2009); *see also* Casey, Burke & Leben, *supra* note 16, at 83–84.

35. Phillip Atiba Goff & Karin Danielle Martin, *Unity Breeds Fairness: The Consortium for Police Leadership in Equity Report on the Las Vegas Metropolitan Police Department* 26–27 (2013), *available at* http://www.lvmpd.com/portals/0/pdfs/lvmpdfinalreport_2013cple .pdf; Rottman, *supra* note 8, at 837.

36. Goff & Martin, *supra* note 35, at 26.

37. Joseph A. Hamm, *An Application of an Integrated Framework of Legitimacy to the Courts Context* (2016) (unpublished manuscript on file with the authors).

Chapter 10
Considering Audience Psychology in the Design of Implicit Bias Education

Victoria C. Plaut and Christina S. Carbone

Chapter Contents

Chapter Highlights

- Care should be taken in designing and implementing implicit bias education, especially given the lack of data regarding effectiveness and the concern about promoting a merely symbolic initiative.

- Be conscious of possible sources of psychological resistance to implicit bias trainings, some of which can be addressed. Among other things, communicate a norm of working against bias, promote individual responsibility and self-efficacy, and don't avoid discomfort.

- Maximize the relevance of the content to people's jobs and organization in order to motivate participants' attention and engagement.

- Be aware that the identity of the presenter and support from organizational leaders can influence effectiveness.

- Manage expectations about the purpose of and skills to be gained in the session.

- Ideally, use an implicit bias session to expand the focus beyond individual bias to appreciate the role of systemic factors.

- Be sensitive to the experience of session participants who are targets of the biases being discussed.

- Implicit bias education has the potential to facilitate cultural change by providing language, tools, and a space for revealing and addressing processes that may otherwise remain hidden from view.

Introduction

On June 27, 2016, the U.S. Department of Justice announced its rollout of a department-wide implicit bias training program.[1] The mandatory program will initially target the 23,000 agents working in its four law enforcement agencies and 5,800 attorneys working in U.S. Attorney's Offices and will eventually expand to include all the department's criminal prosecutors and the Inspector General's Office. This announcement follows the adoption of implicit bias education programs in local and state law enforcement agencies around the country over the past several years.[2] Courts have also taken an interest in implicit bias. Members of the state and federal judiciary and judicial organizations have engaged implicit bias trainers to educate their members on implicit bias.[3] And, the National Center for State Courts has piloted implicit bias education programs in three states and encourages training as a method for reducing bias.[4] Implicit bias training has been implemented by at least one public defender's office.[5] Additionally, the American Bar Association has launched implicit bias initiatives, of which this volume is a part.[6]

By and large these sessions serve an educational function by raising awareness of implicit biases involving a wide range of identities—including not only race and ethnicity, but also gender, sexual orientation, national origin, immigrant status, religion, disability, and socioeconomic status—within the organization. To be sure, whether implicit biases actually predict discriminatory behavior has been hotly debated. According to a group of skeptics, the IAT (Implicit Association Test), one commonly used tool to measure implicit bias, only weakly predicts behavior toward stigmatized groups.[7] But according to a rebuttal, even if one accepts the lower estimates of the magnitude of these relationships, implicit bias can still translate into thousands of people being treated differently because of their race or other characteristics, or the same people being repeatedly subjected to discriminatory treatment.[8] Considering the growing number of studies directly or indirectly implicating implicit biases across many different decisions in legal contexts (e.g., police stops, use of force, detention and release, jury selection, evidence judgments, sentencing, appellate review, and judicial performance evaluations, to name a few), implicit biases could translate into effects that are societally quite significant. Some might even argue that any time implicit bias affects an individual result in a single case, the justice system has not worked properly.

But does training make a difference? Unfortunately, very little research exists on the effectiveness of implicit bias education. In nonlegal contexts, one experimental evaluation of implicit bias training focusing on gender bias among faculty found improvement in workplace climate.[9] Another focusing on racial bias among university students found a decrease in implicit bias and increases in awareness and concern.[10] Related literature on diversity training—although different in many ways from implicit bias trainings[11]—shows more mixed results. Generally, meta-analyses of diversity training have suggested modest positive effects on intergroup attitudes.[12] When it comes to organizational outcomes, however, results are less optimistic. One study of diversity initiatives in over 800 companies across several decades found that diversity training had essentially no effect on the number of White women and Black men managers, and was followed by a decrease in the number of Black women managers.[13]

> As implicit bias presentations proliferate, however, careful thought needs to be given to their content, implementation, and follow-up. Without adequate forethought, organizations risk sponsoring training that is merely symbolic or even counterproductive.

Despite the absence of data, organizations continue to adopt implicit bias education programs; perhaps it is difficult not to adopt this approach while other solutions are lacking and, as discussed throughout this book, the manifestations of racial and other groups' disproportionality remain large. Moreover, these organizations face significant external pressure, as increased public attention to issues of race has brought scrutiny to the behavior of various actors within the justice system, including law enforcement, lawyers, and the judiciary. As implicit bias presentations proliferate, however, careful thought needs to be given to their content, implementation, and follow-up. Without adequate forethought, organizations risk sponsoring training that is merely symbolic or even counterproductive. [14] While symbolic structures[15] afford the organization some legitimacy in the public eye, they may not result in actual, substantive change.

In this chapter we consider factors that could contribute to implicit bias education backlash or ineffectiveness—some specifically related to the nature of the topic and others that are more generic—and strategies for addressing them. Our goal is to surface a set of concerns that could be addressed in order to bolster the effectiveness and avoid possible pitfalls of implicit bias training, particularly given the dearth of data. Our intent is not to suggest that implicit bias education serve as a replacement for other measures that organizations may and ought to take in addressing these systemic issues. We are also not suggesting that implicit bias education be abandoned. In fact, we believe that there is potential for implicit bias sessions to open the door for greater organizational change.

The chapter is divided into six parts. In Strategy 1, we discuss possible sources of psychological resistance to implicit bias trainings and the unintended consequences of addressing such resistance using the dominant "normal cognitive processes" approach.[16] In Strategy 2, we highlight how to motivate participants' attention and engagement by maximizing the relevance of the content to people's jobs and the organizations to which they belong. In Strategy 3, we discuss considerations around forging a connection with participants, including the identity of the presenter and support from organizational leaders. In Strategy 4, we discuss managing expectations about the purpose of and skills to be gained in the session. In Strategy 5, we discuss strategies for broadening the conversation by looking beyond bias as an individual, "bad apple" phenomenon to appreciate the role of systemic factors. Finally, in Strategy 6, we highlight the importance of acknowledging the potential reactions of minority participants—who are often underrepresented and are commonly the targets of the biases being discussed. Where possible, we ground our analysis in empirical social science research, and, where relevant, we provide examples from current initiatives, from the social science literature, and from our experience as implicit bias researchers, teachers, and workshop facilitators and participants.

I.   Strategy 1: Minimizing Reactiveness

> I'm not prejudiced. I treat everyone fairly. Why do I have to listen to this?

As this quote suggests, bias-related content can spark resistance. Negative reactions from participants range from subtle to overt and may involve, for example, questioning the necessity of the training, questioning the competence of the trainer, withdrawal, passive-aggressive behaviors, and outright hostility.[17] After all, biases around race, gender, religion, sexual orientation, and other identities are highly sensitive topics. Moreover, most people think of themselves as egalitarian,[18] and, as we explain below, thinking that one is objective or feeling like one's freedom of thought is being usurped can lead to *more* bias as opposed to less.[19] Notably, studies that have found potential negative effects of similar trainings, such as sexual harassment training[20] and diversity training,[21] attribute these effects to backlash or reactance. In designing an implicit bias session, it is therefore important to consider the potential for defensive reactions.

In this section, we discuss three perceived threats that may serve as sources of resistance. First we discuss the role of threats to autonomy and review evidence that environments that support autonomy are more conducive to decreasing bias than are those that undermine autonomy. Trainings that tell people not to be biased (or are perceived to do so) can create backlash or rebound effects, and trainings that encourage internal motivation (through choice and agency) can decrease threat and bias. Second, we discuss research on racial anxiety and how this anxiety can perpetuate avoidance and deplete mental resources. Third, we discuss research on majority group members' threat reactions to diversity. We then discuss the advantages and disadvantages of a strategy commonly used to mitigate against these reactions—framing implicit bias as a normal process of the mind. We offer suggestions for balancing these considerations in the design of implicit bias sessions, taking into account concerns about the diffusion of responsibility and the role that discomfort can play in fostering change.

A. Threat to Autonomy

According to reactance theory, if people think they have a particular freedom and that freedom is taken away, they are likely to oppose the control over their behavior.[22] People are likely to exhibit psychological reactance if, for example, they feel pressured to act a certain way or to hold a particular opinion. Consider, for example, participants in a session on bias in which the facilitator tells them that they are racist and should change their thoughts or behaviors. The participants may feel the facilitator is imposing on their freedom of thought or questioning their ability to objectively make up their own judgments, and they may in turn get defensive and withdraw or even lash out. According to an anecdotal account of one such training with school teachers, one participant blurted out, "You don't know me. How could you possibly know what I'm thinking?"

Research in the field of health-related persuasion (e.g., communication on alcohol consumption, sunscreen use, contraceptives, and exercise) offers a useful window into the possible effects of messages that are perceived to encroach on people's freedom. When people feel threatened by features of a message, they may feel angry and have negative thoughts, for instance, about the message.[23] The threat may also lead to derogation of the messenger.[24] It can also incite a boomerang effect, where individuals are motivated to perform the very act that is being discouraged, or a related-boomerang effect, where they are motivated to perform a similar act.[25] According to studies on reactance in health-related persuasion, vivid language, such as using graphic words, leads to greater reactance.[26] Forceful, dogmatic language also elicits reactance. For example, using language such as "you must" to persuade people to use sunscreen or exercise leads to more reactance than using language such as "consider" and "up to you."[27]

In the domain of race relations, whether majority group members are internally or externally motivated to reduce prejudice has important implications for their response to pressure imposed by others to react positively to minority group members. White Americans with a combination of low internal motivation and high external motivation to respond without prejudice (i.e., who are motivated to act nonprejudiced not because it is personally important to them but because they want to avoid negative reactions of others) may be especially likely to feel threatened and show backlash to diversity-related requests or initiatives.[28] Thus people's reactance to prejudice-related messages is guided by their motivations.

Prejudice reduction is also sensitive to motivation. Generally, research on self-determination[29] suggests that a sense of autonomy is particularly important for fostering internal motivation. Borrowing from this literature, Legault and colleagues showed non-Black Canadian undergraduates anti-prejudice brochures that either supported or undermined autonomy.[30] The autonomy-supportive brochure encouraged internal motivation by emphasizing the freedom to choose nonprejudice. In contrast, the autonomy-undermining brochure emphasized the need to comply with nonprejudice laws, policies, and norms. Participants reacted with less explicit and implicit prejudice to the autonomy-supportive brochure than to the autonomy-undermining brochure, and this difference was explained by participants' self-determined (internal) motivation to be nonprejudiced.

In part for these reasons, some scholars have suggested that bias reduction interventions provide a nonthreatening context and avoid making participants feel "ashamed of having racial, ethnic, or cultural stereotypes."[31] Others have gone further to suggest that increasing adherence to nondiscrimination norms may be better served by fostering internal motivation than by creating more legal coercion.[32]

Self-determination theory also suggests that a feeling of competence or self-efficacy is an important ingredient of internal motivation. In the context of bias-reduction, this translates into people needing to feel that they can do something to stem bias. For example, experiments that manipulated White undergraduates' sense of efficacy found that positive intergroup attitudes and antidiscrimination behaviors both increased when they were made to feel more efficacious.[33] This is particularly important to remember in the context of bias training, where a message may be communicated that bias is pervasive in the absence of concrete, implementable, and organizationally supported solutions.[34] Some implicit bias interventions have specifically targeted self-efficacy by providing participants with concrete behavioral strategies.[35] In the related context of diversity training, research has found self-efficacy beliefs to be important for following through on diversity-related intentions.[36] Perhaps for this reason, skill-based diversity training has been found to be more effective than awareness-based training in that it is more likely to lead to behavioral change.[37]

There are also other reasons to avoid simply telling people to suppress or avoid their biases. In a classic demonstration of the effects of thought suppression, researchers found that participants instructed to *not* think of a white bear thought about it more.[38] Suppression can also make the expression of bias grow stronger. When people are instructed to avoid thinking about people stereotypically, those stereotypes rebound.[39] Stressing the concept of colorblindness—the idea that people don't or shouldn't see race—has similar effects. For example, it can cause prejudice to come back stronger[40] and generate greater implicit prejudice.[41] Trying to adopt a colorblind interaction strategy also results in Whites appearing more prejudiced toward their other-race interaction partners,[42] putting themselves at a greater distance.[43]

B. Racial Anxiety

The discomfort that people often feel in interracial interactions is called racial anxiety. Racial anxiety can cause people to behave in unintended ways, for example, distancing themselves physically, avoiding eye contact, and even avoiding interactions altogether. Studies have suggested that discussing racially sensitive topics during interracial interaction can exhaust cognitive resources for both Whites and African-Americans[44] and can create physiological stress.[45] One of the sources of racial anxiety for Whites is the concern that they will appear prejudiced. In one study, Whites sat further from Black interaction partners after they were reminded of the stereotype that Whites are prejudiced, which fueled their fear that they would confirm the stereotype.[46] One of the main sources of apprehension for people of color in interracial interactions is the expectation that they will be the targets of prejudice.[47] This anxiety has been documented among Latinos, Asian-Americans, and African-Americans.[48]

The research on racial anxiety is relevant for at least two reasons. First, to the extent that participants are worried about what others will think of them, this could strain inter-group interactions in the session, even in the absence of interracial biases. Second, this literature suggests that discussing racial topics with racially dissimilar others can provoke anxiety. Therefore, racial anxiety is likely to play some role. Remedies for racial anxiety among Whites include increased contact with members of other groups (as contact increases, anxiety tends to decrease) and structure or scripts for interactions. For example, in one study, people who were given scripts or encouraged to develop scripts did not show greater anxiety and discomfort in cross-race interactions.[49] The authors suggest that attending to behavioral scripting in trainings will help curb anxiety, "thereby making other objectives of diversity training (e.g., bias reduction) more attainable."[50] Therefore it could be helpful for the presenter to have scripted questions or, if breaking up the audience into groups, to provide questions to guide their discussion.

C. Other Threats

Other threats have been documented that could be relevant to the delivery of implicit bias sessions. For example, *meritocratic threat* is a threat that Whites in particular might feel when considering "the possibility that their accomplishments in life were not fully earned."[51] Relatedly, *group-image threat* can emanate from "association with a group that has constructed and continues to benefit from unfair social advantages."[52] Both of these can lead to defensive reactions.

An additional source of resistance, at least for majority group members, may come from feeling threatened by racial and ethnic diversity, including threats to belonging, group status and prototypicality, identity and culture, and resources.[53] With respect to belonging, studies have found that Whites feel excluded by multicultural diversity initiatives[54] and show physiological signs of threat in response to those initiatives.[55] Those who identify strongly with being White may feel particularly threatened by multiculturalism, and this threat helps to account for prejudiced reactions.[56] Whites also feel threatened after reading about changing demographics and the decline of the size of their group, which also accounts for increases in prejudice.[57] To help mitigate against the downstream consequences of these threat reactions, some research has pointed to the usefulness of adopting an all-inclusive model of multiculturalism that maximizes inclusion of different groups in diversity initiatives and encourages open communication and learning among employees.[58] At the very least, some of these reactions could be mitigated by not highlighting demographic changes at the start of the session. Our point is not that majority individuals should be catered to, but rather that understanding common sources of threat could improve the design and, therefore, the individual and organizational outcomes of these educational efforts.

D. Framing Bias: A Common Psychological Process?

Grounding implicit bias in common psychological processes has been suggested as a way to improve receptivity to lessons about bias. For example, in their workshop on bias in faculty hiring, Fine and colleagues employ implicit bias research "to avoid stigmatizing or blaming workshop participants for perpetuating discrimination and instead present the influence of implicit or unconscious bias and assumptions as part of normative cognitive processes."[59] Indeed, research on implicit bias grew out of work on basic processes of perception, memory, and learning,[60] and implicit bias researchers and some legal scholars have emphasized that biases in decision making are rooted in processes of categorization and "normal human cognitive functioning."[61] Although there is no research that we know of that empirically tests the assumption that couching bias lessons in normal cognitive functioning helps to decrease defensiveness, it certainly is plausible. And this framework may very well be responsible, at least in part, for the recent popularity of implicit bias training. However, adopters of the "implicit biases are normal" narrative should be aware of at least three important caveats.

First, they must be careful not to pitch it as a norm. Communicating to an audience that stereotyping and prejudice are pervasive (i.e., that nearly everybody does it) can lead to unintended effects. For example, studies have found that communicating the high prevalence of stereotyping leads to *greater* stereotyping, as compared with emphasizing the low prevalence of stereotyping, pointing out the high prevalence of efforts to overcome stereotyping, or not giving any message about prevalence.[62] The culprit is likely the take-home message that "everybody's doing it."[63] Studies in other contexts have also suggested that descriptive norms can encourage undesirable behaviors, such as littering and environmental theft.[64] For example, households that were told that their neighbors used more energy than they did increased their energy use.[65] Cialdini suggests that "[p]ublic service communicators should avoid the tendency to send the normatively muddled message that a targeted activity is socially disapproved but widespread."[66]

> Communicating to an audience that stereotyping and prejudice are pervasive (i.e., that nearly everybody does it) can lead to unintended effects.

Moreover, norms can be particularly powerful when it comes to prejudice. One study found a near-perfect correlation between group norms about the acceptability of expressing prejudice and group members' willingness to express prejudice.[67] In other research, as in the energy consumption study, when told that the majority of students at their university had more negative racial views, the participants' racial views generally became more negative.[68] Other experimental studies have shown that condemnation or confrontation of discrimination by peers fosters anti-prejudice reactions.[69]

Second, they should consider the potential effects of pitching implicit bias as normal on levels of responsibility. Some worry that grounding implicit bias as a normal cognitive process can also lead to the conclusion that "none of us is responsible for our bias or for the discriminatory behavior that results from that bias."[70] Although we know of no direct empirical test of this assertion, social psychological research may offer some insight into the processes that could dismiss bias and inhibit action to address it. A long tradition of research on cognitive dissonance suggests that people change their cognitions to bring them in line with behavior when the two are inconsistent (e.g., conjuring up the thought that "smoking isn't that bad for you" to justify having a cigarette while attempting to quit). "Bias is normal" could similarly act as a rationalizing cognition after a biased thought or action, in order to decrease the dissonance that an egalitarian-minded person might experience. Another set of loosely related concepts comes from literature on helping behavior and the "bystander effect,"[71] which has shown that diffusion of responsibility decreases individuals' propensity to act when people need help. This research also suggests that "pluralistic ignorance" can inhibit helping behavior—if you think that others do not see a problem or a need for intervention, you will likely assume that there really isn't a problem. In other words, even if people think of themselves as egalitarian, social psychological constraints may limit their ability to take responsibility in the face of prejudice.[72]

Third, while framing bias as common may help deflate resistance, it is unclear that discomfort should be avoided altogether. Research on the effects of confrontation suggests that although a confrontation about racial bias can provoke anger and irritation towards the confronter, it also reduces stereotyping and prejudice.[73] And while confrontation in the form of a calm appeal for fairness tends to provoke less negative reactions than a hostile and accusatory confrontation, both appear to reduce bias. Finally, confrontation seems to work at least in part *because* of the discomfort it elicits. Note, however, that this research does not examine the long-term costs of confrontation, which can include costs to interpersonal relationships.

E. Balancing Considerations

In sum, psychological reactance, racial anxiety, and other types of perceived threat could evoke resistance to discussions of bias. To mitigate against such reactions, bias often gets framed as emanating from normal and common psychological processes. While this approach could help diffuse feelings of threat, however, it could also inadvertently communicate a norm, which could lead to increased bias or decreased feelings of responsibility for biased behavior.

Balancing the considerations raised by all of this research, we suggest the following: (1) that implicit bias education programs focus as much as possible on concrete and implementable strategies in order to increase participant self-efficacy, (2) that they avoid communicating that suppression is a useful strategy or telling people to be unbiased, (3) that they avoid framing trainings as externally imposed, (4) that they encourage internal motivation through autonomy and agency, (5) that they communicate a norm of nonprejudice, (6) that they mitigate against diffusion of responsibility, and (7) that although there is value in ensuring that participants do not get defensive, that difficult conversations not be avoided because of discomfort. Many of these suggestions tackle both the effectiveness of implicit bias education and issues of fostering responsibility.

II.   Strategy 2: Maximizing Relevance

> I'll jump through the hoops if that's what you want me to do. But,
> you know, I would much rather be out there on the street trying to
> police and trying to protect the community that I work for.[74]

For some people, trainings can seem like a burden or inconvenience, or a distraction from their jobs. This is especially true when trainings are mandatory and audience members have busy jobs that need to be temporarily set aside in order to attend. Skeptics may see implicit bias training as just another hoop they have to jump through, without appreciating the applicability of the material to them. One of the well-established findings within learning theory literature is that people invest more effort and are intrinsically motivated to learn when a topic is perceived to have personal importance or relevance.[75] A carefully designed session can help trigger an audience's motivation to learn by promoting a task's value. In other words, why should the audience care about implicit bias? How are implicit bias and its effects potentially relevant to their individual jobs and their organization more broadly? Moreover, beyond the content itself, features of delivery, such as opportunities for active participation, can help foster engagement and implementation of lessons learned.

A.   *Mission and Job Relevance*

Increasing a task's value can be done in a couple of different ways. First, the presentation can explicitly tie the material to the organization's values, goals, and mission. How might being attentive to issues of implicit bias within the workplace make employees better and more effective at their jobs? How might lessons from the implicit bias literature connect with and further an organization's goals of justice, equality, fairness, fostering good community relations, meeting ethical standards, and social responsibility? For example, for judges, the value of impartiality may be particularly important, and it coheres with the larger goal of preserving respect for the judiciary.

By framing the training as critical to an organization's purpose and function, members of that organization may come to see the presentation as relevant and important to their jobs and, even further, their identity. Organizational commitment captures not only a congruence between an individual's and organization's values and goals but also "a desire, a need, and/or an obligation to maintain membership in the organization."[76] Research on training effectiveness shows that levels of job involvement and organizational commitment are related to training motivation.[77] Those who psychologically identify with their work and see it as part of their self-image are more motivated during trainings because they see the material as likely to increase their skill level, job performance, and the success of the organization.[78] For these people, linking the implicit bias presentation to the organization's identity will make the session relevant to their own identity and increase their intrinsic motivation to learn and implement the lessons.

Second, one can provide examples of how implicit bias might be operating within the specific organizational context. Taking time to learn about the organization and its actors and tailor the session to the specific context will maximize the relevance of the material to the audience. In tailoring the session, the presenter may also consider which level of the organization he or she is addressing as well as which job functions are represented within the audience. This step is particularly important when the session is led by someone from outside the organization. Obtaining domain-specific knowledge of the organization allows the presenter to make the material self-relevant to audience members. When a topic does not seem directly applicable to a person's job, it may seem like a waste of time to learn about it. To counter this, presenters should incorporate examples pertinent to the daily jobs of participants. Running through hypothetical scenarios, for example, may also make some of the abstract concepts underlying implicit bias research more concrete to audience members.

> By framing the training as critical to an organization's purpose and function, members of that organization may come to see the presentation as relevant and important to their jobs and, even further, their identity.

A word of caution is warranted here. While studies revealing implicit biases have been conducted in a variety of fields, there may not be a study that directly covers the specific, daily decisions and behaviors of the audience. Presenters may want to be careful to not venture too far beyond the existing literature and make claims that are not empirically supported. Yet, with the proper acknowledgments of the limitations of the existing literature, the principles and lessons underlying the research may provide guidance on how implicit bias may be operating in a particular context. For example, are there particular decision points involving a high level of ambiguity and discretion? How might stereotypes or prejudices about different identity groups be triggered in the particular organizational setting? When multiple criteria factor into a decision, are those criteria being weighed and prioritized in a consistent way across cases? How might instances of leniency and second chances toward ingroup members manifest themselves?

A presenter with domain-specific knowledge may come prepared with examples of potential applications of the material to the organizational context. But one way to increase engagement from the audience is to challenge them to reflect on their own jobs and brainstorm about both problems and solutions. We know from the learning theory literature the importance of reflection in the learning process.[79] Reflection can aid learners in the monitoring and controlling of individual cognitive processes.[80] It also encourages self-directed learning and empowers individuals to reach their own conclusions—conclusions that are more likely to be endorsed and followed than ones imposed from an external source.[81] As suggested below in Strategy 4, this challenge to reflect on implicit bias should be aimed not only at the individual level but at the organizational level as well.

B. Active Participation

Research suggests the value of interactive activities for promoting engagement. In the related field of diversity training, most authors agree that experiential learning through active participation is important to the training's effectiveness.[82] Research has shown that including both active and passive forms of instruction has greater impact than trainings with passive instruction only.[83] There are several reasons this is the case. First, designing a dynamic session that includes different ways of conveying the information will likely resonate more broadly than a single, uniform approach. Particularly since most implicit bias sessions are focused on raising awareness, the majority of the session will likely be lecture based, with the presenter educating the audience about implicit bias. But breaking up the session with other types of activities will help keep the audience engaged.

Second, experiential learning presents an opportunity for participants to reach their own conclusions about how the concepts from the session might apply to their own jobs. It takes less work to persuade people of something they generated on their own versus something told to them by another. Interactive activities are a way to activate people's own motivations and attentional resources to address the problem at hand. Also, people are more likely to internalize and commit to ideas that they have worked through on their own accord.[84]

Third, interactive activities may not only reinforce participants' comprehension of the material being presented but also help address the "transfer problem"—that is, the difficulty of transferring the lessons from a training into actual practice.[85] Planned activities during the implicit bias session can challenge participants to extrapolate beyond what is covered in the session itself and apply the new knowledge to their specific roles and jobs. They can aid in translating the generalized, abstract concepts from the implicit bias literature to the concrete realities of participants' daily jobs. Participants may acquire new nodes of knowledge during the session, but the usefulness of this new information will be limited unless those nodes are meaningfully connected to aspects of their job or the organization.

Some of the activities to consider including are (1) small group discussions where participants discuss hypotheticals or brainstorm potential problem areas and solutions, (2) working through case studies or hypotheticals with input from participants, (3) a question-and-answer period where participants can ask for clarification and also highlight points of interest or concern, (4) providing participants the opportunity to anonymously submit question/comment cards at the beginning of a session break and then addressing those questions and comments when the session resumes, and (5) having participants develop an action plan for both themselves and the organization at the end of the session.

One exercise is to have participants write down at the end of the session ideas of how to address implicit bias moving forward. First they write strategies for themselves as individuals, which they take with them from the session. For example, a trial attorney may make a commitment to track the relationship between their peremptory challenges and juror race; a judge may commit to humanizing all defendants by shaking their hand prior to trial; a law firm partner may decide to apportion professional opportunities more equitably among men and women associates. Research has shown that the act of putting ideas to paper has the added benefit of increasing a sense of commitment to follow those strategies.[86] Second, audience members write constructive criticism and suggestions for the organization, including procedural, structural, resource-based, and other institutional factors that could help to curb bias. What areas could the organization evaluate for improvement, and what discussions need to happen beyond the instant session? For example, a prosecutor might suggest that his or her office help confine discretion by setting guidelines for standard offers on cases; an immigration judge might suggest convening a task force to examine caseload and other work factors that exacerbate the expression of implicit biases; an attorney might suggest that his or her general counsel require his or her law firm's legal team be diverse. This second set of ideas is collected by the presenter, who then conveys those ideas to the organization's management or appropriate committee while maintaining the anonymity of the submitter. Because further ideas for the organization may be generated after the session, the organization could also set up a mechanism whereby audience members can continue to submit anonymous comments on an ongoing basis.

In sum, Strategy 2 focuses on two ways to engage an audience during an implicit bias session. First, we suggest increasing the value of the session to participants by tailoring the contents of the presented material to the particular occupation of the audience, including being explicit about how implicit bias is relevant to their personal and organizational values and goals. Second, in designing an implicit bias session, we suggest thinking about how to create opportunities for active participation from the audience so they can already begin the process of translating the lessons of the session into their own jobs.

III. Strategy 3: Cultivating a Connection

Who is this person to tell me how to do my job?

The sentiment reflected in this quote captures one possible reaction that audience members may have to facilitators of implicit bias sessions. In this section we cover issues related to forging a connection with audience members—in terms of not only session leaders but also organizational leaders.

A. *Identity of the Presenter*

We know from the diversity training literature that the identity of the presenter can matter.[87] Consideration of who should lead an implicit bias session might focus on two different factors: (1) whether to have someone from within or outside of the organization or occupational field and (2) demographic characteristics. Both of these factors may be important to the level of trust and perceived legitimacy among participants. When there is a high level of mistrust because the presenter is perceived as an "outsider" or otherwise dissimilar to the participants, we might reasonably expect lower levels of receptiveness to the session's message and less candid conversations or self-disclosures.[88]

Certainly having the session led by a well-respected person within the organization has the benefit of an already developed sense of familiarity and trust with the participants. An organizational insider also has a working knowledge of the nature, demands, and limitations of the job. Thus, participants may be more receptive to a message coming from someone who "gets them." For example, a police agency under scrutiny for the use of force against people of color may more easily write off an external presenter because he or she is not credited with understanding the risk and danger that police officers have to deal with every day on the job. By contrast, a police audience may be more receptive to a presenter with a background in law enforcement who not only understands officer safety concerns but also has a shared identity with them. This is consistent with the approach used by the company contracted to implement the DOJ implicit bias trainings.[89]

The choice of whether the presenter is someone from within or outside the organization may be limited by the existing level of expertise on the topic of implicit bias among organizational members. The presenter must be qualified in knowing the literature on implicit bias in order to adequately provide information and respond to participants' questions and concerns. Thus, recruiting an expert from outside the organization may be necessary. In these situations, however, the presenter can collaborate with key organizational members to develop an understanding of the organizational context and gain domain-specific knowledge that can help frame the implicit bias material. For example, what are the different positions within the organization, what role does each position play in the larger process, what are the key decisional points, which areas are more subject to discretion than others, and in what ways might stereotypes and bias be triggered on the job? As mentioned in the previous section, coming to the table with domain-specific knowledge and concrete examples can be helpful in maximizing the session's relevance to participants.

For a session on implicit bias, the race, gender, and other identity characteristics of the presenter will be salient and may inform an audience's perceptions of the presenter's credibility and effectiveness.[90] Some research suggests that matching the presenter's and audience's demographics may be more critical when the participants are likely to be mistrustful of a demographically dissimilar presenter or when the session focuses on behavioral skills.[91] In the case of implicit bias training, the subject matter may lend itself to initial mistrust, particularly if the session has been prompted by external forces, such as public criticism.

How an audience will react to a particular presenter in the implicit bias context is a complicated matter. On the one hand, presenters from a minority group may come across as more legitimate when speaking about bias because they will be assumed to have had firsthand experience or knowledge about what it is like to be on the receiving end of discrimination. Stereotypes about White male presenters, for example, may include the perception that they have little understanding of institutional discrimination and what it is like to be a member of a minority group.[92] Indeed, some research on diversity training suggests less favorable responses to White male trainers when discussing differences.[93] On the other hand, research also suggests that people often find ingroup members to be more persuasive,[94] and that women and minorities are penalized more than White men for supporting diversity.[95] One suggestion to navigate these complicated dynamics is to have a team that includes presenters from different demographic groups.[96] Whenever possible, this would allow for multiple identities and perspectives to be represented in the room.

B. Organizational Support

Almost all authors writing about training effectiveness in other contexts emphasize that endorsement or buy-in from upper management is critical.[97] For example, researchers have found that diversity initiatives are most effective when organizational leaders directly take on responsibility for them.[98] Arguably, an unequivocal show of support from key leaders is all the more important when the implicit bias session is presented by an external source, and perhaps also when the session is perceived to be initiated as a reaction to external pressures.

> Clear commitment and active participation from the organizational leadership is critical to an effective training session.

A commitment from organizational leaders serves at least two purposes. First, it signals that the organization is taking the issue seriously and that the material being presented matters to the work that it does. Second, it models the desired behavior. When upper management attends and actively participates in the session, they communicate to everyone else that it is appropriate and encouraged in the workplace to grapple with issues of implicit bias. This is the approach taken by the DOJ in announcing its department-wide initiative. According to the Deputy Attorney General's announcement, "Along with the heads of our law enforcement agencies, I'm looking forward to participating in DOJ's very first training session tomorrow morning."[99] In fact, active participation from audience members, including not only leaders but also other organizational members, could signal an interest in discussing and acting on these issues that may not have been salient before. As discussed in Section 1, "pluralistic ignorance" can lead individuals to misperceive the social norm—in this case, misinterpreting silence on issues of bias as disinterest.

In addition, the organizational leadership often drives workplace culture. Therefore, their visible support for issues related to implicit bias can lay the groundwork for an awareness and sensitivity to these issues to become embedded within the organizational culture. Visible support from the leadership can take several forms, including releasing a statement of support in advance of the program, actively participating during the session itself, and releasing participants from their regular duties so they can attend. When thinking about organizational support, however, it is important to keep in mind the adage that "training is a process, not an event." This sentiment should challenge those invested in addressing implicit bias to think beyond a single session. Taking another note from the diversity training literature, research shows that the positive effects of diversity training are greater when done in conjunction with other initiatives.[100] An integrated approach is best. Certainly, implicit bias training should not be thought of as a substitute for other measures. The session should be thought of as the start of an ongoing discussion and, hopefully, action as well. To help ensure that the session does not become a one-shot gesture, how can the organization commit to some type of follow-up, action plan, or form of accountability? For example, after an implicit bias session conducted by one of the authors with a school, the school decided to form a task force to address issues of bias, including racial disparities in discipline. This type of longer-term commitment will keep the materials discussed during the session salient to participants and also reinforce the idea that the organization's support was not merely superficial.

In sum, Strategy 3 raises two things to consider when trying to ensure buy-in from audience members. First, the choice of the presenter—in terms of his or her background experience and identity—may matter to how the message of the implicit bias session is received. Second, because audience members will take a cue from organizational leaders, it is important that these leaders demonstrate through words *and* actions their commitment to implicit bias issues—not only during the session itself but beyond it as well.

IV. Strategy 4: Setting Expectations

> Expectations are premeditated resentments.

As this quote highlights, managing an audience's expectations for an implicit bias session can help prevent people walking away disappointed, frustrated, or feeling like they have wasted their time. As covered in Strategy 1, some participants' expectations about a discussion on implicit bias may predispose them to react negatively or with a closed mind to the session's content. But there are some additional expectations that participants bring with them that can be addressed at the outset. For example, participants may approach the session with some preconceptions about the purpose of the session, the motives of the presenter, the credibility of the material being presented, and what they expect to get out of presentation. We briefly explore each of these expectations below and provide suggestions for how to manage them during the session.

A. Defining the Purpose of the Session

This session should have been used to debias people.

The participant (a law student) making this comment expected that an implicit bias session would focus on "debiasing" participants, possibly because he or she thought participants had biases that needed to be eradicated. Unfortunately, the notion that people can be debiased in a two-hour session on implicit bias is deeply misguided. Studies have shown that changing people's attitudes and associations is no easy feat. For example, stereotype suppression and counter-stereotype production requires tedious and very repetitive training.[101] Although these types of bias-eliminating trainings have been shown to have somewhat persistent effects at least in the short term, people will inevitably be re-exposed to the social contexts that give rise to and reinforce the attitudes and associations underlying bias. Some trainees are in jobs where stereotypes are continuously reinforced. So too we live in a society where stereotypes are continuously reinforced.[102] Bias simply cannot be wiped away in the typical implicit bias session. Apart from the practical difficulties of debiasing people, some would argue that the purpose of training should be to remedy problematic behaviors, not attitudes. There are also concerns that such a tactic is too manipulative or coercive, or that it otherwise compromises people's liberty by imposing a particular worldview on them.[103] Strategies to mitigate the effects of implicit bias, such as greater intergroup contact, changes in motivation, enhanced awareness, and structural or procedural changes to the decision process take time and continual reinforcement.

If debiasing people is not the goal of the implicit bias session, then what is the goal? To manage audience expectations up front, the purpose of the session should be clearly articulated. The types of goals can be varied, ranging from purely educational to starting a larger discussion within an organization to imparting concrete strategies of how to address implicit bias in a particular context. Regardless of the goal, informing the audience at the outset about what to expect is important.

B. Pushing an Agenda

When the only tool you have is a hammer, then every problem is a nail.

This popular saying reflects an expectation that some audience members may bring with them: the presenter is trying to push his or her own agenda and sell us on implicit bias as the source of our problems. Sometimes this expectation may be fueled by assumptions made based on the presenter's background or organizational affiliations (e.g., an advocacy organization). Or it may stem from assumed reasons as to why the session is being put on at all (e.g., politically motivated or in response to public and media attention). One consequence of having this expectation is to be more guarded against the message being delivered, not unlike the reaction people have when they know they are trying to be "sold on something."

To counter this expectation, the presenter should be transparent about his or her motivations with the audience. Relatedly, the presenter

> [T]he presenter may gain credibility from the audience by being explicit about the claims he or she is making and the limitations of those claims.

may gain credibility from the audience by being explicit about the claims he or she is making and the limitations of those claims. If the presenter includes caveats when appropriate, the audience may perceive the presenter as more even-handed in his or her approach to the discussion. As mentioned above in Strategy 2, some degree of extrapolation from the literature may be needed when the presenter is addressing a particular context or decision point not directly covered by the research. The presenter may do well to acknowledge when he or she is doing this and also provide a justification for why it is well founded.

C. Credibility of the Content

I don't have much faith in those results. After all, the materials they used looked so unrealistic!

Even when an implicit bias session is rooted in peer-reviewed, scientific research, some participants will inevitability challenge either the methods or the applicability of the social science. This is, in part, because people will tend to view objective evidence in ways that confirm their previous beliefs or inclinations. For example, Lord, Ross, and Lepper exposed college students with either a pro- or anti-capital punishment stance to the methods and results of one study confirming and one study disconfirming their beliefs about capital punishment.[104] Not only did the students rate the procedures and results of the study that confirmed their belief as more convincing and better methodologically, but they also shifted their capital punishment beliefs in the direction of their original convictions. Similarly, a later study examined the relationship between sociopolitical attitudes and judges' and law students' ratings of admissibility of social science evidence in a pair of Supreme Court death penalty cases.[105] Judges and law students both rated evidence as more admissible when it comported with their own death penalty attitudes, although the effect was less extensive for the judges than for the law students (but judges were more confident that lawyers would agree with them).

Resistance to the science of implicit bias may be mitigated, in part, by placing the research presented within its larger context. For example, the presenter can acknowledge that any individual study will have limitations and shortcomings. However, the points highlighted in the session are supported by a far deeper and broader literature, and the studies presented were chosen as examples and illustrations. The methodological limitations of one study may very well be taken up and addressed in other studies. The presenter can emphasize that it is the repeated finding of implicit bias across various domains and methodologies that makes it a robust phenomenon.

D. What Are They Getting Out of It?

It was interesting information, but I thought since it was a "training" we would be told how we ought to be doing our jobs differently.

The participant (a lawyer) making this comment following an implicit bias training was receptive to the studies and information presented but expressed disappointment in not leaving with more concrete directives about how he should apply the information to his specific job. While some implicit bias sessions do cover concrete strategies specifically directed and tailored to the audience, many sessions are not designed to cover behavioral skill sets. This may be the case for several reasons. The audience may represent such breadth and diversity in occupations that it is not feasible to develop and cover strategies for all the decision points involved. Imagine, for example, an audience comprised of different juvenile justice stakeholders and associated agencies—police, judges, prosecutors, public defenders, probation officers, child welfare workers, school officials, and behavioral health workers. The different focus of each of these groups and the sheer number of decision points represented makes it impossible to identify and solve particular problems relevant to everyone. Rather, the presenter may choose to offer broad strategies and outline the contours of how participants themselves can go about the process of identifying problems and generating solutions.

In managing expectations on this front, the presenter might consider articulating at the beginning of the session what type of skills participants should expect to take away and at what level of detail. If participants are expected to simply leave armed with a better understanding of what implicit bias is and the general science behind it, then this should be made clear up front. In some cases, the presenter may plan simply to leave the audience with a path toward action. That is, while specific issues are not discussed in detail within the session itself, the presenter might give examples of how other organizations tackled a particular issue. Providing guidance as to the *process* of how to identify problematic areas and generate solutions will leave participants with a "take action" mentality that will hopefully extend well past the session itself.

> Providing guidance as to the *process* of how to identify problematic areas and generate solutions will leave participants with a "take action" mentality.

In sum, it is important to be mindful of the expectations that participants may bring with them—for example, regarding the session's purpose, presenter, material, and usefulness. Clearly articulating the purpose and skills to be gained and avoiding the expectation that a session is mean to "debias" people, being transparent about the presenters' motivations, and appropriately acknowledging limitations of the research while also demonstrating the thread that runs through studies from across methodologies and domains can all be used to manage expectations.

V. Strategy 5: Challenging the Bad Apple Mentality by Broadening the Conversation

A "bad apple" mentality—the view that a few bad apples are responsible for problematic behavior—pervades lay thinking about discrimination. According to Sommers and Babbitt, "[O]ne of the many problems with the 'bad apple' view is that it almost inevitably corresponds to a 'not me' mentality, which shifts responsibility for efforts to ameliorate inequity away from the self (and, for that matter, calls into question the necessity of such efforts in the first place)."[106] Implicit bias education might challenge bad apple thinking by simply appealing to the notion that bias emanates from normal cognitive tendencies that we all possess. Earlier in this chapter, however, we discussed the potential downsides of relying on this framing. Another possibility is to utilize implicit bias education to expand the conversation about where bias is located, which could ultimately reduce bad apple thinking.

According to Banks and Ford, "the most worrisome aspect of the unconscious bias discourse is that it is likely to reinforce a misguided preoccupation with individual acts of discrimination."[107] Indeed, the psychological studies comprising much of the implicit bias literature take the individual person as the object of interest. Thus, it is often easy to overlook the ways in which organizational factors create and maintain processes, structures, and environments that make the expression of implicit biases more or less likely,[108] or the ways in which sociocultural or system factors perpetuate bias.[109] Taking a broader sociocultural approach entails "locat[ing] the essence of racism not in biased individuals but instead in the biased 'stuff' of the everyday worlds that these individuals inhabit."[110] It emphasizes, for example, that members from different groups may draw upon divergent bodies of discourse, constructions of reality, lived experiences, and representations of history in making sense of current events.[111] Under this approach, stereotypes are seen as rooted in collectively shared representations and structures rather than simply existing in individual brains.

While research indicates that White Americans tend to view racism as an individual rather than systemic phenomenon,[112] there are some documented benefits to presenting racism from a sociocultural perspective. For example, in a study directly comparing teaching racism from a sociocultural versus individual perspective, students in the sociocultural class showed greater acknowledgment of systemic racism and greater endorsement of policies to address racism.[113] These effects were documented in some instances nearly two months after the lesson. Broadening the conversation to the system level could also help to bring attention to policies or practices that sustain disparate outcomes and may guide legal actors' decisions regardless of their own biases.

Relatedly, it may be useful to consider and acknowledge where the particular audience fits within a larger decision-making system—and how they might view their contribution to existing disparities. Some audiences may feel unjustly targeted by having to attend an implicit bias session because, from their perspective, the effects of implicit bias were already created by other actors—the bad apples—at previous points in the decision-making process. For example, consider an implicit bias session aimed at probation officers. They are one of the last actors in the criminal justice process to handle a particular case. Police, attorneys, lawyers, and juries have already made a host of decisions about a case before it gets assigned to a probation officer. By that point in time, we may very well see disparities in how the case has been treated relative to similarly situated others due to the cumulative effects of implicit bias. The probation officer may be tempted to simply attribute the effects of implicit bias to these other actors and see him- or herself as having inherited someone else's problematic decision making. In addressing this perspective, the presenter may want to acknowledge the contributions made by other entities in the system. However, it is also an opportunity to emphasize that the operation of implicit bias is not limited to any one decision point, and each actor within a larger system is responsible for the decision points under his or her control. Certainly, the decisions made by a particular actor may have differing degrees of significance and impact relative to other actors. In the adult criminal justice system, compared to probation officers, for example, police officers, judges, and prosecutors are involved earlier on in the process, have a greater degree of discretion, and have control over more types of decisions. Regardless of their position in the decision process, however, the audience could be challenged to think critically about their own roles and actions within the larger system and how they may or may not be perpetuating or contributing to the cumulative effects of implicit bias.

Of course, individual members of an organization are constrained and limited to varying degrees by the structures around them and must work within those constraints. As mentioned in the previous section, challenging audience members to consider the potential problems and solutions of implicit bias should include multiple levels of analysis and application, covering both the larger organization as well as instances of individual discretion and action. To reinforce this point, organizational leaders could signal their willingness to critically examine and address the issue of implicit bias at a systemic level, their receptiveness to feedback and ideas from audience members, and their intention to continue discussions on this topic in the future. Feedback mechanisms can be built into the trainings as suggested in Section 2. More broadly, training content will ideally be integrated with other bias-related initiatives that can be referenced during the training.

In sum, implicit bias education could be used to expand the discourse around the roots of bias from a problem of individual minds to a more collective and systemic one, possibly inspiring greater commitment to change. This expanded discussion could also offer opportunities to shed light on policies and practices that sustain discriminatory outcomes. Broadening the focus beyond the individual could also have the added benefit of decreasing defensiveness or a sense of personal attack discussed in preceding sections.

VI. Strategy 6: Taking on Multiple Perspectives

Programs designed to root out biases almost always focus on individuals' judgments of or behaviors toward negatively stereotyped groups. As a result, the focus tends to be on majority groups' thinking about minority groups (e.g., White law firm partners' biased evaluation of a Black versus White associate's work). Psychologists call this taking the perceiver's perspective. Previous sections of this chapter have devoted attention to the reactions of perceivers to bias programming, but it is also crucial to consider a wider range of perspectives, including those of targets. In this section we cover concerns about targets in bias-related sessions and tactics that could be deployed to address these concerns.

> When presenting information about implicit bias, consider and include the perspectives of those who are most often the targets of bias.

The demographics of many audiences result in "solo status" for certain participants, or being the only one or one of few in proportion to other identity groups. For example, a Black woman prosecutor might find herself being the only African-American in a bias training session. Research suggests that solo status increases the feeling that one is a representative of one's group, the feeling that one's sense of self is tied to one's group, and the perception that one's performance will reflect on one's group.[114] In other words, an uncomfortable spotlight gets cast on solo status participants. One Black woman participant once divulged to one of the authors after a bias-related session that while she was grateful that these issues were being discussed, she felt incredibly uncomfortable being the only African-American audience member when racial topics were so salient. To address solo status, conveners of training sessions can consider the diversity of participants and whether there are ways to ensure critical mass of underrepresented groups.[115] Aside from numerical representation, another possible tactic is to ensure a balance of examples so the same groups are not repeatedly presented as the targets of bias. Another is to cover concepts that represent the target's perspective—for example, concepts that capture what it can feel like to be on the receiving end of stereotypes, such as stereotype threat.[116] Stereotype threat is the anxiety people from a negatively stereotyped group feel when they fear they might be viewed through the lens of a negative stereotype or confirm a stereotype about their group. Research also suggests that learning about stereotype threat can help to decrease its negative effects.[117]

Other concerns may include worrying that one's coparticipants will act defensively, will minimize or deny the discriminatory experiences of stigmatized groups, or may say something derogatory. This is consistent with the work on racial anxiety referenced earlier in this chapter highlighting the concern people of color feel about being the targets of prejudice during interracial contact.[118] Moreover, even audience members' perspectives may diverge significantly along race, gender, and other lines. For example, majority and minority group members differ in their conceptions and perceptions of discrimination,[119] and minority groups' perspectives may align more closely with the systemic understanding of bias discussed in Strategy 5.[120] Resources for facilitating intergroup dialogue across these divides[121] could be helpful in fostering respectful spaces and understanding how to address difficult comments in a way that does not alienate people or create a lingering climate of negativity.

Finally, another reaction we have come across among targets is a feeling of despondency when repeatedly confronted with evidence of bias. For example, a law student in a class on implicit bias once shared that while it was gratifying to have her experiences validated, it was also very depressing to see how pervasive bias seemed and how unequipped she felt to dismantle the biases she would face professionally. This is consistent with the research on self-efficacy cited earlier in the chapter (suggesting the value of giving participants implementable strategies), but it suggests that attention needs to be paid to the self-efficacy of targets—not just perceivers. Discussing possible strategies for navigating biases or giving participants the opportunity to offer solutions for dismantling biases in their respective professional settings could help to mitigate this concern. Additional sensitivity is also required in considering the perspective of audience members who might simultaneously feel part of a stigmatized group and that they are seen as perpetrators against that group (e.g., a Black police officer).

In sum, attention should be given to the experiences of audience members who are also the targets of the biases being discussed and who are often underrepresented in these sessions and in their organization or occupational field. Attending to the examples being given in the session, fostering an open and respectful climate of discussion, and offering implementable strategies could help to improve the experience of these individuals.

Conclusion

We began this chapter by highlighting the recent, widespread adoption of implicit bias training by federal, state, and local entities in the justice system. We also stressed that, to date, data on the effectiveness of such programs remain elusive. The purpose of this chapter has been to use the social science literature to provide guidance to architects of implicit bias education on six sets of psychological factors that could increase the receptiveness of audience members to such sessions and enhance their ultimate effectiveness.

Yet the value of this implicit bias education movement may lie not in its ability to effectuate reliable change in individual decision makers. Rather, its value might lie in its ability to facilitate cultural change—in institutions that are often slow to change—by providing shared language, space, and a set of tools on matters of equity and inclusion, and by expressing a normative commitment to addressing issues that are of great concern to many people inside and outside the justice system. These sessions could serve as an institutional vehicle for revealing inequality-sustaining processes that may otherwise remain hidden from view and for increasing accountability for attending to them. Perhaps for these reasons it is all that much more important to ensure the careful and thoughtful design of implicit bias education.

So You'd Like to Know More

- Frank Dobbin and Alexandra Kalev, *Why Diversity Programs Fail* (July–August 2016), https://hbr.org/2016/07/why-diversity-programs-fail?cm_sp=Magazine%20Archive-_-Links-_-Current%20Issue

- Patricia G. Devine, Patrick S. Forscher, Anthony J. Austin & William T.L. Cox, *Long-Term Reduction in Implicit Race Bias: A Prejudice Habit-Breaking Intervention*, 48 Journal of Experimental Social Psychology 1267 (2012)

- Michelle M. Duguid & Melissa C. Thomas-Hunt, *Condoning Stereotyping? How Awareness of Stereotyping Prevalence Impacts Expression of Stereotypes*, 100 Journal of Applied Psychology 343 (2015)

- Victoria C. Plaut, *Diversity Science and Institutional Design*, 1 Policy Insights from Behavioral and Brain Sciences, 72 (2014)

About the Authors

Victoria C. Plaut is Professor of Law and Social Science at the University of California, Berkeley, School of Law, where she also serves as Associate Dean for Equity and Inclusion and Director of the Culture, Diversity, and Intergroup Relations Lab. At Berkeley Law, she teaches, among other things, courses on implicit bias and law and psychology. A social psychologist by training, Dr. Plaut has conducted extensive empirical research on diversity, which has been published in her field's top peer-reviewed journals and funded by the National Science Foundation. She has consulted on implicit bias, diversity, and inclusion with a wide variety of organizations in law, business, health care, and education.

Christina Stevens Carbone earned her J.D. and her Ph.D. in Jurisprudence and Social Policy from Berkeley Law. Her research interests lie at the intersection of law and psychology, including judgment and decision making, race, bias and discrimination, diversity, and organizations. Her dissertation work focused on accountability and its effectiveness in attenuating implicit racial bias in decision-making processes, particularly within the criminal law context. She is currently practicing criminal law as a Deputy District Attorney in Contra Costa County.

ENDNOTES

1. U.S. Dept. of Justice, *Memorandum for All Department Law Enforcement Agents and Prosecutors* (2016), https://www.justice.gov/opa/file/871116/download.
2. For example, in California, the Attorney General's Office announced its implicit bias training initiative in November 2015. Virginia's Attorney General announced an initiative in September 2015. Departments in Seattle, Los Angeles, Baltimore, and New Orleans are among the many that have held implicit bias trainings. *See, e.g.*, Matt Zapotosky, *In Push to Reform Police Work, Officers Examine Their Own Biases*, WASH. POST, Jan. 6, 2016, https://www.washingtonpost.com/local/public-safety/in-push-to-reform -police-work-officers-examine-their-own-biases/2016/01/06/b196ab66-a361-11e5-9c 4e-be37f66848bb_story.html.
3. *See, e.g.*, https://thebettermind.com/.
4. Pamela M. Casey, Roger K. Warren, Fred L. Cheesman II & Jennifer K. Elek, *Helping Courts Address Implicit Bias: Resources for Education*, National Center for State Courts (2012), www.ncsc.org/ibreport.
5. Jeff Adachi, *Public Defenders Can Be Biased, Too, and It Hurts Their Non-White Clients*, WASH. POST, June 7, 2016, https://www.washingtonpost.com/posteverything/wp /2016/06/07/public-defenders-can-be-biased-too-and-it-hurts-their-non-white-clients /?utm_term=.44bde018a5f4.
6. Paulette Brown, *Inclusion Exclusion: Understanding Implicit Bias Is Key to Understanding an Inclusive Profession*, ABA J. (Jan. 1, 2016), http://www.abajournal.com/magazine /article/inclusion_exclusion_understanding_implicit_bias_is_key_to_ensuring.
7. Frederick L Oswald et al., *Predicting Ethnic & Racial Discrimination: A Meta-Analysis of IAT Criterion Studies*, 105 J. PERSONALITY & SOC. PSYCHOL. 171 (2013); *see also* Frederick L. Oswald, Gregory Mitchell, Hart Blanton & James Jaccard, *Using the IAT to Predict Ethnic & Racial Discrimination: Small Effect Sizes of Unknown Societal Significance*, 108 J. PERSONALITY & SOC. PSYCHOL. 562 (2015).
8. Anthony G. Greenwald, Mahzarin R. Banaji & Brian A. Nosek, *Statistically Small Effects of the Implicit Association Test Can Have Societally Large Effects*, 108 J. PERSONALITY & SOC. PSYCHOL. 553 (2015). (The authors provide the analogy of a 1989 report on the link between aspirin and heart attack prevention that found a minuscule correlational effect size. They estimate that when applied to the number of U.S. male residents aged 50 or older, the finding translates into the prevention of 420,000 heart attacks over a five-year period.)
9. Molly Carnes et al., *Effect of an Intervention to Break the Gender Bias Habit for Faculty at One Institution: A Cluster Randomized, Controlled Trial*, 90 ACAD. MED. 221 (2015); *see also* Jessi L. Smith et al., *Now Hiring! Empirically Testing a Three-Step Intervention to Increase Faculty Gender Diversity in STEM*, 65 BIOSCI. 1084, 1085, 1086 (2015) (finding that a three-step intervention that included a 20–30-minute presentation on "the role of implicit gender bias in skewing the candidate-screening and interview processes" resulted in more gender-diverse hiring. It is not possible to ascertain, however, what role the implicit bias component itself played in the results.).

10. Patricia G. Devine, Patrick S. Forscher, Anthony J. Austin & William T.L. Cox, *Long-Term Reduction in Implicit Race Bias: A Prejudice Habit-Breaking Intervention*, 48 J. EXPERIMENTAL SOC. PSYCHOL. 1267 (2012).

11. Diversity trainings have traditionally encompassed a wide variety of approaches, but many do focus on bias. *See, e.g.*, Alexandra Kalev, Frank Dobbin & Erin Kelly, *Best Practices or Best Guesses? Assessing the Efficacy of Corporate Affirmative Action and Diversity Policies*, 71 AM. SOC. REV. 589, 593 (2006) (characterizing diversity training as aiming to reduce bias). *See also* Katerina Bezrukova, Jamie L. Perry, Chester S. Spell & Karen A. Jehn, *A Meta-Analytical Integration of Over 40 Years on Research on Diversity Training Evaluation*, 142 PSYCHOL. BULL. 1227, 1227 (2016) (characterizing diversity training as aiming to "address prejudice, stereotyping and other biases.").

12. *See, e.g.*, Zachary T. Kalinoski et al., *A Meta-Analytic Evaluation of Diversity Training Outcomes*, 31 J. ORG. BEHAV. 1076 (2013); *see also* Bezrukova et al., *supra* note 11, at 1237. (However, this study also found that these effects recede over time.)

13. Kalev et al., *supra* note 11, at 604. They do find diversity training to be more effective when used in conjunction with organizational responsibility structures (such as affirmative action plans and diversity committees), but only for White women. *See id.* at 607.

14. Moreover, the lack of data means that we don't know the potential for these trainings to produce unintended, paradoxical effects. For example, should we be concerned that these trainings may prime stereotypes and hence augment implicit bias? *See, e.g.*, Sandra Graham & Brian S. Lowery, *Priming Unconscious Racial Stereotypes About Adolescent Offenders*, 28 LAW & HUMAN BEHAV. 483 (2004). Should we be concerned about participants walking away from sessions feeling "credentialed"? *See, e.g.*, Benoit Monin & Dale T. Miller, *Moral Credentials & the Expression of Prejudice*, 81 J. PERSONALITY & SOC. PSYCHOL. 33 (2001).

15. *See, e.g.*, Lauren B. Edelman, *Legal Ambiguity & Symbolic Structures: Organizational Mediation of Civil Rights Law*, 91 AM. J. SOC. 1531 (1992) (work on symbolic structures); *see also* Lauren B. Edelman, Howard S. Erlanger & John Lande, *Internal Dispute Resolution: The Transformation of Civil Rights in the Workplace*, 27 L. SOC'Y. REV. 497 (1993); Robert J. MacCoun, *Voice, Control, & Belonging: The Double-Edged Sword of Procedural Fairness*, 1 ANN. REV. L. & SOC. SCI. 171 (2005) ("false consciousness" critiques of procedural justice).

16. What we mean here is the common message inherent in implicit bias education that implicit bias is a normal phenomenon of the human mind.

17. Donna Chrobot-Mason, Rosemary Hays-Thomas & Heather Wishik, *Understanding & Defusing Resistance to Diversity Training & Learning*, in DIVERSITY RESISTANCE IN ORGANIZATIONS 23 (Kecia M. Thomas ed., 2008).

18. Laurie T. O'Brien et al., *But I'm No Bigot: How Prejudiced White Americans Maintain Unprejudiced Self-Images*, 40 J. APPLIED SOC. PSYCHOL. 917 (2010).

19. Eric Luis Uhlmann & Geoffrey L. Cohen, *"I Think It, Therefore It's True": Effects of Self-Perceived Objectivity on Hiring Discrimination*, 104 ORG. BEHAVIOR & HUM. DECISION PROCESSES 207 (2007); *see also* Lisa Legault, Jennifer N. Gutsell & Michael Inzlicht, *Ironic Effects of Antiprejudice Messages: How Motivational Interventions Can Reduce (but Also Increase) Prejudice*, 22 PSYCHOL. SCI. 1472 (2011).

20. Shereen G. Bingham & Lisa L. Scherer, *The Unexpected Effects of a Sexual Harassment Educational Program*, 37 J. APPLIED BEHAV. SCI. 125 (2001).

21. Kalev, Dobbin & Kelly, *supra* note 11, at 611.

22. JACK W. BREHM, A THEORY OF PSYCHOLOGICAL REACTANCE (1966); *see also* SHARON S. BREHM & JACK W. BREHM, PSYCHOLOGICAL REACTANCE: A THEORY OF FREEDOM & CONTROL (1981).

23. James Price Dillard & Lijiang Shen, *On the Nature of Reactance and its Role in Persuasive Health Communication*, 72 COMM. MONOGRAPHS 144 (2005).

24. Claude H. Miller et al., *Psychological Reactance and Promotional Health Messages: The Effects of Controlling Language, Lexical Concreteness, and the Restoration of Freedom*, 33 Hum. Comm. Res. 219 (2007).

25. Brian L. Quick & Michael T. Stephenson, *Examining the Role of Trait Reactance and Sensation Seeking on Perceived Threat, State Reactance, and Reactance Restoration*, 34 Hum. Comm. Res. 448 (2008).

26. *See id.*

27. *See id.*

28. E. Ashby Plant & Patricia G. Devine, *Responses to Other-Imposed Pro-Black Pressure: Acceptance or Backlash?*, 37 J. Experimental Soc. Psychol. 486 (2001).

29. Edward Deci & Richard M. Ryan, Intrinsic Motivation & Self-Determination in Human Behavior (1985).

30. Lisa Legault et al., *supra* note 19.

31. Diana Burgess, Michelle van Ryn, John Dovidio & Somnath Saha, *Reducing Racial Bias among Health Care Providers: Lessons from Social-Cognitive Psychology*, 22 J. Gen. Internal Med. 882 (2007).

32. Katharine T. Bartlett, *Making Good on Good Intentions: The Critical Role of Motivation in Reducing Implicit Workplace Discrimination*, 95 Va L. Rev. 1893 (2009).

33. Tracie L. Stewart, Ioana M. Latu, Nyla R. Branscombe & H. Ted Denney, *Yes We Can! Prejudice Reduction Through Seeing (Inequality) & Believing (in Social Change)*, 21 Psychol. Sci. 1557 (2010).

34. This could also help alleviate the concern that implicit bias has been used as an illness metaphor that contributes to "bias being viewed as ineradicable." *See* Ralph Richard Banks & Richard Thompson Ford, *(How) Does Unconscious Bias Matter?: Law, Politics and Racial Inequality*, 58 Emory L.J. 1053, 1120 (2009).

35. Carnes et al., *supra* note 9; *see also* Devine et al., *supra* note 10.

36. Gwendolyn M. Combs & Fred Luthans, *Diversity Training: Analysis of the Impact of Self-Efficacy*, 18 Dev. Q. 91 (2007).

37. Loriann Roberson, Carol T. Kulik & Molly B. Pepper, *Individual and Environmental Factors Influencing the Use of Transfer Strategies After Diversity Training*, 34 Group Org. Mgmt. 67 (2009).

38. Daniel M. Wegner, David J. Schneider, Samuel R. Carter & Teri L. White, *Paradoxical Effects of Thought Suppression*, 53 J. Personality & Soc. Psychol. 5 (1987).

39. C. Neil Macrae, Galen V. Bodenhausen, Alan B. Milne & Jolanda Jetten, *Out of Mind but Back in Sight: Stereotypes on the Rebound*, 67 J. Personality & Soc. Psychol. 808 (1994).

40. Joshua Correll, Bernadette Park & J. Allegra Smith, *Colorblind & Multicultural Prejudice Reduction Strategies in High-Conflict Situations*, 11 Group Processes & Intergroup Rel. 471 (2008).

41. *See id.; see also* Jennifer A. Richeson & Richard J. Nussbaum, *The Impact of Multiculturalism Versus Color-Blindness on Racial Bias*, 40 J. Experimental Soc. Psychol. 417 (2004).

42. Evan P. Apfelbaum, Samuel R. Sommers & Michael I. Norton, *Seeing Race and Seeming Racist? Evaluating Strategic Colorblindness in Social Interaction*, 95 J. Personality & Soc. Psychol. 918 (2008).

43. Juan M. Madera & Michelle R. Hebl, *"Don't Stigmatize": The Ironic Effects of Equal Opportunity Guidelines in Interviews*, 35 Basic & Applied Soc. Psychol. 123 (2013).

44. Jennifer A. Richeson & J. Nicole Shelton, *When Prejudice Does Not Pay: Effects of Interracial Contact on Executive Function*, 14 Psychol. Sci. 287 (2003); *see also* Jennifer A. Richeson, Sophie Trawalter & J. Nicole Shelton, *African Americans' Implicit Racial Attitudes and the Depletion of Executive Function after Interracial Interactions*, 23 Soc. Cognition 336 (2005).

45. David M. Amodio, *Intergroup Anxiety Effects on the Control of Racial Stereotypes: A Psycho-neuroendocrine Analysis*, 45 J. Experimental Soc. Psychol. 60 (2009).

46. Phillip Atiba Goff, Claude M. Steele & Paul G. Davies, *The Space between Us: Stereotype Threat & Distance in Interracial Contacts*, 94 J. Personality & Soc. Psychol. 91 (2008).

47. J. Nicole Shelton, Jennifer A. Richeson & Jessica Salvatore, *Expecting to Be the Target of Prejudice: Implications for Interethnic Interactions*, 31 Personality & Soc. Psychol. Bull. 1189 (2005).

48. *See id.; see also* Linda R. Tropp, *The Psychological Impact of Prejudice: Implications for Intergroup Contact*, 6 Group Processes & Intergroup Rel. 131 (2003).

49. Derek R. Avery, Jennifer A. Richeson, Michelle R. Hebl & Nalini Ambady, *It Does Not Have to Be Uncomfortable: The Role of Behavior Scripts in Black-White Interracial Interactions*, 94 J. Applied Psychol. 1382 (2009).

50. *See id.* at 1389.

51. Eric D. Knowles, Brian S. Lowery, Rosalind M. Chow & Miguel M. Unzueta, *Deny, Distance, or Dismantle? How White Americans Manage a Privileged Identity*, 9 Persp. Psychol. Sci. 594 (2014).

52. *Id.*

53. Walter G. Stephan & Cookie White Stephan, *Intergroup Anxiety*, 41 J. Soc. Issues 157 (1985); *see also* Felix Danbold & Yuen J. Huo, *No Longer "All-American"? Whites' Defensive Reactions to Their Numerical Decline*, 6 Soc. Psych & Personality Sci. 210 (2015).

54. Victoria C. Plaut, Flanner G. Garnett, Laura E. Buffardi & Jeffrey Sanchez-Burks, *"What about Me?" Perceptions of Exclusion & Whites' Reactions to Multiculturalism*, 101 J. Personality & Soc. Psychol. 337 (2011).

55. Tessa L. Dover, Brenda Major & Cheryl R. Kaiser, *Members of High-Status Groups Are Threatened by Pro-Diversity Organizational Messages*, 62 J. Experimental Soc. Psychol. 58 (2016).

56. Kimberly Rios Morrison, Victoria C. Plaut & Oscar Ybarra, *Predicting Whether Multiculturalism Positively or Negatively Influences White Americans' Intergroup Attitudes: The Role of Ethnic Identification*, 36 Personality & Soc. Psychol. Bull. 1648 (2010).

57. Maureen A. Craig & Jennifer A. Richeson, *More Diverse Yet Less Tolerant? How the Increasingly Diverse Racial Landscape Affects White Americans' Racial Attitudes*, 40 Personality & Soc. Psychol. Bull. 750 (2014); *see also* Danbold & Huo, *supra* note 53.

58. Flannery G. Stevens, Victoria C. Plaut & Jeffrey Sanchez-Burks, *Unlocking the Benefits of Diversity: All-Inclusive Multiculturalism & Positive Organizational Change*, 44 J. Applied Behav. Sci. 116 (2008).

59. Eve Fine et al., *Minimizing the Influence of Gender Bias on the Faculty Search Process*, 19 Gender Transformation in the Acad. 267 (2014).

60. John T. Jost et al., *The Existence of Implicit Bias Is Beyond Reasonable Doubt: A Refutation of Ideological & Methodological Objections & Executive Summary of Ten Studies that No Manager Should Ignore*, 29 Res. Org. Behav. 39 (2009).

61. Linda Hamilton Krieger, *The Content of Our Categories: A Cognitive Bias Approach to Discrimination and Equal Employment Opportunity*, 47 Stan. L. Rev. 1161, 1165 (1995); *see also, e.g.*, Mahzarin R. Banaji, Max H. Bazerman & Dolly Chugh, *How (Un)ethical Are You?*, 81 Harv. L. Rev. 56, 3 (2003) (stating "implicit prejudice arises from the ordinary and unconscious tendency to make associations").

62. Michelle M. Duguid & Melissa C. Thomas-Hunt, *Condoning Stereotyping? How Awareness of Stereotyping Prevalence Impacts Expression of Stereotypes*, 100 J. Applied Psychol. 343 (2015) (these studies focused on gender, age, and weight stigma).

63. Relatedly, Banks and Ford worry that "[t]he fact that most people are found to have some form of implicit bias could bolster the notion that implicit bias is not so bad after all" in Ralph Richard Banks & Richard Thompson Ford, *(How) Does Unconscious Bias Matter?: Law, Politics and Racial Inequality*, 58 Emory L.J. 1053, 1120 (2009).

64. *See, e.g.*, Robert B. Cialdini, *Crafting Normative Messages to Protect the Environment*, 12 Current Directions in Psychol. Sci. 105 (2003).

65. P. Wesley Schultz et al., *The Constructive, Destructive, and Reconstructive Power of Social Norms*, 18 Psychol. Sci. 429 (2007).

66. Cialdini, *supra* note 64.

67. Christian S. Crandall, Amy Eshleman & Lauri O'Brien, *Social Norms & the Expression & Suppression of Prejudice: The Struggle for Internalization*, 82 J. Personality & Soc. Psychol. 359 (2002).

68. Charles Stangor, Gretchen B. Sechrist & John T. Jost, *Changing Racial Beliefs by Providing Consensus Information*, 27 Personality & Soc. Psychol. Bull. 486 (2001).

69. Fletcher A. Blanchard, Christian S. Crandall, John C. Brigham & Leigh Ann Vaughn, *Condemning and Condoning Racism: A Social Context Approach to Interracial Settings*, 79 J. Applied Psychol. 993 (1994); Margo J. Monteith , Nicole E. Deneen & Gregory D. Tooman, *The Effect of Social Norm Activation on the Expression of Opinions Concerning Gay Men and Blacks*, 18 Basic & Applied Soc. Psychol. 267 (1996); Elizabeth Levy Paluck, *Peer Pressure Against Prejudice: A High School Field Experiment Examining Social Network Change*, 47 J. Experimental Soc. Psychol. 350 (2011).

70. Charles Lawrence, *Unconscious Racism Revisited: Reflections on the Impact & Origins of "The Id, the Ego, and Equal Protection,"* 40 U. Conn. L. Rev. 931, 961 (2008); *see also* Banks & Ford, *supra* note 34 (Banks and Ford also express concern about evasion of personal responsibility, though in their view it stems from the perception of implicit bias as a medical problem).

71. Bibb Latané & John M. Darley, The Unresponsive Bystander: Why Doesn't He Help? (1970).

72. For an application of Latané and Darley's (1970) helping behavior model to silence on discrimination, *see* Kecia M. Thomas & Victoria C. Plaut, *The Many Faces of Diversity Resistance in the Workplace, in* Diversity Resistance in Organizations 1 (Kecia M. Thomas ed., 2008).

73. Alexander M. Czopp, Margo J. Monteith & Aimee Y. Mark, *Standing Up for a Change: Reducing Bias through Interpersonal Confrontation*, 90 J. Personality & Soc. Psychol. 784 (2006).

74. *Police Officers Debate Effectiveness of Anti-Bias Training*, NPR, April 6, 2015, http://www.npr.org/2015/04/06/397891177/police-officers-debate-effectiveness-of-anti-bias-training.

75. M.L. de Volder & W. Lens, *Academic Achievement & Future Time Perspective as a Cognitive-Motivational Concept*, 42 J. Personality & Soc. Psychol. 566 (1982); Jenefer Husman & Willy Lens, *The Role of the Future in Student Motivation*, 34 Educ. Psychol. 113 (1999); Raymond B. Miller & Stephanie J. Brickman, *A Model of Future-Oriented Motivation & Self-Regulation*, 16 Educ. Psychol. Rev. 9 (2004); Raymond B. Miller et al., *Engagement in Academic Work: The Role of Learning Goals, Future Consequences, Pleasing Others, and Perceived Ability*, 21 Contemp. Educ. Psychol. 388 (1996); Duane F. Shell & Jenefer Husman, *The Multivariate Dimensionality of Personal Control and Future Time Perspective Beliefs in Achievement and Self-Regulation*, 26 Contemp. Educ. Psychol. 481 (2001); Maarten Vansteenkiste et al., *Examining the Motivational Impact of Intrinsic Versus Extrinsic Goal Framing and Autonomy-Supportive Versus Internally Controlling Communication Style on Early Adolescents' Academic Achievement*, 2 Child Dev. 483 (2005); Allan Wigfield & Jacquelynne S. Eccles, *Expectancy-Value Theory of Achievement Motivation*, 25 Contemp. Educ. Psychol. 68 (2000); Hyungshim Jang, *Supporting Students' Motivation, Engagement, & Learning During an Uninteresting Activity*, 100 J. Educ. Psychol. 798 (2008). This also explains why studies in the diversity training context tend to show larger effect sizes among participants in field studies (employees) compared to laboratory studies (students). *See* Kalinoski et al., *supra* note 12.

76. John P. Meyer & Natalie J. Allen, *A Three-Component Conceptualization of Organizational Commitment*, 1 Hum. Resource Mgmt. Rev. 61, 62 (1991).

77. Jason A. Colquitt, Jeffrey A. LePine & Raymond A. Noe, *Toward an Integrative Theory of Training Motivation: A Meta-Analytic Path Analysis of 20 Years of Research*, 85 J. Applied Psychol. 678 (2000).

78. *See id.*

79. Nian-Shing Chen, Chun-Wang Wei, Kuen-Ting Wu & Lorda Uden, *Effects of High Level Prompts & Peer Assessment on Online Learners' Reflection Levels*, 52 Computers & Educ. 283 (2008); Ali Leijen et al., *Streaming Video to Enhance Students' Reflection in Dance Education*, 52 Computers & Educ. 169 (2009); Sarah Quinton & Teresa Smallbone,

Feeding Forward: Using Feedback to Promote Student Reflection & Learning—A Teaching Model, 47 Innovations in Educ. & Teaching Int'l 125 (2010); Elizabeth A. Davis, *Scaffolding Students' Knowledge Integration: Prompts for Reflection in KIE*, 20 Int'l J. Sci. Educ. 819 (2000); Evelyn M. Boyd & Ann W. Fales, *Reflective Learning: The Key to Learning from Experience*, 23 J. Humanistic Psychol. 99 (1983).

80. Hitomi Saitoa & Kazuhisa Miwa, *Construction of a Learning Environment Supporting Learners' Reflection: A Case of Information Seeking on the Web*, 49 Computers & Educ. 214 (2007).

81. Michael Mobley & Tamara Payne, *Backlash! The Challenge to Diversity Training*, 46 Training & Dev. 45 (1992).

82. Bernardo M. Ferdman & Sari Einy Brody, *Models of Diversity Training*, 2 Handbook of Intercultural Training 282 (1996).

83. Kalinoski et al., *supra* note 12.

84. Deci & Ryan, *supra* note 29.

85. J. Kevin Ford & Daniel A. Weissbein, *Transfer of Training: An Updated Review & Analysis*, 10 Performance Improvement Q. 22 (1997); Brian D. Blume, J. Kevin Ford, Timothy T. Baldwin & Jason L. Huang, *Transfer of Training: A Meta-Analytic Review*, 36 J. Mgmt. 1065 (2010).

86. Robert B. Cialdini, Influence: The Psychology of Persuasion (2006).

87. Courtney L. Holladay & Miguel A. Quiñones, *The Influence of Training Focus & Trainer Characteristics on Diversity Training Effectiveness*, 7 Acad. Mgmt. Learning & Educ. 113 (2008); Loriann Roberson, Carol T. Kulik & Molly B. Pepper, *Using Needs Assessment to Resolve Controversies in Diversity Training Design*, 28 Group Org. Mgmt. 148 (2003).

88. Roberson et al., *supra* note 87.

89. Lorie Fridell, *Fair & Impartial Policing*, http://www.fairimpartialpolicing.com/people/.

90. Benjamin E. Liberman, Caryn J. Block & Sandy M. Koch, *Diversity Trainer Preconceptions: The Effects of Trainer Race and Gender on Perceptions of Diversity Trainer Effectiveness*, 33 Basic & Applied Soc. Psychol. 279 (2011).

91. Roberson et al., *supra* note 87, at 164.

92. Liberman et al., *supra* note 90.

93. Holladay & Quiñones, *supra* note 87.

94. Diane M. Mackie, Leila T. Worth & Arlene G. Asuncion, *Processing of Persuasive In-Group Messages*, 58 J. Personality & Soc. Psychol. 812 (1990).

95. David R. Hekman, Stefanie K. Johnson, Maw-Der Foo & Wei Yang, *Does Diversity-Valuing Behavior Result in Diminished Performance Ratings for Nonwhite and Female Leaders?*, Acad. Mgmt. J. (published online before print Mar. 3, 2016), http://amj.aom.org /content/early/2016/03/03/amj.2014.0538.full.pdf+html.

96. H.B. Karp & Nancy Sutton, *Where the Diversity Training Goes Wrong*, 30 Training 30 (1993); Mobley & Payne, *supra* note 81.

97. Lee Gardenswartz & Anita Rowe, *So You Think You Need Diversity Training?*, Gardenswartz & Rowe (2016), http://www.gardenswartzrowe.com/images/pages/archives/So-You -Think-You-Need-Diversity-Training.pdf; Mobley & Payne, *supra* note 81; Rose Mary Wentling & Nilda Palma-Rivas, *Current Status & Future Trends of Diversity Initiatives in the Workplace: Diversity Experts' Perspective*, 9 Hum. Resources Dev. Q. 235 (1998).

98. Frank Dobbin & Alexandra Kalev, *The Architecture of Inclusion: Evidence from Corporate Diversity Programs*, 30 Harv. J.L. Gender 279 (2007).

99. U.S. Department of Justice, *supra* note 1.

100. Bezrukova, *supra* note 11, at 1238.

101. Kerry Kawakami et al., *Just Say No (to Stereotyping): Effects of Training in the Negation of Stereotype Association on Stereotype Activation*, 78 J. Personality & Soc. Psychol. 871 (2000); Kerry Kawakami, John F. Dovidio & Simone van Kamp, *The Impact of Counterstereotypic Training and Related Correction Processes on the Application of Stereotypes*, 10 Group Process & Intergroup Rel. 139 (2007); Sophie Lebrecht, Lara J. Pierce, Michael

J. Tarr & James W. Tanaka, *Perceptual Other-Race Training Reduces Implicit Racial Bias*, 4 PLoS ONE (2009).

102. *See, e.g.*, Travis L. Dixon, *Understanding How the Internet and Social Media Accelerate Racial Stereotyping and Social Division: The Socially Mediated Stereotyping Model*, in RACE AND GENDER IN ELECTRONIC MEDIA: CONTENT, CONTEXT, CULTURE (Rebecca Ann Lind ed., 2016).

103. Banks & Ford, *supra* note 34.

104. Charles G. Lord, Lee Ross & Mark R. Lepper, *Biased Assimilation & Attitude Polarization: The Effects of Prior Theories on Subsequently Considered Evidence*, 37 J. PERSONALITY & SOC. PSYCHOL. 2098 (1979).

105. Richard E. Redding & N. Dickon Reppucci, *Effects of Lawyers' Socio-Political Attitudes on Their Judgments of Social Science in Legal Decision Making*, 23 L. & HUM. BEHAV. 31 (1999).

106. Samuel R. Sommers & Laura G. Babbitt, *On the Perils of Misplaced Assumptions: Appreciating the Need for Diversity Science*, 21 PSYCHOL. INQUIRY 164 (2010).

107. Banks & Ford, *supra* note 34, at 1120.

108. James N. Baron & Jeffrey Pfeffer, *The Social Psychology of Organizations & Inequality*, 57 SOC. PSYCHOL. Q. 190 (1994); Barbara F. Reskin, *The Proximate Causes of Employment Discrimination*, 29 CONTEMP. SOC. 319 (2000); Barbara F. Reskin, *Modeling Ascriptive Inequality: From Motives to Mechanisms*, 68 AM. SOC. REV. 1 (2003).

109. Glenn Adams et al., *Beyond Prejudice: Toward a Sociocultural Psychology of Racism & Oppression*, in COMMEMORATING BROWN: THE SOCIAL PSYCHOLOGY OF RACISM & DISCRIMINATION 215 (Glenn Adams et al. eds., 2008); JAMES M. JONES, PREJUDICE & RACISM (2d ed. 1997); Victoria C. Plaut, *Diversity Science: Why & How Difference Makes a Difference*, 21 PSYCHOL. INQUIRY 77 (2010).

110. Glenn Adams et al., *Teaching about Racism: Pernicious Implications of the Standard Portrayal*, 30 BASIC & APPLIED SOC. PSYCHOL. 349, 350 (2008).

111. *See also* Russell K. Robinson, *Perceptual Segregation*, 108 COLUM. L. REV. 1093 (2008).

112. Lawrence D. Bobo, *Racial Attitudes & Relations at the Close of the Twentieth Century*, in AMERICA BECOMING: RACIAL TRENDS & THEIR CONSEQUENCES 264 (Neil J. Smelser, William Julius Wilson & Faith Mitchel eds., 2001); Laurie T. O'Brien et al., *Understanding White Americans' Perceptions of Racism in Hurricane Katrina-Related Events*, 12 GROUP PROCESSES & INTERGROUP REL. 431 (2009).

113. Adams et al., *supra* note 110.

114. Denise Sekaquaptewa, Andrew Waldman & Mischa Thompson, *Solo Status & Self-Construal: Being Distinctive Influences Racial Self-Construal & Performance Apprehension in African American Women*, 13 CULTURAL DIVERSITY & ETHNIC MINORITY PSYCHOL. 321 (2007).

115. *See id.*

116. Claude M. Steele & Joshua Aronson, *Stereotype Threat & the Intellectual Test Performance of African Americans*, 69 J. PERSONALITY & SOC. PSYCHOL. 797 (1995).

117. Michael Johns, Toni Schmader & Andy Martens, *Knowing Is Half the Battle: Teaching Stereotype Threat as a Means of Improving Women's Math Performance*, 16 PSYCHOL. SCI. 175 (2005).

118. Shelton et al., *supra* note 47; Tropp et al., *supra* note 48.

119. Pew Research Center, *On Views of Race and Inequality, Blacks and Whites Are Worlds Apart* (June 27, 2016), http://www.pewsocialtrends.org/2016/06/27/on-views-of-race-and-inequality-blacks-and-whites-are-worlds-apart/; Plaut, *supra* note 109; Robinson, *supra* note 111.

120. Adams et al., *supra* note 109.

121. PATRICIA GURIN, BIREN A. NAGDA & XIMENA ZUNIGA, DIALOGUE ACROSS DIFFERENCE: PRACTICE, THEORY & RESEARCH ON INTERGROUP DIALOGUE (2013).

Chapter 11
Awareness as a First Step Toward Overcoming Implicit Bias

Cynthia Lee

Chapter Contents

Introduction

Chapter Highlights

- Awareness is a necessary first step toward reducing implicit bias.

- One way to raise awareness about racial bias in a criminal case is to make race salient.

- Making race salient means calling attention to the possibility that racial stereotypes or racial prejudice may have influenced the actions of the parties in the case.

- Becoming aware of the existence of implicit bias and the fact that everyone is influenced by implicit bias alone is not sufficient to break the prejudice habit.

- One must also be motivated to break the prejudice habit and be trained in ways to overcome bias.

Introduction

For more than half a century, research on bias has focused on the idea that interpersonal contact with diverse others is the best way to reduce prejudice. Perhaps the most well-known proponent of the intergroup contact thesis was Gordon Allport, who argued in his book, *The Nature of Prejudice*, that inter-group interactions involving individuals of equal status from different groups would lead to a reduction in prejudice.[1] Since Allport's book was first published in 1954, much of the empirical research on bias reduction has focused on Allport's intergroup contact hypothesis.[2] This research has confirmed that intergroup contact reduces self-reported measures of prejudice.[3]

Allport's work relied on conscious action and self-reporting. Self-reporting, however, tells only half the story. One can honestly believe it is wrong to discriminate against others and thus have low self-reported measures of prejudice, yet still have biased thoughts and engage in discriminatory behavior. A wealth of research over the past decade has shown that even when individuals do not consciously embrace prejudicial attitudes, they still manifest implicit bias, reflected in the tendency to associate members of different social groups—African-Americans, Latinos, Asian-Americans, gays, elderly people, and women—with stereotypes of these groups. This kind of stereotyping often takes place without conscious thought or awareness.

The existence of implicit bias has been demonstrated by several different measures, including the Implicit Association Test (IAT), which compares response times when individuals are tasked with linking different sets of images and words.[4] The IAT measures implicit bias by comparing the amount of time it takes to hit a specified computer key when one is shown images and words that one expects to go together, such as images of flowers and positive words like "pretty," to response times when one observes images and words that one does not expect to go together, such as pictures of cockroaches and words like "lovely."[5] Time after time, individuals respond more quickly when they see images and words that are typically associated with one another and more slowly when they see images and words that are not commonly linked.[6] For example, most people are quicker to link Black faces with negative words and White faces with positive words, suggesting implicit racial bias in favor of Whites and against Blacks.[7] Most people, including the elderly themselves, are quicker to associate good words with young people and bad words with elderly people, suggesting implicit ageism.[8] Over 14 million IATs measuring bias based on age, gender, ethnicity, and other kinds of biases have been recorded.[9] Seventy-five percent of the individuals who have taken the race IAT have demonstrated implicit bias in favor of Whites over Blacks.[10]

Once social scientists began to recognize that bias can operate without conscious awareness, they began trying to find ways to reduce not simply outward expressions of prejudice but also implicit bias. Reducing implicit bias, however, has proven to be a more difficult task than reducing explicit expressions of prejudice. This is because all of us engage in what Patricia Devine calls the prejudice habit.[11] Devine posits that in order to break the prejudice habit, there must be (1) awareness, (2) desire or motivation to break the prejudice habit,[12] and (3) training in ways that one can overcome bias.[13]

I.   Raising Awareness

This chapter focuses on just the first step in breaking the prejudice habit: making people aware of implicit bias. While some social scientists have questioned whether making people aware of implicit bias can actually reduce bias,[14] social psychologists and others who study racial bias generally agree that awareness of the existence of implicit bias is an important first step towards reducing bias.[15]

A. *Implicit Bias Trainings and Efforts to Educate Jurors about Implicit Bias*

One way to raise awareness about implicit bias is to simply inform individuals about its existence. Lectures and workshops on implicit bias have become more commonplace in various institutional settings, including in workplaces,[16] law schools,[17] law enforcement agencies,[18] and other enterprises. For example, "[m]ore than half of Google's nearly 56,000 employees have attended a 90-minute seminar on unconscious bias," and nearly 2,000 of Google's employees have attended "bias busting" workshops that "give Google employees practical tips on addressing unconscious bias."[19] In response to accusations of racial bias by hosts renting their homes through Airbnb, Airbnb announced in September 2016 that

> [I]n order to break the prejudice habit, there must be (1) awareness, (2) desire or motivation to break the prejudice habit, and (3) training in ways that one can overcome bias.
>
> —Patricia Devine

it would offer implicit bias training to its hosts.[20] In the government sector, on June 27, 2016, the Department of Justice announced that it would require its 23,000 law enforcement agents and 5,800 lawyers in U.S. Attorney's offices across the nation to engage in implicit bias training aimed at getting them to recognize and address implicit bias in their workplace decisions.[21]

Attention to implicit bias training is also present in courtroom settings, where some judges have started informing jurors about the existence of implicit bias and the need to try to guard against such bias. For example, the Honorable Mark Bennett,[22] a federal district court judge in Iowa, routinely tells his jurors,

> Do not decide the case based on "implicit biases." As we discussed in jury selection, everyone, including me, has feelings, assumptions, perceptions, fears, and stereotypes, that is, "implicit biases," that we may not be aware of. These hidden thoughts can impact what we

see and hear, how we remember what we see and hear, and how we make important decisions. Because you are making very important decisions in this case, I strongly encourage you to evaluate the evidence carefully and to resist jumping to conclusions based on personal likes or dislikes, generalizations, gut feelings, prejudices, sympathies, stereotypes, or biases. The law demands that you return a just verdict, based solely on the evidence, your individual evaluation of that evidence, your reason and common sense, and these instructions. Our system of justice is counting on you to render a fair decision based on the evidence, not on biases.[23]

Attorneys are also educating jurors about implicit bias.[24] For example, in one criminal case out of Alaska, defense attorneys representing a Black teenager charged with assaulting a White[25] classmate were worried that their all-White jury would assume their client was guilty because of racial stereotypes linking Blacks with violence and criminality.[26] To combat this potential bias, the attorneys spoke about their own racial biases during voir dire to let potential jurors know that it is normal to have racial bias.[27] They also successfully requested that the judge give the jurors a race-switching jury instruction based on a model jury instruction I first proposed in a law review article.[28] Essentially, the race-switching jury instruction told jurors they should think about the case with the same facts except imagine that the defendant was a White teenage boy and the victim was his Black classmate before deciding whether to find the defendant guilty or not guilty.[29] The jury found the defendant not guilty. Switching as a means of raising awareness about bias can work in other contexts besides race.[30]

Limited research has been done on the effectiveness of implicit bias trainings in general and efforts to educate jurors about implicit bias in particular. The available research, however, suggests that implicit bias training that simply informs or educates individuals about the existence of implicit bias is insufficient. To have any lasting impact, such trainings must give individuals strategies for reducing bias.[31] Similarly, making jurors aware of the existence of implicit bias and the fact that it may affect their own decision making may not be sufficient to make a difference in outcomes.[32] One study, for example, found that jury instructions informing jurors about the existence of implicit bias and instructing jurors to try to resist relying on generalizations and stereotypes had no significant effect on judgments of guilt, belief in the strength of the prosecution's evidence, or length of sentence.[33]

B. Making Race (or Other Types of Bias) Salient

Another way to raise awareness about implicit racial bias in the context of a criminal case is to make the possibility of such bias salient. A wealth of recent research on race salience demonstrates that calling attention to the possibility of racial bias in others can encourage jurors to treat Black and White defendants the same way. Samuel Sommers and Phoebe Ellsworth have conducted numerous experiments studying the possibility that if racial prejudice is made salient to mock jurors in a criminal case, those jurors are more likely to treat similarly situated Black and White defendants the same way.

In one experiment, for example, 196 White individuals were approached by a White experimenter in waiting areas of a major international airport and asked if they would read a written trial summary and complete a questionnaire about legal attitudes while they waited.[34] The trial summary described a case involving a high school basketball player who had an altercation with a fellow teammate in the locker room, resulting in a charge of battery with serious bodily injury.[35] Half the mock jurors were given a trial summary with a White defendant and a Black victim, while half were given the same trial summary with a Black defendant and a White victim. In both the race-salient and non-race-salient conditions, participants were given a description of the defendant and victim, which included the height, weight, race, gender, and age of each.[36] In some of the trial summaries, race was made salient through the testimony of a defense witness who "testified that the defendant was one of the only two Whites (or Blacks) on the team, and had been the 'subject of racial remarks and unfair criticism throughout the season from many of his Black (or White) teammates.'"[37] In others, race was not made salient.[38] In the non-race-salient version of the case, there was no mention of the defendant's race nor any mention of racial remarks.[39] Instead, the defense witness testified that "the defendant had only one other friend on the team and had been the 'subject of obscene remarks and unfair criticism from many of his teammates.'"[40] Other than this testimony, the written trial summaries were the same.[41]

Sommers and Ellsworth found that the White mock jurors were significantly more likely to convict the Black defendant in the non-race-salient condition (90 percent) than in the race-salient condition (70 percent).[42] When race was made salient, conviction rates for the White defendant (69 percent) and the Black defendant (66 percent) were fairly comparable.[43] When participants were asked to rate the strength of the prosecution's case, they rated the prosecution's case against the Black defendant as significantly stronger in the non-race-salient condition than the exact same prosecution case against the Black defendant in the race-salient condition.[44] Participants were also asked to recommend a sentence for the defendant.[45] In the non-race-salient condition, mock jurors recommended a more severe sentence for the Black defendant than the White defendant than in the race-salient condition.[46] Sommers and Ellsworth concluded that when race was made salient, the participants did not demonstrate prejudice "because the racial content of the trial activated a motivation to appear non-prejudiced."[47] On the other hand, "when race was not a salient issue, a motivation to avoid prejudice was not expected among jurors, and White mock jurors did indeed demonstrate racial bias in their judgments."[48]

In another study, Sommers and Ellsworth had 211 individuals who were waiting to depart from gates at a large international airport read a trial summary about a man charged with assault and battery against his girlfriend.[49] The man was at a bar with his coworkers celebrating a recent promotion when his girlfriend stood up and started making fun of his physique and sexual performance.[50] The defendant yelled at his girlfriend, forced her into a chair, and then slapped her.[51] The slap knocked the girlfriend to the ground, injuring her ankle.[52] In the race-salient version of the case, the girlfriend testifies that the defendant yelled, "You know better than to talk that way about a *White* (or *Black*) man in front of his friends."[53] In the non-race-salient version, she testifies that the defendant yelled, "You know better than to talk that way about a man in front of his friends."[54] The only difference between the race-salient and non-race-salient versions of the case was the defendant's mention of his race in this exchange.[55]

In this study, Sommers and Ellsworth found that when race was not made salient, both White and Black mock jurors demonstrated racial bias.[56] White mock jurors gave the Black defendant a significantly higher guilt rating than the White defendant, while Black jurors gave the White defendant a significantly higher guilt rating than the Black defendant.[57] Both White and Black mock jurors were also more punitive in their sentence recommendations toward the other-race defendant when race was not made salient.[58] White mock jurors rated the Black defendant's personality as significantly more aggressive and violent than the White defendant's, and Black mock jurors rated the White defendant's personality as significantly more aggressive and violent than the Black defendant's.[59] When race was made salient, White mock jurors were more likely to treat the Black defendant the same as the White defendant.[60] Black mock jurors, on the other hand, were still more lenient toward the Black defendant than the White defendant.[61] Sommers and Ellsworth theorized that Black jurors may view the criminal justice system as inherently biased, and this belief might motivate them to demonstrate same-race leniency toward Black defendants to compensate for that bias.[62]

Sommers and Ellsworth's research is widely cited, but it is important to note that Sommers himself recognizes significant limitations in the work:

> It remains the case, however, that too little is known regarding the psychological processes underlying the influence of a defendant's race. This gap in the literature prevents conclusions from being drawn regarding, for instance, whether prejudicial attitudes account for the influence of defendant race on White jurors, or whether simple awareness of societal stereotypes regarding race and crime is sufficient to impact judgments.[63]

One concern that judges and others may have is that making race salient might lead jurors to overcompensate. In other words, if judges or attorneys make race salient, then jurors might let guilty Black defendants go free and convict innocent White defendants. The research on race salience, however, suggests that making race salient simply reduces racial bias and results in White jurors treating similarly situated White and Black defendants the same; White mock jurors did not treat White defendants more harshly than similarly situated Black defendants.

The research on race salience . . . suggests that making race salient simply reduces racial bias and results in White jurors treating similarly situated White and Black defendants the same.

C. Awareness Alone Is Not Sufficient to Break the Prejudice Habit

Raising awareness of the possibility of racial bias is a critical first step, but the existing research suggests educating people about implicit bias is not sufficient in and of itself to get them to break the prejudice habit. For example, for years it was thought that merely educating people about the value of cultural diversity and making them aware of the existence of prejudice would help reduce prejudice.[64] While there is some evidence that voluntary enrollment in a class that focuses on the value of diversity can lead to bias reduction,[65] it appears that mandatory enrollment in a diversity training program is not effective at reducing bias.[66] This might be because some people resent being forced to expend time and effort on something they might view as political correctness training.

Similarly, it appears that simply telling people that they should try to avoid relying on stereotypes is not an effective way of permanently reducing bias.[67] While telling people to suppress their stereotype-congruent responses may work in the short term, such interventions may lead to greater reliance on the stereotype when the person stops consciously trying to suppress the stereotype. For example, in one study, participants were shown a photograph of a skinhead and asked to write for five minutes on a day in the life of the person in the photograph.[68] Half of the participants were told to try not to rely on stereotypes about skinheads when writing their narrative.[69] The other half were not given a stereotype-suppression instruction.[70] As might be expected, the narratives by the individuals told not to rely on stereotypes were less stereotypical than the narratives by the individuals in the control group who were given no such instruction.[71] Sometime after this initial exercise, participants were shown a color photograph of another skinhead and asked to write about a day in this skinhead's life.[72] This time, the narratives by the participants who were initially told to suppress stereotypes were more stereotypic than those by the control group.[73]

In a second experiment, which replicated the first part of the experiment described above, each participant was told after writing their narrative that they would meet the person in the photograph, and then the participant was taken to an adjacent room with eight empty chairs.[74] A jacket and a backpack were on the first chair.[75] The participant was told that the person in the photograph, the skinhead, must have gone to the restroom and would be right back.[76] The participant was told to choose any seat.[77] Interestingly, participants who had been given the stereotype-suppression instruction chose seats further away from the seat with the jacket and backpack, whereas participants in the control group who did not receive a stereotype-suppression instruction chose seats closer to the seat where the skinhead presumably had left his belongings.[78] The researchers who conducted the study hypothesized that there is a rebound effect when individuals are told to suppress stereotypic thoughts.[79] In other words, when people attempt to suppress unwanted thoughts, these thoughts will reappear later with even greater insistence than if they had never been suppressed.[80] According to the authors of this study, this rebound effect happens "[a]s a consequence of the ironic monitoring process that occurs during suppression" because "unwanted constructs are continually stimulated or primed."[81]

Other social science research also suggests that calling attention to race, either by asking people not to rely on race or asking them to rely on race, counterintuitively increases the tendency to rely on stereotypes. For example, B. Keith Payne tested whether actively highlighting race prior to the decision to shoot reduced or increased stereotype-congruent errors in the decision to shoot.[82] Participants were told they would see pairs of pictures presented briefly—a face in the first picture and an object, either a gun or a hand tool, in the second picture—and they were to decide quickly whether the object in the second picture was a gun or a tool.[83] Individuals in the control group were given no other instructions.[84] Participants in the "Avoid Race" group were given the same instructions described above but were also told,

> You have been randomly assigned to take the perspective of a completely unbiased person. Regardless of your personal views, we would like you to base your responses only on whether the second object looks more like a gun or tool. Try not to let the race of the face influence your decisions.[85]

Participants in the "Use Race" group were given the same instructions as the control group, but were also told,

> You have been randomly assigned to the "racial profiling" condition. Regardless of your personal views, we would like you to play the role of someone engaged in racial profiling. That is, try to make correct classifications, but we would like you to use the race of the faces to help you identify the gun or tool in question.[86]

All participants misidentified tools as guns more often after seeing a Black face than after seeing a White face.[87] They also misidentified guns as tools more often after seeing a White face than after seeing a Black face.[88] Surprisingly, however, making race salient increased the tendency of individuals to stereotypically misidentify objects regardless of whether participants were told to avoid relying on race or to use race.[89] Participants in both the "Avoid Race" and the "Use Race" conditions were more likely to misidentify harmless objects as guns when held by Blacks and misidentify guns as harmless objects when held by Whites than participants not given any instruction calling attention to race.[90]

What conclusions might we draw from these studies? A skeptic might conclude that making race salient helps reduce bias in some cases but exacerbates bias in other cases, so the best course of action is to do nothing. The research discussed above, however, suggests that salience reduces bias in complex settings where individuals have to make intricate judgments—like jurors deciding whether to find a defendant guilty or not guilty—but such salience may have the opposite effect when individuals have to make a quick decision, such as whether to shoot a suspect who appears to be armed or where to sit before a skinhead who has gone to the restroom returns to the room. In the courtroom setting, where the fact finder has time to consider different arguments and weigh the credibility of witnesses, making race salient is likely to be more beneficial than harmful. Indeed, research on implicit bias and judicial decision making by Jeffrey Rachlinski, one of the authors of Chapter 5, which addresses implicit bias in judicial decision making, lends support to this theory.[91] In Rachlinski's study, White judges who showed a strong preference for Whites were able to mediate their pro-White preference and treat Black defendants fairly when they suspected that their decisions were being evaluated for racial bias.[92]

Conclusion

As discussed above, there are various ways to raise awareness about implicit bias. In the workplace setting, employers can give employees the opportunity to attend implicit bias workshops and lectures. In the courtroom, judges can educate jurors about implicit bias. Attorneys can also make bias salient during voir dire, in opening and closing statements, and through witness testimony.

Raising awareness about implicit bias is an important first step to reducing implicit bias, but it is only the first step. One must be motivated to break the prejudice habit and trained in ways to overcome implicit bias. The ensuing chapters will address various ways to motivate people to break the prejudice habit and overcome the implicit bias that affects us all.

So You'd Like to Know More

- Mahzarin R. Banaji & Anthony G. Greenwald, Blindspot: Hidden Biases of Good People (2013)

- Jerry Kang et al., 59 UCLA Law Review 1124 (2012)

- Patricia G. Devine et al., 48 Journal of Experimental Social Psychology 1267 (2012)

- Carol Izumi, 34 Washington University Journal of Law and Policy 71 (2010)

- Cynthia Lee, 5 UC Irvine Law Review 843 (2015)

ABOUT THE AUTHOR

Cynthia Lee is a law professor at The George Washington University Law School in Washington, D.C., where she teaches criminal law, criminal procedure, and professional responsibility. She is the author of *Murder and the Reasonable Man* (2003), a book that examines the ways that race, gender, and sexual orientation norms can influence verdicts in self-defense and provocation cases. She has also published several articles dealing with implicit racial bias, including "A New Approach to Voir Dire into Racial Bias," 5 *U.C. Irvine L. Rev.* 843 (2015) and "Making Race Salient: Trayvon Martin and Implicit Bias in a Not yet Post-Racial Society," 91 *N.C. L. Rev.* 1557 (2013).[93]

ENDNOTES

1. GORDON W. ALLPORT, THE NATURE OF PREJUDICE (1954).
2. *See, e.g.*, Carmit T. Tadmor et al., *Multicultural Experiences Reduce Intergroup Bias through Epistemic Unfreezing*, 103 J. PERSONALITY & SOC. PSYCHOL. 750 (2012) (finding that exposure to multicultural experiences leads to a reduction in stereotype endorsement even for groups other than the comparative culture); Shawn O. Utsey et al., *Prejudice and Racism, Year 2008—Still Going Strong: Research on Reducing Prejudice with Recommended Methodological Advances*, 86 J. COUNSELING & DEVELOPMENT 339 (2008); Richard Crisp & Sarah R. Beck, *Reducing Intergroup Bias: The Moderating Role of Ingroup Identification*, 8 GROUP PROCESSES & INTERGROUP REL. 173 (2005).
3. Thomas F. Pettigrew & Linda R. Tropp, *A Meta-Analytic Test of Intergroup Contact Theory*, 90 J. PERSONALITY & SOC. PSYCHOL. 751 (2006); Utsey et al., *supra* note 2.
4. Jerry Kang et al., *Implicit Bias in the Courtroom*, 59 UCLA L. REV. 1124, 1130 (2012) (explaining how the IAT works).
5. Anthony G. Greenwald et al., *Measuring Individual Differences in Implicit Cognition: The Implicit Association Test*, 74 J. PERSONALITY & SOC. PSYCHOL. 1464, 1465–68 (1998).
6. *Id.* at 1465–70.
7. *Id.* at 1467, 1474.
8. Becca R. Levy & Mahzarin R. Banaji, *Implicit Ageism, in* AGEISM: STEREOTYPING AND PREJUDICE AGAINST OLDER PERSONS 49, 54–55 (Todd D. Nelson ed., 2002).
9. MAHZARIN R. BANAJI & ANTHONY G. GREENWALD, BLINDSPOT: HIDDEN BIASES OF GOOD PEOPLE 69 (2013).
10. *Id.* at 47.
11. Patricia G. Devine et al., *Long-Term Reduction in Implicit Race Bias: A Prejudice Habit-Breaking Intervention*, 48 J. EXPERIMENTAL SOC. PSYCHOL. 1267, 1268 (2012) (finding that "breaking the habit" of prejudice or implicit bias "requires learning about the contexts that activate the bias and how to replace the biased responses with responses that reflect one's non-prejudiced goals").
12. Motivation to break the prejudice habit can be either internal or external. One is considered internally motivated to break the prejudice habit if one sincerely believes that it is morally wrong to discriminate against others. *Id.* at 1269 (noting that internal motivation to respond without prejudice "is primarily driven by personal values and the belief that prejudice is wrong"). One is considered externally motivated if the primary reason for conforming one's behavior to societal norms is so that one will not be seen as a bigot. *Id.* (noting that external motivation to respond without prejudice is "primarily driven by a desire to escape social sanctions").
13. The most important part of breaking the prejudice habit is training in bias reduction. While many debiasing interventions have been proposed, only a few appear to be effective at reducing implicit bias. In 2014, Calvin Lai and others conducted a comparative investigation of 17 debiasing interventions. Calvin K. Lai et al., *Reducing Implicit Racial Preferences: I. A Comparative Investigation of 17 Interventions*, 143 J. EXPERIMENTAL PSYCHOL. 1765 (2014). The most effective bias-reducing intervention was one in which participants were assigned to be on a dodge ball team in which all of their teammates were Black

and all of the individuals on the opposing team were White. *Id.* at 1771. Members of the all-White team engaged in unfair play. *Id.* At the end of the game, participants were asked to remember how their Black teammates helped them and their White opponents hurt them. *Id.* This intervention resulted in a reduction in implicit racial bias in favor of Whites and against Blacks. *Id.* The second most effective intervention was one in which participants read a story in the second-person narrative in which a White man assaults the participant and a Black man rescues the participant. *Id.* Participants took the race IAT both before and after reading the story. After reading the story, participants were told that the race IAT they would take would affirm that White is bad and Black is good and to keep the story they had just read in mind when taking the IAT. *Id.* This intervention successfully reduced participants' implicit racial preferences. *Id.* The third most successful intervention was one in which participants were shown six positive, well-known Black individual exemplars (one of whom was Bill Cosby, who was viewed positively at that time) and six negative, infamous White individual exemplars, such as Charles Manson. *Id.* Participants practiced taking an IAT that only paired Black faces with good things and White faces with bad things. *Id.* This intervention was also effective at reducing implicit preferences. *Id.* A similar experiment by Nilanjana Dasgupta and Anthony Greenwald found that exposure to pictures of famous admired Black individuals and infamous disliked White individuals resulted in a reduction in automatic implicit racial bias in favor of Whites. Nilanjana Dasgupta & Anthony G. Greenwald, *On the Malleability of Automatic Attitudes: Combating Automatic Prejudice with Images of Admired and Disliked Individuals*, 81 J. Personality & Soc. Psychol. 800 (2001).

14. Masua Sagiv, *Cultural Bias in Judicial Decision Making*, 35 B.C. J.L. & Soc. Just. 229, 254 n.114 (2015) ("Research in the field of law and psychology is divided as to the significance that an individual's awareness of her own bias has in reducing or diminishing it."); Linda Babcock et al., *Creating Convergence: Debiasing Biased Litigants*, 22 Law & Soc. Inquiry 913, 916 (1997) (arguing that merely making someone aware of a bias won't make him or her less biased, but having people think about counterarguments or weaknesses in their position helps reduce self-serving biases).

15. As Carol Izumi notes, "Awareness of bias is critical for mental decontamination success." Carol Izumi, *Implicit Bias and the Illusion of Mediator Neutrality*, 34 Wash. U. J.L. & Pol'y 71, 141 (2010) (citing Laurie A. Rudman et al., *"Unlearning" Automatic Biases: The Malleability of Implicit Prejudice and Stereotypes*, 81 J. Personality & Soc. Psychol. 856 (2001)).

16. Jessica Guynn, *Google's 'Bias-Busting' Workshops Target Hidden Prejudices*, USA Today (May 12, 2015), http://www.usatoday.com/story/tech/2015/05/12/google-unconscious-bias-diversity/27055485/; Farhad Manjoo, *Exposing Hidden Bias at Google*, N.Y. Times, Sept. 24, 2014, http://www.nytimes.com/2014/09/25/technology/exposing-hidden-biases-at-google-to-improve-diversity.html?_r=0.

17. Jennifer Nasser, *Manhire Presents Bias Workshop to Texas A&M Law*, Tex. A&M Univ. Sch. of Law (Oct. 8, 2015), https://law.tamu.edu/media/news-media-resources/story/manhire-presents-bias-workshop-to-tamu-law (discussing workshop on overcoming implicit bias for faculty and staff at Texas A&M Law School).

18. Lorie Fridell, Producing Bias-Free Policing: A Science Based Approach (2016); Lorie Fridell, *Fair and Impartial Policing*, http://www.fairimpartialpolicing.com/; Tami Abdollah, *Police Agencies Line up to Learn about Unconscious Bias*, CNS News (Mar. 9, 2015), http://www.cnsnews.com/news/article/police-agencies-line-learn-about-unconscious-bias. Sarah Green Carmichael, *Training Police Departments to Be Less Biased*, Harv. Bus. Rev. (Mar. 6, 2015), https://hbr.org/2015/03/training-police-departments-to-be-less-biased; Rio Fernandes, *How Bias Training Works in One Campus Police Department*, Chron. Higher Educ., May 16, 2016, http://chronicle.com/article/How-Bias-Training-Works-in-One/236482; Matt Zapotosky, *Can Police Police Their Biases? Training Is Underway*, Wash. Post Mag., Apr. 3, 2016, at 23 (describing some of the videos that were shown in a recent training of Virginia State Troopers near Richmond, Virginia); Lisa Grace Lednicer, *What Police Are Learning*, Wash. Post Mag., Feb. 22, 2015, at 17 (describing the fair and impartial policing training of police officers led by Lorie Fridell).

19. Jessica Guynn, *Diversity Gets Googled*, USA TODAY, May 7, 2015, at B2.
20. Emily Badger, *Airbnb Details Plans to Enrich Nondiscrimination Policy*, WASH. POST, Sept. 9, 2016, at A17.
21. Eric Yoder, *Justice Dept. Employees to Undergo Training on Implicit Bias*, WASH. POST, June 29, 2016, at A17; *see also* Julia Edwards, *Justice Dept. Mandates "Implicit Bias" Training for Agents, Lawyers*, REUTERS.COM, June 27, 2016, http://www.reuters.com/article/us -usa-justice-bias-exclusive-idUSKCN0ZD251.
22. Judge Bennett is the author of Chapter 4, *Manifestations of Implicit Bias in the Courts*, which examines several ways in which implicit bias affects lawyers, jurors, and judges.
23. Anna Roberts, *(Re)forming the Jury: Detection and Disinfection of Implicit Juror Bias*, 44 CONN. L. REV. 827, 859 (2012), *also available at* http://wispd.org/attachments/article /101/ImplicitBiasJuryInstruction.pdf. Jury orientation videos can also inform prospective jurors about implicit bias. *Id.* (proposing that jury orientation videos educate prospective jurors about implicit bias) I was called for jury duty in May 2016 and was pleased to see that D.C. Superior Court had adopted a new jury orientation video, narrated by Andrew Ferguson, Professor of Law at the University of District of Columbia David A. Clarke School of Law and author of WHY JURY DUTY MATTERS: A CITIZEN'S GUIDE TO CONSTITUTIONAL ACTION (2013). The new jury orientation video focuses on the role of the juror in upholding our democratic values, and while it does not address implicit bias per se, it does talk about bias in general and the need to guard against bias. *See We the People: A Call to Duty* (2014), *available at* http://www.dccourts.gov/juryvideo.
24. Cynthia Lee, *A New Approach to Voir Dire into Racial Bias*, 5 UC IRVINE L. REV. 843 (2015).
25. Like many others who write about race, I purposely capitalize the "B" in "Black" and the "W" in "White" to highlight the fact that Blacks and Whites are commonly perceived in the United States as members of clearly defined racial groups.
26. James McComas & Cynthia Stout, *Combating the Effects of Racial Stereotyping in Criminal Cases*, THE CHAMPION 22–23 (Aug. 1999).
27. *Id.*
28. Cynthia Kwei Yung Lee, *Race and Self-Defense: Toward a Normative Conception of Reasonableness*, 81 MINN. L. REV. 367, 482 (1996) (suggesting a model limiting instruction on the impropriety of relying on racial stereotypes); *see also* CYNTHIA LEE, MURDER AND THE REASONABLE MAN: PASSION AND FEAR IN THE CRIMINAL COURTROOM 224–25 (2003) (proposing a race-switching jury instruction in cases involving a risk that racial stereotyping will influence the jury's determination of reasonableness).
29. McComas & Stout, *supra* note 26.
30. Cynthia Lee, *The Gay Panic Defense*, 42 UC DAVIS L. REV. 471, 564–65 (2008); Cynthia Lee & Peter Kwan, *The Trans Panic Defense: Masculinity, Heteronormativity, and the Murder of Transgender Women*, 66 HASTINGS L.J. 77, 105 (2014).
31. Patricia G. Devine, *Stereotypes and Prejudice: Their Automatic and Controlled Components*, 56 J. PERSONALITY & SOC. PSYCHOL. 5, 5–6, 15 (1989) (suggesting five strategies to reduce bias, including counter-stereotypic imaging, obtaining specific information about individuals in a group, taking the perspective of the person in the stereotyped group, and increased opportunities for contact with outgroup members). *See also* Molly Carnes et al., *The Effect of an Intervention to Break the Gender Bias Habit for Faculty at One Institution: A Cluster Randomized, Controlled Trial*, 90 ACADEMIC MED. 221 (2015) (finding that gender bias was reduced when individuals were given specific behavioral strategies to practice, such as replacing a gender stereotype with accurate information, positive counter-stereotype imaging, imagining in detail what it is like to be a person in a stereotyped group, and meeting with counter-stereotypic exemplars, such as senior women faculty).
32. Anna Roberts reports that the "National Center for State Courts attempted the first empirical testing of jury instructions like [Judge Bennett's], and found no significant influence of the instructions on jurors' verdict preferences." Anna Roberts, *Jury Failures and Reform Post-Ferguson* (work-in-progress presented at the 2016 SEALS Annual Meeting, Amelia Island, Florida, on Aug. 4, 2016) (manuscript on file with author), citing Jennifer K. Elek & Paula Hannaford-Agor, *Can Explicit Instructions Reduce Expressions*

of Implicit Bias? New Questions Following a Test of a Specialized Jury Instruction *8, 14 (National Center for State Courts, Apr. 2014), archived at http://perma.cc/ZZD4-XD73.

33. Elek & Hannaford-Agor, *supra* note 32 (finding "no significant effects . . . on judgments of guilt, confidence, strength of the prosecution's evidence, or sentence length" when testing a specialized implicit-bias jury instruction "[b]ased loosely on [the] jury instruction developed and used by Judge Mark Bennett").

34. Samuel R. Sommers & Phoebe C. Ellsworth, *White Juror Bias: An Investigation of Prejudice against Black Defendants in the American Courtroom,* 7 PSYCHOL. PUB. POL'Y & L. 201, 216 (2001).

35. *Id.*

36. *Id.*

37. *Id.* at 214–16.

38. *Id.*

39. *Id.*

40. *Id.*

41. *Id.*

42. *Id.* at 217.

43. *Id.*

44. *Id.* at 218.

45. *Id.* at 219.

46. *Id.*

47. *Id.* at 220.

48. *Id.*

49. Samuel R. Sommers & Phoebe C. Ellsworth, *Race in the Courtroom: Perceptions of Guilt and Dispositioned Attributions,* 26 PERSONALITY & SOC. PSYCHOL. BULL. 1367, 1372–73 (2000). Of the 211 participants, 156 identified themselves as White and 55 identified themselves as Black.

50. *Id.*

51. *Id.* at 1373.

52. *Id.*

53. *Id.*

54. *Id.*

55. *Id.* Because the case raised issues of gender as well as race, Sommers and Ellsworth included gender of the mock juror as an independent variable in their analysis and found no significant main effects. *Id.* at 1377.

56. *Id.* at 1374.

57. *Id.*

58. *Id.*

59. *Id.* at 1375.

60. *Id.* Black mock jurors, on the other hand, were more lenient toward the Black defendant than the White defendant. *Id.* Sommers and Ellsworth theorized that Black jurors may view the criminal justice system as inherently biased, and this belief might motivate them to demonstrate same-race leniency toward Black defendants to compensate for that bias. *Id.* at 1376.

61. *Id.*

62. *Id.* At least one other research team has found results similar to Sommers. *See, e.g., Ellen S. Cohn et al., Reducing White Juror Bias: The Role of Race Salience and Racial Attitudes,* 39 J. APPLIED SOC. PSYCHOL. 1953 (2009); Donald O. Bucolo & Ellen S. Cohn, *Playing the Race Card: Making Race Salient in Defence Opening and Closing Statements,* 15 LEGAL & CRIMINOLOGICAL PSYCHOL. 293 (2010).

63. Samuel Sommers, *Race and the Decision Making of Juries,* 12 LEGAL & CRIMINOLOGICAL PSYCHOL. 171, 174 (2007).

64. Clark McCauley et al., *Diversity Workshops on Campus: A Survey of Current Practice at US Colleges and Universities,* 34 COLLEGE STUDENT J. 100 (2000) (finding that 81 percent of U.S. colleges and universities have held diversity workshops).

65. Lorie A. Rudman et al., *"Unlearning" Automatic Biases: The Malleability of Implicit Prejudice and Stereotypes*, 81 J. PERSONALITY & SOC. PSYCHOL. 856 (2001) (finding that students who voluntarily enrolled in a prejudice and conflict seminar taught by a Black professor showed reduced implicit and explicit anti-Black bias at the end of the semester compared to students who were not enrolled in the seminar).

66. Peter Bregman, *Diversity Training Doesn't Work*, HARV. BUS. REV., https://hbr.org/2012/03/diversity-training-doesnt-work (Mar. 12, 2012), citing Frank Dobbin et al., *Diversity Management in Corporate America*, 6 CONTEXTS 21 (2007); Suzanne Lucas, *Why You Should Stop Attending Diversity Training*, CBS NEWS, http://www.cbsnews.com/news/why-you-should-stop-attending-diversity-training/ (May 2, 2012); Shankar Vedantam, *Most Diversity Training Ineffective, Study Finds*, WASH. POST, Jan. 20, 2008, http://www.washingtonpost.com/wp-dyn/content/article/2008/01/19/AR2008011901899.html.

67. Linda Babcock et al., *Creating Convergence: Debiasing Litigants*, 22 LAW & SOC. INQUIRY 813, 916 (1997) ("many researchers have tried, albeit unsuccessfully, to mitigate various biases by informing subjects about them—for example, by telling subjects about the hindsight bias and its effects").

68. C. Neil Macrae et al., *Out of Mind but Back in Sight: Stereotypes on the Rebound*, 67 J. PERSONALITY & SOC. PSYCHOL. 808, 810 (1994).

69. *Id.*

70. *Id.*

71. *Id.* at 811.

72. *Id.* at 810.

73. *Id.* at 811.

74. *Id.*

75. *Id.*

76. *Id.*

77. *Id.*

78. *Id.* at 812.

79. *Id.* at 813–14.

80. *Id.* at 814 (concluding that "[o]ut of sight . . . does not necessarily mean out of mind, at least where unwanted thoughts are concerned.").

81. *Id.* at 812.

82. B. Keith Payne, Alan J. Lambert & Larry L. Jacoby, *Best Laid Plans: Effects of Goals on Accessibility Bias and Cognitive Control in Race-Based Misperceptions of Weapons*, 38 J. EXPERIMENTAL SOC. PSYCHOL. 384 (2002).

83. *Id.* at 388.

84. *Id.*

85. *Id.*

86. *Id.*

87. *Id.* at 389.

88. *Id.*

89. *Id.* at 390–91.

90. *Id.*

91. Jeffrey J. Rachlinski et al., *Does Unconscious Racial Bias Affect Trial Judges?*, 84 NOTRE DAME L. REV. 1195 (2009).

92. *Id.*

93. Professor Lee thanks Christina Stevens Carbone, Phyllis Pickett, and Jeffrey Rachlinski for enormously helpful comments on this chapter. She also thanks Andrew Hyun, Christine Kulumani, and Madeline DiLascia-Azia for helpful research assistance support on this chapter and Prerna Balasundaram for administrative assistance. Finally, she thanks Sarah Redfield for inviting her to be a contributing author for this book.

Chapter 12

Knowledge-Based Interventions Are More Likely to Reduce Legal Disparities Than Are Implicit Bias Interventions

Dr. Patrick S. Forscher and Patricia G. Devine

Chapter Contents

Introduction
Conclusion

Chapter Highlights

- No current evidence establishes that implicit bias causes disparities in legal outcomes.

- The effects of currently available interventions to change implicit bias are ephemeral, and there is no evidence that their effects generalize to behavior.

- Instead of focusing our efforts on changing implicit bias, we should focus on changing knowledge about the nature of discrimination in society.

Introduction

Scholars have long noted lingering disparities in United States legal outcomes between social groups.[1] These disparities are troubling by themselves because they suggest that some groups are treated unfairly before the law. However, they are especially concerning given that judges and other legal decision makers have a duty to uphold and interpret the law in a way that is neutral with respect to age, race, gender, and other protected categories. If legal actors sincerely intend to uphold their legal duties, the existence of ongoing disparities implies that forces other than intentions contribute to ongoing disparities.

One factor in particular, implicit bias, has received increasing levels of attention. The existence of this volume attests to the fact that legal scholars are both interested in and concerned about how implicit bias may undermine fairness in the judgments of those charged with adjudicating evidence in the legal setting. Defined as automatically activated associations about social groups,[2] implicit biases are theorized to be acquired early in life through repeated exposure to stereotypic information.[3] Over time, implicit biases become so well-rehearsed that, upon one's exposure to information related to a stereotyped group, they activate automatically and without intention. Once activated, these biases are theorized to affect behavior in situations where people lack motivation, awareness, or the ability to think about their responses.[4]

Across a large number of studies, scholars have observed that scores on measures of implicit bias are associated with behavior across a large number of domains.[5] Based on this evidence, many have argued that implicit bias causes biased behavior and that the accumulation of these biased behaviors causes disparities.[6] The mere existence of disparities in legal outcomes is troubling. However, if it is true that implicit bias causes disparities, the existence of implicit bias raises a possibility that is even more disquieting: Well-meaning legal actors who sincerely desire to uphold their duties to the law may nonetheless be complicit in perpetuating these disparities. It is therefore important to evaluate the evidence as to the likely cause of legal disparities, both to determine whether this disquieting possibility has been realized and to evaluate what we can do to alleviate disparities in legal outcomes. Evaluating the cause of outcomes is challenging, but it is especially challenging when the cause is theorized to operate inside people's heads without their conscious awareness. This task is the province of many social scientists but especially psychological scientists.

We should note at the outset that this chapter is different from most others in this volume. Neither author is an expert of the law, legal proceedings, or the criminal justice system more generally. Instead, we are both psychological scientists who specialize in race and unintentional forms of bias. Our goal in this chapter is to review the extant work on implicit bias and interventions to change implicit bias. Though the work in this area is ever burgeoning, the evidence regarding the effectiveness of implicit bias interventions is rather mixed and the goals for the specific research efforts are quite varied. Our hope is to lay out the issues in ways that elucidate what this work can and cannot say about the causes of and remedies to disparities in legal outcomes. We hope that this review will prove helpful to those who choose to investigate the impact of biases, both unintentional and intentional, throughout the legal system.

To wit, in this chapter, we will review the evidence that, in general, is required to establish that implicit bias causes legal disparities. A great deal of the evidence regarding implicit bias and legal disparities is correlational, and, of course, evidence of correlations between measured implicit bias and biased behavior is insufficient to establish cause. We will then conduct a selective review of implicit bias intervention research and argue that this research also does not speak directly to whether interventions to change implicit bias are effective ways to resolve social disparities. Indeed, we will argue that, based on the extant evidence, any intervention that is focused on directly changing scores on measures of implicit bias is unlikely to be effective at changing social disparities. Finally, we will review an approach that we believe is more effective: change people's knowledge about how the structure of the social environment makes them complicit in the perpetuation of bias. We will illustrate this approach with an intervention we have developed, the prejudice habit-breaking intervention.

I. Implicit Bias as a Cause of Disparities

Developing interventions that are effective at reducing disparities requires first identifying and defining the processes that are thought to cause disparities. Any concept without a clear definition becomes hopelessly broad or ambiguous and therefore not useful. In the context of interventions, if the definition of a process that is thought to cause disparities is unclear, it becomes difficult or impossible to craft interventions that might change that process. For these reasons, we are defining in this chapter "implicit bias" precisely as associations between concepts (for example, an association between Black people and negative concepts) that are activated automatically (i.e., without requiring awareness or intention). The measurement of implicit bias therefore requires a procedure that does not require a person to actively retrieve the target association from memory.

There are two major implications of this definition. First, implicit bias is a process that occurs within a person's head. That means that implicit bias is distinct from the disparities it is presumed to cause. Thus, the mere presence of disparities—even disparities in judgments among people, such as judges, who believe in fairness—cannot by itself be taken as evidence that implicit bias causes the disparities. Implicit bias may well cause these disparities, but this must be established through an independent measurement of implicit bias. Second, implicit bias is just one type of bias that can occur unintentionally. We would like to underscore this point because it is often overlooked. Implicit bias has received perhaps more than the lion's share of focus in recent years because many prominent scholars have argued that it could play a strong role in perpetuating social disparities.[7] However, it is quite possible for a bias to occur unintentionally without being caused by the automatic activation of an association between concepts. For example, legal actors can adhere to established laws and procedures, even though they themselves believe that the laws have negative consequences that disproportionately affect certain groups of people. We will revisit these points at the end of this chapter.

After a potential target of change is identified, it is essential to establish that the process actually causes disparities. Providing evidence that firmly establishes cause is quite difficult and is the subject of vigorous academic debate.[8] However, most scholars agree that one must develop a procedure that, in randomized experiments, produces a difference in both the candidate process (i.e., implicit bias) and a behavior (i.e., discrimination). With this procedure in hand, one must show that it is the changes in the candidate process, not changes in other processes brought about by the candidate procedure, that produce the changes in the behavior. This is a challenging task.

What should be clear from this discussion is that mere associations between a process and behavior are insufficient to show that the process causes the behavior. If an intervention targets a process that is associated with disparities but does not cause them, the result will be wasted time, effort, and, possibly, other unintended negative consequences. To illustrate why this is important, consider the following, somewhat whimsical, example. When developing policies to reduce violent crime, one might notice that the number of murders in a city is associated with the city's sales of ice cream, as both occur more frequently in larger cities. In this example, although an association exists, no one would suggest that outlawing ice cream is an effective means of reducing violent crime.

The suggestion that a correlation exists between violent crime and ice cream sales is clearly different from the suggestion that implicit bias causes discrimination (and therefore disparities) in that the latter suggestion is much more plausible than the former. Yet the very plausibility of this proposition makes it all the more important to evaluate it based on evidence rather than intuition. If we use intuition rather than evidence, we run the risk of committing resources to interventions that, though well meaning, may be at best wasteful and at worst harmful. The intuitive appeal of the proposition leads us to commit an error in logic and therefore waste resources on well-meaning interventions that are nonetheless ineffective. For this reason, studies that find an association between measured implicit bias and discrimination, while suggestive, should not be taken as evidence that implicit bias causes discrimination. This is true regardless of the strength of the association and regardless of the size of the sample in which the association is found.[9] Rather, to understand whether implicit bias causes disparities, we must turn to evidence based on interventions that produce changes in implicit bias and evaluate whether these changes in implicit bias bring about changes in behavior.

> [S]tudies that find an association between measured implicit bias and discrimination, while suggestive, should not be taken as evidence that implicit bias causes discrimination.

II.   Implicit Bias Interventions

Fortunately, the extant research on interventions to change implicit bias is voluminous. We can therefore use this literature to assess whether it is possible to change implicit bias and, if so, whether these changes are likely to bring about changes in biased behavior.

Implicit bias intervention research arose out of two separate research traditions. On the one hand are people from a broad array of backgrounds and a broad range of formal research training who are interested in implicit bias as a means of solving social disparities. On the other hand are people, mostly experimental psychologists, who are interested in implicit bias as a means of understanding the inner workings of the human mind. Some background on these research traditions is necessary to understand what they *have* and *have not* taught us about the role of implicit bias in creating social disparities.

The distinct research traditions have led to a division in both methods and research questions.[10] The disparities-focused researchers often conduct their research in the field, use non-experimental designs, and measure outcomes longitudinally.[11] In addition, disparities-focused researchers do not typically measure implicit bias directly, instead focusing on self-reported knowledge or outcomes collected as part of the administrative mission of a given organization.[12] The focus in this research is on deploying methods of solving the problems that are presumed to be caused by implicit bias while respecting the difficulties of working in non-laboratory settings.

For example, Tan, Morris, and Romero developed a training module intended to educate employees of the Federal Aviation Administration (FAA) about issues related to workforce diversity, prevent workforce harassment and discrimination, and increase future FAA workforce diversity.[13] Whether the researchers thought they were producing their effects through changes in implicit bias is unclear, though the workshop shares many features in common with other trainings developed in the disparities-focused research tradition: It explored the primary dimensions of diversity, the values of the employees and how they might conflict with their prejudices and preconceptions, and the readiness of the employees to embrace diversity. The authors evaluated the effectiveness of the diversity training using a single-group, before-after design by asking the workshop participants to rate their knowledge of diversity-related issues. Although a single-group design respects the fact that, as a matter of organizational policy, the diversity training should not be withheld from any employees, a single-group design is not well-suited for drawing conclusions about the causes of an intervention because natural fluctuations in outcomes over time are confounded with the intervention's true effects. In addition, although self-reported knowledge is easy to measure, it is difficult for people to directly assess changes that have occurred due to a given experience.[14] Any apparent improvements in self-reported knowledge may well be due to participants wishing to present themselves as good employees who are engaged with the organizational mission of the FAA.

In contrast, cognition-focused researchers most often conduct their research in the laboratory in single-session experiments, usually using samples of college students[15] who, though they may have psychological characteristics that make them different from the general population,[16] are cheap, easy, and convenient for psychological research. Cognition-focused researchers employ a large array of implicit bias measures but measure explicit bias and behavior less often.[17] The focus of cognition-focused researchers is drawing rigorous conclusions about mental processes.

For example, Phills and colleagues argued that messages presented on backgrounds consistent with the messages' content are more effective in reducing implicit bias than messages presented on inconsistent backgrounds.[18] Accordingly, they compared the implicit bias of people who viewed the message "Say yes to equality" presented alongside images of positive interracial interactions (a consistent pairing of message with background) to the implicit bias of people who viewed the same message presented alongside pictures of the KKK (an inconsistent pairing of message with background). They also compared the implicit bias of people who viewed the message "Say no to prejudice" presented alongside pictures of the KKK (consistent pairing) to the implicit bias of people who viewed the same message presented alongside pictures of positive interracial interactions. As predicted, Phills and colleagues found that consistent pairings produced lower scores on implicit race bias (as measured using an Implicit Association Test or IAT)[19] than inconsistent pairings and interpreted this result as supporting regulatory focus theory,[20] a theory of motivation. Because participants were randomly assigned to condition and because the researchers included an implicit bias measure, this study is well positioned to speak to the causal effects of the manipulation on people's responses on that measure. However, because the researchers did not measure discriminatory behavior, the study does not speak strongly to how to reduce racial disparities. Nor was the study necessarily intended to speak to these issues—the researchers were more interested in revealing insights into the principles of motivation than they were in understanding the causes of and remedies for racial disparities.

The result of this division in method and research question is that much of the research on implicit bias interventions does not speak directly to whether these interventions are effective in resolving social disparities. Because the disparities-focused research is often not experimental, it is silent as to whether the interventions tested cause any change in social disparities. Because implicit bias is often not measured, it is unclear whether these interventions change implicit bias at all, and, if these interventions change outcomes other than implicit bias, it is unclear whether these changes occur *because of* a change in implicit bias. The interventions developed and tested in the cognition-focused tradition usually do use randomized designs and therefore do not have the same causal inference problems as those developed and tested in the disparities-focused tradition. However, these studies have their own limitations: Because they are often conducted among college students, it is unclear whether these interventions would be useful in non-college settings. Because these studies often do not include measures of behavior and often do not test their effects longitudinally, it is also unclear whether these interventions have effects on implicit bias that last and that cause changes in behavior.

Indeed, if we focus more closely on the cognition-focused studies that do measure their outcomes longitudinally, the evidence suggests that the effects of most implicit bias interventions on measures of implicit bias do not endure. For example, in a large-scale evaluation of nine interventions to change measured implicit bias involving over 6,000 participants, all the interventions had immediate effects on implicit bias.[21] Without exception, these effects disappeared one to two days later. Even motivating participants to use these interventions on their own rather than at the request of the experimenter appears to be ineffective; in an evaluation of this approach with over 1,500 participants, it had no enduring effect on measured implicit bias.[22]

If we focus instead on the cognition-focused studies that measure both implicit and behavioral outcomes, the effects of implicit bias interventions on behavior are quite different, in general, from their effects on implicit bias. In addition, based on an analysis of more than 400 studies of methods to change implicit bias, there is no evidence that the changes in implicit bias that these interventions produce are linked to their small to nonexistent effects on behavior. That is, there is no evidence that these interventions change behavior *because of* their changes in implicit bias.[23]

Our review of research on implicit bias interventions is quite revealing. Because of issues with the design of the research (i.e., a lack of randomization, no measurement of implicit bias, no measurement of behavior), many studies that investigate implicit bias interventions do not speak strongly to whether implicit bias causes disparities. If we focus on the studies that speak more strongly to causality, the effects of current interventions to change implicit bias fade quickly, and there is no evidence that these changes in implicit bias produce changes in behavior. In sum, it is unclear whether developing interventions that change implicit bias is a reasonable approach to resolving social disparities, in law or any other domain.

> [I]t is unclear whether developing interventions that change implicit bias is a reasonable approach to resolving social disparities, in law or any other domain.

III. A More Effective Approach: Knowledge-Based Interventions

From the perspective of classic social psychological theory, it is not surprising that interventions that directly target implicit bias appear to be ineffective. Classic social psychological theory holds that each person's conception of him- or herself strongly affects whether psychological processes are easy or difficult to change.[24] According to these theories, psychological processes are organized hierarchically around a person's conceptions of him- or herself. Processes that are more central to the self-concept resist outside change because changing these processes requires changing all the processes that are below them in

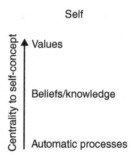

FIGURE 12.1   A simplified model of the self. Psychological processes that are higher in the hierarchy are more central to the self-concept and therefore more resistant to external change. Processes lower in the hierarchy are less central and therefore more susceptible to change.

the hierarchy as well. Processes that are more peripherally located are easier to change, but these changes may not last because the processes higher in the hierarchy remain unchanged.

Because implicit bias is a process that operates independent of awareness and intention, it is, by definition, a process peripheral to the self-concept. This peripheral status implies that brief shifts in implicit bias should be easy to achieve, at least in the short term. However, implicit biases are created and sustained by repeated stereotypic pairings in the social environment. Thus, without changes in processes that are more central to the self-concept, the shifts in implicit bias are likely to be quickly erased soon after the intervention is administered.[25] If the original shifts in implicit bias do not endure, they also would not be able to produce enduring changes in behavior.[26]

If changing implicit bias is ineffective for reducing social disparities because implicit bias is too peripheral to the self-concept, perhaps changing processes that are more central will be correspondingly more effective. However, the process that is the target of intervention should not be so central that it is immune to all but the most dramatic of external changes. Although changes in more central processes such as values do occur, they occur incrementally over long periods of time[27] and may be quite hard to achieve as a result of a relatively brief laboratory procedure.[28] The optimal process to target may thus be one that is moderately central to how people view themselves. One possible candidate is knowledge. People become invested in certain views of themselves and the world,[29] and yet knowledge does change in response to evidence.

Evidence for the effectiveness of a knowledge-based intervention for producing long-term changes in psychological processes related to social disparities stems from work on the prejudice habit-breaking intervention.[30] The habit-breaking intervention is based on the premise that biases that occur unintentionally are like unwanted habits that can be broken through a combination of motivation to reduce unintentional bias, awareness of its existence and the ways it affects minorities, and effort-practicing strategies that reduce unintentional bias.[31] The intervention consists of a semi-interactive, self-paced slideshow composed of feedback, education, and a training section.

During the feedback section, the participants complete a task that can reveal how bias can operate unintentionally, such as a race IAT, and receive feedback about their performance. The implicit measure is thus used to provide participants with a palpable experience of what unintentional bias feels like[32] and a pedagogical tool to make people aware that not all of their responses are consistent with their intentions. Thus, although an implicit measure is an important component of the habit-breaking intervention, its importance stems from its pedagogical usefulness rather than because it is the habit-breaking intervention's primary target of change.

> The habit-breaking intervention is based on the premise that biases that occur unintentionally are like unwanted habits that can be broken through a combination of motivation to reduce unintentional bias, awareness of its existence and the ways it affects minorities, and effort-practicing strategies that reduce unintentional bias. The intervention consists of a semi-interactive, self-paced slideshow composed of feedback, education, and a training section.

During the education section, the participants learn how some of our reactions are inconsistent with intentions. The slideshow applies this general principle to social groups by showing how subtle stereotypic messages pervade the social environment and how these messages can spontaneously pop to mind. The spontaneous reactions can then influence behavior unintentionally. This section then provides evidence that, although they can be subtle, these unintentionally biased behaviors can still lead to adverse outcomes for minorities in a wide variety of domains. The education section is thus designed to leverage the momentary awareness provoked by completing the implicit measure into a more general, enduring awareness of how unintentional biases systematically disadvantage minorities. Following the education section, the participants complete a training section that describes evidence-based strategies, such as stereotype replacement,[33] individuating, perspective-taking,[34] and intergroup contact,[35] that, if practiced, can lead to reductions in unintentional bias.

In our original demonstration of the habit-breaking intervention's effects, people who received the habit-breaking intervention exhibited reductions in measured implicit bias that endured two months after receiving the intervention. In subsequent replications of this study, people who received the habit-breaking intervention were no different in their measured implicit bias than control participants, suggesting that our original results may have been a false positive.[36]

Nevertheless, we have accumulated substantial evidence that the habit-breaking intervention does affect participants' concern about discrimination.[37]

The changes in concern are themselves associated with an increased tendency to notice when others act with bias and to see biased behaviors in themselves and others as wrong.[38] These results suggest that the habit-breaking intervention changes people's knowledge about unintentional bias and its consequences for minorities. These changes lead to changes in how people perceive incidents in the social environment, which in turn can lead to further changes in knowledge. The initial changes in knowledge may thus create a recursive, self-sustaining feedback loop, which may be critical for sustaining any changes that the intervention creates.[39] This feedback loop may explain why the habit-breaking intervention's effects on knowledge endure and may be critical for creating enduring changes in behavior. Indeed, the habit-breaking's effects on behavior may be especially enduring; in one sample, people who received the habit-breaking intervention were more likely to post a comment objecting to an online essay arguing that stereotyping is harmless than were control participants.[40] This difference occurred two years after the intervention was administered.

We have also gathered some evidence that knowledge-based habit breaking may be effective at reducing some kinds of intergroup disparities. This evidence comes from a cluster-randomized trial in 92 academic departments of a 2.5-hour workshop based on the prejudice habit-breaking intervention.[41] The workshop was designed to improve climate for female faculty and thereby improve the representation of women in these departments. Three months after the workshop, faculty in experimental departments reported feeling more self-efficacy to promote gender equity than faculty in control departments.[42] Three years after the workshop, 47 percent of the new hires in experimental departments were women, compared to 29 percent in control departments.[43] In addition, there is evidence that these differences in hiring rates were due to the influence of faculty who attended the habit-breaking workshop; faculty who worked with workshop attenders on department-related affairs (e.g., hiring committees) reported doing more to promote gender equity in their departments.[44]

In sum, because knowledge is moderately related to the self-concept, interventions that change knowledge may be especially useful for reducing intergroup disparities. Knowledge requires less effort to change than do highly central processes, such as values, but is more likely to sustain long-term change than are peripheral processes, such as implicit bias. Indeed, we believe our intervention is effective because it helps people to recognize that wanting to be free of bias is not equivalent to being free of bias. Knowledge that they could be, however unwittingly, complicit in the perpetuation of bias is critical to creating concern about discrimination. And that concern appears to change their understanding of discrimination and encourages them to see bias in themselves and

> Knowledge requires less effort to change than do highly central processes, such as values, but is more likely to sustain long-term change than are peripheral processes, such as implicit bias.

in the world around them (e.g., in others, on TV, etc.). Although we have not directly tested the utility of knowledge-based interventions for changing disparities in legal outcomes, we believe these interventions are more likely to prove useful than are interventions that target implicit bias directly.

Resolving social disparities is not easy. We have argued that addressing issues of such societal importance requires the engagement of the conscious mind.[45] These problems cannot be reduced to responses on any one measure of implicit bias, and assuming that they can respects neither their complexity nor seriousness.

Conclusion

We have argued that the current research on implicit bias does not speak strongly to whether implicit bias causes disparities in legal outcomes, nor does it speak directly to whether implicit bias is a useful target for intervention. In fact, interventions that attempt to directly change responses on measures of implicit bias may be doomed to fail because implicit bias is, by definition, peripheral to the self-concept. This means that, even if an implicit bias intervention reliably produces a change in implicit bias, this change is likely to fade due to the very forces in the social environment that create and sustain the biases in the

> [C]urrent research on implicit bias does not speak strongly to whether implicit bias causes disparities in legal outcomes, nor does it speak directly to whether implicit bias is a useful target for intervention.

first place. We believe that interventions that target processes more central to the self-concept, such as the knowledge-based prejudice habit-breaking intervention, are more likely to produce the type of changes necessary to reduce legal disparities.

To be clear, although we are skeptical as to whether implicit bias plays a central role in creating and sustaining disparities in law, we do not mean to suggest that no forms of unintentional bias contribute to disparities in law. As we noted earlier in the chapter, unintentional biases occur for many reasons besides implicit bias—for example, established laws and procedures that advantage one group at the expense of another, unequal distributions of wealth and education, and/or a lack of awareness of the systematic advantages provided to some groups and not others. However, because each of these potential causes has different implications for which interventions are likely to be effective at resolving social disparities, it is important to distinguish between these potential causes rather than lumping them into the same category.

Finally, although the habit-breaking intervention has proven useful at producing enduring changes in some contexts, it has not yet been tested in a legal context. Indeed, it is quite possible that disparities in legal outcomes are better addressed through changes in policy than through individually targeted psychological interventions. However, we will only discover the approaches that are effective through research that compares the relative effectiveness of different approaches. Considering the social importance of addressing disparities in legal outcomes, conducting this research is a high priority for future work.

ABOUT THE AUTHORS

Dr. Patrick Forscher is a postdoctoral researcher at the University of Wisconsin-Madison Department of Psychology. He collaborated with Dr. Patricia Devine and other members of her lab to develop and test the prejudice habit-breaking intervention (*Long-Term Reduction in Implicit Bias: A Prejudice Habit-Breaking Intervention*, 48 J. EXPERIMENTAL SOC. PSYCHOL. 1267 (2012)) as a means of reducing unintentional biases such as implicit bias. He also conducted the largest quantitative review to date of procedures to change implicit bias (Forscher & Lai et al., under review). Dr. Forscher currently lives in Chicago.

Patricia G. Devine is the Kenneth and Mamie Clark Professor of Psychology at the University of Wisconsin-Madison. Dr. Devine is an internationally recognized expert in the study of stereotyping, prejudice, and intergroup relations. Her original examinations of the dynamics of intergroup relations have educated us about the contemporary manifestations of what Gunnar Myrdal (1944) referred to as the American dilemma—the reality that people's actual (discriminatory) behaviors belie their egalitarian sentiments. In addition, her even-handed blending of psychological theory and social problems has enriched our understanding of the troubling intergroup relations that characterize every society.

ENDNOTES

1. SAMUEL R. GROSS & ROBERT MAURO, DEATH AND DISCRIMINATION: RACIAL DISPARITIES IN CAPITAL SENTENCING (1989); David B. Mustard, *Racial, Ethnic, and Gender Disparities in Sentencing: Evidence from the U.S. Federal Courts*, 44 J.L. & ECON. 285–314 (2001).
2. Patrick S. Forscher et al., *A Meta-Analysis of Changes in Implicit Bias* (unpublished manuscript).
3. Patricia G. Devine, *Stereotypes and Prejudice: Their Automatic and Controlled Components*, 56 J. PERSONALITY & SOC. PSYCHOL. 5–18 (1989).
4. *Id.*
5. C. Daryl Cameron et al., *Sequential Priming Measures of Implicit Social Cognition: A Meta-Analysis of Association with Behavior and Explicit Attitudes*, 16 PERSONALITY & SOC. PSYCHOL. REV. 330–50 (2012); Anthony G. Greenwald et al., *Understanding and Using the Implicit Association Test*, 97 J. PERSONALITY & SOC. PSYCHOL. 17–41 (2009); Frederick L. Oswald et al., *Predicting Ethnic and Racial Discrimination: A Meta-Analysis of IAT Criterion Studies*, 105 J. PERSONALITY & SOC. PSYCHOL. 171–92 (2013).
6. Anthony G. Greenwald et al., *Statistically Small Effects of the Implicit Association Test Can Have Societally Large Effects*, 180 J. PERSONALITY & SOC. PSYCHOL. 553–61 (2015).
7. *Id.*
8. John G. Bullock et al., *Yes, But What's the Mechanism? (Don't Expect an Easy Answer)*, 98 J. PERSONALITY & SOC. PSYCHOL. 550–58 (2010); Steven J. Spencer et al., *Establishing a Causal Chain: Why Experiments Are Often More Effective Than Mediational Analyses in Examining Psychological Processes*, 89 J. PERSONALITY & SOC. PSYCHOL. 845–51 (2005).
9. *See* Cameron et al., *supra* note 5, at 330–50; Greenwald et al., *supra* note 5, at 17–41; Oswald et al., *supra* note 5, at 171–92.

10. Elizabeth Levy Paluck & Donald P. Green, *Prejudice Reduction: What Works? A Review and Assessment of Research and Practice*, 60 ANN. REV. PSYCHOL. 339–67 (2009).

11. *Id.*

12. *Id.*

13. David L. Tan et al., *Changes in Attitude After Diversity Training*, 50 TRAINING & DEV. 54–56 (1996).

14. Richard E. Nisbett & Timothy DeCamp Wilson, *Telling More Than We Can Know: Verbal Reports on Mental Processes*, 84 PSYCHOL. REV. 231–59 (1977).

15. Calvin K. Lai et al., *Reducing Implicit Racial Preferences: II. Intervention Effectiveness Across Time*, 145 J. EXPERIMENTAL SOC. PSYCHOL. 1001 (2016).

16. Joseph Henrich et al., *The Weirdest People in the World?*, 33 BEHAV. & BRAIN SCI. 61 (2010).

17. Forscher et al., *supra* note 2.

18. Curtis E. Phills et al., *Reducing Implicit Prejudice: Matching Approach/Avoidance Strategies to Contextual Valence and Regulatory Focus*, 47 J. EXPERIMENTAL SOC. PSYCHOL. 968–73 (2011).

19. Anthony G. Greenwald et al., *Measuring Individual Differences in Implicit Cognition: The Implicit Association Test*, 74 J. PERSONALITY & SOC. PSYCHOL. 1464–80 (1998).

20. E. Tory Higgins, *Beyond Pleasure and Pain*, 52 AM. PSYCHOL. 1280–1300 (1997).

21. Calvin K. Lai et al., *Reducing Implicit Racial Preferences*, 145 J. EXPERIMENTAL PSYCHOL. 1001–16 (2016).

22. Patrick S. Forscher et al., Breaking the Prejudice Habit: Mechanisms, Timecourse, and Longevity (unpublished manuscript).

23. Forscher et al., *supra* note 2.

24. MILTON ROKEACH, THE NATURE OF HUMAN VALUES (1973).

25. Lai et al., *supra* note 21, at 1001–16.

26. Forscher et al., *supra* note 22.

27. Brent W. Roberts & Wendy F. DelVecchio, *The Rank-Order Consistency of Personality Traits from Childhood to Old Age: A Quantitative Review of Longitudinal Studies*, 126 PSYCHOL. BULL. 3–25 (2000).

28. Rokeach, *supra* note 24.

29. Charles G. Lord et al., *Biased Assimilation and Attitude Polarization: The Effects and Prior Theories on Subsequently Considered Evidence*, 37 J. PERSONALITY & SOC. PSYCHOL. 2098 (1979); William B. Swann, Jr. et al., *The Cognitive-Affective Crossfire: When Self-Consistency Confronts Self-Enhancement*, 52 J. PERSONALITY & SOC. PSYCHOL. 881–89 (1987).

30. Patricia G. Devine et al., *Long-Term Reduction in Implicit Race Bias: A Prejudice Habit-Breaking Intervention*, 48 J. EXPERIMENTAL SOC. PSYCHOL. 1267–78 (2012).

31. Devine, *supra* note 3, at 5–18.

32. Margo J. Monteith et al., *Taking a Look Underground: Detecting, Interpreting, and Reacting to Implicit Racial Biases*, 19 SOC. COGNITION 395–417 (2001).

33. Margo J. Monteith, *Self-Regulation of Prejudiced Responses: Implications for Progress in Prejudice-Reduction Efforts*, 65 J. PERSONALITY & SOC. PSYCHOL. 469–85 (1993).

34. Adam D. Galinsky & Gordon B. Moskowitz, *Perspective-Taking: Decreasing Stereotype Expression, Stereotype Accessibility, and In-Group Favoritism*, 78 J. PERSONALITY & SOC. PSYCHOL. 708–24 (2000); Andrew R. Todd et al., *Perspective Taking Combats Automatic Expressions of Racial Bias*, 100 J. PERSONALITY & SOC. PSYCHOL. 1027–42 (2011).

35. Thomas F. Pettigrew, *Intergroup Contact Theory*, 49 ANN. REV. PSYCHOL. 65–85 (1998); Thomas F. Pettigrew & Linda R. Tropp, *A Meta-Analytic Test of Intergroup Contact Theory*, 90 J. PERSONALITY & SOC. PSYCHOL. 751–83 (2006).

36. Forscher et al., *supra* note 2; Forscher et al., *supra* note 22.

37. Devine et al., *supra* note 30, at 1267–78; Forscher et al., *supra* note 2; Forscher et al., *supra* note 22.

38. Forscher et al., *supra* note 2.

39. *Id.*
40. *Id.*
41. Molly Carnes et al., *The Effect of an Intervention to Break the Gender Bias Habit for Faculty at One Institution: A Cluster Randomized, Controlled Trial*, 90 ACAD. MED. 221–30 (2015).
42. *Id.*
43. Forscher et al., *supra* note 2.
44. Forscher et al., *supra* note 22.
45. Devine, *supra* note 3, at 5–18; Devine et al., *supra* note 30, at 1267–78.

Chapter 13

Assessing Interventions to Reduce Judicial Bias

Fighting Implicit Bias—What Judges and Lawyers Can Do

Lindsay M. Perez, Monica K. Miller,
Alicia Summers, and Shawn C. Marsh

Chapter Contents

Chapter Highlights

- Interventions to reduce implicit bias including increasing awareness, focusing on the decision-making process, and receiving feedback on decisions are described.

- It is critical that intervention be assessed in the most rigorous way possible to ensure that it is effective in reducing bias and improving outcomes.

- Research-based information is provided to bridge the gap between research practitioners seeking to identify the best methods for reducing implicit bias and legal personnel attempting to achieve the same ends.

- Evaluations of varying depths are considered.

Introduction

The American public views the justice system as an institution that is supposed to ensure justice and fairness for everyone it serves, but this is not always the case.[1] Other chapters discuss at length research from various fields demonstrating that implicit bias affects decision making even for individuals such as physicians and legal actors who are expected to remain impartial. Other chapters also review implicit bias and ingroup and outgroup dynamics, and offer possible explanations for the kind of disparities that lead many to question how fair the system may be in practice.

As interest grows in implicit bias and related concepts where responses are nonconscious, efforts to intervene and limit unwanted bias also increase. Because by definition individuals are unaware of the degree to which implicit bias affects their decisions, simply informing legal actors that bias leads to discriminatory outcomes does not necessarily reduce the effect of implicit bias. In this context, a variety of interventions or strategies have been proposed, and some implemented, to potentially reduce implicit bias in legal decision making.[2] Many of these efforts are reviewed and suggested in other chapters, and these all represent a notable effort to eliminate disproportionate outcomes and achieve fairness. However, making an effort to reduce implicit bias is not enough; one has to examine whether these interventions are actually reducing implicit bias and discriminatory outcomes.

Assessing interventions generates information regarding the degree to which interventions are serving their intended purpose as well as whether these strategies should continue or new strategies should be implemented.[3] The purpose of this chapter is to convey the importance of assessing interventions intended to reduce implicit bias in legal decision making and explain potential methods for assessment. Although a reduction of implicit bias in legal decision making is important for a variety of legal actors, this chapter will focus on judges' decisions.

Overall, this chapter offers research-based information to bridge the gap between research practitioners seeking to identify the best methods for reducing implicit bias and legal personnel attempting to implement the best practices for avoiding discriminatory outcomes resulting from biased decision making. Part I briefly recaps the types and effects of implicit bias; Part II briefly recaps some strategies for reducing implicit bias; Part III explains why assessment of these strategies or interventions is necessary and reviews factors to consider during the empirical assessment of interventions; and Part IV offers concluding thoughts on assessment.

I. Types and Effects of Implicit Bias

As previously discussed throughout this book, implicit biases against individuals based on observable characteristics (e.g., race or gender) can influence judgments based upon the degree to which the target (the judged individual) appears to adequately represent stereotypes or assumed characteristics of the group.[4]

A perceived relationship between racial stereotypes and criminality is one example. Researchers have found that harsher outcomes occur in the criminal justice system for Blacks as compared to Whites[5] and that these differences extend to differences in degree; individuals exhibiting more stereotypical physical characteristics of their group receive harsher outcomes than individuals with less stereotypical physical features.[6] For example, a Black defendant with more Afrocentric physical features (e.g., dark skin, wide nose) is more likely to receive negative judgments compared to a Black defendant who has fewer of these features (e.g., light skin).[7] Similar research identifies racial bias in cases in which the defendant is accused of a crime stereotypically associated with his or her race (e.g., Black defendant accused of theft) compared to when the defendant is accused of a crime *not* stereotypically associated with his or her race (e.g., Black defendant accused of embezzlement).[8] Research also suggests implicit racial bias against minorities occurs more frequently when the defendant is accused of a crime that threatens the majority group (e.g., Black

> Research also suggests implicit racial bias against minorities occurs more frequently when the defendant is accused of a crime that threatens the majority group (e.g., Black defendant victimizing a White woman) than when a stereotypical race-based threat does not appear to exist (e.g., Asian defendant victimizing a Hispanic woman).

defendant victimizing a White woman) than when a stereotypical race-based threat does not appear to exist (e.g., Asian defendant victimizing a Hispanic woman).[9] More recent scholarship has approached the disproportionality picture differently, by focusing on bias formed *toward* a group or what Professor Levinson and his colleagues have labeled *implicit favoritism*.[10]

Like race-based bias, implicit gender bias can occur based on the degree to which the target (i.e., person being judged or evaluated) is perceived as conforming to gender norms. For example, a "battered woman defense" is described as passive rather than active or aggressive, suggesting that the defendant's reason for killing her husband is more believable if that particular act seems to be out of character.[11] Unfortunately, implicit gender bias is also evidenced in cases involving rape where individuals have the tendency to evaluate the victim's (in) actions when determining what type of punishment the perpetrator should receive. Individuals assessing punishment for perpetrators of date rape are more likely to recommend harsher sentences when the victim only resisted verbally compared to when the victim engaged in both verbal and physical resistance.[12]

Similar patterns occur where implicit bias is based on socioeconomic status (SES) or social class that relates to the individual's income level.[13] For example, individuals who were provided with a vignette about date rape and were asked to rate the degree to which they blamed the male perpetrator, either a bus driver or a doctor, placed more blame on the bus driver (i.e., low SES male) compared to the doctor (i.e., high SES male).[14]

Implicit bias regarding other demographic characteristics that are morally charged, such as religion, sexual orientation, and gender identity, can also potentially affect legal decision making. Religion-based implicit biases can occur due to the evaluator or the target's religion, as well as in situations more typically associated with an individual's religion (i.e., the crime is associated with a particular religious group).[15] For example, individuals evaluating a bombing case might be more likely to convict a religious defendant compared to a non-religious defendant, due to the perception that bombings are generally motivated by religious beliefs. It is possible that religion-based implicit bias is also determined by an individual's awareness of circumstances in which it is acceptable (or unacceptable) to have bias against particular groups (e.g., terrorists).[16] Implicit bias against the target's sexual orientation or identity can occur due to an individual's lack of acceptance of other lifestyles or moral beliefs regarding whether sexual orientation is a choice versus a genetic trait. For example, individuals who believe sexual orientation is a genetic trait are less likely to exhibit biased attitudes against lesbians and gays compared to those who do not support the genetic explanation.[17]

As discussed in many other chapters, implicit biases can affect legal decisions and outcomes for those interacting with the justice system despite decision makers' commitment to fairness.[18] The intent to remain objective does not sufficiently prevent someone from making decisions that are influenced by implicit bias. This is true at all levels and decision points in the system from early childhood to education attainment and through adulthood. For example, researchers have documented that Black children are more often reported in cases of child abuse and neglect and that the child welfare system generally is disproportionately comprised of racial minorities.[19]

II. Identification of Interventions for Reducing Implicit Bias

Various strategies and interventions have been proposed as methods for reducing implicit bias in legal decision making. Strategies recapped here are those recommended by organizations within the justice system (e.g., specific jurisdictions or court programs) or by other groups and researchers working in collaboration with judges. Some of these interventions have been implemented with judges, and other strategies have not yet been implemented but are supported by research findings within juror decision-making literature. As discussed in the next section, these interventions are important but are only valuable if they are actually serving their intended purpose.

A. Training

Not surprisingly, several organizations and researchers recommend training to improve awareness of implicit bias and reduce its negative impact. Leading among them is the National Campaign to Ensure the Racial and Ethnic Fairness of America's State Courts led by the National Center for State Courts (NCSC).[20] NCSC engaged in and recommended that courts offer legal actors training about implicit bias, diversity, and perspective-taking.[21] The Department of Justice has recently pursued this strategy by mandating implicit bias training for prosecutors and law enforcement officers.[22]

This kind of training typically includes introduction to examples of implicit bias in professional judgments to promote awareness of the issue. This training demonstrates that no one is immune to the effect of implicit bias on decision making, promotes introspection or perspective-taking, and encourages becoming self-aware and more process oriented when attempting to debias judgments.[23] Trainers encourage legal actors to evaluate and improve their decision-making process by reviewing facts and relying less on stereotypes. For example, trainers often offer "decision-support tools" to allow judges to articulate their thought processes through the use of notes, written opinions, or bench cards.

B. Reflection

Interventions also generally focus on reflection. As part of the Call to Action Workshop, the National Council for Juvenile and Family Court Judges (NCJFCJ) collaborated with two other organizations to develop an implicit bias and institutional racism training as well as a judicial bench card.[24] Piloted in three different court sites and ultimately implemented in dozens more around the country, the NCJFCJ approach reviewed implicit bias and institutional racism bias and emphasized the use of reflective decision making and introspective deliberation in order to reduce effects of implicit bias.[25] Reflection was encouraged through the use of a bench card designed to provide judges with references to laws and practices relevant to the specific legal proceeding and to remind them of important procedures and discussion topics particular to their decision, in this case, in preliminary protective court hearings. Providing judges with a bench card that reminds them about best practices can aid in reducing the influence of implicit bias on judges' decisions by increasing the likelihood that they incorporate procedural information into their judgments.

> Providing judges with a bench card that reminds them about best practices can aid in reducing the influence of implicit bias on judges' decisions by increasing the likelihood that they incorporate procedural information into their judgments.

Previous research on the use of reflective, or introspective, thinking during decision-making processes suggests that this procedure can reduce implicit bias by encouraging individuals to more closely consider the information they receive and rely less on quick associations.[26] Findings suggesting that juror deliberation can reduce implicit religious bias[27] also hint at the potential benefit of introspective deliberation in reducing judges' implicit biases. Assessment of the interventions, which will be discussed more extensively in the next section, indicated that the training coupled with the bench card was successful in affecting placement outcomes over an extended period of time.

C. Other Behavioral Approaches

Other strategies identified by the National Center for State Courts and others working in the field involve addressing factors that foster the use of implicit bias and reducing those factors. This involves recommendations such as reducing distractions, sources of stress, and sources of ambiguity.[28] Also recommended is work to increase judges' familiarity with stigmatized groups and counter-stereotypical situations through exercises or interactions.[29]

III. Assessment

Researchers conducting assessments typically examine whether the desired effect has occurred on the outcome variable after the intervention has been introduced. Specifically, researchers assessing interventions aimed to reduce implicit bias would measure judges' level of implicit bias or potential patterns in their legal decisions. For example, researchers seeking to identify the impact of the NCJFCJ training and bench card measured whether there was a difference in judges' juvenile placement decisions after receiving these interventions.[30]

It is important to note that researchers and judges work together using each other's expertise during the assessment process. Researchers offer methodological expertise to assess interventions that help judges continue making objective decisions, and judges offer legal expertise to inform the criteria measured in the assessment. Considering that judges generally do not have specific training or expertise regarding assessment of interventions, judges can work with researchers and organizations, such as the NCJFCJ, to assist in this process. The following section outlines several methods researchers can use to assess interventions for reducing implicit bias.

A. Importance of Assessing Interventions

Assessment determines the degree to which interventions actually reduce the effect of implicit bias in legal decisions and result in a decrease in discriminatory outcomes.[31] Through assessment, organizations learn which strategies are most effective for reducing bias, which strategies are not effective, and which strategies appear to be working but are not actually generating change. Court officials supporting interventions should be interested in determining whether their time, effort, and resources are being used on best practices for reducing implicit bias. In addition to identifying whether biased decision making and discriminatory outcomes are being reduced, assessment also provides information that promotes transparency of the justice system. Conducting assessments of an intervention's effect on legal decisions holds the justice system accountable for upholding practices that best provide resolutions to the problem(s) being addressed by the intervention.[32]

Assessment of interventions potentially generates trust in the justice system[33] because it communicates that legal decision makers are making an active effort to be objective. That is, assessment of judicial practices gives individuals the impression that the justice system is genuinely attempting to address problems with discrimination by implementing changes and ensuring that they work. Assessment of interventions also provides information to stakeholders regarding the degree to which resources are being adequately distributed to efforts that impact decision making.[34] It is possible that stakeholders and the general public develop more confidence in court programs that are actively assessed to determine the degree to which these programs are successful. In fact, stakeholders have begun promoting the use of empirical data to inform decisions within various government programs, suggesting that assessment has been identified as a method for developing evidence-based practices.

B. Empirical Assessment of Interventions (Methodology)

1. Fidelity Assessment

Prior to assessing potential links between an intervention and the outcome of interest, it is important to examine whether the intervention was completed as intended. This initial component of the assessment, called a fidelity assessment, measures whether the judges actually followed the steps indicated in the intervention.[35] For example, an intervention for increasing judges' awareness of implicit bias in legal decisions could involve asking judges to take the IAT. Before assessing that intervention, it would be important to assess *whether* judges took the IAT and whether they received their IAT scores before determining how the intervention affected decision making. If the program is not carried out as designed, a failure to reduce implicit bias might be due to not actually using the program as it was intended, rather than due to program ineffectiveness.[36] Conducting a fidelity assessment can occur over a spectrum from a simple check-in as to whether participants did the assignment to a more in-depth procedure, such as direct court observation of judicial practice and training or re-training on use of intervention instruments.

2. Experiment

Various methodologies can be used to assess the impact of interventions on a particular outcome, such as reducing implicit bias. The most robust assessment technique that researchers use is an experiment. Researchers who use this approach randomly assign the individuals being assessed into different groups; one or more groups typically receive the intervention (i.e., the treatment group), and one group does not receive any intervention (i.e., the control group). This procedure allows for a comparison and an assessment of the effectiveness of the intervention. The experimental approach is robust because it allows the researcher to account for potential outside sources of influence, which are defined as variables that are not part of the experiment but could potentially affect the outcome. For example, outside sources of influence in an experiment might relate to the participant's location (e.g., region of the United States) or the conditions in which the experiment occurs (e.g., if the participant was in a bad mood). However, because experiments involve random assignment, the potential outside sources are randomly distributed among the groups and do not systematically influence results. Random assignment affords researchers with the control necessary to be able to determine causality between an intervention and the outcome measured, which is why an experimental design is the most robust assessment technique.

Some researchers have adopted methodology from experimental research to assess interventions intended to reduce the role of implicit bias on judges' decisions in juvenile dependency hearings. Russell and Summers provided all judges with training on implicit bias and institutional racism.[37] However, judges at each site included in the intervention were randomly assigned into groups to determine who would receive bench cards as part of the intervention (i.e., the manipulation in the experiment). The researchers also examined judges' preliminary protection decisions prior to implementing bench cards and at the adjudication hearing following use of the bench cards.

3. Pre-/Post-Analysis

Conducting an analysis prior to the intervention as well as after the intervention is referred to as a pre-/post-analysis; this method is typically used to establish the effect of the intervention on the outcome by comparing the participants' behavior before and after the manipulation.[38] In the Russell and Summers research discussed above, using random assignment to determine which judges would receive bench cards and conducting pre-/post-analyses allowed the researchers to assess the effect of bench cards on judges' decisions while controlling for other factors that could influence decision making.

Rachlinski and colleagues' research also utilized experimental methods to determine whether increasing race salience could reduce the effect of implicit racial bias on judges' sentencing decisions.[39] These researchers wanted to assess whether increasing race salience by making the defendant's race explicit would reduce the effect of implicit bias (i.e., measured by the IAT) on judges' verdicts. White and Black judges, who had already taken the IAT for another part of the study, were randomly assigned a vignette in which the defendant was described as White or Black (i.e., manipulation). The researchers statistically assessed whether judges were more likely to convict a White or Black defendant based on their implicit racial bias (i.e., level of White preference). Results indicated that White and Black judges were equally as likely to convict the White over the Black defendant for the same crime, which occurred whether the judges exhibited a White or Black preference according to the IAT. The researchers concluded that making race explicitly salient (i.e., noticeable) in the case might motivate judges to become more aware of the influence implicit bias might have on their decisions and subsequently lead them to suppress bias.[40] Although this particular intervention might appear minimal, empirical assessment demonstrated that race salience could be an effective way of reducing the impact of implicit bias on legal decisions. However, it is important to note that increasing race salience in actual court proceedings would require a different method than in the study, because race is typically already explicit.

> [E]mpirical assessment demonstrated that race salience could be an effective way of reducing the impact of implicit bias on legal decisions.

4. Quasi-Experiment

Slightly less rigorous, but more commonly used in applied settings, is a quasi-experimental design. Random assignment to groups may not be practical or feasible in the applied world, but assessments can still occur. Quasi-experimental designs do not typically have random assignment but do find a meaningful comparison group (e.g., comparing recidivism outcomes for a specialty court docket to recidivism outcomes for a regular court docket where all participants in the study are somewhat similar). More often, this design takes the form of pre-/post-assessments, where data is examined prior to and after an intervention to determine changes in behavior and outcomes. For example, in the bench card study, researchers utilized both an experimental and a quasi-experimental design.[41] They compared case outcome decisions prior to and after the intervention for each judge involved in the study. These pre-post types of comparisons provide important information about how practice has changed and how outcomes may have changed. While they may not be able to demonstrate causal connections, they can demonstrate change.

5. Qualitative

A less robust but still meaningful method of assessment is to use a qualitative approach to collect data that describes judges' attitudes or legal decisions after implementing a specific intervention. Using qualitative methods typically involves systematic observation or collecting free response (i.e., non-numerical) data from a survey or interview and identifying themes or commonalities among participant responses. For example, researchers might interview judges who have participated in interventions to reduce implicit bias in order to find out more about judges' experiences with the intervention or changes in their attitudes. Researchers might also review judges' explanations of court decisions in order to find out potential effects of the intervention on judges' decision-making process. Conducting a qualitative analysis of judges' responses can also reveal more specific information regarding judges' experiences with the intervention such as its practicality or potential issues with the implementation, as well as support for the intervention.[42]

C. *Other Methods and Considerations*

Other methods for assessing interventions differ based upon the type of information that is available to researchers regarding attitudes and behavioral outcomes. Although assessing behavioral outcomes before and after introducing an intervention into the courts would be preferred, there are cases in which evaluators do not have access to information regarding individuals' biases and decisions prior to the implementation of the intervention. For example, Marts and colleagues were interested in learning whether the implementation of a community program affected social workers' and community members' attitudes about the child welfare system and the rate at which children entered the welfare system.[43] Although the researchers had data on child welfare rates prior to and after the intervention, they did not have any documented information regarding community or social worker attitudes about the child welfare system prior to the intervention. The researchers conducted focus group interviews with social workers and community members about their opinions of the Department of Children and Family Services (DCFS) after the community program had been implemented. Participants (i.e., social workers and community members) indicated that they believed that the community had a more positive view of DCFS following the intervention, and that it was starting to believe that child welfare initiatives could actually benefit families. Assessing participants' attitudes about child welfare following the implementation of the intervention provided some support for attitude change, even if participants' attitudes about child welfare were not measured before the intervention.

1. Measurement over Time

Another approach to assessing the impact of an intervention is to measure attitude or behavioral change among those who received the specific intervention over an extended period of time (e.g., months or years). Although assessing changes in the attitudes or behavioral outcomes immediately after an intervention is important,[44] it is also important to assess whether these effects last over time. Assessing attitudes or behavioral outcomes over time provides stronger evidence of long-term effects of the intervention on decision making.[45] For example, Marts and colleagues reviewed data on child welfare placement (i.e., removal from family into the child welfare system) for two years following the implementation of a community program. They found that the community program made a long-term impact on community attitudes and child welfare placement decisions. In another study, Devine and colleagues assessed college students' level of implicit racial bias for 12 weeks following an interactive training on strategies to reduce implicit bias, and they determined that the intervention had a long-term attitudinal effect on participants.[46]

2. Developing a Partnership between Researchers and Practitioners

It is important to note that researchers are often delighted to have an opportunity to work on "real-world" issues and appreciate forming partnerships with practitioners in the justice system such as judges. Partnerships between researchers and practitioners involved in court programs provide both parties with resources to develop an intervention assessment that has rigorous methodology and the appropriate data sources to properly evaluate intervention effectiveness.[47] Judges are essential to assessment efforts because they can help researchers understand the legal process and key legal issues. Additionally, judges can provide researchers with information that will aid in making legally relevant measures as well as prevent them from violating any judicial rules. Researchers and system improvement experts at organizations such as the National Council for Juvenile and Family Court Judges, the National Center for State Courts, the American Bar Association, and local universities are eager to work with judges to make positive changes in the justice system.

In order to form a successful assessment partnership, the team of researchers and practitioners should discuss the goals of the program being assessed and tailor the evaluation to produce information regarding attainment of those goals.[48] For example, researchers should speak with practitioners in order to understand how the program is intended to reduce implicit bias and the behavioral outcomes expected from a successful intervention (e.g., less disproportionate sentencing). The team of researchers and practitioners should also outline the information they would like to gain from assessing an intervention and discuss the steps necessary to obtain data for the assessment. Both of these steps should ideally occur before the program is implemented to better inform the content of the materials or measures used to assess the intervention. However, researchers are often asked to conduct an assessment *after* the intervention has been implemented or data has been collected. This situation can present researchers with challenges relating to data quality and the types of conclusions that can be drawn from the assessment. The following section outlines several challenges that researchers might encounter during the assessment of interventions.

3. Challenges Encountered during the Assessment of Interventions

Assessments, particularly those assessing court behaviors and outcomes, are rare, due in large part to the challenges researchers face when trying to gain access to judges, courts, and confidential data associated with legal cases. Some challenges stem from concerns regarding the assessment implications. Other challenges involve the methodology used to conduct the assessment or structural limitations due to requirements within an applied setting.

One challenge in assessing interventions involves addressing judges' potential apprehension regarding the implications of data collected. The political reality is that many judges are appointed or elected and have legitimate concerns about what the data may reveal and how that may be used against them. This is especially true for data that may reveal a potential bias (even a nonconscious bias) among judges who need to be impartial decision makers. This is a huge barrier in assessing the effectiveness of interventions, and more efforts need to be dedicated to reducing this fear and increasing interest in learning about potential biases so that efforts can be made to reduce them.

Another challenge researchers encounter when beginning an assessment of a particular intervention is conceptualizing data sources and data collection in various ways in order to produce informative findings. Researchers must initially determine the types of decisions and behavioral outcomes that should be impacted if the intervention is effective. Theory can help identify the types of changes expected; then researchers can consider how changes in decision making can be measured. Researchers must consider the type of data that is required for the assessment and the degree to which resources available to them can provide this data.[49] In some cases, researchers have access to sentencing data collected before and after the intervention was implemented, which can provide specific information regarding potential changes in legal outcomes.[50] However, it is possible that methods used for secondary data analysis or inconsistencies in documentation can limit the utility of existing data resources. Some data sources are developed from court observations[51] or from other intervention procedures, such as requiring judges to document their thoughts leading up to the legal decision.[52] If researchers determine that they need to collect data in order to access the information required for assessment, they must consider the best method for acquiring desired information as well as the feasibility of data collection. Researchers will often use one or more methods described in the previous section of this chapter (e.g., experiment); researcher's access to judges and limitations relating to legal procedures typically determine this decision.

Researchers asked to assess an intervention already in place can experience particular challenges due to not being involved in the original implementation. When practitioners who implement interventions do not collect pre-test data, researchers presented with the task of assessing the intervention do not have a reference for previous attitudes or behavioral outcomes. Additionally, the intervention might be informed by previous theories or research that the assessment researcher does not find relevant or helpful. If data has already been collected, the measures used for data collection (e.g., survey) often are not designed in the same manner that the researcher assessing the intervention would find most useful. Finally, researchers asked to assess interventions they did not assist in implementing do not typically involve random assignment; therefore, the researcher cannot establish causality between the intervention and any changes in attitudinal or behavioral outcomes.

Researchers assessing interventions in the justice system typically encounter various challenges related to conducting experimental research in applied settings. Experimental researchers conducting intervention assessments need to balance the obligations of justice system personnel with their overall research goals. For example, although researchers use random assignment to establish causality between an intervention and a behavioral outcome, the justice system might have concerns with the disruption of established court procedures or with only some judges receiving the intervention. Additionally, court programs might desire rapid, succinct findings to support future funding efforts,[53] whereas researchers might place less emphasis on these characteristics and are more interested in elaborate theory-based methods that would produce answers to their research questions. Experimental research is also difficult to conduct in a manner that adequately represents the situational characteristics of the applied setting, creating issues with generalizability of results if researchers are too focused on controlling the influence of external factors. Specifically, experimental research allows for control of external factors that likely systematically influence individual defendants' legal outcomes in the real world (e.g., doing an experiment in a laboratory using fictional cases). Yet in doing so, they may have created an environment that is too artificial to be meaningful.

Conclusions

Individuals typically incorporate stereotypes into their assessments of others, leading to the formation of various types of implicit biases relating to group membership,[54] and these implicit biases have contributed to discriminatory outcomes for those seeking fairness in our legal system.[55] Several types of strategies for reducing the effect of implicit bias on judges' decisions have been recommended or implemented to promote fairness and equality within the larger criminal and civil justice system. Interventions reducing implicit bias in judges' decisions also have implications for children and families involved in juvenile proceedings. For example, although there is limited research suggesting a link between implicit racial bias and legal decisions regarding child abuse and neglect cases, statistics indicate that there is racial disparity in the foster care system.[56] Given judges' implicit biases and their influence on child placement into foster care or with a relative, it is likely that at least some portion of racial disparity in the foster care system can be attributed to judges' implicit racial bias. Interventions reducing implicit bias in judges' decisions would likely lead to equality in decisions for child placement. Judges with reduced implicit bias might base their decisions more on factors relating to the case itself rather than outside information. Furthermore, judges might make decisions that are more sensitive to cultural and structural factors affecting children based on their background or consider their decisions in light of underlying risk factors that affect minorities.[57]

Although it is important to implement strategies to reduce implicit bias, it is equally as important to assess the effectiveness of these strategies for producing objective decisions and decreasing discriminatory legal outcomes. Researchers can take several methodological approaches to assess interventions intended to reduce judges' implicit biases but should consider potential issues encountered with empirical research in applied settings. Assessment occurs most effectively through researcher-practitioner partnerships. Therefore, judges with a desire to consistently make fair legal decisions or who seek to implement positive changes in the justice system or make more effective decisions should contact researchers who are eager to make a real-world impact.

APPENDIX
Practical Considerations for Judges

Implicit bias is a completely normal human phenomenon that occurs outside of your awareness. Even judges, who have years of training, keen analytical minds, and make exceptional efforts to be impartial decision makers are still human and can fall prey to this bias. Here are three practical considerations, drawn from this chapter.

1. Awareness of Implicit Biases Is Critical

Consider your own experiences and background. How might that affect your decisions? Some practical tips to increase awareness:

- Think about stereotypes you hold based on race, gender, religion, and sexual orientation. What do you see as *typical* behavior for these groups?
- Take the Implicit Associations Test (IAT) to learn more about implicit biases you may have (https://implicit.harvard.edu/implicit/takeatest.html).

2. Focus on the Process instead of the Outcomes

Consider what tools are available to you to focus more on the process. For example, these reflection questions, from the National Council of Juvenile and Family Court Judges, are meant to help judges focus on the process.

- What assumptions have I made about the cultural identity, genders, and background of this family?
- What is my understanding of this family's unique culture and circumstances?
- How is my decision specific to this child and this family?
- How has the court's past contact and involvement with this family influenced (or how might it influence) my decision-making process and findings?
- What evidence has supported every conclusion I have drawn, and how have I challenged unsupported assumptions?

3. Be Open to Assessments That May Yield Critical Information about Bias and Effective Interventions

No one wants to learn that he or she is biased and may have made decisions in a biased way. However, it is important to be open to understanding what the biases may be and how to reduce them and improve equity. Be *open* to research being conducted within the court. Most researchers can come to agreements with practitioners (e.g., judges) as to *how* the data can be used and *who* will get to see the data. De-identification is an option, to ensure that it cannot be traced to one person or one jurisdiction.

- Look for *evidence-based* interventions or efforts to increase evidence around a specific intervention. The more that we (researchers) know, the better able we are to provide information back to the court in a meaningful way.
- Encourage *use and testing* of tools to reduce bias. Testing interventions can tell us what actually helps improve equity to ensure all families have the opportunity for fair outcomes.

So You'd Like to Know More

- For an example of assessment involving comparison of interventions and behavioral outcomes, see Calvin K. Lai et al., *Reducing Implicit Racial Preferences: I. A Comparative Investigation of 17 Interventions*, 143 Journal of Experimental Psychology General 4 (2014).

- For a review of implicit bias and strategies to reduce its presence in the courtroom, see Pamela M. Casey et al., *Addressing Implicit Bias in the Courtroom*, 49 Court Review, 64–70 (2011); also see Pamela M. Casey et al., *Strategies to Reduce the Influence of Implicit Bias: Resources for Education*, Helping Courts Address Implicit Bias (2012). http://www.ncsc.org/~/media/Files/PDF/Topics/Gender%20and%20Racial%20Fairness/IB_report_033012.ash.

About the Authors

Lindsay M. Perez, Ph.D., is a data analytics consultant in the private sector. The primary focus of her work is to use research and data analysis to inform decision making and strategy development in various contexts. Some of her interests include implicit bias reduction, legal decision making, and social justice issues.

Monica K. Miller, J.D., Ph.D., is a Professor of Criminal Justice and faculty in the Interdisciplinary Social Psychology Ph.D. Program at the University of Nevada, Reno. Her interests lie at the intersection of law and psychology. Specifically, she studies bias in legal decision making, judges' and jurors' stress, and regulation of family relationships and behavior.

Alicia Summers, Ph.D., is an independent consultant working directly with court and court systems. Dr. Summers worked with the National Council of Juvenile and Family Court Judges for 11 years, with efforts focusing on disproportionality and disparity within the dependency court system, including testing of judicial tools meant to reduce implicit bias and improve outcomes for children and families. Dr. Summers has a Ph.D. in social psychology from the University of Nevada, Reno.

Shawn C. Marsh, Ph.D., is the Director of Judicial Studies, Associate Professor of Communication Studies, and faculty in the Interdisciplinary Social Psychology Ph.D. Program at the University of Nevada, Reno. He is the former Chief Program Officer for Juvenile Law at the National Council of Juvenile and Family Court Judges, where he taught and provided technical assistance extensively on topics such as implicit bias and trauma-responsive justice, and oversaw myriad national projects focused on child welfare, juvenile justice, judicial decision making, school engagement, and trauma/victimization.

Endnotes

1. Jerry Kang, Nat'l Ctr. for State Courts, *Implicit Bias: A Primer for Courts* 1, 6 (2009), http://wp.jerrykang.net.s110363.gridserver.com/wp-content/uploads/2010/10/kang-Implicit-Bias-Primer-for-courts-09.pdf; Jerry Kang et al., *Implicit Bias in the Courtroom*, 59 UCLA L. Rev. 1124, 1128–1134 (2012).
2. *See, e.g.,* Jesse Russell & Alicia Summers, *Reflective Decision-Making and Foster Care Placements*, 19 Psychol. Pub. Pol'y & L. 2 (2013).
3. Corey S. Shdaimah & Alicia Summers, *Judiciary-Academic Partnerships: Resources for Evaluation*, 95 Judicature 1, 30–31 (2011).

4. Christopher S. Jones & Martin F. Kaplan, *The Effects of Racially Stereotypical Crimes on Juror Decision-Making and Information-Processing Strategies,* 25 Basic & Applied Soc. Psychol. 1, 1–3 (2003); *see also* Charles G. Lord et al., *Attitude Prototypes as Determinants of Attitude–Behavior Consistency,* 46 J. Personality & Soc. Psychol. 4, 1264–65 (1984).

5. *See, e.g.,* Jennifer L. Eberhardt et al., *Looking Deathworthy: Perceived Stereotypicality of Black Defendants Predicts Capital-Sentencing Outcomes,* 17 Psychol. Sci. 5 (2006); *see also* Kimberly B. Kahn & Paul G. Davies, *Differently Dangerous? Phenotypic Racial Stereotypicality Increases Implicit Bias Among Ingroup and Outgroup Members,* 14 Group Processes & Intergroup Rel. 4 (2010).

6. *Eberhardt et al., supra note 5; see also Kahn & Davies, supra note 5.*

7. *Eberhardt et al., supra note 5; see also Kahn & Davies, supra note 5.*

8. Jones & Kaplan, *supra* note 4, at 9–11.

9. Eberhardt et al., *supra* note 5, at 384–65.

10. Robert J. Smith, Justin D. Levinson & Zoe Robinson, *Implicit White Favoritism in the Criminal Justice System,* 66 Ala. L. Rev. 871, 891 (2014) ("Implicit white favoritism refers to the positive effects of implicit bias on members of privileged groups."); *see also* Monica K. Miller et al., *Exploring the Boundaries of Societally Acceptable Bias Expression Toward Muslims and Atheists* (unpublished manuscript under review 2016).

11. Brenda L. Russell & Linda S. Melillo, *Attitudes Toward Battered Women Who Kill: Defendant Typicality and Judgments of Culpability,* 33 Crim. Justice & Behav. 219, 223–29 (2006).

12. Katherine A. Black & David J. Gold, *Gender Differences and Socioeconomic Status Biases in Judgments About Blame in Date Rape Scenarios,* 23 Violence & Victims 1, 122–25 (2008).

13. *Id.*

14. *Id.*; Neitz provides a more detailed overview of how implicit bias regarding socioeconomic status impact legal decisions in Chapter 6.

15. Monica K. Miller et al., *The Effects of Deliberations and Religious Identity on Mock Jurors' Verdicts,* 14 Group Processes & Intergroup Rel. 4 (2011).

16. Miller et al., *supra* note 10.

17. Toby E. Jayaratne et al., *White Americans' Genetic Lay Theories of Race Differences and Sexual Orientation: Their Relationship with Prejudice Toward Blacks, and Gay Men and Lesbians,* 9 Group Processes & Intergroup Rel. 1, 86–89 (2006).

18. Patricia G. Devine, *Stereotypes and Prejudice: Their Automatic and Controlled Components,* 56 J. Personality & Soc. Psychol. 1–2; *see also* Alexander R. Green et al., *Implicit Bias among Physicians and Its Prediction of Thrombolysis Decisions for Black and White Patients,* J. Gen. Internal Med. (2007).

19. Brett Drake et al., *Racial Bias in Child Protection? A Comparison of Competing Explanations Using National Data,* Pediatrics, 471–72 (2011).

20. Pamela M. Casey et al., *Strategies to Reduce the Influence of Implicit Bias: Resources for Education, Helping Courts Address Implicit Bias* (2012). For full report, *see* http://www.ncsc.org/~/media/Files/PDF/Topics/Gender%20and%20Racial%20Fairness/IB_report_033012.ashx. These strategies were produced as part of a larger report advocating for court education resources, demonstrating interest on behalf of the justice system to enact changes and provide judges with more resources.

21. *Id.* at 5–21.

22. Joe Davidson, *Implicit Bias Training Seeks to Counter Hidden Prejudice in Law Enforcement,* Wash. Post, Aug. 16, 2016, https://www.washingtonpost.com/news/powerpost/wp/2016/08/16/implicit-bias-training-seeks-to-counter-hidden-prejudice-in-law-enforcement/?wpisrc=nl_fed&wpmm=1 (last visited Sept. 8, 2016).

23. Evan R. Seamone, *Understanding the Person Beneath the Robe: Practical Methods for Neutralizing Harmful Judicial Biases,* 42 Willamette L. Rev. 1, 22–30 (2006).

24. National Council of Juvenile and Family Court Judges (NCJFCJ), *Right from the Start: The CCC Preliminary Protective Hearing Benchcard; A Tool for Judicial Decision-Making*

(Reno, NV, 2010), http://www.ncjfcj.org/sites/default/files/CCC%20Benchcard%20 Study%20Report.pdf.

25. Russell & Summers, *supra* note 2, at 129–31.

26. Seamone, *supra* note 23, at 4–10.

27. Miller et al., *supra* note 15.

28. Casey et al., *supra* note 20, at 13–15.

29. Nilanjana Dasgupta & Luis M. Rivera, *When Social Context Matters: The Influence of Long-Term Contact*, 26 Social Cognition 1 (2008).

30. Russell & Summers, *supra* note 25.

31. Susan J. Wells et al., *Bias, Racism, and Evidence-Based Practice: The Case for More Focused Development of the Child Welfare Evidence Base*, 31 Children & Youth Service Rev. 1160–63 (2009).

32. Peter M. Jackson, *Public Service Performance Evaluation: A Strategic Perspective*, 13 Pub. Money & Mgmt. 9 (1993); *see also* Shdaimah et al., *supra* note 3.

33. Jackson, *supra* note 32.

34. Shdaimah et al., *supra* note 3.

35. Carol T. Mowbray et al., *Fidelity Criteria: Development, Measurement, and Validation*, 24 Am. J. Evaluation 315, 316 (2003).

36. *Id.* at 317.

37. Russell & Summers, *supra* note 30.

38. Although a pre-/post-analysis is typically used in a quasi-experimental design (i.e., a method that does not involve random assignment), this particular study did use random assignment to determine which judges received bench cards.

39. Jeffery J. Rachlinski et al., *Does Racial Bias Affect Trial Judges*, 84 Notre Dame L. Rev. 1217–22, (2009).

40. *Id.*

41. See discussion *supra* note 38.

42. Eric J. Marts et al., *Points of Engagement: Reducing Disproportionality and Improving Child and Family Outcomes*, 87 Child Welfare League of America 335, 335–53 (2008).

43. *Id.* at 339–45.

44. One way of assessing the effectiveness of one or more interventions is to measure behavioral outcomes such as IAT scores or attitude survey responses. For an example of assessment involving comparison of interventions and behavioral outcomes, *see* Lai et al., *Reducing Implicit Racial Preferences: I. A Comparative Investigation of 17 Interventions*, 143 J. Experimental Soc. Psychol. 4 (2014).

45. *Id.*

46. Patricia G. Devine, *Stereotypes and Prejudice: Their Automatic and Controlled Components*, 56 J. Personality & Soc. Psychol. 5, 5–6, 15 (1989).

47. Shdaimah et al., *supra* note 3.

48. *Id.*

49. Shdaimah et al., *supra* note 3, at 34–37.

50. *Id.*

51. Russell & Summers, *supra* note 2, at 130–31.

52. This is suggested by Casey et al., *supra* note 20.

53. Shdaimah et al., *supra* note 3.

54. Rachlinski et al., *supra* note 39.

55. Kang, *supra* note 1, at 1135–68.

56. Alicia Summers, *Disproportionality Rates for Children of Color in Foster Care Fiscal Year 2013*, Technical Assistance Bull. 3 (2015), http://www.ncjfcj.org/sites/default/files /NCJFCJ%202013%20Dispro%20TAB%20Final.pdf.

57. Drake et al., *supra* note 19, at 476.

Chapter 14
Combating Bias through Judicial Leadership

Judge Sophia H. Hall

Chapter Contents

Chapter Highlights

- An experienced and thoughtful judge describes her experience learning and teaching about implicit bias.

- Lessons are offered on how to bring others together for training and for community building.

Introduction

Judges are tasked with an extraordinary responsibility—doing justice. Every day we try to follow the law and deliver justice to the parties before us. What if bias blinds our ability to mete out justice? The science of implicit bias suggests that this can happen without our knowing.

As judges, we have an obligation to prevent our biases from denying justice to those we have sworn to serve. Our oath of office compels us, and the Code of Judicial Conduct requires us, to do the best we can to be fair. These codes explicitly require us to be fair and unbiased, and to ensure that those who work in our courtrooms and the lawyers before us do not manifest bias by words or conduct. The prohibited biases listed in the American Bar Association Code of Judicial Conduct, which are mirrored in many state judicial codes of conduct, require that we do not discriminate based on "race, sex, gender, religion, national origin, ethnicity, disability, age, sexual orientation, marital status, socioeconomic status, or political affiliation."[1]

> As judges, we have an obligation to prevent our biases from denying justice to those we have sworn to serve.

As discussed at length in several other chapters, the scientific research into people's views and attitudes suggests that most Americans are unaware of their own cognitive biases.[2] The implications of this science also apply to judges. Our duties, as judges, obligate us to uncover any unconscious biases that might affect our ability to be fair. Uncovering our personal biases is not easy. It can be embarrassing to discover that we might be biased when we thought we were not. It can be humiliating to discover that we may have acted unfairly. But we can take actions to prevent this from happening.

Our obligation to ensure that we treat people fairly and render fair decisions is made even more urgent by the attacks on the fairness of our system of justice. These attacks, often aimed at judges, are fed by the increasing politicization of the judicial selection process, appointive and elective. Public perception that our system of justice is unfair is part and parcel of the explosive national discourse, punctuated by expressions of disgust with all kinds of authority. Public anger is fueled by frustrations driven by the fault lines of race, ethnicity, sexual orientation, gender, and economic inequalities in our society.

The divisive discourse revealed in all forms of media threatens the efficacy and, ultimately, the relevancy of our system of justice. The looming danger is that if the courts are no longer seen as a fair forum to hear sensitive, divisive disputes, then the possibility exists that disagreements will be fought in the streets rather than addressed in the halls of justice.

This chapter provides steps judges can take to uncover and manage their biases so that we can do justice and be perceived as fair. In addition, this chapter discusses how judges, in meetings to improve the administration of justice, can help diverse participants engage in meaningful and civil discourse, even when views conflict and bias threatens to obstruct progress.

I. Learning Our Biases

Learning ourselves and uncovering our biases exposes a far different challenge than learning the law. Most judges, when questioned, will probably say that that they are not biased and accordingly have nothing to learn. Why would we question ourselves? Who would challenge the judge when we might likely take it as a personal affront?

Can we then engage in a searching, constructive conversation about whether we are biased without it being personal? We cannot. The conversation about bias is indisputably personal. The biases that reside within us are there by virtue of our life experiences, including experiences with family and friends and in our communities, schools, and work places. These learned biases are a part of who we all are. Thus, understandably, our journey is difficult as we unveil our biases, scrutinize where they come from, and consider their effects on us.

After ten years on the bench, I had the opportunity to take a deliberate journey into my own biased self. In 1993, as Presiding Judge of the Juvenile Court in Cook County, Illinois, I helped create a diversity management training course for juvenile court judges, probation officers, states attorneys, public defenders, and juvenile detention center employees. I learned through creating and attending the course that, though I assumed I was fair, I could not be sure. This surprised me, because as an African-American and a woman, I felt I knew about discrimination and prejudice.

I did not know what I did not know. That is the lesson taught by the science of implicit bias. You do not know because implicit bias is a bias hidden below conscious awareness, and, most disturbingly, it is automatically activated. Implicit bias is

> the bias in judgment and/or behavior that results from subtle cognitive processes (e.g., implicit attitudes and implicit stereotypes) that often operate at a level below conscious awareness and without intentional control. The underlying implicit attitudes and stereotypes responsible for implicit bias are those beliefs or simple associations that a person makes between an object and its evaluation that ". . . are automatically activated by the mere presence (actual or symbolic) of the attitude object."[3]

The words "without intentional control" and "automatically" are alarming for judges who have sworn an oath to be fair in managing their courtroom and making decisions. It is an anathema to have our actions controlled by something within ourselves, which we do not know and which is automatically affecting our behavior or decisions. It would be a relief if we could do something about it. The seminar I teach shows us that we can and the way in which to accomplish this change.

II.   The Creation of the Implicit Bias Seminar

In 2001, nearly ten years after beginning my personal journey into my biased self, Chief Judge Timothy C. Evans of the Circuit Court of Cook County, Illinois, recognized the need for judges to receive information about bias and asked me to adapt the bias training I had helped to develop at the Juvenile Court for other judges. The seminar I created teaches judges how to recognize and manage their biases as they deal with the people in their courtroom and decide the cases before them. Ever since then, I have taught this seminar as a required part of the Cook County Circuit Court New Judges Training Course. In addition to new judges, I have also taught the seminar to administrative law judges.

The goal of the implicit bias seminar is to teach judges how to find their biases and address them. Having a bench educated in the contours of bias provides judges with the tools to enhance their ability to be fair and improve the public's perception of justice in our court system.

The public's perceptions are significantly informed by the conduct of the judges before whom they appear. Litigants, defendants, and lawyers are scrutinizing us to determine if we can be fair in their cases. They consider whether we are giving the litigants a voice by including them in the process through acknowledging their presence, and, when appropriate, letting them speak. Are we behaving in a neutral manner, as exhibited by our demeanor and willingness to explain when needed? Are we showing respect for everyone by treating people well? Are we trustworthy, as revealed by our honesty, integrity, and sincerity?

These factors were delineated by Professor Tom R. Tyler of New York University, early in his two-decade-long examination into the public's satisfaction with their experiences in the justice system. The terms "procedural fairness" and "procedural justice" are used to embrace the results of his research. Professor Tyler's research showed that three factors—participation, neutrality and respect—contributed to the public's satisfaction with their experience in court. All of these factors influence the public's perception of the fairness of judges.[4]

> Professor Tyler's research showed that three factors—participation, neutrality and respect—contributed to the public's satisfaction with their experience in court.

The first challenge for judges in doing justice and being fair is to master themselves. An important part of that task is to explore the biases we may hold that might interfere with satisfying our sworn duty to treat people fairly and to render fair decisions. The seminar takes judges on that journey.

A.   The Seminar

If we do not know we have biases, then talking to ourselves about bias is futile. More helpful is talking to others about it, but doing so is more uncomfortable because the subject of bias is so sensitive. Yet we cannot see our biased selves as others might until we speak out loud. If we can have this conversation in a diverse group of people who are comfortable with each other, then we can benefit from others' honest reaction to our words. We then learn whether, unknown to us, some of our words are controversial or offensive.

Such a diverse group of people exists on the bench in Cook County, Illinois. Cook County judges come from different backgrounds including race, ethnicity, and sexual orientation and, correspondingly, different life experiences. The seminar opportunity brings these judges together and provides them with a space where only judges are present. Thus, they learn among colleagues who share a motivation to engage in this discussion and who have a common desire to improve their ability to be fair judges and to be perceived as fair.

1. Our Stories

To create an even more comfortable atmosphere in which to speak out loud about bias, we share stories of our experiences with bias. These stories may be our own or ones told to us. This sharing may require some courage since some of the stories may involve painful memories, but, on the other hand, some stories can be self-consciously humorous.

Some of the stories told in the seminar have been extremely moving. I could hear the pain in the voice of one judge who talked about experiencing discrimination due to being of Italian descent. The judge became quite emotional while telling the story. Another judge talked, with humility, about the prejudice the judge had against unemployed people, until the judge had become unemployed. Another defiantly declared, "I have been discriminated against because I am fat, gay, and because of how I dress." Another judge told a success story of overcoming an adverse reaction to people with many visible tattoos. With satisfaction, the judge shared how the techniques learned in one of the seminars I taught for administrative law judges had helped the judge change attitudes toward people who have tattoos.

Sharing these stories of bias allows the judges to know that they are not alone in having these experiences or in feeling uncomfortable in talking out loud about them. Also, in listening to others' stories, the judges may hear something they did not know or hear a story that resonates with their own experiences. Hearing about actual experiences gives real meaning and understanding to the effects of bias on the perpetrators and the victims of bias.

2. Talking about Differences

The most uncomfortable part of talking out loud about bias is the risk of embarrassment. Embarrassment can happen when an innocent statement is met with an unexpected negative reaction. Emotional discomfort is hard, but it is an effective learning tool. Embarrassment is better encountered in a seminar room full of judges than in a courtroom full of lawyers and litigants.

I embarrassed myself once during one of my seminars when I realized the words I was using might be offensive. I was talking about different life experiences and discussed the privileges I have been afforded as a light-skinned African-American because I looked White. As I told the story, I embarrassed myself. In describing color differences, I said "light *down* to black." The commonly used phrase "light down to black" in this racial context can be seen as negative. I immediately caught the term and realized this phrasing might make me appear biased or be offensive to someone. I turned the situation into a teaching moment, explaining the bias trap lurking in the phrases we commonly use when we are describing differences.

3. Discussing Culture and Frame of Reference

To enable the participants to continue to talk about their differences, I lead a discussion of the concepts of "culture" and "frame of reference." This conversation is a means of learning the influences in our lives that cause us to react the way we do to our differences.

a. Culture

Discussing the differences between one culture and another is fertile ground for revealing bias. We have all mastered our own culture but are less likely to be knowledgeable about cultures outside our own. When discussing cultural differences, we may stumble over our ignorance and reveal unknown bias.

Dictionaries and other sources provide definitions breaking out the various aspects of the concept of culture. Merriam-Webster's definition of culture is "the integrated pattern of human knowledge, belief, and behavior that depends upon the capacity for learning and transmitting knowledge to succeeding generations."[5] Another definition from the Center for Advanced Research on Language Acquisition states, "[C]ulture is defined as the shared patterns of behaviors and interaction, cognitive constructs, and affective understanding that are learned through a process of socialization. These shared patterns identify the members of a culture group while also distinguishing those of another group."[6]

Combining and enhancing these definitions, I describe culture as "a total way of life for a group of people. It is developed and communicated consciously and unconsciously through the generations, and also within groups that are created for various reasons. It consists of ideas, beliefs, attitudes, language, customs, and traditions that create the rules for a group of people to coexist."

These definitions reveal the complexity and multilayered aspects of the concept of culture as applied to smaller and larger contexts. Larger contexts include differences across ethnicities. Smaller contexts include differences across families, workplaces, and even the cultures of our individual courtrooms.

Many of us have experienced different ethnic cultures through their cuisine. Discussing food usually does not reveal the more sensitive differences revealed when discussing habits, attitudes, and beliefs. When we discuss any of these differences, we naturally think, for example, that our way of doing something seems correct and acceptable while the way those of another culture do a comparable activity seems strange and absurd. In discussing people different than us, the common phrases we use may surface a bias in characterizing the differences. Using these common phrases risks unknowingly communicating stereotypes and judgments carried in those phrases, which might truly offend another.

For example, the way people of different cultures engage in discussion with each other differs. My family is reserved, and our conversations around the dinner table generally proceed without interruption of the speaker as we explore fairly focused subject matters. A friend's family engages in much more animated conversations, full of interruptions and rapidly moving from topic to topic. It was difficult to get used to their manner of discussion. Describing these differences can appear negative if one uses the common language of stereotypes.

b. Frame of Reference

Another way to gain an understanding of how we react to others is to think about the effect of our distinct and unique individual life experiences. Our personal way of perceiving others' differences and the effect of that perception upon us frames how we make sense of the world around us. Our life experiences provide a filter, like a lens, through which we see the world. The advantage of our lens of life experience is that it helps us to quickly organize the familiar things we think we know. This speed gives us more time to process the unfamiliar. The disadvantage is that our personal lens may exclude information when we are dealing with a lot of information at once. In our hurry, we may not "see" the unfamiliar things and risk missing significant or important facts needed for correct action.

Our personal lens underlies how we relate to everything we do in our courtrooms. For example, a question judges often ask of prospective jurors in criminal cases is, "Would you give more weight to a police officer's testimony than to another's testimony?" The life experience underlying that question is that people have good experiences with police officers and respect them, but nevertheless, they should overcome this bias and assess the credibility of their testimony the same as the testimony of a non-police officer. I used that question early in my career when I was hearing criminal cases, and I did not question it because the question was consistent with my life experiences. One time, however, a prospective juror asked me why I did not ask whether a person would give *less* weight to the police officer's testimony. This question would have acknowledged the experience of some who, unlike me, had not had good experiences with police officers and, therefore, carried an opposite bias.

As judges, as this example illustrates, our personal frame of reference can undermine our efforts to be fair. If we automatically filter out, consciously or unconsciously, significant information offered by litigants, defendants, or witnesses, we may miss information critical to appropriately responding to them or necessary to make a correct legal decision. We also may appear biased because we failed to see the importance of their information.

c. Safe Spaces

Finding safe places and people with whom to speak of differences provides an important opportunity to hear and learn from their reactions to our words. The risk of encountering discomfort and embarrassment is our road to finding our implicit biases. As we stumble and fail and are given grace by others who are subject to the same vulnerability when they speak within the safe space, we are able to learn about our biased selves.

4. Implicit Bias as Automatic

In addition to the opportunity for the participants to speak openly about differences and thus encounter hidden unconscious bias, we also explore the second lesson of implicit bias—how automatic it is. Some might not accept their vulnerability to automatically expressing unconscious biases. To bring them to that realization, I use several exercises to enable the judges to experience just how unconscious their reactions can be.

One exercise explores perceptions of the land masses on our planet Earth. I show a map of the world with the countries of the southern hemisphere at the top and the countries of the northern hemisphere on the bottom. Invariably, the class's reaction is that this map is "upside down" or "wrong." Why that instant reaction? Why that instant judgment?

We react that way because the map we usually see shows the northern hemisphere on top with the United States in the upper left corner, and Europe, Russia, and China to the right. The southern hemisphere is on the bottom, with Mexico and South America below the United States, and to the right Africa, India, and Australia below Europe, Russia, and China. These maps are ubiquitous in our culture and around the world. They also are presumed to be an objective representation of the global landscape. But the assumption that these maps are objectively accurate is flawed. First, the maps distort the sizes of the continents, because the linear navigational lines shown conflict with the curvature of the Earth's surface. In actuality, the United States is smaller and Africa significantly larger than the comparison revealed by the map. Second, Earth, which is undisputedly round, has no top or bottom as depicted on a flat map. The representation of countries on the "top" and those on

[D]ue to our life experiences we automatically accept, without question, information frequently presented to us through our education and the media and confirmed in common phrases we use. We do not explore the embedded attitudes and judgments that might exist in what we constantly see and hear, and so we automatically react according to these persistent images.

the "bottom" reinforces attitudes about the positive value of those countries on the "top" and negative value of those on the "bottom." Nicole De Armendi, assistant professor at George Mason University, in her article "The Map as Political Agent," wrote of the effect that this orientation can have on attitudes of people about those Latin countries on the bottom.[7] People of the "bottom" southern countries of Latin America have more concern about this than those in the "top" Eurocentric countries. The "top" countries are generally perceived by our culture as more powerful, with a "better" location, and as having "wealth." The phrase "down under," referring to Australia, reflects this bias.

The point of the map exercise is to illustrate that due to our life experiences we automatically accept, without question, information frequently presented to us through our education and the media and confirmed in common phrases we use. We do not explore the embedded attitudes and judgments that might exist in what we constantly see and hear, and so we automatically react according to these persistent images.

5. Stereotypes—Carriers of Bias

The judgments made about differences among people are carried in common phrases, including stereotypes, which often have negative connotations. Our language is replete with these stereotypes. As the map example illustrates, at times we may not realize that the casual and common phrases we use actually contain a stereotype.

To allow the class to consciously explore the pervasiveness of these stereotypes, I ask them to select five groups that they know are subject to stereotypes. They make their selection among racial groups, religious groups, and groups characterized by physical characteristics such as being overweight or having a disability. We often will include lawyers or judges as a group. Then the class writes down the stereotypes associated with each group and posts them on the wall for all to see. It is no surprise to find that practically all of the stereotypes posted are stereotypes seen as negative. I ask the class how they felt writing the stereotypes and how they felt looking at them. Their frequent reaction is discomfort.

> Reverend Jesse Jackson revealed his own implicit bias when he noted, "There is nothing more painful to me at this stage in my life than to walk down the street and hear footsteps and start thinking about robbery—then look around and see somebody white and feel relieved."[8]

6. Engaging Our Biases

Having discussed how our personal life experiences populate our judgments of differences among people, having recognized how automatic unconscious judgments of these differences influence us, and reminding ourselves of the pervasive presence of negative stereotypes in our society, I next discuss how we can address our challenge to act fairly. The steps set forth below may enable us to dispel our bias. Until then, however, at an important minimum, we can take effective steps to prevent biases from infecting our treatment of people and the decisions we make in their cases.

a. Step One—Admission

The acceptance of our biased self allows us to be less self-conscious about making an effort to address our particular biases. As discussed, the science of implicit bias proclaims that all of us suffer from some unconscious and automatic biases. The universality of negative stereotypes in our language and institutions confirms the pervasiveness of bias in our society.

We can proactively protect ourselves from our decisions being driven by unconscious and automatic biases. Being self-aware is our primary protection. My red flag, alerting me to possible bias, is when I have an immediate negative reaction to someone about whom I know almost nothing. I then search myself to find out whether that reaction reflects a hidden bias against them.

b. Step Two—Exploration

Our personal search can reach a quick conclusion as to whether we are biased, or it may take longer. How we pursue our search depends on how open we can be with ourselves. One way of approaching this search is to review the history of the contacts we have had with the culture from which the object of our reaction comes. What was the nature of the experience? Did our experiences involve hearing people around us customarily using disparaging characterizations about that group? Sometimes negativity is embedded in a commonly used joke like, "How many (insert ethnic group) does it take to screw in a light bulb?" Ask the question whether you in your heart of hearts believe the implications of this "joke."

Sometimes, we may discount our negative reaction to a member of a group as an indicator of bias because we have a good friend who belongs to that group. Still, we might ask ourselves whether our relationship with our good friend has actually dispelled the possibility of bias to other members of that group. Think seriously about this question and consider how you feel in that group without the presence of your good friend. One way that stereotypes are preserved is by considering that our friend is an "an exception to the rule."

As we search to find out whether our negative reaction is the result of a negative stereotype, we may discover that in fact our reaction springs from an unconscious or an automatic negative stereotype that exists in our communities. On the other hand, we may discover that the root of the bias is more deeply emotional. As an example of what this may feel like, some people are afraid of dogs, even a friendly dog, as a result of a frightening experience with a dog that they repressed. Seeking the emotional roots that might be causing our bias can be disturbing in what it reveals.

Being aware and sensitive to our reactions operates as an important instigator prodding us to search for bias, and if found, to undertake proactive steps to address it.

c. Step Three—Confrontation

The next step involves taking actions to confront our bias. The source of our bias will dictate the nature of our actions.

If the source is simply that I have never had any personal contact with the person or culture and only know the negative things I have heard or seen, then I take an opportunity to learn about the culture. Engage in a conversation with an individual from that culture whom you feel you can talk to as a colleague. This can require a bit of courage and may take you out of your comfort zone, but people generally enjoy talking about themselves.

Using the story of the judge who had a bias against people with visible tattoos, several possibilities present themselves. The judge could have been reacting to the negative stereotype that tattoos may indicate membership in "gangs" that are generally perceived as violent. If an opportunity arises (or you make it happen) to be in the company of someone with tattoos, you might challenge that belief by seeking evidence that disconfirms it.

If the source of your bias is a judgment that certain behaviors are wrong, try finding neutral terms to describe the behavior, thus taking the negative judgment out of your thinking. For example, many people are overweight. One of the stereotypes is that they are not disciplined. An open, non-judgmental attitude might provide an opportunity for a conversation that is respectful or simply provide the possibility that their weight is not for you to judge.

Maybe you still cannot stop your negative reaction or dispel the bias. I have some biases that I cannot dispel because they are emotionally rooted and do not respond to reason, but I know that the bias is there and that my negative reaction is not rational.

d. Step Four—Self-Acceptance

Once you know you have a bias about a particular thing or person, or that it is possible that you are biased because of your persistent negative reaction, there are actions you can take to manage your biases and ensure that you will not be perceived as biased.

You can be deliberate in engaging the person. Choose behavior that enhances the relationship. Maintain eye contact. Nod your head to show you are hearing. Smile appropriately. Be polite and respectful.

I have used these behaviors to allow me time to deal with myself and interact positively with the person. These actions communicate openness. I actually feel more open when I am doing these things because I am really thinking about how the person feels. My role as a judge is not to be judgmental about him or her, but to judge the case, impartially.

By using these interaction techniques, I consciously accept the fact that the cases before me are not about me but are about the people who appear before me. Nevertheless, if I do not manage my biases, then the case can become about me.

The four-step self-examination—admission, exploration, confrontation, and acceptance of self—I have described determines the contours of our biased self. It can be hard work. The result of the conscious and repeated use of these steps can result in your being able to know and control yourself in your interactions with everyone with whom you come in contact. In this way you are able to treat people fairly and decide fairly.

e. Summary

The journey to overcome bias and achieve fairness in treating people and deciding cases is an ongoing effort. We cannot shirk the journey. Learning our biased selves is as important to our judicial responsibility to make fair, just, and correct decision, as is learning the applicable law.

By examining our biased selves, we will satisfy our oath of office and the requirements of the Code of Judicial Conduct that we treat people fairly and decide cases fairly. By examining our biased selves, we can overcome being a victim of our biases and become a survivor of them. None of us were born biased. We learned it. We can change.

B. System Support

In Cook County, Illinois, for some of the kinds of cases the judges hear, the court system has provided some support to aid the judges' ongoing efforts to prevent biases from affecting their decisions. These supports include implicit bias training as well as form orders and bench cards that aid judges in articulating the legal steps they consider in reaching their decisions.

For example, a form order is used to set forth the basis for findings of abuse and neglect, and another form for the issuance of orders of protection. Bench cards provide similar support to judges issuing decisions in other kinds of cases. These aids in setting forth the basis for a decision filter the judge's immediate reactions to the circumstances presented in a case. Reactions and immediate actions are more likely to occur in high-volume courtrooms where time is at a premium. The self-imposed use of support to aid deliberateness, though slowing the judge's decision process, is well worth the benefit of impartiality and the appearance of impartiality in reaching decisions.

In addition to self-directed efforts, judges can provide jurors with recognition of the possibility that they might have biases that could affect their consideration of the evidence and application of the law to the cases they hear. The authors of other chapters of this book call this approach "priming." One of the authors, Judge Mark Bennett, suggests that discussion about bias during jury selection may help jurors to be more aware of their reactions. He also suggests some innovative ways to put into a familiar context the meaning of such legalese such as "innocent until proven guilty" and "proof beyond a reasonable doubt" as a means of preparing jurors to apply the law to the evidence they will hear in criminal cases.

The system support for judges' engagement of their biases and efforts to keep those biases from infecting their decisions recognizes that we all must make a continuing conscious effort to be fair. We must ensure that the best of who we can be as judges intent on satisfying our extraordinary responsibility— doing justice—is provided to the citizens who are in our courtrooms expecting justice to be done.

III. Leading Effective Collaborations

I believe that judges are citizens of our communities and that our responsibilities include improving the administration of justice and being advocates in our communities for an understanding of the role of judges. We can do this by participating in various groups. Our knowledge of our biases and the image of judges as being fair allow us to make valuable contributions to the tenor of these meetings. Using our skills, we can assist in fostering effective, meaningful, and productive collaboration.

A. Engaging Collaboration

Collaboration with others assumes particular importance when we seek to improve the administration of justice in cases involving individuals challenged by drug addiction, mental illness, physical abuse, sexual abuse, or other traumas. Their issues are not amenable to our adversarial process bent on declaring winners and losers. Effectively addressing these social issues in the cases before us requires the services of social service agencies and other groups. Collaboration among all of these interests is not easy.

Many challenges present themselves in collaborative meetings of diverse participants. Since members of our public and private institutions serving the public often operate in silos, we often do not have knowledge of the diverse roles and responsibilities of the others, even if we have met or worked together.

In addition to our diverse roles and responsibilities, we bring our different life experiences to these collaborative meetings. These differences, including race, ethnicity, sexual orientation, and economic status, add to opportunities for misunderstandings. Our different cultures and personal experiences, perhaps even experiences around violence, drug addiction, mental illness, physical and sexual abuse, and racial discrimination, can affect our perspectives and attitudes and can be the source of bias.

In collaborative meetings of such a diversity of participants who may have implicit biases, judges can play a critical and pivotal role and use their understanding of bias to help maintain respect and civility. The judge can model respect for the participants and can monitor for and interrupt expressions of explicit or implicit bias in the discussion of social issues. The skill of listening deeply without your own biases preventing you from hearing what is actually being said and having the understanding of how to break down bias enables the judge to take an appropriate action when disrespect and incivility arise.

In my role as Presiding Judge of the Juvenile Court, and later as Presiding Judge of the Resource Section of the Juvenile Court, I have convened and been invited to collaborative meetings of diverse attendees to improve the court's service to juveniles beset by the trauma of their circumstances. In 2001, as a response to the pressure of these societal issues on the juvenile court, I convened the "Citywide Restorative Justice Committee." In attendance at the Citywide meetings are representatives of the same kinds of systems, including law enforcement and attorneys, social service providers, and community representatives who work with problem-solving courts.

The Citywide Restorative Justice Committee promotes the use of restorative practices as an alternative to punitive processes in responding to youth in trouble. The restorative approach, used as a response to a particular offense, brings together the community affected by the youth's conduct including their family, the victim, their school, and others. Together they discuss the harm the youth has done, everyone's needs with regard to the offense, and the obligations and responsibilities all have to each other. Then the participants, together, determine how the harms can be repaired.

In the same vein, representatives of these multiple stakeholders in the youth's community, local and citywide, are participants in the Citywide Committee. Rather than waiting until an offense is committed, we talk through how members of communities working together can support youth before trouble arises. We discuss bringing together youth, their families, and representatives of schools and police, and others such as businesses, not-for-profits, and government agencies, to work together to build citywide approaches to prevent trouble and violence.

When the Citywide Committee started, there were tensions among some participants. The police representative was not respected, nor was the representative from the Chicago Public Schools. Many of us at the meeting espoused our adherence to restorative practices, and my facilitation forcefully modeled respect and civility. Over time we were able to work through the distrust. This process was advantaged by the regularity of the Citywide meetings, which provided a continuing opportunity for the participants to get to know each other as people and provided an expectation of following the progress of initiatives. The Citywide Committee has become a learning community for restorative justice.

B. Managing the Diversity

Three principles helped me to manage the diversity of views and disagreements in the Citywide meetings. These principles are the same ones judges use to manage their courtrooms. The principles are (1) supporting respectful relationships among the participants, (2) honoring the multiple differences that each participant brings to the conversation, and (3) maintaining a civil discourse.

1. Respectful Relationships

Supporting respectful relationships among the participants at the meeting starts with modeling respect, as I mentioned above. As convener of the meeting, and as a judge, I receive some deference in promoting respect. When I am not the convener, but an invitee to a meeting, I look for indicators of this value. Thus, if I hear speakers being interrupted, I will seek an opportunity to put the value of respectful listening in front of the participants, so they can establish it for their meeting. Because I have taught approaches to finding and managing bias, I more consciously consider and respect the significance of a participant's different life experiences which might affect the differing views they express. I also am aware how difficult it is to listen without interrupting when you strongly disagree with views being expressed.

One method for creating an atmosphere of respect involves ensuring that everyone knows he or she will have the opportunity to participate and will be allowed to speak without interruption. Assuring participants that they will have an opportunity to participate enhances their interest in assisting in moving the meeting along so that others will have that same opportunity. Thus, respect for the speaker's opportunity to speak becomes a value that all will support.

2. Honoring Differences

The second principle, honoring differences, can be challenging with so many different personalities, cultures, roles, and agendas at these meetings. Honoring peoples' differences, as the bias training teaches, means exhibiting a non-judgmental reaction to the different views presented by a participant, even if you do not agree with his or her views.

Honoring the different life experiences and views of all of the participants reinforces a respectful environment. To do this, I find out which organization or group each participant represents and attempt to understand each participant's attitudes and possible biases. I may have such information from prior experiences with the individual, his or her reputation, or what others have said about the person. I continually evaluate what I think I know by listening to the person's comments and considering his or her actions in the meeting.

This information guides how I manage the individual's participation in the meeting and manage the other participants' possible judgmental reactions. One method of intervening when disrespect and discourtesy arise is to deflect a judgmental reaction. The facilitator might interrupt and reframe the reaction into a less confrontational tone by interpreting the reaction using different words or by turning the reaction into a question. This honors the person's reaction while, at the same time, making his or her reaction appear less volatile.

3. Civility

The third principle necessary to maintain an environment of productive conversation is to ensure civility in the discussions. Once a culture of respect for each individual's participation and life experiences is established, and honor is afforded to the individuality of each participant, civility becomes a mutual priority. All the attendees will join in the effort to keep disagreements civil and support talking out differences. Disagreements are critical because they can lead to better outcomes, as long as they are diffused of anger, which can thwart productive discussion.

Distinguishing the source of an uncivil reaction or interruption can guide the facilitator in the manner of intervening. If caused by misunderstanding, then non-interrupted speaking allows for the full explanation of a position. If it appears that people are frustrated, this may come from their belief that they have not been heard or the vexing inability of participants to understand another's point of view.

It is also possible that a participant's uncivil reaction may be an expression of an underlying bias. The judge's ability to approach this possible cause is informed by the implicit bias training that provides an understanding of the contexts and causes of bias and provides techniques to respectfully confront differences.

Ignoring bias impedes the relationships of the participants, resulting in unproductive and contentious meetings.

Depending on the circumstances, one immediate way to address bias based in civility is to steer the conversation toward an opportunity for the participants to share stories about their experiences with the perceived bias. Another possibility is to table the subject that caused the dispute with assurances that the subject will be revisited later in the meeting or at a future meeting.

Needless to say, although the issue of bias is sensitive, and how to approach it is delicate, bias must be addressed. Ignoring bias impedes the relationships of the participants, resulting in unproductive and contentious meetings.

4. Summary

These three principles for managing a meeting of diverse participants—(1) maintaining respect, (2) honoring who people are, and (3) maintaining civil discourse—can result in enhancing the possibility that the conversations will be productive even if the subjects are sensitive. Thus, judges respected for their fairness and neutrality can contribute to the productivity of these potentially difficult collaborative meetings.

These three principles for managing a meeting of diverse participants—(1) maintaining respect, (2) honoring who people are, and (3) maintaining civil discourse—can result in enhancing the possibility that the conversations will be productive even if the subjects are sensitive. Thus, judges respected for their fairness and neutrality can contribute to the productivity of these potentially difficult collaborative meetings.

Conclusion

The ideal judge is wise, intelligent, and compassionate, with a soul that is innocent, a mind that is practical, and a heart that is enduring. We must meet the enormous responsibilities put upon us while managing all the flaws that make us human. We must know and take charge of our flaws, including bias, a condition we share with those we serve. Hopefully, this chapter serves you in satisfying this never-ending task, in and out of court.

ABOUT THE AUTHOR

Presiding Judge Sophia H. Hall is a judge of the Circuit Court of Cook County, Illinois, since 1980. She hears cases in the Chancery Division of the Court. She is a past president of the National Association of Women Judges and a past chair of the Board of Trustees of the National Judicial College. She has taught implicit bias seminars to new judges and administrative law judges since 2001.

ENDNOTES

1. *See* MODEL CODE OF JUDICIAL CONDUCT R. 2.3 (2011); MODEL CODE OF JUDICIAL CONDUCT R. 2.12 (2011).
2. Other chapters in this book set forth scientific research into bias, and thus this author does not include that information herein.

3. Pamela M. Casey et al., *Helping Courts Address Implicit Bias: Resources for Education* (2012), http://www.ncsc.org.

4. Tom R. Tyler, *Procedural Justice and the Courts,* 44 J. AM. JUDGES ASS'N 26, 30–31 (2007–08).

5. *Culture,* http://www.merriam-webster.com/dictionary/culture (last visited June 30, 2016).

6. Center for Advanced Research on Language Acquisition, *What Is Culture?,* http://carla.umn.edu/culture/definitions.html (last visited June 30, 2016).

7. Nicole De Armendi, *The Map as Political Agent: Destabilising the North-South Model and Redefining Identity in Twentieth-Century Latin American Art,* 13 ST. ANDREWS J. ART HISTORY & MUSEUM STUDIES 5, 5–17 (2009).

8. Justice Michael B. Hyman, *Implicit Bias in the Courts,* 102 ILL. BAR J. 40, 41 (January 2014).

Chapter 15
On Being Mindful

Judge Jeremy D. Fogel

Chapter Contents

Chapter Highlight

- An experienced judge offers perspective on being a mindful judge and why it matters.

Judges, as our title implies, make judgments. Sometimes the process of making a judgment is straightforward, as when a clearly written statute plainly applies to undisputed facts. But more often, the meaning or applicability of a statute requires interpretation, or factual disputes can be resolved only by determining the believability of human witnesses or weighing conflicting circumstantial evidence.

If applying the law to the facts also involves the exercise of discretion, whether in resolving issues in a civil action or imposing sentence in a criminal case, the process of making a judgment may become complex and multidimensional. Most cases involve real people with important, sometimes very personal interests at stake. The environment in which these cases play out often is infused with passions that can confound the detached rationality with which decisions—at least in theory—are supposed to be made.

As professional decision makers, judges typically become skilled at thinking reflectively and articulating reasons for their decisions. Most judges try to recognize and account for their reactions to the cases they hear and to avoid ruling impulsively. Judges also strive to treat people fairly. Yet despite these efforts, almost every experienced judge can think of cases in which a judgment missed the mark, in which the emotional impact of the situation made thoughtful reflection difficult or impossible, or in which there was lingering doubt about whether justice truly was done.

Judicial educators have recognized this reality for many years. Many have developed courses intended to help judges hone their decision-making skills and manage occupational stress. Some also have designed courses that explore unconscious psychological and cultural factors that can influence fact finding and decision making.

I. Understanding Mindfulness

Another distinct construct that is only beginning to be explored in connection with judging is mindfulness. Although it has been most deeply understood and articulated in practices such as meditation and yoga, mindfulness actually is a remarkably simple and universal concept. Its value has attracted increasing attention in business, education, medicine, and, in the legal context, mediation. In essence, it involves slowing down one's mental processes enough to allow one to notice as much as possible about a given moment or situation and then acting thoughtfully based on what one has noticed, rather than falling back on preexisting stereotypes. It sometimes is described as approaching each moment with a "beginner's mind" or "thinking about thinking while thinking." While much of the discussion of mindfulness in relation to judges so far has focused on health and wellness, mindfulness also has obvious implications for the actual work that judges do. The following examples may be helpful.

A. A Thoughtful Approach to Repetitive Tasks

Many trial-level judges preside over busy calendars in the course of which they perform repetitive tasks. For instance, they may take multiple guilty pleas. Because appellate courts have provided detailed guidance with respect to the contents of a plea colloquy, and because many criminal cases have similar fact patterns, it is easy for the process of taking a plea to become routine, especially over time. While few judges knowingly "mail the process in," it is not uncommon for such repetitive tasks to receive less focused attention than other judicial work, particularly when a judge is operating in a chronically stressful environment. While it is understandable, this split focus can be problematic, as the discussion in Chapter 9, "Procedural Fairness," suggests.

Mindfully taking a plea involves approaching each plea as a new and unique situation. The judge notices consciously things that otherwise might tend to be noticed only in passing if at all: the defendant's tone of voice and body language, the way the defendant and counsel appear to be communicating (or not communicating) with each other, the defendant's physical appearance, whether friends or family members of the defendant (or victims) appear to be in the courtroom, and so on. None of these things necessarily changes the outcome of the process, yet taken as a whole they can help the judge learn more about the defendant and assess more fully whether the defendant is entering a knowing and voluntary plea. And perhaps just as importantly, the attentiveness shown by the judge is communicated to the defendant and everyone else who is present.

B. A Way of Limiting Unconscious Assumptions

A core competency of trial court judges is assessing credibility. Judges decide regularly whom to believe and how much to believe them, not only in evaluating witnesses who are testifying under oath but also in dealing with lawyers and parties in the course of managing cases. Both consciously and unconsciously, judges draw upon their professional and personal life experience and respond to cues that they believe have been reliable in the past. And again, particularly under stressful circumstances, the process of doing this can become somewhat automatic.

As our society has become increasingly diverse, there are more cases in which a person's behavior may have a different valence when viewed in cultural context (as discussed further in Chapter 8, "Hearing All Voices: Challenges of Cultural Competence and Opportunities for Community Outreach"). For instance, a judge reflexively may view a witness's lack of eye contact when testifying as an indication that the witness is not telling the truth. Yet in some cultures, making direct eye contact in certain settings is seen as disrespectful. Creating additional capacity for reflection can allow the judge to notice his or her reflexive response and to consider what significance, if any, to attach to the witness's manner of testifying. The same is true with respect to a judge's perception of any number of other behavioral differences.

II. Mindfulness and Judicial Demeanor

At least from the perspective of those with whom he or she interacts, perhaps the most important attributes of a judge are demeanor and temperament. While lawyers and parties undoubtedly hope that a judge will rule in their favor, often what matters most to them is the way they are treated: whether they feel listened to, heard, understood, and respected. While judges have a wide range of personalities and dispositions, all judges at one time or another experience states of mind, such as anger, frustration, distraction, or fatigue, that make it difficult or impossible for them to live up to these expectations.

Noticing as fully as possible what is occurring in the moment makes a judge more aware of his or her own physical and mental state. A judge with such awareness is more conscious of his or her emotional reactions to a lawyer, litigant, or situation and is able to choose an appropriate response rather than ignoring the reactions or losing control. Often the optimal response will be to set one's feelings aside, but sometimes an intentional, considered expression of emotion may be exactly what is needed to show that a judge is engaged and respectful. In either case, it is more likely that the judge's demeanor will reflect the seriousness and thoughtfulness that our society hopes for in its judiciary.

III.   The Value of Reflective Thinking

In his best-selling book *Thinking, Fast and Slow,* the Nobel laureate Daniel Kahneman makes a useful distinction between intuition, in which one reacts to stimuli immediately and instinctively, and reflection, in which one thinks consciously about what one is experiencing. Kahneman observes that intuitive ("System 1") thinking is particularly active when one is doing routine tasks or when reflection is inhibited by stress. While intuitive thinking can be an efficient and even necessary response to a given situation, its accuracy can be limited by one's life experience and unchecked assumptions. Kahneman suggests that reflective ("System 2") thinking allows for a more careful assessment of the circumstances, including the ability to notice and, when appropriate, question one's intuitive responses. One is able to be more intentional in the moment as well as after the fact.

Although System 2 would appear to be normative for judges in our professional role, the demands of our job can cause System 1 to operate more frequently than we might want. One way of understanding mindfulness is as a means of strengthening our ability to be in System 2 by heightening our self-awareness and building our capacity to be reflective. Mindfulness can improve judicial functioning not only by mitigating the unbidden intrusion of System 1 thinking but also by increasing the richness of System 2 thinking. While slowing down one's thought processes may result in a given task taking somewhat longer to complete, Kahneman and others point out that the additional time involved typically is relatively minimal. And because reflective thinking can be expected to reduce the "unforced errors" that often are present in System 1, mindfulness actually can improve one's net efficiency.

IV.   The Personal Benefits of Mindfulness

As the current interest in mindfulness in the context of health and wellness suggests, the benefits of mindfulness are not limited to more nuanced decision making and better emotional regulation. One of the consequences of chronic stress is that its symptoms can become one's "new normal." One's mind and body literally can forget how it feels to relax, to breathe deeply, and to appreciate being in the present, which in turn can have significant negative consequences for one's health. Mindfulness is a powerful way of counteracting these effects. It allows one to notice what is happening and think about and take remedial measures.

Fortunately, cultivating and practicing mindfulness is a natural and accessible process. Perhaps because of its popular association with meditation, yoga, and other traditional ways of developing and sustaining it, some may think of mindfulness as an element of a particular cultural style or worldview. But looking at mindfulness in this way misapprehends its nature. Its purpose is not to tell one what to think or do but rather to help one think and act as one chooses with the benefit of deeper reflection and more fully conscious intent. For judges, whose judgments can have profound effects on others, it can be both an enormously effective tool and a key to a more satisfying professional life.

About the Author

Jeremy D. Fogel was appointed U.S. District Judge for the Northern District of California in 1998 after more than 16 years as a judge in the California state courts. He has been Director of the Federal Judicial Center, which oversees professional education and policy research for the federal judiciary, since 2011. As director, he has led a significant revision of the center's curriculum and pedagogy, including a specific focus on the psychology of judicial decision making. He received his B.A. from Stanford University in 1971 and his J.D. from Harvard Law School in 1974.

Epilogue

Collectively by the Advisory Group for *Enhancing Justice: Reducing Bias*—
Judge Karen Arnold-Burger,* Judge Bernice Donald,* Judge Theodore
McKee,* Cynthia Orr, Phyllis Pickett,* Sarah Redfield* and Anna Torres

In October 2014, a special joint committee to fight implicit bias in the court-room was formed by three American Bar Association entities: the Criminal Justice Section, the Section of Litigation, and the Judicial Division. Armed with an ABA Enterprise Grant, the report from the March 2013 Perceptions of Justice Summit, and other research, the ABA entities decided right away to focus on producing a tool that would both inform judges about implicit bias and serve as a resource to combat it. An Advisory Group composed of two members representing each entity took on the task of guiding the direction and content of what is now this book: The Honorable Karen Arnold-Burger, Kansas Court of Appeals; The Honorable Bernice Donald, U.S. Court of Appeals for the Sixth Circuit; The Honorable Theodore A. McKee, Chief Judge, U.S. Court of Appeals for the Third Circuit; Attorney Cynthia Hujar Orr, Goldstein, Goldstein & Hilley, San Antonio, TX; Attorney Phyllis Pickett, North Carolina General Assembly Staff; Professor Sarah Redfield, University of New Hampshire; and Attorney Anna D. Torres, Torres Law Group, West Palm Beach, FL. Judge Donald chaired the group, which selected Professor Redfield to serve as editor.[1]

Each of the Advisory Group members share a deep and unwavering commitment to a justice system that equally and fairly serves every member of society. Each had personal and professional reasons for participating in this effort. The Call for Papers issued by the Advisory Group yielded responses from an array of authors who have an equally strong commitment to justice. The authors brought with them a diverse and rich array of expertise from law and social science. Not surprisingly, they did not agree on all points, but each chapter offers perspective and thought-provoking suggestions from their experience as to how to achieve a more just and fair judicial system. The Advisory Group and each of the authors learned much from the interchange, and their perspectives (and even disagreements) make the book stronger.

*Bios appear with their chapters, the Preface, Chapter 2, and Chapter 8.

> Ancient Greek dramas ended with an epilogue at the end of the play that spoke directly to the audience. The audience was all ears, waiting to hear the final segue to a happy ending or justified tragic one. And, the thematic moral of the story was revealed to all.

Judges comprise the main audience for this book, and implicit bias is the central topic. Its writers range from lawyer- and non-lawyer scientists and academics, to sitting judges and practicing lawyers, and include educators, expert trainers, and private consultants. For all of our readers who are waiting to hear the final segue to a happy ending or even a justified tragic one, we are afraid you will have to wait. The viewpoints presented in the chapters of this book cannot be so smoothly reconciled. After all, this is not a work of fiction, and the stage is the ever-changing stage of the American justice system as it is set daily in courtrooms around the country. Instead, the epilogue for this book will play itself out in the minds and work of the judges, court administrators, lawyers, and others who read it and either begin or continue to grow in awareness of implicit bias and strive to minimize the effects of implicit bias in the courtroom.

While we are not able to write the epilogue in the traditional sense, we can share that the writing of the book has profoundly affected those who guided and worked on the final product. As the book goes to press, we recognize that much of the science, including many of the suggested approaches to debiasing, remains unproven, and, too, much of the law that will come from this is unwritten. Yet recognizing how much we have each grown from the experience of working on the book, we are confident indeed that our readers will grow and change as well, no doubt in ways we cannot yet predict. We trust that even if that change can't be measured, it will come. With this in mind, we close with these personal vignettes:

From Karen Arnold-Burger

Twenty years ago I was referred to the Institute for Faculty Excellence in Judicial Education by our state judicial educator. The institute was operated out of the University of Memphis by an amazing professor, Dr. Patricia Murrell. The program was focused on adult education theory and judicial leadership. We were each to pick a topic to present to the group. It had to be an issue we believed judges needed to know about. To quote Donald Rumsfeld, as judicial educators we had to be aware of the "unknown unknowns"—the things that judges need to know but don't know they don't know. Our task over a six-month timeframe was to develop a program that was classroom ready. A couple recent experiences were fresh in my mind when the time came to pick a topic. I was a municipal judge in a predominately Caucasian county. But when I looked out over my courtroom, I saw many dark faces, many more than resided in my community. I had also recently attended a one-week seminar put on by Dr. Thomas Kochman and Jean Mavrelis on cultural communication styles. There is no other way to describe its impact on me than life changing. I was certain that these communication style differences played a part in racial profiling and disproportionate minority confinement. Dr. Murrell encouraged me to examine the issue in more depth and develop a training program around it. Ever since that day I have been researching and teaching on the topic of racial profiling and disproportionate minority confinement to judges all over the country.

I always kept in the forefront of my research and teaching the things I had learned from Tom and Jean, but most of my presentations centered on national and local statistics, long-term impact, and ways judges could measure their own bias and why it was essential that they do so. I was not an expert in cultural anthropology and didn't feel comfortable making presentations from that perspective. However, even when simply confronting judges with the facts and their contribution to the problem, judges were changed by the information. Judges want to be better judges. They want to be fair and impartial. The fact that people were being treated differently in our justice system was no longer a headline to them but a real issue that called for their action.

Because of my work, I was asked by the chair of the Judicial Division to serve on the ABA Advisory Group for this project. It has reunited me with Tom and Jean and given me a great opportunity to coauthor a chapter integrating the issue of cultural communication styles with implicit bias in our justice system. Working on this book with the other Advisory Group judges and lawyers that have come to this issue from different backgrounds and perspectives has been yet another life-changing experience. There is no doubt that this has made me a better judge and a better judicial educator. I hope the judges and judicial staff members who read the amazing chapters in this book from leading researchers on this topic will also find that it will make them better and more mindful judges.

From Bernice Donald

Much of my experience with bias is described in Chapter 2. I would add here that working with Professor Redfield on education and pipeline issues and writing this book, with its wide diversity of authors and perspectives, have reinforced for me that implicit biases, which partially inform disproportionality, disparate treatment, and disparate outcomes, remain an important barrier to attaining our goals of equal opportunity, equal protection, and equal justice. I have personally seen how training and open discussion of implicit biases can bring about change. I remain committed to this kind of training and hope that all stakeholders in the civil and criminal justice systems will work diligently with us to enhance fairness by reducing bias. I am pleased to be part of the team that has brought to fruition this resource, which defines the issue, frames the discussion, and offers strategies and solutions.

From Theodore McKee

Although I have long been aware of the danger that my own thoughts are not beyond the reach of implicit bias, the first time I recall seeing it on display in others within the court system was several years ago when I was a trial judge about to sentence a white defendant for a residential burglary he had committed to fund a cocaine habit. During the sentencing, he kept insisting that he should not have to serve any time in prison because all of the people in there were criminals and he was no criminal. When I reminded him that he had been convicted of a felony of the first degree that was punishable by up to 20 years imprisonment under Pennsylvania law, he simply reiterated that he was not like the people in prison because, unlike them, he was not a criminal. Of course, the population of Black inmates was then, as now, hugely disproportionate, and it seemed clear that his brief time in custody following his arrest had allowed him to draw a distinction between himself and his fellow inmates. When I persisted in asking the defendant what made him different from the other people imprisoned for crimes—including defendants he had seen me sentence that day before him—he simply reiterated that he was not a criminal. It was impossible for me not to interpret that as him saying that somehow his "Whiteness" set him apart from people who should be sent to jail or prison.

A more blatant example of the extent to which we can become the unwitting hosts of bias was presented by an older White female juror during a trial of a Black man accused of raping a White woman. Defense counsel was considering the defense of consent and asked me to include questions in my voir dire about whether the perspective juror thought that a White woman could ever consent to have sex with a Black man. When that question was asked of this one juror, she looked directly at me (a Black judge sitting less than ten feet from her), smiled, and ever-so-politely assured me that it simply wasn't possible that a White girl would ever agree to have sex with "any of them." I rephrased the question several times to be sure there was no misunderstanding. She remained quite pleasant and quite forthright. I thanked her for her response and then excused her from jury service. Her other answers to my questions were quite innocuous, and there was nothing to suggest that she was merely trying to avoid jury duty. The White assistant district attorney who had vigorously objected to my asking the question ultimately apologized to me and defense counsel for objecting. Moreover, to his credit, he thereafter began making similar inquiries of perspective jurors himself. As he left my courtroom for the day, he simply paused to tell me, "Your honor, if I had not seen and heard that exchange myself, I never would have believed it." I wanted to say "Welcome to the real world," but I just thanked him for his response.

In the many years since my days on the trial court, I have tried to devote all of the resources that I can to informing my colleagues, and myself, about the power of implicit bias and the need to continually guard against it. Shortly after I was confirmed to the Third Circuit, I cochaired a task force that looked into racial and ethnic bias within the Third Circuit. During the years that I had the honor of serving as chief judge of my court, I used bench bar conferences to focus on the subject, and I continue to devote my energies and (to the extent that I now can) the energies of my court to sensitizing those within the judicial system about the implicit biases that lurk in all of us.

From Cynthia Eva Hujar Orr

I defend death penalty cases in the South as part of my pro bono practice. Most of the people I have represented are minorities. The fact that persons of color are most often the persons against whom our system of justice seeks to give the ultimate punishment is wrong. Explicit and implicit biases manifest themselves in the decisions to seek the death penalty, during jury selection, in the testimony of witnesses, and in the courts' decisions before and during trial. Even the actions of the communities in which the trials occur demonstrate that most people are unsuspecting of their own presumptions, assumptions, and stereotyping. In East Texas in the late '90s, I tried a case where White community members protested for "justice" because they were outraged that a Black defendant was entitled to pre-trial hearings, bomb threats were made against the predominantly Black church, and a lynching of a young Black man occurred in the piney woods prior to the trial. The judge treated my cocounsel, the then president of the Texas NAACP, with extreme disrespect. But he treated me, a younger lawyer, with feigned deference. He allowed my client a piece of birthday cake during the trial to show he could be fair, even though he had refused to consider my ex parte motion for expert witness assistance and quashed all of my pre-trial subpoenas. Each of the trial participants felt he or she was being even-handed, fair, and unbiased. None could allow for the possibility that he or she was motivated by internal and unconscious bias. I was not aware of implicit bias then, but it was active and virulent in that case.

I think that our racial biases are remnants of what most of us would like to forget was a part of our national fabric; they are the legacy of slavery. Not gone from our history long enough, this history still affects us. Because we are not comfortable keeping the memory fresh of our deplorable past history, we do not hold the lessons from it dear enough. We think that is in the past and is gone. So we have become complacent about guarding against the wrongs that have come from a time when our nation treated human beings as less than human. For these reasons, we must each allow for the possibility that we are afflicted with wrong thinking and unfair, if unconscious, assumptions about others. This project is taking steps to allow for that possibility, and I expect it will lead us to a more aware and better legal process. It is important work in which I am delighted to take part.

From Phyllis B. Pickett

The Honorable Michael B. Hyman serves on the Appellate Court in Illinois and is known for his exceptional writing and eloquent oratory. But, when I met him in 2008, Judge Hyman was serving as chair of the ABA Judicial Division Lawyers Conference, one of the six conferences that comprise the Judicial Division. In the obligatory "Chair's Column" that accompanies such a position, Judge Hyman, who was just beginning his service on the trial bench in Chicago, wrote about "assumptions of justice," expressing his concern about whether justice is blind and positing that minority members of the community see the court system as unfair. And, Judge Hyman wrote, something must be done about the situation. The Perceptions of Justice (POJ) Initiative resulted from the conversations started by that opinion piece. Subsequently, as chairs of the larger Judicial Division, Retired Judge William Missouri of Maryland and North Carolina Chief Supreme Court Justice Mark Martin continued and expanded the initiative that Judge Hyman and the Lawyers Conference started.

I have been fortunate to participate at every stage of the POJ effort that culminates in, if only for now, the publication of this book—a detailed resource for greater fairness in our court system. Bench and bar must work together, with the community, to dismiss assumptions and transform "Justice for All" into truth rather than rhetoric—from an aspiration into a result. For the opportunity to do so, I am both grateful and humbled. Grateful, because as a member of the legal profession, I can uphold my oath and make a difference by working for justice. Humbled, because I am affected by implicit bias—whether favorably or unfavorably, externally or internally, mine or theirs—like everyone else. I have a better understanding of implicit bias after working with this publication, as well as a better understanding of myself. I believe that any judge, lawyer, court administrator, law enforcement officer, or other reader who approaches this book with an open mind will experience a similar result, and that result will make a difference.

From Sarah Redfield

Like my colleagues who write here, I came to this project with an abiding commitment to fairness and to using my skills to help bring that fairness to others. I wrote in Chapter 2 about my introduction to the ideas of implicit response and how this knowledge has changed my life perspective. I write here to echo what the Advisory Group members say about how powerful an experience this book has been in terms of teaching us all more about introspection, more about being mindful, and more about giving back to our communities. And I write also to thank not only the Advisory Group but also all of the authors who gave so generously of their time, their intellect, and their experience. The book and my life are enriched by their work.

From Anna D. Torres

When I was first provided with the opportunity to serve on this Advisory Group, none of us could have anticipated the turn our country would be taking by the time this book went to press. It seems optimistic, at this point in our history, to be speaking of implicit bias when there has been a visible and raucous resurgence and acceptance of overt bigotry and prejudice. One could understand if the attention of well-intentioned participants in our judicial system was diverted from the topic of implicit bias back to more fundamental issues that we thought we had left behind. It is said that progress does not proceed in a straight line, and so, like hotshot firefighters, our assignment requires that we both battle the main fire and suppress sparks and embers using every possible tool and piece of equipment we have at our disposal.

As a civil litigator, I am not a participant in the criminal justice system, where the consequences of implicit bias have an insidious impact. And yet, as a woman litigator of color, my clients and I are also directly impacted. It is also important to be cognizant that implicit bias is a two-way street, and litigators' perception of our judiciary is also tainted by implicit bias. I have not only noted many of the subtle and not-so-subtle manifestations of judicial bias that are discussed in this book but also noted manifestation of bias toward our sitting judges by litigators when the judge is a woman or a minority. Participating in this project has been tremendously enlightening.

The work of this Advisory Group, concluding with the publication of this book, is important to every actor in the judicial system, as only when we all make a concerted effort to deliver a justice system that lives up to the "just" in its name can we effectuate lasting change. I recently had the opportunity to hear Professor Ronald S. Sullivan, Jr., Director of Harvard Law School's Criminal Justice Institute, deliver a keynote address. I was touched by his comments on justice: "Justice is not something that happens. Justice is something that men and women of goodwill do." The members of this Advisory Group and the contributors to this work are unequivocally men and women of goodwill who are committed to "doing justice." I am privileged to have had the opportunity to work alongside them on this impactful project.

And from Us All

We all invite all of our readers to contact us with questions or insights from your experiences and to stay in touch.

ABOUT THE AUTHORS

Cynthia Eva Hujar Orr is an AV-rated litigator with 28 years of experience. She defends citizens and entities in state and federal trial and in appellate courts and is a past chair of the American Bar Association's Criminal Justice Section and past president of the

National Association of Criminal Defense Lawyers. She is also a member of the ABA's House of Delegates on behalf of the National Association of Criminal Defense Lawyers. Ms. Hujar Orr is licensed to practice in Texas and in federal and appellate courts nationwide. She is recognized in Woodward White's Best Lawyers in America in White Collar Criminal Defense. Ms. Hujar Orr is board certified in both criminal law and criminal appeals by the Texas Board of Legal Specialization.

Anna D. Torres is an AV-rated litigator with over 25 years of experience and the founder and principal of Torres Law Group. She has dedicated her practice to civil and commercial defense litigation and insurance coverage. She attended San Diego State University and Stanford Law School and is admitted to practice in California and Florida state and federal courts. Ms. Torres is an active member of the American Bar Association, Section of Litigation, and currently serves in leadership positions in the Diversity and Inclusion Committee, Legal Opportunity Scholarship Selection Committee, and the Judicial Division's Joint Task Force on Fighting Implicit Bias in the Justice System and is a frequent speaker in continuing education and industry programs.

ENDNOTE

1. Judicial Division Director Peter Koelling and Felice Shur staffed the project for the ABA. In addition, the Advisory Group thanks Kate Duncan Butler, former research attorney for Judge Arnold-Burger, and Jasmine Bolton, Pablo Davis, Crystal Enekwa, Nicole Langston, and Brianna Powell, Judge Donald's clerks, for their excellent and generous help with the manuscript.

Index

Featured Publication from the Judicial Division

 Judicial Division

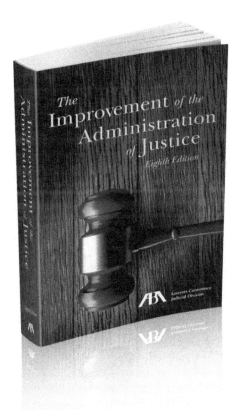

The Improvement of the Administration of Justice, Eighth Edition

To order 🌐 visit **www.ShopABA.org** or call 📞 **(800) 285-2221**.

ABA Publishing